# Classical and Contemporary Readings in the Philosophy of Religion

# 3rd edition

# Classical and Contemporary Readings in the

# Philosophy of Religion

edited by

## John Hick

*Claremont Graduate School*

PRENTICE HALL, Upper Saddle River, New Jersey 07458

Library of Congress Cataloging-in-Publication Data

Classical and contemporary readings in the philosophy of religion /
   edited by John Hick. -- 3rd ed.
      p.   cm.
   ISBN 0-13-136904-0
   1. Religion--Philosophy.   I. Hick, John.
BL51.C558   1990
200'.1--dc20                                         89-38789
                                                        CIP

Editorial/production supervision: Merrill Peterson
Interior design: Joan Stone
Cover design: 20/20 Services Inc.
Manufacturing buyer: Carol Bystrom/Mike Woerner

Printed in the United States of America
11

ISBN 0-13-136904-0

Prentice-Hall International (UK) Limited,London
Prentice-Hall of Australia Pty. Limited, Sydney
Prentice-Hall Canada Inc., Toronto
Prentice-Hall Hispanoamericana, S.A., Mexico
Prentice-Hall of India Private Limited, New Delhi
Prentice-Hall of Japan, Inc., Tokyo
Pearson Education Asia Pte. Ltd., Singapore
Editora Prentice-Hall do Brasil, Ltda., Rio de Janeiro

# Contents

## The Readings

## Immanuel Kant

## Ludwig Feuerbach

## Søren Kierkegaard

## William James

## Ernst Troeltsch

## Bertrand Russell and F. C. Copleston

## Martin Buber

## Paul Tillich

## Ludwig Wittgenstein

## Charles Hartshorne

## H. H. Price

## R. B. Braithwaite

## John Herman Randall, Jr.

## John Wisdom

## Norman Malcolm

## Antony Flew and Others

## John Hick

## Sallie McFague

## William Alston

## Alvin Plantinga

# Appendix: Introductory Notes and Bibliographies

# Topical Contents

## The Theistic Arguments

### THE ONTOLOGICAL ARGUMENT

### THE COSMOLOGICAL ARGUMENT

### THE DESIGN ARGUMENT

### THE MORAL ARGUMENT

# Epistemology of Religion

# The Problem of Evil

# Human Destiny

# The Rejection of Theism and New Forms of Religious Naturalism

# Religious Language

# The Relation Between Religions

# Preface

This book is designed primarily for use in courses in the philosophy of religion. Because such courses are sometimes arranged historically and sometimes in terms of topics or problems the material is presented here in two different tables of contents adapted to these two uses. The readings themselves are printed in chronological sequence, mainly in order that discussions by the same writer of different but related topics may conveniently be studied together—for example, Kant's critique of the three traditional theistic proofs.

Material written in other languages appears here in the best available English translation—for example, the versions of Augustine recently made by J. H. S. Burleigh and Albert Outler; A. C. McGill's translation of the Anselm material; Anton Pegis' Aquinas; the Kemp Smith version of Kant's first Critique and Lewis Beck's version of the second; and so on.

Preparing a volume of readings like this is an enjoyable if sometimes arduous task, involving much re-reading and new reading in a wide field. It has also involved many difficult decisions. At first the space available, in this case a quarter of a million words, seemed ample for everything that could be desired in a book of this kind. But presently the list of apparently basic and inevitable selections had grown to the point at which there was little room left for maneuver, and one was weighing and re-weighing one piece against another and experimenting with alternative plans for trying to achieve the desired result.

But what result is to be desired? Even this is something that has to be chosen from among several possibilities. I have striven to achieve a balance between the two pedagogic interests indicated by the two tables of contents. One made me wish to include selections worthily representative of all of the succession of great thinkers whose work constitutes the long history of the discipline. The other made me desire to present as adequately as possible the main points of view on each of the chief problems encompassed within the subject, as well as important contemporary developments in the discussion of some of them. This has led to the inclusion of a certain proportion of material by living writers. A third concern was to use passages which will be reasonably readily comprehensible to students, or best fitted to introduce them to the various facets of a new topic. This has led me to use, for instance, William James on mysticism even though James was not himself a mystic; for he discusses carefully chosen examples with sensitive appreciation and tries to make their significance clear to the science-oriented twentieth-century reader. A further subsidiary concern has been to use somewhat lengthy selections rather than a scattering of "snippets." (On the other hand an exception seemed called for in the case of the extraordinarily pregnant three final pages of Wittgenstein's *Tractatus*.) Sometimes one of these criteria has been in conflict with one or more of the others. Amid these divergent considerations I have always sought to bear the teaching situation firmly in mind and to treat its needs as paramount.

Many legitimate questions might be raised about the selection of this or that passage or about the omission of some other passage or author. There is a reason for each choice, though whether the reasons are sufficient can only be decided over a period of time by fellow teachers of the subject and their classes.

In order to devote as much space as possible to the main business of the book, which is transacted through the selections themselves, I have narrowly restricted my own editorial contributions. I have not, for example, written an Introduction telling the reader what the philosophy of religion is. In a book designed for use in courses on the subject this hardly seems necessary. Nor have I tried to supplant the living teacher by providing commentaries on the selections. There are brief notes to identify the writers and occasional footnotes, and insertions in square brackets to translate foreign language quotations or otherwise remove hindrances to ready comprehension. In addition I have written a series of short essays on the central topics, to each of which is appended a list of suggestions for further reading. These brief essays are built around the relevant selections and may be of help to some in focusing attention upon the most important points in them. In order not to obtrude them, these notes are printed together in an Appendix at the end of the book.

A word should perhaps be said here about the scope and limitations of the work. It covers most of the topics which are usually discussed in books and courses under the heading of the philosophy of religion. Among the influential contemporary schools of thought which have their place in it are various types of philosophical analysis (selections 22, 23, 25, 26, 27, 29, 32, 33), existentialism (selections 13 and 23), humanism (selections 12 and 24), and process thought (selection 21), as well as traditional Thomism (selections 4–6), modern Protestantism (selection 19), atheism (selections 12 and 16), and other positions in between. The book does not cover comparative religion or the history of religions; and the material is largely confined to the Judaic-Christian tradition. Nor does the book attempt to cover the psychology of religion (although selection 14 is concerned with this), or the sociology of religion, or ethics; for each demands and justifies treatment on its own.

In this new edition various older selections have (regretfully) been omitted to make room for two new ones on the problems of religious pluralism by Ernst Troeltsch (16) and John Hick (30), and three new ones on recent work in the epistemology of religion by Sallie McFague (31), expressing a feminist point of view, and by William Alston (32) and Alvin Plantinga (33). With this new material the book is, I think, now fully up to date.

I am most grateful to all who have helped to try to make this fresh version of the book more useful to teachers and their students during the 1990s.

JOHN HICK
Department of Religion
Claremont Graduate School
Claremont, CA 91711

# Classical and Contemporary Readings in the Philosophy of Religion

# Plato

Plato (428/7–348/7 B.C.E.), one of the first and one of the greatest of Western philosophers, developed the body-soul distinction that underlies so much subsequent thought, both popular and philosophical.

# 1

# *Arguments for Immortality*

## THE PHILOSOPHER'S DETACHMENT FROM THE BODY

SOCRATES: Do we believe that there is such a thing as death?
To be sure, replied Simmias.
Is it not the separation of soul and body? And to be dead is the completion of this; when the soul exists in herself, and is released from the body and the body is released from the soul, what is this but death?
Just so, he replied.
There is another question, which will probably throw light on our present enquiry if you and I can agree about it:—Ought the philosopher to care about the pleasures—if they are to be called pleasures—of eating and drinking?
Certainly not, answered Simmias.
And what about the pleasures of love—should he care for them?
By no means.
And will he think much of the other ways of indulging the body, for example, the acquisition of costly raiment, or sandals, or other adornments of the body? Instead of caring about them, does he not rather despise anything more than nature needs? What do you say?
I should say that the true philosopher would despise them.
Would you not say that he is entirely concerned with the soul and not with the body? He would like, as far as he can, to get away from the body and to turn to the soul.
Quite true.

---

Plato's *Phaedo*, 64C–70A, 72E–80C, 91C–95A Reprinted from *The Dialogues of Plato* translated by Benjamin Jowett (4th ed 1953) by permission of Oxford University Press. This dialogue takes place in prison during the day on which Socrates is to be executed in the evening.

In matters of this sort philosophers, above all other men, may be observed in every sort of way to dissever the soul from the communion of the body.

Very true.

Whereas, Simmias, the rest of the world are of opinion that to him who has no sense of pleasure and no part in bodily pleasure, life is not worth having; and that he who is indifferent about them is as good as dead.

That is also true.

What again shall we say of the actual acquirement of knowledge?—is the body, if invited to share in the enquiry, a hinderer or a helper? I mean to say, have sight and hearing any truth in them? Are they not, as the poets are always telling us, inaccurate witnesses? and yet, if even they are inaccurate and indistinct, what is to be said of the other senses?—for you will allow that they are the best of them?

Certainly, he replied.

Then when does the soul attain truth?—for in attempting to consider anything in company with the body she is obviously deceived.

True.

Then must not true existence be revealed to her in thought, if at all?

Yes.

And thought is best when the mind is gathered into herself and none of these things trouble her—neither sounds nor sights nor pain nor any pleasure,—when she takes leave of the body, and has as little as possible to do with it, when she has no bodily sense or desire, but is aspiring after true being?

Certainly.

And in this the philosopher dishonours the body; his soul runs away from his body and desires to be alone and by herself?

That is true.

Well, but there is another thing, Simmias: Is there or is there not an absolute justice?

Assuredly there is.

And an absolute beauty and absolute good?

Of course.

But did you ever behold any of them with your eyes?

Certainly not.

Or did you ever reach them with any other bodily sense?—and I speak not of these alone, but of absolute greatness, and health, and strength, and of the essence or true nature of everything. Has the reality of them ever been perceived by you through the bodily organs? or rather, is not the nearest approach to the knowledge of their several natures made by him who so orders his intellectual vision as to have the most exact conception of the essence of each thing which he considers?

Certainly.

And he attains to the purest knowledge of them who goes to each with the mind alone, not introducing or intruding in the act of thought sight or any other sense together with reason, but with the very light of the mind in her own clearness searches into the very truth of each; he who has got rid, as far as he can, of eyes and ears and, so to speak, of the whole body, these being in his opinion distracting elements which when they infect the soul hinder her from acquiring truth and knowledge—who, if not he, is likely to attain to the knowledge of true being?

What you say has a wonderful truth in it, Socrates, replied Simmias.

And when real philosophers consider all these things, will they not be led to make a reflection which they will express in words something like the following? 'Have we not found,' they will say, 'a path of thought which seems to bring us and our argument to the conclusion, that while we are in the body, and while the soul is infected with the evils of the body, our desire will not be satisfied? and our desire is of the truth. For the body is a source of endless trouble to us by reason of the mere requirement of food; and is liable also to diseases which overtake and impede us in the search after true being: it fills us full of loves, and lusts, and fears, and fancies of all kinds, and endless foolery, and in fact, as men say, takes away from us the power of thinking at all. Whence come wars, and fightings, and factions? whence but from the body and the lusts of the body? Wars are occasioned by the love of money, and money has to be acquired for the sake and in the service of the body; and by reason of all these impediments we have no time to give to philosophy; and, last and worst of all, even if we are at leisure and betake ourselves to some speculation, the body is always breaking in upon us, causing turmoil and confusion in our enquiries, and so amazing us that we are prevented from seeing the truth. It has been proved to us by experience that if we would have pure knowledge of anything we must be quit of the body—the soul in herself must behold things in themselves: and then we shall attain the wisdom which we desire, and of which we say that we are lovers; not while we live, but after death; for if while in company with the body, the soul cannot have pure knowledge, one of two things follows—either knowledge is not to be attained at all, or, if at all, after death. For then, and not till then, the soul will be parted from the body and exist in herself alone. In this present life, I reckon that we make the nearest approach to knowledge when we have the least possible intercourse or communion with the body, and are not surfeited with the bodily nature, but keep ourselves pure until the hour when God himself is pleased to release us. And thus having got rid of the foolishness of the body we shall be pure and hold converse with the pure, and know of ourselves the clear light everywhere, which is no other than the light of truth.' For the impure are not permitted to approach the pure. These are the sort of words,

Simmias, which the true lovers of knowledge cannot help saying to one another, and thinking. You would agree; would you not?

Undoubtedly, Socrates.

## TRUE AND FALSE VIRTUE

But, O my friend, if this be true, there is great reason to hope that, going whither I go, when I have come to the end of my journey, I shall attain that which has been the pursuit of my life. And therefore I go on my way rejoicing, and not I only, but every other man who believes that his mind has been made ready and that he is in a manner purified.

Certainly, replied Simmias.

And what is purification but the separation of the soul from the body, as I was saying before; the habit of the soul gathering and collecting herself into herself from all sides out of the body; the dwelling in her own place alone, as in another life, so also in this, as far as she can;—the release of the soul from the chains of the body?

Very true, he said.

And this separation and release of the soul from the body is termed death?

To be sure, he said.

And the true philosophers, and they only, are ever seeking to release the soul. Is not the separation and release of the soul from the body their especial study?

That is true.

And, as I was saying at first, there would be a ridiculous contradiction in men studying to live as nearly as they can in a state of death, and yet repining when it comes upon them.

Clearly.

And the true philosophers, Simmias, are always occupied in the practice of dying, wherefore also to them least of all men is death terrible. Look at the matter thus:—if they have been in every way the enemies of the body, and are wanting to be alone with the soul, when this desire of theirs is granted, how inconsistent would they be if they trembled and repined, instead of rejoicing at their departure to that place where, when they arrive, they hope to gain that which in life they desired—and this was wisdom—and at the same time to be rid of the company of their enemy. Many a man has been willing to go to the world below animated by the hope of seeing there an earthly love, or wife, or son, and conversing with them. And will he who is a true lover of wisdom, and is strongly persuaded in like manner that only in the world below he can worthily enjoy her, still repine at death? Will he not depart with joy? Surely he will, O my friend, if he be a true philosopher. For he will have a firm conviction that there, and there only, he can find wisdom in her purity. And if this be true, he would be very absurd, as I was saying, if he were afraid of death.

He would indeed, replied Simmias.

And when you see a man who is repining at the approach of death, is not his reluctance a sufficient proof that he is not a lover of wisdom, but a lover of the body, and probably at the same time a lover of either money or power, or both?

Quite so, he replied.

And is not courage, Simmias, a quality which is specially characteristic of the philosopher?

Certainly.

There is temperance again, which even by the vulgar is supposed to consist in the control and regulation of the passions, and in the sense of superiority to them—is not temperance a virtue belonging to those only who despise the body, and who pass their lives in philosophy?

Most assuredly.

For the courage and temperance of other men, if you will consider them, are really a contradiction.

How so?

Well, he said, you are aware that death is regarded by men in general as a great evil.

Very true, he said.

And do not courageous men face death because they are afraid of yet greater evils?

That is quite true.

Then all but the philosophers are courageous only from fear, and because they are afraid; and yet that a man should be courageous from fear, and because he is a coward, is surely a strange thing.

Very true.

And are not the temperate exactly in the same case? They are temperate because they are intemperate—which might seem to be a contradiction, but is nevertheless the sort of thing which happens with this foolish temperance. For there are pleasures which they are afraid of losing; and in their desire to keep them, they abstain from some pleasures, because they are overcome by others; and although to be conquered by pleasure is called by man intemperance, to them the conquest of pleasure consists in being conquered by pleasure. And that is what I mean by saying that, in a sense, they are made temperate through intemperance.

Such appears to be the case.

Yet the exchange of one fear or pleasure or pain for another fear or pleasure or pain, and of the greater for the less, as if they were coins, is not the exchange of virtue. O my blessed Simmias, is there not one true coin for which all things ought to be exchanged?—and that is wisdom; and only in exchange for this, and in company with this, is anything truly bought or sold, whether courage or temperance or justice. And is not all true virtue the companion of wisdom, no matter what fears or pleasures or other similar goods or evils may or may not attend her? But the virtue which is made up of these goods, when they are severed from wisdom and exchanged with one another, is a shadow of virtue only, nor is there any freedom or health or truth in her; but in the true exchange there is a purging away of all these things, and temperance, and justice, and courage, and wisdom herself are the purgation of them. The founders of the mysteries would appear to have had a real meaning, and were not talking nonsense when they intimated in a figure long ago that he who passes unsanctified and uninitiated into the world below will lie in a slough, but that he who arrives there after initiation and purification will dwell with the gods. For 'many,' as they say in the mysteries, 'are the thyrsus-bearers, but few are the mystics,'—meaning, as I interpret the words, 'the true philosophers.' In the number of whom, during my whole life, I have been seeking, according to my ability, to find a place;—whether I have sought in a right way or not, and whether I have succeeded or not, I shall truly know in a little while, if God will, when I myself arrive in the other world—such is my belief. And therefore I maintain that I am right, Simmias and Cebes, in not grieving or repining at parting from you and my masters in this world, for I believe that I shall equally find good masters and friends in another world. But most men do not believe this saying; if then I succeed in convincing you by my defense better than I did the Athenian judges, it will be well.

Cebes answered: I agree, Socrates, in the greater part of what you say. But in what concerns the soul, men are apt to be incredulous; they fear that when she has left the body her place may be nowhere, and that on the very day of death she may perish and come to an end—immediately on her release from the body, issuing forth dispersed like smoke or air and in her flight vanishing away into nothingness. If she could only be collected into herself after she has obtained release from the evils of which you were speaking, there would be good reason to hope, Socrates, that what you say is true. But surely it requires a great deal of argument and many proofs to show that when the man is dead his soul yet exists, and has any force or intelligence....

## THE THEORY OF RECOLLECTION

Cebes added: Your favourite doctrine, Socrates, that knowledge is simply recollection, if true, also necessarily implies a previous time in which we have learned that which we now recollect. But this would be impossible unless our soul had been in some place before existing in the form of man; here then is another proof of the soul's immortality.

But tell me, Cebes, said Simmias, interposing, what arguments are urged in favour of this doctrine of recollection. I am not very sure at the moment that I remember them.

One excellent proof, said Cebes, is afforded by questions. If you put a question to a person in a right way, he will give a true answer of himself, but how could he do this unless there were knowledge and right reason already in him? And this is most clearly shown when he is taken to a diagram or to anything of that sort.

But if, said Socrates, you are still incredulous, Simmias, I would ask you whether you may not agree with me when you look at the matter in another way;—I mean, if you are still incredulous as to whether knowledge is recollection?

Incredulous I am not, said Simmias; but I want to have this doctrine of recollection brought to my own recollection, and, from what Cebes has said, I am beginning to recollect and be convinced: but I should still like to hear what you were going to say.

This is what I would say, he replied:—We should agree, if I am not mistaken, that what a man recollects he must have known at some previous time.

Very true.

And what is the nature of this knowledge or recollection? I mean to ask, Whether a person who, having seen or heard or in any way perceived anything, knows not only that, but has a conception of something else which is the subject, not of the same but of some other kind of knowledge, may not be fairly said to recollect that of which he has the conception?

What do you mean?

I mean what I may illustrate by the following instance:—The knowledge of a lyre is not the same as the knowledge of a man?

True.

And yet what is the feeling of lovers when they recognize a lyre, or a garment, or anything else which the beloved has been in the habit of using? Do not they, from knowing the lyre, form in the mind's eye an image of the youth to whom the lyre belongs? And this is recollection. In like manner any one who sees Simmias may remember Cebes; and there are endless examples of the same thing.

Endless, indeed, replied Simmias.

And recollection is most commonly a process of recovering that which has been already forgotten through time and inattention.

Very true, he said.

Well; and may you not also from seeing the picture of a house or a lyre remember a man? and from the picture of Simmias, you may be led to remember Cebes?

True.

Or you may also be led to the recollection of Simmias himself?

Quite so.

And in all these cases, the recollection may be derived from things either like or unlike?

It may be.

And when the recollection is derived from like things, then another consideration is sure to arise, which is—whether the likeness in any degree falls short or not of that which is recollected?

Very true, he said.

And shall we proceed a step further, and affirm that there is such a thing as equality, not of one piece of wood or stone with another, but that, over and above this, there is absolute equality? Shall we say so?

Say so, yes, replied Simmias, and swear to it, with all the confidence in life.

And do we know the nature of this absolute essence?

To be sure, he said.

And whence did we obtain our knowledge? Did we not see equalities of material things, such as pieces of wood and stones, and gather from them the idea of an equality which is different from them? For you will acknowledge that there is a difference. Or look at the matter in another way:—Do not the same pieces of wood or stone appear at one time equal, and at another time unequal?

That is certain.

But are real equals ever unequal? or is the idea of equality the same as of inequality?

Impossible, Socrates.

Then these (so-called) equals are not the same with the idea of equality?

I should say, clearly not, Socrates.

And yet from these equals, although differing from the idea of equality, you conceived and attained that idea?

Very true, he said.

Which might be like, or might be unlike them?

Yes.

But that makes no difference: whenever from seeing one thing you conceived another, whether like or unlike, there must surely have been an act of recollection?

Very true.

But what would you say of equal portions of wood and stone, or other material equals? and what is the impression produced by them? Are they equals in the same sense in which absolute equality is equal? or do they fall short of this perfect equality in a measure?

Yes, he said, in a very great measure too.

And must we not allow, that when I or anyone, looking at any object, observes that the thing which he sees aims at being some other thing, but falls short of, and cannot be, that other thing, but is inferior, he who makes this observation must have had a previous knowledge of that to which the other, although similar, was inferior.

Certainly.

And has not this been our own case in the matter of equals and of absolute equality?

Precisely.

Then we must have known equality previously to the time when we first saw the material equals, and reflected that all these apparent equals strive to attain absolute equality, but fall short of it?

Very true.

And we recognize also that this absolute equality has only been known, and can only be known, through the medium of sight or touch, or of some other of the senses, which are all alike in this respect?

Yes, Socrates, as far as the argument is concerned, one of them is the same as the other.

From the senses then is derived the knowledge that all sensible things aim at an absolute equality of which they fall short?

Yes.

Then before we began to see or hear or perceive in any way, we must have had a knowledge of absolute equality, or we could not have referred to that standard the equals which are derived from the senses?—for to that they all aspire, and of that they fall short.

No other inference can be drawn from the previous statements.

And did we not see and hear and have the use of our other senses as soon as we were born?

Certainly.

Then we must have acquired the knowledge of equality at some previous time?

Yes.

That is to say, before we were born, I suppose?

True.

And if we acquired this knowledge before we were born, and were born having the use of it, then we also knew before we were born and at the instant of birth not only the equal or the greater or the less, but all other ideas; for we are not speaking only of equality, but of beauty, goodness, justice, holiness, and of all which we stamp with the name of essence in the dialectical process, both when we ask and when we answer questions. Of all this we may certainly affirm that we acquired the knowledge before birth?

We may.

But if, after having acquired, we have not forgotten what in each case we acquired, then we must always have come into life having knowledge, and shall always continue to know as long as life lasts—for knowing is the acquiring and retaining knowledge and not forgetting. Is not forgetting, Simmias, just the losing of knowledge?

Quite true, Socrates.

But if the knowledge which we acquired before birth was lost by us at birth, and if afterwards by the use of the senses we recovered what we previously knew, will not the process which we call learning be a recovering of the knowledge which is natural to us, and may not this be rightly termed recollection?

Very true.

So much is clear—that when we perceive something, either by the help of sight, or hearing, or some other sense, from that perception we are able to obtain a notion of some other thing like or unlike which is associated with it but has been forgotten. Whence, as I was saying, one of two alternatives follows:—either we had this knowledge at birth, and continued to know through life; or, after birth, those who are said to learn only remember, and learning is simply recollection.

Yes, that is quite true, Socrates.

And which alternative, Simmias, do you prefer? Had we the knowledge at our birth, or did we recollect the things which we knew previously to our birth?

I cannot decide at the moment.

At any rate you can decide whether he who has knowledge will or will not be able to render an account of his knowledge? What do you say?

Certainly, he will.

But do you think that every man is able to give an account of these very matters about which we are speaking?

Would that they could, Socrates, but I rather fear that tomorrow, at this time, there will no longer be anyone alive who is able to give an account of them such as ought to be given.

Then you are not of opinion, Simmias, that all men know these things?

Certainly not.

They are in process of recollecting that which they learned before?

Certainly.

But when did our souls acquire this knowledge?—not since we were born as men?

Certainly not.

And therefore, previously?

Yes.

Then, Simmias, our souls must also have existed without bodies before they were in the form of man, and must have had intelligence.

Unless indeed you suppose, Socrates, that these notions are given us at the very moment of birth; for this is the only time which remains.

Yes, my friend, but if so, when do we lose them? for they are not in us when we are born—that is admitted. Do we lose them at the moment of receiving them, or if not at what other time?

No, Socrates, I perceive that I was unconsciously talking nonsense.

Then may we not say, Simmias, that if, as we are always repeating, there is an absolute beauty, and goodness, and an absolute essence of all things; and if to this, which is now discovered to have existed in our former state, we refer all our sensations, and with this compare them, finding these ideas to be pre-existent and our inborn possession—then our souls must have had a prior existence, but if not, there would be no force in the argument? There is the same proof that these ideas must have existed before we were born, as that our souls existed before we were born; and if not the ideas, then not the souls.

Yes, Socrates; I am convinced that there is precisely the same necessity for the one as for the other; and the argument retreats successfully to the position that the existence of the soul before birth cannot be separated from the existence of the essence of which you speak. For there is nothing which to my mind is so patent as that beauty, goodness, and the other notions of which you were just now speaking, have a most real and absolute existence; and I am satisfied with the proof.

Well, but is Cebes equally satisfied? for I must convince him too.

I think, said Simmias, that Cebes is satisfied: although he is the most incredulous of mortals, yet I believe that he is sufficiently convinced of the existence of the soul before birth. But that after death the soul will continue to exist is not yet proven even to my own satisfaction. I cannot get rid of the feeling of the many to which Cebes was referring—the feeling that when the man dies the soul will be dispersed, and that this may be the extinction of her. For admitting that she may have been born elsewhere, and framed out of other elements, and was in existence before entering the human body, why after having entered in and gone out again may she not herself be destroyed and come to an end?

Very true, Simmias, said Cebes; about half of what was required has been proven; to wit, that our souls existed before we were born:—that the soul will exist after death as well as before birth is the other half of which the proof is still wanting, and has to be supplied; when that is given the demonstration will be complete.

But that proof, Simmias and Cebes, has been already given, said Socrates, if you put the two arguments together—I mean this and the former one, in which we admitted that everything living is born of the dead. For if the soul exists before birth, and in coming to life and being born can be born only from death and dying, must she not after death continue to exist, since she has to be born again?—Surely the proof which you desire has been already furnished. Still I suspect that you and Simmias would be glad to probe the argument further. Like children, you are haunted with a fear that when the soul leaves the body, the wind may really blow her away and scatter her; especially if a man should happen to die in a great storm and not when the sky is calm.

Cebes answered with a smile: Then, Socrates, you must argue us out of our fears—and yet, strictly speaking, they are not our fears, but there is a child within us to whom death is a sort of hobgoblin: him too we must persuade not to be afraid when he is alone in the dark.

Socrates said: Let the voice of the charmer be applied daily until you have charmed away the fear.

And where shall we find a good charmer of our fears, Socrates, when you are gone?

Hellas, he replied, is a large place, Cebes, and has many good men, and there are barbarous races not a few: seek for him among them all, far and wide, sparing neither pains nor money; for there is no better way of spending your money. And you must seek among yourselves too; for you will not find others better able to make the search.

The search, replied Cebes, shall certainly be made. And now, if you please, let us return to the point of the argument at which we digressed.

By all means, replied Socrates; what else should I please?

Very good.


## THE KINSHIP OF SOULS AND IDEAS

Must we not, said Socrates, ask ourselves what that is which, as we imagine, is liable to be scattered, and about which we fear? and what again is that about which we have no fear? And then we may proceed further to inquire whether that which suffers dispersion is or is not of the nature of soul—our hopes and fears as to our own souls will turn upon the answers to these questions.

Very true, he said.

Now the compound or composite may be supposed to be naturally capable, as of being compounded, so also of being dissolved; but that which is uncompounded, and that only, must be, if anything is, indissoluble.

Yes; I should imagine so, said Cebes.

And the uncompounded may be assumed to be the same and unchanging, whereas the compound is always changing and never the same.

I agree, he said.

Then now let us return to the previous discussion. Is that idea or essence, which in the dialectical process we define as essence or true existence—whether essence of equality, beauty, or anything else—are these essences, I say, liable at times to some degree of change? or are they each of them always what they are, having the same simple self-existent and unchanging forms, not admitting of variation at all, or in any way, or at any time?

They must be always the same, Socrates, replied Cebes.

And what would you say of the many beautiful—whether men or horses or garments or any other things which are named by the same names and may be called equal or beautiful,—are they all unchanging and the same always, or quite the reverse? May they not rather be described as almost always changing and hardly ever the same, either with themselves or with one another?

The latter, replied Cebes; they are always in a state of change.

And these you can touch and see and perceive with the senses, but the unchanging things you can only perceive with the mind—they are invisible and are not seen?

That is very true, he said.

Well then, added Socrates, let us suppose that there are two sorts of existences—one seen, the other unseen.

Let us suppose them.

The seen is the changing, and the unseen is the unchanging?

That may be also supposed.

And, further, is not one part of us body, another part soul?

To be sure.

And to which class is the body more alike and akin?

Clearly to the seen—no one can doubt that.

And is the soul seen or not seen?

Not by man, Socrates.

And what we mean by 'seen' and 'not seen' is that which is or is not visible to the eye of man?

Yes, to the eye of man.

And is the soul seen or not seen?

Not seen.

Unseen then?

Yes.

Then the soul is more like to the unseen, and the body to the seen?

That follows necessarily, Socrates.

And were we not saying long ago that the soul when using the body as an instrument of perception, that is to say, when using the sense of sight or hearing or some other sense (for the meaning of perceiving through the body is perceiving through the senses)—were we not saying that the soul too is then dragged by the body into the region of the changeable, and wanders and is confused; the world spins round her, and she is like a drunkard, when she touches change?

Very true.

But when returning into herself she reflects, then she passes into the other world, the region of purity, and eternity, and immortality, and unchangeableness, which are her kindred, and with them she ever lives, when she is by herself and is not let or hindered; then she ceases from her erring ways, and being in communion with the unchanging is unchanging. And this state of the soul is called wisdom?

That is well and truly said, Socrates, he replied.

And to which class is the soul more nearly alike and akin, as far as may be inferred from this argument, as well as from the preceding one?

I think, Socrates, that, in the opinion of everyone who follows the argument, the soul will be infinitely more like the unchangeable—even the most stupid person will not deny that.

And the body is more like the changing?

Yes.

Yet once more consider the matter in another light: When the soul and the body are united, then nature orders the soul to rule and govern, and the body to obey and serve. Now which of these two functions is akin to the divine? and which to the mortal? Does not the divine appear to you to be that which naturally orders and rules, and the mortal to be that which is subject and servant?

True.

And which does the soul resemble?

The soul resembles the divine, and the body the mortal—there can be no doubt of that, Socrates.

Then reflect, Cebes: of all which has been said is not this the conclusion?—that the soul is in the very likeness of the divine, and immortal, and intellectual, and uniform, and indissoluble, and unchangeable; and that the body is in the very likeness of the human, and mortal, and unintellectual, and multiform, and dissoluble, and changeable. Can this, my dear Cebes, be denied?

It cannot.

But if it be true, then is not the body liable to speedy dissolution? and is not the soul almost or altogether indissoluble?

Certainly.

• • •

## THE SOUL'S INDEPENDENCE FROM THE BODY (REFUTATION OF EPIPHENOMENALISM[1]

And now let us proceed, he said. And first of all let me be sure that I have in my mind what you were saying. Simmias, if I remember rightly, has

---

[1]Epiphenomenalism: the theory that consciousness is a by-product of the functioning of the physical brain, but with no independent status or efficacy—like (in a much used analogy) the glow of light generated by a radio tube as the electric current passes through it.

fears and misgivings whether the soul, although a fairer and diviner thing than the body, being as she is in the form of harmony, may not perish first. On the other hand, Cebes appeared to grant that the soul was more lasting than the body, but he said that no one could know whether the soul, after having worn out many bodies, might not perish herself and leave her last body behind her; and that this is death, which is the destruction not of the body but of the soul, for in the body the work of destruction is ever going on. Are not these, Simmias and Cebes, the points which we have to consider?

They both agreed to this statement of them.

He proceeded: And did you deny the force of the whole preceding argument, or of a part only?

Of a part only, they replied.

And what did you think, he said, of that part of the argument in which we said that knowledge was recollection, and hence inferred that the soul must have previously existed somewhere else before she was enclosed in the body?

Cebes said that he had been wonderfully impressed by that part of the argument, and that his conviction remained absolutely unshaken. Simmias agreed, and added that he himself could hardly imagine the possibility of his ever thinking differently.

But, rejoined Socrates, you will have to think differently, my Theban friend, if you still maintain that harmony is a compound, and that the soul is a harmony which is made out of strings set in the frame of the body; for you will surely never allow yourself to say that a harmony is prior to the elements which compose it.

Never, Socrates.

But do you not see that this is what you imply when you say that the soul existed before she took the form and body of man, and was made up of elements which as yet had no existence? For harmony is not like the soul, as you suppose; but first the lyre, and the strings, and the sounds exist in a state of discord, and then harmony is made last of all, and perishes first. And how can such a notion of the soul as this agree with the other?

Not at all, replied Simmias.

And yet, he said, there surely ought to be harmony in a discourse of which harmony is the theme?

There ought, replied Simmias.

But there is no harmony, he said, in the two propositions that knowledge is recollection, and that the soul is a harmony. Which of them will you retain?

I think, he replied, that I have a much stronger faith, Socrates, in the first of the two, which has been fully demonstrated to me, than in the latter, which has not been demonstrated at all, but rests only on probable and plausible grounds; and is therefore believed by the many. I know too well that these arguments from probabilities are impostors, and unless great caution is observed in the use of them, they are apt to be deceptive—in geometry, and in other things too. But the doctrine of knowledge and recollection has been proven to me on trustworthy grounds: and the proof was that the soul must have existed before she came into the body, because to her belongs the essence of which the very name implies existence. Having, as I am convinced, rightly accepted this conclusion, and on sufficient grounds, I must, as I suppose, cease to argue or allow others to argue that the soul is a harmony.

Let me put the matter, Simmias, he said, in another point of view: Do you imagine that a harmony or any other composition can be in a state other than that of the elements, out of which it is compounded?

Certainly not.

Or do or suffer anything other than they do or suffer?

He agreed.

Then a harmony does not, properly speaking, lead the parts or elements which make up the harmony, but only follows them.

He assented.

For harmony cannot possibly have any motion, or sound, or other quality which is opposed to its parts.

That would be impossible, he replied.

And does not the nature of every harmony depend upon the manner in which the elements are harmonized?

I do not understand you, he said.

I mean to say that a harmony admits of degrees, and is more of a harmony, and more completely a harmony, when more truly and fully harmonized, to any extent which is possible; and less of a harmony, and less completely a harmony, when less truly and fully harmonized.

True.

But does the soul admit of degrees? or is one soul in the very least degree more or less, or more or less completely, a soul than another?

Not in the least.

Yet surely of two souls, one is said to have intelligence and virtue, and to be good, and the other to have folly and vice, and to be an evil soul: and this is said truly?

Yes, truly.

But what will those who maintain the soul to be a harmony say of this presence of virtue and vice in the soul?—will they say that here is another harmony, and another discord, and that the virtuous soul is harmonized, and herself being a harmony has another harmony within her, and that the vicious soul is inharmonical and has no harmony within her?

I cannot tell, replied Simmias; but I suppose that something of the sort would be asserted by those who say that the soul is a harmony.

And we have already admitted that no soul is more a soul than another; which is equivalent to admitting that harmony is not more or less harmony, or more or less completely a harmony?

Quite true.

And that which is not more or less a harmony is not more or less harmonized?

True.

And that which is not more or less harmonized cannot have more or less of harmony, but only an equal harmony?

Yes, an equal harmony.

Then one soul not being more or less absolutely a soul than another, is not more or less harmonized?

Exactly.

And therefore has neither more nor less of discord, nor yet of harmony?

She has not.

And having neither more nor less of harmony or of discord, one soul has no more vice or virtue than another, if vice be discord and virtue harmony?

Not at all more.

Or speaking more correctly, Simmias, the soul, if she is a harmony, will never have any vice; because a harmony, being absolutely a harmony, has no part in the inharmonical.

No.

And therefore a soul which is absolutely a soul has no vice?

How can she have, if the previous argument holds?

Then, if all souls are equally by their nature souls, all souls of all living creatures will be equally good?

I agree with you, Socrates, he said.

And can all this be true, think you? he said; for these are the consequences which seem to follow from the assumption that the soul is a harmony?

It cannot be true.

Once more, he said, what ruler is there of the elements of human nature other than the soul, and especially the wise soul? Do you know of any?

Indeed, I do not.

And is the soul in agreement with the affections of the body? or is she at variance with them? For example, when the body is hot and thirsty, does not the soul incline us against drinking? and when the body is hungry, against eating? And this is only one instance out of ten thousand of the opposition of the soul to the things of the body.

Very true.

But we have already acknowledged that the soul, being a harmony, can never utter a note at variance with the tensions and relaxations and vibrations and other affections of the strings out of which she is composed; she can only follow, she cannot lead them?

It must be so, he replied.

And yet do we not now discover the soul to be doing the exact opposite—leading the elements of which she is believed to be composed; almost always opposing and coercing them in all sorts of ways throughout life, sometimes more violently with the pains of medicine and gymnastic; then again more gently; now threatening, now admonishing the desires, passions, fears, as if talking to a thing which is not herself, as Homer in the Odyssey represents Odysseus doing in the words—

> 'He beat his breast, and thus reproached his heart:
> Endure, my heart; far worse hast thou endured!'

Do you think that Homer wrote this under the idea that the soul is a harmony capable of being led by the affections of the body, and not rather of a nature which should lead and master them—herself a far diviner thing than any harmony?

Yes, Socrates, I quite think so.

Then, my friend, we can never be right in saying that the soul is a harmony, for we should contradict the divine Homer, and contradict ourselves.

True, he said.

• • •

# St. Augustine

Saint Augustine (354–430), whose writings have influenced Christian thought more than any others since the Bible, grappled throughout his career with the problem of evil.

# 2

# *The Problem of Evil*

*EVIL AS PRIVATION OF GOOD*

• • •

By this Trinity, supremely and equally and immutably good, were all things created. But they were not created supremely, equally, nor immutably good. Still, each single created thing is good, and taken as a whole they are very good, because together they constitute a universe of admirable beauty.

In this universe, even what is called evil, when it is rightly ordered and kept in place, commends the good more eminently, since good things yield greater pleasure and praise when compared to the bad things. For the Omnipotent God, whom even the heathen acknowledge as the Supreme Power over all, would not allow any evil in His works, unless in His omnipotence and goodness, as the Supreme Good, He is able to bring forth good out of evil. What, after all, is anything we call evil except the privation of good? In animal bodies, for instance, sickness and wounds are nothing but the privation of health. When a cure is effected, the evils which were present (i.e., the sickness and the wounds) do not retreat and go elsewhere. Rather, they simply do not exist any more. For such evil is not a substance; the wound or the disease is a defect of the bodily substance which, as a substance, is good. Evil, then, is an accident, i.e., a privation of that good which is called health. Thus, whatever defects there are in a soul are privations of a natural good. When a cure takes place, they are not transferred elsewhere but, since they are no longer present in the state of health, they no longer exist at all.

All of nature, therefore, is good, since the Creator of all nature is supremely good. But nature is not supremely and immutably good as is the

From *Augustine: Confessions and Enchiridion*, Vol. VII, The Library of Christian Classics. Newly translated and edited by Albert C. Outler. First published MCMLV, Great Britain: SCM Press, Ltd., London and USA: Westminster Press, Philadelphia. Used by permission of Westminster/John Knox Press, Louisville.

Creator of it. Thus the good in created things can be diminished and augmented. For good to be diminished is evil; still, however much it is diminished, something must remain of its original nature as long as it exists at all. For no matter what kind or however insignificant a thing may be, the good which is its "nature" cannot be destroyed without the thing itself being destroyed. There is good reason, therefore, to praise an uncorrupted thing, and if it were indeed an incorruptible thing which could not be destroyed, it would doubtless be all the more worthy of praise. When, however, a thing is corrupted, its corruption is an evil because it is, by just so much, a privation of the good. Where there is no privation of the good, there is no evil. Where there is evil, there is a corresponding diminution of the good. As long, then, as a thing is being corrupted, there is good in it of which it is being deprived; and in this process, if something of its being remains that cannot be further corrupted, this will then be an incorruptible entity [natura incorruptibilis], and to this great good it will have come through the process of corruption. But even if the corruption is not arrested, it still does not cease having some good of which it cannot be further deprived. If, however, the corruption comes to be total and entire, there is no good left either, because it is no longer an entity at all. Wherefore corruption cannot consume the good without also consuming the thing itself. Every actual entity [natura] is therefore good; a greater good if it cannot be corrupted, a lesser good if it can be. Yet only the foolish and unknowing can deny that it is still good even when corrupted. Whenever a thing is consumed by corruption, not even the corruption remains, for it is nothing in itself, having no subsistent being in which to exist.

From this it follows that there is nothing to be called evil if there is nothing good. A good that wholly lacks an evil aspect is entirely good. Where there is some evil in a thing, its good is defective or defectible. Thus there can be no evil where there is no good. This leads us to a surprising conclusion: that, since every being, insofar as it is a being, is good, if we then say that a defective thing is bad, it would seem to mean that we are saying that what is evil is good, that only what is good is ever evil and that there is no evil apart from something good. This is because every actual entity is good [omnis natura bonum est]. Nothing evil exists in itself, but only as an evil aspect of some actual entity. Therefore, there can be nothing evil except something good. Absurd as this sounds, nevertheless the logical connections of the argument compel us to it as inevitable. At the same time, we must take warning lest we incur the prophetic judgment which reads: "Woe to those who call evil good and good evil; who call darkness light and light darkness; who call the bitter sweet and the sweet bitter" [Isaiah 5:20]. Moreover the Lord himself saith: "An evil man brings forth evil out of the evil treasure of his heart" [Matt. 12:35]. What, then, is an evil man but an evil entity [natura mala], since man is an entity? Now, if a man is something good because he is an entity, what, then, is a bad man except an evil good? When, however, we distinguish between these two concepts, we find that the bad man is not bad because he is a man, nor is he good because he is wicked. Rather, he is a good entity insofar as he is a man, evil insofar as he is wicked. Therefore, if anyone says that simply to be a man is evil, or that to be a wicked man is good, he rightly falls under the prophetic judgment: "Woe to him who calls evil good and good evil." For this amounts to finding fault with God's work, because man is an entity of God's creation. It also means that we are praising the defects in this particular man *because* he is a wicked person. Thus, every entity, even if it is a defective one, insofar as it is an entity, is good. Insofar as it is defective, it is evil.

Actually, then, in these two contraries we call evil and good, the rule of the logicians fails to apply.[1] No weather is both dark and bright at the same time; no food or drink is both sweet and sour at the same time; no body is, at the same time and place, both white and black, nor deformed and well formed at the same time. This principle is found to apply in almost all disjunctions: two contraries cannot coexist in a single thing. Nevertheless, while no one maintains that good and evil are not contraries, they can not only coexist, but the evil cannot exist at all without the good, or in a thing that is not a good. On the other hand, the good can exist without evil. For a man or an angel could exist and yet not be wicked, whereas there cannot be wickedness except in a man or an angel. It is good to be a man, good to be an angel; but evil to be wicked. These two contraries are thus coexistent, so that if there were no good in what is evil, then the evil simply could not be, since it can have no mode in which to exist, nor any source from which corruption springs, unless it be something corruptible. Unless this something is good, it cannot be corrupted, because corruption is nothing more than the deprivation of the good. Evils, therefore, have their source in the good, and unless they are parasitic on something good, they are not anything at all. There is no other source whence an evil thing can come to be. If this is the case, then, insofar as a thing is an entity, it is unquestionably good. If it is an incorruptible entity, it is a great good. But even if it is a corruptible entity, it still has no mode of existence except as an aspect of something that is good. Only by corrupting something good can corruption inflict injury.

But when we say that evil has its source in the good, do not suppose that this denies our Lord's judgment: "A good tree cannot bear evil fruit" [Matt. 7:18]. This cannot be, even as the Truth himself declareth: "Men do not gather grapes from thorns" [Lk. 6:44], since thorns cannot bear grapes. Nevertheless, from good soil we can see both vines and thorns spring up. Likewise, just as a bad tree does not grow good fruit, so also an evil will does not produce good deeds. From a human nature, which is good in itself, there

---

[1]This refers to the "law of excluded middle": that anything must be either x or not-x.

can spring forth either a good or an evil will. There was no other place from whence evil could have arisen in the first place except from the nature—good in itself—of an angel or a man. This is what our Lord himself most clearly shows in the passage about the trees and the fruits, for He said: "Make the tree good and the fruits will be good, or make the tree bad and its fruits will be bad" [Cf. Matt. 12:33]. This is warning enough that bad fruit cannot grow on a good tree nor good fruit on a bad one. Yet from that same earth to which He was referring, both sorts of trees can grow.

• • •

### EVIL WILLING AS "DEFICIENT CAUSATION" [2]

Let no one, therefore, look for an efficient cause of the evil will; for it is not efficient, but deficient, as the will itself is not an effecting of something, but a defect. For defection from that which supremely is, to that which has less of being—this is to begin to have an evil will. Now, to seek to discover the causes of these defections—causes, as I have said, not efficient, but deficient—is as if someone sought to see darkness, or hear silence. Yet both of these are known by us, and the former by means only of the eye, the latter only by the ear; but not by their positive actuality [specie], but by their want of it. Let no one, then, seek to know from me what I know that I do not know; unless he perhaps wishes to learn to be ignorant of that of which all we know is, that it cannot be known. For those things which are known not by their actuality, but by their want of it, are known, if our expression may be allowed and understood, by not knowing them, that by knowing them, they may be not known. For when the eyesight surveys objects that strike the sense, it nowhere sees darkness but where it begins not to see. And so no other sense but the ear can perceive silence, and yet it is only perceived by not hearing. Thus, too, our mind perceives intelligible forms by understanding them; but when they are deficient, it knows them by not knowing them; for "who can understand defects?" [Ps. 19:12].

This I do know, that the nature of God can never, nowhere, nowise be defective, and that natures made of nothing can. These latter, however, the more being they have, and the more good they do (for then they do something positive), the more they have efficient causes; but insofar as they are defective in being, and consequently do evil (for then what is their work but vanity?), they have deficient causes. And I know likewise, that the will could not become evil, were it unwilling to become so; and therefore its failings are justly punished, being not necessary, but voluntary. For its defections are not

---

[2]*City of God*, Bk. XII, Chaps. 7–8, translated by Marcus Dods (Edinburgh: T. & T. Clark, 1871).

to evil things, but are themselves evil; that is to say, are not towards things that are naturally and in themselves evil, but the defection of the will is evil, because it is contrary to the order of nature, and an abandonment of that which has supreme being for that which has less. For avarice is not a fault inherent in gold, but in the man who inordinately loves gold, to the detriment of justice, which ought to be held in incomparably higher regard than gold. Neither is luxury the fault of lovely and charming objects, but of the heart that inordinately loves sensual pleasures, to the neglect of temperance, which attaches us to objects more lovely in their spirituality, and more delectable by their incorruptibility. Nor yet is boasting the fault of human praise, but of the soul that is inordinately fond of the applause of men, and that makes light of the voice of conscience. Pride, too, is not the fault of him who delegates power, nor of power itself, but of the soul that is inordinately enamoured of its own power, and despises the more just dominion of a higher authority. Consequently he who inordinately loves the good which any nature possesses, even though he obtain it, himself becomes evil in the good, and wretched because deprived of a greater good.

## THE PRINCIPLE OF PLENITUDE
## AND THE "AESTHETIC" THEME[3]

For, among those beings which exist, and which are not of God the Creator's essence, those which have life are ranked above those which have none; those that have the power of generation, or even of desiring, above those which want this faculty. And, among things that have life, the sentient are higher than those which have no sensation, as animals are ranked above trees. And, among the sentient, the intelligent are above those that have not intelligence—men, e.g., above cattle. And, among the intelligent, the immortal, such as the angels, above the mortal, such as men. These are the gradations according to the order of nature; but according to the utility each man finds in a thing, there are various standards of value, so that it comes to pass that we prefer some things that have no sensation to some sentient beings. And so strong is this preference, that, had we the power, we would abolish the latter from nature altogether, whether in ignorance of the place they hold in nature, or, though we know it, sacrificing them to our own convenience. Who, e.g., would not rather have bread in his house than mice, gold than fleas? But there is little to wonder at in this, seeing that even when valued by men themselves (whose nature is certainly of the highest dignity), more is often given for a horse than for a slave, for a jewel than for a maid. Thus the reason of one contemplating nature prompts very different judgments from those

---

[3]*Ibid.*, Bk. XI, Chaps. 16–18.

dictated by the necessity of the needy, or the desire of the voluptuous; for the former considers what value a thing in itself has in the scale of creation, while necessity considers how it meets its need; reason looks for what the mental light will judge to be true, while pleasure looks for what pleasantly titillates the bodily sense. But of such consequence in rational natures is the weight, so to speak, of will and of love, that though in the order of nature angels rank above men, yet by the scale of justice, good men are of greater value than bad angels.

It is with reference to the nature, then, and not to the wickedness of the devil, that we are to understand these words, "This is the beginning of God's handiwork" [Job 40:14]; for, without doubt, wickedness can be a flaw or vice only where the nature previously was not vitiated. Vice, too, is so contrary to nature, that it cannot but damage it. And therefore departure from God would be no vice, unless in a nature whose property it was to abide with God. So that even the wicked will is a strong proof of the goodness of the nature. But God, as He is the supremely good Creator of good natures, so is He of evil wills the most just Ruler; so that, while they make an ill use of good natures, He makes a good use even of evil wills. Accordingly, He caused the devil (good by God's creation, wicked by his own will) to be cast down from his high position, and to become the mockery of His angels—that is, He caused his temptations to benefit those whom he wished to injure by them. And because God, when He created him, was certainly not ignorant of his future malignity, and foresaw the good which He Himself would bring out of his evil, therefore says the psalm, "This leviathan whom Thou hast made to be a sport therein" [Ps. 104:26], that we may see that even while God in His goodness created him good, He yet had already foreseen and arranged how He would make use of him when he became wicked.

For God would never have created any, I do not say angel, but even man, whose future wickedness He foreknew, unless He had equally known to what uses in behalf of the good He could turn him, thus embellishing the course of the ages, as it were an exquisite poem set off with antitheses. For what are called antitheses are among the most elegant of the ornaments of speech. They might be called in Latin "oppositions," or, to speak more accurately, "contrapositions"; but this word is not in common use among us, though the Latin and indeed the languages of all nations avail themselves of the same ornaments of style. In the Second Epistle to the Corinthians the Apostle Paul also makes a graceful use of antithesis, in that place where he says, "By the armour of righteousness on the right hand and on the left, by honour and dishonour, by evil report and good report: as deceivers, and yet true; as unknown, and yet well known; as dying, and, behold, we live; as chastened, and not killed; as sorrowful, yet always rejoicing; as poor, yet making many rich; as having nothing, and yet possessing all things" [2 Cor. 6:7–10]. As, then, these oppositions of contraries lend beauty to the language, so the beauty of the course of this world is achieved by the opposition of contraries, arranged, as it were, by an eloquence not of words, but of things. This is quite plainly stated in the Book of Ecclesiasticus, in this way: "Good is set against evil, and life against death: so is the sinner against the godly. So look upon all the works of the Most High, and these are two and two, one against another" [Ecclus. 33:15].

### THE "AESTHETIC" THEME AGAIN[4]

To Thee there is no such thing as evil, and even in Thy creation taken as a whole, there is not; because there is nothing from beyond it that can burst in and destroy the order which Thou hast appointed for it. But in the parts of creation, some things, because they do not harmonize with others, are considered evil. Yet those same things harmonize with others and are good, and in themselves are good. And all these things which do not harmonize with each other still harmonize with the inferior part of creation which we call the earth, having its own cloudy and windy sky of like nature with itself. Far be it from me, then, to say, "These things should not be." For if I could see nothing but these, I should indeed desire something better—but still I ought to praise Thee, if only for these created things. For that Thou art to be praised is shown from the fact that "earth, dragons, and all deeps; fire, and hail, snow and vapors, stormy winds fulfilling thy word; mountains, and all hills, fruitful trees, and all cedars; beasts and all cattle; creeping things, and flying fowl; things of the earth, and all people; princes, and all judges of the earth; both young men and maidens, old men and children" [Ps. 148:7–12] praise Thy name! But seeing also that in heaven "all Thy angels praise Thee, O God, praise Thee in the heights, and all Thy hosts, sun and moon, all stars and light, the heavens of heavens, and the waters that are above the heavens" [Ps. 148:1–4] praise Thy name—seeing this, I say, I no longer desire a better world, because my thought ranged over all, and with a sounder judgment I reflected that the things above were better than those below, yet that all creation together was better than the higher things alone.

### THE "AESTHETIC" THEME AND SIN[5]

If it is said: It would not have been difficult or laborious for Almighty God to have seen to it that all His creatures should have observed their proper

---

[4]*Confessions*, Bk. VII, Chap. 13, translated by A. C. Outler in *Augustine: Confessions and Enchiridion*, Library of Christian Classics, Vol. VII (Philadelphia: The Westminster Press, 1955).

[5]*On Free Will*, Bk. III, Chaps. 24–26, translated by J. H. S. Burleigh in *Augustine: Earlier Writings*, Library of Christian Classics, Vol. VI (Philadelphia: The Westminster Press, 1953).

order so that none of them should have come to misery. If He is omnipotent that would not have been beyond His power; and if He is good He would not have grudged it; this is my answer. The order of creatures proceeds from top to bottom by just grades, so that it is the remark of envy to say: That creature should not exist, and equally so to say: *That* one should be different. It is wrong to wish that anything should be like another thing higher in the scale, for it has its being, perfect in its degree, and nothing ought to be added to it. He who says that a thing ought to be different from what it is, either wants to add something to a higher creature already perfect, in which case he lacks moderation and justice; or he wants to destroy the lower creature, and is thereby wicked and grudging. Whoever says that any creature ought not to be is no less wicked and grudging, for he wants an inferior creature not to exist, which he really ought to praise. For example, the moon is certainly far inferior to the sun in the brightness of its light, but in its own way it is beautiful, adorns earthly darkness, and is suited to nocturnal uses. For all these things he should admit that it is worthy of all praise in its own order. If he denies that, he is foolish and contentious. Anyone who said that there should be no light would feel that he deserved to be laughed at. How then will he dare to say there should not be a moon? If instead of saying that the moon should not exist he said that the moon ought to be like the sun, what he is really saying without knowing it is, not that there should be no moon, but that there should be two suns. In this there is a double error. He wants to add something to the perfection of the universe, seeing he desires another sun. But he also wants to take something from that perfection, seeing he wants to do away with the moon.

Perhaps he will reply that he is not complaining about the moon, because though its light is less, it is not unhappy; his trouble does not concern the lack of lustre in souls but their misery. Let him carefully consider that so far as concerns the brightness of the moon and the sun there is no question of happiness or unhappiness. Though these are celestial bodies, they are nonetheless bodies so far as their light is concerned. For it is perceived by the corporeal eyes. Corporeal things in themselves, as such, cannot be happy or unhappy, although they can be the bodies of happy or unhappy creatures. But the analogy suggested from the celestial luminaries teaches us this lesson. When you contemplate the differences between bodies and observe that some are brighter than others, it is wrong to ask that the dimmer ones should be done away or made equal to the brighter ones. All must be contemplated in the light of the perfection of the universe; and you will see that all differences in brightness contribute to the perfection of the whole. You will not be able to imagine a perfect universe unless it contains some greater things and some smaller in perfect relation one to the other. Similarly you must consider the differences between souls. In them also you will discover that the misery you lament has this advantage. The fact that there are souls which ought to be miserable because they willed to be sinful contributes to the perfection of the universe. So far is it from being the case that God ought not to have made such souls, that He ought to be praised for having made other creatures far inferior to miserable souls.

But one who does not quite understand what has been said may have this to urge against our argument: If our being miserable completes the perfection of the universe, it will lose something of its perfection if we should become eternally happy. If the soul does not come to misery save by sinning, our sins also are necessary to the perfection of the universe which God has made. How then does He justly punish sins without which His creation could be neither complete nor perfect? The answer is: Neither the sins nor the misery are necessary to the perfection of the universe, but souls as such are necessary which have power to sin if they so will, and become miserable if they sin. If misery persisted after their sins had been abolished, or if there were misery before there were sins, then it might be right to say that the order and government of the universe were at fault. Again, if there were sins and no consequent misery, that order is equally dishonored by lack of equity. But since there is happiness for those who do not sin, the universe is perfect; and it is no less perfect because there is misery for sinners. Because there are souls whose sins are followed by misery and whose righteous conduct is followed by happiness—because it contains all kinds of natures—the universe is always complete and perfect. Sin and its punishment are not natural objects but states of natural objects, the one voluntary, the other penal. The voluntary state of being sinful is dishonorable. Hence the penal state is imposed to bring it into order, and is therefore in itself not dishonorable. Indeed it compels the dishonorable state to become harmonized with the honor of the universe, so that the penalty of sin corrects the dishonor of sin.

# St. Anselm

St. Anselm (1033--1109) was one of the greatest of Christian philosophical theologians. His subtle and profound ontological argument for the existence of God is still a subject of keen debate.

# 3

# The Ontological Argument for the Existence of God

## The Proslogion, Chaps. II–IV

### CHAPTER II

### THAT GOD TRULY IS

O Lord, you who give understanding to faith, so far as you know it to be beneficial, give me to understand that you are as we believe, and that you are what we believe.

We believe that you are something than which nothing greater can be conceived.

But is there any such nature, since "the fool has said in his heart: God is not"?

However, when this same fool hears what I say, when he hears of this something than which nothing greater can be conceived, he at least understands what he hears.

What he understands stands in relation to his understanding, even if he does not understand that it exists. For it is one thing for a thing to stand in relation to our understanding; it is another thing for us to understand that it really exists. For instance, when a painter imagines what he is about to paint, he has it in relation to his understanding. However, he does not yet understand that it exists, because he has not yet made it. After he paints it, then he both has it in relation to his understanding and understands that it exists. Therefore even the fool is convinced that something than which nothing

Reprinted by permission of Macmillan Publishing Company from Anselm, *The Proslogion*, from Chapters II–IV; Gaunilo, *On Behalf of the Fool*; Anselm, *Reply*; translated by Arthur C. McGill from Arthur C. McGill and John Hick, eds., *The Many-Faced Argument* (New York: The Macmillan Co., 1967). Copyright © 1967 by John H. Hick and Arthur C. McGill.

greater can be conceived at least stands in relation to his understanding, because when he hears of it he understands it, and whatever he understands stands in relation to his understanding.[1]

However, that than which a greater cannot be conceived can certainly not stand only in relation to the understanding. For if it at least stood only in relation to the understanding, it could be conceived to be also in reality, and this would be something greater. Therefore, if that than which a greater cannot be conceived only stood in relation to the understanding, then that than which a greater cannot be conceived would be something than which a greater can be conceived. Obviously this is impossible.

Therefore, something than which a greater cannot be conceived undoubtedly both stands in relation to the understanding and exists in reality.

CHAPTER III

## THAT IT IS IMPOSSIBLE TO CONCEIVE THAT GOD IS NOT

This so truly is that it is impossible to think of it as not existing.

It can be conceived to be something such that we cannot conceive of it as not existing.

This is greater than something which we can conceive of as not existing.

Therefore, if that than which a greater cannot be conceived could be conceived not to be, we would have an impossible contradiction: that than which a greater cannot be conceived would not be that than which a greater cannot be conceived.

Therefore something than which a greater cannot be conceived so truly is that it is impossible even to conceive of it as not existing.

This is you, O Lord our God. You so truly are that you cannot be thought not to be. And rightly so.

For if some mind could conceive of something better than you, the creature would become superior to its Creator and would judge its Creator.

This is obviously absurd. Indeed, whatever else there is, except for you alone, can be conceived not to be.

---

[1]The meaning of Anselm's phrase *esse in intellectu* has been the subject of much discussion. I have found little evidence that the word *intellectus* ever suggested to Anselm, as it does to us, an organ (such as the mind) or a faculty (such as the intellect). It was chiefly the noun form of the verb *intelligere*, and signified the act of understanding. "To be *in intellectu*" therefore does not mean to be located "in the intellect," inside the human head, as if this were a place, but to be located in relation to human thinking, to be present to the human act of understanding. See Adolf Kolping, *Anselm's Proslogion—Beweis der Existenz Gottes* (Bonn, 1939), pp. 114f. In moving from *intelligere* to *esse in intellectu*, Anselm is simply shifting the focus from the human activity, as related to some object, to the presence of that object to the human activity, still without prejudicing the question of the object's actual existence one way or the other. To avoid the peculiar modern overtones associated with the phrase "to be in the understanding," *esse in intellectu* is here translated "to stand in relation to the understanding."—TRANSLATOR

Therefore you alone, of all things, exist in the truest and greatest way (*verissime et maxime esse*), for nothing else so truly exists and therefore everything else has less being.

Why, then, did the fool say in his heart: "God is not," since it is so obvious to the rational mind that you exist supremely above all things? Why, because he is a dim-witted fool.

CHAPTER IV

## HOW THE FOOL SAID IN HIS HEART
## WHAT CANNOT BE CONCEIVED

How was the fool able to "say in his heart" what he was unable to conceive? Or how was it that he could not conceive what he said in his heart? For to "say in one's heart" and to "conceive" are the same thing.

However, if—or rather because—he really did conceive of it (since he said it in his heart) and yet did not really say it in his heart (since he was unable to conceive of it), then there must be more than one way for something to be said in one's heart, or to be conceived.

Indeed, a thing is conceived of in one way when the word signifying it is thought; in another way when the very thing itself is understood. Accordingly God can be conceived not to be in the first way, but not at all in the second.

[For no one who understands what fire and water are]² can think that the reality of fire is the reality of water. At the level of the words, however, this confusion is possible.

No one, therefore, who understands what God is can think that God is not. It is possible, however, for him to say this word in his heart, while giving it either no meaning at all or some alien meaning. God is that than which a greater cannot be conceived. Whoever understands this correctly at least understands that he exists in such a way that even for thought he cannot not exist.

Therefore whoever understands that God is so cannot even conceive that He is not.

My thanksgiving to you, good Lord, my thanksgiving to you. For what I first believed through your giving I now understand through your illumination, so that now, even if I did not want to believe that you exist, I would be unable not to understand it.

---

²Recent manuscript investigations have established that these words in square brackets were not part of Anselm's text, but were interpolated later.—TRANSLATOR

# Gaunilo and Anselm—Criticism and Reply

Of the nineteen extant manuscripts which give us Chapters II–IV of the *Proslogion*, almost half also contain a criticism of Anselm's argument written by one of his contemporaries, and his own reply. Two of the manuscripts attribute the criticism to a monk Gaunilo of the French cloister at Marmoutiere, but nothing is known about him.

According to Gaunilo, Anselm's argument consists of two points. First, anyone who denies God at least understands the phrase "that than which nothing greater can be conceived," so that this stands in relation to his understanding. Secondly, reasoning will show him that this cannot stand only in relation to his understanding but must also exist in reality, for otherwise it would not be "that than which nothing greater can be conceived." Gaunilo attacks each of these steps in turn, speaking in the first person "on behalf of the fool."

Anselm's reply is not a sustained discussion, especially in its later chapters, but has the appearance of a series of notes, each in answer to a particular point made by Gaunilo. The reply is therefore easier to understand when each section of it is placed beside the appropriate passages in Gaunilo's criticism. The translation below follows this arrangement. The page references below refer to Dom Schmitt's Latin edition.

Against the Reasoning that if "That Than Which Nothing Greater Can Be Conceived" Is Understood It Must Also Exist.

*1. Gaunilo argues that for something to stand in relation to the understanding cannot establish its real existence, if that something is doubted.*

## GAUNILO
*Para. 5 (p. 127.25–p. 128.13)*

That this exists necessarily in reality is proved to me in this way: if this does not exist, whatever is in reality will be greater than it, in which case that which has just been proved at least to stand in relation to my understanding will not be greater than all things.

To this I reply. If it is said that this stands in relation to the understanding as something which cannot be conceived on the basis of the truth of any real thing, I do not deny that it does stand in relation to the understanding in this way. However, because it cannot possess real existence simply by standing in relation to the understanding, I certainly do not concede that it really exists—at least not until it is proved to me by an indubitable argument.

He who says that this exists because otherwise that which is greater than all would not be greater than all, does not sufficiently attend to what is being said. I do not yet say—on the contrary I deny or doubt—that this is greater than any real thing. I concede to it no other reality (if this can be called "reality") than of something which is absolutely unknown to the mind, but which the mind tries to conceive of on the basis of a word merely heard. Therefore, how is it proved to me that this "greater" exists in reality, simply because it is held to be greater than all things, when I deny or doubt that this is to be held at all? I deny or doubt it so completely, in fact, that in my view this "greater" does not stand in relation to my understanding or to conception, except in the way in which many doubtful and uncertain things stand there.

It first must be made certain to me that this "greater" is actually somewhere, and only then, from the fact that it is greater than all things, will there be no doubt that it subsists in itself.

### ANSELM

I said that, even if it only stood in relation to the understanding, it could at least be conceived to be also in reality, and that this is greater. Therefore, if it only stood in relation to the understanding, then "that than which a greater cannot be conceived" would be that than which a greater can be conceived. What, I ask, could be more logical? For if it only stood in relation to the understanding, could it not be conceived to be in reality also? And if so, then does not anyone who conceives of this existing also in reality conceive of something greater than that which only stands in relation to the understanding? What therefore could be more logical than this: if "that than which a greater cannot be conceived" only stands in relation to the understanding, then it is that than which a greater can be conceived? But certainly "that than which a greater can be conceived" does not stand in relation to any understanding as "that than which a greater cannot be conceived."

Does it not therefore follow that if "that than which a greater cannot be conceived" stands in relation to *any* understanding, it does not only stand in relation to the understanding? For if it only stood in relation to the understanding alone, it would then be that than which a greater can be conceived, which is a contradiction (Chap. II, p. 132.22–133.2).

• • •

"That which cannot possibly not be" is obviously something that can be conceived and understood. He who conceives of this conceives of something greater than he who conceives of that which has the possibility of not being. Therefore, while he is conceiving of "that than which a greater cannot be conceived," if he conceives that it has the possibility of not being, he is obviously not conceiving of that than which a greater cannot be conceived. However, the same thing cannot be conceived and not be conceived at the same time. Therefore he who conceives of "that than which a greater cannot be conceived" is not conceiving of what can, but of what cannot possibly not be. For that reason what he is conceiving of must necessarily exist, because whatever is able not to exist is not that of which he is conceiving (Chap. IX, p. 138.19–27).

*2. Gaunilo argues that if in the case of God "to be the best conceivable" entails "to exist," then it can also be demonstrated that the best conceivable island must exist.*

### GAUNILO
### *Para. 6 (p. 128.14–32)*

Consider this example. Certain people say that somewhere in the ocean there is an island which they call the "Lost Island," because of the difficulty or, rather, the impossibility of finding what does not exist. They say that it is more abundantly filled with inestimable riches and delights than the Isles of the Blessed, and that although it has no owner or inhabitant, it excels all the lands that men inhabit taken together in the unceasing abundance of its fertility.

When someone tells me that there is such an island, I easily understand what is being said, for there is nothing difficult here. Suppose, however, as a consequence of this, he then goes on to say: you cannot doubt that this island, more excellent than all lands, actually exists somewhere in reality, because it undoubtedly stands in relation to your understanding. Since it is more excellent, not simply to stand in relation to the understanding, but to be in reality as well, therefore this island must necessarily be in reality. Otherwise any other land that exists in reality would be more excellent than this island, and this island, which you understood to be the most excellent of all lands, would then not be the most excellent.

If, I repeat, someone should wish by this argument to demonstrate to me that this island truly exists and is no longer to be doubted, I would think he were joking; or, if I accepted the argument, I do not know whom I would regard as the greater fool, me for accepting it or him for supposing that he had proved the existence of this island with any kind of certainty. He should first show that this excellent island exists as a genuine and undeniably real thing, and not leave it standing in relation to my understanding as a false or uncertain something.

### ANSELM

My reasoning, you claim, is as if someone should say that there is an island in the ocean, which surpasses the whole earth in its fertility, but which is called a "Lost Island" because of the difficulty, or even impossibility, of finding something that does not exist, and as if he should then argue that no one can doubt that it actually does exist because the words describing it are easily understood.

I can confidently say that if anyone discovers for me something existing either in fact or in thought alone, other than "that than which a greater cannot be thought," and is able to apply the logic of my argument to it, I shall find that lost island for him and shall give it to him as something which he will never lose again (Chap. III, p. 133.3–9).

*3. Gaunilo argues that since the existence of "that than which nothing greater can be conceived" has not been proved, it can be conceived not to exist.*

## GAUNILO
### Para. 7 (p. 129.1–10)

When it is asserted to the fool [in *Pros.* III] that this "greater than all things" is such that even to thought it cannot not be, and yet when this is proved to him on no other grounds than that otherwise this greater than all things would not be greater than all things, he can give the same answer and reply: When did *I* ever say that such a being, one that is "greater than all things," exists in reality, so that from this you could prove to me that it exists so fully in reality that it cannot be conceived not to be? First of all it should be proved by some most certain argument that some superior reality, that is, a nature which is greater and better than everything that is, actually exists. From this we can then prove all the other qualities which must not be lacking from that which is greater and better than all things.

## ANSELM[3]

It is now obvious, however, that "that than which a greater cannot be conceived" cannot be conceived not to be, because its existing has such manifest truthfulness. Otherwise, it would not exist at all.

Let us suppose that there is someone who says that he does conceive that this does not exist. In my view, when he is conceiving in this way, he is either conceiving of that than which a greater cannot be conceived, or he is not conceiving of it. If he is not conceiving of it, then it is not this which he thinks does not exist. On the other hand, if he is really conceiving of it, he at least conceives of something which cannot be conceived not to be. For if it could be conceived not to be, it could also be conceived to have a beginning and an end. But this is impossible [for "that than which a greater cannot be

---

[3]In the manuscripts, this passage immediately follows Anselm's remarks on the Lost Island, and in the view of some thinkers it applies to this objection. (See below, pp. 500–01.)

conceived"]. Therefore whoever really conceives of this conceives of something which cannot be conceived not to be. Whoever really conceives of it, then, does not in fact conceive that it is not. Otherwise he would be conceiving of something which cannot be conceived. Therefore "that than which a greater cannot be conceived" cannot be conceived not to be (Chap. III, p. 133.10–20).

4. *Gaunilo argues that it should be said that God's existence cannot be "understood," not that it cannot be "conceived."*

### GAUNILO
#### Para. 7 (p. 129.10–19)

When it is said that this supreme reality cannot be "conceived" (*cogitari*) not to be, it would probably be better to say that it cannot be "understood" (*intelligi*) not to be, or even that it cannot be "understood" to be capable of not being.

According to the proper meaning of this word "understand," false matters cannot be understood, though they can certainly be conceived, just as the fool conceived that God is not. I "know" (*scio*) most certainly that I am, but I also know nonetheless than I am capable of not being. I "understand" without any doubt that the greatest reality which is God both is and cannot not be. However, I do not know whether I can "conceive" of my not existing at the time when I "know" most certainly that I do exist. If I can do this, why can I not also "conceive" as not existing whatever else I "know" to exist with the same certainty [including God]? If I cannot do this, however, then the impossibility of being conceived not to exist will not be the property of God alone.

### ANSELM

Further still you say: while it is said that this greatest reality cannot be "conceived" not to be, it would probably be better to say that its non-existence, or even the possibility of its non-existence, cannot be "understood."

It is more correct, however, to say that this cannot be "conceived." For you yourself say that according to the proper meaning of this word nothing false can be "understood." Therefore, if I had said that this supreme reality itself could not be "understood" not to be, you would probably have made three objections: that nothing which is can be "understood" not to be, for the non-being of that which is is something false [and therefore not a proper object of "understanding"]; that the impossibility of being understood not to be is therefore not a property peculiar to God [but is characteristic of every object of "understanding"]; and finally, that *if* something which most certainly exists can be "understood" not to be, in the same way other certain things can also be "understood" not to be.

If one examines the matter closely, these objections cannot be made against "conceiving." For even if there is nothing existing which can be "understood" not to be, nevertheless *everything* can be "conceived" not to be, except that which is the highest. In fact all those things—and only those things—can be conceived not to be which have a beginning, or an end, or a combination of parts, and, as I have already said, which do not exist completely everywhere and always. But that alone cannot be conceived not to be which has neither beginning nor end nor combination of parts, and which thought finds existing completely always and everywhere.

You must realize that even though you know with complete certainty that you exist, you can "conceive" of yourself as not existing. It surprises me that you say that you do not know this. For we "conceive" of the non-existence of many things which we "know" to exist, and we "conceive" of the existence of many things which we "know" not to exist. We do this, not by making a real judgment, but by imagining that these things are as we conceive of them. In this sense, we can "conceive" that something is not when we "know" that it is, because at one and the same time we can "conceive" of the former and "know" the latter. In another sense, we cannot "conceive" that something is not when we "know" that it is, because we cannot conceive of something as both existing and not existing at the same time.

Therefore, if anyone distinguishes between these two meanings [of "conceive"—conceiving within the limits of what he knows to be actual (meaning A), and conceiving by his own imaginative effort (meaning B)], he will understand that whenever something is "known" to be, it cannot be "conceived" not to be [in the sense of meaning A]; and yet that whatever is, except that than which a greater cannot be conceived, even if it is "known" to be, can still be "conceived" not to be [in the sense of meaning B]. Therefore it is the peculiar property of God that he cannot be "conceived" not to be [in the sense of meaning B], while many things so far as they exist, cannot be "conceived" not to be [in the sense of meaning A] (Chap. IV, p. 133.21–134.19).

# St. Thomas Aquinas

St. Thomas Aquinas (1224/5–1274), the great systematizer of Christian thought in terms of Aristotelian philosophy, has long been regarded by the Roman Catholic Church as its most authoritative theologian and by Christendom in general as one of its most massive and powerful minds.

# 4

# *Five Ways to Prove the Existence of God*

FIRST ARTICLE

*WHETHER THE EXISTENCE OF GOD IS SELF-EVIDENT?*

*We proceed thus to the First Article:—*

*Objection* 1. It seems that the existence of God is self-evident. For those things are said to be self-evident to us the knowledge of which exists naturally in us, as we can see in regard to first principles. But as Damascene says, "the knowledge of God is naturally implanted in all." Therefore the existence of God is self-evident.

*Obj.* 2. Further, those things are said to be self-evident which are known as soon as the terms are known, which the Philosopher [Aristotle] says is true of the first principles of demonstration. Thus, when the nature of a whole and of a part is known, it is at once recognized that every whole is greater than its part. But as soon as the signification of the name *God* is understood, it is at once seen that God exists. For by this name is signified that thing than which nothing greater can be conceived. But that which exists actually and mentally is greater than that which exists only mentally. Therefore, since as soon as the name *God* is understood it exists mentally, it also follows that it exists actually. Therefore the proposition *God exists* is self-evident.

*Obj.* 3. Further, the existence of truth is self-evident. For whoever denies the existence of truth grants that truth does not exist: and, if truth does not exist, then the proposition *Truth does not exist* is true: and if there is anything true, there must be truth. But God is truth itself: "I am the way, the truth, and the life" (John, 14:6). Therefore *God exists* is self-evident.

*On the contrary,* No one can mentally admit the opposite of what is self-evident, as the Philosopher states concerning the first principles of demonstration. But the opposite of the proposition *God is* can be mentally admitted: "The fool said in his heart, There is no God" (Ps. 52:1). Therefore, that God exists is not self-evident.

*I answer that,* A thing can be self-evident in either of two ways: on the one hand, self-evident in itself, though not to us; on the other, self-evident in itself, and to us. A proposition is self-evident because the predicate is included in the essence of the subject: e.g., *Man is an animal,* for animal is contained in the essence of man. If, therefore, the essence of the predicate and subject be known to all, the proposition will be self-evident to all; as is clear with regard to the first principles of demonstration, the terms of which are certain common notions that no one is ignorant of, such as being and non-being, whole and part, and the like. If, however, there are some to whom the essence of the predicate and subject is unknown, the proposition will be self-evident in itself, but not to those who do not know the meaning of the predicate and subject of the proposition. Therefore, it happens, as Boethius says, that there are some notions of the mind which are common and self-evident only to the learned, as that incorporeal substances are not in space. Therefore I say that this proposition, *God exists,* of itself is self-evident, for the predicate is the same as the subject, because God is His own existence as will be hereafter shown. Now because we do not know the essence of God, the proposition is not self-evident to us, but needs to be demonstrated by things that are more known to us, though less known in their nature—namely, by His effects.

*Reply Obj.* 1. To know that God exists in a general and confused way is implanted in us by nature, inasmuch as God is man's beatitude. For man naturally desires happiness, and what is naturally desired by man is naturally known by him. This, however, is not to know absolutely that God exists; just as to know that someone is approaching is not the same as to know that Peter is approaching, even though it is Peter who is approaching; for there are many who imagine that man's perfect good, which is happiness, consists in riches, and others in pleasures, and others in something else.

*Reply Obj.* 2. Perhaps not everyone who hears this name *God* understands it to signify something than which nothing greater can be thought, seeing that some have believed God to be a body. Yet, granted that everyone understands that by this name *God* is signified something than which nothing greater can be thought, nevertheless, it does not therefore follow that he understands that what the name signifies exists actually, but only that it exists mentally. Nor can it be argued that it actually exists, unless it be admitted that there actually exists something than which nothing greater can be thought; and this precisely is not admitted by those who hold that God does not exist.

*Reply Obj.* 3. The existence of truth in general is self-evident, but the existence of a Primal Truth is not self-evident to us.

SECOND ARTICLE

## WHETHER IT CAN BE DEMONSTRATED THAT GOD EXISTS?

*We proceed thus to the Second Article:—*
*Objection* 1. It seems that the existence of God cannot be demonstrated. For it is an article of faith that God exists. But what is of faith cannot be demonstrated, because a demonstration produces scientific knowledge, whereas faith is of the unseen, as is clear from the Apostle (Heb. 11:1). Therefore it cannot be demonstrated that God exists.

*Obj.* 2. Further, essence is the middle term of demonstration. But we cannot know in what God's essence consists, but solely in what it does not consist, as Damascene says. Therefore we cannot demonstrate that God exists.

*Obj.* 3. Further, if the existence of God were demonstrated, this could only be from His effects. But His effects are not proportioned to Him, since He is infinite and His effects are finite, and between the finite and infinite there is no proportion. Therefore, since a cause cannot be demonstrated by an effect not proportioned to it, it seems that the existence of God cannot be demonstrated.

*On the contrary,* The Apostle says: "The invisible things of Him are clearly seen, being understood by the things that are made" (Rom. 1:20). But this would not be unless the existence of God could be demonstrated through the things that are made; for the first thing we must know of anything is whether it exists.

*I answer that,* Demonstration can be made in two ways: One is through the cause, and is called *propter quid,* and this is to argue from what is prior absolutely. The other is through the effect, and is called a demonstration *quia;* this is to argue from what is prior relatively only to us. When an effect is better known to us than its cause, from the effect we proceed to the knowledge of the cause. And from every effect the existence of its proper cause can be demonstrated, so long as its effects are better known to us; because, since every effect depends upon its cause, if the effect exists, the cause must preexist. Hence the existence of God, insofar as it is not self-evident to us, can be demonstrated from those of His effects which are known to us.

*Reply Obj.* 1. The existence of God and other like truths about God, which can be known by natural reason, are not articles of faith, but are preambles to the articles; for faith presupposes natural knowledge, even as grace presupposes nature and perfection the perfectible. Nevertheless, there is nothing to prevent a man, who cannot grasp a proof, from accepting, as a matter of faith, something which in itself is capable of being scientifically known and demonstrated.

*Reply Obj.* 2. When the existence of a cause is demonstrated from an effect, this effect takes the place of the definition of the cause in proving the cause's existence. This is especially the case in regard to God, because, in order to prove the existence of anything, it is necessary to accept as a middle term the meaning of the name, and not its essence, for the question of its essence follows on the question of its existence. Now the names given to God are derived from His effects, as will be later shown. Consequently, in demonstrating the existence of God from His effects, we may take for the middle term the meaning of the name *God*.

*Reply Obj.* 3. From effects not proportioned to the cause no perfect knowledge of that cause can be obtained. Yet from every effect the existence of the cause can be clearly demonstrated, and so we can demonstrate the existence of God from His effects; though from them we cannot know God perfectly as He is in His essence.

THIRD ARTICLE

## WHETHER GOD EXISTS?

*We proceed thus to the Third Article:—*

*Objection* 1. It seems that God does not exist; because if one of two contraries be infinite, the other would be altogether destroyed. But the name *God* means that He is infinite goodness. If, therefore, God existed, there would be no evil discoverable; but there is evil in the world. Therefore God does not exist.

*Obj.* 2. Further, it is superfluous to suppose that what can be accounted for by a few principles has been produced by many. But it seems that everything we see in the world can be accounted for by other principles, supposing God did not exist. For all natural things can be reduced to one principle, which is nature; and all voluntary things can be reduced to one principle, which is human reason, or will. Therefore there is no need to suppose God's existence.

*On the contrary,* it is said in the person of God: "I am Who am" (Exod. 3:14).

*I answer that,* The existence of God can be proved in five ways.

The first and more manifest way is the argument from motion. It is certain, and evident to our senses, that in the world some things are in motion. Now whatever is moved is moved by another, for nothing can be moved except it is in potentiality to that towards which it is moved; whereas a thing moves inasmuch as it is in act. For motion is nothing else than the reduction of something from potentiality to actuality. But nothing can be reduced from potentiality to actuality, except by something in a state of actuality. Thus that which is actually hot, as fire, makes wood, which is potentially hot, to be actually hot, and thereby moves and changes it. Now it is not possible that the same thing should be at once in actuality and potentiality in the same respect, but only in different respects. For what is actually hot cannot simultaneously be potentially hot; but it is simultaneously potentially cold. It is therefore impossible that in the same respect and in the same way a thing should be both mover and moved, i.e., that it should move itself. Therefore, whatever is moved must be moved by another. If that by which it is moved be itself moved, then this also must needs be moved by another, and that by another again. But this cannot go on to infinity, because then there would be no first mover, and, consequently, no other mover, seeing that subsequent movers move only inasmuch as they are moved by the first mover; as the staff moves only because it is moved by the hand. Therefore it is necessary to arrive at a first mover, moved by no other; and this everyone understands to be God.

The second way is from the nature of efficient cause. In the world of sensible things we find there is an order of efficient causes. There is no case known (neither is it, indeed, possible) in which a thing is found to be the efficient cause of itself; for so it would be prior to itself, which is impossible. Now in efficient causes it is not possible to go on to infinity, because in all efficient causes following in order, the first is the cause of the intermediate cause, and the intermediate is the cause of the ultimate cause, whether the intermediate cause be several, or one only. Now to take away the cause is to take away the effect. Therefore, if there be no first cause among efficient causes, there will be no ultimate, nor any intermediate, cause. But if in efficient causes it is possible to go on to infinity, there will be no first efficient cause, neither will there be an ultimate effect, nor any intermediate efficient causes; all of which is plainly false. Therefore it is necessary to admit a first efficient cause, to which everyone gives the name of God.

The third way is taken from possibility and necessity, and runs thus. We find in nature things that are possible to be and not to be, since they are found to be generated, and to be corrupted, and consequently, it is possible for them to be and not to be. But it is impossible for these always to exist, for that which can not-be at some time is not. Therefore, if everything can not-be, then at one time there was nothing in existence. Now if this were true, even now there would be nothing in existence, because that which does not exist begins to exist only through something already existing. Therefore, if at one time nothing was in existence, it would have been impossible for anything to have begun to exist; and thus even now nothing would be in existence—which is absurd. Therefore, not all beings are merely possible, but there must exist something the existence of which is necessary. But every necessary thing either has its necessity caused by another, or not. Now it is impossible to go on to infinity in necessary things which have their necessity caused by another, as has been already proved in regard to efficient causes. Therefore we cannot but admit the existence of some being having of itself its own necessity, and not receiving it from another, but rather causing in others their necessity. This all men speak of as God.

The fourth way is taken from the gradation to be found in things. Among beings there are some more and some less good, true, noble, and the like. But *more* and *less* are predicated of different things according as they resemble in their different ways something which is the maximum, as a thing is said to be hotter according as it more nearly resembles that which is hottest; so that there is something which is truest, something best, something noblest, and, consequently, something which is most being, for those things that are greatest in truth are greatest in being, as it is written in *Metaphysics* II. Now the maximum in any genus is the cause of all in that genus, as fire, which is the maximum of heat, is the cause of all hot things, as is said in the same book. Therefore there must also be something which is to all beings the cause of their being, goodness, and every other perfection; and this we call God.

The fifth way is taken from the governance of the world. We see that things which lack knowledge, such as natural bodies, act for an end, and this is evident from their acting always, or nearly always, in the same way, so as to obtain the best result. Hence it is plain that they achieve their end, not fortuitously, but designedly. Now whatever lacks knowledge cannot move towards an end, unless it be directed by some being endowed with knowledge and intelligence; as the arrow is directed by the archer. Therefore some intelligent being exists by whom all natural things are directed to their end; and this being we call God.

*Reply Obj.* 1. As Augustine says: "Since God is the highest good, He would not allow any evil to exist in His works, unless His omnipotence and goodness were such as to bring good even out of evil" (*Enchiridion*, XI). This is part of the infinite goodness of God, that He should allow evil to exist, and out of it produce good.

*Reply Obj.* 2. Since nature works for a determinate end under the direction of a higher agent, whatever is done by nature must be traced back to God as to its first cause. So likewise whatever is done voluntarily must be traced back to some higher cause other than human reason and will, since these can change and fail; for all things that are changeable and capable of defect must be traced back to an immovable and self-necessary first principle, as has been shown.

# 5

# *The Doctrine of Analogy*

CHAPTER 28

*ON THE DIVINE PERFECTION*

Although the things that exist and live are more perfect than the things that merely exist, nevertheless, God, Who is not other than His being, is a universally perfect being. And I call *universally perfect* that to which the excellence of no genus is lacking.

Every excellence in any given thing belongs to it according to its being. For man would have no excellence as a result of his wisdom unless through it he were wise. So, too, with the other excellences. Hence, the mode of a thing's excellence is according to the mode of its being. For a thing is said to be more or less excellent according as its being is limited to a certain greater or lesser mode of excellence. Therefore, if there is something to which the whole power of being belongs, it can lack no excellence that is proper to some thing. But for a thing that is its own being it is proper to be according to the whole power of being. For example, if there were a separately existing whiteness, it could not lack any of the power of whiteness. For a given white thing lacks something of the power of whiteness through a defect in the receiver of the whiteness, which receives it according to its mode and perhaps not according to the whole power of whiteness. God, therefore, Who is His being, as we have proved above, has being according to the whole power of being itself. Hence, He cannot lack any excellence that belongs to any given thing.

But just as every excellence and perfection is found in a thing according as that thing *is*, so every defect is found in it according as in some way it *is not*. Now, just as God has being wholly, so non-being is wholly absent from Him. For as a thing has being, in that way is it removed from non-being. Hence, all defect is absent from God. He is, therefore, universally perfect.

Those things that merely exist are not imperfect because of an imperfection in absolute being. For they do not possess being according to its whole power; rather, they participate in it through a certain particular and most imperfect mode.

Furthermore, everything that is imperfect must be preceded by something perfect. Thus, the seed is from the animal or the plant. The first being must, therefore, be most perfect. But we have shown that God is the first being. He is, therefore, most perfect.

Again, each thing is perfect according as it is in act, and imperfect according as it is in potency and lacking act. Hence, that which is in no way in potency, but is pure act, must be most perfect. Such, however, is God. God is, therefore, most perfect.

Nothing, moreover, acts except as it is in act. Hence, action follows the mode of act in the agent. It is therefore impossible that an effect brought forth by an action be of a more excellent act than is the act of the agent. On the other hand, it is possible that the act of the effect be less perfect than the act of the efficient cause, since an action can become weakened through the effect in which it terminates. Now, in the genus of the efficient cause there is a reduction to one cause, called God, as is evident from what we have said; and from this cause, as we shall show later on, all things come. Hence, it is necessary that whatever is found in act in anything whatever must be found in God in a more eminent way than in that thing itself. But the converse is not true. God, therefore, is most perfect.

In every genus, furthermore, there is something that is most perfect for that genus, acting as a measure for all other things in the genus. For each thing is shown to be more or less perfect according as it approaches more or less to the measure of its genus. Thus, *white* is said to be the measure among all colors, and the *virtuous man* among all men. Now, the measure of all beings cannot be other than God, Who is His own being. No perfection, consequently, that is appropriate to this or that thing is lacking to Him; otherwise, He would not be the common measure of all things.

This is why, when Moses asked to see the divine countenance or glory, he received this reply from the Lord: "I will show thee all good," as it is written in Exodus (33:18, 19); by which the Lord gave Moses to understand that the fullness of all goodness was in Him. Dionysius likewise says: "God does not exist in a certain way; He possesses, and this before all others, all being within Himself absolutely and limitlessly."[1]

We must note, however, that *perfection* cannot be attributed to God appropriately if we consider the signification of the name according to its origin; for it does not seem that what is not made [*factum*] can be called perfect [*perfectum*]. But everything that comes to be is brought forth from potency to act and from non-being to being when it has been made. That is why it is rightly said to be perfect, as being completely made, at that moment when

---

[1]Pseudo-Dionysius, *De divinis nominibus*, Bk. V. Chap. 4.

the potency is wholly reduced to act, so that it retains no non-being but has a completed being. By a certain extension of the name, consequently, *perfect* is said not only of that which by way of becoming reaches a completed act, but also of that which, without any making whatever, is in complete act. It is thus that, following the words of Matthew (5:48), we say that God is perfect: "Be ye perfect as also your heavenly Father is perfect."

CHAPTER 29

## ON THE LIKENESS OF CREATURES TO GOD

In the light of what we have said, we are able to consider how a likeness to God is and is not possible in things.

Effects that fall short of their causes do not agree with them in name and nature. Yet, some likeness must be found between them, since it belongs to the nature of action that an agent produce its like, since each thing acts according as it is in act. The form of an effect, therefore, is certainly found in some measure in a transcending cause, but according to another mode and another way. For this reason the cause is called an *equivocal cause*. Thus, the sun causes heat among these sublunary bodies by acting according as it is in act. Hence, the heat generated by the sun must bear some likeness to the active power of the sun, through which heat is caused in this sublunary world; and because of this heat the sun is said to be hot, even though not in one and the same way. And so the sun is said to be somewhat like those things in which it produces its effects as an efficient cause. Yet the sun is also unlike all these things insofar as such effects do not possess heat and the like in the same way as they are found in the sun. So, too, God gave things all their perfections and thereby is both like and unlike all of them.

Hence it is that Sacred Scripture recalls the likeness between God and creatures, as when it is said in Genesis (1:26): "Let us make man to our image and likeness." At times the likeness is denied, as in the text of Isaiah (40:18): "To whom then have you likened God, and what image will you make for Him?" or in the Psalm (82:1): "O God, who shall be like to Thee?"

Dionysius is in agreement with this argument when he says: "The same things are both like and unlike God. They are like according as they imitate as much as they can Him Who is not perfectly imitable; they are unlike according as effects are lesser than their causes."[2]

In the light of this likeness, nevertheless, it is more fitting to say that a creature is like God rather than the converse. For that is called *like* something which possesses a quality or form of that thing. Since, then, that which is found in God perfectly is found in other things according to a certain dimin-

---

[2]*Ibid.*, Bk. IX, Chap. 7.

ished participation, the basis on which the likeness is observed belongs to God absolutely, but not to the creature. Thus, the creature has what belongs to God and, consequently, is rightly said to be like God. But we cannot in the same way say that God has what belongs to the creature. Neither, then, can we appropriately say that God is like a creature, just as we do not say that man is like his image, although the image is rightly said to be like him.

All the less proper, moreover, is the expression that God is likened to a creature. For likening expresses a motion towards likeness and thus belongs to the being that receives from another that which makes it like. But a creature receives from God that which makes it like Him. The converse, however, does not hold. God, then, is not likened to a creature; rather, the converse is true.

CHAPTER 30

## THE NAMES THAT CAN BE PREDICATED OF GOD

From what we have said we can further consider what it is possible to say or not to say of God, what is said of Him alone, and also what is said of Him and other things together.

Since it is possible to find in God every perfection of creatures, but in another and more eminent way, whatever names unqualifiedly designate a perfection without defect are predicated of God and of other things: for example, goodness, wisdom, being, and the like. But when any name expresses such perfections along with a mode that is proper to a creature, it can be said of God only according to likeness and metaphor. According to metaphor, what belongs to one thing is transferred to another, as when we say that a man is a *stone* because of the hardness of his intellect. Such names are used to designate the species of a created thing, for example, *man* and *stone*; for to each species belongs its own mode of perfection and being. The same is true of whatever names designate the properties of things, which are caused by the proper principles of their species. Hence, they can be said of God only metaphorically. But the names that express such perfections along with the mode of supereminence with which they belong to God are said of God alone. Such names are the *highest good, the first being,* and the like.

I have said that some of the aforementioned names signify a perfection without defect. This is true with reference to that which the name was imposed to signify; for as to the mode of signification, every name is defective. For by means of a name we express things in the way in which the intellect conceives them. For our intellect, taking the origin of its knowledge from the senses, does not transcend the mode which is found in sensible things, in which the form and the subject of the form are not identical owing to the composition of form and matter. Now, a simple form is indeed found among such things, but one that is imperfect because it is not subsisting; on the other hand, though a subsisting subject of a form is found among sensible things, it is not simple but rather concreted. Whatever our intellect signifies as subsisting, therefore, it signifies in concretion; but what it signifies as simple, it signifies, not as *that which is*, but as *that by which something is*. As a result, with reference to the mode of signification there is in every name that we use an imperfection, which does not befit God, even though the thing signified in some eminent way does befit God. This is clear in the name *goodness* and *good*. For *goodness* has signification as something not subsisting, while *good* has signification as something concreted. And so with reference to the mode of signification no name is fittingly applied to God; this is done only with reference to that which the name has been imposed to signify. Such names, therefore, as Dionysius teaches,[3] can be both affirmed and denied of God. They can be affirmed because of the meaning of the name; they can be denied because of the mode of signification.

Now, the mode of supereminence in which the abovementioned perfections are found in God can be signified by names used by us only through negation, as when we say that God is *eternal* or *infinite*, or also through a relation of God to other things, as when He is called the *first cause* or the *highest good*. For we cannot grasp what God is, but only what He is not and how other things are related to Him, as is clear from what we said above.

CHAPTER 31

### THAT THE DIVINE PERFECTION AND THE PLURALITY OF DIVINE NAMES ARE NOT OPPOSED TO THE DIVINE SIMPLICITY

From what has been said it can likewise be seen that the divine perfection and the plurality of names said of God are not opposed to His simplicity.

We have said that all the perfections found in other things are attributed to God in the same way as effects are found in their equivocal causes. These effects are in their causes virtually, as heat is in the sun. For, unless the power of the sun belonged to some extent to the genus of heat, the sun acting through this power would not generate anything like itself. The sun, then, is said to be hot through this power not only because it produces heat, but also because the power through which it does this has some likeness to heat. But through the same power through which it produces heat, the sun produces also many other effects among sublunary bodies—for example, dryness. And thus heat and dryness, which in fire are diverse qualities, belong to the sun through one and the same power. So, too, the perfections of all things, which belong to the

---

[3]*Ibid.*, Bk. I, Chap. 5. *De caelesti hierarchia*, Bk. II, Chap. 3.

rest of things through diverse forms, must be attributed to God through one and the same power in Him. This power is nothing other than His essence, since, as we have proved, there can be no accident in God. Thus, therefore, God is called *wise* not only insofar as He produces wisdom, but also because, insofar as we are wise, we imitate to some extent the power by which He makes us wise. On the other hand, God is not called a *stone*, even though He has made stones, because in the name *stone* there is understood a determinate mode of being according to which a stone is distinguished from God. But the stone imitates God as its cause in being and goodness, and other such characteristics, as do also the rest of creatures.

A similar situation obtains among the knowing and operative powers of man. For by its single power the intellect knows all the things that the sensitive part of the soul grasps through a diversity of powers—and many other things as well. So, too, the higher an intellect is, the more it can know more things through one likeness, while a lesser intellect manages to know many things only through many likenesses. So, too, a ruling power extends to all those things to which diverse powers under it are ordered. In this way, therefore, through His one simple being God possesses every kind of perfection that all other things come to possess, but in a much more diminished way, through diverse principles.

From this we see the necessity of giving to God many names. For, since we cannot know Him naturally except by arriving at Him from His effects, the names by which we signify His perfection must be diverse, just as the perfections belonging to things are found to be diverse. Were we able to understand the divine essence itself as it is and give to it the name that belongs to it, we would express it by only one name. This is promised to those who will see God through His essence: "In that day there shall be one Lord, and His name shall be one" (Zach. 14:9).

CHAPTER 32

## THAT NOTHING IS PREDICATED UNIVOCALLY OF GOD AND OTHER THINGS

It is thereby evident that nothing can be predicated univocally of God and other things.

An effect that does not receive a form specifically the same as that through which the agent acts cannot receive according to a univocal predication the name arising from that form. Thus, the heat generated by the sun and the sun itself are not called univocally *hot*. Now, the forms of the things God has made do not measure up to a specific likeness of the divine power; for the things that God has made receive in a divided and particular way that which in Him is found in a simple and universal way. It is evident, then, that nothing can be said univocally of God and other things.

If, furthermore, an effect should measure up to the species of its cause, it will not receive the univocal predication of the name unless it receives the same specific form according to the same mode of being. For the house that is in the art of the maker is not univocally the same house that is in matter, for the form of the house does not have the same being in the two locations. Now, even though the rest of things were to receive a form that is absolutely the same as it is in God, yet they do not receive it according to the same mode of being. For, as is clear from what we have said, there is nothing in God that is not the divine being itself, which is not the case with other things. Nothing, therefore, can be predicated of God and other things univocally.

Moreover, whatever is predicated of many things univocally is either a genus, a species, a difference, an accident, or a property. But, as we have shown, nothing is predicated of God as a genus or a difference; and thus neither is anything predicated as a definition, nor likewise as a species, which is constituted of genus and difference. Nor, as we have shown, can there be any accident in God, and therefore nothing is predicated of Him either as an accident or a property, since property belongs to the genus of accidents. It remains, then, that nothing is predicated univocally of God and other things.

Again, what is predicated of many things univocally is simpler than both of them, at least in concept. Now, there can be nothing simpler than God either in reality or in concept. Nothing, therefore, is predicated univocally of God and other things.

Everything, likewise, that is predicated univocally of many things belongs through participation to each of the things of which it is predicated; for the species is said to participate in the genus and the individual in the species. But nothing is said of God by participation, since whatever is participated is determined to the mode of that which is participated and is thus possessed in a partial way and not according to every mode of perfection. Nothing, therefore, can be predicated univocally of God and other things.

Then, too, what is predicated of some things according to priority and posteriority is certainly not predicated univocally. For the prior is included in the definition of the posterior, as *substance* is included in the definition of accident according as an accident is a being. If, then, being were said univocally of substance and accident, substance would have to be included in the definition of being insofar as being is predicated of substance. But this is clearly impossible. Now nothing is predicated of God and creatures as though they were in the same order, but, rather, according to priority and posteriority. For all things are predicated of God essentially. For God is called *being* as being entity itself, and He is called *good* as being goodness itself. But in other beings predications are made by participation, as Socrates is said to be a man, not because he is humanity itself, but because he possesses humanity. It is impossible, therefore, that anything be predicated univocally of God and other things.

### CHAPTER 33

## THAT NOT ALL NAMES ARE SAID OF GOD AND CREATURES IN A PURELY EQUIVOCAL WAY

From what we have said it likewise appears that not everything predicated of God and other things is said in a purely equivocal way, in the manner of equivocals by chance.

For in equivocals by chance there is no order or reference of one to another, but it is entirely accidental that one name is applied to diverse things: the application of the name to one of them does not signify that it has an order to the other. But this is not the situation with names said of God and creatures, since we note in the community of such names the order of cause and effect, as is clear from what we have said. It is not, therefore, in the manner of pure equivocation that something is predicated of God and other things.

Furthermore, where there is pure equivocation, there is no likeness in things themselves; there is only the unity of a name. But, as is clear from what we have said, there is a certain mode of likeness of things to God. It remains, then, that names are not said of God in a purely equivocal way.

Moreover, when one name is predicated of several things in a purely equivocal way, we cannot from one of them be led to the knowledge of another; for the knowledge of things does not depend on words, but on the meaning of names. Now, from what we find in other things, we do arrive at a knowledge of divine things, as is evident from what we have said. Such names, then, are not said of God and other things in a purely equivocal way.

Again, equivocation in a name impedes the process of reasoning. If, then, nothing was said of God and creatures except in a purely equivocal way, no reasoning proceeding from creatures to God could take place. But, the contrary is evident from all those who have spoken about God.

It is also a fact that a name is predicated of some being uselessly unless through that name we understand something of the being. But, if names are said of God and creatures in a purely equivocal way, we understand nothing of God through those names; for the meanings of those names are known to us solely to the extent that they are said of creatures. In vain, therefore, would it be said or proved of God that He is a being, good, or the like.

Should it be replied that through such names we know only what God is not, namely, that God is called *living* because He does not belong to the genus of lifeless things, and so with the other names, it will at least have to be the case that *living* said of God and creatures agrees in the denial of the lifeless. Thus, it will not be said in a purely equivocal way.

CHAPTER 34

## THAT NAMES SAID OF GOD AND CREATURES
## ARE SAID ANALOGICALLY

From what we have said, therefore, it remains that the names said of God and creatures are predicated neither univocally nor equivocally but analogically, that is, according to an order or reference to something one.

This can take place in two ways. In one way, according as many things have reference to something one. Thus, with reference to one *health* we say that an animal is healthy as the subject of health, medicine is healthy as its cause, food as its preserver, urine as its sign.

In another way, the analogy can obtain according as the order or reference of two things is not to something else but to one of them. Thus, *being* is said of substance and accident according as an accident has reference to a substance, and not according as substance and accident are referred to a third thing.

Now, the names said of God and things are not said analogically according to the first mode of analogy, since we should then have to posit something prior to God, but according to the second mode.

In this second mode of analogical predication the order according to the name and according to reality is sometimes found to be the same and sometimes not. For the order of the name follows the order of knowledge, because it is the sign of an intelligible conception. When, therefore, that which is prior in reality is found likewise to be prior in knowledge, the same thing is found to be prior both according to the meaning of the name and according to the nature of the thing. Thus, substance is prior to accident both in nature, insofar as substance is the cause of accident, and in knowledge, insofar as substance is included in the definition of accident. Hence, *being* is said of substance by priority over accident both according to the nature of the thing and according to the meaning of the name. But when that which is prior in nature is subsequent in our knowledge, then there is not the same order in analogicals according to reality and according to the meaning of the name. Thus, the power to heal, which is found in all health-giving things, is by nature prior to the health that is in the animal, as a cause is prior to an effect; but because we know this healing power through an effect, we likewise name it from its effect. Hence it is that the *health-giving* is prior in reality, but animal is by priority called *healthy* according to the meaning of the name.

Thus, therefore, because we come to a knowledge of God from other things, the reality in the names said of God and other things belongs by priority in God according to His mode of being, but the meaning of the name belongs to God by posteriority. And so He is said to be named from His effects.

# 6

# *Faith and Reason*

## Question 1

SECOND ARTICLE

WHETHER THE OBJECT OF FAITH IS SOMETHING
COMPLEX, SUCH AS A PROPOSITION?

*We proceed thus to the Second Article:—*

*Objection* 1. It would seem that the object of faith is not something complex such as a proposition. For the object of faith is the First Truth as was stated above. Now the First Truth is something simple. Therefore the object of faith is not something complex.

*Obj.* 2. Further, The exposition of faith is contained in the symbol. Now the symbol does not contain propositions, but things; for it is not stated therein that God is almighty, but: *I believe in God...almighty.* Therefore the object of faith is not a proposition but a thing.

*Obj.* 3. Further, Faith is succeeded by vision, according to 1 Cor. 13:12: "We see now through a glass in a dark manner, but then face to face. Now I know in part, but then I shall know even as I am known." But the object of the heavenly vision is something simple, for it is the divine essence. Therefore the faith of the wayfarer is also.

*On the contrary,* Faith is a mean between science and opinion. Now the mean is in the same genus as the extremes. Since, then, science and opinion are about propositions, it seems that faith is likewise about propositions; so that its object is something complex.

*I answer that,* The thing known is in the knower according to the mode of the knower. Now the mode proper to the human intellect is to know the truth by composition and division, as was stated in the First Part. Hence things that are simple in themselves are known by the intellect with a certain complexity, just as on the other hand the divine intellect knows, without any complexity, things that are complex in themselves.

Accordingly, the object of faith may be considered in two ways. First, as regards the thing itself which is believed, and thus the object of faith is something simple, namely, the thing itself about which we have faith; secondly, on the part of the believer, and in this respect the object of faith is something complex, such as a proposition.

Hence in the past both opinions have been held with a certain amount of truth.

*Reply Obj.* 1. This argument considers the object of faith on the part of the thing believed.

*Reply Obj.* 2. The symbol mentions the things about which faith is, insofar as the act of the believer is terminated in them, as is evident from the manner of speaking about them. Now the act of the believer does not terminate in a proposition, but in a thing. For we do not form propositions, except in order to have knowledge about things through their means; and this is true of faith as well as of science.

*Reply Obj.* 3. The object of the heavenly vision will be the First Truth seen in itself, according to 1 John 3:2: "We know that when He shall appear, we shall be like to Him: because we shall see Him as He is." Hence that vision will not be by way of a proposition, but by way of simple understanding. On the other hand, by faith, we do not apprehend the First Truth as it is in itself. Hence the comparison fails.

• • •

FOURTH ARTICLE

## WHETHER THE OBJECT OF FAITH CAN BE SOMETHING SEEN?

*We proceed thus to the Fourth Article:—*

*Objection* 1. It would seem that the object of faith is something seen. For our Lord said to Thomas (John 20:29): "Because thou hast seen Me, Thomas, thou hast believed." Therefore vision and faith regard the same object.

*Obj.* 2. Further, The Apostle, while speaking of the knowledge of faith, says (1 Cor. 13:12): "We see now through a glass in a dark manner." Therefore what is believed is seen.

*Obj.* 3. Further, Faith is a spiritual light. Now something is seen under every light. Therefore faith is about things seen.

*Obj.* 4. Further, "Every sense is a kind of sight," as Augustine states (*Sermons*, 112, 6). But faith is of things heard, according to Rom. 10:17: "Faith...cometh by hearing." Therefore faith is about things seen.

*On the contrary*, The Apostle says (Heb. 11:1) that "faith is the evidence of things that appear not."

*I answer that*, Faith signifies the assent of the intellect to that which is believed. Now the intellect assents to a thing in two ways. First, through being moved to assent by its very object, which is known either by itself (as in the case of first principles, which are held by the habit of understanding), or through something else already known (as in the case of conclusions, which are held by the habit of science). Secondly, the intellect assents to something, not through being sufficiently moved to this assent by its proper object, but through an act of choice, whereby it turns voluntarily to one side rather than to the other. Now if this be accompanied by doubt and fear of the opposite side, there will be opinion; while, if there be certainty and no fear of the other side, there will be faith.

Now those things are said to be seen which, of themselves, move the intellect or the senses to knowledge of them. Therefore it is evident that neither faith nor opinion can be of things seen either by the senses or by the intellect.

*Reply Obj.* 1. Thomas *saw one thing, and believed another.* He saw the Man and, believing Him to be God, he made profession of his faith, saying: "My Lord and my God" (John 20:28).

*Reply Obj.* 2. Those things which come under faith can be considered in two ways. First, in particular, and in this way they cannot be seen and believed at the same time, as was shown above. Secondly, in general, that is, under the common aspect of credibility; and in this way they are seen by the believer. For he would not believe unless, on the evidence of signs, or of something similar, he saw that they ought to be believed.

*Reply Obj.* 3. The light of faith makes us see what we believe. For just as, by the habits of the other virtues, man sees what is becoming to him in respect of that habit, so, by the habit of faith, the human mind is inclined to assent to such things as are becoming to a right faith, and not to assent to others.

*Reply Obj.* 4. Hearing is of words signifying what is of faith, but not of the things themselves that are believed. Hence it does not follow that these things are seen.

FIFTH ARTICLE

## WHETHER THOSE THINGS THAT ARE OF FAITH CAN BE AN OBJECT OF SCIENCE?

*We proceed thus to the Fifth Article:*—

*Objection* 1. It would seem that those things that are of faith [*fides*] can be an object of science [*scientia*]. For where science is lacking there is ignorance, since ignorance is the opposite of science. Now we are not in ignorance of those things we have to believe, since ignorance of such things belongs to unbelief, according to 1 Tim. 1:13: "I did it ignorantly in unbelief." Therefore things that are of faith can be an object of science.

*Obj.* 2. Further, Science is acquired by arguments. Now sacred writers employ arguments to inculcate things that are of faith. Therefore such things can be an object of science.

*Obj.* 3. Further, Things which are demonstrated are an object of science, since a *demonstration is a syllogism that produces science*. Now certain matters of faith have been demonstrated by the philosophers, such as the existence and unity of God, and so forth. Therefore things that are of faith can be an object of science.

*Obj.* 4. Further, Opinion is further from science than faith is, since faith is said to stand between opinion and science. Now opinion and science can, in a way, be about the same object, as is stated in *Posterior Analytics* I. Therefore faith and science can be about the same object also.

*On the contrary,* Gregory says that "when a thing is manifest, it is the object, not of faith, but of perception" (*Evangelium* II, homily 26). Therefore things that are of faith are not the object of perception, whereas what is an object of science is the object of perception. Therefore there can be no faith about things which are an object of science.

*I answer that,* All science is derived from self-evident and therefore *seen* principles; and so all objects of science must needs be, in a fashion, seen.

Now, as was stated above, it is impossible that one and the same thing should be believed and seen by the same person. Hence it is equally impossible for one and the same thing to be an object of science and of belief for the same person. It may happen, however, that a thing which is an object of vision or science for one, is believed by another; for we hope to see someday what we now believe about the Trinity, according to 1 Cor. 13:12: "We see now through a glass in a dark manner; but then face to face." And this vision the angels possess already, so that what we believe, they see. In like manner, it may also happen that what is an object of vision or scientific knowledge for one man, even in the state of a wayfarer, is, for another man, an object of faith, because he does not know it by demonstration.

Nevertheless, that which is proposed to be believed equally by all is equally unknown by all as an object of science. Such are the things which are of faith absolutely. Consequently, faith and science are not about the same things.

*Reply Obj.* 1. Unbelievers are in ignorance of things that are of faith, for neither do they see or know them in themselves, nor do they know them to be credible. The faithful, on the other hand, know them, not as by demonstration, but by the light of faith which makes them see that they ought to believe them, as was stated above.

*Reply Obj.* 2. The arguments employed by holy men to prove things that are of faith are not demonstrations; they are either persuasive arguments showing that what is proposed to our faith is not impossible, or else they are proofs drawn from the principles of faith, i.e., from the authority of Holy Scripture, as Dionysius declares. Whatever is based on these principles is as well proved in the eyes of the faithful as a conclusion drawn from self-evident principles is in the eyes of all. Hence, again, theology is a science, as we stated at the outset of this work.

*Reply Obj.* 3. Things which can be proved by demonstration are reckoned among what is of faith, not because they are believed absolutely by all, but because they are a necessary presupposition to matters of faith; so that those who do not know them by demonstration must possess them at least by faith.

*Reply Obj.* 4. As the Philosopher [Aristotle] says, "science and opinion about the same object can certainly be in different men" (*Posterior Analytics* I), as we have stated above about science and faith; yet it is possible for one and the same man to have science and faith about the same thing relatively, i.e., in relation to the object, but not in the same respect. For it is possible for the same person, about one and the same object, to know one thing and to have an opinion about another; and, in like manner, one may know by demonstration the unity of God, and believe that there are three Persons in God. On the other hand, in one and the same man, about the same object, and in the same respect, science is incompatible with either opinion or faith, but for different reasons. For science is incompatible with opinion about the same object absolutely, for the reason that science demands that its object should be deemed impossible to be otherwise, whereas it is essential to opinion that its object should be deemed possible to be otherwise. But that which is the object of faith, because of the certainty of faith, is also deemed impossible to be otherwise; and the reason why science and faith cannot be about the same object, and in the same respect, is because the object of science is something seen, whereas the object of faith is the unseen, as was stated above.

• • •

## Question 2

### FOURTH ARTICLE

### WHETHER IT IS NECESSARY TO BELIEVE THOSE THINGS WHICH CAN BE PROVED BY NATURAL REASON?

*We proceed thus to the Fourth Article:—*

*Objection* 1. It would seem unnecessary to believe those things which can be proved by natural reason. For nothing is superfluous in God's works, much less even than in the works of nature. Now it is superfluous to employ other means, where one already suffices. Therefore it would be superfluous to receive by faith things that can be known by natural reason.

*Obj.* 2. Further, Those things must be believed which are the object of faith. Now science and faith are not about the same object, as was stated above. Since, therefore, all things that can be known by natural reason are an object of science, it seems that there is no need to believe what can be proved by natural reason.

*Obj.* 3. Further, All things knowable by science would seem to have one nature; so that if some of them are proposed to man as objects of faith, in like manner the others should also be believed. But this is not true. Therefore it is not necessary to believe those things which can be proved by natural reason.

*On the contrary*, It is necessary to believe that God is one and incorporeal; which things philosophers prove by natural reason.

*I answer that*, It is necessary for man to receive by faith not only things which are above reason, but also those which can be known by reason; and this for three motives. First, in order that man may arrive more quickly at the knowledge of divine truth. For the science to whose province it belongs to prove the existence of God and many other such truths is the last of all to offer itself to human inquiry, since it presupposes many other sciences; so that it would be far along in life that man would arrive at the knowledge of God. The second reason is, in order that the knowledge of God may be more widespread. For many are unable to make progress in the study of science, either through dullness of ability, or through having a number of occupations and temporal needs, or even through laziness in learning; and all these persons would be altogether deprived of the knowledge of God, unless divine things were brought to their knowledge by way of faith. The third reason is for the sake of certitude. For human reason is very deficient in things concerning God. A sign of this is that philosophers, in their inquiry into human affairs by natural investigation, have fallen into many errors, and have disagreed among themselves. And consequently, in order that men might have knowledge of God, free of doubt and uncertainty, it was necessary for divine truths to be delivered to them by way of faith, being told to them, as it were, by God Himself, Who cannot lie.

*Reply Obj.* 1. The inquiry of natural reason does not suffice mankind for the knowledge of divine truths, even of those that can be proved by reason; and so it is not superfluous if these be believed.

*Reply Obj.* 2. Science and faith cannot be in the same subject and about the same object; but what is an object of science for one can be an object of faith for another, as was stated above.

*Reply Obj.* 3. Although all things that can be known by science have the notion of science in common, they do not all alike lead man to beatitude; and hence they are not all equally proposed to our belief.

FIFTH ARTICLE

## WHETHER MAN IS BOUND TO BELIEVE ANYTHING EXPLICITLY?

*We proceed thus to the Fifth Article:—*

*Objection* 1. It would seem that man is not bound to believe anything explicitly. For no man is bound to do what is not in his power. Now it is not in man's power to believe a thing explicitly, for it is written (Rom. 10:14, 15): "How shall they believe Him, of whom they have not heard? And how shall they hear without a preacher? And how shall they preach unless they be sent?" Therefore man is not bound to believe anything explicitly.

*Obj.* 2. Further, Just as we are directed to God by faith, so also are we by charity. Now man is not bound to keep the precepts of charity, but it is enough if he be ready to fulfill them. This is evidenced by the precept of Our Lord (Matt. 5:39): "If one strike thee on one cheek, turn to him also the other"; and by others of the same kind, according to Augustine's exposition. Therefore neither is man bound to believe anything explicitly, but it is enough if he be ready to believe whatever God proposes to be believed.

*Obj.* 3. Further, The good of faith consists in a certain obedience, according to Rom. 1:5: "For obedience to the faith in all nations." Now the virtue of obedience does not require man to keep certain fixed precepts, but it is enough that his mind be ready to obey, according to Ps. 118:60: "I am ready and am not troubled, that I may keep Thy commandments." Therefore it seems enough for faith, too, that man should be ready to believe whatever God may propose, without believing anything explicitly.

*On the contrary,* It is written (Heb. 11:6): "He that cometh to God must believe that He is, and is a rewarder to them that seek Him."

*I answer that,* The precepts of the Law, which man is bound to fulfill, concern acts of virtue which are the means of attaining salvation. Now an act of virtue, as was stated above, depends on the relation of the habit to its object. But two things may be considered in the object of any virtue, namely, that which is the proper and direct object of that virtue, which is necessarily in every act of virtue, and that which is accidental and consequent to the object. But two things may be considered in the object of any virtue, namely, of fortitude to face the dangers of death, and to charge at the foe with danger to oneself, for the sake of the common good; and yet that, in a just war, a man be armed, or strike another with his sword, and so forth, is reduced to the object of fortitude, but indirectly.

Accordingly, just as a virtuous act is required for the fulfillment of a precept, so is it necessary that the virtuous act should terminate in its proper and direct object; but, on the other hand, the fulfillment of the precept does not require that a virtuous act should terminate in those things which have an accidental or secondary relation to the proper and direct object of that virtue, except in certain places and at certain times.

We must, therefore, say that the direct object of faith is that whereby man is made one of the Blessed, as was stated above; while the indirect and secondary object comprises all things delivered by God to us in Holy Scripture, for instance, that Abraham had two sons, that David was the son of Jesse, and so forth. Therefore, as regards the primary points or articles of faith, man must believe them explicitly, just as he must have faith; but as to other points of faith, man is not bound to believe them explicitly, but only implicitly, or to be ready to believe them, insofar as he is prepared to believe whatever is contained in the divine Scriptures. Then alone is he bound to believe such things explicitly, when it is clear to him that they are contained in the doctrine of faith.

*Reply Obj.* 1. If we understand those things alone to be in a man's power, which we can do without the help of grace, then we are bound to do many things which we cannot do without the aid of healing grace, such as to love God and our neighbor, and likewise to believe the articles of faith. But with the help of grace we can do this, for this help "to whomsoever it is given from above it is mercifully given; and from whom it is withheld it is justly withheld, as a punishment of a previous, or at least of original, sin," as Augustine states (*Epistles*, 190.3).

*Reply Obj.* 2. Man is bound to love definitely those lovable things which are properly and directly the objects of charity, namely, God and neighbor. The objection refers to those precepts of charity which belong, as by a consequence, to the object of charity.

*Reply Obj.* 3. The virtue of obedience is seated, properly speaking, in the will; and hence the promptness of the will, which is subject to authority, suffices for the act of obedience, because it is the proper and direct object of obedience. But this or that precept is accidental or consequent to that proper and direct object.

• • •

NINTH ARTICLE

## WHETHER TO BELIEVE IS MERITORIOUS?

*We proceed thus to the Ninth Article:—*

*Objection* 1. It would seem that to believe is not meritorious. For the principle of all merit is charity, as was stated above. Now faith, like nature, is a preamble to charity. Therefore, just as an act of nature is not meritorious, since we do not merit by our natural gifts, so neither is an act of faith.

*Obj.* 2. Further, Belief is intermediate between opinion and scientific knowledge or the consideration of things known by science. Now the considerations of science are not meritorious, nor on the other hand is opinion. Therefore belief is not meritorious.

*Obj.* 3. Further, He who assents to a point of faith either has a sufficient motive for believing, or he has not. If he has a sufficient motive for his belief, this does not seem to imply any merit on his part, since he is no longer free to believe or not to believe; whereas if he has not a sufficient motive for believing, this is a mark of levity, according to Ecclesiasticus 19:4: "He that is hasty to give credit, is light of heart," so that, seemingly, he gains no merit thereby. Therefore to believe is by no means meritorious.

*On the contrary,* It is written (Heb. 11:33) that the saints "by faith...obtained promises," which would not be the case if they did not merit by believing. Therefore to believe is meritorious.

*I answer that,* As was stated above, our actions are meritorious insofar as they proceed from free choice moved with grace by God. Therefore every human act proceeding from free choice, if it be referred to God, can be meritorious. Now the act of believing is an act of the intellect assenting to divine truth at the command of the will moved by the grace of God, so that it is subject to free choice in relation to God; and consequently the act of faith can be meritorious.

*Reply Obj.* 1. Nature is compared to charity, which is the principle of merit, as matter to form; whereas faith is compared to charity as the disposition which precedes the ultimate form. Now it is evident that the subject or the matter cannot act by virtue of the form, nor can a preceding disposition, before the advent of the form; but after the advent of the form, both the subject and the preceding disposition act by virtue of the form, which is the chief principle of action, even as the heat of fire acts by virtue of the substantial form of fire. Accordingly, neither nature nor faith can, without charity, produce a meritorious act; but, when accompanied by charity, the act of faith is made meritorious thereby, even as an act of nature, and a natural act of free choice.

*Reply Obj.* 2. Two things may be considered in science, namely, the assent of the one who has science to the thing that he knows, and his consideration of that thing. Now the assent of science is not subject to free choice, because the knower is obliged to assent by the force of the demonstration; and so scientific assent is not meritorious. But the actual consideration of what a man knows by science is subject to his free choice, for it is in his power to consider or not to consider. Hence consideration of science may be meritorious if it be referred to the end of charity, i.e., to the honor of God or the good of our neighbor. On the other hand, in the case of faith, both these things are subject to free choice, so that in both respects the act of faith can be meritorious. But in the case of opinion, there is no firm assent, since it is weak and infirm, as the Philosopher observes, so that it does not seem to proceed from a perfect act of the will; and for this reason, as regards the assent, it does not appear to be very meritorious, though it can be as regards the actual consideration.

*Reply Obj.* 3. The believer has sufficient motive for believing, for he is moved by the authority of divine teaching confirmed by miracles, and, what is more, by the inward instigation of the divine invitation; and so he does not believe lightly. He has not, however, sufficient reason for scientific knowledge, and hence he does not lose the merit.

• • •

## Question 6

FIRST ARTICLE

*WHETHER FAITH IS INFUSED INTO MAN BY GOD?*

*We proceed thus to the First Article:—*

*Objection* 1. It would seem that faith is not infused into man by God. For Augustine says that "science begets faith in us, and nourishes, defends and strengthens it" (*De Trinitate*, xiv, 1). Now those things which science begets in us seem to be acquired rather than infused. Therefore faith does not seem to be in us by divine infusion.

*Obj.* 2. Further, That to which man attains by hearing and seeing seems to be acquired by him. Now man attains to belief both by seeing miracles and by hearing the teachings of faith; for it is written (John 4:53): "The father...knew that it was at the same hour, that Jesus said to him, Thy son liveth; and himself believed, and his whole house"; and (Rom. 10:17) it is said that "faith is through hearing." Therefore man attains to faith by acquiring it.

*Obj.* 3. Further, That which depends on a man's will can be acquired by him. But "faith depends on the believer's will," according to Augustine (*De Praedestinatione Sanctorum*, V). Therefore faith can be acquired by man.

*On the contrary*, It is written (Ephes. 2:8, 9): "By grace you are saved through faith, and that not of yourselves...that no man may glory...for it is the gift of God."

*I answer that*, Two things are requisite for faith. First, that the things which are of faith should be proposed to man; and this is necessary in order that man believe something explicitly. The second thing requisite for faith is the assent of the believer to the things which are proposed to him. Accordingly, as regards the first of these, faith must needs be from God. For the things which are of faith surpass human reason, and hence they do not come to man's knowledge, unless God reveal them. To some, indeed, they are revealed by God immediately, as those things which were revealed to the Apostles and prophets, while to some they are proposed by God in sending preachers of the faith, according to Rom. 10:15: "How shall they preach, unless they be sent?"

As regards the second, viz., man's assent to the things which are of faith, we may observe a twofold cause, one of external inducement, such as seeing a miracle, or being persuaded by someone to embrace the faith; neither of which is a sufficient cause, since of those who see the same miracle, or who hear the same sermon, some believe, and some do not. Hence we must assert another and internal cause, which moves man inwardly to assent to what belongs to faith.

The Pelagians held that this cause was nothing else than man's free choice, and consequently they said that the beginning of faith is from ourselves, inasmuch as, namely, it is in our power to be ready to assent to the things which are of faith, but that the consummation of faith is from God, Who proposes to us the things we have to believe. But this is false, for since, by assenting to what belongs to faith, man is raised above his nature, this must needs come to him from some supernatural principle moving him inwardly; and this is God. Therefore faith, as regards the assent which is the chief act of faith, is from God moving man inwardly by grace.

*Reply Obj.* 1. Science begets and nourishes faith by way of external persuasion afforded by some science; but the chief and proper cause of faith is that which moves man inwardly to assent.

*Reply Obj.* 2. This argument likewise refers to the cause that proposes outwardly the things that are of faith, or persuades man to believe by words or deeds.

*Reply Obj.* 3. To believe does indeed depend on the will of the believer; but man's will needs to be prepared by God with grace, in order that he may be raised to things which are above his nature, as was stated above.

# René Descartes

René Descartes (1596–1650), "the father of modern philosophy," author of the *Discourse on Method* and *Meditations,* and founder of the European rationalist tradition, reformulated the ontological argument for the existence of God.

# 7

# *The Ontological Argument Restated*

But now, if just because I can draw the idea of something from my thought, it follows that all which I know clearly and distinctly as pertaining to this object does really belong to it, may I not derive from this an argument demonstrating the existence of God? It is certain that I no less find the idea of God, that is to say, the idea of a supremely perfect Being, in me, than that of any figure or number whatever it is; and I do not know any less clearly and distinctly that an [actual and] eternal existence pertains to this nature than I know that all that which I am able to demonstrate of some figure or number truly pertains to the nature of this figure or number, and therefore, although all that I concluded in the preceding Meditations were found to be false, the existence of God would pass with me as at least as certain as I have ever held the truths of mathematics (which concern only numbers and figures) to be.

This indeed is not at first manifest, since it would seem to present some appearance of being a sophism. For being accustomed in all other things to make a distinction between existence and essence, I easily persuade myself that the existence can be separated from the essence of God, and that we can thus conceive God as not actually existing. But, nevertheless, when I think of it with more attention, I clearly see that existence can no more be separated from the essence of God than can its having its three angles equal to two right angles be separated from the essence of a [rectilinear] triangle, or the idea of a mountain from the idea of a valley; and so there is not any less repugnance to our conceiving a God (that is, a Being supremely perfect) to whom existence

---

"Of God, that He Exists," from *Meditations,* V, in *The Philosophical Works of Descartes,* Vol. I, E. S. Haldane and G. R. T. Ross, trans. (Cambridge: The University Press, 1911). Reprinted by permission of the publisher.

is lacking (that is to say, to whom a certain perfection is lacking), than to conceive of a mountain which has no valley.

But although I cannot really conceive of a God without existence any more than a mountain without a valley, still from the fact that I conceive of a mountain with a valley, it does not follow that there is such a mountain in the world; similarly although I conceive of God as possessing existence, it would seem that it does not follow that there is a God which exists; for my thought does not impose any necessity upon things, and just as I may imagine a winged horse, although no horse with wings exists, so I could perhaps attribute existence to God, although no God existed.

But a sophism is concealed in this objection; for from the fact that I cannot conceive a mountain without a valley, it does not follow that there is any mountain or any valley in existence, but only that the mountain and the valley, whether they exist or do not exist, cannot in any way be separated one from the other. While from the fact that I cannot conceive God without existence, it follows that existence is inseparable from Him, and hence that He really exists; not that my thought can bring this to pass, or impose any necessity on things, but, on the contrary, because the necessity which lies in the thing itself, i.e., the necessity of the existence of God, determines me to think in this way. For it is not within my power to think of God without existence (that is, of a supremely perfect Being devoid of a supreme perfection) though it is in my power to imagine a horse either with wings or without wings.

And we must not here object that it is in truth necessary for me to assert that God exists after having presupposed that He possesses every sort of perfection, since existence is one of these, but that as a matter of fact my original supposition was not necessary, just as it is not necessary to consider that all quadrilateral figures can be inscribed in the circle; for supposing I thought this, I should be constrained to admit that the rhombus might be inscribed in the circle since it is a quadrilateral figure, which, however, is manifestly false. [We must not, I say, make any such allegations because] although it is not necessary that I should at any time entertain the notion of God, nevertheless whenever it happens that I think of a first and a sovereign Being, and, so to speak, derive the idea of Him from the storehouse of my mind, it is necessary that I should attribute to Him every sort of perfection, although I do not get so far as to enumerate them all, or to apply my mind to each one in particular. And this necessity suffices to make me conclude (after having recognized that existence is a perfection) that this first and sovereign Being really exists; just as though it is not necessary for me ever to imagine any triangle, yet, whenever I wish to consider a rectilinear figure composed only of three angles, it is absolutely essential that I should attribute to it all those properties which serve to bring about the conclusion that its three angles are not greater than two right angles, even although I may not then be considering this point in particular. But when I consider which figures are capable of being inscribed in the circle, it is in no wise necessary that I should think that all quadrilateral figures are of this number; on the contrary, I cannot even pretend that this is the case, so long as I do not desire to accept anything which I cannot conceive clearly and distinctly. And in consequence there is a great difference between the false suppositions such as this, and the true ideas born within me, the first and principal of which is that of God. For really I discern in many ways that this idea is not something factitious, and depending solely on my thought, but that it is the image of a true and immutable nature; first of all, because I cannot conceive anything but God Himself to whose essence existence [necessarily] pertains; in the second place because it is not possible for me to conceive two or more Gods in this same position; and, granted that there is one such God who now exists, I see clearly that it is necessary that He should have existed from all eternity, and that He must exist eternally; and finally, because I know an infinitude of other properties in God, none of which I can either diminish or change.

For the rest, whatever proof or argument I avail myself of, we must always return to the point that it is only those things which we conceive clearly and distinctly that have the power of persuading me entirely. And although amongst the matters which I conceive of in this way, some indeed are manifestly obvious to all, while others only manifest themselves to those who consider them closely and examine them attentively; still, after they have once been discovered, the latter are not esteemed as any less certain than the former. For example, in the case of every right-angled triangle, although it does not so manifestly appear that the square of the base is equal to the squares of the two other sides as that this base is opposite to the greatest angle; still, when this has once been apprehended, we are just as certain of its truth as of the truth of the other. And as regards God, if my mind were not preoccupied with prejudices, and if my thought did not find itself on all hands diverted by the continual pressure of sensible things, there would be nothing which I could know more immediately and more easily than Him. For is there anything more manifest than that there is a God, that is to say, a Supreme Being, to whose essence alone existence pertains?[1]

And although for a firm grasp of this truth I have need of a strenuous application of mind, at present I not only feel myself to be as assured of it as of all that I hold as most certain, but I also remark that the certainty of all other things depends on it so absolutely, that without this knowledge it is impossible ever to know anything perfectly.

---

[1] "in the idea of whom alone necessary or external existence is comprised." French version.

For although I am of such a nature that as long as[2] I understand anything very clearly and distinctly, I am naturally impelled to believe it to be true, yet because I am also of such a nature that I cannot have my mind constantly fixed on the same object in order to perceive it clearly, and as I often recollect having formed a past judgment without at the same time properly recollecting the reasons that led me to make it, it may happen meanwhile that other reasons present themselves to me, which would easily cause me to change my opinion, if I were ignorant of the facts of the existence of God, and thus I should have no true and certain knowledge, but only vague and vacillating opinions. Thus, for example, when I consider the nature of a [rectilinear] triangle, I who have some little knowledge of the principles of geometry recognize quite clearly that the three angles are equal to two right angles, and it is not possible for me not to believe this so long as I apply my mind to its demonstration; but so soon as I abstain from attending to the proof, although I still recollect having clearly comprehended it, it may easily occur that I come to doubt its truth, if I am ignorant of there being a God. For I can persuade myself of having been so constituted by nature that I can easily deceive myself even in those matters which I believe myself to apprehend with the greatest evidence and certainty, especially when I recollect that I have frequently judged matters to be true and certain which other reasons have afterwards impelled me to judge to be altogether false.

But after I have recognized that there is a God—because at the same time I have also recognized that all things depend upon Him, and that He is not a deceiver, and from that have inferred that what I perceive clearly and distinctly cannot fail to be true—although I no longer pay attention to the reasons for which I have judged this to be true, provided that I recollect having clearly and distinctly perceived it no contrary reason can be brought forward which could ever cause me to doubt of its truth; and thus I have a true and certain knowledge of it. And this same knowledge extends likewise to all other things which I recollect having formerly demonstrated, such as the truths of geometry and the like; for what can be alleged against them to cause me to place them in doubt? Will it be said that my nature is such as to cause me to be frequently deceived? But I already know that I cannot be deceived in the judgment whose grounds I know clearly. Will it be said that I formerly held many things to be true and certain which I have afterwards recognized to be false? But I had not had any clear and distinct knowledge of these things, and not as yet knowing the rule whereby I assure myself of the truth, I had been impelled to give my assent from reasons which I have since recognized to be less strong than I had at the time imagined them to be. What further objection can then be raised? That possibly I am dreaming (an objection I myself made a little while ago), or that all the thoughts which I now

_____

[2]"from the moment that." French version.

have are no more true than the phantasies of my dreams? But even though I slept the case would be the same, for all that is clearly present to my mind is absolutely true.

And so I very clearly recognize that the certainty and truth of all knowledge depends alone on the knowledge of the true God, insomuch that, before I knew Him, I could not have a perfect knowledge of any other thing. And now that I know Him I have the means of acquiring a perfect knowledge of an infinitude of things, not only of those which relate to God Himself and other intellectual matters, but also of those which pertain to corporeal nature insofar as it is the object of pure mathematics [which have no concern with whether it exists or not].

# David Hume

David Hume (1711–1776) dealt severe blows to philosophical rationalism in his *Treatise* and *Enquiries;* and in his posthumously published *Dialogues Concerning Natural Religion,* written from a standpoint of religious skepticism, he extended the attack to theological rationalism.

# 8

# *Against the Design Argument*

### PART II

I must own, Cleanthes, said Demea, that nothing can more surprise me than the light in which you have all along put this argument. By the whole tenor of your discourse, one would imagine that you were maintaining the Being of a God against the cavils of atheists and infidels, and were necessitated to become a champion for that fundamental principle of all religion. But this, I hope, is not by any means a question among us. No man, no man at least of common sense, I am persuaded, ever entertained a serious doubt with regard to a truth so certain and self-evident. The question is not concerning the *being* but the *nature* of God. This I affirm, from the infirmities of human understanding, to be altogether incomprehensible and unknown to us. The essence of that supreme Mind, His attributes, the manner of His existence, the very nature of His duration—these and every particular which regards so divine a Being are mysterious to men. Finite, weak, and blind creatures, we ought to humble ourselves in His august presence, and, conscious of our frailties, adore in silence His infinite perfections which eye hath not seen, ear hath not heard, neither hath it entered into the heart of man to conceive. They are covered in a deep cloud from human curiosity; it is profaneness to attempt penetrating through these sacred obscurities, and, next to the impiety of denying His existence, is the temerity of prying into His nature and essence, decrees and attributes.

But lest you should think that my *piety* has here got the better of my *philosophy,* I shall support my opinion, if it needs any support, by a very great authority. I might cite all the divines, almost from the foundation of Christianity, who have ever treated of this or any other theological subject; but I shall confine myself, at present, to one equally celebrated for piety and philosophy.

---

*Dialogues Concerning Natural Religion,* Parts II, IV–VIII, XII.

It is Father Malebranche who, I remember, thus expresses himself.[1] "One ought not so much," says he, "to call God a spirit in order to express positively what He is, as in order to signify that He is not matter. He is a Being infinitely perfect—of this we cannot doubt. But in the same manner as we ought not to imagine, even supposing Him corporeal, that He is clothed with a human body, as the anthropomorphites asserted, under colour that that figure was the most perfect of any, so neither ought we to imagine that the spirit of God has human ideas or bears any resemblance to our spirit, under colour that we know nothing more perfect than a human mind. We ought rather to believe that as He comprehends the perfections of matter without being material...He comprehends also the perfections of created spirits without being spirit, in the manner we conceive spirit: that His true name is *He that is,* or, in other words, Being without restriction, All Being, the Being infinite and universal."

After so great an authority, Demea, replied Philo, as that which you have produced, and a thousand more which you might produce, it would appear ridiculous in me to add my sentiment or express my approbation of your doctrine. But surely, where reasonable men treat these subjects, the question can never be concerning the *being* but only the *nature* of the Deity. The former truth, as you well observe, is unquestionable and self-evident. Nothing exists without a cause; and the original cause of this universe (whatever it be) we call God, and piously ascribe to Him every species of perfection. Whoever scruples this fundamental truth deserves every punishment which can be inflicted among philosophers, to wit, the greatest ridicule, contempt, and disapprobation. But as all perfection is entirely relative, we ought never to imagine that we comprehend the attributes of this divine Being, or to suppose that His perfections have any analogy or likeness to the perfections of a human creature. Wisdom, thought, design, knowledge— these we justly ascribe to Him because these words are honourable among men, and we have no other language or other conceptions by which we can express our adoration of Him. But let us beware lest we think that our ideas anywise correspond to His perfections, or that His attributes have any resemblance to these qualities among men. He is infinitely superior to our limited view and comprehension, and is more the object of worship in the temple than of disputation in the schools.

In reality, Cleanthes, continued he, there is no need of having recourse to that affected skepticism so displeasing to you in order to come at this determination. Our ideas reach no farther than our experience. We have no experience of divine attributes and operations. I need not conclude my syllogism, you can draw the inference yourself. And it is a pleasure to me (and I hope to you, too) that just reasoning and sound piety here concur in

---

[1] *Recherche de la Vérité*, Bk. III, Chap. 9.

the same conclusion, and both of them establish the adorably mysterious and incomprehensible nature of the Supreme Being.

Not to lose any time in circumlocutions, said Cleanthes, addressing himself to Demea, much less in replying to the pious declamations of Philo, I shall briefly explain how I conceive this matter. Look round the world, contemplate the whole and every part of it: you will find it to be nothing but one great machine, subdivided into an infinite number of lesser machines, which again admit of subdivisions to a degree beyond what human senses and faculties can trace and explain. All these various machines, and even their most minute parts, are adjusted to each other with an accuracy which ravishes into admiration all men who have ever contemplated them. The curious adapting of means to ends, throughout all nature, resembles exactly, though it much exceeds, the productions of human contrivance—of human design, thought, wisdom, and intelligence. Since therefore the effects resemble each other, we are led to infer, by all the rules of analogy, that the causes also resemble, and that the Author of nature is somewhat similar to the mind of man, though possessed of much larger faculties, proportioned to the grandeur of the work which He has executed. By this argument a posteriori, and by this argument alone, do we prove at once the existence of a Deity and His similarity to human mind and intelligence.

I shall be so free, Cleanthes, said Demea, as to tell you that from the beginning I could not approve of your conclusion concerning the similarity of the Deity to men, still less can I approve of the mediums by which you endeavour to establish it. What! No demonstration of the Being of God! No abstract arguments! No proofs a priori! Are these which have hitherto been so much insisted on by philosophers all fallacy, all sophism? Can we reach no farther in this subject than experience and probability? I will not say that this is betraying the cause of a Deity; but surely, by this affected candour, you give advantages to atheists which they never could obtain by the mere dint of argument and reasoning.

What I chiefly scruple in this subject, said Philo, is not so much that all religious arguments are by Cleanthes reduced to experience, as that they appear not to be even the most certain and irrefragable of that inferior kind. That a stone will fall, that fire will burn, that the earth has solidity, we have observed a thousand and a thousand times; and when any new instance of this nature is presented, we draw without hesitation the accustomed inference. The exact similarity of the cases gives us a perfect assurance of a similar event, and a stronger evidence is never desired nor sought after. But wherever you depart, in the least, from the similarity of the cases, you diminish proportionably the evidence, and may at last bring it to a very weak *analogy*, which is confessedly liable to error and uncertainty. After having experienced the circulation of the blood in human creatures, we make no doubt that it takes place in Titius and Maevius; but from its circulation in frogs and fishes it is only a presumption, though a strong one, from analogy that it takes place in men and other animals. The analogical reasoning is much weaker when we infer the circulation of the sap in vegetables from our experience that the blood circulates in animals; and those who hastily followed that imperfect analogy are found, by more accurate experiments, to have been mistaken.

If we see a house, Cleanthes, we conclude, with the greatest certainty, that it had an architect or builder because this is precisely that species of effect which we have experienced to proceed from that species of cause. But surely you will not affirm that the universe bears such a resemblance to a house that we can with the same certainty infer a similar cause, or that the analogy is here entire and perfect. The dissimilitude is so striking that the utmost you can here pretend to is a guess, a conjecture, a presumption concerning a similar cause; and how that pretension will be received in the world, I leave you to consider.

It would surely be very ill received, replied Cleanthes; and I should be deservedly blamed and detested did I allow that the proofs of a Deity amounted to no more than a guess or conjecture. But is the whole adjustment of means to ends in a house and in the universe so slight a resemblance? the economy of final causes? the order, proportion, and arrangement of every part? Steps of a stair are plainly contrived that human legs may use them in mounting; and this inference is certain and infallible. Human legs are also contrived for walking and mounting; and this inference, I allow, is not altogether so certain because of the dissimilarity which you remark; but does it, therefore, deserve the name only of presumption or conjecture?

Good God! cried Demea, interrupting him, where are we? Zealous defenders of religion allow that the proofs of a Deity fall short of perfect evidence! And you, Philo, on whose assistance I depended in proving the adorable mysteriousness of the Divine Nature, do you assent to all these extravagant opinions of Cleanthes? For what other name can I give them? or, why spare my censure when such principles are advanced, supported by such an authority, before so young a man as Pamphilus?

You seem not to apprehend, replied Philo, that I argue with Cleanthes in his own way, and, by showing him the dangerous consequences of his tenets, hope at last to reduce him to our opinion. But what sticks most with you, I observe, is the representation which Cleanthes has made of the argument a posteriori; and, finding that that argument is likely to escape your hold and vanish into air, you think it so disguised that you can scarcely believe it to be set in its true light. Now, however much I may dissent, in other respects, from the dangerous principle of Cleanthes, I must allow that he has fairly represented that argument, and I shall endeavour so to state the matter to you that you will entertain no further scruples with regard to it.

Were a man to abstract from everything which he knows or has seen, he would be altogether incapable, merely from his own ideas, to determine what kind of scene the universe must be, or to give the preference to one state or situation of things above another. For as nothing which he clearly conceives could be esteemed impossible or implying a contradiction, every chimera of his fancy would be upon an equal footing; nor could he assign any just reason why he adheres to one idea or system, and rejects the others which are equally possible.

Again, after he opens his eyes and contemplates the world as it really is, it would be impossible for him at first to assign the cause of any one event, much less of the whole of things, or of the universe. He might set his fancy a-rambling, and she might bring him in an infinite variety of reports and representations. These would all be possible, but, being all equally possible, he would never of himself give a satisfactory account for his preferring one of them to the rest. Experience alone can point out to him the true cause of any phenomenon.

Now, according to this method of reasoning, Demea, it follows (and is, indeed, tacitly allowed by Cleanthes himself) that order, arrangement, or the adjustment of final causes, is not of itself any proof of design, but only so far as it has been experienced to proceed from that principle. For aught we can know a priori, matter may contain the source or spring of order originally within itself, as well as mind does; and there is no more difficulty in conceiving that the several elements, from an internal unknown cause, may fall into the most exquisite arrangement, than to conceive that their ideas, in the great universal mind, from a like internal unknown cause, fall into that arrangement. The equal possibility of both these suppositions is allowed. But, by experience, we find (according to Cleanthes) that there is a difference between them. Throw several pieces of steel together, without shape or form, they will never arrange themselves so as to compose a watch. Stone and mortar and wood, without an architect, never erect a house. But the ideas in a human mind, we see, by an unknown, inexplicable economy, arrange themselves so as to form the plan of a watch or house. Experience, therefore, proves that there is an original principle of order in mind, not in matter. From similar effects we infer similar causes. The adjustment of means to ends is alike in the universe, as in a machine of human contrivance. The causes, therefore, must be resembling.

I was from the beginning scandalized, I must own, with this resemblance which is asserted between the Deity and human creatures, and must conceive it to imply such a degradation of the Supreme Being as no sound theist could endure. With your assistance, therefore, Demea, I shall endeavour to defend what you justly call the adorable mysteriousness of the Divine Nature, and shall refute this reasoning of Cleanthes, provided he allows that I have made a fair representation of it.

When Cleanthes had assented, Philo, after a short pause, proceeded in the following manner.

That all inferences, Cleanthes, concerning fact are founded on experience, and that all experimental reasonings are founded on the supposition that similar causes prove similar effects, and similar effects similar causes, I shall not at present much dispute with you. But observe, I entreat you, with what extreme caution all just reasoners proceed in the transferring of experiments to similar cases. Unless the cases be exactly similar, they repose no perfect confidence in applying their past observation to any particular phenomenon. Every alteration of circumstances occasions a doubt concerning the event; and it requires new experiments to prove certainly that the new circumstances are of no moment or importance. A change in bulk, situation, arrangement, age, disposition of the air, or surrounding bodies—any of these particulars may be attended with the most unexpected consequences. And unless the objects be quite familiar to us, it is the highest temerity to expect with assurance, after any of these changes, an event similar to that which before fell under our observation. The slow and deliberate steps of philosophers here, if anywhere, are distinguished from the precipitate march of the vulgar, who, hurried on by the smallest similitude, are incapable of all discernment or consideration.

But can you think, Cleanthes, that your usual phlegm and philosophy have been preserved in so wide a step as you have taken when you compared to the universe houses, ships, furniture, machines, and, from their similarity in some circumstances, inferred a similarity in their causes? Thought, design, intelligence, such as we discover in men and other animals, is no more than one of the springs and principles of the universe, as well as heat or cold, attraction or repulsion, and a hundred others which fall under daily observation. It is an active cause by which some particular parts of nature, we find, produce alterations on other parts. But can a conclusion, with any propriety, be transferred from parts to the whole? Does not the great disproportion bar all comparison and inference? From observing the growth of a hair, can we learn anything concerning the generation of a man? Would the manner of a leaf's blowing, even though perfectly known, afford us any instruction concerning the vegetation of a tree?

But allowing that we were to take the *operations* of one part of nature upon another for the foundation of our judgment concerning the *origin* of the whole (which never can be admitted), yet why select so minute, so weak, so bounded a principle as the reason and design of animals is found to be upon this planet? What peculiar privilege has this little agitation of the brain which we call *thought*, that we must thus make it the model of the whole universe? Our partiality in our own favour does indeed present it on all occasions, but sound philosophy ought carefully to guard against so natural an illusion.

So far from admitting, continued Philo, that the operations of a part can afford us any just conclusion concerning the origin of the whole, I will not allow any one part to form a rule for another part if the latter be very remote from the former. Is there any reasonable ground to conclude that the inhabitants of other planets possess thought, intelligence, reason, or anything similar to these faculties in men? When nature has so extremely diversified her manner of operation in this small globe, can we imagine that she incessantly copies herself throughout so immense a universe? And if thought, as we may well suppose, be confined merely to this narrow corner and has even there so limited a sphere of action, with what propriety can we assign it for the original cause of all things? The narrow views of a peasant who makes his domestic economy the rule for the government of kingdoms is in comparison a pardonable sophism.

But were we ever so much assured that a thought and reason resembling the human were to be found throughout the whole universe, and were its activity elsewhere vastly greater and more commanding than it appears in this globe, yet I cannot see why the operations of a world constituted, arranged, adjusted, can with any propriety be extended to a world which is in its embryo state, and is advancing towards that constitution and arrangement. By observation we know somewhat of the economy, action, and nourishment of a finished animal, but we must transfer with great caution that observation to the growth of a fetus in the womb, and still more to the formation of an animalcule in the loins of its male parent. Nature, we find, even from our limited experience, possesses an infinite number of springs and principles which incessantly discover themselves on every change of her position and situation. And what new and unknown principles would actuate her in so new and unknown a situation as that of the formation of a universe, we cannot, without the utmost temerity, pretend to determine.

A very small part of this great system, during a very short time, is very imperfectly discovered to us; and do we thence pronounce decisively concerning the origin of the whole?

Admirable conclusion! Stone, wood, brick, iron, brass, have not, at this time, in this minute globe of earth, an order or arrangement without human art and contrivance; therefore, the universe could not originally attain its order and arrangement without something similar to human art. But is a part of nature a rule for another part very wide of the former? Is it a rule for the whole? Is a very small part a rule for the universe? Is nature in one situation a certain rule for nature in another situation vastly different from the former?

And can you blame me, Cleanthes, if I here imitate the prudent reserve of Simonides, who, according to the noted story, being asked by Hiero what God was, desired a day to think of it, and then two days more; and after that manner continually prolonged the term, without ever bringing in his definition or description? Could you even blame me if I had answered, at first, *that I did not know*, and was sensible that this subject lay vastly beyond the reach of my faculties? You might cry out skeptic and rallier, as much as you pleased; but, having found in so many other subjects much more familiar the imperfections and even contradictions of human reason, I never should expect any success from its feeble conjectures in a subject so sublime and so remote from the sphere of our observation. When two species of objects have always been observed to be conjoined together, I can *infer*, by custom, the existence of one wherever I *see* the existence of the other; and this I call an argument from experience. But how this argument can have place where the objects, as in the present case, are single, individual, without parallel or specific resemblance, may be difficult to explain. And will any man tell me with a serious countenance that an orderly universe must arise from some thought and art like the human because we have experience of it? To ascertain this reasoning it were requisite that we had experience of the origin of worlds; and it is not sufficient, surely, that we have seen ships and cities arise from human art and contrivance.

Philo was proceeding in this vehement manner, somewhat between jest and earnest, as it appeared to me, when he observed some signs of impatience in Cleanthes, and then immediately stopped short. What I had to suggest, said Cleanthes, is only that you would not abuse terms, or make use of popular expressions to subvert philosophical reasonings. You know that the vulgar often distinguish reason from experience, even where the question relates only to matter of fact and existence, though it is found, where that reason is properly analyzed, that it is nothing but a species of experience. To prove by experience the origin of the universe from mind is not more contrary to common speech than to prove the motion of the earth from the same principle. And a caviller might raise all the same objections to the Copernican system which you have urged against my reasonings. Have you other earths, might he say, which you have seen to move? Have . . . .

Yes! cried Philo, interrupting him, we have other earths. Is not the moon another earth, which we see to turn round its center? Is not Venus another earth, where we observe the same phenomenon? Are not the revolutions of the sun also a confirmation, from analogy, of the same theory? All the planets, are they not earths which revolve about the sun? Are not the satellites moons which move round Jupiter and Saturn, and along with these primary planets round the sun? These analogies and resemblances, with others which I have not mentioned, are the sole proofs of the Copernican system; and to you it belongs to consider whether you have any analogies of the same kind to support your theory.

In reality, Cleanthes, continued he, the modern system of astronomy is now so much received by all inquirers, and has become so essential a part even of our earliest education, that we are not commonly very scrupulous in examining the reasons upon which it is founded. It is now become a matter of mere curiosity to study the first writers on that subject who had the full force of prejudice to encounter, and were obliged to turn their arguments on every side in order to render them popular and convincing. But if we peruse

Galileo's famous *Dialogues* concerning the system of the world, we shall find that the great genius, one of the sublimest that ever existed, first bent all his endeavours to prove that there was no foundation for the distinction commonly made between elementary and celestial substances. The schools, proceeding from the illusions of sense, had carried this distinction very far; and had established the latter substances to be ingenerable, incorruptible, unalterable, impassible; and had assigned all the opposite qualities to the former. But Galileo, beginning with the moon, proved its similarity in every particular to the earth: its convex figure, its natural darkness when not illuminated, its density, its distinction into solid and liquid, the variations of its phases, the mutual illuminations of the earth and moon, their mutual eclipses, the inequalities of the lunar surface, etc. After many instances of this kind, with regard to all the planets, men plainly saw that these bodies became proper objects of experience, and that the similarity of their nature enabled us to extend the same arguments and phenomena from one to the other.

In this cautious proceeding of the astronomers you may read your own condemnation, Cleanthes, or rather may see that the subject in which you are engaged exceeds all human reason and inquiry. Can you pretend to show any such similarity between the fabric of a house and the generation of a universe? Have you ever seen nature in any such situation as resembles the first arrangement of the elements? Have worlds ever been formed under your eye, and have you had leisure to observe the whole progress of the phenomenon, from the first appearance of order to its final consummation? If you have, then cite your experience and deliver your theory....

## PART IV

It seems strange to me, said Cleanthes, that you, Demea, who are so sincere in the cause of religion, should still maintain the mysterious, incomprehensible nature of the Deity, and should insist so strenuously that He has no manner of likeness or resemblance to human creatures. The Deity, I can readily allow, possesses many powers and attributes of which we can have no comprehension; but, if our ideas, so far as they go, be not just and adequate and correspondent to His real nature, I know not what there is in this subject worth insisting on. Is the name, without any meaning, of such mighty importance? Or how do you mystics, who maintain the absolute incomprehensibility of the Deity, differ from skeptics or atheists, who assert that the first cause of all is unknown and unintelligible? Their temerity must be very great if, after rejecting the production by a mind—I mean a mind resembling the human (for I know of no other)—they pretend to assign, with certainty, any other specific intelligible cause; and their conscience must be very scrupulous, indeed, if they refuse to call the universal unknown cause a God or Deity, and to bestow on Him as many sublime eulogies and unmeaning epithets as you shall please to require of them.

Who could imagine, replied Demea, that Cleanthes, the calm philosophical Cleanthes, would attempt to refute his antagonists by affixing a nickname to them, and, like the common bigots and inquisitors of the age, have recourse to invective and declamation instead of reasoning? Or does he not perceive that these topics are easily retorted, and that *anthropomorphite* is an appellation as invidious, and implies as dangerous consequences, as the epithet of *mystic* with which he has honoured us? In reality, Cleanthes, consider what it is you assert when you represent the Deity as similar to a human mind and understanding. What is the soul of man? A composition of various faculties, passions, sentiments, ideas—united, indeed, into one self or person, but still distinct from each other. When it reasons, the ideas which are the parts of its discourse arrange themselves in a certain form or order which is not preserved entire for a moment, but immediately gives place to another arrangement. New opinions, new passions, new affections, new feelings arise which continually diversify the mental scene and produce in it the greatest variety and most rapid succession imaginable. How is this compatible with that perfect immutability and simplicity which all true theists ascribe to the Deity? By the same act, say they, He sees past, present, and future; His love and hatred, His mercy and justice, are one individual operation; He is entire in every point of space, and complete in every instant of duration. No succession, no change, no acquisition, no diminution. What He is implies not in it any shadow of distinction or diversity. And what He is this moment He ever has been and ever will be, without any new judgment, sentiment, or operation. He stands fixed in one simple, perfect state; nor can you ever say, with any propriety, that this act of His is different from that other, or that this judgment or idea has been lately formed and will give place, by succession, to any different judgment or idea.

I can readily allow, said Cleanthes, that those who maintain the perfect simplicity of the Supreme Being, to the extent in which you have explained it, are complete mystics, and chargeable with all the consequences which I have drawn from their opinion. They are, in a word, atheists, without knowing it. For though it be allowed that the Deity possesses attributes of which we have no comprehension, yet ought we never to ascribe to Him any attributes which are absolutely incompatible with that intelligent nature essential to Him. A mind whose acts and sentiments and ideas are not distinct and successive, one that is wholly simple and totally immutable, is a mind which has no thought, no reason, no will, no sentiment, no love, no hatred; or, in a word, is no mind at all. It is an abuse of terms to give it that appellation, and we may as well speak of limited extension without figure, or of number without composition.

Pray consider, said Philo, whom you are at present inveighing against. You are honouring with the appellation of *atheist* all the sound, orthodox divines, almost, who have treated of this subject; and you will at last be, yourself, found, according to your reckoning, the only sound theist in the world. But if idolaters be atheists, as, I think, may justly be asserted, and Christian theologians the same, what becomes of the argument, so much celebrated, derived from the universal consent of mankind?

But, because I know you are not much swayed by names and authorities, I shall endeavour to show you, a little more distinctly, the inconveniences of that anthropomorphism which you have embraced, and shall prove that there is no ground to suppose a plan of the world to be formed in the Divine mind, consisting of distinct ideas, differently arranged, in the same manner as an architect forms in his head the plan of a house which he intends to execute.

It is not easy, I own, to see what is gained by this supposition, whether we judge of the matter by *reason* or by *experience*. We are still obliged to mount higher in order to find the cause of this cause which you had assigned as satisfactory and conclusive.

If *reason* (I mean abstract reason derived from inquiries a priori) be not alike mute with regard to all questions concerning cause and effect, this sentence at least it will venture to pronounce: that a mental world or universe of ideas requires a cause as much as does a material world or universe of objects, and, if similar in its arrangement, must require a similar cause. For what is there in this subject which should occasion a different conclusion or inference? In an abstract view, they are entirely alike; and no difficulty attends the one supposition which is not common to both of them.

Again, when we will needs force *experience* to pronounce some sentence, even on these subjects which lie beyond her sphere, neither can she perceive any material difference in this particular between these two kinds of worlds, but finds them to be governed by similar principles, and to depend upon an equal variety of causes in their operations. We have specimens in miniature of both of them. Our own mind resembles the one; a vegetable or animal body the other. Let experience, therefore, judge from these samples. Nothing seems more delicate, with regard to its causes, than thought; and as these causes never operate in two persons after the same manner, so we never find two persons who think exactly alike. Nor indeed does the same person think exactly alike at any two different periods of time. A difference of age, of the disposition of his body, of weather, of food, of company, of books, of passions—any of these particulars, or others more minute, are sufficient to alter the curious machinery of thought and communicate to it very different movements and operations. As far as we can judge, vegetables and animal bodies are not more delicate in their motions, nor depend upon a greater variety or more curious adjustment of springs and principles.

How, therefore, shall we satisfy ourselves concerning the cause of that Being whom you suppose the Author of nature, or, according to your system of anthropomorphism, the ideal world into which you trace the material? Have we not the same reason to trace that ideal world into another ideal world or new intelligent principle? But if we stop and go no farther, why go so far? why not stop at the material world? How can we satisfy ourselves without going on *in infinitum?* And, after all, what satisfaction is there in that infinite progression? Let us remember the story of the Indian philosopher and his elephant. It was never more applicable than to the present subject. If the material world rests upon a similar ideal world, this ideal world must rest upon some other, and so on without end. It were better, therefore, never to look beyond the present material world. By supposing it to contain the principle of its order within itself, we really assert it to be God; and the sooner we arrive at that Divine Being, so much the better. When you go one step beyond the mundane system, you only excite an inquisitive humour which it is impossible ever to satisfy.

To say that the different ideas which compose the reason of the Supreme Being fall into order of themselves and by their own nature is really to talk without any precise meaning. If it has a meaning, I would fain know why it is not as good sense to say that the parts of the material world fall into order of themselves and by their own nature. Can the one opinion be intelligible, while the other is not so?

We have, indeed, experience of ideas which fall into order of themselves and without any *known* cause. But, I am sure, we have a much larger experience of matter which does the same, as in all instances of generation and vegetation where the accurate analysis of the cause exceeds all human comprehension. We have also experience of particular systems of thought and of matter which have no order; of the first in madness, of the second in corruption. Why, then, should we think that order is more essential to one than the other? And if it requires a cause in both, what do we gain by your system, in tracing the universe of objects into a similar universe of ideas? The first step which we make leads us on forever. It were, therefore, wise in us to limit all our inquiries to the present world, without looking farther. No satisfaction can ever be attained by these speculations which so far exceed the narrow bounds of human understanding.

It was usual with the Peripatetics, you know, Cleanthes, when the cause of any phenomenon was demanded, to have recourse to their *faculties* or *occult qualities,* and to say, for instance, that bread nourished by its nutritive faculty, and senna purged by its purgative. But it has been discovered that this subterfuge was nothing but the disguise of ignorance, and that these philosophers, though less ingenuous, really said the same thing with the skeptics or the vulgar who fairly confessed that they knew not the cause of these phenomena. In like manner, when it is asked what cause produces order in the ideas of the Supreme Being, can any other reason be assigned by you, anthropomorphites, than that it is a *rational* faculty, and that such is the nature of the Deity? But why a similar answer will not be equally satisfactory in accounting for the order of the world, without having recourse to any such intelligent Creator as you insist on, may be difficult to determine. It is only to say that *such* is the nature of material objects, and that they are all originally possessed of a *faculty* of order and proportion. These are only more learned and elaborate ways of confessing our ignorance; nor has the one hypothesis any real advantage above the other, except in its greater conformity to vulgar prejudices.

You have displayed this argument with great emphasis, replied Cleanthes: You seem not sensible how easy it is to answer it. Even in common life, if I assign a cause for any event, is it any objection, Philo, that I cannot assign the cause of that cause, and answer every new question which may incessantly be started? And what philosophers could possibly submit to so rigid a rule?—philosophers who confess ultimate causes to be totally unknown, and are sensible that the most refined principles into which they trace the phenomena are still to them as inexplicable as these phenomena themselves are to the vulgar. The order and arrangement of nature, the curious adjustment of final causes, the plain use and intention of every part and organ—all these bespeak in the clearest language an intelligent cause or author. The heavens and the earth join in the same testimony; The whole chorus of nature raises one hymn to the praises of its Creator. You alone, or almost alone, disturb this general harmony. You start abstruse doubts, cavils, and objections; you ask me what is the cause of this cause? I know not; I care not; that concerns not me. I have found a Deity; and here I stop my inquiry. Let those go farther who are wiser or more enterprising.

I pretend to be neither, replied Philo; and for that very reason I should never, perhaps, have attempted to go so far, especially when I am sensible that I must at last be contented to sit down with the same answer which, without further trouble, might have satisfied me from the beginning. If I am still to remain in utter ignorance of causes and can absolutely give an explication of nothing, I shall never esteem it any advantage to shove off for a moment a difficulty which you acknowledge must immediately, in its full force, recur upon me. Naturalists indeed very justly explain particular effects by more general causes, though these general causes themselves should remain in the end totally inexplicable, but they never surely thought it satisfactory to explain a particular effect by a particular cause which was no more to be accounted for than the effect itself. An ideal system, arranged of itself, without a precedent design, is not a whit more explicable than a material one which attains its order in a like manner; nor is there any more difficulty in the latter supposition than in the former.

## PART V

But to show you still more inconveniences, continued Philo, in your anthropomorphism, please to take a new survey of your principles. *Like effects prove like causes.* This is the experimental argument; and this, you say too, is the sole theological argument. Now it is certain that the liker the effects are which are seen and the liker the causes which are inferred, the stronger is the argument. Every departure on either side diminishes the probability and renders the experiment less conclusive. You cannot doubt of the principle; neither ought you to reject its consequences.

All the new discoveries in astronomy which prove the immense grandeur and magnificence of the works of nature are so many additional arguments for a Deity, according to the true system of theism; but, according to your hypothesis of experimental theism, they become so many objections, by removing the effect still farther from all resemblance to the effects of human art and contrivance. For if Lucretius, even following the old system of the world, could exclaim:

> Quis regere immensi summam, quis habere profundi
> Indu manu validas potis est moderanter habenas?
> Quis pariter cœlos omnes convertere? et omnes
> Ignibus ætheriis terras suffire feraces?
> Omnibus inve locis esse omni tempore præsto?[2]

If Tully [Cicero] esteemed this reasoning so natural as to put it into the mouth of his Epicurean:

> Quibus enim oculis animi intueri potuit vester Plato fabricam illam tanti operis, qua construi a Deo atque ædificari mundum facit? quæ molitio? quæ ferramenta? qui vectes? quæ machinæ? qui ministri tanti muneris fuerunt? quemadmodum autem obedire et parere voluntati architecti aer, ignis, aqua, terra potuerunt?[3]

If this argument, I say, had any force in former ages, how much greater must it have at present when the bounds of nature are so infinitely enlarged

---

[2]*De Rerum Natura*, Bk. XI, Chap. 2. "Who can rule the sum, who hold in his hand with controlling force the strong reins, of the immeasurable deep? Who can at once make all the different heavens to roll and warm with ethereal fires all the fruitful earths, or be present in all places at all times?" (Munro's translation).

[3]*De Natura Deorum*, Bk. I, Chap. 8. "For with what eyes of the mind could your Plato see the construction of so vast a work which, according to him, God was putting together and building? What materials, what tools, what bars, what machines, what servants were employed in such gigantic work? How could the air, fire, water, and earth pay obedience and submit to the will of the architect?"

and such a magnificent scene is opened to us? It is still more unreasonable to form our idea of so unlimited a cause from our experience of the narrow productions of human design and invention.

The discoveries by microscopes, as they open a new universe in miniature, are still objections, according to you, arguments, according to me. The further we push our researches of this kind, we are still led to infer the universal cause of all to be vastly different from mankind, or from any object of human experience and observation.

And what say you to the discoveries in anatomy, chemistry, botany? . . . These surely are no objections, replied Cleanthes; they only discover new instances of art and contrivance. It is still the image of mind reflected on us from innumerable objects. Add a mind *like the human*, said Philo. I know of no other, replied Cleanthes. And the liker, the better, insisted Philo. To be sure, said Cleanthes.

Now, Cleanthes, said Philo, with an air of alacrity and triumph, mark the consequences. *First,* by this method of reasoning you renounce all claim to infinity in any of the attributes of the Deity. For, as the cause ought only to be proportioned to the effect, and the effect, so far as it falls under our cognizance, is not infinite, what pretensions have we, upon your suppositions, to ascribe that attribute to the Divine Being? You will still insist that, by removing Him so much from all similarity to human creatures, we give in to the most arbitrary hypothesis, and at the same time weaken all proofs of His existence.

*Secondly,* you have no reason, on your theory, for ascribing perfection to the Deity, even in His finite capacity, or for supposing Him free from every error, mistake, or incoherence, in His undertakings. There are many inexplicable difficulties in the works of nature which, if we allow a perfect Author to be proved a priori, are easily solved, and become only seeming difficulties from the narrow capacity of man, who cannot trace infinite relations. But according to your method of reasoning, these difficulties become all real, and, perhaps, will be insisted on as new instances of likeness to human art and contrivance. At least, you must acknowledge that it is impossible for us to tell, from our limited views, whether this system contains any great faults or deserves any considerable praise if compared to other possible and even real systems. Could a peasant, if the *Æneid* were read to him, pronounce that poem to be absolutely faultless, or even assign to it its proper rank among the productions of human wit, he who had never seen any other production?

But were this world ever so perfect a production, it must still remain uncertain whether all the excellences of the work can justly be ascribed to the workman. If we survey a ship, what an exalted idea must we form of the ingenuity of the carpenter who framed so complicated, useful, and beautiful a machine? And what surprise must we feel when we find him a stupid mechanic who imitated others, and copied an art which, through a long succession of ages, after multiplied trials, mistakes, corrections, deliberations, and controversies, had been gradually improving? Many worlds might have been botched and bungled, throughout an eternity, ere this system was struck out; much labour lost, many fruitless trials made, and a slow but continued improvement carried on during infinite ages in the art of world-making. In such subjects, who can determine where the truth, nay, who can conjecture where the probability, lies, amidst a great number of hypotheses which may be proposed, and a still greater which may be imagined?

And what shadow of an argument, continued Philo, can you produce from your hypothesis to prove the unity of the Deity? A great number of men join in building a house or ship, in rearing a city, in framing a commonwealth; why may not several deities combine in contriving and framing a world? This is only so much greater similarity to human affairs. By sharing the work among several, we may so much further limit the attributes of each, and get rid of that extensive power and knowledge which must be supposed in one deity, and which, according to you, can only serve to weaken the proof of his existence. And if such foolish, such vicious creatures as man can yet often unite in framing and executing one plan, how much more those deities or demons, whom we may suppose several degrees more perfect!

To multiply causes without necessity is indeed contrary to true philosophy, but this principle applies not to the present case. Were one deity antecedently proved by your theory who were possessed of every attribute requisite to the production of the universe, it would be needless, I own (though not absurd), to suppose any other deity exist. But while it is still a question whether all these attributes are united in one subject or dispersed among several independent beings, by what phenomena in nature can we pretend to decide the controversy? Where we see a body raised in a scale, we are sure that there is in the opposite scale, however concealed from sight, some counterpoising weight equal to it; but it is still allowed to doubt whether that weight be an aggregate of several distinct bodies or one uniform united mass. And if the weight requisite very much exceeds anything which we have ever seen conjoined in any single body, the former supposition becomes still more probable and natural. An intelligent being of such vast powers and capacity as is necessary to produce the universe, or, to speak in the language of ancient philosophy, so prodigious an animal exceeds all analogy and even comprehension.

But further, Cleanthes: men are mortal, and renew their species by generation; and this is common to all living creatures. The two great sexes of male and female, says Milton, animate the world. Why must this circumstance, so universal, so essential, be excluded from those numerous and limited deities? Behold, then, the theogeny of ancient times brought back upon us.

And why not become a perfect anthropomorphite? Why not assert the deity or deities to be corporeal, and to have eyes, a nose, mouth, ears, etc.? Epicurus maintained that no man had ever seen reason but in a human figure; therefore, the gods must have a human figure. And this argument, which is deservedly so much ridiculed by Cicero, becomes, according to you, solid and philosophical.

In a word, Cleanthes, a man who follows your hypothesis is able, perhaps, to assert or conjecture that the universe sometime arose from something like design; but beyond that position he cannot ascertain one single circumstance, and is left afterwards to fix every point of his theology by the utmost license of fancy and hypothesis. This world, for aught he knows, is very faulty and imperfect, compared to a superior standard, and was only the first rude essay of some infant deity who afterwards abandoned it, ashamed of his lame performance; it is the work only of some dependent, inferior deity, and is the object of derision to his superiors; it is the production of old age and dotage in some superannuated deity, and ever since his death has run on at adventures, from the first impulse and active force which it received from him. You justly give signs of horror, Demea, at these strange suppositions; but these, and a thousand more of the same kind, are Cleanthes' suppositions, not mine. From the moment the attributes of the Deity are supposed finite, all these have place. And I cannot, for my part, think that so wild and unsettled a system of theology is, in any respect, preferable to none at all.

These suppositions I absolutely disown, cried Cleanthes: they strike me, however, with no horror, especially when proposed in that rambling way in which they drop from you. On the contrary, they give me pleasure when I see that, by the utmost indulgence of your imagination, you never get rid of the hypothesis of design in the universe, but are obliged at every turn to have recourse to it. To this concession I adhere steadily; and this I regard as a sufficient foundation for religion.

## PART VI

It must be a slight fabric, indeed, said Demea, which can be erected on so tottering a foundation. While we are uncertain whether there is one deity or many, whether the deity or deities, to whom we owe our existence, be perfect or imperfect, subordinate or supreme, dead or alive, what trust or confidence can we repose in them? What devotion or worship address to them? What veneration or obedience pay them? To all the purposes of life the theory of religion becomes altogether useless; and even with regard to speculative consequences its uncertainty, according to you, must render it totally precarious and unsatisfactory.

To render it still more unsatisfactory, said Philo, there occurs to me another hypothesis which must acquire an air of probability from the method of reasoning so much insisted on by Cleanthes. That like effects arise from like causes—this principle he supposes the foundation of all religion. But there is another principle of the same kind, no less certain and derived from the same source of experience, that, where several known circumstances are observed to be similar, the unknown will also be found similar. Thus, if we see the limbs of a human body, we conclude that it is also attended with a human head, though hid from us. Thus, if we see, through a chink in a wall, a small part of the sun, we conclude that were the wall removed we should see the whole body. In short, this method of reasoning is so obvious and familiar that no scruple can ever be made with regard to its solidity.

Now, if we survey the universe, so far as it falls under our knowledge, it bears a great resemblance to an animal or organized body, and seems actuated with a like principle of life and motion. A continual circulation of matter in it produces no disorder; a continual waste in every part is incessantly repaired; the closest sympathy is perceived throughout the entire system; and each part or member, in performing its proper offices, operates both to its own preservation and to that of the whole. The world, therefore, I infer, is an animal; and the Deity is the *soul* of the world, actuating it, and actuated by it.

You have too much learning, Cleanthes, to be at all surprised at this opinion which, you know, was maintained by almost all the theists of antiquity, and chiefly prevails in their discourses and reasonings. For though, sometimes, the ancient philosophers reason from final causes, as if they thought the world the workmanship of God, yet it appears rather their favourite notion to consider it as His body whose organization renders it subservient to Him. And it must be confessed that, as the universe resembles more a human body than it does the works of human art and contrivance, if our limited analogy could ever, with any propriety, be extended to the whole of nature, the inference seems juster in favour of the ancient than the modern theory.

There are many other advantages, too, in the former theory which recommended it to the ancient theologians. Nothing more repugnant to all their notions because nothing more repugnant to common experience than mind without body, a mere spiritual substance which fell not under their senses nor comprehension, and of which they had not observed one single instance throughout all nature. Mind and body they knew because they felt both; an order, arrangement, organization, or internal machinery, in both they likewise knew, after the same manner; and it could not but seem reasonable to transfer this experience to the universe, and to suppose the divine mind and body to be also coeval and to have, both of them, order and arrangement naturally inherent in them and inseparable from them.

Here, therefore, is a new species of anthropomorphism, Cleanthes, on which you may deliberate, and a theory which seems not liable to any considerable difficulties. You are too much superior, surely, to *systematical prejudices* to find any more difficulty in supposing an animal body to be, originally, of itself or from unknown causes, possessed of order and organization, than in supposing a similar order to belong to mind. But the *vulgar prejudice* that body and mind ought always to accompany each other ought not, one should think, to be entirely neglected; since it is founded on *vulgar experience*, the only guide which you profess to follow in all these theological inquiries. And if you assert that our limited experience is an unequal standard by which to judge of the unlimited extent of nature, you entirely abandon your own hypothesis, and must thenceforward adopt our mysticism, as you call it, and admit of the absolute incomprehensibility of the Divine Nature.

This theory, I own, replied Cleanthes, has never before occurred to me, though a pretty natural one; and I cannot readily, upon so short an examination and reflection, deliver any opinion with regard to it. You are very scrupulous, indeed, said Philo, were I to examine any system of yours, I should not have acted with half that caution and reserve, in starting objections and difficulties to it. However, if anything occur to you, you will oblige us by proposing it.

Why then, replied Cleanthes, it seems to me that, though the world does, in many circumstances, resemble an animal body, yet is the analogy also defective in many circumstances the most material: no organs of sense; no seat of thought or reason; no one precise origin of motion and action. In short, it seems to bear a stronger resemblance to a vegetable than to an animal, and your inference would be so far inconclusive in favour of the soul of the world.

But, in the next place, your theory seems to imply the eternity of the world; and that is a principle which, I think, can be refuted by the strongest reasons and probabilities. I shall suggest an argument to this purpose which, I believe, has not been insisted on by any writer. Those who reason from the late origin of arts and sciences, though their inference wants not force, may perhaps be refuted by considerations derived from the nature of human society, which is in continual revolution between ignorance and knowledge, liberty and slavery, riches and poverty; so that it is impossible for us, from our limited experience, to foretell with assurance what events may or may not be expected. Ancient learning and history seem to have been in great danger of entirely perishing after the inundation of the barbarous nations; and had these convulsions continued a little longer or been a little more violent, we should not probably have now known what passed in the world a few centuries before us. Nay, were it not for the superstition of the popes, who preserved a little jargon of Latin in order to support the appearance of an ancient and universal church, that tongue must have been utterly lost; in which case the Western world, being totally barbarous, would not have been in a fit disposition for receiving the Greek language and learning, which was conveyed to them after the sacking of Constantinople. When learning and books had been extinguished, even the mechanical arts would have fallen considerably to decay; and it is easily imagined that fable or tradition might ascribe to them a much later origin than the true one. This vulgar argument, therefore, against the eternity of the world seems a little precarious.

But here appears to be the foundation of a better argument. Lucullus was the first that brought cherry trees from Asia to Europe, though that tree thrives so well in many European climates that it grows in the woods without any culture. Is it possible that, throughout a whole eternity, no European had ever passed into Asia and thought of transplanting so delicious a fruit into his own country? Or if the tree was once transplanted and propagated, how could it ever afterwards perish? Empires may rise and fall, liberty and slavery succeed alternately, ignorance and knowledge give place to each other; but the cherry tree will still remain in the woods of Greece, Spain, and Italy, and will never be affected by the revolutions of human society.

It is not two thousand years since vines were transplanted into France, though there is no climate in the world more favourable to them. It is not three centuries since horses, cows, sheep, swine, dogs, corn, were known in America. Is it possible that during the revolutions of a whole eternity there never arose a Columbus who might open the communication between Europe and that continent? We may as well imagine that all men would wear stockings for ten thousand years, and never have the sense to think of garters to tie them. All these seem convincing proofs of the youth or rather infancy of the world, as being founded on the operation of principles more constant and steady than those by which human society is governed and directed. Nothing less than a total convulsion of the elements will ever destroy all the European animals and vegetables which are now to be found in the Western world.

And what argument have you against such convulsions? replied Philo. Strong and almost incontestable proofs may be traced over the whole earth that every part of this globe has continued for many ages entirely covered with water. And though order were supposed inseparable from matter, and inherent in it, yet may matter be susceptible of many and great revolutions, through the endless periods of eternal duration. The incessant changes to which every part of it is subject seem to intimate some such general transformations; though, at the same time, it is observable that all the changes and corruptions of which we have ever had experience are but passages from one state of order to another; nor can matter ever rest in total deformity and confusion. What we see in the parts, we may infer in the whole; at least, that is the method of reasoning on which you rest your whole theory. And were I obliged to defend any particular system of this nature, which I never willingly should do, I esteem none more plausible than that which ascribes an eternal inherent principle of order to the world, though attended with great and continual revolutions and alterations. This at once solves all difficulties; and if the solution, by being so general, is not entirely complete and satisfactory, it is at least a theory that we must sooner or later have recourse to, whatever system we embrace. How could things have been as they are, were there not an original inherent principle of order somewhere, in thought or in matter? And it is very indifferent to which of these we give the preference. Chance has no place, on any hypothesis, skeptical or religious. Everything is surely governed by steady, inviolable laws. And were the inmost essence of things laid open to us, we should then discover a scene of which, at present, we can have no idea. Instead of admiring the order of natural beings, we should clearly see that it was absolutely impossible for them, in the smallest article, ever to admit of any other disposition.

Were anyone inclined to revive the ancient pagan theology which maintained, as we learn from Hesiod, that this globe was governed by 30,000 deities, who arose from the unknown powers of nature, you would naturally object, Cleanthes, that nothing is gained by this hypothesis; and that it is as easy to suppose all men and animals, beings more numerous but less perfect, to have sprung immediately from a like origin. Push the same inference a step further, and you will find a numerous society of deities as explicable as one universal deity who possesses within himself the powers and perfections of the whole society. All these systems, then, of skepticism, polytheism, and theism, you must allow, on your principles, to be on a like footing, and that no one of them has any advantage over the others. You may thence learn the fallacy of your principles.

## PART VII

But here, continued Philo, in examining the ancient system of the soul of the world there strikes me, all of a sudden, a new idea which, if just, must go near to subvert all your reasoning, and destroy even your first inferences on which you repose such confidence. If the universe bears a greater likeness to animal bodies and to vegetables than to the works of human art, it is more probable that its cause resembles the cause of the former than that of the latter, and its origin ought rather to be ascribed to generation or vegetation than to reason or design. Your conclusion, even according to your own principles, is therefore lame and defective.

Pray open up this argument a little further, said Demea, for I do not rightly apprehend it in that concise manner in which you have expressed it.

Our friend Cleanthes, replied Philo, as you have heard, asserts that, since no question of fact can be proved otherwise than by experience, the existence of a Deity admits not of proof from any other medium. The world, says he, resembles the works of human contrivance; therefore its cause must also resemble that of the other. Here we may remark that the operation of one very small part of nature, to wit, man, upon another very small part, to wit, that inanimate matter lying within his reach, is the rule by which Cleanthes judges of the origin of the whole; and he measures objects, so widely disproportioned, by the same individual standard. But to waive all objections drawn from this topic, I affirm that there are other parts of the universe (besides the machines of human invention) which bear still a greater resemblance to the fabric of the world, and which, therefore, afford a better conjecture concerning the universal origin of this system. These parts are animals and vegetables. The world plainly resembles more an animal or a vegetable than it does a watch or a knitting-loom. Its cause, therefore, it is more probable, resembles the cause of the former. The cause of the former is generation or vegetation. The cause, therefore, of the world we may infer to be something similar or analogous to generation or vegetation.

But how is it conceivable, said Demea, that the world can arise from anything similar to vegetation or generation?

Very easily, replied Philo. In like manner as a tree sheds its seed into the neighbouring fields and produces other trees, so the great vegetable, the world, or this planetary system, produces within itself certain seeds which, being scattered into the surrounding chaos, vegetate into new worlds. A comet, for instance, is the seed of a world; and after it has been fully ripened, by passing from sun to sun, and star to star, it is, at last, tossed into the unformed elements which everywhere surround this universe, and immediately sprouts up into a new system.

Or if, for the sake of variety (for I see no other advantage), we should suppose this world to be an animal: a comet is the egg of this animal; and in like manner as an ostrich lays its egg in the sand, which, without any further care, hatches the egg and produces a new animal, so . . . . I understand you, says Demea. But what wild, arbitrary suppositions are these! What data have you for such extraordinary conclusions? And is the slight, imaginary resemblance of the world to a vegetable or an animal sufficient to establish the same inference with regard to both? Objects which are in general so widely different, ought they to be a standard for each other?

Right, cries Philo: This is the topic on which I have all along insisted. I have still asserted that we have no data to establish any system of cosmogony. Our experience, so imperfect in itself and so limited both in extent and duration, can afford us no probable conjecture concerning the whole of things. But if we must needs fix on some hypothesis, by what rule, pray, ought we to determine our choice? Is there any other rule than the greater similarity of the objects compared? And does not a plant or an animal, which springs from vegetation or generation, bear a stronger resemblance to the world than does any artificial machine, which arises from reason and design?

But what is this vegetation and generation of which you talk? said Demea. Can you explain their operations, and anatomize that fine internal structure on which they depend?

As much, at least, replied Philo, as Cleanthes can explain the operations of reason, or anatomize that internal structure on which it depends. But without any such elaborate disquisitions, when I see an animal, I infer that it sprang from generation; and that with as great certainty as you conclude a house to have been reared by design. These words *generation, reason* mark only certain powers and energies in nature whose effects are known, but whose essence is incomprehensible; and one of these principles, more than the other, has no privilege for being made a standard to the whole of nature.

In reality, Demea, it may reasonably be expected that the larger the views are which we take of things, the better will they conduct us in our conclusions concerning such extraordinary and such magnificent subjects. In this little corner of the world alone, there are four principles, *reason, instinct, generation, vegetation,* which are similar to each other, and are the causes of similar effects. What a number of other principles may we naturally suppose in the immense extent and variety of the universe could we travel from planet to planet, and from system to system, in order to examine each part of this mighty fabric? Any one of these four principles above mentioned (and a hundred others which lie open to our conjecture) may afford us a theory by which to judge of the origin of the world; and it is a palpable and egregious partiality to confine our view entirely to that principle by which our own minds operate. Were this principle more intelligible on that account, such a partiality might be somewhat excusable; but reason, in its internal fabric and structure, is really as little known to us as instinct or vegetation; and, perhaps, even that vague, undeterminate word *nature* to which the vulgar refer everything is not at the bottom more inexplicable. The effects of these principles are all known to us from experience; but the principles themselves and their manner of operation are totally unknown; nor is it less intelligible or less conformable to experience to say that the world arose by vegetation, from a seed shed by another world, than to say that it arose from a divine reason or contrivance, according to the sense in which Cleanthes understands it.

But methinks, said Demea, if the world had a vegetative quality and could sow the seeds of new worlds into the infinite chaos, this power would be still an additional argument for design in its Author. For whence could arise so wonderful a faculty but from design? Or how can order spring from anything which perceives not that order which it bestows?

You need only look around you, replied Philo, to satisfy yourself with regard to this question. A tree bestows order and organization on that tree which springs from it, without knowing the order; an animal in the same manner on its offspring; a bird on its nest; and instances of this kind are even more frequent in the world than those of order which arise from reason and contrivance. To say that all this order in animals and vegetables proceeds ultimately from design is begging the question; nor can that great point be ascertained otherwise than by proving, a priori, both that order is, from its nature, inseparably attached to thought and that it can never of itself or from original unknown principles belong to matter.

But further, Demea, this objection which you urge can never be made use of by Cleanthes, without renouncing a defence which he has already made against one of my objections. When I inquired concerning the cause of that supreme reason and intelligence into which he resolves everything, he told me that the impossibility of satisfying such inquiries could never be admitted as an objection in any species of philosophy. "We must stop somewhere," says he; "nor is it ever within the reach of human capacity to explain ultimate causes or show the last connections of any objects. It is sufficient if any steps, so far as we go, are supported by experience and observation." Now that vegetation and generation, as well as reason, are experienced to be principles of order in nature is undeniable. If I rest my system of cosmogony on the former, preferably to the latter, it is at my choice. The matter seems entirely arbitrary. And when Cleanthes asks me what is the cause of my great vegetative or generative faculty, I am equally entitled to ask him the cause of his great reasoning principle. These questions we have agreed to forbear on both sides; and it is chiefly his interest on the present occasion to stick to this agreement. Judging by our limited and imperfect experience, generation has some privileges above reason; for we see everyday the latter arise from the former, never the former from the latter.

Compare, I beseech you, the consequences on both sides. The world, say I, resembles an animal; therefore it is an animal, therefore it arose from generation. The steps, I confess, are wide, yet there is some small appearance of analogy in each step. The world, says Cleanthes, resembles a machine; therefore it is a machine, therefore it arose from design. The steps are here equally wide, and the analogy less striking. And if he pretends to carry on *my* hypothesis a step further, and to infer design or reason from the great principle of generation on which I insist, I may, with better authority, use the same freedom to push further *his* hypothesis, and infer a divine generation or theogony from his principle of reason. I have at least some faint shadow of experience, which is the utmost that can ever be attained in the present subject. Reason, in innumerable instances, is observed to arise from the principle of generation, and never to arise from any other principle.

Hesiod and all the ancient mythologists were so struck with this analogy that they universally explained the origin of nature from an animal birth, and copulation. Plato, too, so far as he is intelligible, seems to have adopted some such notion in his *Timæus*.

The Brahmins assert that the world arose from an infinite spider, who spun this whole complicated mass from his bowels, and annihilates afterwards the whole or any part of it, by absorbing it again and resolving it into his own essence. Here is a species of cosmogony which appears to us ridiculous because a spider is a little, contemptible animal whose operations we are never likely to take for a model of the whole universe. But still here is a new species of analogy, even in our globe. And were there a planet wholly inhabited by spiders (which is very possible), this inference would there appear as natural and irrefragable as that which in our planet ascribes the origin of all things to design and intelligence, as explained by Cleanthes. Why an orderly system may not be spun from the belly as well as from the brain, it will be difficult for him to give a satisfactory reason.

I must confess, Philo, replied Cleanthes, that, of all men living, the task which you have undertaken, of raising doubts and objections, suits you best and seems, in a manner, natural and unavoidable to you. So great is your fertility of invention that I am not ashamed to acknowledge myself unable, on a sudden, to solve regularly such out-of-the-way difficulties as you incessantly start upon me, though I clearly see, in general, their fallacy and error. And I question not, but you are yourself, at present, in the same case, and have not the solution so ready as the objection, while you must be sensible that common sense and reason are entirely against you, and that such whimsies as you have delivered may puzzle but never can convince us.

## PART VIII

What you ascribe to the fertility of my invention, replied Philo, is entirely owing to the nature of the subject. In subjects adapted to the narrow compass of human reason there is commonly but one determination which carries probability or conviction with it; and to a man of sound judgment all other suppositions but that one appear entirely absurd and chimerical. But in such questions as the present, a hundred contradictory views may preserve a kind of imperfect analogy, and invention has here full scope to exert itself. Without any great effort of thought, I believe that I could, in an instant, propose other systems of cosmogony which would have some faint appearance of truth, though it is a thousand, a million to one if either yours or anyone of mine be the true system.

For instance, what if I should revive the old Epicurean hypothesis? This is commonly, and I believe justly, esteemed the most absurd system that has yet been proposed; yet I know not whether, with a few alterations, it might not be brought to bear a faint appearance of probability. Instead of supposing matter infinite, as Epicurus did, let us suppose it finite. A finite number of particles is only susceptible of finite transpositions; and it must happen, in an eternal duration, that every possible order or position must be tried an infinite number of times. This world, therefore, with all its events, even the most minute, has before been produced and destroyed, and will again be produced and destroyed, without any bounds and limitations. No one who has a conception of the powers of infinite, in comparison of finite, will ever scruple this determination.

But this supposes, said Demea, that matter can acquire motion without any voluntary agent or first mover.

And where is the difficulty, replied Philo, of that supposition? Every event, before experience, is equally difficult and incomprehensible; and every event, after experience, is equally easy and intelligible. Motion, in many instances, from gravity, from elasticity, from electricity, begins in matter, without any known voluntary agent; and to suppose always, in these cases, an unknown, voluntary agent is mere hypothesis and hypothesis attended with no advantages. The beginning of motion in matter itself is as conceivable a priori as its communication from mind and intelligence.

Besides, why may not motion have been propagated by impulse through all eternity, and the same stock of it, or nearly the same, be still upheld in the universe? As much is lost by the composition of motion, as much is gained by its resolution. And whatever the causes are, the fact is certain that matter is and always has been in continual agitation, as far as human experience or tradition reaches. There is not probably, at present, in the whole universe, one particle of matter at absolute rest.

And this very consideration, too, continued Philo, which we have stumbled on in the course of the argument suggests a new hypothesis of cosmogony that is not absolutely absurd and improbable. Is there a system, an order, an economy of things, by which matter can preserve that perpetual agitation which seems essential to it, and yet maintain a constancy in the forms which it produces? There certainly is such an economy, for this is actually the case with the present world. The continual motion of matter, therefore, in less than infinite transpositions, must produce this economy or order, and, by its very nature, that order, when once established, supports itself for many ages if not to eternity. But wherever matter is so poised, arranged, and adjusted as to continue in perpetual motion, and yet preserve a constancy in the forms, its situation must, of necessity, have all the same appearance of art and contrivance which we observe at present. All the parts of each form must have a relation to each other and to the whole; and the whole itself must have a relation to the other parts of the universe, to the element in which the form subsists, to the materials with which it repairs its waste and decay, and to every other form which is hostile or friendly. A defect in any of these particulars destroys the form, and the matter of which it is composed is again set loose, and is thrown into irregular motions and fermentations till it unite itself to some other regular form. If no such form be prepared to receive it, and if there be a great quantity of this corrupted matter in the universe, the universe itself is entirely disordered, whether it be the feeble embryo of a world in its first beginnings that is thus destroyed or the rotten carcass of one languishing in old age and infirmity. In either case, a chaos ensues till finite though innumerable revolutions produce, at last, some forms whose parts and organs are so adjusted as to support the forms amidst a continued succession of matter.

Suppose (for we shall endeavour to vary the expression) that matter were thrown into any position by a blind, unguided force; it is evident that this first position must, in all probability, be the most confused and most disorderly imaginable, without any resemblance to those works of human contrivance which, along with a symmetry of parts, discover an adjustment of means to ends and a tendency to self-preservation. If the actuating force cease after this operation, matter must remain forever in disorder and continue an immense chaos, without any proportion or activity. But suppose that the actuating force, whatever it be, still continues in matter, this first position will immediately give place to a second which will likewise, in all probability, be as disorderly as the first, and so on through many successions of changes and revolutions. No particular order or position ever continues a moment unaltered. The original force, still remaining in activity, gives a perpetual restlessness to matter. Every possible situation is produced, and instantly destroyed. If a glimpse or dawn of order appears for a moment, it is instantly hurried away and confounded by that never-ceasing force which actuates every part of matter.

Thus the universe goes on for many ages in a continued succession of chaos and disorder. But is it not possible that it may settle at last, so as not to lose its motion and active force (for that we have supposed inherent in it), yet so as to preserve an uniformity of appearance, amidst the continual motion and fluctuation of its parts? This we find to be the case with the universe at present. Every individual is perpetually changing, and every part of every individual; and yet the whole remains, in appearance, the same. May we not hope for such a position or rather be assured of it from the eternal revolutions of unguided matter; and may not this account for all the appearing wisdom and contrivance which is in the universe? Let us contemplate the subject a little, and we shall find that this adjustment if attained by matter of a seeming stability in the forms, with a real and perpetual revolution or motion of parts, affords a plausible, if not a true, solution of the difficulty.

It is in vain, therefore, to insist upon the uses of the parts in animals or vegetables, and their curious adjustment to each other. I would fain know how an animal could subsist unless its parts were so adjusted? Do we not find that it immediately perishes whenever this adjustment ceases, and that its matter, corrupting, tries some new form? It happens indeed that the parts of the world are so well adjusted that some regular form immediately lays claim to this corrupted matter; and if it were not so, could the world subsist? Must it not dissolve, as well as the animal, and pass through new positions and situations till in great but finite succession it fall, at last, into the present or some such order?

It is well, replied Cleanthes, you told us that this hypothesis was suggested on a sudden, in the course of the argument. Had you had leisure to examine it, you would soon have perceived the insuperable objections to which it is exposed. No form, you say, can subsist unless it possess those powers and organs requisite for its subsistence; some new order or economy must be tried, and so on, without intermission, till at last some order which can support and maintain itself is fallen upon. But according to this hypothesis, whence arise the many conveniences and advantages which men and all animals possess? Two eyes, two ears are not absolutely necessary for the subsistence of the species. Human race might have been propagated and preserved without horses, dogs, cows, sheep, and those innumerable fruits and products which serve to our satisfaction and enjoyment. If no camels had been created for the use of man in the sandy deserts of Africa and Arabia, would the world have been dissolved? If no loadstone had been framed to give that wonderful and useful direction to the needle, would human society and the humankind have been immediately extinguished? Though the maxims of nature be in general very frugal, yet instances of this kind are far from being rare; and any one of them is a sufficient proof of design—and of a benevolent design—which gave rise to the order and arrangement of the universe.

At least, you may safely infer, said Philo, that the foregoing hypothesis is so far incomplete and imperfect, which I shall not scruple to allow. But can we ever reasonably expect greater success in any attempts of this nature? Or can we ever hope to erect a system of cosmogony that will be liable to no exceptions, and will contain no circumstance repugnant to our limited and imperfect experience of the analogy of nature? Your theory itself cannot surely pretend to any such advantage, even though you have run into anthropomorphism, the better to preserve a conformity to common experience. Let us once more put it to trial. In all instances which we have ever seen, ideas are copied from real objects, and are ectypal, not archetypal, to express myself in learned terms. You reverse this order and give thought the precedence. In all instances which we have ever seen, thought has no influence upon matter except where that matter is so conjoined with it as to have an equal reciprocal influence upon it. No animal can move immediately anything but the members of its own body; and, indeed, the equality of action and reaction seems to be an universal law of nature; but your theory implies a contradiction to this experience. These instances, with many more which it were easy to collect (particularly the supposition of a mind or system of thought that is eternal or, in other words, an animal ingenerable and immortal)—these instances, I say, may teach all of us sobriety in condemning each other, and let us see that as no system of this kind ought ever to be received from a slight analogy, so neither ought any to be rejected on account of a small incongruity. For that is an inconvenience from which we can justly pronounce no one to be exempted.

All religious systems, it is confessed, are subject to great and insuperable difficulties. Each disputant triumphs in his turn, while he carries on an offensive war, and exposes the absurdities, barbarities, and pernicious tenets of his antagonist. But all of them, on the whole, prepare a complete triumph for the *skeptic*, who tells them that no system ought ever to be embraced with regard to such subjects: for this plain reason that no absurdity ought ever to be assented to with regard to any subject. A total suspense of judgment is here our only reasonable resource. And if every attack, as is commonly observed, and no defence among theologians is successful, how complete must be *his* victory who remains always, with all mankind, on the offensive, and has himself no fixed station or abiding city which he is ever, on any occasion, obliged to defend?

• • •

## PART XII

After Demea's departure, Cleanthes and Philo continued the conversation in the following manner. Our friend, I am afraid, said Cleanthes, will have little inclination to revive this topic of discourse while you are in company; and to tell the truth, Philo, I should rather wish to reason with either of you apart on a subject so sublime and interesting. Your spirit of controversy, joined to your abhorrence of vulgar superstition, carries you strange lengths when engaged in an argument; and there is nothing so sacred and venerable, even in your own eyes, which you spare on that occasion.

I must confess, replied Philo, that I am less cautious on the subject of natural religion than on any other; both because I know that I can never, on that head, corrupt the principles of any man of common sense and because no one, I am confident, in whose eyes I appear a man of common sense will ever mistake my intentions. You, in particular, Cleanthes, with whom I live in unreserved intimacy, you are sensible that, notwithstanding the freedom of my conversation and my love of singular arguments, no one has a deeper sense of religion impressed on his mind, or pays more profound adoration to the Divine Being, as he discovers himself to reason in the inexplicable contrivance and artifice of nature. A purpose, an intention, a design strikes everywhere the most careless, the most stupid thinker; and no man can be so hardened in absurd systems as at all times to reject it. *That nature does nothing in vain* is a maxim established in all the schools, merely from the contemplation of the works of nature, without any religious purpose; and, from a firm conviction of its truth, an anatomist who had observed a new organ or canal would never be satisfied till he had also discovered its use and intention. One great foundation of the Copernican system is the maxim *that nature acts by the simplest methods, and chooses the most proper means to any end;* and astronomers often, without thinking of it, lay this strong foundation of piety and religion. The same thing is observable in other parts of philosophy; and thus all the sciences almost lead us insensibly to acknowledge a first intelligent Author; and their authority is often so much the greater as they do not directly profess that intention.

It is with pleasure I hear Galen reason concerning the structure of the human body. The anatomy of a man, says he, discovers above 600 different muscles; and whoever duly considers these will find that, in each of them, nature must have adjusted at least ten different circumstances in order to attain the end which she proposed: proper figure, just magnitude, right disposition of the several ends, upper and lower position of the whole, the due insertion of the several nerves, veins, and arteries, so that, in the muscles alone, above 6000 several views and intentions must have been formed and executed. The bones he calculates to be 284; the distinct purposes aimed at in the structure of each, above forty. What a prodigious display of artifice, even in these simple and homogeneous parts! But if we consider the skin, ligaments, vessels, glandules, humours, the several limbs and members of the body, how must our astonishment rise upon us, in proportion to the number and intricacy of the parts so artificially adjusted! The further we advance in these researches, we discover new scenes of art and wisdom; but descry still, at a distance, further scenes beyond our reach: in the fine internal structure of the parts, in the economy of the brain, in the fabric of the seminal vessels. All these artifices are repeated in every different species of animal, with wonderful variety, and with exact propriety, suited to the different intentions of nature in framing each species. And if the infidelity of Galen, even when these natural sciences were still imperfect, could not withstand such striking appearances, to what pitch of pertinacious obstinacy must a philosopher in this age have attained who can now doubt of a Supreme Intelligence!

Could I meet with one of these species (who, I thank God, are very rare), I would ask him: Supposing there were a God who did not discover himself immediately to our senses, were it possible for Him to give stronger proofs of His existence than what appear on the whole face of nature? What indeed could such a Divine Being do but copy the present economy of things, render many of His artifices so plain that no stupidity could mistake them, afford glimpses of still greater artifices which demonstrate His prodigious superiority above our narrow apprehensions, and conceal altogether a great many from such imperfect creatures? Now, according to all rules of just reasoning, every fact must pass for undisputed when it is supported by all the arguments which its nature admits of, even though these arguments be not, in themselves, very numerous or forcible—how much more in the present case where no human imagination can compute their number, and no understanding estimate their cogency!

I shall further add, said Cleanthes, to what you have so well urged, that one great advantage of the principle of theism is that it is the only system of cosmogony which can be rendered intelligible and complete, and yet can throughout preserve a strong analogy to what we everyday see and experience in the world. The comparison of the universe to a machine of human contrivance is so obvious and natural, and is justified by so many instances of order and design in nature, that it must immediately strike all unprejudiced apprehensions and procure universal approbation. Whoever attempts to weaken this theory cannot pretend to succeed by establishing in its place any other that is precise and determinate; it is sufficient for him if he start doubts and difficulties, and, by remote and abstract views of things, reach that suspense of judgment which is here the utmost boundary of his wishes. But, besides that this state of mind is in itself unsatisfactory, it can never be steadily maintained against such striking appearances as continually engage us into the religious hypothesis. A false, absurd system, human nature, from the force of prejudice, is capable of adhering to with obstinacy and perseverance; but no system at all, in opposition to a theory supported by strong and obvious reason, by natural propensity, and by early education, I think it absolutely impossible to maintain or defend.

So little, replied Philo, do I esteem this suspense of judgment in the present case to be possible that I am apt to suspect there enters somewhat of a dispute of words into this controversy, more than is usually imagined. That the works of nature bear a great analogy to the productions of art is evident, and, according to all the rules of good reasoning, we ought to infer, if we argue at all concerning them, that their causes have a proportional analogy. But as there are also considerable differences, we have reason to suppose a proportional difference in the causes, and, in particular, ought to attribute a much higher degree of power and energy to the Supreme Cause than any we have ever observed in mankind. Here, then, the existence of a *Deity* is plainly ascertained by reason; and if we make it a question whether, on account of these analogies, we can properly call Him a *Mind* or *Intelligence*, notwithstanding the vast difference which may reasonably be supposed between Him and human minds, what is this but a mere verbal controversy? No man can deny the analogies between the effects; to restrain ourselves from inquiring concerning the causes is scarcely possible. From this inquiry the legitimate conclusion is that the causes have also an analogy; and if we are not contented with calling the First and Supreme Cause a *God* or *Deity*, but desire to vary the expression, what can we call Him but *Mind* or *Thought* to which He is justly supposed to bear a considerable resemblance?

All men of sound reason are disgusted with verbal disputes, which abound so much in philosophical and theological inquiries; and it is found that the only remedy for this abuse must arise from clear definitions, from the precision of those ideas which enter into any argument, and from the strict and uniform use of those terms which are employed. But there is a species of controversy which, from the very nature of language and of human ideas, is involved in perpetual ambiguity, and can never, by any precaution or any definitions, be able to reach a reasonable certainty or precision. These are the controversies concerning the degrees of any quality or circumstance. Men may argue to all eternity whether Hannibal be a great, or a very great, or a superlatively great man, what degree of beauty Cleopatra possessed, what epithet of praise Livy or Thucydides is entitled to, without bringing the controversy to any determination. The disputants may here agree in their sense and differ in the terms, or vice versa, yet never be able to define their terms so as to enter into each other's meaning; because the degrees of these qualities are not, like quantity or number, susceptible of any exact mensuration, which may be the standard in the controversy. That the dispute concerning theism is of this nature, and consequently is merely verbal, or, perhaps, if possible, still more incurably ambiguous, will appear upon the slightest inquiry. I ask the theist if he does not allow that there is a great and immeasurable, because incomprehensible, difference between the *human* and the *divine* mind; the more pious he is, the more readily will he assent to the affirmative, and the more will he be disposed to magnify the difference; he will even assert that the difference is of a nature which cannot be too much magnified. I next turn to the atheist, who, I assert, is only nominally so and can never possibly be in earnest, and I ask him whether, from the coherence and apparent sympathy in all the parts of this world, there be not a certain degree of analogy among all the operations of nature, in every situation and in every age; whether the rotting of a turnip, the generation of an animal, and the structure of human thought, be not energies that probably bear some remote analogy to each other. It is impossible he can deny it; he will readily acknowledge it. Having obtained this concession, I push him still further in his retreat, and I ask him if it be not probable that the principle which first arranged and still maintains order in this universe bears not also some remote inconceivable analogy to the other operations of nature and, among the rest, to the economy of human mind and thought. However reluctant, he must give his assent. Where then, cry I to both these antagonists, is the subject of your dispute? The theist allows that the original intelligence is very different from human reason; the atheist allows that the original principle of order bears some remote analogy to it. Will you quarrel, gentlemen, about the degrees, and enter into a controversy which admits not of any precise meaning, nor consequently of any determination? If you should be so obstinate, I should not be surprised to find you insensibly change sides; while the theist, on the one hand, exaggerates the dissimilarity between the Supreme Being and frail, imperfect, variable, fleeting, and mortal creatures; and the atheist, on the other, magnifies the analogy among all the operations of nature, in every period, every situation, and every position. Consider then where the real point of controversy lies; and if you cannot lay aside your disputes, endeavour, at least, to cure yourselves of your animosity.

And here I must also acknowledge, Cleanthes, that, as the works of nature have a much greater analogy to the effects of *our* art and contrivance than to those of *our* benevolence and justice, we have reason to infer that the natural attributes of the Deity have a greater resemblance to those of man than His morals have to human virtues. But what is the consequence? Nothing but this, that the moral qualities of man are more defective in their kind than his natural abilities. For, as the Supreme Being is allowed to be absolutely and entirely perfect, whatever differs most from Him departs the farthest from the supreme standard of rectitude and perfection.[4]

These, Cleanthes, are my unfeigned sentiments on this subject; and these sentiments, you know, I have ever cherished and maintained. But in proportion to my veneration for true religion is my abhorrence of vulgar superstitions; and I indulge a peculiar pleasure, I confess, in pushing such principles sometimes into absurdity, sometimes into impiety. And you are sensible that all bigots, notwithstanding their great aversion to the latter above the former, are commonly equally guilty of both.

My inclination, replied Cleanthes, lies, I own, a contrary way. Religion, however corrupted, is still better than no religion at all. The doctrine of a future state is so strong and necessary a security to morals that we never ought to abandon or neglect it. For if finite and temporary rewards and punishments have so great an effect, as we daily find, how much greater must be expected from such as are infinite and eternal?

How happens it then, said Philo, if vulgar superstition be so salutary to society, that all history abounds so much with accounts of its pernicious consequences on public affairs? Factions, civil wars, persecutions, subversions of government, oppression, slavery—these are the dismal consequences which always attend its prevalence over the minds of men. If the religious spirit be ever mentioned in any historical narration, we are sure to meet afterwards with a detail of the miseries which attend it. And no period of time can be happier or more prosperous than those in which it is never regarded or heard of.

---

[4]It seems evident that the dispute between the skeptics and dogmatists is entirely verbal, or, at least, regards only the degrees of doubt and assurance which we ought to indulge with regard to all reasoning; and such disputes are commonly, at the bottom, verbal and admit not of any precise determination. No philosophical dogmatist denies that there are difficulties both with regard to the senses and to all science, and that these difficulties are, in a regular, logical method, absolutely insolvable. No skeptic denies that we lie under an absolute necessity, notwithstanding these difficulties, of thinking, and believing, and reasoning, with regard to all kinds of subjects, and even of frequently assenting with confidence and security. The only difference, then, between these sects, if they merit that name, is that the skeptic, from habit, caprice, or inclination, insists most on the difficulties, the dogmatist, for like reasons, on the necessity.

The reason of this observation, replied Cleanthes, is obvious. The proper office of religion is to regulate the heart of men, humanize their conduct, infuse the spirit of temperance, order, and obedience; and, as its operation is silent and only enforces the motives of morality and justice, it is in danger of being overlooked and confounded with these other motives. When it distinguishes itself, and acts as a separate principle over men, it has departed from its proper sphere and has become only a cover to faction and ambition.

And so will all religion, said Philo, except the philosophical and rational kind. Your reasonings are more easily eluded than my facts. The inference is not just—because finite and temporary rewards and punishments have so great influence that therefore such as are infinite and eternal must have so much greater. Consider, I beseech you, the attachment which we have to present things, and the little concern which we discover for objects so remote and uncertain. When divines are declaiming against the common behaviour and conduct of the world, they always represent this principle as the strongest imaginable (which indeed it is), and describe almost all human kind as lying under the influence of it, and sunk into the deepest lethargy and unconcern about their religious interest. Yet these same divines, when they refute their speculative antagonists, suppose the motives of religion to be so powerful that, without them, it were impossible for civil society to subsist, nor are they ashamed of so palpable a contradiction. It is certain, from experience, that the smallest grain of natural honesty and benevolence has more effect on men's conduct than the most pompous views suggested by theological theories and systems. A man's natural inclination works incessantly upon him; it is forever present to the mind, and mingles itself with every view and consideration; whereas religious motives, where they act at all, operate only by starts and bounds, and it is scarcely possible for them to become altogether habitual to the mind. The force of the greatest gravity, say the philosophers, is infinitely small, in comparison of that of the least impulse, yet it is certain that the smallest gravity will, in the end, prevail above a great impulse because no strokes or blows can be repeated with such constancy as attraction and gravitation.

Another advantage of inclination: it engages on its side all the wit and ingenuity of the mind, and, when set in opposition to religious principles, seeks every method and art of eluding them; in which it is almost always successful. Who can explain the heart of man, or account for those strange salvos and excuses with which people satisfy themselves when they follow their inclinations in opposition to their religious duty? This is well understood in the world; and none but fools ever repose less trust in a man because they hear that, from study and philosophy, he has entertained some speculative doubts with regard to theological subjects. And when we have to do with a man who makes a great profession of religion and devotion, has this any other effect upon several who pass for prudent than to put them on their guard, lest they be cheated and deceived by him?

We must further consider that philosphers, who cultivate reason and reflection, stand less in need of such motives to keep them under the restraint of morals, and that the vulgar, who alone may need them, are utterly incapable of so pure a religion as represents the Deity to be pleased with nothing but virtue in human behaviour. The recommendations to the Divinity are generally supposed to be either frivolous observances or rapturous ecstasies or a bigoted credulity. We need not run back into antiquity or wander into remote regions to find instances of this degeneracy. Amongst ourselves, some have been guilty of that atrociousness, unknown to the Egyptian and Grecian superstitions, of declaiming, in express terms, against morality, and representing it as a sure forfeiture of the Divine favour if the least trust or reliance be laid upon it.

But even though superstition or enthusiasm should not put itself in direct opposition to morality, the very diverting of the attention, the raising up a new and frivolous species of merit, the preposterous distribution which it makes of praise and blame, must have the most pernicious consequences, and weaken extremely men's attachment to the natural motives of justice and humanity.

Such a principle of action likewise, not being any of the familiar motives of human conduct, acts only by intervals on the temper, and must be roused by continual efforts in order to render the pious zealot satisfied with his own conduct and make him fulfill his devotional task. Many religious exercises are entered into with seeming fervour where the heart, at the time, feels cold and languid. A habit of dissimulation is by degrees contracted, and fraud and falsehood become the predominant principle. Hence the reason of that vulgar observation that the highest zeal in religion and the deepest hypocrisy, so far from being inconsistent, are often or commonly united in the same individual character.

The bad effects of such habits, even in common life, are easily imagined, but, where the interests of religion are concerned, no morality can be forcible enough to bind the enthusiastic zealot. The sacredness of the cause sanctifies every measure which can be made use of to promote it.

The steady attention alone to so important an interest as that of eternal salvation is apt to extinguish the benevolent affections, and beget a narrow, contracted selfishness. And when such a temper is encouraged, it easily eludes all the general precepts of charity and benevolence.

Thus the motives of vulgar superstition have no great influence on general conduct, nor is their operation favourable to morality, in the instances where they predominate.

Is there any maxim in politics more certain and infallible than that both the number and authority of priests should be confined within very narrow limits, and that the civil magistrate ought, forever, to keep his *fasces* and *axes* from such dangerous hands? But if the spirit of popular religion were so salutary to society, a contrary maxim ought to prevail. The greater number of priests and their greater authority and riches will always augment the religious spirit. And though the priests have the guidance of this spirit, why may we not expect a superior sanctity of life and greater benevolence and moderation from persons who are set apart for religion, who are continually inculcating it upon others, and who must themselves imbibe a greater share of it? Whence comes it then that, in fact, the utmost a wise magistrate can propose with regard to popular religions is, as far as possible, to make a saving game of it, and to prevent their pernicious consequences with regard to society? Every expedient which he tries for so humble a purpose is surrounded with inconveniences. If he admits only one religion among his subjects, he must sacrifice, to an uncertain prospect of tranquillity, every consideration of public liberty, science, reason, industry, and even his own independence. If he gives indulgence to several sects, which is the wiser maxim, he must preserve a very philosophical indifference to all of them and carefully restrain the pretensions of the prevailing sect, otherwise he can expect nothing but endless disputes, quarrels, factions, persecutions, and civil commotions.

True religion, I allow, has no such pernicious consequences; but we must treat of religion as it has commonly been found in the world, nor have I anything to do with that speculative tenet of theism which, as it is a species of philosophy, must partake of the beneficial influence of that principle, and, at the same time, must lie under a like inconvenience of being always confined to very few persons.

Oaths are requisite in all courts of judicature, but it is a question whether their authority arises from any popular religion. It is the solemnity and importance of the occasion, the regard to reputation, and the reflecting on the general interests of society, which are the chief restraints upon mankind. Customhouse oaths and political oaths are but little regarded even by some who pretend to principles of honesty and religion; and a Quaker's asseveration is with us justly put upon the same footing with the oath of any other person. I know that Polybius ascribes the infamy of Greek faith to the prevalence of the Epicurean philosophy; but I know also that Punic faith had as bad a reputation in ancient times as Irish evidence has in modern, though we cannot account for these vulgar observations by the same reason. Not to mention that Greek faith was infamous before the rise of the Epicurean philosophy; and Euripides, in a passage which I shall point out to you, has glanced a remarkable stroke of satire against his nation, with regard to this circumstance.

Take care, Philo, replied Cleanthes, take care: push not matters too far, allow not your zeal against false religion to undermine your veneration for the true. Forfeit not this principle—the chief, the only great comfort in life and our principal support amidst all the attacks of adverse fortune. The most agreeable reflection which it is possible for human imagination to suggest is that of genuine theism, which represents us as the workmanship of a Being perfectly good, wise, and powerful; who created us for happiness; and who, having implanted in us immeasurable desires of good, will prolong our existence to all eternity, and will transfer us into an infinite variety of scenes, in order to satisfy those desires and render our felicity complete and durable. Next to such a Being Himself (if the comparison be allowed), the happiest lot which we can imagine is that of being under His guardianship and protection.

These appearances, said Philo, are most engaging and alluring, and, with regard to the true philosopher, they are more than appearances. But it happens here, as in the former case, that, with regard to the greater part of mankind, the appearances are deceitful, and that the terrors of religion commonly prevail above its comforts.

It is allowed that men never have recourse to devotion so readily as when dejected with grief or depressed with sickness. Is not this a proof that the religious spirit is not so nearly allied to joy as to sorrow?

But men, when afflicted, find consolation in religion, replied Cleanthes. Sometimes, said Philo; but it is natural to imagine that they will form a notion of those unknown beings, suitable to the present gloom and melancholy of their temper, when they betake themselves to the contemplation of them. Accordingly, we find the tremendous images to predominate in all religions; and we ourselves, after having employed the most exalted expression in our descriptions of the Deity, fall into the flattest contradiction in affirming that the damned are infinitely superior in number to the elect.

I shall venture to affirm that there never was a popular religion which represented the state of departed souls in such a light as would render it eligible for human kind that there should be such a state. These fine models of religion are the mere product of philosophy. For as death lies between the eye and the prospect of futurity, that event is so shocking to nature that it must throw a gloom on all the regions which lie beyond it, and suggest to the generality of mankind the idea of Cerberus and Furies, devils, and torrents of fire and brimstone.

It is true, both fear and hope enter into religion because both these passions, at different times, agitate the human mind, and each of them forms a species of divinity suitable to itself. But when a man is in a cheerful disposition, he is fit for business, or company, or entertainment of any kind; and he naturally applies himself to these and thinks not of religion. When melancholy and dejected, he has nothing to do but brood upon the terrors of the invisible world, and to plunge himself still deeper in affliction. It may indeed happen that, after he has, in this manner, engraved the religious opinions deep into his thought and imagination, there may arrive a change of health or circumstances which may restore his good humour and, raising cheerful prospects of futurity, make him run into the other extreme of joy and triumph. But still it must be acknowledged that, as terror is the primary principle of religion, it is the passion which always predominates in it, and admits but of short intervals of pleasure.

Not to mention that these fits of excessive, enthusiastic joy, by exhausting the spirits, always prepare the way for equal fits of superstitious terror and dejection, nor is there any state of mind so happy as the calm and equable. But this state it is impossible to support where a man thinks that he lies in such profound darkness and uncertainty, between an eternity of happiness and an eternity of misery. No wonder that such an opinion disjoints the ordinary frame of the mind and throws it into the utmost confusion. And though that opinion is seldom so steady in its operation as to influence all the actions, yet it is apt to make a considerable breach in the temper, and to produce that gloom and melancholy so remarkable in all devout people.

It is contrary to common sense to entertain apprehensions or terrors upon account of any opinion whatsoever, or to imagine that we run any risk hereafter, by the freest use of our reason. Such a sentiment implies both an *absurdity* and an *inconsistency*. It is an absurdity to believe that the Deity has human passions, and one of the lowest of human passions, a restless appetite for applause. It is an inconsistency to believe that, since the Deity has this human passion, He has not others also, and, in particular, a disregard to the opinions of creatures so much inferior.

"To know God," says Seneca, "is to worship Him." All other worship is indeed absurd, superstitious, and even impious. It degrades Him to the low condition of mankind, who are delighted with entreaty, solicitation, presents, and flattery. Yet is this impiety the smallest of which superstition is guilty. Commonly, it depresses the Deity far below the condition of mankind, and represents Him as a capricious demon who exercises his power without reason and without humanity! And were that Divine Being disposed to be offended at the vices and follies of silly mortals, who are His own workmanship, ill would it surely fare with the votaries of most popular superstitions. Nor would any of human race merit His *favour* but a very few, the philosophical theists, who entertain or rather indeed endeavour to entertain suitable notions of His Divine perfections. As the only persons entitled to His *compassion* and *indulgence* would be the philosophical skeptics, a sect almost equally rare, who, from a natural diffidence of their own capacity, suspend or endeavour to suspend all judgment with regard to such sublime and such extraordinary subjects.

If the whole of natural theology, as some people seem to maintain, resolves itself into one simple, though somewhat ambiguous, at least undefined, proposition, *that the cause or causes of order in the universe probably bear some remote analogy to human intelligence*—if this proposition be not capable of extension, variation, or more particular explication, if it affords no inference that affects human life, or can be the source of any action or forbearance, and if the analogy, imperfect as it is, can be carried no further than to the human intelligence, and cannot be transferred, with any appearance of probability, to the other qualities of the mind, if this really be the case, what can the most inquisitive, contemplative, and religious man do more than give a plain, philosophical assent to the proposition, as often as it occurs, and believe that the arguments on which it is established exceed the objections which lie against it? Some astonishment, indeed, will naturally arise from the greatness of the object, some melancholy from its obscurity, some contempt of human reason that it can give no solution more satisfactory with regard to so extraordinary and magnificent a question. But believe me, Cleanthes, the most natural sentiment which a well-disposed mind will feel on this occasion is a longing desire and expectation that Heaven would be pleased to dissipate, at least alleviate, this profound ignorance by affording some more particular revelation to mankind, and making discoveries of the nature, attributes, and operations of the Divine object of our faith. A person, seasoned with a just sense of the imperfections of natural reason, will fly to revealed truth with the greatest avidity, while the haughty dogmatist, persuaded that he can erect a complete system of theology by the mere help of philosophy, disdains any further aid and rejects this adventitious instructor. To be a philosophical skeptic is, in a man of letters, the first and most essential step towards being a sound, believing Christian—a proposition which I would willingly recommend to the attention of Pamphilus; and I hope Cleanthes will forgive me for interposing so far in the education and instruction of his pupil.

Cleanthes and Philo pursued not this conversation much further; and as nothing ever made greater impression on me than all the reasonings of that day, so I confess that, upon a serious review of the whole, I cannot but think that Philo's principles are more probable than Demea's, but that those of Cleanthes approach still nearer to the truth.

# 9

# *Miracles*

## PART I

There is, in Dr. Tillotson's writings, an argument against the *real pres-ence*, which is as concise, and elegant, and strong as any argument can possibly be supposed against a doctrine so little worthy of a serious refuta-tion. It is acknowledged on all hands, says that learned prelate, that the authority, either of the scripture or of tradition, is founded merely in the testimony of the apostles, who were eye-witnesses to those miracles of our Saviour, by which he proved his divine mission. Our evidence, then, for the truth of the *Christian* religion is less than the evidence for the truth of our senses; because, even in the first authors of our religion, it was no greater; and it is evident it must diminish in passing from them to their disciples; nor can anyone rest such confidence in their testimony, as in the immediate object of his senses. But a weaker evidence can never destroy a stronger; and therefore, were the doctrine of the real presence ever so clearly revealed in scripture, it were directly contrary to the rules of just reasoning to give our assent to it. It contradicts sense, though both the scripture and tradition, on which it is supposed to be built, carry not such evidence with them as sense; when they are considered merely as external evidences, and are not brought home to everyone's breast, by the immediate operation of the Holy Spirit.

Nothing is so convenient as a decisive argument of this kind, which must at least *silence* the most arrogant bigotry and superstition, and free us from their impertinent solicitations. I flatter myself, that I have discovered an argument of a like nature, which, if just, will, with the wise and learned, be an everlasting check to all kinds of superstitious delusion, and consequently, will be useful as long as the world endures. For so long, I presume, will the accounts of miracles and prodigies be found in all history, sacred and profane.

Though experience be our only guide in reasoning concerning matters of fact; it must be acknowledged, that this guide is not altogether infallible, but in some cases is apt to lead us into errors. One, who in our climate, should expect better weather in any week of June than in one of December, would reason justly, and conformably to experience; but it is certain that he may happen, in the event, to find himself mistaken. However, we may observe,

---

*An Enquiry Concerning Human Understanding*, Sec. X.

that, in such a case, he would have no cause to complain of experience; because it commonly informs us beforehand of the uncertainty, by that contrariety of events, which we may learn from a diligent observation. All effects follow not with like certainty from their supposed causes. Some events are found, in all countries and all ages, to have been constantly conjoined together: Others are found to have been more variable, and sometimes to disappoint our expectations; so that, in our reasonings concerning matter of fact, there are all imaginable degrees of assurance, from the highest certainty to the lowest species of moral evidence.

A wise man, therefore, proportions his belief to the evidence. In such conclusions as are founded on an infallible experience, he expects the event with the last degree of assurance, and regards his past experience as a full *proof* of the future existence of that event. In other cases, he proceeds with more caution: he weighs the opposite experiments: he considers which side is supported by the greater number of experiments: to that side he inclines, with doubt and hesitation; and when at last he fixes his judgement, the evidence exceeds not what we properly call *probability*. All probability, then, supposes an opposition of experiments and observations, where the one side is found to overbalance the other, and to produce a degree of evidence, proportioned to the superiority. A hundred instances or experiments on one side, and fifty on another, afford a doubtful expectation of any event; though a hundred uniform experiments, with only one that is contradictory, reasonably beget a pretty strong degree of assurance. In all cases, we must balance the opposite experiments, where they are opposite, and deduct the smaller number from the greater, in order to know the exact force of the superior evidence.

To apply these principles to a particular instance; we may observe, that there is no species of reasoning more common, more useful, and even necessary to human life, than that which is derived from the testimony of men, and the reports of eye-witnesses and spectators. This species of reasoning, perhaps, one may deny to be founded on the relation of cause and effect. I shall not dispute about a word. It will be sufficient to observe that our assurance in any argument of this kind is derived from no other principle than our observation of the veracity of human testimony, and of the usual conformity of facts to the reports of witnesses. It being a general maxim that no objects have any discoverable connection together, and all the inferences, which we can draw from one to another, are founded merely on our experience of their constant and regular conjunction; it is evident, that we ought not to make an exception to this maxim in favour of human testimony, whose connection with any event seems, in itself, as little necessary as any other. Were not the memory tenacious to a certain degree; had not men commonly an inclination to truth and a principle of probity; were they not sensible to shame, when detected in a falsehood: were not these, I say, discovered by *experience* to be qualities inherent in human nature, we should never repose the least confidence in human testimony. A man delirious, or noted for falsehood and villainy, has no manner of authority with us.

And as the evidence, derived from witnesses and human testimony, is founded on past experience, so it varies with the experience, and is regarded either as a *proof* or a *probability*, according as the conjunction between any particular kind of report and any kind of object has been found to be constant or variable. There are a number of circumstances to be taken into consideration in all judgements of this kind; and the ultimate standard, by which we determine all disputes that may arise concerning them, is always derived from experience and observation. Where this experience is not entirely uniform on any side, it is attended with an unavoidable contrariety in our judgements, and with the same opposition and mutual destruction of argument as in every other kind of evidence. We frequently hesitate concerning the reports of others. We balance the opposite circumstances, which cause any doubt or uncertainty; and when we discover a superiority on any side, we incline to it; but still with a diminution of assurance, in proportion to the force of its antagonist.

This contrariety of evidence, in the present case, may be derived from several different causes from the opposition of contrary testimony; from the character or number of the witnesses; from the manner of their delivering their testimony; or from the union of all these circumstances. We entertain a suspicion concerning any matter of fact, when the witnesses contradict each other; when they are but few, or of a doubtful character; when they have an interest in what they affirm; when they deliver their testimony with hesitation, or on the contrary, with too violent asseverations. There are many other particulars of the same kind, which may diminish or destroy the force of any argument, derived from human testimony.

Suppose, for instance, that the fact, which the testimony endeavours to establish, partakes of the extraordinary and the marvellous; in that case, the evidence, resulting from the testimony, admits of a diminution, greater or less, in proportion as the fact is more or less unusual. The reason why we place any credit in witnesses and historians, is not derived from any *connection*, which we perceive a priori, between testimony and reality, but because we are accustomed to find a conformity between them. But when the fact attested is such a one as has seldom fallen under our observation, here is a contest of two opposite experiences; of which the one destroys the other, as far as its force goes, and the superior can only operate on the mind by the force, which remains. The very same principle of experience, which gives us a certain degree of assurance in the testimony of witnesses, gives us also, in this case, another degree of assurance against the fact, which they endeavour to establish; from which contradiction there necessarily arises a counterpoise, and mutual destruction of belief and authority.

"I should not believe such a story were it told me by Cato" was a proverbial saying in Rome, even during the lifetime of that philosophical patriot. The incredibility of a fact, it was allowed, might invalidate so great an authority.

The Indian prince, who refused to believe the first relations concerning the effects of frost, reasoned justly; and it naturally required very strong testimony to engage his assent to facts that arose from a state of nature, with which he was unacquainted, and which bore so little analogy to those events, of which he had had constant and uniform experience. Though they were not contrary to his experience, they were not conformable to it.[1]

But in order to increase the probability against the testimony of witnesses, let us suppose that the fact, which they affirm, instead of being only marvellous, is really miraculous; and suppose also, that the testimony considered apart and in itself, amounts to an entire proof; in that case, there is proof against proof, of which the strongest must prevail, but still with a diminution of its force, in proportion to that of its antagonist.

A miracle is a violation of the laws of nature; and as a firm and unalterable experience has established these laws, the proof against a miracle, from the very nature of the fact, is as entire as any argument from experience can possibly be imagined. Why is it more than probable that all men must die; that lead cannot, of itself, remain suspended in the air; that fire consumes wood, and is extinguished by water; unless it be that these events are found agreeable to the laws of nature, and there is required a violation of these laws, or in other words, a miracle to prevent them? Nothing is esteemed a miracle, if it ever happen in the common course of nature. It is no miracle that a man, seemingly in good health, should die on a sudden: because such a kind of death, though more unusual than any other, has yet been frequently observed to happen. But it is a miracle that a dead man should come to life; because that has never been observed in any age or country. There must, therefore, be a uniform experience against every miraculous event, otherwise the event

---

[1] No Indian, it is evident, could have experience that water did not freeze in cold climates. This is placing nature in a situation quite unknown to him; and it is impossible for him to tell a priori what will result from it. It is making a new experiment, the consequence of which is always uncertain. One may sometimes conjecture from analogy what will follow; but still this is but conjecture. And it must be confessed that, in the present case of freezing, the event follows contrary to the rules of analogy, and is such as a rational Indian would not look for. The operations of cold upon water are not gradual, according to the degrees of cold; but whenever it comes to the freezing point, the water passes in a moment from the utmost liquidity to perfect hardness. Such an event, therefore, may be denominated *extraordinary*, and requires a pretty strong testimony to render it credible to people in a warm climate. But still it is not *miraculous*, nor contrary to uniform experience of the course of nature in cases where all the circumstances are the same. The inhabitants of Sumatra have always seen water fluid in their own climate, and the freezing of their rivers ought to be deemed a prodigy. But they never saw water in Muscovy during the winter; and therefore they cannot reasonably be positive what would there be the consequence.

would not merit that appellation. And as a uniform experience amounts to a proof, there is here a direct and full *proof*, from the nature of the fact, against the existence of any miracle; nor can such a proof be destroyed, or the miracle rendered credible, but by an opposite proof, which is superior.[2]

The plain consequence is (and it is a general maxim worthy of our attention) "that no testimony is sufficient to establish a miracle, unless the testimony be of such a kind that its falsehood would be more miraculous than the fact which it endeavours to establish; and even in that case there is a mutual destruction of arguments, and the superior only gives us an assurance suitable to that degree of force, which remains, after deducting the inferior." When anyone tells me that he saw a dead man restored to life, I immediately consider with myself whether it be more probable that this person should either deceive or be deceived, or that the fact, which he relates, should really have happened. I weigh the one miracle against the other; and according to the superiority which I discover, I pronounce my decision, and always reject the greater miracle. If the falsehood of his testimony would be more miraculous than the event which he relates; then, and not till then, can he pretend to command my belief or opinion.

## PART II

In the foregoing reasoning we have supposed that the testimony, upon which a miracle is founded, may possibly amount to an entire proof, and that the falsehood of that testimony would be a real prodigy. But it is easy to show that we have been a great deal too liberal in our concession, and that there never was a miraculous event established on so full an evidence.

For *first*, there is not to be found, in all history, any miracle attested by a sufficient number of men, of such unquestioned good sense, education, and learning, as to secure us against all delusion in themselves; of such undoubted

---

[2]Sometimes an event may not, *in itself, seem* to be contrary to the laws of nature, and yet, if it were real, it might, by reason of some circumstances, be denominated a miracle; because, in *fact*, it is contrary to these laws. Thus if a person, claiming a divine authority, should command a sick person to be well, a healthful man to fall down dead, the clouds to pour rain, the winds to blow, in short, should order many natural events, which immediately follow upon his command; these might justly be esteemed miracles, because they are really, in this case, contrary to the laws of nature. For if any suspicion remain that the event and command concurred by accident, there is no miracle and no transgression of the laws of nature. If this suspicion be removed, there is evidently a miracle, and a transgression of these laws; because nothing can be more contrary to nature than that the voice or command of a man should have such an influence. A miracle may be accurately defined, *a transgression of a law of nature by a particular volition of the Deity, or by the interposition of some invisible agent*. A miracle may either be discoverable by men or not. This alters not its nature and essence. The raising of a house or ship into the air is a visible miracle. The raising of a feather, when the wind wants ever so little of a force requisite for that purpose, is as real a miracle, though not so sensible with regard to us.

integrity, as to place them beyond all suspicion of any design to deceive others; of such credit and reputation in the eyes of mankind, as to have a great deal to lose in case of their being detected in any falsehood; and at the same time, attesting facts performed in such a public manner and in so celebrated a part of the world, as to render the detection unavoidable. All which circumstances are requisite to give us a full assurance in the testimony of men.

*Secondly.* We may observe in human nature a principle which, if strictly examined, will be found to diminish extremely the assurance, which we might, from human testimony, have, in any kind of prodigy. The maxim, by which we commonly conduct ourselves in our reasonings, is that the objects of which we have no experience resemble those of which we have; that what we have found to be most usual is always most probable; and that where there is an opposition of arguments, we ought to give the preference to such as are founded on the greatest number of past observations. But though, in proceeding by this rule, we readily reject any fact which is unusual and incredible in an ordinary degree; yet in advancing farther, the mind observes not always the same rule; but when anything is affirmed utterly absurd and miraculous, it rather the more readily admits of such a fact, upon account of that very circumstance, which ought to destroy all its authority. The passion of *surprise* and *wonder*, arising from miracles, being an agreeable emotion, gives a sensible tendency towards the belief of those events, from which it is derived. And this goes so far, that even those who cannot enjoy this pleasure immediately, nor can believe those miraculous events, of which they are informed, yet love to partake of the satisfaction at second-hand or by rebound, and place a pride and delight in exciting the admiration of others.

With what greediness are the miraculous accounts of travellers received, their descriptions of sea and land monsters, their relations of wonderful adventures, strange men, and uncouth manners? But if the spirit of religion join itself to the love of wonder, there is an end of common sense; and human testimony, in these circumstances, loses all pretensions to authority. A religionist may be an enthusiast, and imagine he sees what has no reality: he may know his narrative to be false, and yet persevere in it, with the best intentions in the world, for the sake of promoting so holy a cause: or even where this delusion has not place, vanity, excited by so strong a temptation, operates on him more powerfully than on the rest of mankind in any other circumstances; and self-interest with equal force. His auditors may not have, and commonly have not, sufficient judgement to canvass his evidence: what judgement they have, they renounce by principle, in these sublime and mysterious subjects: or if they were ever so willing to employ it, passion and a heated imagination disturb the regularity of its operations. Their credulity increases his impudence: and his impudence overpowers their credulity.

Eloquence, when at its highest pitch, leaves little room for reason or reflection; but addressing itself entirely to the fancy or the affections, captivates the willing hearers, and subdues their understanding. Happily, this pitch it seldom attains. But what a Tully or a Demosthenes could scarcely effect over a Roman or Athenian audience, every *Capuchin*, every itinerant or stationary teacher can perform over the generality of mankind, and in a higher degree, by touching such gross and vulgar passions.

The many instances of forged miracles, and prophecies, and supernatural events, which, in all ages, have either been detected by contrary evidence, or which detect themselves by their absurdity, prove sufficiently the strong propensity of mankind to the extraordinary and the marvellous, and ought reasonably to beget a suspicion against all relations of this kind. This is our natural way of thinking, even with regard to the most common and most credible events. For instance: There is no kind of report which rises so easily, and spreads so quickly, especially in country places and provincial towns, as those concerning marriages; insomuch that two young persons of equal condition never see each other twice, but the whole neighborhood immediately join them together. The pleasure of telling a piece of news so interesting, of propagating it, and of being the first reporters of it, spreads the intelligence. And this is so well known, that no man of sense gives attention to these reports, till he find them confirmed by some greater evidence. Do not the same passions, and others still stronger, incline the generality of mankind to believe and report, with the greatest vehemence and assurance, all religious miracles?

*Thirdly.* It forms a strong presumption against all supernatural and miraculous relations, that they are observed chiefly to abound among ignorant and barbarous nations; or if a civilized people has ever given admission to any of them, that people will be found to have received them from ignorant and barbarous ancestors, who transmitted them with that inviolable sanction and authority, which always attend received opinions. When we peruse the first histories of all nations, we are apt to imagine ourselves transported into some new world; where the whole frame of nature is disjointed, and every element performs its operations in a different manner from what it does at present. Battles, revolutions, pestilence, famine, and death are never the effect of those natural causes, which we experience. Prodigies, omens, oracles, judgements, quite obscure the few natural events that are intermingled with them. But as the former grow thinner every page, in proportion as we advance nearer the enlightened ages, we soon learn that there is nothing mysterious or supernatural in the case, but that all proceeds from the usual propensity of mankind towards the marvellous, and that, though this inclination may at intervals receive a check from sense and learning, it can never be thoroughly extirpated from human nature.

"It is strange," a judicious reader is apt to say, upon the perusal of these wonderful historians, "that such prodigious events never happen in our days." But it is nothing strange, I hope, that men should lie in all ages. You must surely have seen instances enough of that frailty. You have yourself heard many such marvellous relations started, which, being treated with scorn by all the wise and judicious, have at last been abandoned even by the vulgar. Be assured that those renowned lies, which have spread and flourished to such a monstrous height, arose from like beginnings but being sown in a more proper soil, shot up at last into prodigies almost equal to those which they relate.

It was a wise policy in that false prophet, Alexander, who though now forgotten, was once so famous, to lay the first scene of his impostures in Paphlagonia, where, as Lucian tells us, the people were extremely ignorant and stupid, and ready to swallow even the grossest delusion. People at a distance, who are weak enough to think the matter at all worth inquiry, have no opportunity of receiving better information. The stories come magnified to them by a hundred circumstances. Fools are industrious in propagating the imposture; while the wise and learned are contented, in general, to deride its absurdity, without informing themselves of the particular facts, by which it may be distinctly refuted. And thus the impostor above mentioned was enabled to proceed, from his ignorant Paphlagonians, to the enlisting of votaries, even among the Grecian philosophers, and men of the most eminent rank and distinction in Rome: nay, could engage the attention of that sage emperor Marcus Aurelius; so far as to make him trust the success of a military expedition to his delusive prophecies.

The advantages are so great, of starting an imposture among an ignorant people, that, even though the delusion should be too gross to impose on the generality of them (*which, though seldom, is sometimes the case*) it has a much better chance for succeeding in remote countries than if the first scene had been laid in a city renowned for arts and knowledge. The most ignorant and barbarous of these barbarians carry the report abroad. None of their countrymen have a large correspondence, or sufficient credit and authority to contradict and beat down the delusion. Men's inclination to the marvellous has full opportunity to display itself. And thus a story, which is universally exploded in the place where it was first started, shall pass for certain at a thousand miles distance. But had Alexander fixed his residence at Athens, the philosophers of that renowned mart of learning had immediately spread, throughout the whole Roman empire, their sense of the matter; which, being supported by so great authority, and displayed by all the force of reason and eloquence, had entirely opened the eyes of mankind. It is true; Lucian, passing by chance through Paphlagonia, had an opportunity of performing this good office. But, though much to be wished, it does not always happen that every Alexander meets with a Lucian, ready to expose and detect his impostures.

I may add as a *fourth* reason, which diminishes the authority of prodigies, that there is no testimony for any, even those which have not been expressly detected, that is not opposed by an infinite number of witnesses; so that not only the miracle destroys the credit of testimony, but the testimony destroys itself. To make this the better understood, let us consider that, in matters of religion, whatever is different is contrary; and that it is impossible the religions of ancient Rome, of Turkey, of Siam, and of China should, all of them, be established on any solid foundation. Every miracle, therefore, pretended to have been wrought in any of these religions (and all of them abound in miracles), as its direct scope is to establish the particular system to which it is attributed; so has it the same force, though more indirectly, to overthrow every other system. In destroying a rival system, it likewise destroys the credit of those miracles, on which that system was established; so that all the prodigies of different religions are to be regarded as contrary facts, and the evidences of these prodigies, whether weak or strong, as opposite to each other. According to this method of reasoning, when we believe any miracle of Mahomet or his successors, we have for our warrant the testimony of a few barbarous Arabians: and on the other hand, we are to regard the authority of Titus Livius, Plutarch, Tacitus, and, in short, of all the authors and witnesses, Grecian, Chinese, and Roman Catholic, who have related any miracle in their particular religion; I say, we are to regard their testimony in the same light as if they had mentioned that Mahometan miracle, and had in express terms contradicted it, with the same certainty as they have for the miracle they relate. This argument may appear over subtle and refined; but is not in reality different from the reasoning of a judge, who supposes that the credit of two witnesses, maintaining a crime against anyone, is destroyed by the testimony of two others, who affirm him to have been two hundred leagues distant, at the same instant when the crime is said to have been committed.

One of the best attested miracles in all profane history, is that which Tacitus reports of Vespasian, who cured a blind man in Alexandria, by means of his spittle, and a lame man by the mere touch of his foot; in obedience to a vision of the god Serapis, who had enjoined them to have recourse to the emperor, for these miraculous cures. The story may be seen in that fine historian; where every circumstance seems to add weight to the testimony, and might be displayed at large with all the force of argument and eloquence, if anyone were now concerned to enforce the evidence of that exploded and idolatrous superstition. The gravity, solidity, age, and probity of so great an emperor, who, through the whole course of his life, conversed in a familiar manner with his friends and courtiers, and never affected those extraordinary airs of divinity assumed by Alexander and Demetrius. The historian, a contemporary writer, noted for candour and veracity, and withal, the greatest and most penetrating genius, perhaps, of all antiquity; and so free from any tendency to credulity, that he even lies under the contrary imputation, of atheism and profaneness: the persons, from whose authority he related the miracle, of established character for judgement and veracity, as we may well presume; eye-witnesses of the fact, and confirming their testimony, after the Flavian family was despoiled of the empire, and could no longer give any reward, as the price of a lie. *Utrumque, qui interfuere, nunc quoque memorant, postquam nullum mendacio pretium.* [Now those who were present remember afterwards, when there is no reward for lying.] To which if we add the public nature of the facts, as related, it will appear that no evidence can well be supposed stronger for so gross and so palpable a falsehood.

There is also a memorable story related by Cardinal de Retz, which may well deserve our consideration. When that intriguing politician fled into Spain, to avoid the persecution of his enemies, he passed through Saragossa, the capital of Arragon, where he was shown, in the cathedral, a man, who had served seven years as a doorkeeper, and was well known to everybody in town, that had ever paid his devotions at that church. He had been seen, for so long a time, wanting a leg; but recovered that limb by the rubbing of holy oil upon the stump; and the cardinal assures us that he saw him with two legs. This miracle was vouched by all the canons of the church; and the whole company in town were appealed to for a confirmation of the fact; whom the cardinal found, by their zealous devotion, to be thorough believers of the miracle. Here the relater was also contemporary to the supposed prodigy, of an incredulous and libertine character, as well as of great genius; the miracle of so *singular* a nature as could scarcely admit of a counterfeit, and the witnesses very numerous, and all of them, in a manner, spectators of the fact, to which they gave their testimony. And what adds mightily to the force of the evidence, and may double our surprise on this occasion, is that the cardinal himself, who relates the story, seems not to give any credit to it, and consequently cannot be suspected of any concurrence in the holy fraud. He considered justly that it was not requisite, in order to reject a fact of this nature, to be able accurately to disprove the testimony, and to trace its falsehood, through all the circumstances of knavery and credulity which produced it. He knew that, as this was commonly altogether impossible at any small distance of time and place; so was it extremely difficult, even where one was immediately present, by reason of the bigotry, ignorance, cunning, and roguery of a great part of mankind. He therefore concluded, like a just reasoner, that such an evidence carried falsehood upon the very face of it, and that a miracle, supported by any human testimony, was more properly a subject of derision than of argument.

There surely never was a greater number of miracles ascribed to one person than those which were lately said to have been wrought in France upon the tomb of Abbé Paris, the famous Jansenist, with whose sanctity the people were so long deluded. The curing of the sick, giving hearing to the deaf, and sight to the blind, were everywhere talked of as the usual effects of that holy sepulchre. But what is more extraordinary; many of the miracles were immediately proved upon the spot, before judges of unquestioned integrity, attested by witnesses of credit and distinction, in a learned age, and on the most eminent theatre that is now in the world. Nor is this all: a relation of them was published and dispersed everywhere; nor were the *Jesuits*, though a learned body, supported by the civil magistrate, and determined enemies to those opinions, in whose favour the miracles were said to have been wrought, ever able distinctly to refute or detect them. Where shall we find such a number of circumstances, agreeing to the corroboration of one fact? And what have we to oppose to such a cloud of witnesses, but the absolute impossibility or miraculous nature of the events which they relate? And this surely, in the eyes of all reasonable people, will alone be regarded as a sufficient refutation.

Is the consequence just, because some human testimony has the utmost force and authority in some cases, when it relates the battle of Philippi or Pharsalia for instance; that therefore all kinds of testimony must, in all cases, have equal force and authority? Suppose that the Cæsarean and Pompeian factions had, each of them, claimed the victory in these battles, and that the historians of each party had uniformly ascribed the advantage to their own side; how could mankind, at this distance, have been able to determine between them? The contrariety is equally strong between the miracles related by Herodotus or Plutarch, and those delivered by Mariana, Bede, or any monkish historian.

The wise lend a very academic faith to every report which favours the passion of the reporter; whether it magnifies his country, his family, or himself, or in any other way strikes in with his natural inclinations and propensities. But what greater temptation than to appear a missionary, a prophet, an ambassador from heaven? Who would not encounter many dangers and difficulties, in order to attain so sublime a character? Of if, by the help of vanity and a heated imagination, a man has first made a convert of himself, and entered seriously into the delusion; who ever scruples to make use of pious frauds, in support of so holy and meritorious a cause?

The smallest spark may here kindle into the greatest flame; because the materials are always prepared for it. The *avidum genus auricularum*, the gazing populace, receive greedily, without examination, whatever sooths superstition, and promotes wonder.

How many stories of this nature have, in all ages, been detected and exploded in their infancy? How many more have been celebrated for a time, and have afterwards sunk into neglect and oblivion? Where such reports, therefore, fly about, the solution of the phenomenon is obvious; and we judge in conformity to regular experience and observation, when we account for it by the known and natural principles of credulity and delusion. And shall we, rather than have a recourse to so natural a solution, allow of a miraculous violation of the most established laws of nature?

I need not mention the difficulty of detecting a falsehood in any private or even public history, at the place, where it is said to happen; much more when the scene is removed to ever so small a distance. Even a court of judicature, with all the authority, accuracy, and judgement, which they can employ, find themselves often at a loss to distinguish between truth and falsehood in the most recent actions. But the matter never comes to any issue, if trusted to the common method of altercations and debate and flying rumours; especially when men's passions have taken part on either side.

In the infancy of new religions, the wise and learned commonly esteem the matter too inconsiderable to deserve their attention or regard. And when afterwards they would willingly detect the cheat, in order to undeceive the deluded multitude, the season is now past, and the records and witnesses, which might clear up the matter, have perished beyond recovery.

No means of detection remain, but those which must be drawn from the very testimony itself of the reporters: and these, though always sufficient with the judicious and knowing, are commonly too fine to fall under the comprehension of the vulgar.

Upon the whole, then, it appears that no testimony for any kind of miracle has ever amounted to a probability, much less to a proof; and that, even supposing it amounted to a proof, it would be opposed by another proof; derived from the very nature of the fact, which it would endeavour to establish. It is experience only which gives authority to human testimony; and it is the same experience which assures us of the laws of nature. When, therefore, these two kinds of experience are contrary, we have nothing to do but subtract the one from the other, and embrace an opinion, either on one side or the other, with that assurance which arises from the remainder. But according to the principle here explained, this subtraction, with regard to all popular religions, amounts to an entire annihilation; and therefore we may establish it as a maxim that no human testimony can have such force as to prove a miracle, and make it a just foundation for any such system of religion.

I beg the limitations here made may be remarked, when I say that a miracle can never be proved, so as to be the foundation of a system of religion. For I own that otherwise there may possibly be miracles, or violations of the usual course of nature, of such a kind as to admit of proof from human testimony; though, perhaps, it will be impossible to find any such in all the records of history. Thus, suppose all authors, in all languages, agree that, from the first of January 1600, there was a total darkness over the whole earth for eight days: suppose that the tradition of this extraordinary event is still strong and lively among the people: that all travellers, who return from foreign countries, bring us accounts of the same tradition, without the least variation or contradiction: it is evident that our present philosophers, instead of doubting the fact, ought to receive it as certain, and ought to search for the causes whence it might be derived. The decay, corruption, and dissolution of nature is an event rendered probable by so many analogies, that any phenomenon, which seems to have a tendency towards that catastrophe, comes within the reach of human testimony, if that testimony be very extensive and uniform.

But suppose that all the historians who treat of England should agree that, on the first of January 1600, Queen Elizabeth died; that both before and after her death she was seen by her physicians and the whole court, as is usual with persons of her rank; that her successor was acknowledged and proclaimed by the parliament; and that, after being interred a month, she again appeared, resumed the throne, and governed England for three years: I must confess that I should be surprised at the concurrence of so many odd circumstances, but should not have the least inclination to believe so miraculous an event. I should not doubt of her pretended death, and of those other public circumstances that followed it: I should only assert it to have been pretended, and that it neither was, nor possibly could be real. You would in vain object to me the difficulty, and almost impossibility of deceiving the world in an affair of such consequence; the wisdom and solid judgement of that renowned queen; with the little or no advantage which she could reap from so poor an artifice. All this might astonish me; but I would still reply that the knavery and folly of men are such common phenomena, that I should rather believe the most extraordinary events to arise from their concurrence than admit of so signal a violation of the laws of nature.

But should this miracle be ascribed to any new system of religion; men, in all ages, have been so much imposed on by ridiculous stories of that kind, that this very circumstance would be a full proof of a cheat, and sufficient, with all men of sense, not only to make them reject the fact, but even reject it without further examination. Though the Being to whom the miracle is ascribed, be, in this case, Almighty, it does not, upon that account, become a whit more probable; since it is impossible for us to know the attributes or actions of such a Being, otherwise than from the experience which we have of His productions, in the usual course of nature. This still reduces us to past observation, and obliges us to compare the instances of the violation of truth in the testimony of men, with those of the violation of the laws of nature by miracles, in order to judge which of them is most likely and probable. As the violations of truth are more common in the testimony concerning religious miracles than in that concerning any other matter of fact; this must diminish very much the authority of the former testimony, and make us form a general resolution, never to lend any attention to it, with whatever specious pretence it may be covered.

Lord Bacon seems to have embraced the same principles of reasoning. "We ought," says he, "to make a collection or particular history of all monsters and prodigious births or productions, and in a word of everything new, rare, and extraordinary in nature. But this must be done with the most severe scrutiny, lest we depart from truth. Above all, every relation must be considered as suspicious, which depends in any degree upon religion, as the prodigies of Livy: and no less so, everything that is to be found in the writers of natural magic or alchimy, or such authors, who seem, all of them, to have an unconquerable appetite for falsehood and fable."[3]

I am the better pleased with the method of reasoning here delivered, as I think it may serve to confound those dangerous friends or disguised enemies to the *Christian religion*, who have undertaken to defend it by the principles of human reason. Our most holy religion is founded on *faith*, not on reason; and it is a sure method of exposing it to put it to such a trial as it is, by no means, fitted to endure. To make this more evident, let us examine those miracles related in scripture; and not to lose ourselves in too wide a field, let us confine ourselves to such as we find in the *Pentateuch*, which we shall examine, according to the principles of these pretended Christians, not as the word or testimony of God Himself, but as the production of a mere human writer and historian. Here then we are first to consider a book, presented to us by a barbarous and ignorant people, written in an age when they were still more barbarous, and in all probability long after the facts which it relates, corroborated by no concurring testimony, and resembling those fabulous accounts, which every nation gives of its origin. Upon reading this book, we find it full of prodigies and miracles. It gives an account of a state of the world and of human nature entirely different from the present: of our fall from that state: of the age of man, extended to near a thousand years: of the destruction of the world by a deluge: of the arbitrary choice of one people, as the favourites of heaven; and that people the countrymen of the author: of their deliverance from bondage by prodigies the most astonishing imaginable: I desire anyone to lay his hand upon his heart, and after a serious consideration declare whether he thinks that the falsehood of such a book, supported by such a testimony, would be more extraordinary and miraculous than all the miracles it relates; which is, however, necessary to make it be received, according to the measures of probability above established.

What we have said of miracles may be applied, without any variation, to prophecies; and indeed, all prophecies are real miracles, and as such only, can be admitted as proofs of any revelation. If it did not exceed the capacity of human nature to foretell future events, it would be absurd to employ any prophecy as an argument for a divine mission or authority from heaven. So that, upon the whole, we may conclude, that the *Christian religion* not only was at first attended with miracles, but even at this day cannot be believed by any reasonable person without one. Mere reason is insufficient to convince us of its veracity: and whoever is moved by *faith* to assent to it is conscious of a continued miracle in his own person, which subverts all the principles of his understanding, and gives him a determination to believe what is most contrary to custom and experience.

---

[3]*Novum Organum*, Bk. II, Aphorism 19.

# Immanuel Kant

Immanuel Kant (1724–1804), one of the most penetrating minds in the
history of philosophy, created a new intellectual situation. His account
in the *Critique of Pure Reason* of the nature and limits of human
knowledge constitutes a watershed, and everyone thinking about
these problems since Kant's day has had to do so in the light of his
arguments.

# 10

# *Critique of the Theistic Proofs*

*There are only three possible ways of proving the existence of God by means of
speculative reason.*

All the paths leading to this goal begin either from determinate experience and the specific constitution of the world of sense as thereby known, and
ascend from it, in accordance with laws of causality, to the supreme cause
outside the world; or they start from experience which is purely indetermi-
nate, that is, from experience of existence in general; or finally they abstract
from all experience, and argue completely a priori, from mere concepts, to
the existence of a supreme cause. The first proof is the *physico-theological*, the
second the *cosmological*, the third the *ontological*. There are, and there can be,
no others.

I propose to show that reason is as little able to make progress on the
one path, the empirical, as on the other path, the transcendental, and that it
stretches its wings in vain in thus attempting to soar above the world of sense
by the mere power of speculation. As regards the order in which these
arguments should be dealt with, it will be exactly the reverse of that which
reason takes in the progress of its own development, and therefore of that
which we have ourselves followed in the above account. For it will be shown
that, although experience is what first gives occasion to this enquiry, it is the
*transcendental concept* which in all such endeavours marks out the goal that
reason has set itself to attain, and which is indeed its sole guide in its efforts
to achieve that goal. I shall therefore begin with the examination of the
transcendental proof, and afterwards enquire what effect the addition of the
empirical factor can have in enhancing the force of the argument.

CHAPTER III

*Section 4:*

## THE IMPOSSIBILITY OF AN ONTOLOGICAL PROOF
## OF THE EXISTENCE OF GOD

It is evident, from what has been said, that the concept of an absolutely necessary being is a concept of pure reason, that is, a mere idea the objective reality of which is very far from being proved by the fact that reason requires it. For the idea instructs us only in regard to a certain unattainable completeness, and so serves rather to limit the understanding than to extend it to new objects. But we are here faced by what is indeed strange and perplexing, namely, that while the inference from a given existence in general to some absolutely necessary being seems to be both imperative and legitimate, all those conditions under which alone the understanding can form a concept of such a necessity are so many obstacles in the way of our doing so.

In all ages men have spoken of an *absolutely necessary* being, and in so doing have endeavoured, not so much to understand whether and how a thing of this kind allows even of being thought, but rather to prove its existence. There is, of course, no difficulty in giving a verbal definition of the concept, namely, that it is something the non-existence of which is impossible. But this yields no insight into the conditions which make it necessary to regard the non-existence of a thing as absolutely unthinkable. It is precisely these conditions that we desire to know, in order that we may determine whether or not, in resorting to this concept, we are thinking anything at all. The expedient of removing all those conditions which the understanding indispensably requires in order to regard something as necessary, simply through the introduction of the word *unconditioned*, is very far from sufficing to show whether I am still thinking anything in the concept of the unconditionally necessary, or perhaps rather nothing at all.

Nay more, this concept, at first ventured upon blindly, and now become so completely familiar, has been supposed to have its meaning exhibited in a number of examples; and on this account all further inquiry into its intelligibility has seemed to be quite needless. Thus the fact that every geometrical proposition, as, for instance, that a triangle has three angles, is absolutely necessary, has been taken as justifying us in speaking of an object which lies entirely outside the sphere of our understanding as if we understood perfectly what it is that we intend to convey by the concept of that object.

All the alleged examples are, without exception, taken from *judgments*, not from *things* and their existence. But the unconditioned necessity of judgments is not the same as an absolute necessity of things. The absolute necessity of the judgment is only a conditioned necessity of the thing, or of the predicate in the judgment. The above proposition does not declare that three angles are absolutely necessary, but that, under the condition that there is a triangle (that is, that a triangle is given), three angles will necessarily be found in it. So great, indeed, is the deluding influence exercised by this logical necessity that, by the simple device of forming an a priori concept of a thing in such a manner as to include existence within the scope of its meaning, we have supposed ourselves to have justified the conclusion that because existence necessarily belongs to the object of this concept—always under the condition that we posit the thing as given (as existing)—we are also of necessity, in accordance with the law of identity, required to posit the existence of its object, and that this being is therefore itself absolutely necessary—and this, to repeat, for the reason that the existence of this being has already been thought in a concept which is assumed arbitrarily and on condition that we posit its object.

If, in an identical proposition, I reject the predicate while retaining the subject, contradiction results; and I therefore say that the former belongs necessarily to the latter. But if we reject subject and predicate alike, there is no contradiction; for nothing is then left that can be contradicted. To posit a triangle, and yet to reject its three angles, is self-contradictory; but there is no contradiction in rejecting the triangle together with its three angles. The same holds true of the concept of an absolutely necessary being. If its existence is rejected, we reject the thing itself with all its predicates; and no question of contradiction can then arise. There is nothing outside it that would then be contradicted, since the necessity of the thing is not supposed to be derived from anything external; nor is there anything internal that would be contradicted, since in rejecting the thing itself we have at the same time rejected all its internal properties. "God is omnipotent" is a necessary judgment. The omnipotence cannot be rejected if we posit a Deity, that is, an infinite being; for the two concepts are identical. But if we say, "There is no God," neither the omnipotence nor any other of its predicates is given; they are one and all rejected together with the subject, and there is therefore not the least contradiction in such a judgment.

We have thus seen that if the predicate of a judgment is rejected together with the subject, no internal contradiction can result, and that this holds no matter what the predicate may be. The only way of evading this conclusion is to argue that there are subjects which cannot be removed, and must always remain. That, however, would only be another way of saying that there are absolutely necessary subjects; and that is the very assumption which I have called in question, and the possibility of which the above argument professes to establish. For I cannot form the least concept of a thing which, should it be rejected with all its predicates, leaves behind a contradiction; and in the absence of contradiction I have, through pure a priori concepts alone, no criterion of impossibility.

Notwithstanding all these general considerations, in which everyone must concur, we may be challenged with a case which is brought forward as proof that in actual fact the contrary holds, namely, that there is one concept, and indeed only one, in reference to which the not-being or rejection of its object is in itself contradictory, namely, the concept of the *ens realissimum*. It is declared that it possesses all reality, and that we are justified in assuming that such a being is possible (the fact that a concept does not contradict itself by no means proves the possibility of its object: but the contrary assertion I am for the moment willing to allow).[1] Now [the argument proceeds] "all reality" includes existence; existence is therefore contained in the concept of a thing that is possible. If, then, this thing is rejected, the internal possibility of the thing is rejected—which is self-contradictory.

My answer is as follows. There is already a contradiction in introducing the concept of existence—no matter under what title it may be disguised—into the concept of a thing which we profess to be thinking solely in reference to its possibility. If that be allowed as legitimate, a seeming victory has been won; but in actual fact nothing at all is said: the assertion is a mere tautology. We must ask: Is the proposition that *this or that thing* (which, whatever it may be, is allowed as possible) *exists*, an analytic or a synthetic proposition? If it is analytic, the assertion of the existence of the thing adds nothing to the thought of the thing; but in that case either the thought, which is in us, is the thing itself, or we have presupposed an existence as belonging to the realm of the possible, and have then, on that pretext, inferred its existence from its internal possibility—which is nothing but a miserable tautology. The word "reality," which in the concept of the thing sounds other than the word "existence" in the concept of the predicate, is of no avail in meeting this objection. For if all positing (no matter what it may be that is posited) is entitled reality, the thing with all its predicates is already posited in the concept of the subject, and is assumed as actual; and in the predicate this is merely repeated. But if, on the other hand, we admit, as every reasonable person must, that all existential propositions are synthetic, how can we profess to maintain that the predicate of existence cannot be rejected without contradiction? This is a feature which is found only in analytic propositions, and is indeed precisely what constitutes their analytic character.

I should have hoped to put an end to these idle and fruitless disputations in a direct manner, by an accurate determination of the concept of existence, had I not found that the illusion which is caused by the confusion

---

[1]A concept is always possible if it is not self-contradictory. This is the logical criterion of possibility, and by it the object of the concept is distinguishable from the *nihil negativum*. But it may nonetheless be an empty concept, unless the objective reality of the synthesis through which the concept is generated has been specifically proved; and such proof, as we have shown above, rests on principles of possible experience, and not on the principle of analysis (the law of contradiction). This is a warning against arguing directly from the logical possibility of concepts to the real possibility of things.

of a logical with a real predicate (that is, with a predicate which determines a thing) is almost beyond correction. Anything we please can be made to serve as a logical predicate; the subject can even be predicated of itself; for logic abstracts from all content. But a *determining* predicate is a predicate which is added to the concept of the subject and enlarges it. Consequently, it must not be already contained in the concept.

*Being* is obviously not a real predicate; that is, it is not a concept of something which could be added to the concept of a thing. It is merely the positing of a thing, or of certain determinations, as existing in themselves. Logically, it is merely the copula of a judgment. The proposition, "God is omnipotent," contains two concepts, each of which has its object—God and omnipotence. The small word "is" adds no new predicate, but only serves to posit the predicate *in its relation* to the subject. If, now, we take the subject (God) with all its predicates (among which is omnipotence), and say "God is," or "There is a God," we attach no new predicate to the concept of God, but only posit the subject in itself with all its predicates, and indeed posit it as being an *object* that stands in relation to my *concept*. The content of both must be one and the same; nothing can have been added to the concept, which expresses merely what is possible, by my thinking its object (through the expression "it is") as given absolutely. Otherwise stated, the real contains no more than the merely possible. A hundred real thalers do not contain the least coin more than a hundred possible thalers. For as the latter signify the concept, and the former the object and the positing of the object, should the former contain more than the latter, my concept would not, in that case, express the whole object, and would not therefore be an adequate concept of it. My financial position is, however, affected very differently by a hundred real thalers than it is by the mere concept of them (that is, of their possibility). For the object, as it actually exists, is not analytically contained in my concept, but is added to my concept (which is a determination of my state) synthetically; and yet the conceived hundred thalers are not themselves in the least increased through thus acquiring existence outside my concept.

By whatever and by however many predicates we may think a thing—even if we completely determine it—we do not make the least addition to the thing when we further declare that this thing *is*. Otherwise, it would not be exactly the same thing that exists, but something more than we had thought in the concept; and we could not, therefore, say that the exact object of my concept exists. If we think in a thing every feature of reality except one, the missing reality is not added by my saying that this defective thing exists. On the contrary, it exists with the same defect with which I have thought it, since otherwise what exists would be something different from what I thought. When, therefore, I think a being as the supreme reality, without any defect, the question still remains whether it exists or not. For though, in my concept, nothing may be lacking of the possible real content of a thing in general, something is still lacking in its relation to my whole state of thought, namely, [insofar as I am unable to assert] that knowledge of this object is also possible a posteriori. And here we find the source of our present difficulty. Were we dealing with an object of the senses, we could not confound the existence of the thing with the mere concept of it. For through the concept the object is thought only as conforming to the *universal conditions* of possible empirical knowledge in general, whereas through its existence it is thought as belonging to the context of experience as a whole. In being thus connected with the *content* of experience as a whole, the concept of the object is not, however, in the least enlarged; all that has happened is that our thought has thereby obtained an additional possible perception. It is not, therefore, surprising that, if we attempt to think existence through the pure category alone, we cannot specify a single mark distinguishing it from mere possibility.

Whatever, therefore, and however much, our concept of an object may contain, we must go outside it, if we are to ascribe existence to the object. In the case of objects of the senses, this takes place through their connection with some one of our perceptions, in accordance with empirical laws. But in dealing with objects of pure thought, we have no means whatsoever of knowing their existence, since it would have to be known in a completely a priori manner. Our consciousness of all existence (whether immediately through perception, or mediately through inferences which connect something with perception) belongs exclusively to the unity of experience; any [alleged] existence outside this field, while not indeed such as we can declare to be absolutely impossible, is of the nature of an assumption which we can never be in a position to justify.

The concept of a supreme being is in many respects a very useful idea; but just because it is a mere idea, it is altogether incapable, by itself alone, of enlarging our knowledge in regard to what exists. It is not even competent to enlighten us as to the *possibility* of any existence beyond that which is known in and through experience. The analytic criterion of possibility, as consisting in the principle that bare positives (realities) give rise to no contradiction, cannot be denied to it. But since the realities are not given to us in their specific characters; since even if they were, we should still not be in a position to pass judgment; since the criterion of the possibility of synthetic knowledge is never to be looked for save in experience, to which the object of an idea cannot belong, the connection of all real properties in a thing is a synthesis, the possibility of which we are unable to determine a priori. And thus the celebrated Leibniz is far from having succeeded in what he plumed himself on achieving—the comprehension a priori of the possibility of this sublime ideal being.

The attempt to establish the existence of a supreme being by means of the famous ontological argument of Descartes is therefore merely so much labour and effort lost; we can no more extend our stock of [theoretical] insight by mere ideas, than a merchant can better his position by adding a few noughts to his cash account.

CHAPTER III

*Section 5:*

## THE IMPOSSIBILITY OF A COSMOLOGICAL PROOF OF THE EXISTENCE OF GOD

To attempt to extract from a purely arbitrary idea the existence of an object corresponding to it is a quite unnatural procedure and a mere innovation of scholastic subtlety. Such an attempt would never have been made if there had not been antecedently, on the part of our reason, the need to assume as a basis of existence in general something necessary (in which our regress may terminate); and if, since this necessity must be unconditioned and certain a priori, reason had not, in consequence, been forced to seek a concept which would satisfy, if possible, such a demand, and enable us to know an existence in a completely a priori manner. Such a concept was supposed to have been found in the idea of an *ens realissimum*; and that idea was therefore used only for the more definite knowledge of that necessary being, of the necessary existence of which we were already convinced, or persuaded, on other grounds. This natural procedure of reason was, however, concealed from view, and instead of ending with this concept, the attempt was made to begin with it, and so to deduce from it that necessity of existence which it was only fitted to supplement. Thus arose the unfortunate ontological proof, which yields satisfaction neither to the natural and healthy understanding nor to the more academic demands of strict proof.

The *cosmological proof*, which we are now about to examine, retains the connection of absolute necessity with the highest reality, but instead of reasoning, like the former proof, from the highest reality to necessity of existence, it reasons from the previously given unconditioned necessity of some being to the unlimited reality of that being. It thus enters upon a course of reasoning which, whether rational or only pseudo-rational, is at any rate natural, and the most convincing not only for common sense but even for speculative understanding. It also sketches the first outline of all the proofs in natural theology, an outline which has always been and always will be followed, however much embellished and disguised by superfluous additions. This proof, termed by Leibniz the proof *a contingentia mundi*, we shall now proceed to expound and examine.

It runs thus: If anything exists, an absolutely necessary being must also exist. Now I, at least, exist. Therefore an absolutely necessary being exists.

The minor premise contains an experience, the major premise the inference from there being any experience at all to the existence of the necessary.[2] The proof therefore really begins with experience, and is not wholly a priori or ontological. For this reason, and because the object of all possible experience is called the world, it is entitled the *cosmological* proof. Since, in dealing with the objects of experience, the proof abstracts from all special properties through which this world may differ from any other possible world, the title also serves to distinguish it from the physico-theological proof, which is based upon observations of the particular properties of the world disclosed to us by our senses.

The proof then proceeds as follows: The necessary being can be determined in one way only, that is, by one out of each possible pair of opposed predicates. It must therefore be *completely* determined through its own concept. Now there is only one possible concept which determines a thing completely a priori, namely, the concept of the *ens realissimum*. The concept of the *ens realissimum* is therefore the only concept through which a necessary being can be thought. In other words, a supreme being necessarily exists.

In this cosmological argument there are combined so many pseudo-rational principles that speculative reason seems in this case to have brought to bear all the resources of its dialectical skill to produce the greatest possible transcendental illusion. The testing of the argument may meantime be postponed while we detail in order the various devices whereby an old argument is disguised as a new one, and by which appeal is made to the agreement of two witnesses, the one with credentials of pure reason and the other with those of experience. In reality the only witness is that which speaks in the name of pure reason; in the endeavour to pass as a second witness it merely changes its dress and voice. In order to lay a secure foundation for itself, this proof takes its stand on experience, and thereby makes profession of being distinct from the ontological proof, which puts its entire trust in pure a priori concepts. But the cosmological proof uses this experience only for a single step in the argument, namely, to conclude the existence of a necessary being. What properties this being may have, the empirical premise cannot tell us. Reason therefore abandons experience altogether, and endeavours to discover from mere concepts what properties an absolutely necessary being must have, that is, which among all possible things contains in itself the conditions (*requisita*) essential to absolute necessity. Now these, it is supposed, are nowhere to be found save in the concept of an *ens realissimum;* and the conclusion is therefore drawn that the *ens realissimum* is the absolutely necessary being. But it is evident that we are here presupposing that the

---

[2]This inference is too well known to require a detailed statement. It depends on the supposedly transcendental law of natural causality: that everything contingent has a cause, which, if itself contingent, must likewise have a cause, till the series of subordinate causes ends with an absolutely necessary cause, without which it would have no completeness.

concept of the highest reality is completely adequate to the concept of absolute necessity of existence; that is, that the latter can be inferred from the former. Now this is the proposition maintained by the ontological proof; it is here being assumed in the cosmological proof, and indeed made the basis of the proof; and yet it is an assumption with which this latter proof has professed to dispense. For absolute necessity is an existence determined from mere concepts. If I say, the concept of the *ens realissimum* is a concept, and indeed the only concept, which is appropriate and adequate to necessary existence, I must also admit that necessary existence can be inferred from this concept. Thus the so-called cosmological proof really owes any cogency which it may have to the ontological proof from mere concepts. The appeal to experience is quite superfluous; experience may perhaps lead us to the concept of absolute necessity, but is unable to demonstrate this necessity as belonging to any determinate thing. For immediately we endeavour to do so, we must abandon all experience and search among pure concepts to discover whether any one of them contains the conditions of the possibility of an absolutely necessary being. If in this way we can determine the possibility of a necessary being, we likewise establish its existence. For what we are then saying is this: that of all possible beings there is one which carries with it absolute necessity, that is, that this being exists with absolute necessity.

Fallacious and misleading arguments are most easily detected if set out in correct syllogistic form. This we now proceed to do in the instance under discussion.

If the proposition, that every absolutely necessary being is likewise the most real of all beings, is correct (and this is the *nervus probandi* of the cosmological proof), it must, like all affirmative judgments, be convertible, at least *per accidens*. It therefore follows that some *entia realissima* are likewise absolutely necessary beings. But one *ens realissimum* is in no respect different from another, and what is true of *some* under this concept is true also of *all*. In this case, therefore, I can convert the proposition *simpliciter*, not only *per accidens*, and say that every *ens realissimum* is a necessary being. But since this proposition is determined from its a priori concepts alone, the mere concept of the *ens realissimum* must carry with it the absolute necessity of that being; and this is precisely what the ontological proof has asserted and what the cosmological proof has refused to admit, although the conclusions of the latter are indeed covertly based on it.

Thus the second path upon which speculative reason enters in its attempt to prove the existence of a supreme being is not only as deceptive as the first, but has this additional defect, that it is guilty of an *ignoratio elenchi*. It professes to lead us by a new path, but after a short circuit brings us back to the very path which we had deserted at its bidding.

I have stated that in this cosmological argument there lies hidden a whole nest of dialectical assumptions, which the transcendental critique can easily detect and destroy. These deceptive principles I shall merely enumerate, leaving to the reader, who by this time will be sufficiently expert in these matters, the task of investigating them further, and of refuting them.

We find, for instance, (1) the transcendental principle whereby from the contingent we infer a cause. This principle is applicable only in the sensible world; outside that world it has no meaning whatsoever. For the mere intellectual concept of the contingent cannot give rise to any synthetic proposition, such as that of causality. The principle of causality has no meaning and no criterion for its application save only in the sensible world. But in the cosmological proof it is precisely in order to enable us to advance beyond the sensible world that it is employed. (2) The inference to a first cause, from the impossibility of an infinite series of causes, given one after the other, in the sensible world. The principles of the employment of reason do not justify this conclusion even within the world of experience, still less beyond this world in a realm into which this series can never be extended. (3) The unjustified self-satisfaction of reason in respect of the completion of this series. The removal of all the conditions without which no concept of necessity is possible is taken by reason to be a completion of the concept of the series, on the ground that we can then conceive nothing further. (4) The confusion between the logical possibility of a concept of all reality united into one (without inner contradiction) and the transcendental possibility of such a reality. In the case of the latter there is needed a principle to establish the practicability of such a synthesis, a principle which itself, however, can apply only to the field of possible experiences, etc.

The procedure of the cosmological proof is artfully designed to enable us to escape having to prove the existence of a necessary being a priori through mere concepts. Such proof would require to be carried out in the ontological manner, and that is an enterprise for which we feel ourselves to be altogether incompetent. Accordingly, we take as the starting-point of our inference an actual existence (an experience in general), and advance, in such manner as we can, to some absolutely necessary condition of this existence. We have then no need to show the possibility of this condition. For if it has been proved to exist, the question as to its possibility is entirely superfluous. If now we want to determine more fully the nature of this necessary being, we do not endeavour to do so in the manner that would be really adequate, namely, by discovering from its concept the necessity of its existence. For could we do that, we should be in no need of an empirical starting-point. No, all we seek is the negative condition (*conditio sine qua non*), without which a being would not be absolutely necessary. And in all other kinds of reasoning from a given consequence to its ground this would be legitimate; but in the present case it unfortunately happens that the condition which is needed for absolute necessity is only to be found in one single being. This being must therefore contain in its concept all that is required for absolute necessity, and consequently it enables me to infer this absolute necessity a priori. I must therefore be able also to reverse the inference, and to say: Anything to which this concept (of supreme reality) applies is absolutely necessary. If I cannot make this inference (as I must concede, if I am to avoid admitting the ontological proof), I have come to grief in the new way that I have been following, and am back again at my starting-point. The concept of the supreme being satisfies all questions a priori which can be raised regarding the inner determinations of a thing, and is therefore an ideal that is quite unique, in that the concept, while universal, also at the same time designates an individual as being among the things that are possible. But it does not give satisfaction concerning the question of its own existence—though this is the real purpose of our enquiries—and if anyone admitted the existence of a necessary being but wanted to know which among all [existing] things is to be identified with that being, we could not answer: "This, not that, is the necessary being."

We may indeed be allowed to *postulate* the existence of an all-sufficient being, as the cause of all possible effects, with a view to lightening the task of reason in its search for the unity of the grounds of explanation. But in presuming so far as to say that such a being *necessarily exists*, we are no longer giving modest expression to an admissible hypothesis, but are confidently laying claim to apodeictic certainty. For the knowledge of what we profess to know as absolutely necessary must itself carry with it absolute necessity.

The whole problem of the transcendental ideal amounts to this: either, given absolute necessity, to find a concept which possesses it, or, given the concept of something, to find that something to be absolutely necessary. If either task be possible, so must the other; for reason recognizes that only as absolutely necessary which follows of necessity from its concept. But both tasks are quite beyond our utmost efforts to *satisfy* our understanding in this matter; and equally unavailing are all attempts to induce it to acquiesce in its incapacity.

Unconditioned necessity, which we so indispensably require as the last bearer of all things, is for human reason the veritable abyss. Eternity itself, in all its terrible sublimity, as depicted by a Haller,[3] is far from making the same overwhelming impression on the mind; for it only *measures* the duration of things, it does not *support* them. We cannot put aside, and yet also cannot endure the thought, that a being, which we represent to ourselves as supreme amongst all possible beings, should, as it were, say to itself: "I am from eternity to eternity, and outside me there is nothing save what is through my will, *but whence then am I?*" All support here fails us; and the *greatest* perfection, no less than the *least* perfection, is unsubstantial and baseless for the merely

---

[3] Albrecht von Haller (1708–1777), a writer on medical and kindred subjects, author of *Die Alpen* and other poems.

speculative reason, which makes not the least effort to retain either the one or the other, and feels indeed no loss in allowing them to vanish entirely.

Many forces in nature, which manifest their existence through certain effects, remain for us inscrutable; for we cannot track them sufficiently far by observation. Also, the transcendental object lying at the basis of appearances (and with it the reason why our sensibility is subject to certain supreme conditions rather than to others) is and remains for us inscrutable. The thing itself is indeed given, but we can have no insight into its nature. But it is quite otherwise with an ideal of pure reason; it can never be said to be inscrutable. For since it is not required to give any credentials of its reality save only the need on the part of reason to complete all synthetic unity by means of it; and since, therefore, it is in no wise given as thinkable *object*, it cannot be inscrutable in the manner in which an object is. On the contrary it must, as a mere idea, find its place and its solution in the nature of reason, and must therefore allow of investigation. For it is of the very essence of reason that we should be able to give an account of all our concepts, opinions, and assertions, either upon objective or, in the case of mere illusion, upon subjective grounds.

## DISCOVERY AND EXPLANATION
### of the Dialectical Illusion in All Transcendental Proofs of the Existence of a Necessary Being

Both the above proofs were transcendental, that is, were attempted independently of empirical principles. For although the cosmological proof presupposes an experience in general, it is not based on any particular property of this experience but on pure principles of reason, as applied to an existence given through empirical consciousness in general. Further, it soon abandons this guidance and relies on pure concepts alone. What, then, in these transcendental proofs is the cause of the dialectical but natural illusion which connects the concepts of necessity and supreme reality, and which realizes and hypostatizes what can be an idea only? Why are we constrained to assume that some one among existing things is in itself necessary, and yet at the same time to shrink back from the existence of such a being as from an abyss? And how are we to secure that reason may come to an agreement with itself in this matter, and that from the wavering condition of a diffident approval, ever again withdrawn, it may arrive at settled insight?

There is something very strange in the fact that once we assume something to exist we cannot avoid inferring that something exists necessarily. The cosmological argument rests on this quite natural (although not therefore certain) inference. On the other hand, if I take the concept of anything, no matter what, I find that the existence of this thing can never be represented by me as absolutely necessary, and that, whatever it may be that exists, nothing prevents me from thinking its non-existence. Thus while I may indeed be obliged to assume something necessary as a condition of the existent in general, I cannot think any particular thing as in itself necessary. In other words, I can never *complete* the regress to the conditions of existence save by assuming a necessary being, and yet am never in a position to *begin* with such a being.

If I am constrained to think something necessary as a condition of existing things, but am unable to think any particular thing as in itself necessary, it inevitably follows that necessity and contingency do not concern the things themselves; otherwise there would be a contradiction. Consequently, neither of these two principles can be objective. They may, however, be regarded as subjective principles of reason. The one calls upon us to seek something necessary as a condition of all that is given as existent, that is, to stop nowhere until we have arrived at an explanation which is complete a priori; the other forbids us ever to hope for this completion, that is, forbids us to treat anything empirical as unconditioned and to exempt ourselves thereby from the toil of its further derivation. Viewed in this manner, the two principles, as merely heuristic and *regulative,* and as concerning only the formal interest of reason, can very well stand side by side. The one prescribes that we are to philosophize about nature as if there were a necessary first ground for all that belongs to existence—solely, however, for the purpose of bringing systematic unity into our knowledge, by always pursuing such an idea, as an imagined ultimate ground. The other warns us not to regard any determination whatsoever of existing things as such an ultimate ground, that is, as absolutely necessary, but to keep the way always open for further derivation, and so to treat each and every determination as always conditioned by something else. But if everything which is perceived in things must necessarily be treated by us as conditioned, nothing that allows of being empirically given can be regarded as absolutely necessary.

Since, therefore, the absolutely necessary is only intended to serve as a principle for obtaining the greatest possible unity among appearances, as being their ultimate ground; and since—inasmuch as the second rule commands us always to regard all empirical causes of unity as themselves derived—we can never reach this unity within the world, it follows that we must regard the absolutely necessary as being *outside* the world.

While the philosophers of antiquity regard all form in nature as contingent, they follow the judgment of the common man in their view of matter as original and necessary. But if, instead of regarding matter relatively, as *substratum* of appearances, they had considered it *in itself,* and as regards its existence, the idea of absolute necessity would at once have disappeared. For there is nothing which absolutely binds reason to accept such an existence; on the contrary it can always annihilate it in thought, without contradiction;

absolute necessity is a necessity that is to be found in thought alone. This belief must therefore have been due to a certain regulative principle. In fact extension and impenetrability (which between them make up the concept of matter) constitute the supreme empirical principle of the unity of appearances; and this principle, so far as it is empirically unconditioned, has the character of a regulative principle. Nevertheless, since every determination of the matter which constitutes what is real in appearances, including impenetrability, is an effect (action) which must have its cause and which is therefore always derivative in character, matter is not compatible with the idea of a necessary being as a principle of all derived unity. (For its real properties, being derivative, are one and all only conditionally necessary, and so allow of being removed—wherewith the whole existence of matter would be removed.) If this were not the case, we should have reached the ultimate ground of unity by empirical means—which is forbidden by the second regulative principle. It therefore follows that matter, and in general whatever belongs to the world, is not compatible with the idea of a necessary original being, even when the latter is regarded simply as a principle of the greatest empirical unity. That being or principle must be set outside the world, leaving us free to derive the appearances of the world and their existence from other appearances, with unfailing confidence, just as if there were no necessary being, while yet we are also free to strive unceasingly towards the completeness of that derivation, just as if such a being were presupposed as an ultimate ground.

As follows from these considerations, the ideal of the supreme being is nothing but a regulative principle of reason, which directs us to look upon all connection in the world *as if* it originated from an all-sufficient necessary cause. We can base upon the ideal the rule of a systematic and, in accordance with universal laws, necessary unity in the explanation of that connection; but the ideal is not an assertion of an existence necessary in itself. At the same time we cannot avoid the transcendental subreption, by which this formal principle is represented as constitutive, and by which this unity is hypostatized. We proceed here just as we do in the case of space. Space is only a principle of sensibility, but since it is the primary source and condition of all shapes, which are only so many limitations of itself, it is taken as something absolutely necessary, existing in its own right, and as an object given a priori in itself. In the same way, since the systematic unity of nature cannot be prescribed as a principle for the empirical employment of our reason, except insofar as we presuppose the idea of an *ens realissimum* as the supreme cause, it is quite natural that this latter idea should be represented as an actual object, which, in its character of supreme condition, is also necessary—thus changing a *regulative* into a *constitutive* principle. That such a substitution has been made becomes evident, when we consider this supreme being, which relatively to the world is absolutely (unconditionally) necessary, as a thing in and by itself. For we are then unable to conceive what can be meant by its ne-cessity. The concept of necessity is only to be found in our reason, as a formal condition of thought; it does not allow of being hypostatized as a material condition of thought; it does not allow of being hypostatized as a material condition of existence.

CHAPTER III

*Section 6:*

## THE IMPOSSIBILITY OF THE PHYSICO-THEOLOGICAL PROOF

If, then, neither the concept of things in general nor the experience of any *existence in general* can supply what is required, it remains only to try whether a *determinate experience*, the experience of the things of the present world, and the constitution and order of these, does not provide the basis of a proof which may help us to attain to an assured conviction of a supreme being. Such proof we propose to entitle the *physico-theological*. Should this attempt also fail, it must follow that no satisfactory proof of the existence of a being corresponding to our transcendental idea can be possible by pure speculative reason.

In view of what has already been said, it is evident that we can count upon a quite easy and conclusive answer to this enquiry. For how can any experience ever be adequate to an idea? The peculiar nature of the latter consists just in the fact that no experience can ever be equal to it. The transcendental idea of a necessary and all-sufficient original being is so overwhelmingly great, so high above everything empirical, the latter being always conditioned, that it leaves us at a loss, partly because we can never find in experience material sufficient to satisfy such a concept, and partly because it is always in the sphere of the conditioned that we carry out our search, seeking there ever vainly for the unconditioned—no law of any empirical synthesis giving us an example of any such unconditioned or providing the least guidance in its pursuit.

If the supreme being should itself stand in this chain of conditions, it would be a member of the series, and like the lower members which it precedes, would call for further enquiry as to the still higher ground from which it follows. If, on the other hand, we propose to separate it from the chain, and to conceive it as a purely intelligible being, existing apart from the series of natural causes, by what bridge can reason contrive to pass over to it? For all laws governing the transition from effects to causes, all synthesis and extension of our knowledge, refer to nothing but possible experience, and therefore solely to objects of the sensible world, and apart from them can have no meaning whatsoever.

This world presents to us so immeasurable a stage of variety, order, purposiveness, and beauty, as displayed alike in its infinite extent and in the unlimited divisibility of its parts, that even with such knowledge as our weak understanding can acquire of it, we are brought face to face with so many marvels immeasurably great, that all speech loses its force, all numbers their power to measure, our thoughts themselves all definiteness, and that our judgment of the whole resolves itself into an amazement which is speechless, and only the more eloquent on that account. Everywhere we see a chain of effects and causes, of ends and means, a regularity in origination and dissolution. Nothing has of itself come into the condition in which we find it to exist, but always points to something else as its cause, while this in turn commits us to repetition of the same enquiry. The whole universe must thus sink into the abyss of nothingness, unless, over and above this infinite chain of contingencies, we assume something to support it—something which is original and independently self-subsistent, and which as the cause of the origin of the universe secures also at the same time its continuance. What magnitude are we to ascribe to this supreme cause—admitting that it is supreme in respect of all things in the world? We are not acquainted with the whole content of the world, still less do we know how to estimate its magnitude by comparison with all that is possible. But since we cannot, as regards causality, dispense with an ultimate and supreme being, what is there to prevent us ascribing to it a degree of perfection that sets it *above everything else that is possible*? This we can easily do—though only through the slender outline of an abstract concept—by representing this being to ourselves as combining in itself all possible perfection, as in a single substance. This concept is in conformity with the demand of our reason for parsimony of principles; it is free from self-contradiction, and is never decisively contradicted by any experience; and it is likewise of such a character that it contributes to the extension of the employment of reason within experience, through the guidance which it yields in the discovery of order and purposiveness.

This proof always deserves to be mentioned with respect. It is the oldest, the clearest, and the most accordant with the common reason of mankind. It enlivens the study of nature, just as it itself derives its existence and gains ever new vigour from that source. It suggests ends and purposes, where our observation would not have detected them by itself, and extends our knowledge of nature by means of the guiding-concept of a special unity, the principle of which is outside nature. This knowledge again reacts on its cause, namely, upon the idea which has led to it, and so strengthens the belief in a supreme Author [of nature] that the belief acquires the force of an irresistible conviction.

It would therefore not only be uncomforting but utterly vain to attempt to diminish in any way the authority of this argument. Reason, constantly upheld by this ever-increasing evidence, which, though empirical, is yet so powerful, cannot be so depressed through doubts suggested by subtle and abstruse speculation, that it is not at once aroused from the indecision of all melancholy reflection, as from a dream, by one glance at the wonders of nature and the majesty of the universe—ascending from height to height up to the all-highest, from the conditioned to its conditions, up to the supreme and unconditioned Author [of all conditioned being].

But although we have nothing to bring against the rationality and utility of this procedure, but have rather to commend and to further it, we still cannot approve the claims, which this mode of argument would fain advance, to apodeictic certainty and to an assent founded on no special favour or support from other quarters. It cannot hurt the good cause, if the dogmatic language of the overweening sophist be toned down to the more moderate and humble requirements of a belief adequate to quiet our doubts, though not to command unconditional submission. I therefore maintain that the physico-theological proof can never by itself establish the existence of a supreme being, but must always fall back upon the ontological argument to make good its deficiency. It only serves as an introduction to the ontological argument; and the latter therefore contains (insofar as a speculative proof is possible at all) *the one possible ground of proof* with which human reason can never dispense.

The chief points of the physico-theological proof are as follows: (1) In the world we everywhere find clear signs of an order in accordance with a determinate purpose, carried out with great wisdom; and this in a universe which is indescribably varied in content and unlimited in extent. (2) This purposive order is quite alien to the things of the world, and only belongs to them contingently; that is to say, the diverse things could not of themselves have cooperated, by so great a combination of diverse means, to the fulfilment of determinate final purposes, had they not been chosen and designed for these purposes by an ordering rational principle in conformity with underlying ideas. (3) There exists, therefore, a sublime and wise cause (or more than one), which must be the cause of the world not merely as a blindly working all-powerful nature, by *fecundity*, but as intelligence, through *freedom*. (4) The unity of this cause may be inferred from the unity of the reciprocal relations existing between the parts of the world, as members of an artfully arranged structure—inferred with certainty insofar as our observation suffices for its verification, and beyond these limits with probability, in accordance with the principles of analogy.

We need not here criticize natural reason too strictly in regard to its conclusion from the analogy between certain natural products and what our human art produces when we do violence to nature, and constrain it to proceed not according to its own ends but in conformity with ours—appealing to the similarity of these particular natural products with houses, ships, watches. Nor need we here question its conclusion that there lies at the basis of nature a causality similar to that responsible for artificial products, namely, an understanding and a will; and that the inner possibility of a self-acting nature (which is what makes all art, and even, it may be, reason itself, possible) is therefore derived from another, though superhuman, art—a mode of reasoning which could not perhaps withstand a searching transcendental criticism. But at any rate we must admit that, if we are to specify a cause at all, we cannot here proceed more securely than by analogy with those purposive productions of which alone the cause and mode of action are fully known to us. Reason could never be justified in abandoning the causality which it knows for grounds of explanation which are obscure, of which it does not have any knowledge, and which are incapable of proof.

On this method of argument, the purposiveness and harmonious adaptation of so much in nature can suffice to prove the contingency of the form merely, not of the matter, that is, not of the substance in the world. To prove the latter we should have to demonstrate that the things in the world would not of themselves be capable of such order and harmony, in accordance with universal laws, if they were not *in their substance* the product of supreme wisdom. But to prove this we should require quite other grounds of proof than those which are derived from the analogy with human art. The utmost, therefore, that the argument can prove is an *architect* of the world who is always very much hampered by the adaptability of the material in which he works, not a *creator* of the world to whose idea everything is subject. This, however, is altogether inadequate to the lofty purpose which we have before our eyes, namely, the proof of an all-sufficient primordial being. To prove the contingency of matter itself, we should have to resort to a transcendental argument, and this is precisely what we have here set out to avoid.

The inference, therefore, is that the order and purposiveness everywhere observable throughout the world may be regarded as a completely contingent arrangement, and that we may argue to the existence of a cause *proportioned* to it. But the concept of this cause must enable us to know something quite *determinate* about it, and can therefore be no other than the concept of a being who possesses all might, wisdom, etc., in a word, all the perfection which is proper to an all-sufficient being. For the predicates— "very great," "astounding," "immeasurable" in power and excellence—give no determinate concept at all, and do not really tell us what the thing is in itself. They are only relative representations of the magnitude of the object, which the observer, in contemplating the world, compares with himself and with his capacity of comprehension, and which are equally terms of eulogy whether we be magnifying the object or be depreciating the observing subject in relation to that object. Where we are concerned with the magnitude (or the perfection) of a thing, there is no determinate concept except that which comprehends all possible perfection; and in that concept only the allness (*omnitudo*) of the reality is completely determined.

Now no one, I trust, will be so bold as to profess that he comprehends the relation of the magnitude of the world as he has observed it (alike as regards both extent and content) to omnipotence, of the world order to supreme wisdom, of the world unity to the absolute unity of its Author, etc. Physico-theology is therefore unable to give any determinate concept of the supreme cause of the world, and cannot therefore serve as the foundation of a theology which is itself in turn to form the basis of religion.

To advance to absolute totality by the empirical road is utterly impossible. Nonetheless this is what is attempted in the physico-theological proof. What, then, are the means which have been adopted to bridge this wide abyss?

The physico-theological argument can indeed lead us to the point of admiring the greatness, wisdom, power, etc., of the Author of the world, but can take us no further. Accordingly, we then abandon the argument from empirical grounds of proof, and fall back upon the contingency which, in the first steps of the argument, we had inferred from the order and purposiveness of the world. With this contingency as our sole premise, we then advance, by means of transcendental concepts alone, to the existence of an absolutely necessary being, and [as a final step] from the concept of the absolute necessity of the first cause to the completely determinate or determinable concept of that necessary being, namely, to the concept of an all-embracing reality. Thus the physico-theological proof, failing in its undertaking, has in face of this difficulty suddenly fallen back upon the cosmological proof; and since the latter is only a disguised ontological proof, it has really achieved its purpose by pure reason alone—although at the start it disclaimed all kinship with pure reason and professed to establish its conclusions on convincing evidence derived from experience.

Those who propound the physico-theological argument have therefore no ground for being so contemptuous in their attitude to the transcendental mode of proof, posing as clear-sighted students of nature, and complacently looking down upon that proof as the artificial product of obscure speculative refinements. For were they willing to scrutinize their own procedure, they would find that, after advancing some considerable way on the solid ground of nature and experience, and finding themselves just as far distant as ever from the object which discloses itself to their reason, they suddenly leave this ground, and pass over into the realm of mere possibilities, where they hope upon the wings of ideas to draw near to the object—the object that has refused itself to all their *empirical* enquiries. For after this tremendous leap, when they have, as they think, found firm ground, they extend their concept—the *determinate* concept, into the possession of which they have now come, they know not how—over the whole sphere of creation. And the ideal [which this reasoning thus involves, and] which is entirely a product of pure reason, they then elucidate by reference to experience, though inadequately enough, and in a manner far below the dignity of its object; and throughout they persist in refusing to admit that they have arrived at this knowledge or hypothesis by a road quite other than that of experience.

Thus the physico-theological proof of the existence of an original or supreme being rests upon the cosmological proof, and the cosmological upon the ontological. And since, besides these three, there is no other path open to speculative reason, the ontological proof from pure concepts of reason is the only possible one, if indeed any proof of a proposition so far exalted above all empirical employment of the understanding is possible at all.

# 11

# God and Immortality as Postulates of Practical Reason

CHAPTER II
*The Dialectic of Pure Reason in Defining the Concept of the Highest Good*

The concept of the "highest" contains an ambiguity which, if not attended to, can occasion unnecessary disputes. The "highest" can mean the "supreme" (*supremum*) or the "perfect" (*consummatum*). The former is the unconditional condition, i.e., the condition which is subordinate to no other (*originarium*); the latter is that whole which is no part of a yet larger whole of the same kind (*perfectissimum*). That virtue (as the worthiness to be happy) is the supreme condition of whatever appears to us to be desirable and thus of all our pursuit of happiness and, consequently, that it is the supreme good have been proved in the Analytic. But these truths do not imply that virtue is the entire and perfect good as the object of the faculty of desire of rational finite beings. For this, happiness is also required, and indeed not merely in the partial eyes of a person who makes himself his end but even in the judgment of an impartial reason, which impartially regards persons in the world as ends-in-themselves. For to be in need of happiness and also worthy of it and yet not to partake of it could not be in accordance with the complete volition of an omnipotent rational being, if we assume such only for the sake of the argument. Inasmuch as virtue and happiness together constitute the possession of the highest good for one person, and happiness in exact proportion to morality (as the worth of a person and his worthiness to be happy) constitutes that of a possible world, the highest good means the whole, the perfect good, wherein virtue is always the supreme good, being the condition having no condition superior to it, while happiness, though something always pleasant to him who possesses it, is not of itself absolutely good in every respect but always presupposes conduct in accordance with the moral law as its condition . . . .

### THE IMMORTALITY OF THE SOUL AS A POSTULATE OF PURE PRACTICAL REASON

The achievement of the highest good in the world is the necessary object of a will determinable by the moral law. In such a will, however, the complete fitness of intentions to the moral law is the supreme condition of the highest good. This fitness, therefore, must be just as possible as its object, because it is contained in the command that requires us to promote the latter. But complete fitness of the will to the moral law is holiness, which is a perfection of which no rational being in the world of sense is at any time capable. But since it is required as practically necessary, it can be found only in an endless progress to that complete fitness; on principles of pure practical reason, it is necessary to assume such a practical progress as the real object of our will.

This infinite progress is possible, however, only under the presupposition of an infinitely enduring existence and personality of the same rational being; this is called the immortality of the soul. Thus the highest good is practically possible only on the supposition of the immortality of the soul, and the latter, as inseparably bound to the moral law, is a postulate of pure practical reason. By a postulate of pure practical reason, I understand a theoretical proposition which is not as such demonstrable, but which is an inseparable corollary of an a priori unconditionally valid practical law.

The thesis of the moral destiny of our nature, viz., that it is able only in an infinite progress toward complete fitness to the moral law, is of great use, not merely for the present purpose of supplementing the impotence of speculative reason, but also with respect to religion. Without it, either the moral law is completely degraded from its holiness, by being made out as lenient (indulgent) and thus compliant to our convenience, or its call and its demands are strained to an unattainable destination, i.e., a hoped-for complete attainment of holiness of will, and are lost in fanatical theosophical dreams which completely contradict our knowledge of ourselves. In either case, we are only hindered in the unceasing striving toward the precise and persistent obedience to a command of reason which is stern, unindulgent, truly commanding, really and not just ideally possible.

Only endless progress from lower to higher stages of moral perfection is possible to a rational but finite being. The Infinite Being, to whom the temporal condition is nothing, sees in this series, which is for us without end, a whole conformable to the moral law; holiness, which His law inexorably commands in order to be true to His justice in the share He assigns to each in the highest good, is to be found in a single intellectual intuition of the existence of rational beings. All that can be granted to a creature with respect to hope for this share is consciousness of his tried character. And on the basis of his previous progress from the worse to the morally better, and of the immutability of intention which thus becomes known to him, he may hope for a further uninterrupted continuance of this progress, however long his existence may last, even beyond this life.[1] But he cannot hope here or at any foreseeable point of his future existence to be fully adequate to God's will, without indulgence or remission which would not harmonize with justice. This he can do only in the infinity of his duration which God alone can survey.

## THE EXISTENCE OF GOD AS A POSTULATE OF PURE PRACTICAL REASON

The moral law led, in the foregoing analysis, to a practical problem which is assigned solely by pure reason and without any concurrence of sensuous incentives. It is the problem of the completeness of the first and principal part of the highest good, viz., morality; since this problem can be

---

[1]The conviction of the immutability of character in progress toward the good may appear to be impossible for a creature. For this reason, Christian doctrine lets it derive from the same Spirit which works sanctification, i.e., this firm intention and therewith the consciousness of steadfastness in moral progress. But naturally one who is conscious of having persisted, from legitimate moral motives, to the end of a long life in a progress to the better may very well have the comforting hope, though not the certainty, that he will be steadfast in these principles in an existence continuing beyond this life. Though he can never be justified in his own eyes either here or in the hoped-for increase of natural perfection together with an increase of his duties, nevertheless in this progress toward a goal infinitely remote (a progress which in God's sight is regarded as equivalent to possession) he can have prospect of a blessed future. For "blessed" is the word which reason uses to designate a perfect well-being independent of all contingent causes in the world. Like holiness, it is an idea which can be contained only in an infinite progress and its totality and thus is never fully reached by any creature.

solved only in eternity, it led to the postulate of immortality. The same law must also lead us to affirm the possibility of the second element of the highest good, i.e., happiness proportional to that morality; it must do so just as disinterestedly as heretofore, by a purely impartial reason. This it can do on the supposition of the existence of a cause adequate to this effect, i.e., it must postulate the existence of God as necessarily belonging to the possibility of the highest good (the object of our will which is necessarily connected with the moral legislation of pure reason). We proceed to exhibit this connection in a convincing manner.

Happiness is the condition of a rational being in the world, in whose whole existence everything goes according to wish and will. It thus rests on the harmony of nature with his entire end and with the essential determining ground of his will. But the moral law commands as a law of freedom through motives wholly independent of nature and of its harmony with our faculty of desire (as incentives). Still, the acting rational being in the world is not at the same time the cause of the world and of nature itself. Hence there is not the slightest ground in the moral law for a necessary connection between the morality and proportionate happiness of a being which belongs to the world as one of its parts and as thus dependent on it. Not being nature's cause, his will cannot by its own strength bring nature, as it touches on his happiness, into complete harmony with his practical principles. Nevertheless, in the practical task of pure reason, i.e., in the necessary endeavor after the highest good, such a connection is postulated as necessary: we *should* seek to further the highest good (which therefore must be at least possible). Therefore also the existence is postulated of a cause of the whole of nature, itself distinct from nature, which contains the ground of the exact coincidence of happiness with morality. This supreme cause, however, must contain the ground of the agreement of nature not merely with a law of the will of rational beings but with the idea of this law so far as they make it the supreme ground of determination of the will. Thus it contains the ground of the agreement of nature not merely with actions moral in their form but also with their morality as the motives to such actions, i.e., with their moral intention. Therefore, the highest good is possible in the world only on the supposition of a supreme cause of nature which has a causality corresponding to the moral intention. Now a being which is capable of actions by the idea of laws is an intelligence (a rational being), and the causality of such a being according to this idea of laws is his will. Therefore, the supreme cause of nature, insofar as it must be presupposed for the highest good, is a being which is the cause (and consequently the author) of nature through understanding and will, i.e., God. As a consequence, the postulate of the possibility of a highest derived good (the best world) is at the same time the postulate of the reality of a highest original good, namely, the existence of God. Now it was our duty to promote the highest good; and it is not merely our privilege but a necessity connected with duty as a requisite to presuppose the possibility of this highest good. This presupposition is made only under the condition of the existence of God, and this condition inseparably connects this supposition with duty. Therefore, it is morally necessary to assume the existence of God.

It is well to notice here that this moral necessity is subjective, i.e., a need, and not objective, i.e., duty itself. For there cannot be any duty to assume the existence of a thing, because such a supposition concerns only the theoretical use of reason. It is also not to be understood that the assumption of the existence of God is necessary as a ground of all obligation in general (for this rests, as has been fully shown, solely on the autonomy of reason itself). All that here belongs to duty is the endeavor to produce and to further the highest good in the world, the existence of which may thus be postulated though our reason cannot conceive it except by presupposing a highest intelligence. To assume its existence is thus connected with the consciousness of our duty, though this assumption itself belongs to the realm of theoretical reason. Considered only in reference to the latter, it is a hypothesis, i.e., a ground of explanation. But in reference to the comprehensibility of an object (the highest good) placed before us by the moral law, and thus as a practical need, it can be called *faith* and even pure *rational faith*, because pure reason alone (by its theoretical as well as practical employment) is the source from which it springs.

From this deduction it now becomes clear why the Greek schools could never succeed in solving their problem of the practical possibility of the highest good. It was because they made the rule of the use which the human will makes of its freedom the sole and self-sufficient ground of its possibility, thinking that they had no need of the existence of God for this purpose. They were certainly correct in establishing the principle of morals by itself, independently of this postulate and merely from the relation of reason to the will, thus making the principle of morality the *supreme* practical condition of the highest good; but this principle was not the *entire* condition of its possibility. The Epicureans had indeed raised a wholly false principle of morality, i.e., that of happiness, into the supreme one, and for law had substituted a maxim of arbitrary choice of each according to his inclination. But they proceeded consistently enough, in that they degraded their highest good in proportion to the baseness of their principle and expected no greater happiness than that which could be attained through human prudence (wherein both temperance and the moderation of inclinations belong), though everyone knows prudence to be scarce enough and to produce diverse results according to circumstances, not to mention the exceptions which their maxims continually had to admit and which made them worthless as laws. The Stoics, on the other hand, had chosen their supreme practical principle, virtue, quite correctly as the condition of the highest good. But as they imagined the degree of virtue which is required for its pure law as completely attainable in this life, they not only exaggerated the moral capacity of man, under the name of "sage," beyond all the limits of his nature, making it into something which is contradicted by all our knowledge of men; they also refused to accept the second component of the highest good, i.e., happiness, as a special object of human desire. Rather, they made their sage like a god in the consciousness of the excellence of his person, wholly independent of nature (as regards his own contentment), exposing him to the evils of life but not subjecting him to them. (They also represented him as free from everything morally evil.) Thus they really left out of the highest good the second element (personal happiness), since they placed the highest good only in acting and in contentment with one's own personal worth, including it in the consciousness of moral character. But the voice of their own nature could have sufficiently refuted this.

The doctrine of Christianity,[2] even when not regarded as a religious doctrine, gives at this point a concept of the highest good (the Kingdom of God) which is alone sufficient to the strictest demand of practical reason. The moral law is holy (unyielding) and demands holiness of morals, although all moral perfection to which man can attain is only virtue, i.e., a law-abiding disposition resulting from respect for the law and thus implying consciousness of a continuous propensity to transgress it or at least to a defilement, i.e., to an admixture of many spurious (not moral) motives to obedience to the law; consequently, man can achieve only a self-esteem combined with humility. And thus with respect to the holiness required by the Christian law, nothing remains to the creature but endless progress, though for the same

---

[2]The view is commonly held that the Christian precept of morals has no advantage over the moral concept of the Stoics in respect to its purity; but the difference between them is nevertheless obvious. The Stoic system makes the consciousness of strength of mind the pivot around which all moral intentions should turn; and, if the followers of this system spoke of duties and even defined them accurately, they nevertheless placed the incentives and the real determining ground of the will in an elevation of character above the base incentives of the senses which have their power only through weakness of the mind. Virtue was, therefore, for them a certain heroism of the sage who, raising himself above the animal nature of man, was sufficient to himself, subject to no temptation to transgress the moral law, and elevated above duties though he propounded duties to others. But all this they could not have done had they conceived this law in the same purity and rigor as does the precept of the Gospel. If I understand by "idea" a perfection to which the senses can give nothing adequate, the moral ideas are not transcendent, i.e., of such a kind that we cannot even sufficiently define the concept or of which we are uncertain whether there is a corresponding object (as are the ideas of speculative reason); rather, they serve as models of practical perfection, as an indispensable rule of moral conduct, and as a standard for comparison. If I now regard Christian morals from their philosophical side, it appears in comparison with the ideas of the Greek schools as follows: the ideas of the Cynics, Epicureans, Stoics, and Christians are, respectively, the simplicity of nature, prudence, wisdom, and holiness. In respect to the way they achieve them, the Greek schools differ in that the Cynics found common sense sufficient, while the others found it in the path of science, and thus all held it to lie in the mere use of man's natural powers. Christian ethics, because it formulated its precept as pure and uncompromising (as befits a moral precept), destroyed man's confidence of being wholly adequate to it, at least in this life; but it re-established it by enabling us to hope that, if we act as well as lies in our power, what is not in our power will come to our aid from another source, whether we know in what way or not. Aristotle and Plato differed only as to the origin of our moral concepts.

reason hope of endless duration is justified. The worth of a character completely accordant with the moral law is infinite, because all possible happiness in the judgment of a wise and omnipotent dispenser of happiness has no other limitation than the lack of fitness of rational beings to their duty. But the moral law does not of itself promise happiness, for the latter is not, according to concepts of any order of nature, necessarily connected with obedience to the law. Christian ethics supplies this defect of the second indispensable component of the highest good by presenting a world wherein reasonable beings single-mindedly devote themselves to the moral law; this is the Kingdom of God, in which nature and morality come into a harmony, which is foreign to each as such, through a holy Author of the world, who makes possible the derived highest good. The holiness of morals is prescribed to them even in this life as a guide to conduct, but the well-being proportionate to this, which is bliss, is thought of as attainable only in eternity. This is due to the fact that the former must always be the pattern of their conduct in every state, and progressing toward it is even in this life possible and necessary, whereas the latter, under the name of happiness, cannot (as far as our own capacity is concerned) be reached in this life and therefore is made only an object of hope. Nevertheless, the Christian principle of morality is not theological and thus heteronomous, being rather the autonomy of pure practical reason itself, because it does not make the knowledge of God and His will the basis of these laws but makes such knowledge the basis only of succeeding to the highest good on condition of obedience to these laws; it places the real incentive for obedience to the law not in the desired consequences of obedience but in the conception of duty alone, in true observance of which the worthiness to attain the latter alone consists.

In this manner, through the concept of the highest good as the object and final end of pure practical reason, the moral law leads to religion. Religion is the recognition of all duties as divine commands, not as sanctions, i.e., arbitrary and contingent ordinances of a foreign will, but as essential laws of any free will as such. Even as such, they must be regarded as commands of the Supreme Being because we can hope for the highest good (to strive for which is our duty under the moral law) only from a morally perfect (holy and beneficent) and omnipotent will; and, therefore, we can hope to attain it only through harmony with this will. But here again everything remains disinterested and based only on duty, without being based on fear or hope as incentives, which, if they became principles, would destroy the entire moral worth of the actions. The moral law commands us to make the highest possible good in a world the final object of all our conduct. This I cannot hope to effect except through the agreement of my will with that of a holy and beneficent Author of the world. And although my own happiness is included in the concept of the highest good as a whole wherein the greatest happiness is thought of as connected in exact proportion to the greatest degree of moral perfection possible to creatures, still it is not happiness but the moral law (which, in fact, sternly places restricting conditions upon my boundless longing for happiness) which is proved to be the ground determining the will to further the highest good.

Therefore, morals is not really the doctrine of how to make ourselves happy but of how we are to be *worthy* of happiness. Only if religion is added to it can the hope arise of someday participating in happiness in proportion as we endeavored not to be unworthy of it.

One is worthy of possessing a thing or a state when his possession is harmonious with the highest good. We can easily see now that all worthiness is a matter of moral conduct, because this constitutes the condition of everything else (which belongs to one's state) in the concept of the highest good, i.e., participation in happiness. From this there follows that one must never consider morals itself as a doctrine of happiness, i.e., as an instruction in how to acquire happiness. For morals has to do only with the rational condition (*conditio sine qua non*) of happiness and not with means of achieving it. But when morals (which imposes only duties instead of providing rules for selfish wishes) is completely expounded, and a moral wish has been awakened to promote the highest good (to bring the Kingdom of God to us), which is a wish based on law and one to which no selfish mind could have aspired, and when for the sake of this wish the step to religion has been taken—then only can ethics be called a doctrine of happiness, because the *hope* for it first arises with religion.

From this it can also be seen that, if we inquire into God's final end in creating the world, we must name not the happiness of rational beings in the world but the highest good, which adds a further condition to the wish of rational beings to be happy, viz., the condition of being worthy of happiness, which is the morality of these beings, for this alone contains the standard by which they can hope to participate in happiness at the hand of a *wise* creator. For since wisdom, theoretically regarded, means the knowledge of the highest good and, practically, the suitability of the will to the highest good, one cannot ascribe to a supreme independent wisdom an end based merely on benevolence. For we cannot conceive the action of this benevolence (with respect to the happiness of rational beings) except as conformable to the restrictive conditions of harmony with the holiness[3] of His will as the highest original good. Then perhaps those who have placed the end of creation in the

---

[3]Incidentally, and in order to make the peculiarity of this concept clear, I make the following remark. Since we ascribe various attributes to God, whose quality we find suitable also to creatures (e.g., power, knowledge, presence, goodness, etc.), though in God they are present in a higher degree under such names as omnipotence, omniscience, omnipresence, and perfect goodness, etc., there are three which exclusively and without qualification of magnitude are ascribed to God, and they are all moral. He is the only holy, the only blessed, and the only wise being, because these concepts of themselves imply unlimitedness. By the arrangement of these He is thus the holy lawgiver (and creator), the beneficent ruler (and sustainer), and the just judge. These three attributes contain everything whereby God is the object of religion, and in conformity to them the metaphysical perfections of themselves arise in reason.

glory of God, provided this is not thought of anthropomorphically as an inclination to be esteemed, have found the best term. For nothing glorifies God more than what is the most estimable thing in the world, namely, respect for His command, the observance of sacred duty which His law imposes on us, when there is added to this His glorious plan of crowning such an excellent order with corresponding happiness. If the latter, to speak in human terms, makes Him worthy of love, by the former He is an object of adoration. Human beings can win love by doing good, but by this alone even they never win respect; the greatest well-doing does them honor only by being exercised according to worthiness.

It follows of itself that, in the order of ends, man (and every rational being) is an end-in-himself, i.e., he is never to be used merely as a means for someone (even for God) without at the same time being himself an end, and that thus the humanity in our person must itself be holy to us, because man is subject to the moral law and therefore subject to that which is of itself holy, and it is only on account of this and in agreement with this that anything can be called holy. For this moral law is founded on the autonomy of his will as a free will, which by its universal laws must necessarily be able to agree with that to which it subjects itself.

# Ludwig Feuerbach

Ludwig Feuerbach (1804–1872), a learned and independent nine-teenth-century German thinker, was responsible for the most impressive version of the view of the belief in God as a projection of the human mind. His *Essence of Christianity* was translated into English by the novelist George Eliot.

# 12

# *Religion as Illusion*

CHAPTER I

## § 2. THE ESSENCE OF RELIGION CONSIDERED GENERALLY

What we have hitherto been maintaining generally, even with regard to sensational impressions, of the relation between subject and object, applies especially to the relation between the subject and the religious object.

In the perceptions of the senses consciousness of the object is distinguishable from consciousness of self; but in religion, consciousness of the object and self-consciousness coincide. The object of the senses is out of man, the religious object is within him, and therefore as little forsakes him as his self-consciousness or his conscience; it is the intimate, the closest object. "God," says Augustine, for example, "is nearer, more related to us, and therefore more easily known by us, than sensible, corporeal things." The object of the senses is in itself indifferent—independent of the disposition or of the judgment; but the object of religion is a selected object; the most excellent, the first, the supreme being; it essentially presupposes a critical judgment, a discrimination between the divine and the non-divine, between that which is worthy of adoration and that which is not worthy. And here may be applied, without any limitation, the proposition: the object of any subject is nothing else than the subject's own nature taken objectively. Such as are a man's thoughts and dispositions, such is his God; so much worth as a man has, so much and no more has his God. Consciousness of God is self-consciousness, knowledge of God is self-knowledge. By his God thou knowest the man, and by the man his God; the two are identical. Whatever is God to a man, that is his heart and soul; and conversely, God is the manifested inward nature, the expressed self of a man—religion the solemn

---

Ludwig Feuerbach, *The Essence of Christianity*, George Eliot, trans.

unveiling of a man's hidden treasures, the revelation of his intimate thoughts, the open confession of his love-secrets.

But when religion—consciousness of God—is designated as the self-consciousness of man, this is not to be understood as affirming that the religious man is directly aware of this identity; for, on the contrary, ignorance of it is fundamental to the peculiar nature of religion. To preclude this misconception, it is better to say, religion is man's earliest and also indirect form of self-knowledge. Hence, religion everywhere precedes philosophy, as in the history of the race, so also in that of the individual. Man first of all sees his nature as if *out of* himself, before he finds it in himself. His own nature is in the first instance contemplated by him as that of another being. Religion is the childlike condition of humanity; but the child sees his nature—man—out of himself; in childhood a man is an object to himself, under the form of another man. Hence the historical progress of religion consists in this: that what by an earlier religion was regarded as objective, is now recognized as subjective; that is, what was formerly contemplated and worshiped as God is now perceived to be something *human*. What was at first religion becomes at a later period idolatry; man is seen to have adored his own nature. Man has given objectivity to himself, but has not recognized the object as his own nature: a later religion takes this forward step; every advance in religion is therefore a deeper self-knowledge. But every particular religion, while it pronounces its predecessors idolatrous excepts itself—and necessarily so, otherwise it would no longer be religion—from the fate, the common nature of all religions: it imputes only to other religions what is the fault, if fault it be, of religion in general. Because it has a different object, a different tenor, because it has transcended the ideas of preceding religions, it erroneously supposes itself exalted above the necessary eternal laws which constitute the essence of religion—it fancies its object, its ideas, to be superhuman. But the essence of religion, thus hidden from the religious, is evident to the thinker, by whom religion is viewed objectively, which it cannot be by its votaries. And it is our task to show that the antithesis of divine and human is altogether illusory, that it is nothing else than the antithesis between the human nature in general and the human individual; that, consequently, the object and contents of the Christian religion are altogether human.

Religion, at least the Christian, is the relation of man to himself, or more correctly to his own nature (i.e., his subjective nature); but a relation to it, viewed as a nature apart from his own. The divine being is nothing else than the human being, or, rather, the human nature purified, freed from the limits of the individual man, made objective—i.e., contemplated and revered as another, a distinct being. All the attributes of the divine nature are, therefore, attributes of the human nature.

In relation to the attributes, the predicates, of the Divine Being, this is admitted without hesitation, but by no means in relation to the subject of these predicates. The negation of the subject is held to be irreligion, nay, atheism; though not so the negation of the predicates. But that which has no predicates or qualities has no effect upon me; that which has no effect upon me has no existence for me. To deny all the qualities of a being is equivalent to denying the being himself. A being without qualities is one which cannot become an object to the mind, and such a being is virtually non-existent. Where man deprives God of all qualities, God is no longer anything more to him than a negative being. To the truly religious man, God is not a being without qualities, because to him he is a positive, real being. The theory that God cannot be defined, and consequently cannot be known by man, is therefore the offspring of recent times, a product of modern unbelief.

As reason is and can be pronounced finite only where man regards sensual enjoyment, or religious emotion, or aesthetic contemplation, or moral sentiment, as the absolute, the true; so the proposition that God is unknowable or undefinable, can only be enunciated and become fixed as a dogma, where this object has no longer any interest for the intellect; where the real, the positive, alone has any hold on man, where the real alone has for him the significance of the essential, of the absolute, divine object, but where at the same time, in contradiction with this purely worldly tendency, there yet exist some old remains of religiousness. On the ground that God is unknowable, man excuses himself to what is yet remaining of his religious conscience for his forgetfulness of God, his absorption in the world: he denies God practically by his conduct—the world has possession of all his thoughts and inclinations—but he does not deny him theoretically, he does not attack his existence; he lets that rest. But this existence does not affect or incommode him; it is a merely negative existence, an existence without existence, a self-contradictory existence—a state of being which, as to its effects, is not distinguishable from nonbeing. The denial of determinate, positive predicates concerning the divine nature is nothing else than a denial of religion, with, however, an appearance of religion in its favour, so that it is not recognized as a denial; it is simply a subtle, disguised atheism. The alleged religious horror of limiting God by positive predicates is only the irreligious wish to know nothing more of God, to banish God from the mind. Dread of limitation is dread of existence. All real existence, i.e., all existence which is truly such, is qualitative, determinative existence. He who earnestly believes in the Divine existence is not shocked at the attributing even of gross sensuous qualities to God. He who dreads an existence that may give offence, who shrinks from the grossness of a positive predicate, may as well renounce existence altogether. A God who is injured by determinate qualities has not the courage and the strength to exist. Qualities are the fire, the vital breath, the oxygen, the salt of existence. An existence in general, an existence without qualities, is an insipidity, an absurdity. But there can be no more in God than is supplied by religion. Only where man loses his taste for religion, and thus religion itself becomes insipid, does the existence of God become an insipid existence—an existence without qualities.

There is, however, a still milder way of denying the divine predicates than the direct one just described. It is admitted that the predicates of the divine nature are finite, and, more particularly, human qualities, but their rejection is rejected; they are even taken under protection, because it is necessary to man to have a definite conception of God, and since he is man he can form no other than a human conception of him. In relation to God, it is said, these predicates are certainly without any objective validity; but to me, if he is to exist for me, he cannot appear otherwise than as he does appear to me, namely, as a being with attributes analogous to the human. But this distinction between what God is in himself, and what he is for me destroys the peace of religion, and is besides in itself an unfounded and untenable distinction. I cannot know whether God is something else in himself or for himself than he is for me; what he is to me is to me all that he is. For me, there lies in these predicates under which he exists for me, what he is in himself, his very nature; he is for me what he can alone ever be for me. The religious man finds perfect satisfaction in that which God is in relation to himself; of any other relation he knows nothing, for God is to him what he can alone be to man. In the distinction above stated, man takes a point of view above himself, i.e., above his nature, the absolute measure of his being; but this transcendentalism is only an illusion; for I can make the distinction between the object as it is in itself, and the object as it is for me, only where an object can really appear otherwise to me, not where it appears to me such as the absolute measure of my nature determines it to appear—such as it must appear to me. It is true that I may have a merely subjective conception, i.e., one which does not arise out of the general constitution of my species; but if my conception is determined by the constitution of my species, the distinction between what an object is in itself, and what it is for me ceases; for this conception is itself an absolute one. The measure of the species is the absolute measure, law, and criterion of man. And, indeed, religion has the conviction that its conceptions, its predicates of God, are such as every man ought to have, and must have, if he would have the true ones—that they are the conceptions necessary to human nature; nay, further, that they are objectively true, representing God as he is. To every religion the gods of *other* religions are only notions concerning God, but its own conception of God is to it God himself, the true God—God such as he is in himself. Religion is satisfied only with a complete Deity, a God without reservation; it will not have a mere phantasm of God; it demands God himself. Religion gives up its own existence when it gives up the nature of God; it is no longer a truth when it renounces the possession of the true God. Skepticism is the arch-enemy of religion; but the distinction between object and conception—between God as he is in himself, and God as he is for me—is a skeptical distinction, and therefore an irreligious one.

That which is to man the self-existent, the highest being, to which he can conceive nothing higher—that is to him the Divine Being. How then should he inquire concerning this being, what he is in himself? If God were an object to the bird, he would be a winged being: the bird knows nothing higher, nothing more blissful, than the winged condition. How ludicrous would it be if this bird pronounced: To me God appears as a bird, but what he is in himself I know not. To the bird the highest nature is the bird-nature; take from him the conception of this, and you take from him the conception of the highest being. How, then, could he ask whether God in himself were winged? To ask whether God is in himself what he is for me is to ask whether God is God, is to lift oneself above one's God, to rise up against him.

Wherever, therefore, this idea, that the religious predicates are only anthropomorphisms, has taken possession of a man, there has doubt, has unbelief, obtained the mastery of faith. And it is only the inconsequence of faint-heartedness and intellectual imbecility which does not proceed from this idea to the formal negation of the predicates, and from thence to the negation of the subject to which they relate. If thou doubtest the objective truth of the predicates, thou must also doubt the objective truth of the subject whose predicates they are. If thy predicates are anthropomorphisms, the subject of them is an anthropomorphism too. If love, goodness, personality, etc., are human attributes, so also is the subject which thou presupposest, the existence of God, the belief that there is a God, an anthropomorphism—a presupposition purely human. Whence knowest thou that the belief in a God at all is not a limitation of man's mode of conception? Higher beings—and thou supposest such—are perhaps so blest in themselves, so at unity with themselves, that they are not hung in suspense between themselves and a yet higher being. To know God and not oneself to be God, to know blessedness and not oneself to enjoy it, is a state of disunity, of unhappiness. Higher beings know nothing of this unhappiness; they have no conception of that which they are not.

Thou believest in love as a divine attribute because thou thyself lovest; thou believest that God is a wise, benevolent being because thou knowest nothing better in thyself than benevolence and wisdom; and thou believest that God exists, that therefore he is a subject—whatever exists is a subject, whether it be defined as substance, person, essence, or otherwise—because thou thyself existest, art thyself a subject. Thou knowest no higher human good than to love, than to be good and wise; and even so thou knowest no higher happiness than to exist, to be a subject; for the consciousness of all reality, of all bliss, is for thee bound up in the consciousness of being a subject, of existing. God is an existence, a subject to thee, for the same reason that he is to thee a wise, a blessed, a personal being. The distinction between the divine predicates and the divine subject is only this, that to thee the subject, the existence, does not appear an anthropomorphism, because the conception of it is necessarily involved in thy own existence as a subject, whereas the predicates do appear anthropomorphisms, because their necessity—the necessity that God should be conscious, wise, good, etc.—is not an immediate necessity, identical with the being of man, but is evolved by his self-consciousness, by the activity of his thought. I am a subject, I exist, whether I be wise or unwise, good or bad. To exist is to man the first datum; it constitutes the very idea of the subject; it is presupposed by the predicates. Hence man relinquishes the predicates, but the existence of God is to him a settled, irrefragable, absolutely certain, objective truth. But, nevertheless, this distinction is merely an apparent one. The necessity of the subject lies only in the necessity of the predicate. Thou art a subject only insofar as thou art a human subject; the certainty and reality of thy existence lie only in the certainty and reality of thy human attributes. What the subject is lies only in the predicate; the predicate is the *truth* of the subject—the subject only the personified, existing predicate, the predicate conceived as existing. Subject and predicate are distinguished only as existence and essence. The negation of the predicates is therefore the negation of the subject. What remains of the human subject when abstracted from the human attributes? Even in the language of common life the divine predicates—providence, omniscience, omnipotence—are put for the divine subject.

The certainty of the existence of God, of which it has been said that it is as certain, nay, more certain to man than his own existence, depends only on the certainty of the qualities of God—it is in itself no immediate certainty. To the Christian the existence of the Christian God only is a certainty; to the heathen that of the heathen God only. The heathen did not doubt the existence of Jupiter, because he took no offence at the nature of Jupiter, because he could conceive of God under no other qualities, because to him these qualities were a certainty, a divine reality. The reality of the predicate is the sole guarantee of existence.

Whatever man conceives to be true, he immediately conceives to be real (that is, to have an objective existence), because, originally, only the real is true to him—true in opposition to what is merely conceived, dreamed, imagined. The idea of being, of existence, is the original idea of truth; or, originally, man makes truth dependent on existence, subsequently, existence dependent on truth. Now God is the nature of man regarded as absolute truth—the truth of man; but God, or, what is the same thing, religion, is as various as are the conditions under which man conceives this his nature, regards it as the highest being. These conditions, then, under which man conceives God, are to him the truth, and for that reason they are also the highest existence, or rather they are existence itself; for only the emphatic, the highest existence, is existence, and deserves this name. Therefore, God is an existent, real being, on the very same ground that he is a particular, definite being; for the qualities of God are nothing else than the essential qualities of man himself, and a particular man is what he is, has his existence, his reality, only in his particular conditions. Take away from the Greek the quality of being Greek, and you take away his existence. On this ground it is true that for a definite positive religion—that is, relatively—the certainty of the existence of God is *immediate;* for just as involuntarily, as necessarily, as the Greek was a Greek, so necessarily were his Gods beings, so necessarily were they real, existent beings. Religion is that conception of the nature of the world and of man which is essential to, i.e., identical with, a man's nature. But man does not stand above this his necessary conception; on the contrary, it stands above him; it animates, determines, governs him. The necessity of a proof, of a middle term to unite qualities with existence, the possibility of a doubt, is abolished. Only that which is apart from my own being is capable of being doubted by me. How then can I doubt of God, who is my being? To doubt of God is to doubt myself. Only when God is thought of abstractly, when his predicates are the result of philosophic abstraction, arises the distinction or separation between subject and predicate, existence and nature—arises the fiction that the existence or the subject is something else than the predicate, something immediate, indubitable, in distinction from the predicate, which is held to be doubtful. But this is only a fiction. A God who has abstract predicates has also an abstract existence. Existence, being, varies with varying qualities.

The identity of the subject and predicate is clearly evidenced by the progressive development of religion, which is identical with the progressive development of human culture. So long as man is in a mere state of nature, so long is his god a mere nature-god—a personification of some natural force. Where man inhabits houses, he also encloses his gods in temples. The temple is only a manifestation of the value which man attaches to beautiful buildings. Temples in honour of religion are in truth temples in honour of architecture. With the emerging of man from a state of savagery and wildness to one of culture, with the distinction between what is fitting for man and what is not fitting, arises simultaneously the distinction between that which is fitting and that which is not fitting for God. God is the idea of majesty, of the highest dignity: the religious sentiment is the sentiment of supreme fitness. The later, more cultured artists of Greece were the first to embody in the statues of the gods the ideas of dignity, of spiritual grandeur, of imperturbable repose and serenity. But why were these qualities in their view attributes, predicates of God? Because they were in themselves regarded by the Greeks as divinities. Why did those artists exclude all disgusting and low passions? Because they perceived them to be unbecoming, unworthy, unhuman, and consequently ungodlike. The Homeric gods eat and drink—that implies eating and drinking is a divine pleasure. Physical strength is an attribute of the Homeric gods:

Zeus is the strongest of the gods. Why? Because physical strength, in and by itself, was regarded as something glorious, divine. To the ancient Germans the highest virtues were those of the warrior; therefore their supreme god was the god of war, Odin—war, "the original or oldest law." Not the attribute of the divinity, but the divineness or deity of the attribute, is the first true Divine Being. Thus what theology and philosophy have held to be God, the Absolute, the Infinite, is not God; but that which they have held not to be God is God: namely, the attribute, the quality, whatever has reality. Hence he alone is the true atheist to whom the predicates of the Divine Being—for example, love, wisdom, justice—are nothing; not he to whom merely the subject of these predicates is nothing. And in no wise is the negation of the subject necessarily also a negation of the predicates considered in themselves. These have an intrinsic, independent reality; they force their recognition upon man by their very nature; they are self-evident truths to him; they prove, they attest themselves. It does not follow that goodness, justice, wisdom, are chimæras because the existence of God is a chimæra, nor truths because this is a truth. The idea of God is dependent on the idea of justice, of benevolence; a God who is not benevolent, not just, not wise, is no God; but the converse does not hold. The fact is not that a quality is divine because God has it, but that God has it because it is in itself divine: because without it God would be a defective being. Justice, wisdom, in general every quality which constitutes the divinity of God, is determined and known by itself independently, but the idea of God is determined by the qualities which have thus been previously judged to be worthy of the divine nature; only in the case in which I identify God and justice, in which I think of God immediately as the reality of the idea of justice, is the idea of God self-determined. But if God as a subject is the determined, while the quality, the predicate, is the determining, then in truth the rank of the godhead is due not to the subject, but to the predicate.

Not until several, and those contradictory, attributes are united in one being, and this being is conceived as personal—the personality being thus brought into especial prominence—not until then is the origin of religion lost sight of, is it forgotten that what the activity of the reflective power has converted into a predicate distinguishable or separable from the subject, was originally the true subject. Thus the Greeks and Romans deified accidents as substances; virtues, states of mind, passions, as independent beings. Man, especially the religious man, is to himself the measure of all things, of all reality. Whatever strongly impresses a man, whatever produces an unusual effect on his mind, if it be only a peculiar, inexplicable sound or note, he personifies as a divine being. Religion embraces all the objects of the world: everything existing has been an object of religious reverence; in nature and consciousness of religion there is nothing else than what lies in the nature of man and in his consciousness of himself and of the world. Religion has no material exclusively its own. In Rome even the passions of fear and terror had their temples. The Christians also made mental phenomena into independent beings, their own feelings into qualities of things, the passions which governed them into powers which governed the world, in short, predicates of their own nature, whether recognized as such or not, into independent subjective existences. Devils, cobolds, witches, ghosts, angels, were sacred truths as long as the religious spirit held undivided sway over mankind.

In order to banish from the mind the identity of the divine and human predicates, and the consequent identity of the divine and human nature, recourse is had to the idea that God, as the absolute, real Being, has an infinite fullness of various predicates, of which we here know only a part, and those such as are analogous to our own; while the rest, by virtue of which God must thus have quite a different nature from the human or that which is analogous to the human, we shall only know in the future—that is, after death. But an infinite plentitude or multitude of predicates which are really different, so different that the one does not immediately involve the other, is realized only in an infinite plentitude or multitude of different beings or individuals. Thus the human nature presents an infinite abundance of different predicates, and for that very reason it presents an infinite abundance of different individuals. Each new man is a new predicate, a new phasis of humanity. As many as are the men, so many are the powers, the properties of humanity. It is true that there are the same elements in every individual, but under such various conditions and modifications that they appear new and peculiar. The mystery of the inexhaustible fullness of the divine predicates is therefore nothing else than the mystery of human nature considered as an infinitely varied, infinitely modifiable, but, consequently, phenomenal being. Only in the realm of the senses, only in space and time, does there exist a being of really infinite qualities or predicates. Where there are really different predicates there are different times. One man is a distinguished musician, a distinguished author, a distinguished physician; but he cannot compose music, write books, and perform cures in the same moment of time. Time, and not the Hegelian dialectic, is the medium of uniting opposites, contradictories, in one and the same subject. But distinguished and detached from the nature of man, and combined with the idea of God, the infinite fullness of various predicates is a conception without reality, a mere phantasy, a conception derived from the sensible world, but without the essential conditions, without the truth of sensible existence, a conception which stands in direct contradiction with the Divine Being considered as a spiritual, i.e., an abstract, simple, single being; for the predicates of God are precisely of this character, that one involves all the others, because there is no real difference between them. If, therefore, in the present predicates I have not the future, in the present God not the future

God, then the future God is not the present, but they are two distinct beings.[1] But this distinction is in contradiction with the unity and simplicity of the theological God. Why is a given predicate a predicate of God? Because it is divine in its nature, i.e., because it expresses no limitation, no defect. Why are other predicates applied to him? Because, however various in themselves, they agree in this, that they all alike express perfection, unlimitedness. Hence I can conceive innumerable predicates of God, because they must all agree with the abstract idea of the Godhead, and must have in common that which constitutes every single predicate a divine attribute. Thus it is in the system of Spinoza. He speaks of an infinite number of attributes of the divine substance, but he specifies none except Thought and Extension. Why? Because it is a matter of indifference to know them? Nay, because they are in themselves indifferent, superfluous; for with all these innumerable predicates, I yet always mean to say the same thing as when I speak of Thought and Extension. Why is Thought an attribute of substance? Because, according to Spinoza, it is capable of being conceived by itself, because it expresses something indivisible, perfect, infinite. Why Extension or Matter? For the same reason. Thus, substance can have an indefinite number of predicates, because it is not their specific definition, their difference, but their identity, their equivalence, which makes them attributes of substance. Or rather, substance has innumerable predicates only because (how strange!) it has properly no predicate; that is, no definite, real predicate. The indefinite unity which is the product of thought completes itself by the indefinite multiplicity which is the product of the imagination. Because the predicate is not *multum*, it is *multa*. In truth, the positive predicates are Thought and Extension. In these two infinitely more is said than in the nameless innumerable predicates; for they express something definite—in them I have something. But substance is too indifferent, too apathetic to be *something*; that is, to have qualities and passions; that it may not be something; it is rather nothing.

Now, when it is shown that what the subject is lies entirely in the attributes of the subject; that is, that the predicate is the true subject; it is also proved that if the divine predicates are attributes of the human nature, the subject of those predicates is also of the human nature. But the divine predicates are partly general, partly personal. The general predicates are the metaphysical, but these serve only as external points of support to religion; they are not the characteristic definitions of religion. It is the personal predicates alone which constitute the essence of religion—in which the Divine Being is the object of religion. Such are, for example, that God is a Person, that he is the moral Lawgiver, the Father of mankind, the Holy One, the Just, the

---

[1] For religious faith there is no other distinction between the present and future God than that the former is an object of faith, of conception, of imagination, while the latter is to be an object of immediate, that is, personal, sensible perception. In this life and in the next he is the same God; but in the one he is incomprehensible, in the other comprehensible.

Good, the Merciful. It is, however, at once clear, or it will at least be clear in the sequel, with regard to these and other definitions, that, especially as applied to a personality, they are purely human definitions, and that consequently man in religion—in his relation to God—is in relation to his own nature; for to the religious sentiment these predicates are not mere conceptions, mere images, which man forms of God, to be distinguished from that which God is in himself, but truths, facts, realities. Religion knows nothing of anthropomorphisms; to it they are not anthropomorphisms. It is the very essence of religion that to it these definitions express the nature of God. They are pronounced to be images only by the understanding, which reflects on religion, and which while defending them yet before its own tribunal denies them. But to the religious sentiment God is a real Father, real Love and Mercy; for to it he is a real, living, personal being, and therefore his attributes are also living and personal. Nay, the definitions which are the most sufficing to the religious sentiment are precisely those which give the most offence to the understanding, and which in the process of reflection on religion it denies. Religion is essentially emotion; hence, objectively also, emotion is to it necessarily of a divine nature. Even anger appears to it an emotion not unworthy of God, provided only there be a religious motive at the foundation of this anger.

But here it is also essential to observe, and this phenomenon is an extremely remarkable one, characterizing the very core of religion, that in proportion as the divine subject is in reality human, the greater is the apparent difference between God and man; that is, the more, by reflection on religion, by theology, is the identity of the divine and human denied, and the human, considered as such, is depreciated. The reason of this is, that as what is positive in the conception of the divine being can only be human, the conception of man, as an object of consciousness, can only be negative. To enrich God, man must become poor; that God may be all, man must be nothing. But he desires to be nothing in himself, because what he takes from himself is not lost to him, since it is preserved in God. Man has his being in God; why then should he have it in himself? Where is the necessity of positing the same thing twice, of having it twice? What man withdraws from himself, what he renounces in himself, he only enjoys in an incomparably higher and fuller measure in God.

The monks made a vow of chastity to God; they mortified the sexual passion in themselves, but therefore they had in heaven, in the Virgin Mary, the image of woman—an image of love. They could the more easily dispense with real woman in proportion as an ideal woman was an object of love to them. The greater the importance they attached to the denial of sensuality, the greater the importance of the heavenly virgin for them: she was to them in the place of Christ, in the stead of God. The more the sensual tendencies are renounced, the more sensual is the God to whom they are sacrificed. For whatever is made an offering to God has an especial value attached to it; in it God is supposed to have especial pleasure. That which is the highest in the estimation of man is naturally the highest in the estimation of his God; what pleases man pleases God also. The Hebrews did not offer to Jehovah unclean, ill-conditioned animals; on the contrary, those which they most highly prized, which they themselves ate, were also the food of God (Lev. 3:2). Wherever, therefore, the denial of the sensual delights is made a special offering, a sacrifice well-pleasing to God, there the highest value is attached to the senses, and the sensuality which has been renounced is unconsciously restored, in the fact that God takes the place of the material delights which have been renounced. The nun weds herself to God; she has a heavenly bridegroom, the monk a heavenly bride. But the heavenly virgin is only a sensible presentation of a general truth, having relation to the essence of religion. Man denies as to himself only what he attributes to God. Religion abstracts from man, from the world, but it can only abstract from the limitations, from the phenomena; in short, from the negative, not from the essence, the positive, of the world and humanity: hence, in the very abstraction and negation it must recover that from which it abstracts, or believes itself to abstract. And thus, in reality, whatever religion consciously denies—always supposing that what is denied by it is something essential, true, and consequently incapable of being ultimately denied—it unconsciously restores in God. Thus, in religion man denies his reason; of himself he knows nothing of God, his thoughts are only worldly, earthly; he can only believe what God reveals to him. But on this account the thoughts of God are human, earthly thoughts: like man, he has plans in his mind, he accommodates himself to circumstances and grades of intelligence, like a tutor with his pupils; he calculates closely the effect of his gifts and revelations; he observes man in all his doings; he knows all things, even the most earthly, the commonest, the most trivial. In brief, man in relation to God denies his own knowledge, his own thoughts, that he may place them in God. Man gives up his personality; but in return, God, the Almighty, infinite, unlimited being, is a person; he denies human dignity, the human ego; but in return God is to him a selfish, egoistical being, who in all things seeks only himself, his own honour, his own ends; he represents God as simply seeking the satisfaction of his own selfishness, while yet he frowns on that of every other being; his God is the very luxury of egoism. Religion further denies goodness as a quality of human nature; man is wicked, corrupt, incapable of good; but, on the other hand, God is only good—the Good Being. Man's nature demands as an object goodness, personified as God; but is it not hereby declared that goodness is an essential tendency of man? If my heart is wicked, my understanding perverted, how can I perceive and feel the holy to be holy, the good to be good? Could I perceive the beauty of a fine picture if my mind were æsthetically an absolute piece of perversion? Though I may not be a painter, though I may not have the power of producing what is beautiful myself, I must yet have æsthetic feeling, æsthetic comprehension, since I perceive the beauty that is presented to me externally. Either goodness does not exist at all for man, or, if it does exist, therein is revealed to the individual man the holiness and goodness of human nature. That which is absolutely opposed to my nature, to which I am united by no bond of sympathy, is not even conceivable or perceptible by me. The holy is in opposition to me only as regards the modifications of my personality, but as regards my fundamental nature it is in unity with me. The holy is a reproach to my sinfulness; in it I recognize myself as a sinner; but in so doing, while I blame myself, I acknowledge what I am not, but ought to be, and what, for that very reason, I, according to my destination, can be; for an "ought" which has no corresponding capability does not affect me, is a ludicrous chimæra without any true relation to my mental constitution. But when I acknowledge goodness as my destination, as my law, I acknowledge it, whether consciously or unconsciously, as my own nature. Another nature than my own, one different in quality, cannot touch me. I can perceive sin as sin, only when I perceive it to be a contradiction of myself with myself—that is, of my personality with my fundamental nature. As a contradiction of the absolute, considered as another being, the feeling of sin is inexplicable, unmeaning.

The distinction between Augustinianism and Pelagianism[2] consists only in this, that the former expresses after the manner of religion what the latter expresses after the manner of rationalism. Both say the same thing, both vindicate the goodness of man; but Pelagianism does it directly, in a rationalistic and moral form; Augustinianism indirectly, in a mystical, that is, a religious form. For that which is given to man's God is in truth given to man himself; what a man declares concerning God, he in truth declares concerning himself. Augustinianism would be a truth, and a truth opposed to Pelagianism, only if man had the devil for his God, and, with the consciousness that he was the devil, honoured, reverenced, and worshiped him as the highest being. But so long as man adores a good being as his God, so long does he contemplate in God the goodness of his own nature.

As with the doctrine of the radical corruption of human nature, so is it with the identical doctrine, that man can do nothing good—i.e., in truth, nothing of himself—by his own strength. For the denial of human strength and spontaneous moral activity to be true, the moral activity of God must also be denied; and we must say, with the Oriental nihilist or pantheist: the Divine

---

[2]Pelagius, a contemporary of Augustine, opposed Augustine's teaching that fallen man is wholly wicked and powerless to do good. As Feuerbach says in a footnote: "Augustinianism denies man; but, as a consequence of this, it reduces God to the level of man, even to the ignominy of the cross, for the sake of man. The former puts man in the place of God, the latter puts God in the place of man; both lead to the same result—the distinction is only apparent, a pious illusion. Augustinianism is only an inverted Pelagianism; what to the latter is a subject, is to the former an object."—EDITOR

Being is absolutely without will or action, indifferent, knowing nothing of the discrimination between evil and good. But he who defines God as an active being, and not only so, but as morally active and morally critical—as a being who loves, works, and rewards good, punishes, rejects, and condemns evil—he who thus defines God only in appearance denies human activity, in fact, making it the highest, the most real activity. He who makes God act humanly, declares human activity to be divine; he says: A god who is not active, and not morally or humanly active, is no god; and thus he makes the idea of the Godhead dependent on the idea of activity, that is, of human activity, for a higher he knows not.

Man—this is the mystery of religion—projects his being into objectivity, and then again makes himself an object to this projected image of himself thus converted into a subject, he thinks of himself as an object to himself, but as the object of an object, of another being than himself. Thus here. Man is an object of God. That man is good or evil is not indifferent to God; no! He has a lively, profound interest in man's being good; he wills that man should be good, happy—for without goodness there is no happiness. Thus the religious man virtually retracts the nothingness of human activity, by making his dispositions and actions an object to God, by making man the end of God—for that which is an object to the mind is an end in action—by making the divine activity a means of human salvation. God acts, that man may be good and happy. Thus man, while he is apparently humiliated to the lowest degree, is in truth exalted to the highest. Thus, in and through God, man has in view himself alone. It is true that man places the aim of his action in God, but God has no other aim of action than the moral and eternal salvation of man: thus man has in fact no other aim than himself. The divine activity is not distinct from the human.

How could the divine activity work on me as its object, nay, work in me, if it were essentially different from me; how could it have a human aim, the aim of ameliorating and blessing man, if it were not itself human? Does not the purpose determine the nature of the act? When man makes his moral improvement an aim to himself, he has divine resolutions, divine projects; but also, when God seeks the salvation of man, he has human ends and a human mode of activity corresponding to these ends. Thus in God man has only his own activity as an object. But for the very reason that he regards his own activity as objective, goodness only as an object, he necessarily receives the impulse, the motive not from himself, but from this object. He contemplates his nature as external to himself, and this nature as goodness; thus it is self-evident, it is mere tautology to say that the impulse to good comes only from thence where he places the good.

God is the highest subjectivity of man abstracted from himself; hence man can do nothing of himself, all goodness comes from God. The more subjective God is, the more completely does man divest himself of his subjectivity, because God is, per se, his relinquished self, the possession of which he however again vindicates to himself. As the action of the arteries drives the blood into the extremities, and the action of the veins brings it back again, as life in general consists in a perpetual systole and diastole; so is it in religion. In the religious systole man propels his own nature from himself, he throws himself outward; in the religious diastole he receives the rejected nature in his heart again. God alone is the being who acts of himself—this is the force of repulsion in religion; God is the being who acts in me, with me, through me, upon me, for me, is the principle of my salvation, of my good dispositions and actions, consequently my own good principle and nature—this is the force of attraction in religion.

The course of religious development which has been generally indicated consists specifically in this, that man abstracts more and more from God, and attributes more and more to himself. This is especially apparent in the belief in revelation. That which to a later age or a cultured people is given by nature or reason, is to an earlier age, or to a yet uncultured people, given by God. Every tendency of man, however natural, even the impulse to cleanliness—was conceived by the Israelites as a positive divine ordinance. From this example we again see that God is lowered, is conceived more entirely on the type of ordinary humanity, in proportion as man detracts from himself. How can the self-humiliation of man go further than when he disclaims the capability of fulfilling spontaneously the requirements of common decency?[3] The Christian religion, on the other hand, distinguished the impulses and passions of man according to their quality, their character; it represented only good emotions, good dispositions, good thoughts, as revelations, operations—that is, as dispositions, feelings, thoughts—of God; for what God reveals is a quality of God himself; that of which the heart is full overflows the lips; as is the effect such is the cause; as the revelation, such the being who reveals himself. A God who reveals himself in good dispositions is a God whose essential attribute is only moral perfection. The Christian religion distinguishes inward moral purity from external physical purity; the Israelites identified the two.[4] In relation to the Israelitish religion, the Christian religion is one of criticism and freedom. The Israelite trusted himself to do nothing except what was commanded by God; he was without will even in external things; the authority of religion extended itself even to his food. The Christian religion, on the other hand, in all these external things made man dependent on himself, i.e., placed in man what the Israelite placed out of himself in God. Israel is the most complete presentation of Positivism in religion. In relation to the Israelite, the Christian is an *esprit fort*, a free-thinker. Thus do things change. What yesterday was still religion is no longer such today; and what today is atheism, tomorrow will be religion.

---

[3]Deut. 23:12–13.
[4]See, for example, Gen. 35:2; Lev. 11:44, 20:26.

# Søren Kierkegaard

Søren Kierkegaard (1813–1855), the father of modern existentialism, has had a profound influence upon twentieth-century theology. In his *Philosophical Fragments* and *Concluding Unscientific Postscript*, Kierkegaard attacked the rationalist desire for proofs as an evasion of the claim of revelation.

# 13

# *Against Proofs in Religion*

But what is this unknown something with which the Reason collides when inspired by its paradoxical passion, with the result of unsettling even man's knowledge of himself? It is the Unknown. It is not a human being, insofar as we know what man is; nor is it any other known thing. So let us call this unknown something: *God*. It is nothing more than a name we assign to it. The idea of demonstrating that this unknown something (God) exists could scarcely suggest itself to the Reason. For if God does not exist it would of course be impossible to prove it; and if he does exist it would be folly to attempt it. For at the very outset, in beginning my proof, I will have presupposed it, not as doubtful but as certain (a presupposition is never doubtful, for the very reason that it is a presupposition), since otherwise I would not begin, readily understanding that the whole would be impossible if he did not exist. But if when I speak of proving God's existence I mean that I propose to prove that the Unknown, which exists, is God, then I express myself unfortunately. For in that case I do not prove anything, least of all an existence, but merely develop the content of a conception. Generally speaking, it is a difficult matter to prove that anything exists; and what is still worse for the intrepid souls who undertake the venture, the difficulty is such that fame scarcely awaits those who concern themselves with it. The entire demonstration always turns into something very different from what it assumes to be, and becomes an additional development of the consequences that flow from [our] having assumed that the object in question exists. Thus I always reason from existence, not toward existence, whether I move in the sphere of

Søren Kierkegaard, *Philosophical Fragments*, trans. by David Swenson, Copyright 1936. © 1962 by Princeton University Press. Excerpt, pp. 31-36, reprinted by permission of Princeton University Press.

palpable sensible fact or in the realm of thought. I do not, for example, prove that a stone exists, but that some existing thing is a stone. The procedure in a court of justice does not prove that a criminal exists, but that the accused, whose existence is given, is a criminal. Whether we call existence an *accessorium* or the eternal *prius*, it is never subject to demonstration. Let us take ample time for consideration. We have no such reason for haste as have those who from concern for themselves or for God or for some other thing, must make haste to get its existence demonstrated. Under such circumstances there may indeed be need for haste, especially if the prover sincerely seeks to appreciate the danger that he himself, or the thing in question, may be non-existent unless the proof is finished; and does not surreptitiously entertain the thought that it exists whether he succeeds in proving it or not.

If it were proposed to prove Napoleon's existence from Napoleon's deeds, would it not be a most curious proceeding? His existence does indeed explain his deeds, but the deeds do not prove his existence, unless I have already understood the word "his" so as thereby to have assumed his existence. But Napoleon is only an individual, and insofar there exists no absolute relationship between him and his deeds; some other person might have performed the same deeds. Perhaps this is the reason why I cannot pass from the deeds to existence. If I call these deeds the deeds of Napoleon, the proof becomes superfluous, since I have already named him; if I ignore this, I can never prove from the deeds that they are Napoleon's, but only in a purely ideal manner that such deeds are the deeds of a great general, and so forth. But between God and his works there exists an absolute relationship; God is not a name but a concept. Is this perhaps the reason that his *essentia involvit existentiam* [essence involves existence]? The works of God are such that only God can perform them. Just so, but where then are the works of God? The works from which I would deduce his existence are not immediately given. The wisdom of God in nature, his goodness, his wisdom in the governance of the world—are all these manifest, perhaps, upon the very face of things? Are we not here confronted with the most terrible temptations to doubt, and is it not impossible finally to dispose of all these doubts? But from such an order of things I will surely not attempt to prove God's existence; and even if I began I would never finish, and would in addition have to live constantly in suspense, lest something so terrible should suddenly happen that my bit of proof would be demolished. From what works then do I propose to derive the proof? From the works as apprehended through an ideal interpretation, i.e., such as they do not immediately reveal themselves. But in that case it is not from the works that I prove God's existence. I merely develop the ideality I have presupposed, and because of my confidence in *this* I make so bold as to defy all objections, even those that have not yet been made. In beginning my proof I presuppose the ideal interpretation, and also that I will be successful in carrying it through; but what else is this but to presuppose that God exists, so that I really begin by virtue of confidence in him?

And how does God's existence emerge from the proof? Does it follow straightway, without any breach of continuity? Or have we not here an analogy to the behaviour of these toys, the little Cartesian dolls? As soon as I let go of the doll it stands on its head. As soon as I let it go—I must therefore let it go. So also with the proof for God's existence. As long as I keep my hold on the proof, i.e., continue to demonstrate, the existence does not come out, if for no other reason than that I am engaged in proving it; but when I let the proof go, the existence is there. But this act of letting go is surely also something; it is indeed a contribution of mine. Must not this also be taken in to account, this little moment, brief as it may be—it need not be long, for it is a *leap*. However brief this moment, if only an instantaneous now, this "now" must be included in the reckoning. If anyone wishes to have it ignored, I will use it to tell a little anecdote, in order to show that it really does exist. Chrysippus was experimenting with a sorites to see if he could not bring about a break in its quality, either progressively or retrogressively. But Carneades could not get it in his head when the new quality actually emerged. Then Chrysippus told him to try making a little pause in the reckoning, and so—so it would be easier to understand. Carneades replied: "With the greatest pleasure, please do not hesitate on my account; you may not only pause, but even lie down to sleep, and it will help you just as little; for when you awake we will begin again where you left off. Just so; it boots as little to try to get rid of something by sleeping as to try to come into the possession of something in the same manner."

Whoever therefore attempts to demonstrate the existence of God (except in the sense of clarifying the concept, and without the *reservatio finalis* noted above, that the existence emerges from the demonstration by a leap) proves in lieu thereof something else, something which at times perhaps does not need a proof, and in any case needs none better; for the fool says in his heart that there is no God, but whoever says in his heart or to men: "Wait just a little and I will prove it"—what a rare man of wisdom is he![1] If in the moment of beginning his proof it is not absolutely undetermined whether God exists or not, he does not prove it; and if it is thus undetermined in the beginning he will never come to begin, partly from fear of failure, since God perhaps does not exist, and partly because he has nothing with which to begin. A project of this kind would scarcely have been undertaken by the ancients. Socrates at least, who is credited with having put forth the physico-teleological proof for God's existence, did not go about it in any such manner. He always presupposes God's existence, and under this presupposition seeks to interpenetrate nature with the idea of purpose. Had he been asked why he

---

[1]What an excellent subject for a comedy of the higher lunacy!

pursued this method, he would doubtless have explained that he lacked the courage to venture out upon so perilous a voyage of discovery without having made sure of God's existence behind him. At the word of God he casts his net as if to catch the idea of purpose; for nature herself finds many means of frightening the inquirer, and distracts him by many a digression.

The paradoxical passion of the Reason thus comes repeatedly into collision with the Unknown, which does indeed exist, but is unknown, and insofar does not exist. The Reason cannot advance beyond this point, and yet it cannot refrain in its paradoxicalness from arriving at this limit and occupying itself therewith. It will not serve to dismiss its relation to it simply by asserting that the Unknown does not exist, since this itself involves a relationship. But what then is the Unknown, since the designation of it as God merely signifies for us that it is unknown? To say that it is the Unknown because it cannot be known, and even if it were capable of being known, it could not be expressed, does not satisfy the demands of passion, though it correctly interprets the Unknown as a limit; but a limit is precisely a torment for passion, though it also serves as an incitement. And yet the Reason can come no further, whether it risks an issue *via negationis* or *via eminentia*.[2]

What then is the Unknown? It is the limit to which the Reason repeatedly comes, and insofar, substituting a static form of conception for the dynamic, it is the different, the absolutely different. But because it is absolutely different, there is no mark by which it could be distinguished. When qualified as absolutely different it seems on the verge of disclosure, but this is not the case; for the Reason cannot even conceive an absolute unlikeness. The Reason cannot negate itself absolutely, but uses itself for the purpose, and thus conceives only such an unlikeness within itself as it can conceive by means of itself; it cannot absolutely transcend itself, and hence conceives only such a superiority over itself as it can conceive by means of itself. Unless the Unknown (God) remains a mere limiting conception, the single idea of difference will be thrown into a state of confusion, and become many ideas of many differences. The Unknown is then in a condition of dispersion (διασπορά), and the Reason may choose at pleasure from what is at hand and the imagination may suggest (the monstrous, the ludicrous, etc.).

But it is impossible to hold fast to a difference of this nature. Every time this is done it is essentially an arbitrary act, and deepest down in the heart of piety lurks the mad caprice which knows that it has itself produced its God. If no specific determination of difference can be held fast, because there is no distinguishing mark, like and unlike finally become identified with one another, thus sharing the fate of all such dialectical opposites. The unlikeness clings to the Reason and confounds it, so that the Reason no longer knows

---

[2]I.e., by the method of making negative statements about God or by the method of attributing human qualities to God in a higher degree.—EDITOR

itself and quite consistently confuses itself with the unlikeness. On this point paganism has been sufficiently prolific in fantastic inventions. As for the last-named supposition, the self-irony of the Reason, I shall attempt to delineate it merely by a stroke or two, without raising any question of its being historical. There lives an individual whose appearance is precisely like that of other men; he grows up to manhood like others, he marries, he has an occupation by which he earns his livelihood, and he makes provision for the future as befits a man. For though it may be beautiful to live like the birds of the air, it is not lawful, and may lead to the sorriest of consequences: either starvation if one has enough persistence, or dependence on the bounty of others. This man is also God. How do I know? I cannot know it, for in order to know it I would have to know God, and the nature of the difference between God and man; and this I cannot know, because the Reason has reduced it to likeness with that from which it was unlike. Thus God becomes the most terrible of deceivers, because the Reason had deceived itself. The Reason has brought God as near as possible, and yet he is as far away as ever.

# William James

William James (1842–1910), perhaps America's most eminent philosopher and a leading developer of the philosophy of Pragmatism, was deeply and sympathetically interested in religion, about which he wrote the classic *Varieties of Religious Experience*. In his famous essay, "The Will to Believe," the second of our two selections, he offered an influential defense of religious belief.

# 14

# *Mysticism*

One may say truly, I think, that personal religious experience has its root and centre in mystical states of consciousness; so for us, who in these lectures are treating personal experience as the exclusive subject of our study, such states of consciousness ought to form the vital chapter from which the other chapters get their light. Whether my treatment of mystical states will shed more light or darkness, I do not know, for my own constitution shuts me out from their enjoyment almost entirely, and I can speak of them only at second hand. But though forced to look upon the subject so externally, I will be as objective and receptive as I can; and I think I shall at least succeed in convincing you of the reality of the states in question, and of the paramount importance of their function.

First of all, then, I ask, What does the expression "mystical states of consciousness" mean? How do we part off mystical states from other states?

The words "mysticism" and "mystical" are often used as terms of mere reproach, to throw at any opinion which we regard as vague and vast and sentimental, and without a base in either facts or logic. For some writers a "mystic" is any person who believes in thought-transference, or spirit-return. Employed in this way the word has little value: there are too many less ambiguous synonyms. So, to keep it useful by restricting it, I will . . . simply propose to you four marks which, when an experience has them, may justify us in calling it mystical for the purpose of the present lectures. In this way we shall save verbal disputation, and the recriminations that generally go therewith.

1. *Ineffability.* The handiest of the marks by which I classify a state of mind as mystical is negative. The subject of it immediately says that it defies

---

*The Varieties of Religious Experience* (1902), Lectures XVI–XVII.

expression, that no adequate report of its contents can be given in words. It follows from this that its quality must be directly experienced; it cannot be imparted or transferred to others. In this peculiarity mystical states are more like states of feeling than like states of intellect. No one can make clear to another who has never had a certain feeling in what the quality or worth of it consists. One must have musical ears to know the values of a symphony; one must have been in love oneself to understand a lover's state of mind. Lacking the heart or ear, we cannot interpret the musician or the lover justly, and are even likely to consider him weak-minded or absurd. The mystic finds that most of us accord to his experiences an equally incompetent treatment.

2. *Noetic quality*. Although so similar to states of feeling, mystical states seem to those who experience them to be also states of knowledge. They are states of insight into depths of truth unplumbed by the discursive intellect. They are illuminations, revelations, full of significance and importance, all inarticulate though they remain; and as a rule they carry with them a curious sense of authority for after-time.

These two characters will entitle any state to be called mystical, in the sense in which I use the word. Two other qualities are less sharply marked, but are usually found. These are:

3. *Transiency*. Mystical states cannot be sustained for long. Except in rare instances, half an hour, or at most an hour or two, seems to be the limit beyond which they fade into the light of common day. Often, when faded, their quality can but imperfectly be reproduced in memory; but when they recur it is recognized; and from one recurrence to another it is susceptible of continuous development in what is felt as inner richness and importance.

4. *Passivity*. Although the oncoming of mystical states may be facilitated by preliminary voluntary operations, as by fixing the attention, or going through certain bodily performances, or in other ways which manuals of mysticism prescribe; yet when the characteristic sort of consciousness once has set in, the mystic feels as if his own will were in abeyance, and indeed sometimes as if he were grasped and held by a superior power. This latter peculiarity connects mystical states with certain definite phenomena of secondary or alternative personality, such as prophetic speech, automatic writing, or the mediumistic trance. When these latter conditions are well pronounced, however, there may be no recollection whatever of the phenomenon, and it may have no significance for the subject's usual inner life, to which, as it were, it makes a mere interruption. Mystical states, strictly so called, are never merely interruptive. Some memory of their content always remains, and a profound sense of their importance. They modify the inner life of the subject between the times of their recurrence. Sharp divisions in this region are, however, difficult to make, and we find all sorts of gradations and mixtures.

These four characteristics are sufficient to mark out a group of states of consciousness peculiar enough to deserve a special name and to call for careful study. Let it then be called the mystical group.

Our next step should be to gain acquaintance with some typical examples. Professional mystics at the height of their development have often elaborately organized experiences and a philosophy based thereupon. But . . . phenomena are best understood when placed within their series, studied in their germ and in their over-ripe decay, and compared with their exaggerated and degenerated kindred. The range of mystical experience is very wide, much too wide for us to cover in the time at our disposal. Yet the method of serial study is so essential for interpretation that if we really wish to reach conclusions we must use it. I will begin, therefore, with phenomena which claim no special religious significance, and end with those of which the religious pretensions are extreme.

The simplest rudiment of mystical experience would seem to be that deepened sense of the significance of a maxim or formula which occasionally sweeps over one. "I've heard that said all my life," we exclaim, "but I never realized its full meaning until now." "When a fellow-monk," said Luther, "one day repeated the words of the Creed: 'I believe in the forgiveness of sins,' I saw the Scripture in an entirely new light; and straightway I felt as if I were born anew. It was as if I had found the door of paradise thrown wide open." This sense of deeper significance is not confined to rational propositions. Single words, and conjunctions of words, effects of light on land and sea, odors and musical sounds, all bring it when the mind is tuned aright. Most of us can remember the strangely moving power of passages in certain poems read when we were young, irrational doorways as they were through which the mystery of fact, the wildness and the pang of life, stole into our hearts and thrilled them. The words have not perhaps become mere polished surfaces for us; but lyric poetry and music are alive and significant only in proportion as they fetch these vague vistas of a life continuous with our own, beckoning and inviting, yet ever eluding our pursuit. We are alive or dead to the eternal inner message of the arts according as we have kept or lost this mystical susceptibility.

A more pronounced step forward on the mystical ladder is found in an extremely frequent phenomenon, that sudden feeling, namely, which sometimes sweeps over us, of having "been here before," as if at some indefinite past time, in just this place, with just these people, we were already saying just these things. As Tennyson writes [in "The Two Voices"]:

> Moreover, something is or seems,
> That touches me with mystic gleams,
> Like glimpses of forgotten dreams—

> Of something felt, like something here;
> Of something done, I know not where;
> Such as no language may declare.

Sir James Crichton-Browne has given the technical name of "dreamy states" to these sudden invasions of vaguely reminiscent consciousness. They bring a sense of mystery and of the metaphysical duality of things, and the feeling of an enlargement of perception which seems imminent but which never completes itself. In Dr. Crichton-Browne's opinion they connect themselves with the perplexed and scared disturbances of selfconsciousness which occasionally precede epileptic attacks. I think that this learned alienist takes a rather absurdly alarmist view of an intrinsically insignificant phenomenon. He follows it along the downward ladder, to insanity; our path pursues the upward ladder chiefly. The divergence shows how important it is to neglect no part of a phenomenon's connections, for we make it appear admirable or dreadful according to the context by which we set if off.

Somewhat deeper plunges into mystical consciousness are met with in yet other dreamy states. Such feelings as these which Charles Kingsley describes are surely far from being uncommon, especially in youth:

> When I walk the fields, I am oppressed now and then with an innate feeling that everything I see has a meaning, if I could but understand it. And this feeling of being surrounded with truths which I cannot grasp amounts to indescribable awe sometimes . . . . Have you not felt that your real soul was imperceptible to your mental vision, except in a few hallowed moments?[1]

A much more extreme state of mystical consciousness is described by J. A. Symonds; and probably more persons than we suspect could give parallels to it from their own experience.

> Suddenly at church, or in company, or when I was reading, and always, I think, when my muscles were at rest, I felt the approach of the mood. Irresistibly it took possession of my mind and will, lasted what seemed an eternity, and disappeared in a series of rapid sensations which resembled the awakening from anæsthetic influence. One reason why I disliked this kind of trance was that I could not describe it to myself. I cannot even now find words to render it intelligible. It consisted in a gradual but swiftly progressive obliteration of space, time, sensation, and the multitudinous factors of experience which seem to qualify what we are pleased to call our Self. In proportion as these conditions or ordinary consciousness were subtracted, the sense of an underlying or essential consciousness acquired intensity. At last nothing remained but a pure, absolute, abstract Self. The universe became without form and void of content.

---

[1]Quoted in Inge, *Christian Mysticism* (London: Methuen & Co., Ltd., 1899), p. 341.

But Self persisted, formidable in its vivid keenness, feeling the most poignant doubt about reality, ready, as it seemed, to find existence break as breaks a bubble round about it. And what then? The apprehension of a coming dissolution, the grim conviction that this state was the last state of the conscious Self, the sense that I had followed the last threat of being to the verge of the abyss, and had arrived at demonstration of eternal Maya or illusion, stirred or seemed to stir me up again. The return to ordinary conditions of sentient existence began by my first recovering the power of touch, and then by the gradual though rapid influx of familiar impressions and diurnal interests. At last I felt myself once more a human being; and though the riddle of what is meant by life remained unsolved, I was thankful for this return from the abyss—this deliverance from so awful an initiation into the mysteries of skepticism.

This trance recurred with diminishing frequency until I reached the age of twenty-eight. It served to impress upon my growing nature the phantasmal unreality of all the circumstances which contribute to a merely phenomenal consciousness. Often have I asked myself with anguish, on waking from that formless state of denuded, keenly sentient being, "This is the unreality?"—the trance of fiery, vacant, apprehensive, skeptical Self from which I issue, or these surrounding phenomena and habits which veil that inner Self and build a self of flesh-and-blood conventionality? Again, are men the factors of some dream, the dream-like unsubstantiality of which they comprehend at such eventful moments? What would happen if the final stage of the trance were reached?[2]

In a recital like this there is certainly something suggestive of pathology. The next step into mystical states carries us into a realm that public opinion and ethical philosophy have long since branded as pathological, though private practice and certain lyric strains of poetry seem still to bear witness to its ideality. I refer to the consciousness produced by intoxicants and anæsthetics, especially by alcohol. The sway of alcohol over mankind is unquestionably due to its power to stimulate the mystical faculties of human nature, usually crushed to earth by the cold facts and dry criticisms of the sober hour. Sobriety diminishes, discriminates, and says no; drunkenness expands, unites, and says yes. It is in fact the great exciter of the *Yes* function in man. It brings its votary from the chill periphery of things to the radiant core. It makes him for the moment one with truth. Not through mere perversity do men run after it. To the poor and unlettered it stands in the place of symphony concerts and of literature; and it is part of the deeper mystery and tragedy of life that whiffs and gleams of something that we immediately recognize as excellent should be vouchsafed to so many of us only in the fleeting earlier phases of what in its totality is so degrading a poisoning. The drunken consciousness is one bit of the mystic consciousness, and our total opinion of it must find its place in our opinion of that larger whole.

---

[2]H. F. Brown, *J. A. Symonds: A Biography* (London, 1895), pp. 29–31.

Nitrous oxide and ether, especially nitrous oxide, when sufficiently diluted with air, stimulate the mystical consciousness in an extraordinary degree. Depth beyond depth of truth seems revealed to the inhaler. This truth fades out, however, or escapes, at the moment of coming to; and if any words remain over in which it seemed to clothe itself, they prove to be the veriest nonsense. Nevertheless, the sense of profound meaning having been there persists; and I know more than one person who is persuaded that in the nitrous oxide trance we have a genuine metaphysical revelation.

Some years ago I myself made some observations on this aspect of nitrous oxide intoxication, and reported them in print. One conclusion was forced upon my mind at that time, and my impression of its truth has ever since remained unshaken. It is that our normal waking consciousness, rational consciousness as we call it, is but one special type of consciousness, whilst all about it, parted from it by the filmiest of screens, there lie potential forms of consciousness entirely different. We may go through life without suspecting their existence; but apply the requisite stimulus, and at a touch they are there in all their completeness, definite types of mentality which probably somewhere have their field of application and adaptation. No account of the universe in its totality can be final which leaves these other forms of consciousness quite disregarded. How to regard them is the question—for they are so discontinuous with ordinary consciousness. Yet they may determine attitudes though they cannot furnish formulas, and open a region though they fail to give a map. At any rate, they forbid a premature closing of our accounts with reality. Looking back on my own experiences, they all converge towards a kind of insight to which I cannot help ascribing some metaphysical significance. The keynote of it is invariably a reconciliation. It is as if the opposites of the world, whose contradictoriness and conflict make all our difficulties and troubles, were melted into unity. Not only do they, as contrasted species, belong to one and the same genus, but *one of the species*, the nobler and better one, *is itself the genus, and so soaks up and absorbs its opposite into itself.* This is a dark saying, I know, when thus expressed in terms of common logic, but I cannot wholly escape from its authority. I feel as if it must mean something, something like what the Hegelian philosophy means, if one could only lay hold of it more clearly. Those who have ears to hear, let them hear; to me the living sense of its reality only comes in the artificial mystic state of mind.

I just now spoke of friends who believe in the anæsthetic revelation. For them too it is a monistic insight, in which the *other* in its various forms appears absorbed into the One. [Writes one of them:]

Into this pervading genius we pass, forgetting and forgotten, and thenceforth each is all, in God. There is no higher, no deeper, no other, than the life in which we are founded. "The One remains, the many change and pass"; and each and every one of us *is* the One that remains . . . . This is the ultimatum . . . . As sure as being—whence is all our care—so sure is content, beyond duplexity, antithesis, or trouble, where I have triumphed in a solitude that God is not above.[3]

This has the genuine religious mystic ring! I just now quoted J. A. Symonds. He also records a mystical experience with chloroform, as follows:

After the choking and stifling had passed away, I seemed at first in a state of utter blankness; then came flashes of intense light, alternating with blackness, and with a keen vision of what was going on the room around me, but no sensation of touch. I thought that I was near death; when, suddenly, my soul became aware of God, who was manifestly dealing with me, handling me, so to speak, in an intense personal present reality. I felt him streaming in like light upon me . . . . I cannot describe the ecstasy I felt. Then, as I gradually awoke from the influence of the anæsthetics, the old sense of my relation to the world began to return, the new sense of my relation to God began to fade. I suddenly lept to my feet on the chair where I was sitting, and shrieked out, "It is too horrible, it is too horrible, it is too horrible," meaning that I could not bear this disillusionment. Then I flung myself on the ground, and at last awoke covered with blood, calling to the two surgeons (who were frightened), "Why did you not kill me? Why would you not let me die?" Only think of it. To have felt for that long dateless ecstasy of vision the very God, in all purity and tenderness and truth and absolute love, and then to find that I had after all had no revelation, but that I had been tricked by the abnormal excitement of my brain.

Yet, this question remains, Is it possible that the inner sense of reality which succeeded when my flesh was dead to impressions from without to the ordinary sense of physical relations, was not a delusion but an actual experience? Is it possible that I, in that moment, felt what some of the saints have said they always felt, the undemonstrable but irrefragable certainty of God?[4]

With these we make connection with religious mysticism pure and simple. ". . . [The] sudden realization of the immediate presence of God . . . in one shape or another is not uncommon," writes Mr. Ralph Waldo Trine:

I know an officer on our police force who has told me that many times when off duty, and on his way home in the evening, there comes to him such a vivid and vital realization of his oneness with this Infinite Power, and this Spirit of Infinite Peace so takes hold of and so fills him, that it seems as if his feet could hardly keep to the pavement, so buoyant and so exhilarated does he become by reason of this inflowing tide.[5]

---

[3]Benjamin Paul Blood, *The Anæsthetic Revelation and the Gist of Philosophy* (Amsterdam, N.Y., 1874), pp. 35, 36.

[4]Brown, *op cit.*, pp. 78–80.

[5]Ralph Waldo Trine, *In Tune with the Infinite* (London, 1900), p. 137.

Certain aspects of nature seem to have a peculiar power of awakening such mystical moods. Most of the striking cases which I have collected have occurred out of doors. Literature has commemorated this fact in many passages of great beauty—this extract, for example, from Ameil's *Journal Intime:*

> Shall I ever again have any of those prodigious reveries which sometimes came to me in former days? One day, in youth, at sunrise, sitting in the ruins of the castle of Faucigny; and again in the mountains, under the noonday sun, above Lavey, lying at the foot of a tree and visited by three butterflies; once more at night upon the shingly shore of the Northern Ocean, my back upon the sand and my vision ranging through the milky way—such grand and spacious, immortal, cosmogonic reveries, when one reaches to the stars, when one owns the infinite! Moments divine, ecstatic hours; in which our thought flies from world to world, pierces the great enigma, breathes with a respiration broad, tranquil, and deep as the respiration of the ocean, serene and limitless as the blue firmament; . . . instants of irresistible intuition in which one feels oneself great as the universe, and calm as a god . . . . What hours, what memories! The vestiges they leave behind are enough to fill us with belief and enthusiasm, as if they were visits of the Holy Ghost.[6]

Here is a similar record from the memoirs of that interesting German idealist, Malwida von Meysenbug:

> I was alone upon the seashore as all these thoughts flowed over me, liberating and reconciling; and now again, as once before in distant days in the Alps of Dauphineé, I was impelled to kneel down, this time before the illimitable ocean, symbol of the Infinite. I felt that I prayed as I had never prayed before, and knew now what prayer really is: to return from the solitude of individuation into the consciousness of unity with all that is, to kneel down as one that passes away, and to rise up as one imperishable. Earth, heaven, and sea resounded as in one vast world-encircling harmony. It was as if the chorus of all the great who had ever lived were about me. I felt myself one with them, and it appeared as if I heard their greeting: "Thou too belongest to the company of those who over-come."[7]

The well-known passage from Walt Whitman is a classical expression of this sporadic type of mystical experience.

> I believe in you, my Soul . . .
> Loaf with me on the grass, loose the stop from your throat; . . .
> Only the lull I like, the hum of your valved voice.
> I mind how once we lay, such a transparent summer morning.

---

[6]*Op. cit.,* pp. 43–44.
[7]*Memoiren einer Idealistin,* 5th ed. (1900, Vol. III, 166).

Swiftly arose and spread around me the peace and knowledge that pass all
the argument of the earth,
And I know that the hand of God is the promise of my own,
And I know that the spirit of God is the brother of my own,
And that all the men ever born are also my brothers and the women my
sisters and lovers,
And that a kelson of the creation is love.

I could easily give more instances, but one will suffice. I take it from the
Autobiography of J. Trevor.

One brilliant Sunday morning, my wife and boys went to the Unitarian Chapel
in Macclesfield. I felt it impossible to accompany them—as though to leave the
sunshine on the hills, and go down there to the chapel, would be for the time an
act of spiritual suicide. And I felt such need for new inspiration and expansion
in my life. So, very reluctantly and sadly, I left my wife and boys to go down
into the town, while I went further up into the hills with my stick and my dog.
In the loveliness of the morning, and the beauty of the hills and valleys, I soon
lost my sense of sadness and regret. For nearly an hour I walked along the road
to the "Cat and Fiddle," and then returned. On the way back, suddenly, without
warning, I felt that I was in Heaven—an inward state of peace and joy and
assurance indescribably intense, accompanied with a sense of being bathed in
a warm glow of light, as though the external condition had brought about the
internal effect—a feeling of having passed beyond the body, though the scene
around me stood out more clearly and as if nearer to me than before, by reason
of the illumination in the midst of which I seemed to be placed. This deep
emotion lasted, though with decreasing strength, until I reached home, and for
some time after, only gradually passing away.[8]

The writer adds that having had further experiences of a similar sort, he
now knows them well.

The spiritual life justifies itself to those who live it; but what can we say to those
who do not understand? This, at least, we can say, that it is a life whose
experiences are proved real to their possessor, because they remain with him
when brought closest into contact with the objective realities of life. Dreams
cannot stand this test. We wake from them to find that they are but dreams.
Wanderings of an overwrought brain do not stand this test. These highest
experiences that I have had of God's presence have been rare and brief—flashes
of consciousness which have compelled me to exclaim with surprise—God is
*here!*—or conditions of exaltation and insight, less intense, and only gradually
passing away. I have severely questioned the worth of these moments. To no
soul have I named them, lest I should be building my life and work on mere
phantasies of the brain. But I find that, after every questioning and test, they

---

[8] *My Quest for God* (London, 1897), pp. 268–69.

stand out today as the most real experiences of my life, and experiences which have explained and justified and unified all past experiences and all past growth. Indeed, their reality and their far-reaching significance are ever becoming more clear and evident. When they came, I was living the fullest, strongest, sanest, deepest life. I was not seeking them. What I was seeking, with resolute determination, was to live more intensely my own life, as against what I knew would be the adverse judgment of the world. It was in the most real seasons that the Real Presence came, and I was aware that I was immersed in the infinite ocean of God.[9]

Even the least mystical of you must by this time be convinced of the existence of mystical moments as states of consciousness of an entirely specific quality, and of the deep impression which they make on those who have them. A Canadian psychiatrist, Dr. R. M. Bucke, gives to the more distinctly characterized of these phenomena the name of cosmic consciousness. "Cosmic consciousness in its more striking instances is not," Dr. Bucke says, "simply an expansion or extension of the self-conscious mind with which we are all familiar, but the superaddition of a function as distinct from any possessed by the average man as *self*-consciousness is distinct from any function possessed by one of the higher animals."

The prime characteristic of cosmic consciousness is a consciousness of the cosmos, that is, of the life and order of the universe. Along with the consciousness of the cosmos there occurs an intellectual enlightenment which alone would place the individual on a new plane of existence—would make him almost a member of a new species. To this is added a state of moral exaltation, an indescribable feeling of elevation, elation, and joyousness, and a quickening of the moral sense, which is fully as striking, and more important than is the enhanced intellectual power. With these come what may be called a sense of immortality, a consciousness of eternal life, not a conviction that he shall have this, but the consciousness that he has it already.[10]

It was Dr. Bucke's own experience of a typical onset of cosmic consciousness in his own person which led him to investigate it in others. He has printed his conclusions in a highly interesting volume, from which I take the following account of what occurred to him:

I had spent the evening in a great city, with two friends, reading, and discussing poetry and philosophy. We parted at midnight. I had a long drive in a hansom to my lodging. My mind, deeply under the influence of the ideas, images, and emotions called up by the reading and talk, was calm and peaceful. I was in a state of quiet, almost passive enjoyment, not actually thinking, but letting ideas,

---

[9]*Ibid.*, pp. 256–57.

[10]*Cosmic Consciousness: A Study in the Evolution of the Human Mind* (Philadelphia, 1901), p. 2.

images, and emotions flow of themselves, as it were, through my mind. All at once, without warning of any kind, I found myself wrapped in a flame-colored cloud. For an instant I thought of fire, an immense conflagration somewhere close by in that great city; the next, I knew that the fire was within myself. Directly afterward there came upon me a sense of exultation, of immense joyousness accompanied or immediately followed by an intellectual illumination impossible to describe. Among other things, I did not merely come to believe, but I saw that the universe is not composed of dead matter, but is, on the contrary, a living Presence; I became conscious in myself of eternal life. It was not a conviction that I would have eternal life, but a consciousness that I possessed eternal life then; I saw that all men are immortal; that the cosmic order is such that without any peradventure all things work together for the good of each and all; that the foundation principle of the world, of all the worlds, is what we call love, and that the happiness of each and all is in the long run absolutely certain. The vision lasted a few seconds and was gone; but the memory of it and the sense of the reality of what it taught has remained during the quarter of a century which has since elapsed. I knew that what the vision showed was true. I had attained to a point of view from which I saw that it must be true. That view, that conviction, I may say that consciousness, has never, even during periods of the deepest depression, been lost.[11]

We have not seen enough of this cosmic or mystic consciousness, as it comes sporadically. We must next pass to its methodical cultivation as an element of the religious life. Hindus, Buddhists, Mohammedans, and Christians all have cultivated it methodically.

In India, training in mystical insight has been known from time immemorial under the name of yoga. Yoga means the experimental union of the individual with the divine. It is based on persevering exercise; and the diet, posture, breathing, intellectual concentration, and moral discipline vary slightly in the different systems which teach it. The yogi, or disciple, who has by these means overcome the obscurations of his lower nature sufficiently, enters into the condition termed *samadhi*, "and comes face to face with facts which no instinct or reason can ever know." He learns—

That the mind has a higher state of existence, beyond reason, a superconscious state, and that when the mind gets to that higher state, then this knowledge beyond reasoning comes . . . . All the different steps in yoga are intended to bring us scientifically to the superconscious state or samadhi . . . . Just as unconscious work is beneath consciousness, so there is another work which is above consciousness, and which, also, is not accompanied with the feeling of egoism . . . . There is no feeling of *I*, and yet the mind works, desireless, free from restlessness, objectless, bodiless. Then the Truth shines in its full effulgence, and we know ourselves—for samadhi lies potential in us all—for what we truly are, free,

---

[11]*Ibid.*, pp. 7–8.

immortal, omnipotent, loosed from the finite, and its contrasts of good and evil altogether, and identical with the Atman or Universal Soul.[12]

The Vedantists say that one may stumble into superconsciousness sporadically, without the previous discipline, but it is then impure. Their test of its purity, like our test of religion's value, is empirical: its fruits must be good for life. When a man comes out of samadhi, they assure us that he remains "enlightened, a sage, a prophet, a saint, his whole character changed, his life changed, illumined."

The Buddhists use the word "samadhi" as well as the Hindus; but "dhyana" is their special word for higher states of contemplation. There seem to be four stages recognized in dhyana. The first stage comes through concentration of the mind upon one point. It excludes desire but not discernment or judgment; it is still intellectual. In the second stage the intellectual functions drop off, and the satisfied sense of unity remains. In the third stage the satisfaction departs, and indifference begins, along with memory and self-consciousness. In the fourth stage the indifference, memory, and self-consciousness are perfected. (Just what "memory" and "self-consciousness" mean in this connection is doubtful. They cannot be the faculties familiar to us in the lower life.) Higher stages still of contemplation are mentioned—a region where there exists nothing, and where the meditator says: "There exists absolutely nothing," and stops. Then he reaches another region where he says: "There are neither ideas nor absence of ideas," and stops again. Then another region where, "having reached the end of both idea and perception, he stops finally." This would seem to be, not yet Nirvana, but as close an approach to it as this life affords.[13]

In the Mohammedan world the Sufi sect and various dervish bodies are the possessors of the mystical tradition. The Sufis have existed in Persia from the earliest times, and as their pantheism is so at variance with the hot and rigid monotheism of the Arab mind, it has been suggested that Sufism must have been inoculated into Islam by Hindu influences. We Christians know little of Sufism, for its secrets are disclosed only to those initiated. To give its existence a certain liveliness in your minds, I will quote a Moslem document, and pass away from the subject.

Al-Ghazzali, a Persian philosopher and theologian, who flourished in the eleventh century, and ranks as one of the greatest doctors of the Moslem church, has left us one of the few autobiographies to be found outside of Christian literature. Strange that a species of book so abundant among ourselves should be so little represented elsewhere—the absence of strictly

---

[12]My quotations are from Vivekananda, *Raja Yoga* (London, 1896). The completest source of information on Yoga is the work translated by Vihari Lala Mitra, *Yoga Vasishta Maha Ramayana*, 4 vols. (Calcutta, 1891–1899).

[13]I follow the account in C. F. Koeppen, *Die Religion des Buddha* (Berlin, 1857), Vol. I, 585 ff.

personal confessions is the chief difficulty to the purely literary student who would like to become acquainted with the inwardness of religions other than the Christian.

M. Schmölders has translated a part of Al-Ghazzali's autobiography into French:

The Science of the Sufis aims at detaching the heart from all that is not God, and at giving to it for sole occupation the meditation of the divine being. Theory being more easy for me than practice, I read [certain books] until I understood all that can be learned by study and hearsay. Then I recognized that what pertains most exclusively to their method is just what no study can grasp, but only transport, ecstasy, and the transformation of the soul. How great, for example, is the difference between knowing the definitions of health, of satiety, with their causes and conditions, and being really healthy or filled. How different to know in what drunkenness consists—as being a state occasioned by a vapor that rises from the stomach—and *being* drunk effectively. Without doubt, the drunken man knows neither the definition of drunkenness nor what makes it interesting for science. Being drunk, he knows nothing; whilst the physician, although not drunk, knows well in what drunkenness consists, and what are its predisposing conditions. Similarly there is a difference between knowing the nature of abstinence, and *being* abstinent or having one's soul detached from the world. Thus I had learned what words could teach of Sufism, but what was left could be learned neither by study nor through the ears, but solely by giving oneself up to ecstasy and leading a pious life.

Reflecting on my situation, I found myself tied down by a multitude of bonds—temptations on every side. Considering my teaching, I found it was impure before God. I saw myself struggling with all my might to achieve glory and to spread my name. [Here follows an account of his six months' hesitation to break away from the conditions of his life at Baghdad, at the end of which he fell ill with a paralysis of the tongue.] Then, feeling my own weakness, and having entirely given up my own will, I repaired to God like a man in distress who has no more resources. He answered, as he answers the wretch who invokes him. My heart no longer felt any difficulty in renouncing glory, wealth, and my children. So I quitted Baghdad, and reserving from my fortune only what was indispensable for my subsistence, I distributed the rest. I went to Syria, where I remained about two years, with no other occupation than living in retreat and solitude, conquering my desires, combating my passions, training myself to purify my soul, to make my character perfect, to prepare my heart for meditating on God—all according to the methods of the Sufis, as I had read of them.

This retreat only increased my desire to live in solitude, and to complete the purification of my heart and fit it for meditation. But the vicissitudes of the times, the affairs of the family, the need for subsistence, changed in some respects my primitive resolve, and interfered with my plans for a purely solitary life. I had never yet found myself completely in ecstasy, save in a few single hours; nevertheless, I kept the hope of attaining this state. Every time that the accidents led me astray, I sought to return; and in this situation I spent ten years. During this solitary state things were revealed to me which it is impossible either to describe or to point out. I recognized for certain that the Sufis are assuredly walking in the path of God. Both in their acts and in their inaction, whether internal or external, they are illumined by the light which proceeds from the prophetic source. The first condition for a Sufi is to purge his heart entirely of all that is not God. The next key of the contemplative life consists in the humble prayers which escape from the fervent soul, and in the meditations on God in which the heart is swallowed up entirely. But in reality this is only the beginning of the Sufi life, the end of Sufism being total absorption in God. The intuitions and all that precede are, so to speak, only the threshold for those who enter. From the beginning, revelations take place in so flagrant a shape that the Sufis see before them, whilst wide awake, the angels and the souls of the prophets. They hear their voices and obtain their favors. Then the transport rises from the perception of forms and figures to a degree which escapes all expression, and which no man may seek to give an account of without his words involving sin.

Whoever has had no experience of the transport knows of the true nature of prophetism nothing but the name. He may meanwhile be sure of its existence, both by experience and by what he hears the Sufis say. As there are men endowed only with the sensitive faculty who reject what is offered them in the way of objects of the pure understanding, so there are intellectual men who reject and avoid the things perceived by the prophetic faculty. A blind man can understand nothing of colors save what he has learned by narration and hearsay. Yet God has brought prophetism near to men in giving them all a state analogous to it in its principal characters. This state is sleep. If you were to tell a man who was himself without experience of such a phenomenon that there are people who at times swoon away so as to resemble dead men, and who [in dreams] yet perceive things that are hidden, he would deny it [and give his reasons]. Nevertheless, his arguments would be refuted by actual experience. Wherefore, just as the understanding is a stage of human life in which an eye opens to discern various intellectual objects uncomprehended by sensation; just so in the prophetic the sight is illumined by a light which uncovers hidden things and objects which the intellect fails to reach. The chief properties of prophetism are perceptible only during the transport, by those who embrace the Sufi life. The prophet is endowed with qualities to which you possess nothing analogous, and which consequently you cannot possibly understand. How should you know their true nature, since one knows only what one can comprehend? But the transport which one attains by the method of the Sufis is like an immediate perception, as if one touched the objects with one's hand.[14]

This incommunicableness of the transport is the keynote of all mysticism. Mystical truth exists for the individual who has the transport, but for no one else. In this, as I have said, it resembles the knowledge given to us in sensations more than that given by conceptual thought. Thought, with its remoteness and abstractness, has often enough in the history of philosophy been contrasted unfavorably with sensation. It is a commonplace of meta-

---

[14]A. Schmölders, *Essai sur les écoles philosophiques chez les Arabes* (Paris, 1842), pp. 54–68, abridged.

physics that God's knowledge cannot be discursive but must be intuitive, that is, must be constructed more after the pattern of what in ourselves is called immediate feeling, than after that of proposition and judgment. But *our* immediate feelings have no content but what the five senses supply; and we have seen and shall see again that mystics may emphatically deny that the senses play any part in the very highest type of knowledge which their transports yield.

In the Christian church there have always been mystics. Although many of them have been viewed with suspicion, some have gained favor in the eyes of the authorities. The experiences of these have been treated as precedents, and a codified system of mystical theology has been based upon them, in which everything legitimate finds its place. The basis of the system is "orison" or meditation, the methodical elevation of the soul towards God. Through the practice of orison the higher levels of mystical experience may be attained. It is odd that Protestantism, especially evangelical Protestantism, should seemingly have abandoned everything methodical in this line. Apart from what prayer may lead to, Protestant mystical experience appears to have been almost exclusively sporadic. It has been left to our mind-curers to reintroduce methodical meditation into our religious life.

The first thing to be aimed at in orison is the mind's detachment from outer sensations, for these interfere with its concentration upon ideal things. Such manuals as Saint Ignatius' *Spiritual Exercises* recommend the disciple to expel sensation by a graduated series of efforts to imagine holy scenes. The acme of this kind of discipline would be a semi-hallucinatory mono-ideism—an imaginary figure of Christ, for example, coming fully to occupy the mind. Sensorial images of this sort, whether literal or symbolic, play an enormous part in mysticism. But in certain cases imagery may fall away entirely, and in the very highest raptures it tends to do so. The state of consciousness becomes then insusceptible of any verbal description. Mystical teachers are unanimous as to this. Saint John of the Cross, for instance, one of the best of them, thus describes the condition called the "union of love," which, he says, is reached by "dark contemplation." In this the Deity compenetrates the soul, but in such a hidden way that the soul—

> ... finds no terms, no means, no comparison whereby to render the sublimity of the wisdom and the delicacy of the spiritual feeling with which she is filled .... We receive this mystical knowledge of God clothed in none of the kinds of images, in none of the sensible representations, which our mind makes use of in other circumstances. Accordingly in this knowledge, since the senses and the imagination are not employed, we get neither form nor impression, nor can we give any account or furnish any likeness, although the mysterious and sweet-tasting wisdom comes home so clearly to the inmost parts of our soul. Fancy a man seeing a certain kind of thing for the first time in his life. He can understand it, use and enjoy it, but he cannot apply a name to it, nor communi-

cate any idea of it, even though all the while it be a mere thing of sense. How much greater will be his powerlessness when it goes beyond the senses! This is the peculiarity of the divine language. The more infused, intimate, spiritual, and supersensible it is, the more does it exceed the senses, both inner and outer, and impose silence upon them . . . . The soul then feels as if placed in a vast and profound solitude, to which no created thing has access, in an immense and boundless desert, desert the more delicious the more solitary it is. There, in this abyss of wisdom, the soul grows by what it drinks in from the well-springs of the comprehension of love, . . . and recognizes, however sublime and learned may be the terms we employ, how utterly vile, insignificant, and improper they are, when we seek to discourse of divine things by their means.[15]

I cannot pretend to detail to you the sundry stages of the Christian mystical life. Our time would not suffice, for one thing; and moreover, I confess that the subdivisions and names which we find in the Catholic books seem to me to represent nothing objectively distinct. So many men, so many minds: I imagine that these experiences can be as infinitely varied as are the idiosyncrasies of individuals.

The cognitive aspects of them, their value in the way of revelation, is what we are directly concerned with, and it is easy to show by citation how strong an impression they leave of being revelations of new depths of truth. Saint Teresa is the expert of experts in describing such conditions, so I will turn immediately to what she says of one of the highest of them, the "orison of union."

In the orison of union, the soul is fully awake as regards God, but wholly asleep as regards things of this world and in respect of herself. During the short time the union lasts, she is as it were deprived of every feeling, and even if she would, she could not think of any single thing. Thus she needs to employ no artifice in order to arrest the use of her understanding: it remains so stricken with inactivity that she neither knows what she loves, nor in what manner she loves, nor what she wills. In short, she is utterly dead to the things of the world and lives solely in God . . . . I do not even know whether in this state she has enough life left to breathe. It seems to me she has not; or at least that if she does breathe, she is unaware of it. Her intellect would fain understand something of what is going on within her, but it has so little force now that it can act in no way whatsoever. So a person who falls into a deep faint appears as if dead . . . .

Thus does God, when he raises a soul to union with himself, suspend the natural action of all her faculties. She neither sees, hears, nor understands, so long as she is united with God. But this time is always short, and it seems even shorter than it is. God establishes himself in the interior of this soul in such a way, that when she returns to herself, it is wholly impossible for her to doubt that she has been in God, and God in her. This truth remains so strongly

---

[15]Saint John of the Cross, *The Dark Night of the Soul*, Bk. II, Chap. 17, in *Vie et Œuvres*, 3rd ed. (Paris, 1893), pp. 428–32.

impressed on her that, even though many years should pass without the condition returning, she can neither forget the favor she received, nor doubt of its reality. If you, nevertheless, ask how it is possible that the soul can see and understand that she has been in God, since during the union she has neither sight nor understanding, I reply that she does not see it then, but that she sees it clearly later, after she has returned to herself, not by any vision, but by a certitude which abides with her and which God alone can give her. I knew a person who was ignorant of the truth that God's mode of being in everything must be either by presence, by power, or by essence, but who, after having received the grace of which I am speaking, believed this truth in the most unshakable manner. So much so that, having consulted a half-learned man who was ignorant on this point as she had been before she was enlightened, when he replied that God is in us only by "grace," she disbelieved his reply, so sure she was of the true answer; and when she came to ask wiser doctors, they confirmed her in her belief, which much consoled her . . . .

But how, you will repeat, *can* one have such certainty in respect to what one does not see? This question, I am powerless to answer. These are secrets of God's omnipotence which it does not appertain to me to penetrate. All that I know is that I tell the truth; and I shall never believe that any soul who does not possess this certainty has ever been really united to God.[16]

The kinds of truth communicable in mystical ways, whether these be sensible or supersensible, are various. Some of them relate to this world—visions of the future, the reading of hearts, the sudden understanding of texts, the knowledge of distant events, for example—but the most important revelations are theological or metaphysical.

Saint Ignatius confessed one day to Father Laynez that a single hour of meditation at Manresa had taught him more truths about heavenly things than all the teachings of all the doctors put together could have taught him . . . . One day in orison, on the steps of the choir of the Dominican church, he saw in a distinct manner the plan of divine wisdom in the creation of the world. On another occasion, during a procession, his spirit was ravished in God, and it was given him to contemplate, in a form and images fitted to the weak understanding of a dweller on the earth, the deep mystery of the holy Trinity. This last vision flooded his heart with such sweetness, that the mere memory of it in after times made him shed abundant tears.[17]

Similarly with Saint Teresa. "One day, being in orison," she writes, "it was granted me to perceive in one instant how all things are seen and contained in God. I did not perceive them in their proper form, and nevertheless the view I had of them was of a sovereign clearness, and has remained vividly impressed upon my soul. It is one of the most signal of all the graces which the Lord has

---

[16]*The Interior Castle*, Fifth Abode, Chap. 1, in *Œuvres*, translated by Bouix, pp. 421–24.
[17]Bartoli-Michel, *Vie de Saint Ignace de Loyola*, pp. 34–36.

granted me . . . . The view was so subtle and delicate that the understanding cannot grasp it.[18]

She goes on to tell how it was as if the Deity were an enormous and sovereignly limpid diamond, in which all our actions were contained in such a way that their full sinfulness appeared evident as never before. On another day, she relates, while she was reciting the Athanasian Creed—

> Our Lord made me comprehend in what way it is that one God can be in three Persons. He made me see it so clearly that I remained as extremely surprised as I was comforted,...and now, when I think of the holy Trinity, or hear It spoken of, I understand how the three adorable Persons form only one God and I experience an unspeakable happiness.

On still another occasion, it was given to Saint Teresa to see and understand in what wise the Mother of God had been assumed into her place in Heaven.[19]

The deliciousness of some of these states seems to be beyond anything known in ordinary consciousness. It evidently involves organic sensibilities, for it is spoken of as something too extreme to be borne, and as verging on bodily pain. But it is too subtle and piercing a delight for ordinary words to denote. God's touches, the wounds of his spear, references to ebriety and to nuptial union have to figure in the phraseology by which it is shadowed forth. Intellect and senses both swoon away in these highest states of ecstasy. "If our understanding comprehends," says Saint Teresa, "it is in a mode which remains unknown to it, and it can understand nothing of what it comprehends. For my own part, I do not believe that it does comprehend, because, as I said, it does not understand itself to do so. I confess that it is all a mystery in which I am lost."[20] In the condition called *raptus* or ravishment by theologians, breathing and circulation are so depressed that it is a question among the doctors whether the soul be or be not temporarily dissevered from the body. One must read Saint Teresa's descriptions and the very exact distinctions which she makes, to persuade oneself that one is dealing, not with imaginary experiences, but with phenomena which, however rare, follow perfectly definite psychological types.

To the medical mind these ecstasies signify nothing but suggested and imitated hypnoid states, on an intellectual basis of superstition, and a corporeal one of degeneration and hysteria. Undoubtedly these pathological conditions have existed in many and possibly in all the cases, but that fact tells

---

[18]*Vie*, pp. 581–82.
[19]*Ibid.*, p. 574.
[20]*Ibid.*, p. 198.

us nothing about the value for knowledge of the consciousness which they induce. To pass a spiritual judgment upon these states, we must not content ourselves with superficial medical talk, but inquire into their fruits for life.

Their fruits appear to have been various. Stupefaction, for one thing, seems not to have been altogether absent as a result . . . . Many . . . ecstatics would have perished but for the care taken of them by admiring followers. The "other-worldliness" encouraged by the mystical consciousness makes this over-abstraction from practical life peculiarly liable to befall mystics in whom the character is naturally passive and the intellect feeble; but in natively strong minds and characters we find quite opposite results. The great Spanish mystics, who carried the habit of ecstasy as far as it has often been carried, appear for the most part to have shown indomitable spirit and energy, and all the more so for the trances in which they indulged.

Saint Ignatius was a mystic, but his mysticism made him assuredly one of the most powerfully practical human engines that ever lived. Saint John of the Cross, writing of the intuitions and touches by which God reaches the substance of the soul, tells us that—

> They enrich it marvelously. A single one of them may be sufficient to abolish at a stroke certain imperfections of which the soul during its whole life had vainly tried to rid itself, and to leave it adorned with virtues and loaded with supernatural gifts. A single one of these intoxicating consolations may reward it for all the labors undergone in its life—even were they numberless. Invested with an invincible courage, filled with an impassioned desire to suffer for its God, the soul is then seized with a strange torment—that of not being allowed to suffer enough.[21]

Saint Teresa is as emphatic, and much more detailed . . . . Where in literature is a more evidently veracious account of the formation of a new centre of spiritual energy, than is given in her description of the effects of certain ecstasies which in departing leave the soul upon a higher level of emotional excitement?

> Often, infirm and wrought upon with dreadful pains before the ecstasy, the soul emerges from it full of health and admirably disposed for action...as if God had willed that the body itself, already obedient to the soul's desires, should share in the soul's happiness . . . . The soul after such a favor is animated with a degree of courage so great that if at that moment its body should be torn to pieces for the cause of God, it would feel nothing but the liveliest comfort. Then it is that promises and heroic resolutions spring up in profusion in us, soaring desires, horror of the world, and the clear perception of our proper nothingness . . . . What empire is comparable to that of a soul who, from this sublime summit to

---

[21]*Œuvres, op. cit.*, p. 320.

which God has raised her, sees all the things of earth beneath her feet, and is captivated by no one of them? How ashamed she is of her former attachments! How amazed at her blindness! What lively pity she feels for those whom she recognizes still shrouded in the darkness! . . . She groans at having ever been sensitive to points of honor, at the illusion that made her ever see as honor what the world calls by that name. Now she sees in this name nothing more than an immense lie of which the world remains a victim. She discovers, in the new light from above, that in genuine honor there is nothing spurious, that to be faithful to this honor is to give our respect to what deserves to be respected really, and to consider as nothing, or as less than nothing, whatsoever perishes and is not agreeable to God . . . . She laughs when she sees grave persons, persons of orison, caring for points of honor for which she now feels profoundest contempt. It is suitable to the dignity of their rank to act thus, they pretend, and it makes them more useful to others. But she knows that in despising the dignity of their rank for the pure love of God they would do more good in a single day than they would effect in ten years by preserving it . . . . She laughs at herself that there should ever have been a time in her life when she made any case of money, when she ever desired it . . . . Oh! if human beings might only agree together to regard it as so much useless mud, what harmony would then reign in the world! With what friendship we would all treat each other if our interest in honor and in money could but disappear from earth! For my own part, I feel as if it would be a remedy for all our ills.[22]

Mystical conditions may, therefore, render the soul more energetic in the lines which their inspiration favors. But this could be reckoned an advantage only in case the inspiration were a true one. If the inspiration were erroneous, the energy would be all the more mistaken and misbegotten. So we stand once more before that problem of truth which confronted us at the end of the lectures on saintliness. You will remember that we turned to mysticism precisely to get some light on truth. Do mystical states establish the truth of those theological affections in which the saintly life has its root?

In spite of their repudiation of articulate self-description, mystical states in general assert a pretty distinct theoretic drift. It is possible to give the outcome of the majority of them in terms that point in definite philosophical directions. One of these directions is optimism, and the other is monism. We pass into mystical states from out of ordinary consciousness as from a less into a more, as from a smallness into a vastness, and at the same time as from an unrest to a rest. We feel them as reconciling, unifying states. They appeal to the yes-function more than to the no-function in us. In them the unlimited absorbs the limits and peacefully closes the account. Their very denial of every adjective you may propose as applicable to the ultimate truth—He, the

---

[22]*Vie, op. cit.,* pp.200, 229, 231–33, 243.

Self, the Atman, is to be described by "No! no!" only, say the Upanishads[23]—though it seems on the surface to be a no-function, is a denial made on behalf of a deeper yes. Whoso calls the Absolute anything in particular, or says that it is *this*, seems implicitly to shut it off from being *that*—it is as if he lessened it. So we deny the "this," negating the negation which it seems to us to imply, in the interests of the higher affirmative attitude by which we are possessed. The fountainhead of Christian mysticism is Dionysius the Areopagite. He describes the absolute truth by negatives exclusively.

> The cause of all things is neither soul nor intellect; nor has it imagination, opinion, or reason, or intelligence; nor is it reason or intelligence; nor is it spoken or thought. It is neither number, nor order, nor magnitude, nor littleness, nor equality, nor inequality, nor similarity, nor dissimilarity. It neither stands, nor moves, nor rests.... It is neither essence, nor eternity, nor time. Even intellectual contact does not belong to it. It is neither science nor truth. It is not even royalty or wisdom; not one; not unity; not divinity or goodness; nor even spirit as we know it....[24]

But these qualifications are denied by Dionysius, not because the truth falls short of them, but because it so infinitely excels them. It is above them. It is *super*-lucent, *super*-splendent, *super*-essential, *super*-sublime, *super* everything that can be named. Like Hegel in his logic, mystics journey towards the positive pole of truth only by the *Methode der Absoluten Negativität*.

Thus come the paradoxical expressions that so abound in mystical writings. As when Eckhart tells of the still desert of the Godhead, "where never was seen difference, neither Father, Son, nor Holy Ghost, where there is no one at home, yet where the spark of the soul is more at peace than in itself."[25] As when Boehme writes of the Primal Love, that "it may fitly be compared to Nothing, for it is deeper than any Thing, and is as nothing with respect to all things, forasmuch as it is not comprehensible by any of them. And because it is nothing respectively, it is therefore free from all things, and is that only good, which a man cannot express or utter what it is, there being nothing to which it may be compared, to express it by."[26] Or as when Angelus Silesius sings:

> *Gott ist ein lauter Nichts, ihn rührt kein Nun noch Hier;*
> *je mehr du nach ihm greifst, je mehr entwind er dir.*[27]

---

[23]Müller's translation, Part II, p. 180.

[24]T. Davidson's translation, in *Journal of Speculative Philosophy* (1893), Vol. XXII, 339.

[25]J. Royce, *Studies in Good and Evil*, p. 282.

[26]Jacob Behmen, *Dialogues on the Supersensual Life*, translated by Bernard Holland, London, 1901, p. 48.

[27]*Cherubinischer Wandersmann*, Strophe 25. [God is a mere Nothing, no now or here touches Him; the more you grasp at Him the more He evades you.]

To this dialectical use, by the intellect, of negation as a mode of passage towards a higher kind of affirmation, there is correlated the subtlest of moral counterparts in the sphere of the personal will. Since denial of the finite self and its wants, since asceticism of some sort, is found in religious experience to be the only doorway to the larger and more blessed life, this moral mystery intertwines and combines with the intellectual mystery in all mystical writings.

> Love [is Nothing, for] when thou art gone forth wholly from the Creature and from that which is visible, and art become Nothing to all that is Nature and Creature, then thou are in that eternal One, which is God himself, and then thou shalt feel within thee the highest virtue of Love . . . . The treasure of treasures for the soul is where she goeth out of the Somewhat into that Nothing out of which all things may be made. The soul here saith, *I have nothing*, for I am utterly stripped and naked; *I can do nothing*, for I have no manner of power, but am as water poured out; *I am nothing*, for all that I am is no more than an image of Being, and only God is to me I AM; and so, sitting down in my own Nothingness, I give glory to the eternal Being, and *will nothing* of myself, that so God may will all in me, being unto me my God and all things.[28]

In Paul's language, I live, yet not I, but Christ liveth in me. Only when I become as nothing can God enter in and no difference between his life and mine remain outstanding.

This overcoming of all the usual barriers between the individual and the Absolute is the great mystic achievement. In mystic states we both become one with the Absolute and we become aware of our oneness. This is the everlasting and triumphant mystical tradition, hardly altered by differences of clime or creed. In Hinduism, in Neoplatonism, in Sufism, in Christian mysticism, in Whitmanism, we find the same recurring note, so that there is about mystical utterances an eternal unanimity which ought to make a critic stop and think, and which brings it about that the mystical classics have, as has been said, neither birthday nor native land. Perpetually telling of the unity of man with God, their speech antedates languages, and they do not grow old.

"That art Thou!" say the Upanishads, and the Vedantists add: "Not a part, not a mode of That, but identically That, that absolute Spirit of the World." "As pure water poured into pure water remains the same, thus, O Gautama, is the Self of a thinker who knows. Water in water, fire in fire, ether in ether, no one can distinguish them; likewise a man whose mind has entered into the Self."[29] "Every man," says the Sufi Gulshan-Raz, "whose heart is no longer shaken by any doubt, knows with certainty that there is no being save

---

[28]*Op. cit.*, pp. 42, 74.
[29]*Upanishads, op. cit.*, pp. 17, 334.

only One .... In his divine majesty the *me*, the *we*, the *thou*, are not found, for in the One there can be no distinction. Every being who is annulled and entirely separated from himself, hears resound outside of him this voice and this echo: *I am God:* he has an eternal way of existing, and is no longer subject to death."[30] In the vision of God, says Plotinus, "what sees is not our reason, but something prior and superior to our reason .... He who thus sees does not properly see, does not distinguish or imagine two things. He changes, he ceases to be himself, preserves nothing of himself. Absorbed in God, he makes but one with him, like a centre of a circle coinciding with another centre."[31] "Here," writes Suso, "the spirit dies, and yet is all alive in the marvels of the Godhead ... and is lost in the stillness of the glorious dazzling obscurity and of the naked simple unity. It is in this modeless *where* that the highest bliss is to be found."[32] "*Ich bin so gross als Gott,*" sings Angelus Silesius again, "*Er ist als ich so klein; Er kann nicht über mich, ich unter ihm nicht sein.*"[33]

In mystical literature such self-contradictory phrases as "dazzling obscurity," "whispering silence," "teeming desert," are continually met with. They prove that not conceptual speech, but music rather, is the element through which we are best spoken to by mystical truth. Many mystical scriptures are indeed little more than musical compositions.

> He who would hear the voice of Nada, "the Soundless Sound," and comprehend it, he has to learn the nature of Dharana .... When to himself his form appears unreal, as do on waking all the forms he sees in dreams; when he has ceased to hear the many, he may discern the ONE—the inner sound which kills the outer .... For then the soul will hear, and will remember. And then to the inner ear will speak THE VOICE OF THE SILENCE .... And now thy *Self* is lost in SELF, *thyself* unto THYSELF, merged in that SELF from which thou first didst radiate .... Behold! thou has become the Light, thou has become the Sound, thou are thy Master and thy God. Thou are THYSELF the object of thy search: the VOICE unbroken, that resounds throughout eternities, exempt from change, from sin exempt, the seven sounds in one, the VOICE OF THE SILENCE. *Om tat Sat.*[34]

These words, if they do not awaken laughter as you receive them, probably stir chords within you which music and language touch in common. Music gives us ontological messages which non-musical criticism is unable to contradict, though it may laugh at our foolishness in minding them. There is a verge of the mind which these things haunt; and whispers therefrom

---

[30]Schmölders, *op. cit.*, p. 210.

[31]*Enneads*, Bouillier's translation, Paris, 1861, Vol. III, 561. Compare p⟨ 473–77, and Vol. I, 27.

[32]*Autobiography*, pp. 309–10.

[33]*Op. cit.*, Strophe 10 [I am as great as God. He is as small as me; He cannot exceed me, nor am I beneath Him].

[34]H. P. Blavatsky, *The Voice of the Silence.*

mingle with the operations of our understanding, even as the waters of the infinite ocean send their waves to break among the pebbles that lie upon our shores.

> Here begins the sea that ends not till the world's end. Where we stand,
> Could we know the next high sea-mark set beyond these waves that gleam,
> We should know what never man hath known, nor eye of man hath
>   scanned . . . .
> Ah, but here man's heart leaps, yearning towards the gloom with venturous
>   glee,
> From the shore that hath no shore beyond it, set in all the sea.[35]

That doctrine, for example, that eternity is timeless, that our "immortality," if we live in the eternal, is not so much future as already now and here, which we find so often expressed today in certain philosophic circles, finds its support in a "hear, hear!" or an "amen," which floats up from that mysteriously deeper level. We recognize the passwords to the mystical region as we hear them, but we cannot use them ourselves; it alone has the keeping of "the password primeval."

I have now sketched with extreme brevity and insufficiency, but as fairly as I am able in the time allowed, the general traits of the mystic range of consciousness. *It is on the whole pantheistic and optimistic, or at least the opposite of pessimistic. It is anti-naturalistic, and harmonizes best with twice-bornness and so-called other-worldly states of mind.*

My next task is to inquire whether we can invoke it as authoritative. Does it furnish any *warrant for the truth* of the twice-bornness and supernaturality and pantheism which it favors? I must give my answer to this question as concisely as I can.

In brief my answer is this—and I will divide it into three parts:

1. Mystical states, when well developed, usually are, and have the right to be, absolutely authoritative over the individuals to whom they come.

2. No authority emanates from them which should make it a duty for those who stand outside of them to accept their revelations uncritically.

3. They break down the authority of the non-mystical or rationalistic consciousness, based upon the understanding and the senses alone. They show it to be only one kind of consciousness. They open out the possibility of other orders of truth, in which, so far as anything in us vitally responds to them, we may freely continue to have faith.

I will take up these points one by one.

---

[35]Swinburne, "On the Verge," in *A Midsummer Vacation.*

1. As a matter of psychological fact, mystical states of a well-pronounced and emphatic sort *are* usually authoritative over those who have them. They have been "there," and know. It is vain for rationalism to grumble about this. If the mystical truth that comes to a man proves to be a force that he can live by, what mandate have we of the majority to order him to live in another way? We can throw him into a prison or a madhouse, but we cannot change his mind—we commonly attach it only the more stubbornly to its beliefs. It mocks our utmost efforts, as a matter of fact, and in point of logic it absolutely escapes our jurisdiction. Our own more "rational" beliefs are based on evidence exactly similar in nature to that which mystics quote for theirs. Our senses, namely, have assured us of certain states of fact, but mystical experiences are as direct perceptions of fact for those who have them as any sensations ever were for us. The records show that even though the five senses be in abeyance in them, they are absolutely sensational in their epistemological quality, if I may be pardoned the barbarous expression—that is, they are face-to-face presentations of what seems immediately to exist.

The mystic is, in short, *invulnerable,* and must be left, whether we relish it or not, in undisturbed enjoyment of his creed. Faith, says Tolstoy, is that by which men live. And faith state and mystic state are practically convertible terms.

2. But I now proceed to add that mystics have no right to claim that we ought to accept the deliverance of their peculiar experiences, if we are ourselves outsiders and feel no private call thereto. The utmost they can ever ask of us in this life is to admit that they establish a presumption. They form a consensus and have an unequivocal outcome; and it would be odd, mystics might say, if such a unanimous type of experience should prove to be altogether wrong. At bottom, however, this would only be an appeal to numbers, like the appeal of rationalism the other way; and the appeal to numbers has no logical force. If we acknowledge it, it is for "suggestive," not for logical reasons: we follow the majority because to do so suits our life.

But even this presumption from the unanimity of mystics is far from being strong. In characterizing mystic states as pantheistic, optimistic, etc., I am afraid I over-simplified the truth. I did so for expository reasons, and to keep the closer to the classic mystical tradition. The classic religious mysticism, it now must be confessed, is only a "privileged case." It is an *extract,* kept true to type by the selection of the fittest specimens and their preservation in "schools." It is carved out from a much larger mass; and if we take the larger mass as seriously as religious mysticism has historically taken itself, we find that the supposed unanimity largely disappears. To begin with, even religious mysticism itself, the kind that accumulates traditions and makes schools, is much less unanimous than I have allowed. It has been both ascetic and antinomianly self-indulgent within the Christian church. It is dualistic in Sankhya, and monistic in Vedanta philosophy. I called it pantheistic; but the great Spanish mystics are anything but pantheists. They are with few exceptions non-metaphysical minds, for whom "the category of personality" is absolute. The "union" of man with God is for them much more like an occasional miracle than like an original identity. How different again, apart from the happiness common to all, is the mysticism of Walt Whitman, Edward Carpenter, Richard Jefferies, and other naturalistic pantheists, from the more distinctively Christian sort. The fact is that the mystical feeling of enlargement, union, and emancipation has no specific intellectual content whatever of its own. It is capable of forming matrimonial alliances with material furnished by the most diverse philosophies and theologies, provided only they can find a place in their framework for its peculiar emotional mood. We have no right, therefore, to invoke its prestige as distinctively in favor of any special belief, such as that in absolute idealism, or in the absolute monistic identity, or in the absolute goodness, of the world. It is only relatively in favor of all these things—it passes out of common human consciousness in the direction in which they lie.

So much for religious mysticism proper. But more remains to be told, for religious mysticism is only one half of mysticism. The other half has no accumulated traditions except those which the textbooks on insanity supply. Open any one of these, and you will find abundant cases in which "mystical ideas" are cited as characteristic symptoms of enfeebled or deluded states of mind. In delusional insanity, paranoia, as they sometimes call it, we may have a *diabolical* mysticism, a sort of religious mysticism turned upside down. The same sense of ineffable importance in the smallest events, the same texts and words coming with new meanings, the same voices and visions and leadings and missions, the same controlling by extraneous powers; only this time the emotion is pessimistic: instead of consolations we have desolations; the meanings are dreadful; and the powers are enemies to life. It is evident that from the point of view of their psychological mechanism, the classic mysticism and these lower mysticisms spring from the same mental level, from that great subliminal or transmarginal region of which science is beginning to admit the existence, but of which so little is really known. That region contains every kind of matter: "seraph and snake" abide there side by side. To come from thence is no infallible credential. What comes must be sifted and tested, and run the gauntlet of confrontation with the total context of experience, just like what comes from the outer world of sense. Its value must be ascertained by empirical methods, so long as we are not mystics ourselves.

Once more, then, I repeat that non-mystics are under no obligation to acknowledge in mystical states a superior authority conferred on them by their intrinsic nature.

3. Yet, I repeat once more, the existence of mystical states absolutely overthrows the pretension of non-mystical states to be the sole and ultimate dictators of what we may believe. As a rule, mystical states merely add a

supersensuous meaning to the ordinary outward data of consciousness. They are excitements like the emotions of love or ambition, gifts to our spirit by means of which facts already objectively before us fall into a new expressiveness and make a new connection with our active life. They do not contradict these facts as such, or deny anything that our senses have immediately seized. It is the rationalistic critic rather who plays the part of denier in the controversy, and his denials have no strength, for there never can be a state of facts to which new meaning may not truthfully be added, provided the mind ascend to a more enveloping point of view. It must always remain an open question whether mystical states may not possibly be such superior points of view, windows through which the mind looks out upon a more extensive and inclusive world. The difference of the views seen from the different mystical windows need not prevent us from entertaining this supposition. The wider world would in that case prove to have a mixed constitution like that of this world, that is all. It would have its celestial and its infernal regions, its tempting and its saving moments, its valid experiences and its counterfeit ones, just as our world has them; but it would be a wider world all the same. We should have to use its experiences by selecting and subordinating and substituting just as is our custom in this ordinary naturalistic world; we should be liable to error just as we are now; yet the counting in of that wider world of meanings, and the serious dealing with it, might, in spite of all the perplexity, be indispensable stages in our approach to the final fullness of the truth.

In this shape, I think, we have to leave the subject. Mystical states indeed wield no authority due simply to their being mystical states. But the higher ones among them point in directions to which the religious sentiments even of non-mystical men incline. They tell of the supremacy of the ideal, of vastness, of union, of safety, and of rest. They offer us *hypotheses*, hypotheses which we may voluntarily ignore, but which as thinkers we cannot possibly upset. The supernaturalism and optimism to which they would persuade us may, interpreted in one way or another, be after all the truest of insights into the meaning of this life . . . .

# 15

## *The Will to Believe*

In the recently published Life by Leslie Stephen of his brother, Fitz-James, there is an account of a school to which the latter went when he was a boy. The teacher, a certain Mr. Guest, used to converse with his pupils in this wise: "Gurney, what is the difference between justification and sanctification? Stephen, prove the omnipotence of God!" etc. In the midst of our Harvard freethinking and indifference we are prone to imagine that here at your good old orthodox College conversation continues to be somewhat upon this order; and to show you that we at Harvard have not lost all interest in these vital subjects, I have brought with me tonight something like a sermon on justification by faith to read to you—I mean an essay in justification of faith, a defense of our right to adopt a believing attitude in religious matters, in spite of the fact that our merely logical intellect may not have been coerced. "The Will to Believe," accordingly, is the title of my paper.

I have long defended to my own students the lawfulness of voluntarily adopted faith; but as soon as they have got well imbued with the logical spirit, they have as a rule refused to admit my contention to be lawful philosophically, even though in point of fact they were personally all the time chock-full of some faith or other themselves. I am all the while, however, so profoundly convinced that my own position is correct, that your invitation has seemed to me a good occasion to make my statements more clear. Perhaps your minds will be more open than those with which I have hitherto had to deal. I will be as little technical as I can, though I must begin by setting up some technical distinctions that will help us in the end.

Let us give the name of *hypothesis* to anything that may be proposed to our belief; and just as the electricians speak of live and dead wires, let us speak of any hypothesis as either *live* or *dead*. A live hypothesis is one which appeals as a real possibility to him to whom it is proposed. If I ask you to believe in the Mahdi, the notion makes no electric connection with your nature—it refuses to scintillate with any credibility at all. As an hypothesis it is completely dead. To an Arab, however (even if he be not one of the Mahdi's followers), the hypothesis is among the mind's possibilities: it is alive. This

---

*The Will to Believe and Other Essays* (1897), Chap. 1.

shows that deadness and liveness in an hypothesis are not intrinsic properties, but relations to the individual thinker. They are measured by his willingness to act. The maximum of liveness in an hypothesis means willingness
to act irrevocably. Practically, that means belief; but there is some believing
tendency wherever there is willingness to act at all.

Next, let us call the decision between two hypotheses an *option*. Options
may be of several kinds. They may be (1) *living* or *dead*, (2) *forced* or *avoidable*,
(3) *momentous* or *trivial*; and for our purposes we may call an option a *genuine*
option when it is of the forced, living, and momentous kind.

1. A living option is one in which both hypotheses are live ones. If I say
to you: "Be a theosophist or be a Mohammedan," it is probably a dead option,
because for you neither hypothesis is likely to be alive. But if I say: "Be an
agnostic or be a Christian," it is otherwise: trained as you are, each hypothesis
makes some appeal, however small, to your belief.

2. Next, if I say to you: "Choose between going out with your umbrella
or without it," I do not offer you a genuine option, for it is not forced. You
can easily avoid it by not going out at all. Similarly, if I say, "Either love me
or hate me," "Either call my theory true or call it false," your option is
avoidable. You may remain indifferent to me, neither loving nor hating, and
you may decline to offer any judgment as to my theory. But if I say, "Either
accept this truth or go without it," I put on you a forced option, for there is
no standing place outside of the alternative. Every dilemma based on a
complete logical disjunction, with no possibility of not choosing, is an option
of this forced kind.

3. Finally, if I were Dr. Nansen and proposed to you to join my North Pole
expedition, your option would be momentous; for this would probably be your
only similar opportunity, and your choice now would either exclude you from
the North Pole sort of immortality altogether or put at least the chance of it into
your hands. He who refuses to embrace a unique opportunity loses the prize as
surely as if he tried and failed. *Per contra*, the option is trivial when the opportunity is not unique, when the stake is insignificant, or when the decision is
reversible if it later prove unwise. Such trivial options abound in the scientific
life. A chemist finds an hypothesis live enough to spend a year in its verification:
he believes in it to that extent. But if his experiments prove inconclusive either
way, he is quit for his loss of time, no vital harm being done.

It will facilitate our discussion if we keep all these distinctions well in
mind.

The next matter to consider is the actual psychology of human opinion.
When we look at certain facts, it seems as if our passional and volitional nature
lay at the root of all our convictions. When we look at others, it seems as if
they could do nothing when the intellect had once said its say. Let us take the
latter facts up first.

Does it not seem preposterous on the very face of it to talk of our opinions being modifiable at will? Can our will either help or hinder our intellect in its perceptions of truth? Can we, by just willing it, believe that Abraham Lincoln's existence is a myth, and that the portraits of him in *McClure's Magazine* are all of someone else? Can we, by any effort of our will, or by any strength of wish that it were true, believe ourselves well and about when we are roaring with rheumatism in bed, or feel certain that the sum of the two one-dollar bills in our pocket must be a hundred dollars? We can *say* any of these things, but we are absolutely impotent to believe them; and of just such things is the whole fabric of the truths that we do believe in made up—matters of fact, immediate or remote, as Hume said, and relations between ideas, which are either there or not there for us if we see them so, and which if not there cannot be put there by any action of our own.

In Pascal's *Thoughts* there is a celebrated passage known in literature as Pascal's wager.[1] In it he tries to force us into Christianity by reasoning as if our concern with truth resembled our concern with the stakes in a game of chance. Translated freely his words are these: You must either believe or not believe that God is—which will you do? Your human reason cannot say. A game is going on between you and the nature of things which at the day of judgment will bring out either heads or tails. Weigh what your gains and your losses would be if you should stake all you have on heads, or God's existence: if you win in such case, you gain eternal beatitude; if you lose, you lose nothing at all. If there were an infinity of chances, and only one for God in this wager, still you ought to stake your all on God; for though you surely risk a finite loss by this procedure, any finite loss is reasonable, even a certain one is reasonable, if there is but the possibility of infinite gain. Go, then, and take holy water, and have masses said; belief will come and stupefy your scruples—*Cela vous fera croire et vous abêtira.* Why should you not? At bottom, what have you to lose?

You probably feel that when religious faith expresses itself thus, in the language of the gaming-table, it is put to its last trumps. Surely Pascal's own personal belief in masses and holy water had far other springs; and this celebrated page of his is but an argument for others, a last desperate snatch at a weapon against the hardness of the unbelieving heart. We feel that a faith in masses and holy water adopted wilfully after such a mechanical calculation would lack the inner soul of faith's reality; and if we were ourselves in the place of the Deity, we should probably take particular pleasure in cutting off believers of this pattern from their infinite reward. It is evident that unless there be some pre-existing tendency to believe in masses and holy water, the option offered to the will by Pascal is not a living option. Certainly no Turk ever took to masses and holy water on its account; and even to us Protestants

---

[1]Blaise Pascal, *Pensées,* J. Chevalier, ed. (Paris, 1954) No. 451. In the English translation by F. W. Trotter (New York: E. P. Dutton & Co., 1932), No. 233.

these means of salvation seem such foregone impossibilities that Pascal's logic, invoked for them specifically, leaves us unmoved. As well might the Mahdi write to us, saying, "I am the Expected One whom God has created in his effulgence. You shall be infinitely happy if you confess me; otherwise you shall be cut off from the light of the sun. Weigh, then, your infinite gain if I am genuine against your finite sacrifice if I am not!" His logic would be that of Pascal; but he would vainly use it on us, for the hypothesis he offers us is dead. No tendency to act on it exists in us to any degree.

The talk of believing by our volition seems, then, from one point of view, simply silly. From another point of view it is worse than silly, it is vile. When one turns to the magnificent edifice of the physical sciences, and sees how it was reared; what thousands of disinterested moral lives of men lie buried in its mere foundations; what patience and postponement, what choking down of preference, what submission to the icy laws of outer fact are wrought into its very stones and mortar, how absolutely impersonal it stands in its vast augustness—then how besotted and contemptible seems every little sentimentalist who comes blowing his voluntary smoke-wreaths, and pretending to decide things from out of his private dream! Can we wonder if those bred in the rugged and manly school of science should feel like spewing such subjectivism out of their mouths? The whole system of loyalties which grow up in the schools of science go dead against its toleration; so that it is only natural that those who have caught the scientific fever should pass over to the opposite extreme, and write sometimes as if the incorruptibly truthful intellect ought positively to prefer bitterness and unacceptableness to the heart in its cup.

> It fortifies my soul to know
> That, though I perish, Truth is so—

sings Clough, while Huxley exclaims:

> My only consolation lies in the reflection that, however bad our posterity may become, so far as they hold by the plain rule of not pretending to believe what they have no reason to believe, because it may be to their advantage so to pretend [the word "pretend" is surely here redundant], they will not have reached the lowest depth of immorality.

And that delicious *enfant terrible*, Clifford, writes:

> Belief is desecrated when given to unproved and unquestioned statements for the solace and private pleasure of the believer . . . . Whoso would deserve well of his fellows in this matter will guard the purity of his belief with a very fanaticism of jealous care, lest at any time it should rest on an unworthy object, and catch a stain which can never be wiped away . . . . If [a] belief has been accepted on insufficient evidence [even though the belief be true, as Clifford on

the same page explains] the pleasure is a stolen one . . . . It is sinful because it is stolen in defiance of our duty to mankind. That duty is to guard ourselves from such beliefs as from a pestilence which may shortly master our own body and then spread to the rest of the town . . . . It is wrong always, everywhere, and for everyone, to believe anything upon insufficient evidence.

All this strikes one as healthy, even when expressed, as by Clifford, with somewhat too much of robustious pathos in the voice. Free-will and simple wishing do seem, in the matter of our credences, to be only fifth wheels to the coach. Yet if anyone should thereupon assume that intellectual insight is what remains after wish and will and sentimental preference have taken wing, or that pure reason is what then settles our opinions, he would fly quite as directly in the teeth of the facts.

It is only our already dead hypotheses that our willing nature is unable to bring to life again. But what has made them dead for us is for the most part a previous action of our willing nature of an antagonistic kind. When I say "willing nature," I do not mean only such deliberate volitions as may have set up habits of belief that we cannot now escape from—I mean all such factors of belief as fear and hope, prejudice and passion, imitation and partisanship, the circumpressure of our caste and set. As a matter of fact we find ourselves believing, we hardly know how or why. Mr. Balfour gives the name of "authority" to all those influences, born of the intellectual climate, that make hypotheses possible or impossible for us, alive or dead. Here in this room, we all of us believe in molecules and the conservation of energy, in democracy and necessary progress, in Protestant Christianity and the duty of fighting for "the doctrine of the immortal Monroe," all for no reasons worthy of the name. We see into these matters with no more inner clearness, and probably with much less, than any disbeliever in them might possess. His unconventionality would probably have some grounds to show for its conclusions; but for us, not insight, but the *prestige* of the opinions, is what makes the spark shoot from them and light up our sleeping magazines of faith. Our reason is quite satisfied, in nine hundred and ninety-nine cases out of every thousand of us, if it can find a few arguments that will do to recite in case our credulity is criticized by someone else. Our faith is faith in someone else's faith, and in the greatest matters this is most the case. Our belief in truth itself, for instance, that there is a truth, and that our minds and it are made for each other—what is it but a passionate affirmation of desire, in which our social system backs us up? We want to have a truth; we want to believe that our experiments and studies and discussions must put us in a continually better and better position towards it; and on this line we agree to fight out our thinking lives. But if a pyrrhonistic skeptic asks us *how we know* all this, can our logic find a reply? No! certainly it cannot. It is just one volition against another—we willing to go in for life upon a trust or assumption which he, for his part, does not care to make.

As a rule we disbelieve all facts and theories for which we have no use. Clifford's cosmic emotions find no use for Christian feelings. Huxley belabors the bishops because there is no use for sacerdotalism in his scheme of life. Newman, on the contrary, goes over to Romanism, and finds all sorts of reasons good for staying there, because a priestly system is for him an organic need and delight. Why do so few "scientists" even look at the evidence for telepathy, so called? Because they think, as a leading biologist, now dead, once said to me, that even if such a thing were true, scientists ought to band together to keep it suppressed and concealed. It would undo the uniformity of Nature and all sorts of other things without which scientists cannot carry on their pursuits. But if this very man had been shown something which as a scientist he might *do* with telepathy, he might not only have examined the evidence, but even have found it good enough. This very law which the logicians would impose upon us—if I may give the name of logicians to those who would rule out our willing nature here—is based on nothing but their own natural wish to exclude all elements for which they, in their professional quality of logicians, can find no use.

Evidently, then, our non-intellectual nature does influence our convictions. There are passional tendencies and volitions which run before and others which come after belief, and it is only the latter that are too late for the fair; and they are not too late when the previous passional work has been already in their own direction. Pascal's argument, instead of being powerless, then seems a regular clincher, and is the last stroke needed to make our faith in masses and holy water complete. The state of things is evidently far from simple; and pure insight and logic, whatever they might do ideally, are not the only things that really do produce our creeds.

Our next duty, having recognized this mixed-up state of affairs, is to ask whether it be simply reprehensible and pathological, or whether, on the contrary, we must treat it as a normal element in making up our minds. The thesis I defend is, briefly stated, this: *Our passional nature not only lawfully may, but must, decide an option between propositions, whenever it is a genuine option that cannot by its nature be decided on intellectual grounds; for to say, under such circumstances, "Do not decide, but leave the question open," is itself a passional decision—just like deciding yes or no—and is attended with the same risk of losing the truth.* The thesis thus abstractly expressed will, I trust, soon become quite clear. But I must first indulge in a bit more of preliminary work.

It will be observed that for the purposes of this discussion we are on "dogmatic" ground—ground, I mean, which leaves systematic philosophical skepticism altogether out of account. The postulate that there is truth, and that it is the destiny of our minds to attain it, we are deliberately resolving to make, though the skeptic will not make it. We part company with him, therefore, absolutely, at this point. But the faith that truth exists, and that our minds can find it, may be held in two ways. We may talk of the *empiricist* way and of the *absolutist* way of believing in truth. The absolutists in this matter say that we not only can attain to knowing truth, but we can *know when* we have attained to knowing it; while the empiricists think that although we may attain it, we cannot infallibly know when. To *know* is one thing, and to know for certain *that* we know is another. One may hold to the first being possible without the second; hence the empiricists and the absolutists, although neither of them is a skeptic in the usual philosophic sense of the term, show very different degrees of dogmatism in their lives.

If we look at the history of opinions, we see that the empiricist tendency has largely prevailed in science, while in philosophy the absolutist tendency has had everything its own way. The characteristic sort of happiness, indeed, which philosophies yield has mainly consisted in the conviction felt by each successive school or system that by it bottom-certitude had been attained. "Other philosophies are collections of opinions, mostly false; *my* philosophy gives standing-ground forever"—who does not recognize in this the keynote of every system worthy of the name? A system, to be a system at all, must come as a *closed* system, reversible in this or that detail, perchance, but in its essential features never!

Scholastic orthodoxy, to which one must always go when one wishes to find perfectly clear statement, has beautifully elaborated this absolutist conviction in a doctrine which it calls that of "objective evidence." If, for example, I am unable to doubt that I now exist before you, that two is less than three, or that if all men are mortal then I am mortal too, it is because these things illumine my intellect irresistibly. The final ground of this objective evidence possessed by certain propositions is the *adaequatio intellectûs nostri cum re* [conformity of our minds to fact]. The certitude it brings involves an *aptitudinem ad extorquendum certum assensum* [a power to compel sure assent] on the part of the truth envisaged, and on the side of the subject a *quietem in cognitione* [assurance in knowing], when once the object is mentally received, that leaves no possibility of doubt behind; and in the whole transaction nothing operates but the *entitas ipsa* [reality] of the object and the *entitas ipsa* [reality] of the mind. We slouchy modern thinkers dislike to talk in Latin—indeed, we dislike to talk in set terms at all; but at bottom our own state of mind is very much like this whenever we uncritically abandon ourselves: You believe in objective evidence, and I do. Of some things we feel that we are certain: we know, and we know that we do know. There is something that gives a click inside of us, a bell that strikes twelve, when the hands of our mental clock have swept the dial and meet over the meridian hour. The greatest empiricists among us are only empiricists on reflection: when left to their instincts, they dogmatize like infallible popes. When the Cliffords tell us how sinful it is to be Christian on such "insufficient evidence," insufficiency is really the last thing they have in mind. For them the evidence is absolutely sufficient, only it makes the other way. They believe so completely in an anti-Christian order of the universe that there is no living option: Christianity is a dead hypothesis from the start.

But now, since we are all such absolutists by instinct, what in our quality of students of philosophy ought we to do about the fact? Shall we espouse and indorse it? Or shall we treat it as a weakness of our nature from which we must free ourselves, if we can?

I sincerely believe that the latter course is the only one we can follow as reflective men. Objective evidence and certitude are doubtless very fine ideals to play with, but where on this moonlit and dream-visited planet are they found? I am, therefore, myself a complete empiricist so far as my theory of human knowledge goes. I live, to be sure, by the practical faith that we must go on experiencing and thinking over our experience, for only thus can our opinions grow more true; but to hold any one of them—I absolutely do not care which—as if it never could be reinterpretable or corrigible, I believe to be a tremendously mistaken attitude, and I think that the whole history of philosophy will bear me out. There is but one indefectibly certain truth, and that is the truth that pyrrhonistic skepticism itself leaves standing—the truth that the present phenomenon of consciousness exists. That, however, is the bare starting-point of knowledge, the mere admission of a stuff to be philosophized about. The various philosophies are but so many attempts at expressing what this stuff really is. And if we repair to our libraries what disagreement do we discover! Where is a certainly true answer found? Apart from abstract propositions of comparison (such as two and two are the same as four), propositions which tell us nothing by themselves about concrete reality, we find no proposition ever regarded by anyone as evidently certain that has not either been called a falsehood, or at least had its truth sincerely questioned, by someone else. The transcending of the axioms of geometry, not in play but in earnest, by certain of our contemporaries (as Zöllner and Charles H. Hinton), and the rejection of the whole Aristotelian logic by the Hegelians, are striking instances in point.

No concrete test of what is really true has ever been agreed upon. Some make the criterion external to the moment of perception, putting it either in revelation, the *consensus gentium*, the instincts of the heart, or the systematized experience of the race. Others make the perceptive moment its own test—Descartes, for instance, with his clear and distinct ideas guaranteed by the veracity of God; Reid with his "common-sense"; and Kant with his forms of synthetic judgment a priori. The inconceivability of the opposite; the capacity to be verified by sense; the possession of complete organic unity or self-relation, realized when a thing is its own other—are standards which, in turn, have been used. The much lauded objective evidence is never triumphantly there; it is a mere aspiration or *Grenzbegriff*, marking the infinitely remote ideal of our thinking life. To claim that certain truths now possess it, is simply to say that when you think them true and they *are* true, then their evidence is objective, otherwise it is not. But practically one's conviction that the evidence one goes by is of the real objective brand, is only one more subjective opinion added to the lot. For what a contradictory array of opinions have objective evidence and absolute certitude been claimed! The world is rational through and through—its existence is an ultimate brute fact; there is a personal God—a personal God is inconceivable; there is an extra-mental physical world immediatley known—the mind can only know its own ideas; a moral imperative exists—obligation is only the resultant of desires; a permanent spiritual principle is in everyone—there are only shifting states of mind; there is an endless chain of causes—there is an absolute first cause; an eternal necessity—a freedom; a purpose—no purpose; a primal One—a primal Many; a universal continuity—an essential discontinuity in things; an infinity—no infinity. There is this—there is that; there is indeed nothing which someone has not thought absolutely true, while his neighbor deemed it absolutely false; and not an absolutist among them seems ever to have considered that the trouble may all the time be essential, and that the intellect, even with truth directly in its grasp, may have no infallible signal for knowing whether it be truth or no. When, indeed, one remembers that the most striking practical application to life of the doctrine of objective certitude has been the conscientious labors of the Holy Office of the Inquisition, one feels less tempted than ever to lend the doctrine a respectful ear.

But please observe, now, that when as empiricists we give up the doctrine of objective certitude, we do not thereby give up the quest or hope of truth itself. We still pin our faith on its existence, and still believe that we gain an ever better position towards it by systematically continuing to roll up experiences and think. Our great difference from the scholastic lies in the way we face. The strength of his system lies in the principles, the origin, the *terminus a quo* of his thought; for us the strength is in the outcome, the upshot, the *terminus ad quem*. Not where it comes from but what it leads to is to decide. It matters not to an empiricist from what quarter an hypothesis may come to him: he may have acquired it by fair means or by foul; passion may have whispered or accident suggested it; but if the total drift of thinking continues to confirm it, that is what he means by its being true.

One more point, small but important, and our preliminaries are done. There are two ways of looking at our duty in the matter of opinion—ways entirely different, and yet ways about whose difference the theory of knowledge seems hitherto to have shown very little concern. *We must know the truth;* and *we must avoid error*—these are our first and great commandments as would-be knowers; but they are not two ways of stating an identical commandment, they are two separable laws. Although it may indeed happen that when we believe the truth A, we escape as an incidental consequence from believing the falsehood B, it hardly ever happens that by merely disbelieving B we necessarily believe A. We may in escaping B fall into believing other falsehoods, C or D, just as bad as B; or we may escape B by not believing anything at all, not even A.

Believe truth! Shun error!—these, we see, are two materially different laws; and by choosing between them we may end by coloring differently our whole intellectual life. We may regard the chase for truth as paramount, and the avoidance of error as secondary; or we may, on the other hand, treat the avoidance of error as more imperative, and let truth take its chance. Clifford, in the instructive passage which I have quoted, exhorts us to the latter course. Believe nothing, he tells us, keep your mind in suspense forever, rather than by closing it on insufficient evidence incur the awful risk of believing lies. You, on the other hand, may think that the risk of being in error is a very small matter when compared with the blessings of real knowledge, and be ready to be duped many times in your investigation rather than postpone indefinitely the chance of guessing true. I myself find it impossible to go with Clifford. We must remember that these feelings of our duty about either truth or error are in any case only expressions of our passional life. Biologically considered, our minds are as ready to grind out falsehood as veracity, and he who says, "Better go without belief forever than believe a lie!" merely shows his own preponderant private horror of becoming a dupe. He may be critical of many of his desires and fears, but this fear he slavishly obeys. He cannot imagine anyone questioning its binding force. For my own part, I have also a horror of being duped; but I can believe that worse things than being duped may happen to a man in this world: so Clifford's exhortation has to my ears a thoroughly fantastic sound. It is like a general informing his soldiers that it is better to keep out of battle forever than to risk a single wound. Not so are victories either over enemies or over nature gained. Our errors are surely not such awfully solemn things. In a world where we are so certain to incur them in spite of all our caution, a certain lightness of heart seems healthier than this excessive nervousness on their behalf. At any rate, it seems the fittest thing for the empiricist philosopher.

And now, after all this introduction, let us go straight at our question. I have said, and now repeat it, that not only as a matter of fact do we find our passional nature influencing us in our opinions, but that there are some options between opinions in which this influence must be regarded both as an inevitable and as a lawful determinant of our choice.

I fear here that some of you my hearers will begin to scent danger, and lend an inhospitable ear. Two first steps of passion you have indeed had to admit as necessary—we must think so as to avoid dupery, and we must think so as to gain truth; but the surest path to those ideal consummations, you will probably consider, is from now onwards to take no further passional step.

Well, of course, I agree as far as the facts will allow. Wherever the option between losing truth and gaining it is not momentous, we can throw the chance of *gaining truth* away, and at any rate save ourselves from any chance of *believing falsehood*, by not making up our minds at all till objective evidence has come. In scientific questions, this is almost always the case; and even in human affairs in general, the need of acting is seldom so urgent that a false belief to act on is better than no belief at all. Law courts, indeed, have to decide on the best evidence attainable for the moment, because a judge's duty is to make law as well as to ascertain it, and (as a learned judge once said to me) few cases are worth spending much time over: the great thing is to have them decided on *any* acceptable principle, and got out of the way. But in our dealings with objective nature we obviously are recorders, not makers, of the truth; and decisions for the mere sake of deciding promptly and getting on to the next business would be wholly out of place. Throughout the breadth of physical nature facts are what they are quite independently of us, and seldom is there any such hurry about them that the risks of being duped by believing a premature theory need be faced. The questions here are always trivial options, the hypotheses are hardly living (at any rate not living for us spectators), the choice between believing truth or falsehood is seldom forced. The attitude of skeptical balance is therefore the absolutely wise one if we would escape mistakes. What difference, indeed, does it make to most of us whether we have or have not a theory of the Röntgen rays, whether we believe or not in mind-stuff, or have a conviction about the causality of conscious states? It makes no difference. Such options are not forced on us. On every account it is better not to make them, but still keep weighing reasons *pro et contra* with an indifferent hand.

I speak, of course, here of the purely judging mind. For purposes of discovery such indifference is to be less highly recommended, and science would be far less advanced than she is if the passionate desires of individuals to get their own faiths confirmed had been kept out of the game. See, for example, the sagacity which Spencer and Weismann now display. On the other hand, if you want an absolute duffer in an investigation, you must, after all, take the man who has no interest whatever in its results: he is the warranted incapable, the positive fool. The most useful investigator, because the most sensitive observer, is always he whose eager interest in one side of the question is balanced by an equally keen nervousness lest he become deceived. Science has organized this nervousness into a regular *technique*, her so-called method of verification; and she has fallen so deeply in love with the method that one may even say she has ceased to care for truth by itself at all. It is only truth as technically verified that interests her. The truth of truths might come in merely affirmative form, and she would decline to touch it.

Such truth as that, she might repeat with Clifford, would be stolen in defiance of her duty to mankind. Human passions, however, are stronger than technical rules. *"Le coeur a ses raisons,"* as Pascal says, *"que la raison ne connaît pas"*; and however indifferent to all but the bare rules of the game the umpire, the abstract intellect, may be, the concrete players who furnish him the materials to judge of are usually, each one of them, in love with some pet "live hypothesis" of his own. Let us agree, however, that wherever there is no forced option, the dispassionately judicial intellect with no pet hypothesis, saving us, as it does, from dupery at any rate, ought to be our ideal.

The question next arises: Are there not somewhere forced options in our speculative questions, and can we (as men who may be interested at least as much in positively gaining truth as in merely escaping dupery) always wait with impunity till the coercive evidence shall have arrived? It seems a priori improbable that the truth should be so nicely adjusted to our needs and powers as that. In the great boarding-house of nature, the cakes and the butter and the syrup seldom come out so even and leave the plates so clean. Indeed, we should view them with scientific suspicion if they did.

*Moral questions* immediately present themselves as questions whose solution cannot wait for sensible proof. A moral question is a question not of what sensibly exists, but of what is good, or would be good if it did exist. Science can tell us what exists; but to compare the *worths*, both of what exists and of what does not exist, we must consult not science, but what Pascal calls our heart. Science herself consults her heart when she lays it down that the infinite ascertainment of fact and correction of false belief are the supreme goods for man. Challenge the statement, and science can only repeat it oracularly, or else prove it by showing that such ascertainment and correction bring man all sorts of other goods which man's heart in turn declares. The question of having moral beliefs at all or not having them is decided by our will. Are our moral preferences true or false, or are they only odd biological phenomena, making things good or bad for *us*, but in themselves indifferent? How can your pure intellect decide? If your heart does not *want* a world of moral reality, your head will assuredly never make you believe in one. Mephistophelian skepticism, indeed, will satisfy the head's play-instincts much better than any rigorous idealism can. Some men (even at the student age) are so naturally cool-hearted that the moralistic hypothesis never has for them any pungent life, and in their supercilious presence the hot young moralist always feels strangely ill at ease. The appearance of knowingness is on their side, of naïveté and gullibility on his. Yet, in the inarticulate heart of him, he clings to it that he is not a dupe, and that there is a realm in which (as Emerson says) all their wit and intellectual superiority is no better than the cunning of a fox. Moral skepticism can no more be refuted or proved by logic than intellectual skepticism can. When we stick to it that there *is* truth (be it of either kind), we do so with our whole nature, and resolve to stand or fall by the results. The skeptic with his whole nature adopts the doubting attitude; but which of us is the wiser, Omniscience only knows.

Turn now from these wide questions of good to a certain class of questions of fact, questions concerning personal relations, states of mind between one man and another. *Do you like me or not?*—for example. Whether you do or not depends, in countless instances, on whether I meet you half-way, am willing to assume that you must like me, and show you trust and expectation. The previous faith on my part in your liking's existence is in such cases what makes your liking come. But if I stand aloof, and refuse to budge an inch until I have objective evidence, until you shall have done something apt, as the absolutists say, *ad extorquendum assensum meum* [to compel my assent], ten to one your liking never comes. How many women's hearts are vanquished by the mere sanguine insistence of some man that they *must* love him! he will not consent to the hypothesis that they cannot. The desire for a certain kind of truth here brings about that special truth's existence; and so it is in innumerable cases of other sorts. Who gains promotions, boons, appointments, but the man in whose life they are seen to play the part of live hypotheses, who discounts them, sacrifices other things for their sake before they have come, and takes risks for them in advance? His faith acts on the powers above him as a claim, and creates its own verification.

A social organism of any sort whatever, large or small, is what it is because each member proceeds to his own duty with a trust that the other members will simultaneously do theirs. Wherever a desired result is achieved by the cooperation of many independent persons, its existence as a fact is a pure consequence of the precursive faith in one another of those immediately concerned. A government, an army, a commercial system, a ship, a college, an athletic team, all exist on this condition, without which not only is nothing achieved, but nothing is even attempted. A whole train of passengers (individually brave enough) will be looted by a few highwaymen, simply because the latter can count on one another, while each passenger fears that if he makes a movement of resistance, he will be shot before anyone else backs him up. If we believed that the whole car-full would rise at once with us, we should each severally rise, and train-robbing would never even be attempted. There are, then, cases where a fact cannot come at all unless a preliminary faith exists in its coming. *And where faith in a fact can help create the fact*, that would be an insane logic which should say that faith running ahead of scientific evidence is the "lowest kind of immorality" into which a thinking being can fall. Yet such is the logic by which our scientific absolutists pretend to regulate our lives!

In truths dependent on our personal action, then, faith based on desire is certainly a lawful and possibly an indispensable thing.

But now, it will be said, these are all childish human cases, and have nothing to do with great cosmical matters, like the question of religious faith. Let us then pass on to that. Religions differ so much in their accidents that in discussing the religious question we must make it very generic and broad. What then do we now mean by the religious hypothesis? Science says things are; morality says some things are better than other things; and religion says essentially two things.

First, she says that the best things are the more eternal things, the overlapping things, the things in the universe that throw the last stone, so to speak, and say the final word. "Perfection is eternal"—this phrase of Charles Secrétan seems a good way of putting this first affirmation of religion, an affirmation which obviously cannot yet be verified scientifically at all.

The second affirmation of religion is that we are better off even now if we believe her first affirmation to be true.

Now, let us consider what the logical elements of this situation are *in case the religious hypothesis in both its branches be really true.* (Of course, we must admit that possibility at the outset. If we are to discuss the question at all, it must involve a living option. If for any of you religion be a hypothesis that cannot, by any living possibility, be true, then you need go no further. I speak to the "saving remnant" alone.) So proceeding, we see, first, that religion offers itself as a *momentous* option. We are supposed to gain, even now, by our belief, and to lose by our non-belief, a certain vital good. Secondly, religion is a *forced* option, so far as that good goes. We cannot escape the issue by remaining skeptical and waiting for more light, because, although we do avoid error in that way *if religion be untrue,* we lose the good, *if it be true,* just as certainly as if we positively chose to disbelieve. It is as if a man should hesitate indefinitely to ask a certain woman to marry him because he was not perfectly sure that she would prove an angel after he brought her home. Would he not cut himself off from that particular angel-possibility as decisively as if he went and married someone else? Skepticism, then, is not avoidance of option; it is option of a certain particular kind of risk. *Better risk loss of truth than chance of error*—that is your faith-vetoer's exact position. He is actively playing his stake as much as the believer is; he is backing the field against the religious hypothesis, just as the believer is backing the religious hypothesis against the field. To preach skepticism to us as a duty until "sufficient evidence" for religion be found, is tantamount therefore to telling us, when in presence of the religious hypothesis, that to yield to our fear of its being error is wiser and better than to yield to our hope that it may be true. It is not intellect against all passions, then; it is only intellect with one passion laying down its law. And by what, forsooth, is the supreme wisdom of this passion warranted? Dupery for dupery, what proof is there that dupery through hope is so much worse than dupery through fear? I, for one, can see no proof; and I simply refuse obedience to the scientist's command to imitate his kind of option, in a case where my own stake is important enough to give me the right to choose my own form of risk. If religion be true and the evidence for it be still insufficient, I do not wish, by putting your extinguisher upon my nature (which feels to me as if it had after all some business in this matter), to forfeit my sole chance in life of getting upon the winning side—that chance depending, of course, on my willingness to run the risk of acting as if my passional need of taking the world religiously might be prophetic and right.

All this is on the supposition that it really may be prophetic and right, and that, even to us who are discussing the matter, religion is a live hypothesis which may be true. Now, to most of us religion comes in a still further way that makes a veto on our active faith even more illogical. The more perfect and more eternal aspect of the universe is represented in our religions as having personal form. The universe is no longer a mere *It* to us, but a *Thou*, if we are religious; and any relation that may be possible from person to person might be possible here. For instance, although in one sense we are passive portions of the universe, in another we show a curious autonomy, as if we were small, active centres on our own account. We feel, too, as if the appeal of religion to us were made to our own active goodwill, as if evidence might be forever withheld from us unless we met the hypothesis half-way. To take a trivial illustration: just as a man who in a company of gentlemen made no advances, asked a warrant for every concession, and believed no one's word without proof, would cut himself off by such churlishness from all the social rewards that a more trusting spirit would earn—so here, one who should shut himself up in snarling logicality and try to make the gods extort his recognition willy-nilly, or not get it at all, might cut himself off forever from his only opportunity of making the gods' acquaintance. This feeling, forced on us we know not whence, that by obstinately believing that there are gods (although not to do so would be so easy both for our logic and our life) we are doing the universe the deepest service we can, seems part of the living essence of the religious hypothesis. If the hypothesis *were* true in all its parts, including this one, then pure intellectualism, with its veto on our making willing advances, would be an absurdity; and some participation of our sympathetic nature would be logically required. I, therefore, for one, cannot see my way to accepting the agnostic rules for truth-seeking, or wilfully agree to keep my willing nature out of the game. I cannot do so for this plain reason, that *a rule of thinking which would absolutely prevent me from acknowledging certain kinds of truth if those kinds of truth were really there, would be an irrational rule.* That for me is the long and short of the formal logic of the situation, no matter what the kinds of truth might materially be.

I confess I do not see how this logic can be escaped. But sad experience makes me fear that some of you may still shrink from radically saying with me, *in abstracto*, that we have the right to believe at our own risk any hypothesis that is live enough to tempt our will. I suspect, however, that if this is so, it is because you have got away from the abstract logical point of view altogether, and are thinking (perhaps without realizing it) of some particular religious hypothesis which for you is dead. The freedom to "believe what we will" you apply to the case of some patent superstition; and the faith you think of is the faith defined by the schoolboy when he said, "Faith is when you believe something that you know ain't true." I can only repeat that this is misapprehension. *In concreto*, the freedom to believe can only cover living options which the intellect of the individual cannot by itself resolve; and living options never seem absurdities to him who has them to consider. When I look at the religious question as it really puts itself to concrete men, and when I think of all the possibilities which both practically and theoretically it involves, then this command that we shall put a stopper on our heart, instincts, and courage, and *wait*—acting of course meanwhile more or less as if religion were *not* true—till doomsday, or till such time as our intellect and senses working together may have raked in evidence enough—this command, I say, seems to me the queerest idol ever manufactured in the philosophic cave. Were we scholastic absolutists, there might be more excuse. If we had an infallible intellect with its objective certitudes, we might feel ourselves disloyal to such a perfect organ of knowledge in not trusting to it exclusively, in not waiting for its releasing word. But if we are empiricists, if we believe that no bell in us tolls to let us know for certain when truth is in our grasp, then it seems a piece of idle fantasticality to preach so solemnly our duty of waiting for the bell. Indeed we *may* wait if we will—I hope you do not think that I am denying that—but if we do so, we do so at our peril as much as if we believed. In either case we *act*, taking our life in our hands. No one of us ought to issue vetoes to the other, nor should we bandy words of abuse. We ought, on the contrary, delicately and profoundly to respect one another's mental freedom: then only shall we bring about the intellectual republic; then only shall we have that spirit of inner tolerance without which all our outer tolerance is soulless, and which is empiricism's glory; then only shall we live and let live, in speculative as well as in practical things.

I began by a reference to Fitz-James Stephen; let me end by a quotation from him.

> What do you think of yourself? What do you think of the world? . . . These are questions with which all must deal as it seems good to them. They are riddles of the Sphinx, and in some way or other we must deal with them . . . . In all important transactions of life we have to take a leap in the dark . . . . If we decide to leave the riddles unanswered, that is a choice; if we waver in our answer, that, too, is a choice: but whatever choice we make, we make it at our peril. If a man chooses to turn his back altogether on God and the future, no one can prevent him; no one can show beyond reasonable doubt that he is mistaken. If a man thinks otherwise and acts as he thinks, I do not see that anyone can prove that

*he* is mistaken. Each must act as he thinks best; and if he is wrong, so much the worse for him. We stand on a mountain pass in the midst of whirling snow and blinding mist, through which we get glimpses now and then of paths which may be deceptive. If we stand still we shall be frozen to death. If we take the wrong road we shall be dashed to pieces. We do not certainly know whether there is any right one. What must we do? "Be strong and of good courage." Act for the best, hope for the best, and take what comes . . . . If death ends all, we cannot meet death better.[2]

---

[2]*Liberty, Equality, Fraternity*, 2nd ed. (London, 1874), p. 353.

# Ernst Troeltsch

Ernst Troeltsch (1865–1923) was not only a philosopher of religion
and theologian but also, with his contemporary, Max Weber, a founder
of the modern sociology of religion.

# 16

# *The Place of Christianity Among the World Religions*

*This lecture was written for delivery before the University of Oxford in 1923, but Troeltsch died before it could be given. After some opening remarks (omitted here), Troeltsch refers to his earlier work,* The Absolute Validity of Christianity, *now reissued as* The Absoluteness of Christianity (London, 1972).

To put it briefly, the central meaning of this book consists in a deep and vivid realization of the clash between historical reflection and the determination of standards of truth and value. The problem thus arising presented itself to me at a very early age. I had had a predominantly humanistic and historical education, from which I had been led to extend my studies and interests over a wide field of historical investigation, using the terms "history" and "humanity" in the sense we in Germany have been wont to attribute to them in our best periods—namely, in the objective sense of a contemplation of objects which covers as far as possible the whole extent of human existence, and which finds its delight in all the abundant diversity and ceaseless movement characteristic of human existence, and this without seeking any precise practical ends. It seems to us that it is the wealth of moral life and development that manifests itself in this endlessly diversified world of history, and imparts some of its own loftiness and solemnity to the soul of the observer.

I was, however, inspired by another interest, which was quite as strong and quite as much a part of my natural endowment as the first, I mean the interest in reaching a vital and effective religious position, which could alone furnish my life with a center of reference for all practical questions, and could alone give meaning and purpose to reflection upon the things of this world. This need of mine led me to theology and philosophy, which I devoured with an equally passionate interest. I soon discovered, however, that the historical

From Troeltsch's posthumous *Christian Thought: Its History and Application* (London: 1923).

studies which had so largely formed me, and the theology and philosophy in which I was now immersed, stood in sharp opposition, indeed even in conflict, with one another. I was confronted, upon the one hand, with the perpetual flux of the historian's data, and the distrustful attitude of the historical critic towards conventional traditions, the real events of the past being, in his view, discoverable only as a reward of ceaseless toil, and then only with approximate accuracy. And, upon the other hand, I perceived the impulse in men towards a definite practical standpoint—the eagerness of the trusting soul to receive the divine revelation and to obey the divine commands. It was largely out of this conflict, which was no hypothetical one, but a fact of my own practical experience, that my entire theoretical standpoint took its rise.

Though this conflict was a personal one, however, it was no mere accident of my personal experience. It was rather the personal form in which a vital problem characteristic of the present stage of human development presented itself to me. I am of course aware that the sting of this problem is not equally felt in all parts of the civilized world of Europe and America. As Bouquet has explained in the work I have already mentioned, we must not apply without reservation to England, still less to America with its very underdeveloped historical sense, what is true, in this respect, of other countries.

Nevertheless, there exists at bottom, everywhere, an impression that historical criticism and the breadth of historical interest are fraught with danger to the recognition of simple standards of value, be they of rational or traditional origin. In the Anglo-Saxon countries it is especially ethnography and the comparative study of religion, together with careful philosophical criticism, that produce this attitude. In my own country it is primarily an examination of European civilization itself that has impressed us with the relativity and transitoriness of all things, even of the loftiest values of civilization. The effect, however, is very similar in the two cases. Whether we approach it from the standpoint of Herbert Spencer and the theory of evolution, or from that of Hegel and Ranke and German Romanticism, history presents a spectacle of bewildering diversity, and of historical institutions as all in a perpetual state of movement from within.

Indeed, the comparative study of religion, which gives an additional impulse to the tendency to relativity produced by historical reflection, has been pre-eminently the work of the great colonizing nations, especially of the English and the Dutch. And the criticism of the Bible and of dogma is not without representatives in England; and thus a growing feeling of uncertainty has been created here in this department also. The difference between this English line of reflection and the historical thought of Germany really consists simply in the fact that the latter is less wont to consider the practical needs and interests of society, while in theory it is determined more by the concept of individuality than by sociological or evolutionary principles which tend to regard all processes as leading to a single goal presented by nature.

Important as these differences are, however, they are all but different aspects of the one fundamental conflict between the spirit of critical scepticism generated by the ceaseless flux and manifold contradictions within the sphere of history and the demand of the religious consciousness for certainty, for unity, and for peace. Whether this conflict becomes more apparent in the critical analysis of details or in the challenging of fundamental principles, the cause and the general effect remain very much the same.

In my book on *The Absolute Validity of Christianity* I examined the means whereby theology is able to defend itself against these difficulties. This of course involved an examination of the fundamental concepts of theology as such. I believed that I could here determine two such concepts, both of which claimed to establish the ultimate validity of the Christian revelation in opposition to the relativities revealed by the study of history.

The first of these concepts was the theory that the truth of Christianity is guaranteed by miracles. In our times we are no longer primarily concerned here with miracles in the external world, i.e., with the so-called "nature miracles," involving an infringement of natural law, but with the miracles of interior conversion and the attainment of a higher quality of life through communion with Jesus and his community. In this connection, it is claimed, an entirely different type of causation comes into operation from that which is operative anywhere else in the world. The Christian life may indeed be compared to an island in the midst of the stream of history, exposed to all the storms of secular life, and lured by all its wiles, yet constituting, in reality, a stronghold of experience of quite another order. The absolute validity of Christianity rests upon the absoluteness of God himself, who is made manifest here directly in miracles but who manifested himself beyond this island only as a *causa remota*—as the ground of the interconnection of all relative things. In this way both a natural and a supernatural theology are possible, the latter resting upon the new birth and experience of the inner man, whilst natural theology is based upon the facts and forces of the external world. This theory is simply a restatement of the old miracle apologetic in the more intimate and spiritual form which it acquired under the influence of Methodism and Pietism.

The second fundamental concept of theology, which I have called the concept of evolution, presents a considerable contrast to the first. Its most important exponent is Hegel. According to this view Christianity is simply the perfected expression of religion as such. In the universal process of the unfolding of Spirit, the fundamental impulse towards salvation and communion with God overcomes all the limitations of sense experience, of the natural order, of mythological form, until it attains perfect expression in Christianity, and enters into combination with the loftiest and most spiritual of all philosophies, namely, that of Platonism. Christianity, it is maintained, is not *a particular* religion, it is *religion*. It is no isolated manifestation of Spirit, but the flower of spiritual life itself. All religion implies salvation and re-birth, but outside Christianity these are subject to the limitations of physical nature and are balked by human selfishness. In the prophets and in Christ the Divine Life breaks through these limits and flows unrestrained into the thirsty world, which finds therein the solution of all its conflicts and the goal of all its striving. The whole history of religion and its obvious trend are thus a completely adequate proof of Christianity. The historical process does not stand in opposition to it. When regarded as a whole, and as one process, it rather affords a demonstration of its supreme greatness and all-embracing power. The miracles which attend its development are partly explicable, as in other religions, as mythical elements, accumulated during the growth of tradition, but they are partly effects of the shock produced by the spiritual revolution traceable here. They are thus not so much its credentials as its attendant phenomena, and as such they may be left without anxiety in the hands of the historical critic.

I found myself obliged to dismiss both these views as untenable. The former I rejected on the ground that an inward miracle, though it is indeed a powerful psychical upheaval, is not a miracle in the strict sense of the term. Are we justified in tracing the Platonic *Eros* to a natural cause, whilst we attribute a supernatural origin to the Christian *Agape?* And how can we prove such origin, even if we care to assume it? This would only be possible by having recourse once more to the visible signs which accompany these inward miracles, which would be again to treat the accompaniment as if it were itself the melody. Moreover, we should then be faced with the competition furnished by similar miracles in the non-Christian religions, not to mention the negative results of historical criticism and the trouble attendant upon every theory of miracles.

If, however, we turn for this reason to the second view, we find the difficulties to be different, indeed, but no less formidable. The actual history of religion knows nothing of the common character of all religions, or of their natural upward trend towards Christianity. It perceives a sharp distinction between the great world religions and the national religions of heathen tribes, and further discovers certain irresolvable contradictions between these world religions themselves which render their ultimate fusion and reconciliation in Christianity highly improbable, either in theory or in practice. Moreover, Christianity is itself a theoretical abstraction. It presents no historical uniformity, but displays a different character in every age, and is, besides, split up into many different denominations, hence it can in no wise be represented as the finally attained unity and explanation of all that has gone before, such as religious speculation seeks. It is rather a particular, independent, historical principle, containing, similarly to the other principles, very diverse possibilities and tendencies.

This leads us finally to a conception which has, I think, obtained less recognition in other countries than in Germany—I mean the conception which dominates the whole sphere of history, viz., Individuality. History cannot be regarded as a process in which a universal and everywhere similar principle is confined and obscured. Nor is it a continual mixing and remixing of elemental psychical powers, which indicate a general trend of things towards a rational end or goal of evolution. It is rather an immeasurable, incomparable profusion of always-new, unique, and hence individual tendencies, welling up from undiscovered depths, and coming to light in each case in unsuspected places and under different circumstances. Each process works itself out in its own way, bringing ever-new series of unique transformations in its train, until its powers are exhausted, or until it enters a component material into some new combination. Thus the universal law of history consists precisely in this, that the Divine Reason, or the Divine Life, within history, constantly manifests itself in always-new and always-peculiar individualizations—and hence that its tendency is not towards unity or universality at all, but rather towards the fulfilment of the highest potentialities of each separate department of life. It is this law which, beyond all else, makes it quite impossible to characterize Christianity as the reconciliation and goal of all the forces of history, or indeed to regard it as anything else than a historical individuality.

These are the historical ideas which have been handed down to us from German Romanticism, the great opposition movement to Rationalism and to all the clumsy miracle apologetic. They illustrate the special character and significance of German Romanticism, considered as part of the great Romantic Movement of Europe. They form the starting point of all the German history and most of the German theology of the nineteenth century. They present our problem in its most crucial form, and explain why it became a more burning problem in Germany than elsewhere, except where it was envisaged in the same way, either as a result of independent reflection or under German influence.

What, then, is the solution? This is the question which I attempted to answer in my book. I first endeavored to show that it was in any case impossible to return to the old miracle apologetic. This has been rendered untenable, not by theories, but by documents, by discoveries, by the results of exploration. The force of such evidence cannot be resisted by anyone whose sense of truth has been educated by philology, or even by anyone possessing an average amount of ordinary "common sense." I then submitted that the mere fact of the universality of Christianity—of its presence in all the other religions—would, even if true—be irrelevant. The point at issue was not whether Christianity was as a matter of fact universal, or at least implicit in all religion, but whether it possessed ultimate truth, a truth which might easily depend upon a single instance of itself.

This formed a position for further reflection. It is quite possible, I maintained, that there is an element of truth in every religion, but that this is combined with innumerable transitory, individual features. This element of truth can only be disentangled through strife and disruption, and it should be our constant endeavor to assist in this process of disentanglement. The recognition of this truth is, however, an intuition which is born of deep personal experience and a pure conscientiousness. No strict proof of it is possible, for to demonstrate the actual presence of this truth in all the other cases would not be to establish its validity, even if this demonstration were easier than it is. Such an intuition can only be confirmed retrospectively and indirectly by its practical fruits, and by the light that it sheds upon all the problems of life. Thus in relation to Christianity such an intuition can only arise from immediate impression and personal conviction. Its claim to universal validity can only be felt and believed, in the first instance, and must be confirmed retrospectively through its genuine ability to furnish a solution of the various problems of life.

Now, validity of this kind seems always to rest upon the fine point of personal conviction. We still require a broader foundation upon actual, objective facts. I believed that I had discovered such a foundation for Christianity in the terms in which its claim to ultimate validity finds instinctive and immediate expression; in other words, in its faith in revelation and in the kind of claim it makes to truth. I thought it necessary to compare it from this point of view with other religions, whose belief in revelation and claim to validity were in every case of quite a different kind. If we examine any of the great world religions we shall find that all of them, Judaism, Islam, Zoroastrianism, Buddhism, Christianity, even Confucianism, indeed claim absolute validity, but quite naïvely, and that in a very different manner in each case, the differences being illustrative of differences in their inner structure. These claims are always naïve—simple and direct. They are not the outcome of an apologetic reasoning, and the differences they exhibit in their naïve claims to absolute validity indicate the varying degree of such absolute validity as they really mean and intend within their own minds. This seemed to me to be nearly the most important point in every comparison between the religions, and the one which furnished the most searching test of the character of the dogmatic contents to be compared—contents which, in themselves, reveal so little as to the manner of their foundation in immediate religious experience.

A similar line of thought is to be found in the excellent book on *National and Universal Religions*, by the Dutch writer Abraham Kuenen. If we make his distinction the basis of our investigation and comparison, we at once perceive that Judaism and Zoroastrianism were explicitly national religions, associated with a particular country and concerned with tasks presented by a particular type of civilization—in the case of the Jews primarily with questions of national loyalty and national aspiration. Islam, too, is at the bottom the national religion of the Arab peoples, compelling by the sword recognition of the prophetic claims of Mohammed in all the countries to which the Arab races have penetrated. Where, on the other hand, it has spread beyond the boundaries of Arabian territory, it has not as a rule attempted to convert unbelievers, but has simply maintained them as a source of revenue. And where Islam has developed great missionary activity, as, for example, in Africa and in the islands of the Malay Archipelago, it shows itself to be bound to certain conditions of civilization which render it more readily acceptable to primitive races than Christianity, but which prove it, at the same time, to be indissolubly connected with a particular type of civilization. Finally, where it has adopted Persian or Indian mysticism, or Greek or modern philosophy, it loses its essential character, and becomes no more than a sign and a proof of national autonomy. Confucianism and Buddhism again are rather philosophies than religions, and owe their claim to absolute validity more to the common character of thought than to belief in a specific religious revelation, whilst Confucianism is essentially a national movement and Buddhism is, as a matter of fact, bound to the conditions of life in tropical countries.

Now, the naïve claim to absolute validity made by Christianity is of quite a different kind. All limitation to a particular race or nation is excluded on principle, and this exclusion illustrates the purely human character of its religious ideal, which appeals only to the simplest, the most general, the most personal and spiritual needs of mankind. Moreover, it does not depend in any way upon human reflection or a laborious process of reasoning, but upon an overwhelming manifestation of God in the persons and lives of the great prophets. Thus it was not a theory but a life—not a social order but a power. It owes its claim to universal validity not to the correctness of its reasoning nor to the conclusiveness of its proofs, but to God's revelation of himself in human hearts and lives. Thus the naïve claim to absolute validity of Christianity is as unique as its conception of God. It is indeed a corollary of its belief in a revelation within the depths of the soul, awakening men to a new and higher quality of life, breaking down the barriers which the sense of guilt would otherwise set up, and making a final breach with the egoism obstinately centred in the individual self. It is from this point of view that its claim to absolute validity, following as it does from the content of its religious ideal, appears to be vindicated. It possesses the highest claim to universality of all the religions, for this its claim is based upon the deepest foundations, the nature of God and of man.

Hence we may simply leave aside the question of the measure of validity possessed by the other religions. Nor need we trouble ourselves with the question of the possible further development of religion itself. It suffices that Christianity is itself a developing religion, constantly striving towards a fresh and fuller expression. We may content ourselves with acknowledging that it possesses the highest degree of validity attained among all the historical religions which we are able to examine. We shall not wish to become Jews, nor Zoroastrians, nor Mohammedans, nor again Confucianists nor Buddhists. We shall rather strive continually to bring our Christianity into harmony with the changing conditions of life, and to bring its human and divine potentialities to the fullest possible fruition. It is the loftiest and most spiritual revelation we know at all. It has the highest validity. Let that suffice.

Such was the conclusion I reached in the book which I wrote some twenty years ago, and, from the practical standpoint at least, it contains nothing that I wish to withdraw. From the point of view of theory, on the other hand, there are a number of points which I should wish to modify today, and these modifications are, of course, not without some practical effects.

My scruples arise from the fact that, while the significance for history of the concept of Individuality impresses me more forcibly every day, I no longer believe this to be so easily reconcilable with that of supreme validity. The further investigations, especially into the history of Christianity, of which I have given the results in my *Social Doctrines* (*Die Soziallehren der christlichen Kirchen und Gruppen*, 1912), have shown me how thoroughly individual is historical Christianity after all, and how invariably its various phases and denominations have been due to varying circumstances and conditions of life. Whether you regard it as a whole or in its several forms, it is a purely historical, individual, relative phenomenon, which could, as we actually find it, only have arisen in the territory of the classical culture, and among the Latin and Germanic races. The Christianity of the Oriental peoples—the Jacobites, Nestorians, Armenians, Abyssinians—is of quite a different type, indeed even that of the Russians is a world of its own. The inference from all that is, however, that a religion, in the several forms assumed by it, always depends upon the intellectual, social, and national conditions among which it exists. On the other hand, a study of the non-Christian religions convinced me more and more that their naïve claims to absolute validity are also genuinely such. I found Buddhism and Brahminism especially to be really humane and spiritual religions, capable of appealing in precisely the same way to the inner certitude and devotion of their followers as Christianity, though the particular character of each has been determined by the historical, geographical, and social conditions of the countries in which it has taken shape.

The subject to which I devoted most attention, however, was that of the relation of individual historical facts to standards of value within the entire domain of history in connection with the development of political, social, ethical, aesthetic, and scientific ideas. I have only lately published the results of these investigations in my new book on *The Historical Temper and Its Problems (Der Historismus und seine Probleme*, 1922). I encountered the same difficulties in each of these provinces—they were not confined to religion. Indeed, even the validity of science and logic seemed to exhibit, under different skies and upon different soil, strong individual differences present even in their deepest and innermost rudiments. What was really common to mankind, and universally valid for it, seemed, in spite of a general kinship and capacity for mutual understanding, to be at bottom exceedingly little, and to belong more to the province of material goods than to the ideal values of civilization.

The effect of these discoveries upon the conclusions reached in my earlier book was as follows.

The individual character of European civilization, and of the Christian religion which is intimately connected with it, receives now much greater emphasis, whilst the somewhat rationalistic concept of validity, and specifically of *supreme validity*, falls considerably into the background. It is impossible to deny facts or to resist the decrees of fate. And it is historical facts that have welded Christianity into the closest connection with the civilizations of Greece, Rome and Northern Europe. All our thoughts and feelings are impregnated with Christian motives and Christian presuppositions; and, conversely, our whole Christianity is indissolubly bound up with elements of the ancient and modern civilizations of Europe. From being a Jewish sect Christianity has become the religion of all Europe. It stands or falls with European civilization; while on its own part, it has entirely lost its Oriental character and has become Hellenized and Westernized. Our European conceptions of personality and its eternal, divine right, and of progress towards a kingdom of the spirit and of God, our enormous capacity for expansion and for the interconnection of spiritual and temporal, our whole social order, our science, our art—all these rest, whether we know it or not, whether we like it or not, upon the basis of this deorientalized Christianity.

Its primary claim to validity is thus the fact that only through it have we become what we are, and that only in it can we preserve the religious forces that we need. Apart from it we lapse either into a self-destructive titanic attitude, or into effeminate trifling, or into crude brutality. And at the same time our life is a consistent compromise, as little unsatisfactory as we can manage, between its lofty spirituality and our practical everyday needs—a compromise that has to be renewed at every fresh ascent and every bend of the road. This tension is characteristic of our form of human life and rouses us to many a heroic endeavor, though it may also lead us into the most terrible mendacity and crime. Thus we are, and thus we shall remain, as long as we survive. We cannot live without a religion, yet the only religion that we can endure is Christianity, for Christianity has grown up with us and has become a part of our very being.

Now, obviously we cannot remain in these matters at the level of brute fact. Christianity could not be the religion of such a highly developed racial group if it did not possess a mighty spiritual power and truth; in short, if it were not, in some degree, a manifestation of the Divine Life itself. The evidence we have for this remains essentially the same, whatever may be our theory concerning absolute validity—it is the evidence of a profound inner experience. This experience is undoubtedly the criterion of its validity, but, be it noted, only of its validity *for us*. It is God's countenance as revealed to us; it is the way in which, being what we are, we receive, and react to, the revelation of God. It is binding upon us, and it brings us deliverance. It is final and unconditional for us, because we have nothing else, and because in what we have we can recognize the accents of the divine voice.

But this does not preclude the possibility that other racial groups, living under entirely different cultural conditions, may experience their contact with the Divine Life in quite a different way, and may themselves also possess a religion which has grown up with them, and from which they cannot sever themselves so long as they remain what they are. And they may quite sincerely regard this as absolutely valid for them, and give expression to this absolute validity according to the demands of their own religious feeling. We shall, of course, assume something of this kind only among nations which have reached a relatively high stage of civilization, and whose whole mental life has been intimately connected with their religion through a long period of discipline. We shall not assume it among the less developed races, where many religious cults are followed side by side, nor in the simple animism of heathen tribes, which is so monotonous in spite of its many variations. These territories are gradually conquered by the great world religions which possess a real sense of their own absolute validity. But among the great spiritual religions themselves the fundamental spiritual positions which destiny has assigned to them persist in their distinctness. If we wish to determine their relative value, it is not the religions alone that we must compare, but always only the civilizations of which the religion in each case constitutes a part incapable of severance from the rest. But who will presume to make a really final pronouncement here? Only God himself, who has determined these differences, can do that. The various racial groups can only seek to purify and enrich their experience, each within its own province and according to its own standards, and to win the weaker and less developed races for their own faith, always remembering that the religion thus adopted by another people will individualize itself anew.

The practical bearing of this new manner of thinking differs but little from that of my earlier view, or indeed from that of any theology which seeks to retain the essential basis of Christianity, and intends merely to substantiate and to interpret it. Its detailed application, however, brings to light one or two important consequences.

In the first place, it has a considerable influence upon the question of foreign missions. Missionary enterprise has always been in part simply a concomitant of the political, military, and commercial expansion of a state or nation, but in part also an outcome of the religious enthusiast's zeal for conversion. The former aspect is exceedingly important as a factor in human history, but is irrelevant in the present connection. The latter aspect, on the other hand, is intimately connected with the claim to absolute validity. But here we have to maintain, in accordance with all our conclusions hitherto, that directly religious missionary enterprise must stand in quite a different relation to the great philosophical world religions from that in which it stands to the crude heathenism of smaller tribes. There can be always only a spiritual wrestling of missionary Christianity with the other world religions, possibly a certain contact with them. The heathen races, on the other hand, are being morally and spiritually disintegrated by the contact with European civilization; hence they demand a substitute from the higher religion and culture. We have a missionary duty towards these races, and our enterprise is likely to meet with success amongst them, although Christianity, be it remembered, is by no means the only religion which is taking part in this missionary campaign. Islam and Buddhism are also missionary religions. But in relation to the great world religions we need to recognize that they are expressions of the religious consciousness corresponding to certain definite types of culture, and that it is their duty to increase in depth and purity by means of their own interior impulses, a task in which the contact with Christianity may prove helpful, to them as to us, in such processes of development from within. The great religions might indeed be described as crystallizations of the thought of great races, as these races are themselves crystallizations of the various biological and anthropological forms. There can be no conversion or transformation of one into the other, but only a measure of agreement and of mutual understanding.

The second practical consequence of my new trend of thought concerns the inner development of Christianity itself. If my theory is correct, this development is closely related to the whole spiritual and cultural development of European civilization. True, the religious consciousness, whose object is God and eternal peace, is less exposed to restlessness and change than are the purely temporal constituents of the movement; hence it has become institutionalized in the various large denominations which, because of these internal reasons, constitute the most conservative element in the life of Europe. Nevertheless, Christianity is drawn into the stream of spiritual development even within the churches, and still more outside and beyond them, in the free speculation of literature and philosophy. Moreover, it contains, like all the world religions, and perhaps more than any other world religion, the impulse and the power to a continual self-purification and self-deepening, for it has been assigned to that Spirit which shall lead men into all truth, and which seeks its fulfilment in the coming of the Kingdom of God; and again, because it has been bound up from the first with all the intellectual forces of Hellenism.

Under these circumstances the course of its development is unpredictable, for it is capable of assuming always new individualizations. A new era in the world's history is beginning for it at this moment. It has to ally itself anew to a new conception of nature, a new social order, and a profound interior transformation of the spiritual outlook, and has to bring to the suffering world a new peace and a new brotherhood. How this can be accomplished it is not for me to say here; indeed, the answer is as yet very far from clear. All that is certain is that Christianity is at a critical moment of its further development, and that very bold and far-reaching changes are necessary, transcending anything that has yet been achieved by any denomination. I have, in this respect, become more and more radical and super-denominational, while, at the same time, I have come more and more to regard the specific kernel of religion as a unique and independent source of life and power.

Can we, then, discover no common goal of religion, nothing at all that is absolute, in the objective sense of constituting a common standard for mankind? Instinctive conviction makes us reluctant to admit such a sceptical conclusion, and it will especially be combated on the ground of the reality of the subjective validities which we have discovered. These are not simply illusions or the products of human vanity. They are products of the impulse towards absolute objective truth, and take effect in the practical sphere under constant critical self-purification and effort at self-improvement. I have already drawn attention to this fact in my earlier work. I only wish to emphasize now more strongly than I did then that this synthesis cannot as yet be already attained in any one of the historical religions, but that they all are tending in the same direction, and that all seem impelled by an inner force to strive upward towards some unknown final height, where alone the ultimate unity and the final objective validity can lie. And, as all religion has thus a common goal in the Unknown, the Future, perchance in the Beyond, so too it has a common ground in the Divine Spirit ever pressing the finite mind onward towards further light and fuller consciousness, a Spirit which indwells the finite spirit, and whose ultimate union with it is the purpose of the whole many-sided process.

Between these two poles, however—the divine Source and the divine Goal—lie all the individual differentiations of race and civilization, and, with them also, the individual differences of the great, comprehensive religions.

There may be mutual understanding between them, if they are willing to renounce those sorry things, self-will and the spirit of violent domination. If each strives to fulfil its own highest potentialities, and allows itself to be influenced therein by the similar striving of the rest, they may approach and find contact with each other. Some striking examples of such contact are recorded in Canon Streeter's *The Sadhu*, and in a book called *On the Edge of the Primeval Forest*, by the Alsatian physician and writer on the philosophy of religion, Albert Schweitzer. But, so far as human eye can penetrate into the future, it would seem probable that the great revelations to the various civilizations will remain distinct, in spite of a little shifting of their several territories at the fringes, and that the question of their several relative values will never be capable of objective determination, since every proof thereof will presuppose the special characteristics of the civilization in which it arises. The conception of personality itself is, for instance, different in the East and in the West, hence arguments starting from it will lead to different conclusions in the two cases. Yet there is no other concept which could furnish a basis for argument concerning practical values and truths save this concept of personality, which is always itself already one of the fundamental positions of the several religions, and is determined by them according to those respective general attitudes of theirs.

This is what I wish to say in modification of my former theories. I hope you feel that I am not speaking in any spirit of scepticism or uncertainty. A truth which, in the first instance, is *a truth for us* does not cease, because of this, to be very truth and life. What we learn daily through our love for our fellow men, viz., that they are independent beings with standards of their own, we ought also to be able to learn through our love for mankind as a whole—that here too there exist autonomous civilizations with standards of their own. This does not exclude rivalry, but it must be a rivalry for the attainment of interior purity and clearness of vision. If each racial group strives to develop its own highest potentialities, we may hope to come nearer to one another. This applies to the great world religions, but it also applies to the various religious denominations, and to individuals in their intercourse with one another. In our earthly experience the Divine Life is not one, but many. But to apprehend the one in the many constitutes the special character of love.

# Bertrand Russell
# and F. C. Copleston

Bertrand Russell (1872–1970), the most famous western philosopher of the twentieth century, was throughout his long and highly productive adult life a convinced atheist. Fr. F. C. Copleston, S.J. (1907–  ) is author of the multi-volume *History of Philosophy*.

# 17

# The Existence of God

*A debate between Bertrand Russell
and Father F. C. Copleston, S.J.*

COPLESTON: As we are going to discuss the existence of God, it might perhaps be as well to come to some provisional agreement as to what we understand by the term "God." I presume that we mean a supreme personal being—distinct from the world and creator of the world. Would you agree—provisionally at least—to accept this statement as the meaning of the term "God"?

RUSSELL: Yes, I accept this definition.

COPLESTON: Well, my position is the affirmative position that such a being actually exists, and that His existence can be proved philosophically. Perhaps you would tell me if your position is that of agnosticism or of atheism. I mean, would you say that the non-existence of God can be proved?

RUSSELL: No, I should not say that: my position is agnostic.

COPLESTON: Would you agree with me that the problem of God is a problem of great importance? For example, would you agree that if God does not exist, human beings and human history can have no other purpose than the purpose they choose to give themselves, which—in practice—is likely to mean the purpose which those impose who have the power to impose it?

RUSSELL: Roughly speaking, yes, though I should have to place some limitation on your last clause.

Extract taken from the Third Programme of the British Broadcasting Corporation, by F.C. Copleston and Bertrand Russell reproduced by kind permission of Unwin Hyman Ltd. Copyright © 1948.

COPLESTON: Would you agree that if there is no God—no absolute Being—there can be no absolute values? I mean, would you agree that if there is no absolute good that the relativity of values results?

RUSSELL: No, I think these questions are logically distinct. Take, for instance, G. E. Moore's *Principia Ethica*, where he maintains that there is a distinction of good and evil, that both of these are definite concepts. But he does not bring in the idea of God to support that contention.

COPLESTON: Well, suppose we leave the question of good till later, till we come to the moral argument, and I give first a metaphysical argument. I'd like to put the main weight on the metaphysical argument based on Leibniz's argument from "Contingency" and then later we might discuss the moral argument. Suppose I give a brief statement on the metaphysical argument and that then we go on to discuss it?

RUSSELL: That seems to me to be a very good plan.

## THE ARGUMENT FROM CONTINGENCY

COPLESTON: Well, for clarity's sake, I'll divide the argument into distinct stages. First of all, I should say, we know that there are at least some beings in the world which do not contain in themselves the reason for their existence. For example, I depend on my parents, and now on the air, and on food, and so on. Now, secondly, the world is simply the real or imagined totality or aggregate of individual objects, none of which contain in themselves alone the reason for their existence. There isn't any world distinct from the objects which form it, any more than the human race is something apart from the members. Therefore, I should say, since objects or events exist, and since no object of experience contains within itself the reason of its existence, this reason, the totality of objects, must have a reason external to itself. That reason must be an existent being. Well, this being is either itself the reason for its own existence, or it is not. If it is, well and good. If it is not, then we must proceed farther. But if we proceed to infinity in that sense, then there's no explanation of existence at all. So, I should say, in order to explain existence, we must come to a being which contains within itself the reason for its own existence, that is to say, which cannot not-exist.

RUSSELL: This raises a great many points and it is not altogether easy to know where to begin, but I think that, perhaps, in answering your argument, the best point at which to begin is the question of necessary being. The word "necessary" I should maintain, can only be applied significantly to propositions. And, in fact, only to such as are analytic—that is to say—such as it is self-contradictory to deny. I could only admit a necessary being if there were a being whose existence it is self-contradictory to deny. I should like to know whether you would accept Leibniz's division of propositions into truths of reason and truths of fact. The former—the truths of reason—being necessary.

COPLESTON: Well, I certainly should not subscribe to what seems to be Leibniz's idea of truths of reason and truths of fact, since it would appear that, for him, there are in the long run only analytic propositions. It would seem that for Leibniz truths of fact are ultimately reducible to truths of reason. That is to say, to analytic propositions, at least for an omniscient mind. Well, I couldn't agree with that. For one thing, it would fail to meet the requirements of the experience of freedom. I don't want to uphold the whole philosophy of Leibniz. I have made use of his argument from contingent to necessary being, basing the argument on the principle of sufficient reason, simply because it seems to me a brief and clear formulation of what is, in my opinion, the fundamental metaphysical argument for God's existence.

RUSSELL: But, to my mind, "a necessary proposition" has got to be analytic. I don't see what else it can mean. And analytic propositions are always complex and logically somewhat late. "Irrational animals are animals" is an analytic proposition; but a proposition such as "This is an animal" can never be analytic. In fact, all the propositions that can be analytic are somewhat late in the build-up of propositions.

COPLESTON: Take the proposition "If there is a contingent being then there is a necessary being." I consider that that proposition hypothetically expressed is a necessary proposition. If you are going to call every necessary proposition an analytic proposition, then—in order to avoid a dispute in terminology—I would agree to call it analytic, though I don't consider it a tautological proposition. That there is a contingent being actually existing has to be discovered by experience, and the proposition that there is a contingent being is certainly not an analytic proposition, though once you know, I should maintain, that there is a contingent being, it follows of necessity that there is a necessary being.

RUSSELL: The difficulty of this argument is that I don't admit the idea of a necessary being and I don't admit that there is any particular meaning in calling other beings "contingent." These phrases don't for me have a significance except within a logic that I reject.

COPLESTON: Do you mean that you reject these terms because they won't fit in with what is called "modern logic"?

RUSSELL: Well, I can't find anything that they could mean. The word "necessary," it seems to me, is a useless word, except as applied to analytic propositions, not to things.

COPLESTON: In the first place, what do you mean by "modern logic"? As far as I know, there are somewhat differing systems. In the second place, not all modern logicians surely would admit the meaninglessness of metaphysics. We both know, at any rate, one very eminent modern thinker whose knowledge of modern logic was profound, but who certainly did not think that metaphysics are meaningless or, in particular, that the problem of God is meaningless. Again, even if all modern logicians held that metaphysical terms are meaningless, it would not follow that they were right. The proposition that metaphysical terms are meaningless seems to me to be a proposition based on an assumed philosophy. The dogmatic position behind it seems to be this: What will not go into my machine is non-existent, or it is meaningless; it is the expression of emotion. I am simply trying to point out that anybody who says that a particular system of modern logic is the sole criterion of meaning is saying something that is over dogmatic; he is dogmatically insisting that a part of philosophy is the whole of philosophy. After all, a "contingent" being is a being which has not in itself the complete reason for its existence, that's what I mean by a contingent being. You know, as well as I do, that the existence of neither of us can be explained without reference to something or somebody outside us, our parents, for example. A "necessary" being, on the other hand, means a being that must and cannot not-exist. You may say that there is no such being, but you will find it hard to convince me that you do not understand the terms I am using. If you do not understand them, then how can you be entitled to say that such a being does not exist, if that is what you do say?

RUSSELL: Well, there are points here that I don't propose to go into at length. I don't maintain the meaninglessness of metaphysics in general at all. I maintain the meaninglessness of certain particular terms—not on any general ground, but simply because I've not been able to see an interpretation of those particular terms. It's not a general dogma—it's a particular thing. But those points I will leave out for the moment. And I will say that what you have been saying brings us back, it seems to me, to the ontological argument that there is a being whose essence involves existence, so that his existence is analytic. That seems to me to be impossible, and it raises, of course, the question what one means by existence, and as to this, I think a subject named can never be significantly said to exist but only a subject described. And that existence, in fact, quite definitely is not a predicate.

COPLESTON: Well, you say, I believe, that it is bad grammar, or rather bad syntax to say for example "T. S. Eliot exists"; one ought to say, for example, "He, the author of Murder in the Cathedral, exists." Are you going to say that the proposition, "The cause of the world exists," is without meaning? You may say that the world has no cause; but I fail to see how you can say that the proposition that "the cause of the world exists" is meaningless. Put it in the form of a question: "Has the world a cause?" or "Does a cause of the world exist?" Most people surely would understand the question, even if they don't agree about the answer.

RUSSELL: Well, certainly the question "Does the cause of the world exist?" is a question that has meaning. But if you say "Yes, God is the cause of the world" you're using God as a proper name; then "God exists" will not be a statement that has meaning; that is the position that I'm maintaining. Because, therefore, it will follow that it cannot be an analytic proposition ever to say that this or that exists. For example, suppose you take as your subject "the existent round-square," it would look like an analytic proposition that "the existent round-square exists," but it doesn't exist.

COPLESTON: No, it doesn't, then surely you can't say it doesn't exist unless you have a conception of what existence is. As to the phrase "existent round-square," I should say that it has no meaning at all.

RUSSELL: I quite agree. Then I should say the same thing in another context in reference to a "necessary being."

COPLESTON: Well, we seem to have arrived at an impasse. To say that a necessary being is a being that must exist and cannot not-exist has for me a definite meaning. For you it has no meaning.

RUSSELL: Well, we can press the point a little, I think. A being that must exist and cannot not-exist, would surely, according to you, be a being whose essence involves existence.

COPLESTON: Yes, a being the essence of which is to exist. But I should not be willing to argue the existence of God simply from the idea of His essence because I don't think we have any clear intuition of God's essence as yet. I think we have to argue from the world of experience to God.

RUSSELL: Yes, I quite see the distinction. But, at the same time, for a being with sufficient knowledge it would be true to say "Here is this being whose essence involves existence!"

COPLESTON: Yes, certainly if anybody saw God, he would see that God must exist.

RUSSELL: So that I mean there is a being whose essence involves existence although we don't know that essence. We only know there is such a being.

COPLESTON: Yes, I should add we don't know the essence *a priori*. It is only *a posteriori* through our experience of the world that we come to a knowledge of the existence of that being. And then one argues, the essence and existence must be identical. Because if God's essence and God's existence was not identical, then some sufficient reason for this existence would have to be found beyond God.

RUSSELL: So it all turns on this question of sufficient reason, and I must say you haven't defined "sufficient reason" in a way that I can understand— what do you mean by sufficient reason? You don't mean cause?

COPLESTON: Not necessarily. Cause is a kind of sufficient reason. Only contingent being can have a cause. God is His own sufficient reason; and He is not cause of Himself. By sufficient reason in the full sense I mean an explanation adequate for the existence of some particular being.

RUSSELL: But when is an explanation adequate? Suppose I am about to make a flame with a match. You may say that the adequate explanation of that is that I rub it on the box.

COPLESTON: Well, for practical purposes—but theoretically, that is only a partial explanation. An adequate explanation must ultimately be a total explanation, to which nothing further can be added.

RUSSELL: Then I can only say that you're looking for something which can't be got, and which one ought not to expect to get.

COPLESTON: To say that one has not found it is one thing; to say that one should not look for it seems to me rather dogmatic.

RUSSELL: Well, I don't know. I mean, the explanation of one thing is another thing which makes the other thing dependent on yet another, and you have to grasp this sorry scheme of things entire to do what you want, and that we can't do.

COPLESTON: But are you going to say that we can't, or we shouldn't even raise the question of the existence of the whole of this sorry scheme of things—of the whole universe?

RUSSELL: Yes, I don't think there's any meaning in it at all. I think the word "universe" is a handy word in some connections, but I don't think it stands for anything that has a meaning.

COPLESTON: If the word is meaningless, it can't be so very handy. In any case, I don't say that the universe is something different from the objects which compose it (I indicated that in my brief summary of the proof), what I'm doing is to look for the reason, in this case the cause of the objects—the real or imagined totality of which constitute what we call the universe. You say, I think that the universe—or my existence if you prefer, or any other existence—is unintelligible?

RUSSELL: First may I take up the point that if a word is meaningless it can't be handy. That sounds well but isn't in fact correct. Take, say, such a word as "the" or "than." You can't point to any object that those words mean, but they are very useful words; I should say the same of "universe." But leaving that point, you ask whether I consider that the universe is unintelligible. I shouldn't say unintelligible—I think it is without explanation. Intelligible, to my mind, is a different thing. Intelligible has to do with the thing itself intrinsically and not with its relations.

COPLESTON: Well, my point is that what we call the world is intrinsically unintelligible, apart from the existence of God. You see, I don't believe that the infinity of the series of events—I mean a horizontal series, so to speak—if such an infinity could be proved, would be in the slightest degree relevant to the situation. If you add up chocolates you get chocolates after all and not a sheep. If you add up chocolates to infinity, you presumably get an infinite number of chocolates. So if you add up contingent beings to infinity, you still get contingent beings, not a necessary being. An infinite series of contingent beings will be, to my way of thinking, as unable to cause itself as one contingent being. However, you say, I think, that it is illegitimate to raise the question of what will explain the existence of any particular object?

RUSSELL: It's quite all right if you mean by explaining it, simply finding a cause for it.

COPLESTON: Well, why stop at one particular object? Why shouldn't one raise the question of the cause of the existence of all particular objects?

RUSSELL: Because I see no reason to think there is any. The whole concept of cause is one we derive from our observation of particular things; I see no reason whatsoever to suppose that the total has any cause whatsoever.

COPLESTON: Well, to say that there isn't any cause is not the same thing as saying that we shouldn't look for a cause. The statement that there isn't any cause should come, if it comes at all, at the end of the enquiry, not the beginning. In any case, if the total has no cause, then to my way of thinking it must be its own cause, which seems to me impossible. Moreover, the statement that the world is simply there, if in answer to a question, presupposes that the question has meaning.

RUSSELL: No, it doesn't need to be its own cause, what I'm saying is that the concept of cause is not applicable to the total.

COPLESTON: Then you would agree with Sartre that the universe is what he calls "gratuitous"?

RUSSELL: Well, the word "gratuitous" suggests that it might be something else; I should say that the universe is just there, and that's all.

COPLESTON: Well, I can't see how you can rule out the legitimacy of asking the question how the total, or anything at all comes to be there. Why something rather than nothing, that is the question? The fact that we gain our knowledge of causality empirically, from particular causes, does not rule out the possibility of asking what the cause of the series is. If the word "cause" were meaningless or if it could be shown that Kant's view of the matter were correct, the question would be illegitimate I agree; but you don't seem to hold that the word "cause" is meaningless, and I do not suppose you are a Kantian.

RUSSELL: I can illustrate what seems to me your fallacy. Every man who exists has a mother, and it seems to me your argument is that therefore the human race must have a mother, but obviously the human race hasn't a mother—that's a different logical sphere.

COPLESTON: Well, I can't really see any parity. If I were saying "every object has a phenomenal cause, therefore, the whole series has a phenomenal cause," there would be a parity; but I'm not saying that; I'm saying, every object has a phenomenal cause if you insist on the infinity of the series—but the series of phenomenal causes is an insufficient explanation of the series. Therefore, the series has not a phenomenal cause but a transcendent cause.

RUSSELL: That's always assuming that not only every particular thing in the world, but the world as a whole must have a cause. For that assumption I see no ground whatever. If you'll give me a ground I'll listen to it.

COPLESTON: Well, the series of events is either caused or it's not caused. If it is caused, there must obviously be a cause outside the series. If it's not caused then it's sufficient to itself, and if it's sufficient to itself it is what I call necessary. But it can't be necessary since each member is contingent, and we've agreed that the total is no reality apart from its members, therefore, it can't be necessary. Therefore, it can't be uncaused, therefore it must have a cause. And I should like to observe in passing that the statement "the world is simply there and is inexplicable" can't be got out of logical analysis.

RUSSELL: I don't want to seem arrogant, but it does seem to me that I can conceive things that you say the human mind can't conceive. As for things not having a cause, the physicists assure us that individual quantum transition in atoms have no cause.

COPLESTON: Well, I wonder now whether that isn't simply a temporary inference.

RUSSELL: It may be, but it does show that physicists' minds can conceive it.

COPLESTON: Yes, I agree, some scientists—physicists—are willing to allow for indetermination within a restricted field. But very many scientists are not so willing. I think that Professor Dingle, of London University, maintains that the Heisenberg uncertainty principle tells us something about the success (or the lack of it) of the present atomic theory in correlating observations, but not about nature in itself, and many physicists would accept this view. In any case, I don't see how physicists can fail to accept the theory in practice, even if they don't do so in theory. I cannot see how science could be conducted on any other assumption than that of order and intelligibility in nature. The physicist presupposes, at least tacitly, that there is some sense in investigating nature and looking for the causes of events, just as the detective presupposes that there is some sense in looking for the cause of a murder. The metaphysician assumes that there is sense in looking for the reason or cause of phenomena, and, not being a Kantian, I consider that the metaphysician is as justified in his assumption as the physicist. When Sartre, for example, says that the world is gratuitous, I think that he has not sufficiently considered what is implied by "gratuitous."

RUSSELL: I think—there seems to me a certain unwarrantable extension here; a physicist looks for causes; that does not necessarily imply that there are causes everywhere. A man may look for gold without assuming that there is gold everywhere; if he finds gold, well and good, if he doesn't he's had bad luck. The same is true when the physicists look for causes. As for Sartre, I don't profess to know what he means, and I shouldn't like to be thought to interpret him, but for my part, I do think the notion of the world having an explanation is a mistake. I don't see why one should expect it to have, and I think what you say about what the scientist assumes is an over-statement.

COPLESTON: Well, it seems to me that the scientist does make some such assumption. When he experiments to find out some particular truth, behind that experiment lies the assumption that the universe is not simply discontinuous. There is the possibility of finding out a truth by experiment. The experiment may be a bad one, it may lead to no result, or not to the result that he wants, but that at any rate there is the possibility, through experiment, of finding out the truth that he assumes. And that seems to me to assume an ordered and intelligible universe.

RUSSELL: I think you're generalising more than is necessary. Undoubtedly the scientist assumes that this sort of thing is likely to be found and will often be found. He does not assume that it will be found, and that's a very important matter in modern physics.

COPLESTON: Well, I think he does assume or is bound to assume it tacitly in practice. It may be that, to quote Professor Haldane, "when I light the gas under the kettle, some of the water molecules will fly off as vapour, and there is no way of finding out which will do so," but it doesn't follow necessarily that the idea of chance must be introduced except in relation to our knowledge.

RUSSELL: No it doesn't—at least if I may believe what he says. He's finding out quite a lot of things—the scientist is finding out quite a lot of things that are happening in the world, which are, at first, beginnings of causal chains—first causes which haven't in themselves got causes. He does not assume that everything has a cause.

COPLESTON: Surely that's a first cause within a certain selected field. It's a relatively first cause.

RUSSELL: I don't think he'd say so. If there's a world in which most events, but not all, have causes, he will then be able to depict the probabilities and uncertainties by assuming that this particular event you're interested in probably has a cause. And since in any case you won't get more than probability that's good enough.

COPLESTON: It may be that the scientist doesn't hope to obtain more than probability, but in raising the question he assumes that the question of explanation has a meaning. But your general point then, Lord Russell, is that it's illegitimate even to ask the question of the cause of the world?

RUSSELL: Yes, that's my position.

COPLESTON: If it's a question that for you has no meaning, it's of course very difficult to discuss it, isn't it?

RUSSELL: Yes, it is very difficult. What do you say—shall we pass on to some other issue?

## RELIGIOUS EXPERIENCE

COPLESTON: Let's. Well, perhaps I might say a word about religious experience, and then we can go on to moral experience. I don't regard religious experience as a strict proof of the existence of God, so the character of the discussion changes somewhat, but I think it's true to say that the best explanation of it is the existence of God. By religious experience I don't mean simply feeling good. I mean a loving, but unclear, awareness of some object which irresistibly seems to the experiencer as something transcending the self, something transcending all the normal objects of experience, something which cannot be pictured or conceptualized, but of the reality of which doubt is impossible—at least during the experience. I should claim that cannot be explained adequately and without residue, simply subjectively. The actual basic experience at any rate is most easily explained on the hypotheses that there is actually some objective cause of that experience.

RUSSELL: I should reply to that line of argument that the whole argument from our own mental states to something outside us, is a very tricky affair. Even where we all admit its validity, we only feel justified in doing so, I think, because of the consensus of mankind. If there's a crowd in a room and there's a clock in a room, they can all see the clock. The fact that they can all see it tends to make them think that it's not an hallucination: whereas these religious experiences do tend to be very private.

COPLESTON: Yes, they do. I'm speaking strictly of mystical experience proper, and I certainly don't include, by the way, what are called visions. I mean simply the experience, and I quite admit it's indefinable, of the transcendent object or of what seems to be a transcendent object. I remember Julian Huxley in some lecture saying that religious experience, or mystical experience, is as much a real experience as falling in love or appreciating poetry and art. Well, I believe that when we appreciate poetry and art we appreciate definite poems or a definite work of art. If we fall in love, well, we fall in love with somebody and not with nobody.

RUSSELL: May I interrupt for a moment here. That is by no means always the case. Japanese novelists never consider that they have achieved a success unless large numbers of real people commit suicide for love of the imaginary heroine.

COPLESTON: Well, I must take your word for these goings on in Japan. I haven't committed suicide, I'm glad to say, but I have been strongly influenced in the taking of two important steps in my life by two biographies. However, I must say I see little resemblance between the real influence of those books on me and the mystic experience proper, so far, that is, as an outsider can obtain an idea of that experience.

RUSSELL: Well, I mean we wouldn't regard God as being on the same level as the characters in a work of fiction. You'll admit there's a distinction here?

COPLESTON: I certainly should. But what I'd say is that the best explanation seems to be the not purely subjectivist explanation. Of course, a subjectivist explanation is possible in the case of certain people in whom there is little relation between the experience and life, in the case of deluded people and hallucinated people, and so on. But when you get what one might call the pure type, say St. Francis of Assisi, when you get an experience that results in an overflow of dynamic and creative love, the best explanation of that it seems to me is the actual existence of an objective cause of the experience.

RUSSELL: Well, I'm not contending in a dogmatic way that there is not a God. What I'm contending is that we don't know that there is. I can only take what is recorded as I should take other records and I do find that a very great many things are reported, and I am sure you would not accept things about demons and devils and what not—and they're reported in exactly the same tone of voice and with exactly the same conviction. And the mystic, if his vision is veridical, may be said to know that there are devils. But I don't know that there are.

COPLESTON: But surely in the case of the devils there have been people speaking mainly of visions, appearances, angels or demons and so on. I should rule out the visual appearances, because I think they can be explained apart from the existence of the object which is supposed to be seen.

RUSSELL: But don't you think there are abundant recorded cases of people who believe that they've heard Satan speaking to them in their hearts, in just the same way as the mystics assert God—and I'm not talking now of an external vision, I'm talking of a purely mental experience. That seems to be an experience of the same sort as mystics' experience of God, and I don't see that from what mystics tell us you can get any argument for God which is not equally an argument for Satan.

COPLESTON: I quite agree, of course, that people have imagined or thought they have heard or seen Satan. And I have no wish in passing to deny the existence of Satan. But I do not think that people have claimed to have experienced Satan in the precise way in which mystics claim to have experienced God. Take the case of a non-Christian, Plotinus. He admits the experience is something inexpressible, the object is an object of love, and therefore, not an object that causes horror and disgust. And the effect of that experience is, I should say, borne out, or I mean the validity of the experience is borne out in the records of the life of Plotinus. At any rate it is more reasonable to suppose that he had that experience if we're willing to accept Porphyry's account of Plotinus's general kindness and benevolence.

RUSSELL: The fact that a belief has a good moral effect upon a man is no evidence whatsoever in favour of its truth.

COPLESTON: No, but if it could actually be proved that the belief was actually responsible for a good effect on a man's life, I should consider it a presumption in favour of some truth, at any rate of the positive part of the belief not of its entire validity. But in any case I am using the character of the life as evidence in favour of the mystic's veracity and sanity rather than as a proof of the truth of his beliefs.

RUSSELL: But even that I don't think is any evidence. I've had experiences myself that have altered my character profoundly. And I thought at the time at any rate that it was altered for the good. Those experiences were important, but they did not involve the existence of something outside me, and I don't think that if I'd thought they did, the fact that they had a wholesome effect would have been any evidence that I was right.

COPLESTON: No, but I think that the good effect would attest your veracity in describing your experience. Please remember that I'm not saying that a mystic's mediation or interpretation of his experience should be immune from discussion or criticism.

RUSSELL: Obviously the character of a young man may be—and often is—immensely affected for good by reading about some great man in history, and it may happen that the great man is a myth and doesn't exist, but the boy is just as much affected for good as if he did. There have been such people. Plutarch's *Lives* take Lycurgus as an example, who certainly did not exist, but you might be very much influenced by reading Lycurgus under the impression that he had previously existed. You would then be influenced by an object that you'd loved, but it wouldn't be an existing object.

COPLESTON: I agree with you on that, of course, that a man may be influenced by a character in fiction. Without going into the question of what it is precisely that influences him (I should say a real value) I think that the situation of that man and of the mystic are different. After all the man who is influenced by Lycurgus hasn't got the irresistible impression that he's experienced in some way the ultimate reality.

RUSSELL: I don't think you've quite got my point about these historical characters—these unhistorical characters in history. I'm not assuming what you call an effect on the reason. I'm assuming that the young man reading about this person and believing him to be real loves him—which is quite easy to happen, and yet he's loving a phantom.

COPLESTON: In one sense he's loving a phantom that's perfectly true, in the sense, I mean, that he's loving X or Y who doesn't exist. But at the same time, it is not, I think, the phantom as such that the young man loves; he perceives a real value, an idea which he recognises as objectively valid, and that's what excites his love.

RUSSELL: Well, in the same sense we had before about the characters in fiction.

COPLESTON: Yes, in one sense the man's loving a phantom—perfectly true. But in another sense he's loving what he perceives to be a value.

## THE MORAL ARGUMENT

RUSSELL: But aren't you now saying in effect, I mean by God whatever is good or the sum total of what is good—the system of what is good, and, therefore, when a young man loves anything that is good he is loving God. Is that what you're saying, because if so, it wants a bit of arguing.

COPLESTON: I don't say, of course, that God is the sum-total or system of what is good in the pantheistic sense; I'm not a pantheist, but I do think that all goodness reflects God in some way and proceeds from Him, so that in a sense the man who loves what is truly good, loves God even if he doesn't advert to God. But still I agree that the validity of such an interpretation of a man's conduct depends on the recognition of God's existence, obviously.

RUSSELL: Yes, but that's a point to be proved.

COPLESTON: Quite so, but I regard the metaphysical argument as probative, but there we differ.

RUSSELL: You see, I feel that some things are good and that other things are bad. I love the things that are good, that I think are good, and I hate the things that I think are bad. I don't say that these things are good because they participate in the Divine goodness.

COPLESTON: Yes, but what's your justification for distinguishing between good and bad or how do you view the distinction between them?

RUSSELL: I don't have any justification any more than I have when I distinguish between blue and yellow. What is my justification for distinguishing between blue and yellow? I can see they are different.

COPLESTON: Well, that is an excellent justification, I agree. You distinguish blue and yellow by seeing them, so you distinguish good and bad by what faculty?

RUSSELL: By my feelings.

COPLESTON: By your feelings. Well, that's what I was asking. You think that good and evil have reference simply to feeling?

RUSSELL: Well, why does one type of object look yellow and another look blue? I can more or less give an answer to that thanks to the physicists, and as to why I think one sort of thing good and another evil, probably there is an answer of the same sort, but it hasn't been gone into in the same way and I couldn't give it you.

COPLESTON: Well, let's take the behaviour of the Commandant of Belsen. That appears to you as undesirable and evil and to me too. To Adolf Hitler we suppose it appeared as something good and desirable. I suppose you'd have to admit that for Hitler it was good and for you it is evil.

RUSSELL: No, I shouldn't quite go so far as that. I mean, I think people can make mistakes in that as they can in other things. If you have jaundice you see things yellow that are not yellow. You're making a mistake.

COPLESTON: Yes, one can make mistakes, but can you make a mistake if it's simply a question of reference to a feeling or emotion? Surely Hitler would be the only possible judge of what appealed to his emotions.

RUSSELL: It would be quite right to say that it appealed to his emotions, but you can say various things about that among others, that if that sort of thing makes that sort of appeal to Hitler's emotions, then Hitler makes quite a different appeal to my emotions.

COPLESTON: Granted. But there's no objective criterion outside feeling then for condemning the conduct of the Commandant of Belsen, in your view?

RUSSELL: No more than there is for the colour-blind person who's in exactly the same state. Why do we intellectually condemn the colour-blind man? Isn't it because he's in the minority?

COPLESTON: I would say because he is lacking in a thing which normally belongs to human nature.

RUSSELL: Yes, but if he were in the majority, we shouldn't say that.

COPLESTON: Then you'd say that there's no criterion outside feeling that will enable one to distinguish between the behaviour of the Commandant of Belsen and the behaviour, say, of Sir Stafford Cripps or the Archbishop of Canterbury.

RUSSELL: The feeling is a little too simplified. You've got to take account of the effects of actions and your feelings towards those effects. You see, you can have an argument about it if you say that certain sorts of occurrences are the sort you like and certain others the sort you don't like. Then you have to take account of the effects of actions. You can very well say that the effects of the actions of the Commandant of Belsen were painful and unpleasant.

COPLESTON: They certainly were, I agree, very painful and unpleasant to all the people in the camp.

RUSSELL: Yes, but not only to the people in the camp, but to outsiders contemplating them also.

COPLESTON: Yes, quite true in imagination. But that's my point. I don't approve of them, and I know you don't approve of them, but I don't see what ground you have for not approving of them, because after all, to the Commandant of Belsen himself, they're pleasant, those actions.

RUSSELL: Yes, but you see I don't need any more ground in that case than I do in the case of colour perception. There are some people who think everything is yellow, there are people suffering from jaundice, and I don't agree with these people. I can't prove that the things are not yellow, there isn't any proof, but most people agree with me that they're not yellow, and most people agree with me that the Commandant of Belsen was making mistakes.

COPLESTON: Well, do you accept any moral obligation?

RUSSELL: Well, I should have to answer at considerable length to answer that. Practically speaking—yes. Theoretically speaking I should have to define moral obligation rather carefully.

COPLESTON: Well, do you think that the word "ought" simply has an emotional connotation?

RUSSELL: No, I don't think that, because you see, as I was saying a moment ago, one has to take account of the effects, and I think right conduct is that which would probably produce the greatest possible balance in intrinsic value of all the acts possible in the circumstances, and you've got to take account of the probable effects of your action in considering what is right.

COPLESTON: Well, I brought in moral obligation because I think that one can approach the question of God's existence in that way. The vast majority of the human race will make, and always have made, some distinction between right and wrong. The vast majority I think has some consciousness of an obligation in the moral sphere. It's my opinion that the perception of values and the consciousness of moral law and obligation are best explained through the hypothesis of a transcendent ground of value and of an author of the moral law. I do mean by "author of the moral law" an arbitrary author of the moral law. I think, in fact, that those modern atheists who have argued in the converse way "there is no God; therefore, there are no absolute values and no absolute law," are quite logical.

RUSSELL: I don't like the word "absolute." I don't think there is anything absolute whatever. The moral law, for example, is always changing. At one period in the development of the human race, almost everybody thought cannibalism was a duty.

COPLESTON: Well, I don't see that differences in particular moral judgments are any conclusive argument against the universality of the moral law. Let's assume for the moment that there are absolute moral values, even on that hypothesis it's only to be expected that different individuals and different groups should enjoy varying degrees of insight into those values.

RUSSELL: I'm inclined to think that "ought," the feeling that one has about "ought" is an echo of what has been told one by one's parents or one's nurses.

COPLESTON: Well, I wonder if you can explain away the idea of the "ought" merely in terms of nurses and parents. I really don't see how it can be conveyed to anybody in other terms than itself. It seems to me that if there is a moral order bearing upon the human conscience, that that moral order is unintelligible apart from the existence of God.

RUSSELL: Then you have to say one or other of two things. Either God only speaks to a very small percentage of mankind—which happens to include yourself—or He deliberately says things that are not true in talking to the consciences of savages.

COPLESTON: Well, you see, I'm not suggesting that God actually dictates moral precepts to the conscience. The human being's ideas of the content of the moral law depends certainly to a large extent on education and environment, and a man has to use his reason in assessing the validity of the actual moral ideas of his social group. But the possibility of criticising the accepted moral code presupposes that there is an objective standard, that there is an ideal moral order, which imposes itself (I mean the obligatory character of which can be recognised). I think that the recognition of this ideal moral order is part of the recognition of contingency. It implies the existence of a real foundation of God.

RUSSELL: But the law-giver has always been, it seems to me, one's parents or someone like. There are plenty of terrestrial law-givers to account for it, and that would explain why people's consciences are so amazingly different in different times and places.

COPLESTON: It helps to explain differences in the perception of particular moral values, which otherwise are inexplicable. It will help to explain changes in the matter of the moral law in the content of the precepts as accepted by this or that nation, or this or that individual. But the form of it, what Kant calls the categorical imperative, the "ought," I really don't see how that can possibly be conveyed to anybody by nurse or parent because there aren't any possible terms, so far as I can see, with which it can be explained. It can't be defined in other terms than itself, because once you've defined it in other terms than itself you've explained it away. It's no longer a moral "ought." It's something else.

RUSSELL: Well, I think the sense of "ought" is the effect of somebody's imagined disapproval, it may be God's imagined disapproval, but it's somebody's imagined disapproval. And I think that is what is meant by "ought."

COPLESTON: It seems to me to be external customs and taboos and things of that sort which can most easily be explained simply through environment and education, but all that seems to me to belong to what I call the matter of the law, the content. The idea of the "ought" as such can never be conveyed to a man by the tribal chief or by anybody else, because there are no other terms in which it could be conveyed. It seems to me entirely—[Russell breaks in].

RUSSELL: But I don't see any reason to say that—I mean we all know about conditioned reflexes. We know that an animal, if punished habitually for a certain sort of act, after a time will refrain. I don't think the animal refrains from arguing within himself, "Master will be angry if I do this." He has a feeling that that's not the thing to do. That's what we can do with ourselves and nothing more.

COPLESTON: I see no reason to suppose that an animal has a consciousness of moral obligation; and we certainly don't regard an animal as morally responsible for his acts of disobedience. But a man has a consciousness of obligation and of moral values. I see no reason to suppose that one could condition all men as one can "condition" an animal, and I don't suppose you'd really want to do so even if one could. If "behaviourism" were true, there would be no objective moral distinction between the emperor Nero and St. Francis of Assisi. I can't help feeling, Lord Russell, you know, that you regard the conduct of the Commandant at Belsen as morally reprehensible, and that you yourself would never under any circumstances act in that way, even if you thought, or had reason to think, that possibly the balance of the happiness of the human race might be increased through some people being treated in that abominable manner.

RUSSELL: No. I wouldn't imitate the conduct of a mad dog. The fact that I wouldn't do it doesn't really bear on this question we're discussing.

COPLESTON: No, but if you were making a utilitarian explanation of right and wrong in terms of consequences, it might be held, and I suppose some of the Nazis of the better type would have held that although it's lamentable to have to act in this way, yet the balance in the long run leads to greater happiness. I don't think you'd say that, would you? I think you'd say that that sort of action is wrong—and in itself, quite apart from whether the general balance of happiness is increased or not. Then, if you're prepared to say that, then I think you must have some criterion of right and wrong, that is outside the criterion of feeling, at any rate. To me, that admission would ultimately result in the admission of an ultimate ground of value in God.

RUSSELL: I think we are perhaps getting into confusion. It is not direct feeling about the act by which I should judge, but rather a feeling as to the effects. And I can't admit any circumstances in which certain kinds of behaviour, such as you have been discussing, would do good. I can't imagine circumstances in which they would have a beneficial effect. I think the persons who think they do are deceiving themselves. But if there were circumstances in which they would have a beneficial effect, then I might be obliged, however reluctantly, to say—"Well, I don't like these things, but I will acquiesce in them," just as I acquiesce in the Criminal Law, although I profoundly dislike punishment.

COPLESTON: Well, perhaps it's time I summed up my position. I've argued two things. First, that the existence of God can be philosophically proved by a metaphysical argument; secondly, that it is only the existence of God that will make sense of man's moral experience and of religious experience. Personally, I think that your way of accounting for man's moral judgments leads inevitably to a contradiction between what your theory demands and your own spontaneous judgments. Moreover, your theory explains moral obligation away, and explaining away is not explanation. As regards the metaphysical argument, we are apparently in agreement that what we call the world consists simply of contingent beings. That is, of beings no one of which can account for its own existence. You say that the series of events needs no explanation: I say that if there were no necessary being, no being which must exist and cannot not-exist, nothing would exist. The infinity of the series of contingent beings, even if proved, would be irrelevant. Something does exist; therefore, there must be something which accounts for this fact, a being which is outside the series of contingent beings. If you had admitted this, we could then have discussed whether that being is personal, good, and so on. On the actual point discussed, whether there is or is not a necessary being, I find myself, I think, in agreement with the great majority of classical philosophers.

You maintain, I think, that existing beings are simply there, and that I have no justification for raising the question of the explanation of their existence. But I would like to point out that this position cannot be substantiated by logical analysis; it expresses a philosophy which itself stands in need of proof. I think we have reached an impasse because our ideas of philosophy are radically different; it seems to me that what I call a part of philosophy, that you call the whole, insofar at least as philosophy is rational. It seems to me, if you will pardon my saying so, that besides your own logical system—which you call "modern" in opposition to antiquated logic (a tendentious adjective)—you maintain a philosophy which cannot be substantiated by logical analysis. After all, the problem of God's existence is an existential problem whereas logical analysis does not deal directly with problems of existence. So it seems to me, to declare that the terms involved in one set of problems are meaningless because they are not required in dealing with another set of problems, is to settle from the beginning the nature and extent of philosophy, and that is itself a philosophical act which stands in need of justification.

RUSSELL: Well, I should like to say just a few words by way of summary on my side. First, as to the metaphysical argument: I don't admit the connotations of such a term as "contingent" or the possibility of explanation in Fr. Copleston's sense. I think the word "contingent" inevitably suggests the possibility of something that wouldn't have this what you might call accidental character of just being there, and I don't think is true except in the purely causal sense. You can sometimes give a causal explanation of one thing as being the effect of something else, but that is merely referring one thing to another thing and there's no—to my mind—explanation in Fr. Copleston's sense of anything at all, nor is there any meaning in calling things "contingent" because there isn't anything else they could be. That's what I should say about that, but I should like to say a few words about Fr. Copleston's accusation that I regard logic as all philosophy—that is by no means the case. I don't by any means regard logic as all philosophy. I think logic is an essential part of philosophy and logic has to be used in philosophy, and in that I think he and I are at one. When the logic that he uses was new—namely, in the time of Aristotle, there had to be a great deal of fuss made about it; Aristotle made a lot of fuss about that logic. Nowadays it's become old and respectable, and you don't have to make so much fuss about it. The logic that I believe in is comparatively new, and therefore I have to imitate Aristotle in making a fuss about it; but it's not that I think it's all philosophy by any means—I don't think so. I think it's an important part of philosophy, and when I say that, I don't find a meaning for this or that word, that is a position of detail based upon what I've found out about that particular word, from thinking about it. It's not a general position that all words that are used in metaphysics are nonsense, or anything like that which I don't really hold.

As regards the moral argument, I do find that when one studies anthropology or history, there are people who think it their duty to perform acts which I think abominable, and I certainly can't, therefore, attribute Divine origin to the matter of moral obligation, which Fr. Copleston doesn't ask me to; but I think even the form of moral obligation, when it takes the form of enjoining you to eat your father or what not, doesn't seem to me to be such a very beautiful and noble thing; and, therefore, I cannot attribute a Divine origin to this sense of moral obligation, which I think is quite easily accounted for in quite other ways.

# Martin Buber

Martin Buber (1878–1965), original Jewish thinker and student of
Hasidism, has exerted, through *I and Thou* and other works, a tremendous influence upon contemporary Christian as well as Jewish
thought.

# 18

# *The Eternal Thou*

The extended lines of relations meet in the eternal *Thou*.

Every particular *Thou* is a glimpse through to the eternal *Thou;* by means of every particular *Thou* the primary word addresses the eternal *Thou*. Through this mediation of the *Thou* of all beings fulfilment, and non-fulfilment, of relations comes to them: the inborn *Thou* is realized in each relation and consummated in none. It is consummated only in the direct relation with the *Thou* that by its nature cannot become *It*.

Men have addressed their eternal *Thou* with many names. In singing of Him who was thus named they always had the *Thou* in mind: the first myths were hymns of praise. Then the names took refuge in the language of *It;* men were more and more strongly moved to think of and to address their eternal *Thou* as an *It*. But all God's names are hallowed, for in them He is not merely spoken about, but also spoken to.

Many men wish to reject the word God as a legitimate usage, because it is so misused. It is indeed the most heavily laden of all the words used by men. For that very reason it is the most imperishable and most indispensable. What does all mistaken talk about God's being and works (though there has been, and can be, no other talk about these) matter in comparison with the one truth that all men who have addressed God had God Himself in mind? For he who speaks the word God and really has *Thou* in mind (whatever the illusion by which he is held), addresses the true *Thou* of his life, which cannot be limited by another *Thou*, and to which he stands in a relation that gathers up and includes all others.

But when he, too, who abhors the name, and believes himself to be godless, gives his whole being to addressing the *Thou* of his life, as a *Thou* that cannot be limited by another, he addresses God . . . .

Every real relation with a being or life in the world is exclusive. Its *Thou* is freed, steps forth, is single, and confronts you. It fills the heavens. This does not mean that nothing else exists; but all else lives in *its* light. As long as the presence of the relation continues, this its cosmic range is inviolable. But as soon as a *Thou* becomes *It*, the cosmic range of the relation appears as an offence to the world, its exclusiveness as an exclusion of the universe.

In the relation with God unconditional exclusiveness and unconditional inclusiveness are one. He who enters on the absolute relation is concerned with nothing isolated anymore, neither things nor beings, neither earth nor heaven; but everything is gathered up in the relation. For to step into pure relation is not to disregard everything but to see everything in the *Thou*, not to renounce the world but to establish it on its true basis. To look away from the world, or to stare at it, does not help a man to reach God; but he who sees the world in Him stands in His presence. "Here world, there God" is the language of *It*; "God in the world" is another language of *It*; but to eliminate or leave behind nothing at all, to include the whole world in the *Thou*, to give the world its due and its truth, to include nothing beside God but everything in Him—this is full and complete relation.

Men do not find God if they stay in the world. They do not find Him if they leave the world. He who goes out with his whole being to meet his *Thou* and carries to it all being that is in the world, finds Him who cannot be sought.

Of course God is the "wholly Other": but He is also the wholly Same, the wholly Present. Of course He is the *mysterium tremendum* that appears and overthrows; but He is also the mystery of the self-evident, nearer to me than my *I*.

If you explore the life of things and of conditioned being you come to the unfathomable, if you deny the life of things and of conditioned being you stand before nothingness, if you hallow this life you meet the living God.

Man's sense of *Thou*, which experiences in the relations with every particular *Thou* the disappointment of the change to *It*, strives out but not away from them all to its eternal *Thou*; but not as something is sought: actually there is no such thing as seeking God, for there is nothing in which He could not be found. How foolish and hopeless would be the man who turned aside from the course of his life in order to seek God; even though he won all the wisdom of solitude and all the power of concentrated being he would miss God. Rather is it as when a man goes his way and simply wishes that it might be the way: in the strength of his wish his striving is expressed. Every relational event is a stage that affords him a glimpse into the consummating event. So in each event he does not partake, but also (for he is w ?ting) does partake, of the one event. Waiting, not seeking, he goes his way; hence he is composed before all things, and makes contact with them which helps them. But when he has *found*, his heart is not turned from them, though everything now meets him in the one event. He blesses every cell that sheltered him, and every cell into which he will yet turn. For this finding is not the end, but only the eternal middle, of the way.

It is a finding without seeking, a discovering of the primal, of origin. His sense of *Thou*, which cannot be satiated till he finds the endless *Thou*, had the *Thou* present to it from the beginning; the presence had only to become wholly real to him in the reality of the hallowed life of the world.

God cannot be inferred in anything—in nature, say, as its author, or in history as its master, or in the subject as the self that is thought in it. Something else is not "given" and God then elicited from it; but God is the Being that is directly, most nearly, and lastingly, over against us, that may properly only be addressed, not expressed . . . .

Every real relation in the world is exclusive, the Other breaks in on it and avenges its exclusion. Only in the relation with God are unconditioned exclusiveness and unconditioned inclusiveness one and the same, in which the whole universe is implied.

Every real relation in the world rests on individuation, this is its joy—for only in this way is mutual knowledge of different beings won—and its limitation—for in this way perfect knowledge and being known are foregone. But in the perfect relation my *Thou* comprehends but is not my Self, my limited knowledge opens out into a state in which I am boundlessly known.

Every real relation in the world is consummated in the interchange of actual and potential being; every isolated *Thou* is bound to enter the chrysalis state of the *It* in order to take wings anew. But in pure relation potential being is simply actual being as it draws breath, and in it the *Thou* remains present. By its nature the eternal *Thou* is eternally *Thou*; only our nature compels us to draw it into the world and the talk of *It*.

The world of *It* is set in the context of space and time.

The world of *Thou* is not set in the context of either of these.

Its context is in the Centre, where the extended lines of relations meet—in the eternal *Thou*.

In the great privilege of pure relation the privileges of the world of *It* are abolished. By virtue of this privilege there exists the unbroken world of *Thou*: the isolated moments of relations are bound up in a life of world solidarity. By virtue of this privilege formative power belongs to the world of *Thou*: spirit can penetrate and transform the world of *It*. By virtue of this privilege we are not given up to alienation from the world and the loss of reality by the *I*—to domination by the ghostly. Turning is the recognition of the Centre and the act of turning again to it. In this act of the being the buried relational power of man rises again, the wave that carries all the spheres of relation swells in living streams to give new life to our world.

Perhaps not to our world alone. For this double movement, of estrangement from the primal Source, in virtue of which the universe is sustained in the process of becoming, and of turning towards the primal Source, in virtue of which the universe is released in being, may be perceived as the metacosmical primal form that dwells in the world as a whole in its relation to that which is not the world—form whose twofold nature is represented among men by the twofold nature of their attitudes, their primary words, and their aspects of the world. Both parts of this movement develop, fraught with destiny, in time, and are compassed by grace in the timeless creation that is, incomprehensibly, at once emancipation and preservation, release and binding. Our knowledge of twofold nature is silent before the paradox of the primal mystery.

The spheres in which the world of relation is built are three.

First, our life with nature, in which the relation clings to the threshold of speech.

Second, our life with men, in which the relation takes on the form of speech.

Third, our life with spiritual beings, where the relation, being without speech, yet begets it.

In every sphere in its own way, through each process of becoming that is present to us, we look out toward the fringe of the eternal *Thou;* in each we are aware of a breath from the eternal *Thou;* in each *Thou* we address the eternal *Thou.*

Every sphere is compassed in the eternal *Thou,* but it is not compassed in them.

Through every sphere shines the one present.

We can, however, remove each sphere from the present.

From our life with nature we can lift out the "physical" world, the world of consistency, from our life with men the "psychical" world, the world of sensibility, and from our life with spiritual beings the "noetic" world, the world of validity. But now their transparency, and with it their meaning, has been taken from them; each sphere has become dull and capable of being used—and remains dull even though we light it up with the names of Cosmos and Eros and Logos. For actually there is a cosmos for man only when the universe becomes his home, with its holy hearth whereon he offers sacrifice; there is Eros for man only when beings become for him pictures of the eternal, and community is revealed along with them; and there is Logos for man only when he addresses the mystery with work and service for the spirit.

Form's silent asking, man's loving speech, the mute proclamation of the creature, are all gates leading into the presence of the Word.

But when the full and complete meeting is to take place, the gates are united in one gateway of real life, and you no longer know through which you have entered . . . .

What is the eternal, primal phenomenon, present here and now, of that which we term revelation? It is the phenomenon that a man does not pass, from the moment of the supreme meeting, the same being as he entered into it. The moment of meeting is not an "experience" that stirs in the receptive soul and grows to perfect blessedness; rather, in that moment something happens to the man. At times it is like a light breath, at times like a wrestling-bout, but always—it *happens*. The man who emerges from the act of pure relation that so involves his being has now in his being something more that has grown in him, of which he did not know before and whose origin he is not rightly able to indicate. However the source of this new thing is classified in scientific orientation of the world, with its authorized efforts to establish an unbroken causality, we, whose concern is real consideration of the real, cannot have our purpose served with subconsciousness or any other apparatus of the soul. The reality is that we receive what we did not hitherto have, and receive it in such a way that we know it has been given to us. In the language of the Bible, "Those who wait upon the Lord shall renew their strength." In the language of Nietzsche, who in his account remains loyal to reality, "We take and do not ask who it is there that gives."

Man receives, and he receives not a specific "content" but a Presence, a Presence as power. This Presence and this power include three things, undivided, yet in such a way that we may consider them separately. First, there is the whole fulness of real mutual action, of the being raised and bound up in relation: the man can give no account at all of how the binding in relation is brought about, nor does it in any way lighten his life—it makes life heavier, but heavy with meaning. Secondly, there is the inexpressible confirmation of meaning. Meaning is assured. Nothing can any longer be meaningless. The question about the meaning of life is no longer there. But were it there, it would not have to be answered. You do not know how to exhibit and define the meaning of life, you have no formula or picture for it, and yet it has more certitude for you than the perceptions of your senses. What does the revealed and concealed meaning purpose with us, desire from us? It does not wish to be explained (nor are we able to do that) but only to be done by us. Thirdly, this meaning is not that of "another life," but that of this life of ours, not one of a world "yonder" but that of this world of ours, and it desires its confirmation in this life and in relation with this world. This meaning can be received, but not experienced; it cannot be experienced but it can be done, and this is its purpose with us. The assurance I have of it does not wish to be sealed within me, but it wishes to be born by me into the world. But just as the meaning itself does not permit itself to be transmitted and made into knowledge generally current and admissible, so confirmation of it cannot be transmitted as a valid Ought; it is not prescribed, it is not specified on any tablet, to be raised above all men's heads. The meaning that has been received can be proved true by each man only in the singleness of his being and the singleness of his life. As no prescription can lead us to the meeting, so none leads from it. As only acceptance of the Presence is necessary for the approach to the meeting, so in a new sense is it so when we emerge from it. As we reach the meeting with the simple *Thou* on our lips, so with the *Thou* on our lips we leave it and return to the world.

That before which, in which, out of which, and into which we live, even the mystery, has remained what it was. It has become present to us and in its presentness has proclaimed itself to us as salvation; we have "known" it, but we acquire no knowledge from it which might lessen or moderate its mysteriousness. We have come near to God, but not nearer to unveiling being or solving its riddle. We have felt release, but not discovered a "solution." We cannot approach others with what we have received, and say "You must know this, you must do this." We can only go, and confirm its truth. And this, too, is no "ought," but we can, we *must*.

This is the eternal revelation that is present here and now. I know of no revelation and believe in none whose primal phenomenon is not precisely this. I do not believe in a self-naming of God, a self-definition of God before men. The Word of revelation is *I am that I am*. That which reveals is that which reveals. That which is *is*, and nothing more. The eternal source of strength streams, the eternal contact persists, the eternal voice sounds forth, and nothing more.

# Paul Tillich

Paul Tillich (1886–1965), German-born theologian most of whose career was spent in the United States, is the author of numerous well-
known and widely influential works, including his three-volume
*Systematic Theology.*

# 19

# *Two Types of Philosophy of Religion*

One can distinguish two ways of approaching God: the way of overcoming estrangement and the way of meeting a stranger. In the first way man
discovers *himself* when he discovers God; he discovers something that is
identical with himself although it transcends him infinitely, something from
which he is estranged, but from which he never has been and never can be
separated. In the second way man meets a *stranger* when he meets God. The
meeting is accidental. Essentially they do not belong to each other. They may
become friends on a tentative and conjectural basis. But there is no certainty
about the stranger man has met. He may disappear, and only *probable* statements can be made about His nature.

The two ways symbolize the two possible types of philosophy of
religion: the ontological type and the cosmological type. The way of overcoming estrangement symbolizes the ontological method in the philosophy of
religion. The way of meeting a stranger symbolizes the cosmological method.
It is the purpose of this essay to show: (1) that the ontological method is basic
for every philosophy of religion, (2) that the cosmological method without
the ontological as its basis leads to a destructive cleavage between philosophy
and religion, and (3) that on the basis of the ontological approach and with a
dependent use of the cosmological way, philosophy of religion contributes
to the reconciliation between religion and secular culture. These three points
shall be discussed on the basis of extensive references to the classic expressions of the two types of philosophy of religion in the thirteenth century.

"Two Types of Philosophy of Religion," *Union Seminary Quarterly Review*, May, 1964, pp.
3–13. Copyright, Union Theological Seminary, New York, and used by permission of the
publisher.

## THE WORLD HISTORICAL PROBLEM

In two developments Western humanity has overcome its age-old bondage under the "powers": those half religious-half magical, half divine-half demonic, half superhuman-half subhuman, half abstract-half concrete beings who are the genuine material of the *mythos*. These "powers" were conquered *religiously* by their subjection to one of them, the god of the prophets of Israel; His quality as the god of justice enabled Him to become the universal God. The "powers" were conquered *philosophically* by their subjection to a principle more real than all of them; its quality as embracing all qualities enabled it to become the universal principle. In this process the "powers" lost their sacred character and with it their hold on the human consciousness. All holiness was transferred to the absolute God or to the absolute principle. The gods disappeared and became servants of the absolute God, or appearances of the absolute principle. But the "powers," although subjected and transformed, were not extinguished. They could and can return and establish a reign of superstition and fear; and even the absolute God can become *one* power beside others, perhaps the highest, but not the absolute. It is one of the tasks of the philosophy of religion to protect religion as well as the scientific interpretation of reality against the return of the "powers" who threaten both at the same time.

The problem created by the subjection of the "powers" to the absolute God and to the absolute principle is *the problem of the two Absolutes*. How are they related to each other? The religious and the philosophical Absolutes, *Deus* and *esse* cannot be unconnected! What is their connection from the point of view of being as well as of knowing? In the simple statement "God *is*," the connection is achieved; but the character of this connection is *the* problem in all problems of the philosophy of religion. The different answers given to this question are milestones on the road of Western religious consciousness; and this road is a road towards ever-increasing *loss* of religious consciousness. Philosophy of religion, although not primarily responsible for this development, must ask itself whether according to its principles this was an unavoidable development and whether a reversal is possible.

## THE AUGUSTINIAN SOLUTION

Augustine, after he had experienced all the implications of ancient skepticism, gave a classical answer to the problem of the two Absolutes: They coincide in the nature of truth. *Veritas* is presupposed in every philosophical argument; and *veritas* is God. You cannot deny truth as such because you could do it only in the name of truth, thus establishing truth. And if you establish truth you affirm God. "Where I have found the truth, there I have found my God, the truth itself," Augustine says. The question of the two Ultimates is solved in such a way that the religious Ultimate is presupposed in every philosophical question, including the question of God. *God is the presupposition of the question of God.* This is the ontological solution of the problem of the philosophy of religion. God can never be reached if He is the *object* of a question, and not its *basis*.

The Franciscan school of the thirteenth-century Scholasticism, represented by Alexander of Hales, Bonaventura, and Matthew of Aquasparta, developed the Augustinian solution into a doctrine of the principles of theology, and maintained, in spite of some Aristotelian influences, the ontological type of the philosophy of religion. Their whole emphasis was on the immediacy of the knowledge of God. According to Bonaventura, "God is most truly present to the very soul and immediately knowable"; He is knowable in Himself without media as the one which is common to all. For He is the principle of knowledge, the first truth, in the light of which everything else is known, as Matthew says. As such He is the identity of subject and object. He is not subjected to doubt, which is possible only if subjectivity and objectivity are separated. Psychologically, of course, doubt is possible; but logically, the Absolute is affirmed by the very act of doubt, because it is implied in every statement about the relation between subject and predicate. *Ecce tibi est ipsa veritas. Amplectere illam.* (Thine is truth itself; embrace it.) These ultimate principles and knowledge of them are independent of the changes and relativities of the individual mind; they are the unchangeable, eternal light, appearing in the logical and mathematical axioms as well as in the first categories of thought. These principles are not created functions *of* our mind, but the presence of truth itself and therefore of God, *in* our mind. The Thomistic method of knowledge through sense perception and abstraction may be useful for scientific purposes, but it never can reach the Absolute. Anticipating the consequent development Matthew says about the Aristotelian-Thomistic approach: "For even if this method builds the way of science, it utterly destroys the way of wisdom." Wisdom, *sapientia*, is the knowledge of the principles, of truth itself. And this knowledge is either immediate or it is non-existent. It is distinguished from *humana rationatio*, human reasoning, as well as from *scripturarum autoritas*, the authority of the Holy Scripture. It is *certitudo ex se ipsis*, certainly out of the things themselves, without a medium. Perceiving and accepting the eternal truth are identical, as Alexander of Hales states.

The truth which is presupposed in every question and in every doubt precedes the cleavage into subject and object. Neither of them is an ultimate power. But they participate in the ultimate power above them, in Being itself, in *primum esse*. "Being is what first appears in the intellect" (*Quod primum cadit in intellectu*). And this Being (which is not *a* being) is pure actuality and therefore divine. We always see it, but we do not always notice it; as we see everything in the light without always noticing the light as such.

According to Augustine and his followers the *verum ipsum* is also the *bonum ipsum* because nothing which is less than the ultimate power of Being can be the ultimate power of good. No changeable or conditioned good can overcome the fear that it may be lost. Only in the Unchangeable can be found the *prius* of all goodness. In relation to *esse ipsum* no difference between the cognitive and the appetitive is possible, because a separation of the functions presupposes a separation of subject and object.

The Augustinian tradition can rightly be called mystical, if mysticism is defined as the experience of the identity of subject and object in relation to Being itself. In terms of our ideas of stranger and estrangement, Meister Eckart says: "There is between God and the soul neither strangeness nor remoteness, therefore the soul is not only equal with God but it is . . . the same that He is." This is, of course, a paradoxical statement, as Eckart and all mystics knew; for in order to *state* the identity, an element of non-identity must be presupposed. This proved to be the dynamic and critical point in the ontological approach.

On this basis the ontological argument for the existence of God must be understood. It is neither an argument, nor does it deal with the existence of God, although it often has been expressed in this form. It is the rational description of the relation of our mind to Being as such. Our mind implies *principia per se nota* [self-evident principles] which have immediate evidence whenever they are noticed: the transcendentalia, *esse, verum, bonum* [being, truth, good]. They constitute the Absolute in which the difference between knowing and known is not actual. This Absolute as the principle of Being has absolute certainty. It is a necessary thought because it is the presupposition of all thought. "The divine substance is known in such a way that it cannot be thought not to be," says Alexander of Hales. The fact that people turn away from this thought is based on individual defects but not on the essential structure of the mind. The mind is able to turn away from what is nearest to the ground of its own structure. This is the nerve of the ontological argument. But Anselm, on the basis of his epistemological realism, transformed the *primum esse* into an *ens realissimum*, the principle into a universal being. In doing so he was open to all attacks, from Gaunilo and Thomas to Kant, who rightly deny that there is a logical transition from the necessity of Being itself to a highest being, from a principle which is beyond essence and existence to something that exists.

But even in this insufficient form the meaning of the ontological answer to the question of the two Absolutes is visible. *Deus est esse*, and the certainty of God is identical with the certainty of Being itself: God is the presupposition of the question of God.

## THE THOMISTIC DISSOLUTION

The ontological approach as elaborated by Augustine and his school had led to difficulties, as they appeared in the Anselmian form of the ontological argument and in the theological use of it by the great Franciscans. Here the criticism of Aquinas starts. But this criticism in Thomas himself and more radically in Duns Scotus and William of Occam, goes far beyond the abuses and difficulties. It has, for the larger part of Western humanity, undermined the ontological approach and with it the immediate religious certainty. It has replaced the first type of philosophy of religion by the second type.

The general character of the Thomistic approach to the philosophy of religion is the following: The rational way to God is not immediate, but mediated. It is a way of inference which, although correct, does not give unconditional certainty; therefore it must be completed by the way of authority. This means that the immediate rationality of the Franciscans is replaced by an argumentative rationality, and that beside this rational element stands non-rational authority. In order to make this step, Thomas had to dismiss the Augustinian solution. So he says:

> There are two ways in which something is known: by itself and by us. Therefore I say that this proposition "God is" known by itself insofar as He is in Himself, because the predicate is the same as the subject. For God is His own being . . . . But since we do not know about God, what He is, that proposition is not known by itself, but must be demonstrated through those things which are more known with respect to us, that is, through His effects.

In these words Aquinas cuts the nerve of the ontological approach. Man is excluded from the *primum esse* and the *prima veritas*. It is impossible for him to adhere to the uncreated truth. For the principles, the transcendentalia, are *not* the presence of the divine in us, they are *not* the "uncreated light" through which we see everything, but they are the created structure of our mind. It is obvious that in this way the immediate knowledge of the Absolute is destroyed. *Sapientia*, the knowledge of the principles, is qualitatively not different from *scientia*. As a student of music has to accept the propositions of the mathematicians, even if he does not understand their full meaning, so man has to accept the propositions of that science which God has of Himself and which the angels fully understand. They are given us by authority. "Arguing out of authority is most appropriate to this doctrine (theology)," Thomas says. The Bible, consequently, becomes a collection of true propositions, instead of being a guide book to contemplation as in Bonaventura. And while the Franciscans, especially Alexander, distinguish between (a) those doctrines which belong to the eternal truth and are immediately evident (as, for instance, God as *esse, verum, bonum*), and (b) those doctrines which are secondary, embodying the eternal truth in temporal forms, and are contingent and not evident (as, for instance, the Incarnation and the doctrine of the Church), Thomas puts all theological statements on the same level, namely that of authority. This has the consequence that *credere* and *intelligere* are torn asunder. According to Thomas the same object cannot be the object of faith and of knowledge; for faith does not imply an immediate contact with its object. Faith is less than knowledge. "So far as vision is lacking to it, faith falls short of the order of knowledge which is present in science," says Thomas; and vision, according to him, is not possible in our bodily existence. Here are the roots of that deteriorization of the term "faith" by which it is understood as belief with a low degree of evidence and which makes its use today almost impossible. The separation of faith in the sense of subjection to authority, and knowledge in the sense of science, entails the separation of the psychological functions which in Augustine are expressions of the same psychic substance. The intellect is moved by the will to accept contents which are accidental to the intellect; without the command of the will, assent to the transcendent science cannot be reached. The will fills the gap which the intellect cannot bridge, after the ontological immediacy has been taken away.

For Thomas all this follows from his sense-bound epistemology: "The human intellect cannot reach by natural virtue the divine substance, because, according to the way of the present life the cognition of our intellect starts with the senses." From there we must ascend to God with the help of the category of causality. This is what the philosophy of religion can do, and can do fairly easily in cosmological terms. We can see that there must be pure actuality, since the movement from potentiality to actuality is dependent on actuality, so that an actuality, preceding every movement, must exist. The ontological argument is impossible, not only in its doubtful form, but in its very substance. Gilson puts it this way: "It is indeed incontestable that in God essence and existence are identical. But this is true of the existence in which God subsists eternally in Himself; not of the existence to which our finite mind can rise when, by demonstration, it establishes that God is." It is obvious that this second concept of existence brings God's existence down to the level of that of a stone or a star, and it makes atheism not only possible, but almost unavoidable, as the later development has proved.

The first step in this direction was taken by Duns Scotus, who asserted an insuperable gap between man as finite and God as the infinite being, and who derived from this separation that the cosmological arguments as *demonstrationes ex finito* [demonstrations from the finite] remain within the finite and cannot reach the infinite. They cannot transcend the idea of a self-moving, teleological universe. Only authority can go beyond this rational probability of God which is a mere possibility. The concept of being loses its ontological character; it is a word, covering the entirely different realms of the finite and the infinite. God ceases to be Being itself and becomes a particular being, who must be known, *cognitione particulari*. Occam, the father of later nominalism, calls God a *res singularissima*. He can be approached neither by intuition nor by abstraction; that means not at all, except through an unnoticeable habit of grace in the unconscious which is supposed to move the will towards subjection to authority. This is the final outcome of the Thomistic *dissolution* of the Augustinian *solution*. The question of the two Ultimates is answered in such a way that the religious Absolute has become a singular being of overwhelming power, while the philosophical Absolute is formalized into a given structure of reality in which everything is contingent and individual. Early Protestantism was rather wise when under these philosophical presuppositions it restrained itself from developing any philosophy of religion, and elaborated in the power of its religious experience a concept of faith in which the disrupted elements of later scholasticism entered a new synthesis. For this was the gain of the Thomistic turn, that the nature of faith was thoroughly discussed and the naïve identification of immediate evidence with faith was overcome, so that the contingent element in religion became visible.

## CONFLICTS AND MIXTURES OF THE TWO TYPES IN THE MODERN PHILOSOPHY OF RELIGION

The material which could be collected under this heading is immense. But its originality, in comparison with the classical answers, is small. These answers return again and again, separated or in mixture. While the general trend is determined by the cosmological type and its final self-negation, ontological reactions against it occur in all centuries and have become more frequent in recent years.

It has often been said that the moral type of philosophy of religion (which follows Kant's so-called moral argument for the existence of God) represents a new type. But this is not the case. The moral argument must be either interpreted cosmologically or ontologically. If it is understood cosmologically, the fact of moral valuation is the basis of an inference, leading to a highest being who guarantees the ultimate unity of value and perfection or to the belief in the victorious power of value-creating processes. If the moral argument is interpreted in the ontological way, the experience of the unconditional character of the moral command is immediately, without any inference, the awareness of the Absolute, though not of a highest being. It is interesting to notice in this connection that even the ontological argument can be formulated cosmologically, as for instance, when Descartes, following Duns Scotus, makes an inference from the idea of an infinite being in our mind to his existence as the cause of this idea. This is the basic difference between the Augustinian and Cartesian starting point; it is rooted in the removal of the mystical element of Augustine's idea of ultimate evidence by Descartes' concept of rationality.

Obviously, German idealism belongs to the ontological type of philosophy of religion. It was not wrong in re-establishing the *prius* of subject and object, but it was wrong in deriving from the Absolute the whole of contingent contents, an attempt from which the Franciscans were protected by their religious positivism. This overstepping of the limits of the ontological approach has discredited it in Protestantism, while the same mistake of the Neo-Scholastic ontologists has discredited it in Catholicism.

No new type has been produced by the so-called empirical or experimental philosophy of religion. Most of its representatives belong to the cosmological type. They argue for God as "the best explanation of man's general experiences" or for "the theistic hypothesis" as the "most reasonable belief," etc., in innumerable variations; adding to it, as the cosmological type always must, remnants of the Old-Protestant idea of personal faith, which remain unrelated to the cosmological probabilities. Often, however, an idea of religious experience is used which has little in common with an empirical approach, and uses Franciscan terms and assertions. If the idea of God is to be formulated "in such a way that the question of God's existence becomes a dead issue" (Wieman); if Lyman speaks of "the innermost center of man which is in kinship with the Deepest Reality in the Universe"; if Baillie denies the possibility of genuine atheism; if the concept of vision is used again and again, for our knowledge of God, we are in an ontological atmosphere, although the ontological approach is not clearly stated and its relation to the cosmological approach and to faith is not adequately explained.

More consciously ontological are philosophies of religion like that of Hocking, who emphasizes the immediate experience of "Wholeness" as the *prius* of all objective knowledge with respect to being and value, or of [Alfred N.] Whitehead who calls the primordial nature of God the principle of concretion, or of [Charles] Hartshorne, who tries to reestablish the ontological argument and to combine it with the "contingent" in God. With respect to genuine pragmatism, it belongs to the ontological line insofar as it clearly rejects the cosmological argumentation and refuses to accept the cleavage between subject and object as final. It is, however, not free from remnants of the cosmological type, as James's Scotistic doctrine of the "will to believe," and the widespread assumption that the end of the cosmological way is the end of any rational approach to religion, indicate.

The systematic solution here suggested is stated in a merely affirmative and constructive form. The arguments on which this systematic attempt is based are implied in the classical discussion of the two ways of a philosophy of religion and its modern repercussions. They clearly show why, after the destruction of the ontological approach, religion itself was destroyed.

## THE ONTOLOGICAL AWARENESS
## OF THE UNCONDITIONAL

The question of the two Absolutes can be answered only by the identification of the philosophical Absolute with the *one* element of the religious
Absolute. The *Deus est esse* is the basis of all philosophy of religion. It is the
condition of a unity between thought and religion which overcomes their, so
to speak, schizophrenic cleavages in personal and cultural life.

The ontological principle in the philosophy of religion may be stated in
the following way: *Man is immediately aware of something unconditional which
is the prius of the separation and interaction of subject and object, theoretically as
well as practically.*

"Awareness," in this proposition, is used as the most neutral term,
avoiding the connotations of the terms "intuition," "experience," "knowledge." Awareness of the Unconditioned has not the character of "intuition,"
for the Unconditioned does not appear in this awareness as a *Gestalt* to be
intuited, but as an element, a power, a demand. Thomas was right in denying
that the vision of God is a human possibility, insofar as men in time and space
are concerned. Neither should the word "experience" be used, because it
ordinarily describes the observed presence of one reality to another reality,
and because the Unconditioned is not a matter of experiential observation.
"Knowledge" finally presupposes the separation of subject and object, and
implies an isolated theoretical act, which is just the opposite of awareness of
the Unconditioned. But this terminological question is not of primary importance. It is obvious that the ontological awareness is immediate, and not
mediated by inferential processes. It is present, whenever conscious attention
is focussed on it, in terms of an unconditional certainty.

Awareness, of course, is also a cognitive term. But awareness of the
Unconditional is itself unconditional, and therefore beyond the division of
the psychological functions. It was a main interest of Augustinian psychology
to show the mutual immanence of the functions of the soul and the impossibility of separating them in their relation to the *esse, verum, bonum*. It is
impossible to be aware of the Unconditioned as if it did not exclude by its
very presence any observer who was not conditioned by it in his whole being.
Thomas injured the understanding of religion when he dissolved the substantial unity of the psychological functions, and attributed to the will in isolation
what the intellect alone is not able to perform. And Schleiermacher injured
the understanding of religion when in his great fight against the cosmological
approach of Protestant Enlightenment he cut "feeling" (as the religious
function) off from will and intellect, thus excluding religion from the totality
of personal existence and delivering it to emotional subjectivity. *Man*, not his
cognitive function alone, is aware of the Unconditioned. It would therefore
be possible to call this awareness "existential" in the sense in which existential

philosophy has used the word, namely the participation of man as a whole in the cognitive act. In fact, this is probably the only point where this term could adequately be used in philosophy. The reason it is not used here is the essential unity of the unconditional and the conditioned in the ontological awareness; while in the word "existential," separation and decision are indicated. And the latter are elements of faith. While theology is directly and intentionally existential, philosophy is so only indirectly and unintentionally through the existential situation of the philosopher.

The term "unconditional" needs some interpretation. Although in the historical part of the phrase "the two Absolutes" is applied, in order to explain the problem, the word is replaced by "unconditional" in the constructive part. "Absolute," if taken literally, means "without relation"; if taken traditionally, it connotates the idealistic, self-developing principle. Both meanings are avoided in the concept "unconditional," which implies the unconditional demand upon those who are aware of something unconditional, and which cannot be interpreted as the principle of a rational deduction. But even here wrong connotations must be prevented: Neither "The Unconditioned" nor "something unconditional" is meant as a being, not even the highest being, not even God. God is unconditioned, that makes him God; but the "unconditional" is not God. The word "God" is filled with the concrete symbols in which mankind has expressed its ultimate concern—its being grasped by something unconditional. And this "something" is not just a thing, but the power of being in which every being participates.

This power of being is the *prius* of everything that has being. It precedes all special contents logically and ontologically. It precedes every separation and makes every interaction possible, because it is the point of identity without which neither separation nor interaction can be thought. This refers basically to the separation and interaction of subject and object, in knowing as well as in acting. The *prius* of subject and object cannot become an object to which man as a subject is theoretically and practically related. God is no object for us as subjects. He is always that which precedes this division. But, on the other hand, we speak about Him and we act upon Him, and we cannot avoid it, because everything which becomes real to us enters the subject-object correlation. Out of this paradoxical situation the half-blasphemous and mythological concept of the "existence of God" has arisen. And so have the abortive attempts to prove the existence of this "object." To such a concept and to such attempts atheism is the right religious and theological reply. This was well known to the most intensive piety of all times. The atheistic terminology of mysticism is striking. It leads beyond God to the Unconditioned, transcending any fixation of the divine as an object. But we have the same feeling of the inadequacy of all limiting names for God in nonmystical religion. Genuine religion without an element of atheism cannot be imagined. It is not by chance that not only Socrates, but also the Jews and the early

Christians were persecuted as atheists. For those who adhered to the powers, they were atheists.

The ontological approach transcends the discussion between nominalism and realism, if it rejects the concept of the *ens realissimum*, as it must do. Being itself, as present in the ontological awareness, is power of Being but not the most powerful Being; it is neither *ens realissimum* nor *ens singularissimum*. It is the power in everything that has power, be it a universal or an individual, a thing or an experience.

## THE COSMOLOGICAL RECOGNITION OF THE UNCONDITIONED

History and analysis have shown that the cosmological approach to religion leads to the self-destruction of religion, except as it is based on the ontological approach. If this basis is given, the cosmological principle can be stated in the following way: *The Unconditioned of which we have an immediate awareness, without inference, can be recognized in the cultural and natural universe.*

The cosmological approach has usually appeared in two forms, the first determined by the cosmological and the second by the teleological argument. After having denied radically the argumentative method applied in this kind of cosmology, we can rediscover the real and extremely productive meaning of the cosmological way in the philosophy of religion. From two points of view this can be done and has to be done, more than ever since the Franciscan period, in the last decades of our time. The one kind of cosmological recognition follows the first step of the old cosmological argument, namely the analysis of the finitude of the finite in the light of the awareness of the Unconditioned. In concepts like contingency, insecurity, transitoriness, and their psychological correlates, anxiety, care, meaninglessness, a new cosmological approach has developed. Medical psychology, the doctrine of man, and the existential philosophy have contributed to this negative way of recognizing the unconditional element in man and his world. It is the most impressive way of introducing people into the meaning of religion—if the fallacious inference to a highest being is avoided.

The other kind of cosmological recognition is affirmative and follows the first step of the teleological argument, namely, the tracing of the unconditional element in the creativity of nature and culture. With respect to nature this has been done in the elaboration and ultimate valuation of ideas such as "wholeness," "élan vital," "principle of concretion," *Gestalt*, etc., in all of which something unconditional, conditioning any special experience, is implied. With respect to culture this has been done by a religious interpretation of the autonomous culture and its development, a "theology of culture" as it could be called. The presupposition of this many-sided attempt is that in every cultural creation—a picture, a system, a law, a political movement (however secular it may appear)—an ultimate concern is expressed, and that it is possible to recognize the unconscious theological character of it.

This, of course, is possible only on the basis of the ontological awareness of the Unconditioned, i.e., on the basis of the insight that secular culture is essentially as impossible as atheism, because both presuppose the unconditional element and both express ultimate concerns.

## ONTOLOGICAL CERTAINTY AND THE RISK OF FAITH

The immediate awareness of the Unconditioned has not the character of faith but of self-evidence. Faith contains a contingent element and demands a risk. It combines the ontological certainty of the Unconditioned with the uncertainty about everything conditioned and concrete. This, of course, does not mean that faith is belief in something which has higher or lower degrees of probability. The risk of faith is not that it accepts assertions about God, man and world, which cannot be fully verified, but might be or might not be in the future. The risk of faith is based on the fact that the unconditional element can become a matter of ultimate concern only if it appears in a concrete embodiment. It can appear in purified and rationalized mythological symbols like God as highest personal being, and like most of the other traditional theological concepts. It can appear in ritual and sacramental activities for the adherents of a priestly and authoritarian religion. It can appear in concrete formulas and a special behavior, expressing the ineffable, as it always occurs in living mysticism. It can appear in prophetic-political demands for social justice, if they are the ultimate concern of religious and secular movements. It can occur in the honesty and ultimate devotion of the servants of scientific truth. It can occur in the universalism of the classical idea of personality and in the Stoic (ancient and modern) attitude of elevation over the vicissitudes of existence. In all these cases the risk of faith is an existential risk, a risk in which the meaning and fulfilment of our lives is at stake, and not a theoretical judgment which may be refuted sooner or later.

The risk of faith is not arbitrariness; it is a unity of fate and decision. And it is based on a foundation which is not risk: the awareness of the unconditional element in ourselves and our world. Only on this basis is faith justified and possible. There are many examples of people of the mystical as well as of the prophetic and secular types who in moments (and even periods) of their lives experienced the failure of the faith they had risked, and who preserved the ontological certainty, the unconditional element in their faith. The profoundest doubt could not undermine the presupposition of doubt, the awareness of something unconditional.

Although faith is a matter of fate and decision, the question must be raised whether there is a criterion for the element of decision in faith. The answer is: The unconditional of which we are immediately aware, if we turn our minds to it. The criterion of every concrete expression of our ultimate concern is the degree to which the concreteness of the concern is in unity with its ultimacy. It is the danger of every embodiment of the unconditional element, religious and secular, that it elevates something conditioned, a symbol, an institution, a movement as such to ultimacy. This danger was well known to the religious leaders of all types; and the whole work of theology can be summed up in the statement, that it is the permanent guardian of the unconditional against the aspiration of its own religious and secular appearances.

The ontological approach to philosophy of religion as envisaged by Augustine and his followers, as reappearing in many forms in the history of thought, if critically reinterpreted by us, is able to do for our time what it did in the past, both for religion and culture: to overcome as far as it is possible by mere thought the fateful gap between religion and culture, thus reconciling concerns which are not strange to each other but have been estranged from each other.

# Ludwig Wittgenstein

Ludwig Wittgenstein (1889–1951), Austrian-born philosopher who taught at Cambridge University, has through his personal teaching, his *Tractatus* and his *Philosophical Investigations* and other posthumously published writings, exerted a tremendous influence upon contemporary philosophy.

# 20

# *On Death and the Mystical*

6.4 All propositions are of equal value.

6.41 The sense of the world must lie outside the world. In the world everything is as it is, and everything happens as it does happen: *in* it no value exists—and if it did, it would have no value.

If there is any value that does have value, it must lie outside the whole sphere of what happens and is the case. For all that happens and is the case is accidental.

What makes it non-accidental cannot lie *within* the world, since if it did it would itself be accidental.

It must lie outside the world.

6.42 And so it is impossible for there to be propositions of ethics.
Propositions can express nothing of what is higher.

6.421 It is clear that ethics cannot be put into words.
Ethics is transcendental.
(Ethics and aesthetics are one and the same.)

6.422 When an ethical law of the form, "Thou shalt...," is laid down, one's first thought is, "And what if I do not do it?" It is clear, however, that ethics has nothing to do with punishment and reward in the usual sense of the terms. So our question about the *consequences* of an action must be unimportant.—At least those consequences should not be events. For there must be something right about the question we posed. There must indeed be some kind of ethical reward and ethical punishment, but they must reside in the action itself.

*Tractatus Logico—Philosophicus*, D. F. Pears and B. F. McGuinness, trans. (London: Routledge & Kegan Paul, Ltd., 1961), pp. 144–51. Reprinted by permission of Routledge & Kegan Paul, Ltd., and by The Humanities Press International, Inc.

(And it is also clear that the reward must be something pleasant and the punishment something unpleasant.)

6.423     It is impossible to speak about the will insofar as it is the subject of ethical attributes.

And the will as a phenomenon is of interest only to psychology.

6.43      If good or bad acts of will do alter the world, it can only be the limits of the world that they alter, not the facts, not what can be expressed by means of language.

In short their effect must be that it becomes an altogether different world. It must, so to speak, wax and wane as a whole.

The world of the happy man is a different one from that of the unhappy man.

6.431     So too at death the world does not alter, but comes to an end.

6.4311    Death is not an event in life: we do not live to experience death.

If we take eternity to mean not infinite temporal duration but timelessness, then eternal life belongs to those who live in the present.

Our life has no end in just the way in which our visual field has no limits.

6.4312    Not only is there no guarantee of the temporal immortality of the human soul, that is to say of its eternal survival after death; but, in any case, this assumption completely fails to accomplish the purpose for which it has always been intended. Or is some riddle solved by my surviving forever? Is not this eternal life itself as much of a riddle as our present life? The solution of the riddle of life in space and time lies *outside* space and time.

(It is certainly not the solution of any problems of natural science that is required.)

6.432     *How* things are in the world is a matter of complete indifference for what is higher. God does not reveal Himself *in* the world.

6.4321    The facts all contribute only to setting the problem, not to its solution.

6.44      It is not *how* things are in the world that is mystical, but *that* it exists.

6.45      To view the world *sub specie aeterni* is to view it as a whole—a limited whole.

Feeling the world as a limited whole—it is this that is mystical.

6.5       When the answer cannot be put into words, neither can the question be put into words.

*The riddle* does not exist.

If a question can be framed at all, it is also *possible* to answer it.

6.51      Skepticism is *not* irrefutable, but obviously nonsensical, when it tries to raise doubts where no questions can be asked.

For doubt can exist only where a question exists, a question only where an answer exists, and an answer only where something *can be said.*

6.52       We feel that even when *all possible* scientific questions have been answered, the problems of life remain completely untouched. Of course there are then no questions left, and this itself is the answer.

6.521      The solution of the problem of life is seen in the vanishing of the problem.

(Is not this the reason why those who have found after a long period of doubt that the sense of life became clear to them have then been unable to say what constituted that sense?)

6.522      There are, indeed, things that cannot be put into words. They *make themselves manifest.* They are what is mystical.

6.53       The correct method in philosophy would really be the following: to say nothing except what can be said, i.e., propositions of natural science—i.e., something that has nothing to do with philosophy—and then, whenever someone else wanted to say something metaphysical, to demonstrate to him that he had failed to give a meaning to certain signs in his propositions. Although it would not be satisfying to the other person—he would not have the feeling that we were teaching him philosophy—*this* method would be the only strictly correct one.

6.54       My propositions serve as elucidations in the following way: anyone who understands me eventually recognizes them as nonsensical, when he has used them—as steps—to climb up beyond them. (He must, so to speak, throw away the ladder after he has climbed up it.)

He must transcend these propositions, and then he will see the world aright.

7          What we cannot speak about we must consign to silence.

# Charles Hartshorne

Charles Hartshorne (1897–    ), a close student of the philosophy of
A. N. Whitehead and the author of many influential books, is the leading exponent of process theology.

# 21

# *Time, Death,*
# *and Everlasting Life*

*"We are such stuff as dreams are made on, and our little life is rounded with a sleep."*
—SHAKESPEARE, *in* The Tempest.

Our lives on earth are finite in space and in time. That we are finite in
space perhaps means only that we are not the universe but constituents of it.
True, the universe itself may, according to some speculations, be finite, but
that is a different sort of finitude. Our finitude is our fragmentariness with
respect to what exists; the finitude of the universe, if it be finite, is its
limitedness with respect to the possibilities, rather than the actualities, of
existence. The fact that we are spatially limited means that we have neighbors
around us; but the universe has no neighbors. A conscious individual without
neighbors seems conceivable only as deity. God has no environment, unless
an internal one. Thus either He is infinite, or He is finite somewhat as the
universe perhaps is, but certainly not as we are.

The conclusion so far is that our spatial finitude is the truism that we
are neither the total universe nor deity. If we were the total universe or deity,
we should not be "we"; and so our spatial limitedness is analytic. There is in
principle no alternative.

How is it with temporal finitude? It seems clear that, had we never been
born but instead had always existed throughout past time, we should not
have been human beings and should not have been "we" ourselves at all.
How could any one of us have been the same individual at all times past,
down to the present? Either he must have forgotten all but the most recent
times or else he must be conscious of a personal continuity through the most

radical cultural diversities, changes of beliefs, attitudes, and events. But is it not precisely in our limitations that our personal identity consists? To be simply an individual among many rather than, like God, *the* individual is to leave to others all but a few of the actual attitudes, beliefs, patterns of living. Just as one cannot integrate into the unity of one's consciousness perceptions from multitudes of localities, but only from one locality in space, and not from many but only from one set of sense organs, so one cannot focus into this human personality the ideas and purposes of diverse centuries, let alone all centuries.

It seems, then, that temporal and spatial finitude have in some respects the same truistic meaning. I am not the universe or God, hence of course I am not everywhere, and of course I am not primordial, but rather a being whose existence began at a certain moment of time. However, when we consider temporal limitation with regard to the future than the past, there seems to be an additional question at issue. Something that exists in a small corner of the world nevertheless does exist there. It is not everything, but it is certainly something. But what once existed, and now has "ceased to exist," is apparently not only limited in scope, it even appears not to exist at all. Is it something, or is it nothing? If you reply that it *once* was something but that now it is nothing, you have scarcely clarified the matter. For something cannot literally become nothing. The word "nothing" and the word "Washington" clearly do not have the same referent. Surely, even now when I say "Washington," what I refer to is not mere non-entity. And yet, in what sense is the no-longer-existent nevertheless still something?

There are two basically contrasting attitudes toward this question. According to the one view, not only after the death of Washington is he still something, still a reality, since he can be referred to by a term whose reference is not the same as that of the term "nothing," but also in any time prior to the birth of Washington there was already a something which may be described as the Washington who was "going to live" on earth, just as our present Washington is the one who "once lived" on earth. Thus, according to this theory, prior to birth, the individual is there behind the stage entrance ready to come on the stage, and after death he is there beyond the exit through which he has passed off the stage. According to the other view, prior to birth there just is no such individual as Washington. No one refers to any individual whose life lies centuries in the future, as many of us do refer to individuals who lived centuries in the past. Where there is no reference there need be no referent; and thus the argument that "Washington must still be something" cannot be used to prove that thousands of years ago he was already something.

According to either of the views just outlined death is not sheer destruction, the turning of being into not-being. To me at least it is a truism, though one often forgotten, that whatever death may mean it cannot mean that a man is first something real and then something unreal. He may first be something unreal and then something real (the second of the views presented); but this is only an unnecessarily paradoxical way of saying that once there was neither the name "George Washington" (for example) with the meaning which that term now has, nor any such individual person as the one we now call "George Washington." As soon as there was this particular he, there was a real he. Every he or she is real, but there are new he's and she's each moment. But once an individual is there to refer to, he continues to be there even after death, as object of reference, as a life which really has been lived. The only question is: Was it there all along as a life that was going to be lived?

One argument for this latter notion is based on relativity physics. Since there is held to be no unique simultaneous present moment dividing past from future for the cosmos, it is not easy to see how there can be objective validity in the idea of an individual's coming into reality at a certain moment in cosmic history. The correct conclusion, some say, is to regard all happenings as forming a single complex totality, the whole of what happens, whether in what to us now is the past or in what to us now is the future or in the region intermediate between our past and our future. This whole of space-time as a single complex entity is real, not now or then but just eternally. In our ignorance we may know it chiefly in those parts which are past relative to us, but its total reality is not now or then. It does not happen or become; it just is. This view does seem to fit more painlessly into the general theory of relativity than the view that happenings form no final totality since new individual lives or event-sequences are added to reality from moment to moment. For from the standpoint of the cosmos it seems impossible to find any such "moments."

In spite of this difficulty, a means of escape from which I hope to present elsewhere, I agree with Peirce and many others that the contrast between past and future is that between actual and potential individualities. *Being* is intelligible as the abstract fixed aspect in *becoming*, and eternity as the identical element in all temporal diversity. To hold that happenings form a totality which simply is and never becomes is to seek, on the contrary, to put all the reality of becoming into a being. This attempt is as old as Parmenides and Shankara. It does not necessarily lose its artificial and paradoxical character by being given a modern scientific dress.

Apart from relativity problems, there seems to be no paradox in the view that becoming contains being. For if $Ey$ succeeds $Ex$, $E$ persists as fixed item, although the total, $Ey$, is new. The novel can contain the non-novel. But if the whole were non-novel, then nothing would be novel. For then we could have only $Exy$ and $Exy$ and $Exy$. Change would be the shifting of our consciousness from one portion of the whole to another; but does this not repeat the problem? On the other hand, if $Ey$ succeeds $Ex$, as total state of reality, then the second state is in fact $Ey$ ($Ex$), where the parenthesis indicates that $Ey$

contains *Ex* as its predecessor. In this way, if process is conceived as cumulative change, the having-occurred of previous events may become a fixed item in later events, and so the reality of the past as object of reference in the present can be accounted for. And one may argue that in order to house temporal relations it is enough if events contain earlier ones as their referents, for if *b* follows *a* and *c* follows *b* as following *a*, and so on, every item is given a place in the chain, even though there is not in *a* a real reference to *b* as something which is going to follow, or in *b* to *c* as its successor-to-be. Nay, if the reference were to run both ways, then temporal relations would find a home in events only by ceasing to be temporal, ceasing to be relations of becoming, since they must then be viewed as timelessly there in a total reality which is not subject to addition and at no time has been actualized.

If temporal relations are not real as references running either way in time, then it is hard to see what they can be. For then it is not true either that Washington (before he is born) is something with the character of what is going to be or that (after he is dead) he is something with the character of having been. But then there just is no truth about the temporal process at all. Only as something happens could it be referred to. The implication is that there is nothing to refer to, since the passing moment can hardly speak concerning itself.

If we drop this impossible extreme, then we must also break once for all with the idea of death as simple destruction of an individual. Either individuals are eternal realities—items in a complex of events (so called, for on this view they seem to lose their character as happenings) which as a whole never came to be and cannot cease to be but simply is—or else individuals are not eternal, since there are new ones from time to time, but yet, once in the total reality, no individual can pass from this total. An individual becomes, he does not de-become or unbecome; he is created, he is not destroyed or de-created.

And yet death seems correlative to birth. Fragments assemble into a man and then de-assemble into atoms again. But this language is on a different level from that which we have been using. It assumes individuals whose origin is not considered (atoms), and it never really arrives at the human individual in question. Prior to my first experiences, "I" was not "I," the individual which I am. This ego is not identical with a multitude of atomic individuals, however assembled, in spite of the apparent fact that this ego and the assembly are not found apart from each other. According to the view I adopt, there was once no such individual as myself, even as something that was "going to exist." But centuries after my death, there will have been that very individual which I am. This is creation, with no corresponding de-creation. But, again, what then is death?

Death is the last page of the last chapter of the book of one's life, as birth is the first page of the first chapter. Without a first page there is no book. But given the first page there is, in so far, a book. The question of death then is, How rich and how complete is the book to be? It is not a question of reality. The book is already real as soon as the possibility of my death arises; and, as we have argued, reality, whether or not it is created, is indestructible. But truncated books, without suitable extent and proper conclusions, are always possible, until life has continued long enough for the individuals' basic purposes to be carried out. Such truncation can be tragic. But it is not even tragic if the entire book is to be annihilated; for then there will have been nothing, not even something tragically broken off and brief. The evil of death presupposes indestructibility of the individual as such. Washington having died is at least Washington. Not just a certain corpse, for by "Washington" we mean a unique unity of experience and decision and thought, and that is no corpse. So those are right who say to themselves upon the death of the loved one: It cannot be that that beloved human reality is now nothing or is now something not human at all.

We must, however, distinguish between continuing reality, in the form of retained actuality, and reality in the form of further actualization. The realized actuality of the beloved one lay in his or her thoughts, feelings, decisions, perceptions. These are evermore as real as when they occurred. But it does not follow that new thoughts, feelings, decisions, are occurring "in heaven," having the stamp of the same individuality; or that friends who died earlier are now being conversed with in new dialogues, and so on. This would be new reality, not the indestructibility of the old. Perhaps such views of heaven are only mythical ways of trying to grasp the truth that death is not ultimate destruction but simply termination, finitude.

To say that the book of life, be it long or short, is indestructible suggests at least a potential reader of that book for any time in the future. A book which neither is nor could be read is scarcely a book; a chain of events which cannot be known by any possible mind is doubtfully distinguishable from nonentity. Who are the at least potential readers of the book of our lives after they have reached their final chapter in death? The answer nearest to hand is, of course, future human beings, posterity. Immortality as thus constituted has been termed "social immortality." Our children, or the readers of books (in the literal sense) which we have written, or the spectators of the buildings we have erected, or those who recall words we have spoken or the expression of our features—is it these who furnish the actual or at least potential realization of our future reality as an individual with the status we describe as that of "having-existed"? There are two severe limitations to this kind of immortality. No human being will, it seems fairly clear, strictly speaking, "read" even a page in the book we will have written by the act of living, the book of our experiences, thoughts, intentions, decisions, emotions, and the like. Even while we live no one else quite sees the content of our own experience at this or that moment. I see that you smile at me, but I do not see that in the fringe of consciousness you feel a slight discomfort from being too warmly dressed or that you have just recalled that I need sympathy because of some misfortune which you know is to happen to me though I do not yet know it or—any one of a million other complications which your smile cannot distinctly convey to me. If such things are missed even by the closest of our contemporaries, they are even more missed by posterity. For though some hidden facts later come to light, many more are lost forever, since posterity will not have seen my actual gestures, heard the tones of my voice just as they occurred in the context which gave them meaning. And at best one never intuits the exact quality of another's experience. Thus the reality of one's life, as a stream of experiences, sensations, ideas, emotions, recollections, anticipations, decisions, indecisions, is a target at which the perception of others may be aimed but which they never literally reach. The reality of Washington as an individual having-really-lived-thus-and-thus is not a reality by virtue of any experience which we either do or even could now have. The only positive account of this reality which can be imagined, so far as I can see, is that there is an individual who is not subject to the incurable ignorances of human perception, understanding, and memory but who from the time Washington was born has been fully aware of all that he felt, sensed, thought, or dreamed, and of just how he felt, sensed, thought, or dreamed it.

In short, our adequate immortality can only be God's omniscience of us. He to whom all hearts are open remains evermore open to any heart that ever has been apparent to Him. What we once were to Him, less than that we never can be, for otherwise He Himself as knowing us would lose something of His own reality; and this loss of something that has been must be final, since, if deity cannot furnish the abiding reality of events, there is, as we have seen, no other way, intelligible to us at least, in which it can be furnished. Now the meaning of omniscience is a knowledge which is coextensive with reality, which can be taken as the measure of reality. Hence, if we can never be less than we have been to God, we can in reality never be less than we have been. Omniscience and the indestructibility of every reality are correlative aspects of one truth. Death cannot mean the destruction, or even the fading, of the book of one's life; it can mean only the fixing of its concluding page. Death writes "The End" upon the last page, but nothing further happens to the book, by way of either addition or subtraction.

That there can be no subtraction is, in my opinion, more certain than that there can be no addition. For personal survival after death with memory of personal life before death is hardly an absolute absurdity. Perhaps personal existence without a body is indeed impossible, yet the analogy to a butterfly with its succession of bodies, while remote and implausible, is not necessarily strictly inapplicable. But we need to distinguish two meanings of survival. It is one thing to say that death is not the end, in the sense of the closing page, of the book of life, that there will be further chapters; it is another thing to say that there will never be any end, that the chapters will be infinite. This looks to me like a genuine impossibility. For if I am to be I, and not you and not the universe and not God, then I must be limited, a fragment of reality, not the whole. And, as we saw at the beginning of our discussion, temporal limitedness seems to have the same basic meaning as spatial, in that it is an aspect of our individuality as such, as nondivine individuality. If our capacity to assimilate new future content and yet remain ourselves, as much united with our past selves as in contrast to them, is unlimited, then in that respect we are exactly as God is. (For it is one of the divine attributes that no novelty of content can be too much for God's personal continuity or integrity.) In unlimited future time, unlimited novelty must accrue (unless there is to be ever increasing monotony or boredom), and yet one is always to be oneself, just that individual and no other, and not identical with God. (For, if you say that we are to become God, you merely utter a contradiction.) As for metaphors like being "absorbed into deity," they merely evade alternatives that can be stated more directly. Such crude physical images are surely not the best our spiritual insight can suggest.

A popular idea of immortality is that after death the artist will paint new pictures in some finer medium; by the same principle, the statesman will have some finer mode of group leadership opened to him, and so on. I wonder. The chance to paint pictures or lead groups seems to be here and now, and there will not, I suspect, be another—for us. Our chance to do right and not wrong, to love God and in God all creatures, is here and now. Not only will there be "no marrying and giving in marriage" in the heavenly mansions, there will, I imagine, be no personal actions of yours and mine other than those we enact before we die. And there will be no such thing as our feeling (with a feeling we lacked while on earth) pain or sorrow as punishment for misdeeds, or bliss as reward for good ones. The time and place to look for the rewards of virtue are now and here. If you cannot on earth find good in being good and ill in being or doing ill, then I doubt whether you will find it in any heaven or hell. After all, if love is to be the motive, then scheming for reward or avoidance of punishment must not be the motive; and what should not be motive is irrelevant.

But words are slippery and inadequate. While I have the notion that the theory of heaven and hell is in good part a colossal error and one of the most dangerous that ever occurred to the human mind, I also think that it was closely associated with certain truths and that it requires intellectual and spiritual effort to purify these truths from the error.

First, as explained above, I believe it to be true that death is not destruction of an individual's reality but merely the affixing of the quantum of that individual's reality. Death only says to us: "More than you already have been you will not be. For instance, the virtues you have failed to acquire, you will now never acquire. It is too late. You had your chance." This may be thought to be expressed in the notion of the Last Judgment. Our lives will be definitively estimated, the account will be closed, nothing can be added or taken away. But this applies to punishments and rewards also. If you have no objection in advance to having been an ugly soul, lacking in the deeper harmonies of will and love and understanding, then no further punishment will be meted out to you. Sadistic or vengeful men may wish that you should be further punished; but God is not sadistic and he is not vengeful, and the attempt to combine such things with divine mercy should be given up. Each of us has the options: first, of despising himself all his days; second, of avoiding this by achieving a sufficient degree of stupidity and illusion so that he does not know how contemptible he is but also does not know what life at its best really is or what the best lives around him are really like; or, finally, of living a life of loving insight into self and others. The heaven of a life rich in love and understanding, the hell of a life poor in these respects—between these you may choose (of course intermediate states are possible), and you will not escape judgment. But God does not stamp on the bodies or the souls of those who have lived ill; nor does He insult those who found love its own reward with post mortem rewards so out of proportion to all the goods of this life that a reasonable man could think of nothing else if he really took them seriously.

That there are (in my opinion) no post mortem rewards or punishments does not imply that there are no good or bad results to be anticipated from our lives after they have been terminated (not destroyed). It is natural to find inspiration in the thought that another will live more richly because I have lived, and in this thought one may find a reward for courageous and generous actions. But this reward is *now*, while I am performing the actions. I aim at a future result, namely, good to another who survives my death, but this aiming is my present joy. In a sense, the future good to the other will be my reward, but it is one that I never shall enjoy save in anticipation. I shall not be there to share in the future joys that I will have made possible. My participation must be now. Moses must enjoy the promised land through devoted imagination or not at all. But this enjoyment through devoted imagination is not to be despised. The nobler the spirit the more such vicarious participation suffices. Moses perhaps did not especially mind not entering the promised land, so long as he could know it would be entered and that this entering was his doing or, at least, that he had done his part toward it.

Let us take another analogy. There are many men and many women who cannot bear the thought that they are growing too old for the joys of young love. This is no doubt one motive which leads men to divorce their wives, middle-aged like themselves, and marry girls who might be their children. Thus they want to escape, or imagine they escape, growing old. They are in some cases deceived, I really think, by a metaphysical confusion.

Seeing that young love is beautiful, they draw the conclusion that it is good that they should have it. The right conclusion is: It is good that young love should be had, by those best able to have it, presumably the young. Much of the art of life, I suggest, lies in being able to distinguish between "this possible beauty of life ought to be actualized," and "it ought to be actualized by and for me." The "by and for me" is irrelevant, in last analysis. "There is a certain good in the life of A" means that there is that certain good. If, instead, the same good is in the life of B, then also there is that certain good. From the standpoint of God it must be the same. We are to love God unreservedly, and this is nonsense unless it means that we are to try to understand that that is good which is good in the eyes of God. The old man or a young man, but not both, can occupy the central place in a young girl's life. As a rule, it should be the young man. The old men who make exceptions for themselves either have very unusual reasons or imagine that a good is not good unless they enjoy it themselves. I honestly think there is an element of intellectual confusion here in many cases. Such persons do not quite understand and take to heart the truth that the closing of their lives is not the closing of life, the ending of their youth the ending of youth, and that the secret of living consists in the service of life and good as life and as good rather than as essentially my life and my good. The devoted imagination can win such reward as it needs from joys that only others are to possess directly.

For the nontheist, the ultimate future good we aim at must, it seems, be a good for our human posterity. But our promotion of this is always more or less problematic. Perhaps we misjudge or have poor luck. And, also, it is just not possible to live for posterity in every moment of life with every act and breath. How can I know what it will mean to posterity that I now listen to Mozart for an hour? Perhaps nothing of any significance. And this applies to much of my life. But there is One to whom it may mean something. For while God is already familiar with Mozart He is not already familiar with the experience *I* may now have of Mozart, which is bound to be a variation on the theme, human experiences of Mozart—how significant a variation depends on my alertness, sensitivity, and imagination. All of one's life can be a "reasonable, holy, and living sacrifice" to deity, a sacrifice whose value depends on the quality of the life, and this depends on the depth of the devotion to all good things, to all life's possibilities, neither as mine nor as not mine but as belonging to God's creatures and thus to God. A poor, thin, or discordant life, made so by lack of generous openness to others, to the beauty of the world and the divine harmony pervading all sad and seemingly insignificant things, is a poor gift to the divine valuer of all things.

It is difficult to avoid onesidedness when trying to think analytically or clearly. It is onesided to contrast social immortality, the nonreligious form of everlasting life, to immortality in the divine awareness, as though to accept one is to reject the other. This is not so. If I do nothing to posterity, then I have no gift to offer deity except just my own life or those I immediately benefit. But if I can inspire multitudes who will never see me in the flesh, then the incense I send up to God will continue to rise anew for many generations. As a theist, I have all the reason the nontheist can have for devoting myself to such a result, if it is within my power. The nontheist at his best loves his fellows for themselves, for what they are. The theist in no sense lacks this ground for love. But the theist has a positive imagination of what it means to say, "what men are." He envisages no mere neutral "truth" as containing all lives and all values, but an all-perceptive, all-participating living receptacle of reality and value. How can this belief make one love creatures the less—the belief that they are integral to the supreme creation, the divine life as newly enriched each moment by the lives of all?

In this sense we can interpret "heaven" as the conception which God forms of our actual living, a conception which we partly determine by our free decisions but which is more than all our decisions and experiences, since it is the synthesis of God's participating responses to these experiences. It is the book which is never read by any man save in unclear, fragmentary glimpses; but is the clearly given content of the divine appreciation. Hell is, in the same terms, simply whatever of ugliness is inherent in the content because of my perversity, which even the divine synthesis cannot remove but can only make the best of, bringing out of it whatever good is possible. In this hell God Himself participates, in the sense that there is because of it a tinge of tragedy even in the divine experiences. No mere peace is the divine self-realization, but a joy containing somehow an element of sorrow.

Thus we escape the horrible dilemma: either God is lacking in love for sinners in hell or He loses His divinity by participating sympathetically in their sorrow. He does participate in it, but His divinity is not so defined that participation means loss of it. Rather it is the absoluteness of participation that is divine. I wish to repeat that, for myself, there is no sinner in hell, if that means an individual suffering from this location, save for those who really feel themselves in hell while on earth. Afterward, only God or other men will know that one has presented himself as a poor excuse for a human being to the immortal memory of deity. But one will one's self forever have known this while still living, or else will have stupefied one's self so that not knowing it will have been part and parcel with not knowing many among the things most worth knowing.

Lequier said that we "make our fame before God." He also said: "God has made us makers of ourselves," and pointed out that in making ourselves we, in so far, decide what God is to contemplate in us. One might say that we mold the picture which forever will hang in the divine mansion. God will make as much out of the picture in beholding it as can be made; but how much can be made depends partly upon the picture and not merely upon the divine insight in seeing relations and meanings. The true immortality is everlasting fame before God.

It may be felt that the consolations of the old faith are lost in this doctrine. What, no chance to make amends for errors in this life! No chance to grow deeper in insight and devotion beyond the grave! No compensation for bad luck in one's earthly career! My suggestion is that these objections involve the confusion spoken of above, between my good and good or between my life and creaturely life in general. Others will make amends, will develop deeper insight and devotion, will be lucky where I was not. All good cannot be my good; only God is heir to all good. Of course there should be higher modes of life than those which we now achieve on earth. But, if present-day astronomy is right, there are hundreds of thousands of inhabitable planets. Who knows how many of them support wiser or more saintly creatures than the best of us human beings? And who knows what the future of the race or the universe may make possible? But that you or I must be there to say, "This good is mine," seems to me as unnecessary as that it must be I who marries this delightful young girl. Renunciation of the claim to put the stamp of myness on everything, save as through devoted imagination I make it mine, is the principle which either case seems to call for. Without this renunciation the argument is not on a level that deserves much consideration. With it, what is left of the argument?

It is said that while we should not demand personal survival for ourselves, it is all right to ask it for others. But yet I do not demand that the other middle-aged man have a young wife any more than I demand that I should have. Similarly there is no essential difference between saying that I ought to have another chance to avoid my mistakes, to grow wiser and nobler than I do in this life, and saying that my neighbor ought to have this chance. The essential question is whether the human personality, or any nondivine personality, is not, just in being non-divine, limited in a sense that is contradicted by the notion that there will always be another chapter to the book of life as lived by that individual.

It is said that if God loves us He will not suffer us to be destroyed. But death, we have seen, is not destruction. It is the setting of a definite limit, not the obliteration of what is limited. If God cannot suffer us to be limited, then He cannot suffer us to be at all, as limited creatures or as other than Himself. Moreover, does God love us as we are on earth merely for the sake of ourselves as we will be in some future life, or does He love us as we are on earth for the sake of ourselves as we are on earth, that is, as we really are? For we really do live on earth and have just certain qualities of experience and thought and intention and decision in this life. I believe that God loves us in our present reality for the sake of that reality. And this reality will never be destroyed. Postponing death indefinitely would only add new realities, not preserve this one.

The best argument for personal survival in the conventional sense is perhaps this: life is cumulative, and many potentialities are lost when a man dies, so that it is wasteful for life always to begin over again with a new individual as a child. Yet children continue to be born! And the argument seems weak. Potentialities were lost when men ceased to write Shakespearian dramas; no art form is fully exhausted when abandoned for new forms. But the further variations would have been less significant than those already actual; it is better to turn to a new art form than to exhaust possible variations on the old. Each of us is a theme with infinity of variations. No theme other than that of the divine nature can admit an infinity of variations all significant enough to be worth making a place for in reality. Life is cumulative; but it is just as true that it is self-exhaustive. "In the prime of life" is no mere expression or false theory; it is truth. Those who deny it will, if they live long enough, only illustrate it with unnecessary obviousness. We must accept as our destiny the probability that one's personality will be less rather than more in the closing years of life, if one lives exceptionally long. Miraculous rejuvenations or resurrections might change matters somewhat; but if they are to keep us the same individuals, and yet to enable us to avoid the monotony of insignificant variations on the theme of our personality, they cannot go on forever, so far at least as I can grasp the problem. And I see no reason why we should quarrel with this or think it unjust or sad. Living without zest is sad, and to do so forever—

On the other hand, if "resurrection" means the synthesis of one's life in God, the divine act of envisagement that keeps adding up the story of one's terrestrial existence, producing a total reality that is invisible to us on earth, which moth and rust cannot corrupt and from which naught may ever be stolen, then in such resurrection one may believe without falling into any confusion between my good and good, or between ourselves and deity, and without denying the fact that our life is a balance between cumulative and self-exhaustive tendencies. For the divine theme is the one theme which need not be self-exhaustive, since it is an unrestricted theme, universally relevant, absolute in flexibility. We are individuated by our localization in the world; but God is individuated by containing the world in Himself. Only He does that, and so long as He does it He is distinguished from all other individuals. Were He to exhaust His personality, He would thereby prove that He never was the divine, the strictly cosmic individual; just as, if we were to become inexhaustible, we would prove we never were less than divine or cosmic, never were other than God.

God acquires novelty by acquiring us as novel individuals. Our function is then to be novel, not to be ever-persistent in the sense of ourselves enjoying ever additional novelties. Such persistence is fully supplied by the divine inexhaustibility. We, as themes, are essentially variations on *the* theme. True, inasmuch as the divine awareness is concretely new each moment, God must reform His awareness of us forever, so that we function as a theme for literally endless variations in the use God makes of us as objects of His awareness to be synthesized with ever additional objects. But these endless variations are nothing we shall experience, save in principle and in advance through our devoted imagination, our love of God. Devoted imagination is the better alternative to unlimited claims for one's self or for such as we are. To live everlastingly, as God does, can scarcely be our privilege; but we may earn everlasting places as lives well lived within the one life that not only evermore will have been lived, but evermore and inexhaustibly will be lived in ever new ways.

## H. H. Price

H. H. Price (1899–1984) of Oxford University wrote many influential books and articles on the problems of sense perception and of epistemology generally, including *Perception, Thinking and Experience* and *Belief*.

# 22

# *Personal Survival and the Idea of Another World*

As you all know, this year is the seventieth anniversary of the foundation of the Society for Psychical Research. From the very beginning, the problem of survival has been one of the main interests of the Society; and that is my excuse, if any excuse is needed, for discussing some aspects of the problem this evening. I shall not, however, talk about the evidence for survival. In this lecture I am concerned only with the conception of survival; with the *meaning* of the Survival Hypothesis, and not with its truth or falsity. When we consider the Survival Hypothesis, whether we believe it or disbelieve it, what is it that we have in mind? Can we form any idea, even a rough and provisional one, of what a disembodied human life might be like? Supposing we cannot, it will follow that what is called the Survival Hypothesis is a mere set of words and not a hypothesis at all. The evidence adduced in favour of it might still be evidence for something, and perhaps for something important, but we should no longer have the right to claim that it is evidence for survival. There cannot be evidence for something which is completely unintelligible to us.

Now let us consider the situation in which we find ourselves after seventy years of psychical research. A very great deal of work has been done on the problem of survival, and much of the best work by members of our Society. Yet there are the widest differences of opinion about the results. A number of intelligent persons would maintain that we now have a very large mass of evidence in favour of survival; that some of it is of very good quality indeed, and cannot be explained away unless we suppose that the supernor-

"Survival and the Idea of 'Another World,' " *Proceedings of the Society for Psychical Research*, Vol. L, Part 182 (January, 1953), 1-25. Reprinted by permission of the publisher.

mal cognitive powers of some embodied human minds are vastly more extensive and more accurate than we can easily believe them to be; in short, that on the evidence available the Survival Hypothesis is more probable than not. Some people—and not all of them are silly or credulous—would even maintain that the Survival Hypothesis is proved, or as near to being so as any empirical hypothesis can be. On the other hand, there are also many intelligent persons who entirely reject these conclusions. Some of them, no doubt, have not taken the trouble to examine the evidence. But others of them have; they may even have given years of study to it. They would agree that the evidence is evidence of *something*, and very likely of something important. But, they would say, it cannot be evidence of survival; there *must* be some alternative explanation of it, however difficult it may be to find out. Why do they take this line? I think it is because they find the very conception of survival unintelligible. The very idea of a "discarnate human personality" seems to them a muddled or absurd one; indeed not an idea at all, but just a phrase—an emotionally exciting one, no doubt—to which no clear meaning can be given.

Moreover, we cannot just ignore the people who have not examined the evidence. Some of our most intelligent and most highly educated contemporaries are among them. These men are well aware, by this time, that the evidence does exist, even if their predecessors fifty years ago were not. If you asked them why they do not trouble to examine it in detail, they would be able to offer reasons for their attitude. And one of their reasons, and not the least weighty in their eyes, is the contention I mentioned just now, that the very idea of survival is a muddled or absurd one. To borrow an example from Whately Carington, we know pretty well what we mean by asking whether Jones has survived a shipwreck. We are asking whether he continues to live after the shipwreck has occurred. Similarly it makes sense to ask whether he survived a railway accident, or the bombing of London. But if we substitute "his own death" for "a shipwreck" and ask whether he has survived it, our question (it will be urged) becomes unintelligible. Indeed, it *looks* self-contradictory, as if we were asking whether Jones is still alive at a time when he is no longer alive—whether Jones is both alive and not alive at the same time. We may try to escape from this logical absurdity by using phrases like "discarnate existence," "alive, but disembodied." But such phrases, it will be said, have no clear meaning. No amount of facts, however well established, can have the slightest tendency to support a meaningless hypothesis, or to answer an unintelligible question. It would therefore be a waste of time to examine such facts in detail. There are other and more important things to do.

If I am right so far, questions about the meaning of the word "survival" or of the phrase "life after death" are not quite so arid and academic as they may appear. Anyone who wants to maintain that there is empirical evidence for survival ought to consider these questions, whether he thinks the evidence strong or weak. Indeed, anyone who thinks there is a *problem* of survival at all should ask himself what his conception of survival is.

Now why should it be thought that the very idea of life after death is unintelligible? Surely it is easy enough to conceive (whether or not it is true) that experiences might occur after Jones's death which are linked with experiences which he had before his death, in such a way that his personal identity is preserved? But, it will be said, the idea of after-death *experiences* is just the difficulty. What kind of experiences could they conceivably be? In a disembodied state, the supply of sensory stimuli is perforce cut off, because the supposed experient has no sense organs and no nervous system. There can therefore be no sense-perception. One has no means of being aware of material objects any longer; and if one has not, it is hard to see how one could have any emotions or wishes either. For all the emotions and wishes we have in this present life are concerned directly or indirectly with material objects, including of course our own organisms and other organisms, especially other human ones. In short, one could only be said to have experiences at all, if one is aware of some sort of a *world*. In this way, the idea of survival is bound up with the idea of "another world" or a "next world." Anyone who maintains that the idea of survival is after all intelligible must also be claiming that we can form some conception, however rough and provisional, of what "the next world" or "the other world" might be like. The skeptics I have in mind would say that we can form no such conception at all; and this, I think, is one of the main reasons why they hold that the conception of survival itself is unintelligible. I wish to suggest, on the contrary, that we *can* form some conception, in outline at any rate, of what a "next world" or "another world" might be like, and consequently of the kind of experiences which disembodied minds, if indeed there are such, might be supposed to have.

The thoughts which I wish to put before you on this subject are not at all original. Something very like them is to be found in the chapter on survival in Whately Carington's book *Telepathy*,[1] and in the concluding chapter of Professor C. J. Ducasse's book *Nature, Mind and Death*.[2] Moreover, if I am not mistaken, the Hindu conception of *Kama Loka* (literally, "the world of desire") is essentially the same as the one I wish to discuss; and something very similar is to be found in Mahayana Buddhism. In these two religions, of course, there is not just one "other world" but several different "other worlds," which we are supposed to experience in succession; not merely the next world, but the next but one, and another after that. But I think it will be quite enough for us to consider just the next world, without troubling ourselves about any

---

[1]Whately Carington, *Telepathy* (London: Methuen & Co., Ltd., 1945).

[2]C. J. Ducasse, *Nature, Mind and Death* (La Salle, Ill.: Open Court Publishing Co., 1951).

additional other worlds which there might be. It is a sufficiently difficult task, for us Western people, to convince ourselves that it makes sense to speak of any sort of after-death world at all. Accordingly, with your permission, I shall use the expressions "next world" and "other world" interchangeably. If anyone thinks this is an oversimplification, it will be easy for him to make the necessary corrections.

The next world, I think, might be conceived as a kind of dream-world. When we are asleep, sensory stimuli are cut off, or at any rate are prevented from having their normal effects upon our brain-centres. But we still manage to have experiences. It is true that sense-perception no longer occurs, but something sufficiently like it does. In sleep, our image-producing powers, which are more or less inhibited in waking life by a continuous bombardment of sensory stimuli, are released from this inhibition. And then we are provided with a multitude of objects of awareness, about which we employ our thoughts and towards which we have desires and emotions. These objects which we are aware of behave in a way which seems very queer to us when we wake up. The laws of their behaviour are not the laws of physics. But however queer their behaviour is, it does not at all disconcert us at the time and our personal identity is not broken.

In other words, my suggestion is that the next world, if there is one, might be a world of mental images. Nor need such a world be so "thin and insubstantial" as you might think. Paradoxical as it may sound, there is nothing imaginary about a mental image. It is an actual entity, as real as anything can be. The seeming paradox arises from the ambiguity of the verb "to imagine." It does sometimes mean "to have mental images." But more usually it means "to entertain propositions without believing them"; and very often they are false propositions, and moreover we *dis*believe them in the act of entertaining them. This is what happens, for example, when we read Shakespeare's play *The Tempest*, and that is why we say that Prospero and Ariel are "imaginary characters." Mental images are not in this sense imaginary at all. We do actually experience them, and they are no more imaginary than sensations. To avoid the paradox, though at the cost of some pedantry, it would be well to distinguish between *imagining* and *imaging*, and to have two different adjectives "imaginary" and "imagy." In this terminology, it is imaging, and not imagining, that I wish to talk about; and the next world, as I am trying to conceive of it, is an *imagy* world, but not on that account an imaginary one.

Indeed, to those who experienced it an image-world would be just as "real" as this present world is; perhaps so like it, that they would have considerable difficulty in realizing that they were dead. We are, of course, sometimes told in mediumistic communications that quite a lot of people do find it difficult to realize that they are dead; and this is just what we should expect if the next world is an image-world. Lord Russell and other philosophers have maintained that a material object in this present physical world is nothing more nor less than a complicated system of *appearances*. So far as I can see, there might be a set of visual images related to each other perspectivally, with front views and side views and back views all fitting neatly together in the way that ordinary visual appearances do now. Such a group of images might contain tactual images too. Similarly it might contain auditory images and smell images. Such a family of interrelated images would make a pretty good object. It would be quite a satisfactory substitute for the material objects which we perceive in this present life. And a whole world composed of such families of mental images would make a perfectly good world.

It is possible, however, and indeed likely, that some of those images would be what Francis Galton called *generic* images. An image representing a dog or a tree need not necessarily be an exact replica of some individual dog or tree one has perceived. It might rather be a representation of a *typical* dog or tree. Our memories are more specific on some subjects than on others. How specific they are depends probably on the degree of interest we had in the individual objects or events at the time when we perceived them. An event which moved us deeply is likely to be remembered specifically and in detail; and so is an individual object to which we were much attached (for example, the home of our childhood). But with other objects which interested us less and were less attended to, we retain only a "general impression" of a whole class of objects collectively. Left to our own resources, as we should be in the other world, with nothing but our memories to depend on, we should probably be able to form only generic images of such objects. In this respect, an image-world would not be an exact replica of this one, not even of those parts of this one which we have actually perceived. To some extent it would be, so to speak, a generalized picture, rather than a detailed reproduction.

Let us now put our question in another way, and ask what kind of experience a disembodied human mind might be supposed to have. We can then answer that it might be an experience in which *imaging* replaces sense-perception; "replaces" it, in the sense that imaging would perform much the same function as sense-perception performs now, by providing us with objects about which we could have thoughts, emotions and wishes. There is no reason why we should not be "as much alive," or at any rate *feel* as much alive, in an image-world as we do now in this present material world, which we perceive by means of our sense-organs and nervous systems. And so the use of the word "survival" ("life after death") would be perfectly justifiable.

It will be objected, perhaps, that one cannot be said to be alive unless one has a body. But what is meant here by "alive"? It is surely conceivable (whether or not it is true) that *experiences* should occur which are not causally connected with a physical organism. If they did, should we or should we not say that "life" was occurring. I do not think it matters much whether we answer Yes or No. It is purely a question of definition. If you define "life" in terms of certain very complicated physico-chemical processes, as some people would, then of course life after death is by definition impossible, because there is no longer anything to be alive. In that case, the problem of survival (*life* after bodily death) is misnamed. Instead, it ought to be called the problem of after-death *experiences*. And this is in fact the problem with which all investigators of the subject have been concerned. After all, what people want to know, when they ask whether we survive death, is simply whether experiences occur after death, or what likelihood, if any, there is that they do; and whether such experiences, if they do occur, are linked with each other and with *ante mortem* ones in such a way that personal identity is preserved. It is not physico-chemical processes which interest us, when we ask such questions. But there is another sense of the words "life" and "alive" which may be called the psychological sense; and in this sense "being alive" just *means* "having experiences of certain sorts." In this psychological sense of the word "life," it is perfectly intelligible to ask whether there is life after death, even though life in the physiological sense does *ex hypothesi* come to an end when someone dies. Or, if you like, the question is whether one could *feel* alive after bodily death, even though (by hypothesis) one would not *be* alive at the time. It will be just enough to satisfy most of us if the *feeling* of being alive continues after death. It will not make a halfpennyworth of difference that one will not then *be* alive in the physiological or biochemical sense of the word.

It may be said, however, that "feeling alive" (life in the psychological sense) cannot just be equated with having experiences in general. Feeling alive, surely, consists in having experiences of a special sort, namely *organic sensations*—bodily feelings of various sorts. In our present experience, these bodily feelings are not as a rule separately attended to unless they are unusually intense or unusually painful. They are a kind of undifferentiated mass in the background of consciousness. All the same, it would be said, they constitute our feeling of being alive; and if they were absent (as surely they must be when the body is dead) the feeling of being alive could not be there.

I am not at all sure that this argument is as strong as it looks. I think we should still feel alive—or alive enough—provided we experienced emotions and wishes, even if no organic sensations accompanied these experiences, as they do now. But in case I am wrong here, I would suggest that *images* or organic sensations could perfectly well provide what is needed. We can quite well image to ourselves what it feels like to be in a warm bath, even when we are not actually in one; and a person who has been crippled can image what it felt like to climb a mountain. Moreover, I would ask whether we do not feel alive when we are dreaming. It seems to me that we obviously do—or at any rate quite alive enough to go on with.

This is not all. In an image-world, a dream-like world such as I am trying to describe, there is no reason at all why there should not be *visual* images resembling the body which one had in this present world. In this present life (for all who are not blind) visual percepts of one's own body form as it were the constant centre of one's perceptual world. It is perfectly possible that visual images of one's own body might perform the same function in the next. They might form the continuing centre or nucleus of one's image world, remaining more or less constant while other images altered. If this were so, we should have an additional reason for expecting that recently dead people would find it difficult to realize that they were dead, that is, disembodied. To all appearances they *would* have bodies just as they had before, and pretty much the same ones. But, of course, they might discover in time that these image-bodies were subject to rather peculiar causal laws. For example, it might be found that in an image-world our wishes tend *ipso facto* to fulfil themselves in a way they do not now. A wish to go to Oxford might be immediately followed by the occurrence of a vivid and detailed set of Oxford-like images; even though, at the moment before, one's images had resembled Piccadilly Circus or the palace of the Dalai Lama in Tibet. In that case, one would realize that "going somewhere"—transferring one's body from one place to another—was a rather different process from what it had been in the physical world. Reflecting on such experiences, one might come to the conclusion that one's body was not after all the same as the physical body one had before death. One might conclude perhaps that it must be a "spiritual" or "psychical" body, closely resembling the old body in appearance, but possessed of rather different causal properties. It has been said, of course, that phrases like "spiritual body" or "psychical body" are utterly unintelligible, and that no conceivable empirical meaning could be given to such expressions. But I would rather suggest that they might be a way (rather a misleading way perhaps) of referring to a set of body-like images. If our supposed dead empiricist continued his investigations, he might discover that his whole world—not only his own body, but everything else he was aware of—had different causal properties from the physical world, even though everything in it had shape, size, colour, and other qualities which material objects have now. And so eventually, by the exercise of ordinary inductive good sense, he could draw the conclusion that he was in "the next world" or "the other world" and no longer in this one. If, however, he were a very dogmatic philosopher, who distrusted inductive good sense and preferred a priori reasoning, I do not know what condition he would be in. Probably he would never discover that he was dead at all. Being persuaded, on a priori ground, that life after death was impossible, he might insist on thinking that he must still be in this world, and refuse to pay any attention to the new and strange causal laws which more empirical thinkers would notice.

I think, then, that there is no difficulty in conceiving that the experience of feeling alive could occur in the absence of a physical organism; or, if you prefer to put it so, a disembodied personality could *be* alive in the psychological sense, even though by definition it would not be alive in the physiological or biochemical sense.

Moreover, I do not see why disembodiment need involve the destruction of personal identity. It is, of course, sometimes supposed that personal identity depends on the continuance of a background of organic sensation—the "mass of bodily feeling" mentioned before. (This may be called the somato-centric analysis of personal identity.) We must notice, however, that this background of organic sensation is not literally the same from one period of time to another. The very most that can happen is that the organic sensations which form the background of my experience now should be *exactly similar* to those which were the background of my experience a minute ago. And as a matter of fact, the present ones need not *all* be exactly similar to the previous ones. I might have a twinge of toothache now which I did not have then. I may even have an over-all feeling of lassitude now which I did not have a minute ago, so that the whole mass of bodily feeling, and not merely part of it, is rather different; and this would not interrupt my personal identity at all. The most that is required is only that the majority (not all) of my organic sensations should be closely (not exactly) similar to those I previously had. And even this is only needed if the two occasions are close together in my private time series; the organic sensations I have now might well be very unlike those I used to have when I was one year old. I say "in my private time series." For when I wake up after eight hours of dreamless sleep my personal identity is not broken, though in the physical or public time series there has been a long interval between the last organic sensations I experienced before falling asleep, and the first ones I experience when I wake up. But if similarity, and not literal sameness, is all that is required of this "continuing organic background," it seems to me that the continuity of it could be perfectly well preserved if there were organic *images* after death very like the organic *sensations* which occurred before death.

As a matter of fact, this whole "somato-centric" analysis of personal identity appears to me highly disputable. I should have thought that Locke was much nearer the truth when he said that personal identity depends on memory. But I have tried to show that even if the "somato-centric" theory of personal identity is right, there is no reason why personal identity need be broken by bodily death, provided there are images after death which sufficiently resemble the organic sensations one had before; and this is very like what happens when one falls asleep and begins dreaming.

There is, however, another argument against the conceivability of a disembodied person, to which some present-day linguistic philosophers would attach great weight. It is neatly expressed by Mr. A. G. N. Flew when he says, "people are what you meet."[3] By "a person" we are supposed to mean

---

[3]*University*, Vol. II, No. 2, 38, in a symposium on "Death" with Professor D. M. Mackinnon. Mr. Flew obviously uses "people" as the plural of "person"; but if we are to be linguistic, I am inclined to think that the nuances of "people" are not quite the same as those of "person." When we use the word "person," in the singular or the plural, the notion of consciousness is more prominently before our minds than it is when we use the word "people."

a human organism which behaves in certain ways, and especially one which speaks and can be spoken to. And when we say, "this is the same person whom I saw yesterday," we are supposed to mean just that it is the same human organism which I saw yesterday, and also that it behaves in a recognizably similar way.

"People are what you meet." With all respect to Mr. Flew, I would suggest that he does not in this sense "meet" *himself*. He might indeed have had one of those curious out-of-body experiences which are occasionally mentioned in our records, and he might have seen his body from outside (if he has, I heartily congratulate him); but I do not think we should call this "meeting." And surely the important question is, what constitutes my personal identity for *myself*. It certainly does not consist in the fact that other people can "meet" me. It might be that I was for myself the same person as before, even at a time when it was quite impossible for others to meet me. No one can "meet" me when I am dreaming. They can, of course, come and look at my body lying in bed; but this is not "meeting," because no sort of social relations are possible between them and me. Yet, although temporarily "unmeetable," during my dreams I am still, for myself, the same person that I was. And if I went on dreaming *in perpetuum*, and could never be "met" again, this need not prevent me from continuing to be, for myself, the same person.

As a matter of fact, however, we can quite easily conceive that "meeting" of a kind might still be possible between discarnate experients. And therefore, even if we do make it part of the definition of "a person," that he is capable of being met by others, it will still make sense to speak of "discarnate persons," provided we allow that telepathy is possible between them. It is true that a special sort of telepathy would be needed; the sort which in life produces *telepathic apparitions*. It would not be sufficient that A's thoughts or emotions should be telepathically affected by B's. If such telepathy were sufficiently prolonged and continuous, and especially if it were reciprocal, it would indeed have some of the characteristics of social intercourse; but I do not think we should call it "meeting," at any rate in Mr. Flew's sense of the word. It would be necessary, in addition, that A should be aware of something which could be called "B's body," or should have an experience not too unlike the experience of *seeing* another person in this life. This additional condition would be satisfied if A experienced a telepathic apparition of B. It would be necessary, further, that the telepathic apparition by means of which B "announces himself" (if one may put it so) should be recognizably similar on different occasions. And if it were a case of meeting some person *again* whom one had previously known in this world, the telepathic apparition would have to be recognizably similar to the physical body which that person had when he was still alive.

There is no reason why an image-world should not contain a number of images which are telepathic apparitions; and if it did, one could quite intelligently speak of "meeting other persons" in such a world. All the experiences I have when I meet another person in this present life could still occur, with only this difference, that percepts would be replaced by images. It would also be possible for another person to "meet" me in the same manner, if I, as a telepathic agent could cause him to experience a suitable telepathic apparition, sufficiently resembling the body I used to have when he formerly "met" me in this life.

I now turn to another problem which may have troubled some of you. If there be a next world, *where* is it? Surely it must be somewhere. But there does not seem to be any room for it. We can hardly suppose that it is up in the sky (i.e., outside the earth's atmosphere) or under the surface of the earth, as Homer and Vergil seemed to think. Such suggestions may have contented our ancestors, and the Ptolemaic astronomy may have made them acceptable, for some ages, even to the learned; but they will hardly content us. Surely the next world, if it exists, must be somewhere; and yet, it seems, there is nowhere for it to be.

The answer to this difficulty is easy if we conceive of the next world in the way I have suggested, as a dream-like world of mental images. Mental images, including dream images, are in a space of their own. They do have spatial properties. Visual images, for another, have extension and shape, and they have spatial relations to one another. But they have no spatial relation to objects in the physical world. If I dream of a tiger, my tiger-image has extension and shape. The dark stripes have spatial relation to the yellow parts, and to each other; the nose has a spatial relation to the tail. Again, the tiger image as a whole may have spatial relations to another image in my dream, for example to an image resembling a palm tree. But suppose we have to ask how far it is from the foot of my bed, whether it is three inches long, or longer or shorter; is it not obvious that these questions are absurd ones? We cannot answer them, not because we lack the necessary information or find it impracticable to make the necessary measurements, but because the questions themselves have no meaning. In the space of the physical world these images are nowhere at all. But in relation to other images of mine, each of them is somewhere. Each of them is extended, and its parts are in spatial relations to one another. There is no a priori reason why all extended entities must be in physical space.

If we now apply these considerations to the next world, as I am conceiving of it, we see that the question "where is it?" simply does not arise. An image-world would have a space of its own. We could not find it anywhere in the space of the physical world, but this would not in the least prevent it from being a spatial world all the same. If you like, it would be its own "where."[4]

I am tempted to illustrate this point by referring to the fairy-tale of Jack and the Beanstalk. I am not of course suggesting that we should take the story seriously. But if we were asked to try to make sense of it, how should we set about it? Obviously the queer world which Jack found was not at the top of the beanstalk in the literal, spatial sense of the words "at the top of." Perhaps he found some very large pole rather like a beanstalk, and climbed up it. But (we shall say) when he got to the top he suffered an abrupt change of consciousness, and began to have a dream or waking vision of a strange country with a giant in it. To choose another and more respectable illustration: In Book VI of Vergil's *Aeneid*, we are told how Aeneas descended into the Cave of Avernus with the Sibyl and walked from there into the other world. If we wished to make the narrative of the illustrious poet intelligible, how should we set about it? We should suppose that Aeneas did go down into the cave, but that once he was there he suffered a change of consciousness, and all the strange experiences which happened afterwards—seeing the River Styx, the Elysian Fields and the rest—were part of a dream or vision which he had. The space he passed through in his journey was an image-space, and the River Styx was not three Roman miles, or any other number of miles, from the cave in which his body was.

It follows that when we speak of "passing" from this world to the next, this passage is not to be thought of as any sort of movement in space. It should rather be thought of as a change of consciousness, analogous to the change which occurs when we "pass" from waking experience to dreaming. It would be a change from the perceptual type of consciousness to another type of consciousness in which perception ceases and imaging replaces it, but unlike the change from waking consciousness to dreaming in being irreversible. I suppose that nearly everyone nowadays who talks of "passing" from this world to the other does think of the transition in this way, as some kind of irreversible change of consciousness, and not as a literal spatial transition in which one goes from one place to another place.

So much for the question "where the next world is," if there be one. I have tried to show that if the next world is conceived of as a world of mental images, the question simply does not arise. I now turn to another difficulty. It may be felt that an image-world is somehow a deception and a sham, not a *real* world at all. I have said that it would be a kind of dream-world. Now when one has a dream in this life, surely the things one is aware of in the

---

[4]Conceivably its geometrical structure might also be different from the geometrical structure of the physical world. In that case the space of the next world would not only be other than the space of the physical world, but would also be a different *sort* of space.

dream are not *real* things. No doubt the dreamer really does have various mental images. These images do actually occur. But this is not all that happens. As a result of having these images, the dreamer believes, or takes for granted, that various material objects exist and various physical events occur; and these beliefs are mistaken. For example, he believes that there is a wall in front of him and that by a mere effort of will he succeeds in flying over the top of it. But the wall did not really exist, and he did not really fly over the top of it. He was in a state of delusion. Because of the images which he really did have, there *seemed* to him to be various objects and events which did not really exist at all. Similarly, you may argue, it may *seem* to discarnate minds (if indeed there are such) that there is a world in which they live, and a world not unlike this one. If they have mental images of the appropriate sort, it may even *seem* to them that they have bodies not unlike the ones they had in this life. But surely they will be mistaken. It is all very well to say, with the poet, that "dreams are real while they last"—that dream-objects are only called "unreal" when one wakes up, and normal sense-perceptions begin to occur with which the dream experiences can be contrasted. And it is all very well to conclude from this that if one did *not* wake up, if the change from sense-perception to imaging were irreversible, one would not call one's dream objects unreal, because there would then be nothing with which to contrast them. But would they not still *be* unreal for all that? Surely discarnate minds, according to my account of them, would be in a state of permanent delusion; whereas a dreamer in this life (fortunately for him) is only in a temporary one. And the fact that a delusion goes on for a long time, even forever and ever, does not make it any less delusive. Delusions do not turn themselves into realities just be going on and on. Nor are they turned into realities by the fact that their victim is deprived of the power of detecting their delusiveness.

Now, of course, if it were true that the next life (supposing there is one) is a condition of permanent delusion, we should just have to put up with it. We might not like it; we might think that a state of permanent delusion is a bad state to be in. But our likes and dislikes are irrelevant to the question. I would suggest, however, that this argument about the "delusiveness" or "unreality" of an image-world is based on confusion.

One may doubt whether there is any clear meaning in using the words "real" and "unreal" *tout court*, in this perfectly general and unspecified way. One may properly say, "this is real silver, and that is not," "this is a real pearl and that is not," or again "this is a real pool of water, and that is only a mirage." The point here is that something X is mistakenly believed to be something else Y, because it does resemble Y in some respects. It makes perfectly good sense, then, to say that X is not really Y. This piece of plated brass is not real silver, true enough. It only looks like silver. But for all that, it cannot be called "unreal" in the unqualified sense, in the sense of not existing at all. Even the mirage is something, though it is not the pool of water you took it to be. It is a perfectly good set of visual appearances, though it is not related to other appearances in the way you thought it was; for example, it does not have the relations to tactual appearances, or to visual appearances from other places, which you expected it to have. You may properly say that the mirage is not a real pool of water, or even that it is not a real physical object, and that anyone who thinks it is must be in a state of delusion. But there is no clear meaning in saying that it is just "unreal" *tout court*, without any further specification or explanation. In short, when the word "unreal" is applied to something, one means that it is different from something else, with which it might be mistakenly identified; what that something else is may not be explicitly stated, but it can be gathered from the context.

What, then, could people mean by saying that a next world such as I have described would be "unreal"? If they are saying anything intelligible, they must mean that it is different from something else, something else which it does resemble in some respects, and might therefore be confused with. And what is that something else? It is the present physical world in which we now live. An image-world, then, is only "unreal" in the sense that it is not really physical, though it might be mistakenly thought to be physical by some of those who experience it. But this only amounts to saying that the world I am describing would be an *other* world, other than this present physical world, which is just what it ought to be; other than this present physical world, and yet sufficiently like it to be possibly confused with it, because images do resemble percepts. And what would this otherness consist in? First, in the fact that it is in a *space* which is other than physical space; secondly, and still more important, in the fact that the *causal laws* of an image-world would be different from the laws of physics. And this is also our ground for saying that the events we experience in dreams are "unreal," that is, not really physical, though mistakenly believed by the dreamer to be so. They do in some ways closely resemble physical events, and that is why the mistake is possible. But the causal laws of their occurrence are quite different, as we recognize when we wake up; and just occasionally we recognize it even while we are still asleep.

Now let us consider the argument that the inhabitants of the other world, as I have described it, would be in a state of delusion. I admit that some of them might be. That would be the condition of the people described in the mediumistic communications already referred to—the people who "do not realize that they are dead." Because their images are so like the normal percepts they were accustomed to in this life, they believe mistakenly that they are still living in the physical world. But, as I have already tried to explain, their state of delusion need not be permanent and irremediable. By attending to the relations between one image and another, and applying the ordinary inductive methods by which we ourselves have discovered the causal laws of this present world in which *we* live, they too could discover in time what the causal laws of *their* world are. These laws, we may suppose, would be more like the laws of Freudian psychology than the laws of physics. And once the discovery was made, they would be cured of their delusion. They would find out, perhaps with surprise, that the world they were experiencing was *other* than the physical world which they experienced before, even though like it in some respects.

Let us now try to explore the conception of a world of mental images a little more fully. Would it not be a *"subjective"* world? And surely there would be many *different* next worlds, not just one; and each of them would be private. Indeed, would there not be as many next worlds as there are discarnate minds, and each of them wholly private to the mind which experiences it? In short, it may seem that each of us, when dead, would have his own dream-world, and there would be no common or public next world at all.

"Subjective," perhaps, is a rather slippery world. Certainly, an image-world would have to be subjective in the sense of being mind-dependent, dependent for its existence upon mental processes of one sort or another; images, after all, are mental entities. But I do not think that such a world need be completely private, if telepathy occurs in the next life. I have already mentioned the part which telepathic apparitions might play in it in connection with Mr. Flew's contention that "people are what you meet."[5] But there is more to be said. It is reasonable to suppose that in a disembodied state telepathy would occur more frequently than it does now. It seems likely that in this present life our telepathic powers are constantly being inhibited by our need to adjust ourselves to our physical environment. It even seems likely that many telepathic "impressions" which we receive at the unconscious level are shut out from consciousness by a kind of biologically motivated censorship. Once the pressure of biological needs is removed, we might expect that telepathy would occur continually, and manifest itself in consciousness by modifying and adding to the images which one experiences. (Even in this life, after all, some dreams are telepathic.)

If this is right, an image-world such as I am describing would not be the product of one single mind only, nor would it be purely private. It would be the joint product of a group of telepathically interacting minds and public to all of them. Nevertheless, one would not expect it to have unrestricted publicity. It is likely that there would still be *many* next worlds, a different one for each group of like-minded personalities. I admit I am not quite sure what might be meant by "like-minded" and "unlike-minded" in this connection. Perhaps we could say that two personalities are like-minded if their memories or their characters are sufficiently similar. It might be that Nero

---

[5]Cf. p. 287, above.

and Marcus Aurelius do not have a world in common, but Socrates and Marcus Aurelius do.

So far, we have a picture of many "semi-public" next worlds, if one may put it so; each of them composed of mental images, and yet not wholly private for all that, but public to a limited group of telepathically interacting minds. Or, if you like, after death everyone does have his own dream, but there is still some overlap between one person's dream and another's, because of telepathy.

I have said that such a world would be mind-dependent, even though dependent on a group of minds rather than a single mind. In what way would it be mind-dependent? Presumably in the same way as dreams are now. It would be dependent on the *memories* and the *desires* of the persons who experienced it. Their memories and their desires would determine what sort of images they had. If I may put it so, the "stuff" or "material" of such a world would come in the end from one's memories, and the "form" of it from one's desires. To use another analogy, memory would provide the pigments, and desire would paint the picture. One might expect, I think, that desires which had been unsatisfied in one's early life would play a specially important part in the process. That may seem an agreeable prospect. But there is another which is less agreeable. Desires which had been *repressed* in one's earthly life, because it was too painful or too disgraceful to admit that one had them, might also play a part, and perhaps an important part, in determining what images one would have in the next. And the same might be true of repressed memories. It may be suggested that what Freud (in one stage of his thought) called "the censor"—the force or barrier or mechanism which keeps some of our desires and memories out of consciousness, or only lets them in when they disguise themselves in symbolic and distorted forms—operates only in this present life and not in the next. However we conceive of "the censor," it does seem to be a device for enabling us to adapt ourselves to our environment. And when we no longer have an environment, one would expect that the barrier would come down.

We can now see that an after-death world of mental images can also be quite reasonably described in the terminology of the Hindu thinkers as "a world of desire" (Kama Loka). Indeed, this is just what we should expect if we assume that dreams, in this present life, are the best available clue to what the next life might be like. Such a world could also be described as "a world of memories"; because imaging, in the end, is a function of memory, one of the ways in which our memory-dispositions manifest themselves. But this description would be less apt, even though correct as far as it goes. To use the same rather inadequate language as before, the "materials" out of which an image-world is composed would have to come from the memories of the mind or group of minds whose world it is. But it would be their desires (including those repressed in earthly life) which determined the way in which these memories were used, the precise kind of dream which was built up out of them or on the basis of them.

It will, of course, be objected that memories cannot exist in the absence of a physical brain, nor yet desires, nor images either. But this proposition, however plausible, is after all just an empirical hypothesis, not a necessary truth. Certainly there is empirical evidence in favour of it. But there is also empirical evidence against it. Broadly speaking one might say, perhaps, that the "normal" evidence tends to support this materialistic or epiphenomenalist theory of memories, images, and desires, whereas the "supernormal" evidence on the whole tends to weaken the materialist or epiphenomenalist theory of human personality (of which this hypothesis about the brain-dependent character of memories, images, and desires is a part). Moreover, any evidence which directly supports the Survival Hypothesis (and there is quite a lot of evidence which does, provided we are prepared to admit that the Survival Hypothesis is intelligible at all) is *pro tanto* evidence against the materialistic conception of human personality.

In this lecture, I am not of course trying to argue in favour of the Survival Hypothesis. I am only concerned with the more modest task of trying to make it intelligible. All I want to maintain, then, is that there is nothing self-contradictory or logically absurd in the hypothesis that memories, desires, and images can exist in the absence of a physical brain. The hypothesis may, of course, be false. My point is only that it is not absurd; or if you like, that it is at any rate intelligible, whether true or not. To put the question in another way, when we are trying to work out for ourselves what sort of thing a discarnate life might conceivably be (if there is one) we have to ask what kind of *equipment*, so to speak, a discarnate mind might be supposed to have. It cannot have the power of sense-perception, nor the power of acting on the physical world by means of efferent nerves, muscles, and limbs. What would it have left? What could we take out with us, as it were, when we pass from this life to the next? What we take out with us, I suggest, can only be our memories and desires, and the power of constructing out of them an image world to suit us. Obviously we cannot take our material possessions out with us; but I do not think this is any great loss, for if we remember them well enough and are sufficiently attached to them, we shall be able to construct image-replicas of them which will be just as good, and perhaps better.

In this connection I should like to mention a point which has been made several times before. Both Whately Carington and Professor Ducasse have referred to it, and no doubt other writers have. But I believe it is of some importance and worth repeating. Ecclesiastically minded critics sometimes speak rather scathingly of the "materialistic" character of mediumistic communications. They are not at all edified by these descriptions of agreeable houses, beautiful landscapes, gardens, and the rest. And then, of course, there is Raymond Lodge's notorious cigar.[6] These critics complain that the next world as described in these communications is no more than a reproduction of this one, slightly improved perhaps. And the argument apparently is that the "materialistic" character of the communications is evidence against their genuineness. On the contrary, as far as it goes, it is evidence *for* their genuineness. Most people in this life do like material objects and are deeply interested in them. This may be deplorable, but there it is. If so, the image-world they would create for themselves in the next life might be expected to have just the "materialistic" character of which these critics complain. If one had been fond of nice houses and pleasant gardens in this life, the image-world one would create for oneself in the next might be expected to contain image-replicas of such objects, and one would make these replicas as like "the real thing" as one's memories permitted; with the help, perhaps, of telepathic influences from other minds whose tastes were similar. This would be all the more likely to happen if one had not been able to enjoy such things in this present life as much as one could wish.

But possibly I have misunderstood the objection which these ecclesiastical critics are making. Perhaps they are saying that if the next world is like this, life after death is not worth having. Well and good. If they would prefer a different sort of next world, and find the one described in these communications insipid and unsatisfying to their aspirations, then they can expect to get a different one—in fact, just the sort of next world they want. They have overlooked a crucial point which seems almost obvious; that if there is an after-death life at all, there must surely be many next worlds, separate from and as it were impenetrable to one another, corresponding to the *different* desires which different groups of discarnate personalities have.

The belief in life after death is often dismissed as "mere wish-fulfilment." Now it will be noticed that the next world as I have been trying to conceive of it is precisely a wish-fulfilment world, in much the same sense in which some dreams are described as wish-fulfilments. Should not this make a rational man very suspicious of the ideas I am putting before you? Surely this account of the other world is "too good to be true"? I think not. Here we must distinguish two different questions. The question whether human personality continues to exist after death is a question of fact, and wishes have nothing to do with it one way or the other. But *if* the answer to this factual question were "Yes" (and I emphasise the "if"), wishes might have a very great deal to do with the kind of world which discarnate beings would live in. Perhaps it may be helpful to consider a parallel case. It is a question of fact whether dreams occur in this present life. It has been settled by empirical investigation, and the wishes of the instigators have nothing to do with it. It is just a question of what the empirical facts are, whether one likes them or

---

[6]See: Sir Oliver Lodge, *Raymond Revised* (London: Methuen & Co., Ltd., 1922), p. 113.

not. Nevertheless, granting that dreams do occur, a man's wishes might well have a very great deal to do with determining what the content of his dreams is to be; especially unconscious wishes on the one hand, and on the other, conscious wishes which are not satisfied in waking life. Of course the parallel is not exact. There is one very important difference between the two cases. With dreams, the question of fact is settled. It is quite certain that many people do have dreams. But in the case of survival, the question of fact is not settled, or not at present. It is still true, however, that though wishes have nothing to do with it, they have a very great deal to do with the kind of world we should live in after death, *if* we survive death at all.

But perhaps this does not altogether dispose of the objection that my account of the other world is "too good to be true." Surely a sober-minded and cautious person would be very shy of believing that there is, or even could be, a world in which all our wishes are fulfilled? How very suspicious we are about travellers' tales of Eldorado or descriptions of idyllic South Sea islands! Certainly we are, and on good empirical grounds. For they are tales about this present material world; and we know that matter is very often recalcitrant to human wishes. But in a dream-world Desire is king. This objection would only hold good if the world I am describing were supposed to be some part of the *material* world—another planet perhaps, or the Earthly Paradise of which some poets have written. But the next world as I am trying to conceive of it (or rather next worlds, for we have seen that there would be many different ones) is not of course supposed to be part of the material world at all. It is a dream-like world of mental images. True enough, some of these images might be expected to resemble some of the material objects with which we are familiar now; but only if, and to the extent that, their percipients *wanted* this resemblance to exist. There is every reason, then, for being suspicious about descriptions of this present material world, or alleged parts of it, on the ground that they are "too good to be true"; but when it is a "country of the mind" (if one may say so) which is being described, these suspicions are groundless. A purely mind-dependent world, if such a world there be, would *have* to be a wish-fulfilment world.

Nevertheless, likes and dislikes, however irrelevant they may be, do of course have a powerful psychological influence upon us when we consider the problem of survival; not only when we consider the factual evidence for or against, but also when we are merely considering the theoretical implications of the Survival Hypothesis itself, as I am doing now. It is therefore worthwhile to point out that the next world as I am conceiving of it need not necessarily be an agreeable place at all. If arguments about what is good or what is bad did have any relevance, a case could be made out for saying that this conception of the next world is "too bad to be true," rather than too good. As we have seen, we should have to reckon with many different next worlds, not just with one. The world you experience after death would depend upon the kind of person you are. And if what I have said so far has any sense in it, we can easily conceive that some people's next worlds would be much more like purgatories than paradises—and pretty unpleasant purgatories too.

This is because there are *conflicting* desires within the same person. Few people, if any, are completely integrated personalities, though some people come nearer to it than others. And sometimes when a man's desires appear (even to himself) to be more or less harmonious with one another, the appearance is deceptive. His conscious desires do not conflict with one another or not much; but this harmony has only been achieved at the cost of repression. He has unconscious desires which conflict with the neatly organized pattern of his conscious life. If I was right in suggesting that repression is a biological phenomenon, if the "threshold" between conscious and unconscious no longer operates in a disembodied state, or operates much less effectively, this seeming harmony will vanish after the man is dead. To use scriptural language, the secrets of his heart will be revealed—at any rate to himself. These formerly repressed desires will manifest themselves by appropriate images, and these images might be exceedingly horrifying—as some dream-images are in this present life, and for the same reason. True enough, they will be "wish-fulfilment" images, like everything else that he experiences in the next world as I am conceiving it. But the wishes they fulfil will conflict with other wishes which he also has. And the emotional state which results might be worse than the worst nightmare; worse, because the dreamer cannot wake up from it. For example, in his after-death dream world he finds himself doing appallingly cruel actions. He never did them in his earthly life. Yet the desire to do them was there, even though repressed and unacknowledged. And now the lid is off, and this cruel desire fulfils itself by creating appropriate images. But unfortunately for his comfort, he has benevolent desires as well, perhaps quite strong ones; and so he is distressed and even horrified by these images, even though there is also a sense in which they are just the ones he wanted. Of course his benevolent desires too may be expected to manifest themselves by appropriate wish-fulfilment images. But because there is this conflict in his nature, they will not wholly satisfy him either. There will be something in him which rejects them as tedious and insipid. It is a question of the point of view, if one cares to put it so. Suppose a person has two conflicting desires A and B. Then from the point of view of desire A, the images which fulfil desire B will be unsatisfying, or unpleasant, or even horrifying; and vice versa from the point of view of desire B. And unfortunately, both points of view belong to the same person. He occupies them both at once.

This is not all. If psychoanalysts are right, there is such a thing as a desire to be punished. Most people, we are told, have guilt-feelings which are more or less repressed; we have desires, unacknowledged or only half-acknowledged, to suffer for the wrongs we have done. These desires too will have their way in the next world, if my picture of it is right, and will manifest themselves by images which fulfil them. It is not a very pleasant prospect, and I need not elaborate it. But it looks as if everyone would experience an image-purgatory which exactly suits him. It is true that his unpleasant experiences would not literally be punishments, any more than terrifying dreams are in this present life. They would not be inflicted upon him by an external judge; though, of course, if we are theists, we shall hold that the laws of nature, in other worlds as in this one, are in the end dependent on the will of a Divine Creator. Each man's purgatory would be just the automatic consequence of his own desires; if you like, he would punish himself by having just those images which his own good feelings demand. But, if there is any consolation in it, he would have these unpleasant experiences because he *wanted* to have them; exceedingly unpleasant as they might be, there would still be something in him which was satisfied by them.

There is another aspect of the conflict of desires. Every adult person has what we call "a character"; a set of more or less settled and permanent desires, with the corresponding emotional dispositions, expressing themselves in a more or less predictable pattern of thoughts, feelings, and actions. But it is perfectly possible to desire that one's character should be different, perhaps very different, from what it is at present. This is what philosophers call a "second-order" desire, a desire that some of one's own desires should be altered. Such second-order desires are not necessarily ineffective, as New Year resolutions are supposed to be. People can within limits alter their own characters, and sometimes do; and if they succeed in doing so, it is in the end because they *want* to. But these "second-order" desires—desires to alter one's own character—are seldom effective immediately; and even when they appear to be, as in some cases of religious conversion, there has probably been a long period of subconscious or unconscious preparation first. To be effective, desires of this sort must occur again and again. I must go on wishing to be more generous or less timid, and not just wish it on New Year's day; I must train myself to act habitually—and think too—in the way that I should act and think if I possessed the altered character for which I wish. From the point of view of the present moment, however, one's character is something fixed and given. The wish I have at half-past twelve today will do nothing, or almost nothing, to alter it.

These remarks may seem very remote from the topic I am supposed to be discussing. But they have a direct bearing on a question which has been mentioned before:[7] whether, or in what sense, the next world as I am conceiving of it should be called a "subjective" world. As I have already said, a next world such as I have described *would* be subjective, in the sense of mind-dependent. The minds which experience it would also have created it. It

[7]See p. 293 above.

would just be the manifestation of their own memories and desires, even though it might be the joint creation of a number of telepathically interacting minds, and therefore not wholly private. But there is a sense in which it might have a certain objectivity all the same. One thing we mean by calling something "objective" is that it is so whether we like it or not, and even if we dislike it. This is also what we mean by talking about "hard facts" or "stubborn facts."

At first sight it may seem that in an image-world such as I have described there could be no hard facts or stubborn facts, and nothing objective in this sense of the word "objective." How could there be, if the world we experience is itself a wish-fulfilment world? But a man's character *is* in this sense "objective"; objective in the sense that he has it whether he likes it or not. And facts about his character are as "hard" or "stubborn" as any. Whether I like it or not, and even though I dislike it, it is a hard fact about me that I am timid or spiteful, that I am fond of eating oysters or averse from talking French. I may wish sometimes that these habitual desires and aversions of mine were different, but at any particular moment this wish will do little or nothing to alter them. In the short run, a man's permanent and habitual desires are something "given" which he must accept and put up with as best he can, even though in the very long run they are alterable.

Now in the next life, according to my picture of it, it would be these permanent and habitual desires which would determine the nature of the world in which a person has to live. His world would be, so to speak, the outgrowth of his character; it would be his own character represented before him in the form of dream-like images. There is therefore a sense in which he gets exactly the sort of world he wants, whatever internal conflicts there may be between one of these wants and another. Yet he may very well dislike having the sort of character he does have. In the short run, as I have said, his character is something fixed and given, and objective in the sense that he has that character whether he likes it or not. Accordingly his image-world is also objective in the same sense. It is objective in the sense that it insists on presenting itself to him whether he likes it or not.

To look at the same point in another way: the next world as I am picturing it may be a very queer sort of world, but still it would be subject to causal laws. The laws would not, of course, be the laws of physics. As I have suggested already, they might be expected to be more like the laws of Freudian psychology. But they would be laws all the same, and objective in the sense that they hold good whether one liked it or not. And if we do dislike the image-world which our desires and memories create for us—if, when we get what we want, we are horrified to discover what things they were which we wanted—we shall have to set about altering our characters, which might be a very long and painful process.

Some people tell us, of course, that all desires, even the most permanent and habitual ones, will wear themselves out in time by the mere process of being satisfied. It may be so, and perhaps there is comfort in the thought. In that case the dream-like world of which I have been speaking would only be temporary, and we should have to ask whether after the next world there is a next but one. The problem of survival would then arise again in a new form. We should have to ask whether personal identity could still be preserved when we were no longer even dreaming. It could, I think, be preserved through the transition from this present, perceptible world to a dream-like image world of the kind I have been describing. But if even imaging were to cease, would there be anything left of human personality at all? Or would the state of existence—if any—which followed be one to which the notion of personality, at any rate our present notion, no longer had any application? I think that these are questions upon which it is unprofitable and perhaps impossible to speculate. (If anyone wishes to make the attempt, I can only advise him to consult the writings of the mystics, both Western and Oriental.) It is quite enough for us to consider what the *next* world might conceivably be like, and some of you may think that even this is too much.

Before I end, I should like to make one concluding remark. You may have noticed that the next world, according to my account of it, is not at all unlike what some metaphysicians say *this* world is. In the philosophy of Schopenhauer, this present world itself, in which we now live, is a world of "will and idea." And so it is in Berkeley's philosophy too; material objects are just collections of "ideas," though according to Berkeley the will which presents these ideas to us is the will of God, acting directly upon us in a way which is in effect telepathic. Could it be that these idealist metaphysicians have given us a substantially correct picture of the next world, though a mistaken picture of this one? The study of metaphysical theories is out of fashion nowadays. But perhaps students of psychical research would do well to pay some attention to them. *If* there are other worlds than this (again I emphasize the "if") who knows whether with some stratum of our personalities we are not living in them now, as well as in this present one which conscious sense-perception discloses? Such a repressed and unconscious awareness of a world different from this one might be expected to break through into consciousness occasionally in the course of human history, very likely in a distorted form, and this might be the source of those very queer ideas which we read of with so much incredulity and astonishment in the writings of some speculative metaphysicians. Not knowing their source, they mistakenly applied these ideas to this world in which we now live, embellishing them sometimes with an elaborate façade of deductive reasoning. Viewed in cold blood and with a skeptical eye, their attempts may appear extremely unconvincing and their deductive reasoning fallacious. But perhaps, without knowing it, they may have valuable hints to give us if we are trying to form some conception, however tentative, of "another world." And this is something we must try to do if we take the problem of survival seriously.

# R. B. Braithwaite

R. B. Braithwaite (1900– ), Cambridge philosopher, is the author of *Scientific Explanation* and of numerous articles on ethics, epistemology, and religion.

## 23

# An Empiricist's View of the Nature of Religious Belief

The meaning of any statement . . . will be taken as being given by the way it is used. The kernel for an empiricist of the problem of the nature of religious belief is to explain, in empirical terms, how a religious statement is used by a man who asserts it in order to express his religious conviction.

Since I shall argue that the primary element in this use is that the religious assertion is used as a moral assertion, I must first consider how moral assertions are used. According to the view developed by various moral philosophers since the impossibility of regarding moral statements as verifiable propositions was recognized, a moral assertion is used to express an *attitude* of the man making the assertion. It is not used to assert the proposition that he has the attitude—a verifiable psychological proposition; it is used to show forth or evince his attitude. The attitude is concerned with the action which he asserts to be right or to be his duty, or the state of affairs which he asserts to be good; it is a highly complex state, and contains elements to which various degrees of importance have been attached by moral philosophers who have tried to work out an "ethics without propositions." One element in the attitude is a feeling of approval toward the action; this element was taken as the fundamental one in the first attempts, and views of ethics without propositions are frequently lumped together as "emotive" theories of ethics. But discussion of the subject during the last twenty years has made it clear, I think, that no emotion or feeling of approval is fundamental to the use of

R. B. Braithwaite, *An Empiricist's View of the Nature of Religious Belief* (Cambridge: Cambridge University Press, 1955), pp. 11–28, 30–35. Reprinted by permission of the publisher.

moral assertions; it may be the case that the moral asserter has some specific feeling directed on to the course of action said to be right, but this is not the most important element in his "pro-attitude" towards the course of action: what is primary is his intention to perform the action when the occasion for it arises.

The form of ethics without propositions which I shall adopt is therefore a conative rather than an emotive theory: it makes the primary use of a moral assertion that of expressing the intention of the asserter to act in a particular sort of way specified in the assertion. A utilitarian, for example, in asserting that he ought to act so as to maximize happiness, is thereby declaring his intention to act, to the best of his ability, in accordance with the policy of utilitarianism: he is not asserting any proposition, or necessarily evincing any feeling of approval; he is subscribing to a policy of action. There will doubtless be empirical propositions which he may give as reasons for his adherence to the policy (e.g., that happiness is what all, or what most people, desire), and his having the intention will include his understanding what is meant by pursuing the policy, another empirically verifiable proposition. But there will be no specifically moral proposition which he will be asserting when he declares his intention to pursue the policy. This account is fully in accord with the spirit of empiricism, for whether or not a man has the intention of pursuing a particular behaviour policy can be empirically tested, both by observing what he does and by hearing what he replies when he is questioned about his intentions.

Not all expressions of intentions will be moral assertions: for the notion of morality to be applicable it is necessary either that the policy of action intended by the asserter should be a general policy (e.g., the policy of utilitarianism) or that it should be subsumable under a general policy which the asserter intends to follow and which he would give as the reason for his more specific intention. There are difficulties and vaguenesses in the notion of a general policy of action, but these need not concern us here. All that we require is that, when a man asserts that he ought to do so-and-so, he is using the assertion to declare that he resolves, to the best of his ability, to do so-and-so. And he will not necessarily be insincere in his assertion if he suspects, at the time of making it, that he will not have the strength of character to carry out his resolution.

The advantage this account of moral assertions has over all others, emotive non-propositional ones as well as cognitive propositional ones, is that it alone enables a satisfactory answer to be given to the question: What is the reason for my doing what I think I ought to do? The answer it gives is that, since my thinking that I ought to do the action is my intention to do it if possible, the reason why I do the action is simply that I intend to do it, if possible. On every other ethical view there will be a mysterious gap to be filled somehow between the moral judgment and the intention to act in accordance with it: there is no such gap if the primary use of a moral assertion is to declare such an intention.

Let us now consider what light this way of regarding moral assertions throws upon assertions of religious conviction. The idealist philosopher McTaggart described religion as "an emotion resting on a conviction of a harmony between ourselves and the universe at large"[1] and many educated people at the present time would agree with him. If religion is essentially concerned with emotion, it is natural to explain the use of religious assertions on the lines of the original emotive theory of ethics and to regard them as primarily evincing religious feelings or emotions. The assertion, for example, that God is our Heavenly Father will be taken to express the asserter's feeling secure in the same way as he would feel secure in his father's presence. But explanations of religion in terms of feeling, and of religious assertions as expressions of such feelings, are usually propounded by people who stand outside any religious system; they rarely satisfy those who speak from inside. Few religious men would be prepared to admit that their religion was a matter merely of feeling: feelings—of joy, of consolation, of being at one with the universe—may enter into their religion, but to evince such feelings is certainly not the primary use of their religious assertions.

This objection, however, does not seem to me to apply to treating religious assertions in the conative way in which recent moral philosophers have treated moral statements—as being primarily declarations of adherence to a policy of action, declarations of commitment to a way of life. That the way of life led by the believer is highly relevant to the sincerity of his religious conviction has been insisted upon by all the moral religions, above all, perhaps, by Christianity. "By their fruits ye shall know them." The view which I put forward for your consideration is that the intention of a Christian to follow a Christian way of life is not only the criterion for the sincerity of his belief in the assertions of Christianity; it is the criterion for the meaningfulness of his assertions. Just as the meaning of a moral assertion is given by its use in expressing the asserter's intention to act, so far as in him lies, in accordance with the moral principle involved, so the meaning of a religious assertion is given by its use in expressing the asserter's intention to follow a specified policy of behaviour. To say that it is belief in the dogmas of religion which is the cause of the believer's understanding to behave as he does is to put the cart before the horse: it is the intention to behave which constitutes what is known as religious conviction.

But this assimilation of religious to moral assertions lays itself open to an immediate objection. When a moral assertion is taken as declaring the intention of following a policy, the form of the assertion itself makes it clear

----

[1] J. M. E. McTaggart, *Some Dogmas of Religion* (London, 1906), p. 3.

what the policy is with which the assertion is concerned. For a man to assert that a certain policy ought to be pursued, which on this view is for him to declare his intention of pursuing the policy, presupposes his understanding what it would be like for him to pursue the policy in question. I cannot resolve not to tell a lie without knowing what a lie is. But if a religious assertion is the declaration of an intention to carry out a certain policy, what policy does it specify? The religious statement itself will not explicitly refer to a policy, as does a moral statement; how then can the asserter of the statement know what is the policy concerned, and how can he intend to carry out a policy if he does not know what the policy is? I cannot intend to do something I know not what.

The reply to this criticism is that, if a religious assertion is regarded as representative of a large number of assertions of the same religious system, the body of assertions of which the particular one is a representative specimen is taken by the asserter as implicitly specifying a particular way of life. It is no more necessary for an empiricist philosopher to explain the use of a religious statement taken in isolation from other religious statements than it is for him to give a meaning to a scientific hypothesis in isolation from other scientific hypotheses. We understand scientific hypotheses, and the terms that occur in them, by virtue of the relation of the whole system of hypotheses to empirically observable facts; and it is the whole system of hypotheses, not one hypothesis in isolation, that is tested for its truth-value against experience. So there are good precedents, in the empiricist way of thinking, for considering a system of religious assertions as a whole, and for examining the way in which the whole system is used.

If we do this, the fact that a system of religious assertions has a moral function can hardly be denied. For to deny it would require any passage from the assertion of a religious system to a policy of action to be mediated by a moral assertion. I cannot pass from asserting a fact, of whatever sort, to intending to perform an action, without having the hypothetical intention to intend to do the action if I assert the fact. This holds however widely fact is understood—whether as an empirical fact or as a non-empirical fact about goodness or reality. Just as the intention-to-act view of moral assertions is the only view that requires no reason for my doing what I assert to be my duty, so the similar view of religious assertions is the only one which connects them to ways of life without requiring an additional premise. Unless a Christian's assertion that God is love (*agape*)—which I take to epitomize the assertions of the Christian religion—be taken to declare his intention to follow an agapeistic way of life, he could be asked what is the connection between the assertion and the intention, between Christian belief and Christian practice. And this question can always be asked if religious assertions are separated from conduct. Unless religious principles are moral principles, it makes no sense to speak of putting them into practice.

The way to find out what are the intentions embodied in a set of religious assertions, and hence what is the meaning of the assertions, is by discovering what principles of conduct the asserter takes the assertions to involve. These may be ascertained both by asking him questions and by seeing how he behaves, each test being supplemental to the other. If what is wanted is not the meaning of the religious assertions made by a particular man but what the set of assertions would mean were they to be made by anyone of the same religion (which I will call their *typical* meaning), all that can be done is to specify the form of behaviour which is in accordance with what one takes to be the fundamental moral principles of the religion in question. Since different people will take different views as to what these fundamental moral principles are, the typical meaning of religious assertions will be different for different people. I myself take the typical meaning of the body of Christian assertions as being given by their proclaiming intentions to follow an agapeistic way of life, and for a description of this way of life—a description in general and metaphorical terms, but an empirical description nevertheless—I should quote most of the Thirteenth Chapter of I Corinthians. Others may think that the Christian way of life should be described somewhat differently, and will therefore take the typical meaning of the assertions of Christianity to correspond to their different view of its fundamental moral teaching.

My contention then is that the primary use of religious assertions is to announce allegiance to a set of moral principles: without such allegiance there is no "true religion." This is borne out by all the accounts of what happens when an unbeliever becomes converted to a religion. The conversion is not only a change in the propositions believed—indeed there may be no specifically intellectual change at all; it is a change in the state of will. An excellent instance is C. S. Lewis's . . . account of his conversion from an idealist metaphysic—"a religion (as he says) that cost nothing"—to a theism where he faced (and he quotes George MacDonald's phrase) "something to be neither more nor less nor other than *done*." There was no intellectual change, for (as he says) "there had long been an ethic (theoretically) attached to my Idealism": it was the recognition that he had to do something about it, that "an attempt at complete virtue must be made."[2] His conversion was a reorientation of the will.

In assimilating religious assertions to moral assertions I do not wish to deny that there are any important differences. One if the fact already noticed that usually the behaviour policy intended is not specified by one religious assertion in isolation. Another difference is that the fundamental moral teaching of the religion is frequently given, not in abstract terms, but by means of concrete examples—of how to behave, for instance, if one meets a man set

---

[2]C. S. Lewis, *Surprised by Joy* (London, 1955), pp. 198, 212–13.

upon by thieves on the road to Jericho. A resolution to behave like the good Samaritan does not, in itself, specify the behaviour to be resolved upon in quite different circumstances. However, absence of explicitly recognized general principles does not prevent a man from acting in accordance with such principles; it only makes it more difficult for a questioner to discover upon what principles he is acting. And the difficulty is not only one way round. If moral principles are stated in the most general form, as most moral philosophers have wished to state them, they tend to become so far removed from particular courses of conduct that it is difficult, if not impossible, to give them any precise content. It may be hard to find out what exactly is involved in the imitation of Christ; but it not very easy to discover what exactly is meant by the pursuit of Aristotle's *eudaemonia* or of Mill's *happiness*. The tests for what it is to live agapeistically are as empirical as are those for living in quest of happiness; but in each case the tests can best be expounded in terms of examples of particular situations.

A more important difference between religious and purely moral principles is that, in the higher religions at least, the conduct preached by the religion concerns not only external but also internal behaviour. The conversion involved in accepting a religion is a conversion, not only of the will, but of the heart. Christianity requires not only that you should behave towards your neighbour as if you loved him as yourself: it requires that you should love him as yourself. And though I have no doubt that the Christian concept of *agape* refers partly to external behaviour—the agapeistic behaviour for which there are external criteria—yet being filled with *agape* includes more than behaving agapeistically externally: it also includes an agapeistic frame of mind. I have said that I cannot regard the expression of a feeling of any sort as the primary element in religious assertion; but this does not imply that intention to feel in a certain way is not a primary element, nor that it cannot be used to discriminate religious declarations of policy from declarations which are merely moral. Those who say that Confucianism is a code of morals and not, properly speaking, a religion are, I think, making this discrimination.

The resolution proclaimed by a religious assertion may then be taken as referring to inner life as well as to outward conduct. And the superiority of religious conviction over the mere adoption of a moral code in securing conformity to the code arises from a religious conviction changing what the religious man wants. It may be hard enough to love your enemy, but once you have succeeded in doing so it is easy to behave lovingly towards him. But if you continue to hate him, it requires a heroic perseverance continually to behave as if you loved him. Resolutions to feel, even if they are only partly fulfilled, are powerful reinforcements of resolutions to act.

But though these qualifications may be adequate for distinguishing religious assertions from purely moral ones, they are not sufficient to discriminate between assertions belonging to one religious system and those belonging to another system in the case in which the behaviour policies, both of inner life and of outward conduct, inculcated by the two systems are identical. For instance, I have said that I take the fundamental moral teaching of Christianity to be the preaching of an agapeistic way of life. But a Jew or a Buddhist may, with considerable plausibility, maintain that the fundamental moral teaching of his religion is to recommend exactly the same way of life. How then can religious assertions be distinguished into those which are Christian, those which are Jewish, those which are Buddhist, by the policies of life which they respectively recommend if, on examination, these policies turn out to be the same?

Many Christians will, no doubt, behave in a specifically Christian manner in that they will follow ritual practices which are Christian and neither Jewish nor Buddhist. But though following certain practices may well be the proper test for membership of a particular religious society, a church, not even the most ecclesiastically minded Christian will regard participation in a ritual as the fundamental characteristic of a Christian way of life. There must be some more important difference between an agapeistically policied Christian and an agapeistically policied Jew than that the former attends a church and the latter a synagogue.

The really important difference, I think, is to be found in the fact that the intentions to pursue the behaviour policies, which may be the same for different religions, are associated with thinking of different *stories* (or sets of stories). By a story I shall here mean a proposition or set of propositions which are straightforwardly empirical propositions capable of empirical test and which are thought of by the religious man in connection with his resolution to follow the way of life advocated by his religion. On the assumption that the ways of life advocated by Christianity and by Buddhism are essentially the same, it will be the fact that the intention to follow this way of life is associated in the mind of a Christian with thinking of one set of stories (the Christian stories) while it is associated in the mind of a Buddhist with thinking of another set of stories (the Buddhist stories) which enables a Christian assertion to be distinguished from a Buddhist one.

A religious assertion will, therefore, have a propositional element which is lacking in a purely moral assertion, in that it will refer to a story as well as to an intention. The reference to the story is not an assertion of the story taken as a matter of empirical fact: it is a telling of the story, or an alluding to the story, in the way in which one can tell, or allude to, the story of a novel with which one is acquainted. To assert the whole set of assertions of the Christian religion is both to tell the Christian doctrinal story and to confess allegiance to the Christian way of life.

The story, I have said, is a set of empirical propositions, and the language expressing the story is given a meaning by the standard method of understanding how the story-statements can be verified. The empirical story-statements will vary from Christian to Christian; the doctrines of Christianity are capable of different empirical interpretations, and Christians will differ in the interpretations they put upon the doctrines. But the interpretations will all be in terms of empirical propositions. Take, for example, the doctrine of Justification by means of the Atonement. Matthew Arnold imagined it in terms of

> ... a sort of infinitely magnified and improved Lord Shaftesbury, with a race of vile offenders to deal with, whom his natural goodness would incline him to let off, only his sense of justice will not allow it; then a younger Lord Shaftesbury, on the scale of his father and very dear to him, who might live in grandeur and splendour if he liked, but who prefers to leave his home, to go and live among the race of offenders, and to be put to an ignominious death, on condition that his merits shall be counted against their demerits, and that his father's goodness shall be restrained no longer from taking effect, but any offender shall be admitted to the benefit of it on simply pleading the satisfaction made by the son—and then, finally, a third Lord Shaftesbury, still on the same high scale, who keeps very much in the background, and works in a very occult manner, but very efficaciously nevertheless, and who is busy in applying everywhere the benefits of the son's satisfaction and the father's goodness.[3]

Arnold's "parable of the three Lord Shaftesburys" got him into a lot of trouble: he was "indignantly censured" (as he says) for wounding "the feelings of the religious community by turning into ridicule an august doctrine, the subject of their solemn faith."[4] But there is no other account of the Anselmian doctrine of the Atonement that I have read which puts it in so morally favourable a light. Be that as it may, the only way in which the doctrine can be understood verificationally is in terms of human beings—mythological beings, it may be, who never existed, but who nevertheless would have been empirically observable had they existed.

For it is not necessary, on my view, for the asserter of a religious assertion to believe in the truth of the story involved in the assertions: what is necessary is that the story should be entertained in thought, i.e., that the statement of the story should be understood as having a meaning. I have secured this by requiring that the story should consist of empirical propositions. Educated Christians of the present day who attach importance to the doctrine of the Atonement certainly do not believe an empirically testable story in Matthew Arnold's or any other form. But it is the fact that entertainment in thought of this and other Christian stories forms the context in which Christian resolutions are made which serves to distinguish Christian assertions from those made by adherents of another religion, or of no religion.

---

[3]Matthew Arnold, *Literature and Dogma* (1873), pp. 306–7.
[4]Matthew Arnold, *God and the Bible* (1875), pp. 18–19.

What I am calling a *story* Matthew Arnold called a *parable* and a *fairytale*. Other terms which might be used are *allegory, fable, tale, myth*. I have chosen the word "story" as being the most neutral term, implying neither that the story is believed nor that it is disbelieved. The Christian stories include straightforward historical statements about the life and death of Jesus of Nazareth; a Christian (unless he accepts the unplausible Christ-myth theory) will naturally believe some or all of theses. Stories about the beginning of the world and of the Last Judgment as facts of past or of future history are believed by many unsophisticated Christians. But my contention is that belief in the truth of the Christian stories is not the proper criterion for deciding whether or not an assertion is a Christian one. A man is not, I think, a professing Christian unless he both proposes to live according to Christian moral principles and associates his intention with thinking of Christian stories; but he need not believe that the empirical propositions presented by the stories correspond to empirical fact.

But if the religious stories need not be believed, what function do they fulfil in the complex state of mind and behaviour known as having a religious belief? How is entertaining the story related to resolving to pursue a certain way of life? My answer is that the relation is a psychological and causal one. It is an empirical psychological fact that many people find it easier to resolve upon and to carry through a course of action which is contrary to their natural inclinations if this policy is associated in their minds with certain stories. And in many people the psychological link is not appreciably weakened by the fact that the story associated with the behaviour policy is not believed. Next to the Bible and the Prayer Book the most influential work in English Christian religious life has been a book whose stories are frankly recognized as fictitious—Bunyan's *Pilgrim's Progress;* and some of the most influential works in setting the moral tone of my generation were the novels of Dostoievsky. It is completely untrue, as a matter of psychological fact, to think that the only intellectual considerations which affect action are beliefs: it is *all* the thoughts of a man that determine his behaviour; and these include his phantasies, imaginations, ideas of what he would wish to be and do, as well as the propositions which he believes to be true ...

There is one story common to all the moral theistic religions which has proved of great psychological value in enabling religious men to persevere in carrying out their religious behaviour policies—the story that in so doing they are doing the will of God. And here it may look as if there is an intrinsic connection between the story and the policy of conduct. But even when the story is literally believed, when it is believed that there is a magnified Lord Shaftesbury who commands or desires the carrying out of the behaviour policy, that in itself is no reason for carrying out the policy: it is necessary also to have the intention of doing what the magnified Lord Shaftesbury commands or desires. But the intention to do what a person commands or desires, irrespective of what this command or desire may be, is no part of a higher religion; it is when the religious man finds that what the magnified Lord Shaftesbury commands or desires accords with his own moral judgement that he decides to obey or to accede to it. But this is no new decision, for his own moral judgement is a decision to carry out a behaviour policy; all that is happening is that he is describing his old decision in a new way. In religious conviction the resolution to follow a way of life is primary; it is not derived from believing, still less from thinking of, any empirical story. The story may psychologically support the resolution, but it does not logically justify it.

In this lecture I have been sparing in my use of the term "religious belief" (although it occurs in the title), preferring instead to speak of religious assertions and of religious conviction. This was because for me the fundamental problem is that of the meaning of statements used to make religious assertions, and I have accordingly taken my task to be that of explaining the use of such assertions, in accordance with the principle that meaning is to be found by ascertaining use. In disentangling the elements of this use I have discovered nothing which can be called "belief" in the senses of this word applicable either to an empirical or to a logically necessary proposition. A religious assertion, for me, is the assertion of an intention to carry out a certain behaviour policy, subsumable under a sufficiently general principle to be a moral one, together with the implicit or explicit statement, but not the assertion, of certain stories. Neither the assertion of the intention nor the reference to the stories includes belief in its ordinary senses. But in avoiding the term "belief" I have had to widen the term "assertion," since I do not pretend that either the behaviour policy intended or the stories entertained are adequately specified by the sentences used in making isolated religious assertions. So assertion has been extended to include elements not explicitly expressed in the verbal form of the assertion. If we drop the linguistic expression of the assertion altogether the remainder is what may be called religious belief. Like moral belief, it is not a species of ordinary belief, of belief in a proposition. A moral belief is an intention to behave in a certain way: a religious belief is an intention to behave in a certain way (a moral belief) together with the entertainment of certain stories associated with the intention in the mind of the believer. This solution of the problem of religious belief seems to me to do justice both to the empiricist's demand that meaning must be tied to empirical use and to the religious man's claim for his religious beliefs to be taken seriously.

Seriously, it will be retorted, but not objectively. If a man's religion is all a matter of following the way of life he sets before himself and of strengthening his determination to follow it by imagining exemplary fairytales, it is purely subjective: his religion is all in terms of his own private ideals and of his own private imaginations. How can he even try to convert others to his religion if there is nothing objective to convert them to? How can he argue in its defence if there is no religious proposition which he believes, nothing which he takes to be the fundamental truth about the universe? And is it of any public interest what mental techniques he uses to bolster up his will? Discussion about religion must be more than the exchange of autobiographies.

But we are all social animals; we are all members one of another. What is profitable to one man in helping him to persevere in the way of life he has decided upon may well be profitable to another man who is trying to follow a similar way of life; and to pass on information that might prove useful would be approved by almost every morality. The autobiography of one man may well have an influence upon the life of another, if their basic wants are similar.

But suppose that these are dissimilar, and that the two men propose to conduct their lives on quite different fundamental principles. Can there be any reasonable discussion between them? This is the problem that has faced the many moral philosophers recently who have been forced, by their examination of the nature of thinking, into holding non-propositional theories of ethics. All I will here say is that to hold that the adoption of a set of moral principles is a matter of the personal decision to live according to these principles does not imply that beliefs as to what are the practical consequences of following such principles are not relevant to the decision. An intention, it is true, cannot be logically based upon anything except another intention. But in considering what conduct to intend to practice, it is highly relevant whether or not the consequences of practicing that conduct are such as one would intend to secure. As R. M. Hare has well said, an ultimate decision to accept a way of life, "far from being arbitrary, . . . would be the most well-founded of decisions, because it would be based upon a consideration of everything upon which it could possibly be founded."[5] And in this consideration there is a place for every kind of rational argument.

Whatever may be the case with other religions, Christianity has always been a personal religion demanding personal commitment to a personal way of life. In the words of another Oxford philosopher, "the questions 'What shall I do?' and 'What moral principles should I adopt?' must be answered by each man for himself."[6] Nowell-Smith takes this as part of the meaning of morality: whether or not this is so, I am certain that it is of the very essence of the Christian religion.

---

[5]R. M. Hare, *The Language of Morals* (Oxford, 1952), p. 69.
[6]P. H. Nowell-Smith, *Ethics* (1954), p. 320.

# J. H. Randall, Jr.

John Hermann Randall, Jr. (1899–1980), of Columbia University, was
the author of a number of influential works in the history of philosophy.

# 24

# *A Form of Religious Naturalism*

We are now in a position to ask once more our major question. What,
in the light of this long history of relations intimate if not always legitimatized
between them, is the rightful place of knowledge in religion? At the outset
we can, I think, agree on certain preliminary negative conclusions. Note well
this "preliminary": for as we push our exploratory investigation we shall be
forced to introduce significant qualifications. But, accepting the main features
of the analysis of the institution of religion worked out by our cultural
sciences, we can say, religion and knowledge are clearly not rivals for our
intellectual respect, though they may well be for our affections. This holds
whether that "knowledge" be taken as the deliverances of the enterprise of
science, as the findings of the thoughtful philosophical interpretation of
experience, or as the opinions of mere sound common sense. These are the
three major kinds of formulated assertions or propositions capable of being
tested by evidence and of being judged to be true. As thus susceptible to
verification, they are commonly agreed to constitute "knowledge"; they
include both descriptions of facts and explanations of those facts, for both
take the form of statements *that* such and such is the case. This is the sense of
"knowledge" whose role in religion we are questioning. It is necessary to be
precise about just what we mean by "knowledge," lest our arguments turn
into quarrels about the mere use of words. It is beyond doubt, there can be
no serious conflict between religion and "knowledge" in this sense, "knowledge" taken as factual descriptions or theoretical explanations of anything,
as propositions that are "warrantedly assertible" or "true."

For religion offers no descriptions and no explanations whatever independent of men's best secular knowledge—though its presence and its chal-

---

"Knowledge, Intelligence, and Religious Symbols," Chap. 4 in Randall, *The Role of Knowledge in Western Religion* (Boston: Beacon Press, 1958). Reprinted by permission of the author.

lenge may, and historically has, come to influence that knowledge profoundly. Religion is rather itself a human activity that demands careful observation and description, explanation, reflective understanding, and intelligent criticism. A religion, we have seen, may well embrace in the body of beliefs associated with it an explanation, a truth, drawn from some nonreligious source. The religious thought of those interested in explanations normally does, and certainly in the Christian tradition has done so from the beginning. These explanations embodied in religious beliefs then may well come later to conflict with new and better secular explanations: this too has happened again and again, and in some areas of inquiry is still happening today. But the conflict will then arise between different explanations within the common intellectual enterprise of discovering truth. It will not break out between the religious life and fresh explanation or knowledge.

We can assume, therefore, that all religious beliefs without exceptions are "mythology." That is, they are all religious "symbols." If such symbols can be said to possess any kind of "truth," they certainly do not possess the literal truth of the factual statements of the descriptive sciences or of common sense, or the "warranted assertibility" and explanatory value of the well founded theories of science and philosophy.

In passing, we might well ask, are scientific beliefs, the hypotheses, theories and laws that go beyond mere descriptive statements of fact, any the less "mythological," any the less "symbols" or instruments of the techniques of inquiry? If they too be indeed symbols, then they are symbols of something else, surely, and perhaps in a significantly different way. But the same Goodenough[1] already quoted goes on to insist, rightly enough, that if religious beliefs and symbols are "wish projections," so too are scientific hypotheses and theories. Neither can rightly claim to be literal statements of the nature of things.

To this negative conclusion, that there is no literal description of fact or explanatory truth to be found in religion in general or in Christianity in particular, there would today be widespread agreement. It would be found not only among scientific and philosophic students of religion, but also among the many Christian theologians and philosophers who would not pride themselves on holding to the letter of orthodoxy. The full implications of this position, however, seem not always to be realized. It means, for instance, not only that the "existence of God" is a "myth" or symbol; Neo-Orthodox theologians can easily take this in their stride. It means also that the doctrine of Original Sin is likewise a "myth" or symbol, and supplies no literal truth about man that other adequate analyses of human nature can not and have not been able to arrive at. Between a religious, even a Christian, view of

---

[1]Edwin R. Goodenough, *Towards a Mature Faith* (Englewood-Cliffs, N.J.: Prentice-Hall, Inc., 1955).—EDITOR

human nature, and a sound psychological analysis, there can be no conflict—as explanations, as truth. In practice this seems a much harder doctrine to take seriously. It is by no means clear that all the Neo-Orthodox would countenance it.

The reason, no doubt, is that adequate analyses of human nature and sound psychological judgments are not easy to come by—as yet. For it is not very difficult to suspect certain limitations in behavioristic psychology. Graham Wallas once remarked that it had gotten along swimmingly as far up the scale as the decorticated white rat; but since then of course it has gone on to Pavlov's dog. Indeed, even Joseph Wood Krutch has a certain justification in his distrust of the adequacy of all laboratory methods to deal with the nature of man. And as for depth psychology, despite the spate of candidates, it has still to give birth to its Newton; as yet we have had only a number of rival Keplers. In this far from stabilized climate of psychological opinion, it is not surprising that genuine insight is still to be won from poets like Paul or Augustine. But poetic insight into human nature, however revealing in particular, is inherently far from exhaustive or balanced. And sensitive religious students of the nature of man might well pause to recollect that if Kierkegaard be an authentic and gifted poet whose insights are to be taken seriously, so too is Jesus of Nazareth.

At the moment, indeed, the severest specific intellectual conflict between newer ideas and the older ones enshrined in religious thought is raised when religious men confront some of our recent psychological theories. It is not the world but the nature of man that so-called "science" today seems to be distorting. Since for all their suggestiveness and their promise that they will lead to future knowledge, these speculative theories and approaches to the analysis of human nature of our psychological Keplers are not notorious for their sobriety, sanity, or general wisdom and judicious appraisals, the religious men who are shocked would do well to exercise a little toleration, and patience. The morrow will bring new theories of man.

We can agree, secondly, that if no truth is to be found in religion that can possibly conflict with the explanations of science, neither does religion furnish men with any *additional* "truth" discoverable by specifically religious methods that will supplement the conclusions of patient inquiry. It provides no further "truth" about the world or man not attainable by the intellectual methods we ordinarily call "scientific." By this time liberal Christians and Jews have pretty well reconstructed their beliefs so that they no longer come into open conflict with any of the verified conclusions of the scientists. But they are still apt to hold that their faith adds further knowledge, either explanations of a realm inaccessible to scientific inquiry, or an additional kind of explanation of the same realm from which that inquiry selects. This assumption is historically a holdover from the days of idealistic philosophy, when the narrow and limited methods and assumptions of natural science were obviously inapplicable to human experience, and hence inevitably drove men on to other methods and assumptions for inquiring into those richer and more concrete fields. The apologetic strategy of these belated idealists is to point to the obvious fact that mathematical and laboratory techniques do not yield significant results when applied to the moral and spiritual activities of men. But these are only the *techniques* and *procedures* of physical science; they are emphatically not "scientific method" and "logic" themselves. Of course practical procedures differ from field to field, but the logic and method of inquiry are the same for all fields, as well as the rules of evidence.

Nor can the view be sustained that "religious experience" is a specific and distinctive cognitive activity of man, involving unique factors or materials, and hence bringing a knowledge of its special objects which is to be gained in no other manner. "Religious experience" is not unique. In this respect it is not like the "mystic experience," so exploited in this century as an apologetic for a distinctive and "higher" religious knowledge. If we take "mystic" as an immediate quality of experience—or as a quality of immediate experience— viewed from the personal side, this unique quality can indeed function religiously, it can indeed play an important part in the religious life. But it is clearly by no means necessary to that life. And it can occur quite apart from the religious situation, as the effect of certain drugs, for example. The specifically religious function of the mystic experience is to strengthen religious commitment, conviction, and vision, but not to give theoretical knowledge, of God or anything else.

"Functioning religiously" is indeed very much like "functioning aesthetically": any set of factors can be involved in the practice of the religious life, in "functioning religiously." Just as no one type of material alone possesses aesthetic qualities or powers, but any type can on occasion function aesthetically, just so, no one type of activity or "experience" alone possesses religious qualities or powers, but any type can on occasion function religiously. The qualities or powers become "religious" in character if they function in the specifically religious way. What such religious functioning involves as its essential components we attempted to characterize briefly at the close of the previous chapter.

Indeed, "mystic experience," or any other similar type of immediate experience, like Otto's experience of "the Holy" or "the Numinous," or like the "Thou"[2] of the "I-Thou experience," while genuine enough, does not and cannot by itself tell us what its object "really is," what its relations are to other objects in experience, what are its causes and conditions, what are its values

---

[2]Martin Buber has made it clear that he does not pretend to know what God or the Divine "really is"—what God may be apart from his relations to man. He reports rather that in his own experience, and in the experience of the Hebrew people he finds recorded in the "Biblical religion" of the Hebrew Scripture, God is always encountered in the guise of a person.

and consequences. For that we have to turn to intellectual inquiry, to scientific methods.

Again, while "religious experience" can be supremely valuable, it is clearly not an experience of "values" about which we can come to learn in no other way. It can not tell us what those values "are": their nature, their consequences, their relations to their causes and conditions and to other values. Only inquiry can do that. Scientific method and logic can of course deal with values, in answering precisely these questions about them. Indeed, science is essentially a method for the *criticism* of values, for determining which beliefs are *better than* others.

Nor does there seem to be any such thing as "existential truth," quite different from and irrelevant to "nonparticipating detached scientific truth."[3] Devotion—"existential commitment"—to something may bring many fruits: sympathy, understanding of its appeal from within, sensitive feeling, awareness of qualities, and many others. But none of these consequences is "knowledge" or "truth." We cannot indeed become "acquainted with" a painting without looking at it with our eyes. But eyes alone are not sufficient for an understanding of the painting, for knowledge of its aesthetic or other "meaning." Likewise, sharing a belief may be essential to becoming acquainted with what it is—"with what it means," we say. But mere sharing hardly establishes the truth of the belief. Many a German through sharing and commitment found "existential truth" in the Nazi ideology. Commitment may be a necessary condition of some kinds of truth, though there is such a thing as imaginative sympathy or empathy. But it is clearly not a sufficient criterion. Here too only patient inquiry and checking will suffice.

Religion, then, furnishes no additional "truth" about the world or man or the Divine. What it does furnish—and here the "extranaturalists" or "transcendentalists" are clearly right—is additional subject matter, experiences and qualities that are found and enjoyed, visions that are seen. Religion gives men more, and how much more only the participant can realize. In this it is like art, which likewise furnishes no supplementary truth, but does open whole worlds to be explored, whole heavens to be enjoyed. What the poet, the artist, the prophet or the saint beholds, is genuine and important enough, if his vision be actually authentic. But visions are not understood by vision. They may not, and perhaps need not, be understood at all, in order to live by them. But if we do seek to understand visions, we can only understand and interpret them by patient inquiry. The intellectual clarification of religious insight and vision is one of the most important of all contributions which intelligence can make to the religious life. It is the essential and necessary condition of the most valuable of all the functions of intelligence in religion,

---

[3]The phrase is Paul Tillich's.

the criticism of the activities and visions of man's spiritual experience of the Divine.

If the function of religious beliefs is not to generate knowledge and truth, what is their function? Very early in every great religious tradition, reflective men came to see that the ordinary ideas entertained and used in worship, prayer and ritual could not be "literally" true. The idea of God, for example, employed by the unreflective in the actual practice of the religious arts, could not be adequate to the true nature of the Divine. God could not be "really" the animal, or natural force, or carved image, the imaginative picture, in which the average man conceives the Divine. He could not be even the highest human image, the "Father," or the kind of "person" who in the present fashion seems appropriately approached in terms of the "I-Thou" experience. Important and even indispensable in religious practice as are these ways of imagining the Divine, they are all, reflective men soon came to realize, attempts to fit the idea of God in somehow with the rest of men's experience. But they are not adequate definitions or descriptions of the religious dimension of that experience. They cannot be taken as literal accounts of the Divine. They are imaginative and figurative ways of conceiving the relations of men and their ideals to the nature of things, and to its religious dimensions. We have seen how the Greeks came to this insight, that all ideas of the Divine are necessarily imaginative and symbolic. We have seen how Philo of Alexandria worked out the consequences of this notion for the Hebraic tradition, and how the Alexandrian Doctors and Augustine carried the same realization into Christian theology.

All ideas of God, like all other religious beliefs, are without exception *religious symbols*. This means that they perform what is primarily a religious function. They are employed in religious experience, and serve to carry on the religious life. They are techniques, instruments, in terms of which ritual and the other religious arts are conducted.

But not all conceptions of God are imaginative images drawn from men's experience of their fellows. There is a notorious difference between ideas of God whose primary function is to serve in religious practice, which are employed in the actual conduct of religious techniques, worship, prayer and the rest—ideas like those of God as a loving Father, God as a stern Judge, God as the "Thou" of the "I-Thou" relationship—and a quite different set of ideas of God worked out for very different purposes by philosophic theologians. The function of these latter ideas, as we have seen, is not so much to serve in the practical living of the religious life as to introduce intellectual consistency between the different areas of men's experience. We have examined the long history of this philosophic enterprise in the Western tradition. Men have tried to elaborate notions of God that would fit in with their own reflective understanding of the world and of their experience. They have tried to find conceptions of the Divine that would construe and interpret religious insight in terms of their particular philosophy and science, and adjust it to the rest of their experience in ways that would be consistent with their other beliefs. We have seen how for the Jews and the Christians rational theology began with the interpretation of the Hebrew and Christian symbols in the light of the Neoplatonic philosophy of the Hellenistic world.

Western philosophic theology has conceived God in terms of the ultimate intellectual ideal enshrined in the successive schemes of understanding, the changing philosophies, our Western culture has developed. In each scheme the highest object of knowledge has been identified with the highest good; and thus has been achieved, for that philosophy, a harmony between men's moral and religious faith and their way of understanding the world, between "faith" and "reason." God, we have seen, has been thus identified successively with the ultimate conception of the Platonic science of the Hellenistic age, the Logos or objective rational structure of the cosmos; with the first principle of the Aristotelian science of the Middle Ages, the ultimate Final Cause or Prime Mover; with the mathematical Order of Nature of Cartesian science; with the original Force or Creator of Newtonian science; with the Absolute or Unconditioned of idealistic philosophy; with the first principle of creative evolution, with Alexander's "nisus toward Deity," or with Whitehead's "principle of concretion," with the *Sein* of Heidegger's existential ontology. The intellectual and religious success of these rational theologies has depended upon the power of the particular scheme of science employed to understand and illuminate man and his various activities and values. The attempts have been least successful when, as with Newtonian science, there was provided no adequate way of understanding human life.

But broadly, experience makes clear that any philosopher worth his salt can find in the thought of his day such an intellectual symbol for God. Or rather, any philosophy that has not found such an intellectual symbol for the religious dimension of the world, for the Divine, is a truncated philosophy— and what such a "philosophy" is like may be observed in many widely professed at the present time. But with our deepened knowledge of how beliefs actually function in religion, we have come to realize today that these successive philosophical ideas of God, though they have all managed to play a useful and indeed an essential part in the different schemes of understanding by which men have organized their intellectual experience, are themselves all symbols too. They are of course quite different from the concrete images that have been employed in the religious arts, and would hardly serve in the actual practice of worship or prayer. Despite the apocryphal story, it is doubtful whether even a disciple of [Henry Nelson] Wieman ever really prayed to the principle of concretion. Such ideas are *intellectual symbols* rather than symbols of religious practice. They have a religious function only in the lives of those who must understand. Only the Gods of metaphysicians are metaphysical principles.

All ideas of God, indeed, like all religious beliefs, are religious symbols. This is as true of the subtle and intellectualized conceptions of the philosophers as of the simple, concrete and familiar images the unreflective man borrows from his experience with his fellows. It is not that the philosopher is right while the average man is wrong, that the former's conceptions are true while the latter's are false. It is not even that the thinker'sideas are more adequate than the images of the practical man. The two sets of concepts of God we have been distinguishing both perform necessary and fundamental religious functions. But the two functions are so different that they do not compete. The concrete images of religious practice are in nowise discredited by the refined concepts of the philosophical theologian. In the religious life they are indeed more fundamental. For without them men could hardly worship or pray at all, while the great majority could and do easily dispense with the concepts which reflective men find necessary in the interests of intellectual consistency. Only for intellectuals are intellectual symbols a religious necessity.

But different as their functions are, both sets of ideas serve as religious symbols. What this means negatively is clear: neither set is literally true, neither is correct, neither gives exact knowledge. To think that either set of ideas does function to produce knowledge and literal truth leads to muddles, mistakes and confusions. Above all, it generates that intolerance which leads men to judge that all ideas of God save their own are false and blasphemous, and to insist that to be saved all men must subscribe to creeds embodying their own prejudices and partial insights.

But what religious symbols do not do is after all not so important as the functions they do perform. This latter is a complex matter difficult to formulate and state satisfactorily. In answering our questions as to the role of knowledge and truth in the religious life, it is necessary to dwell for a little on the positive functions of religious symbols, and on the way in which even those symbols whose primary role is clearly noncognitive nevertheless do contribute to what has always been described as a "revelation" of truth. In this attempt to elucidate a very complicated matter, I shall state some of the conclusions to which I have been led, if not always he, as a result of various seminars I have been privileged to conduct jointly with Paul Tillich.

At the outset it is necessary to draw a sharp distinction between a symbol and a sign. A sign is something which provokes the same human response as some other thing, for which it can hence stand as a kind of surrogate or substitute. A sign hence stands for or represents something other than itself: it is always a sign *of* something else. In contrast, a symbol is in no sense representative: it does not stand for or take the place of anything other than itself. Rather, it *does* something in its own right: it provokes a characteristic response in men. The terminology is not yet settled on this point; but the distinction is fundamental, though the particular way of expressing it is in the present state of usage arbitrary. It is important to realize that religious symbols are not signs; they belong rather with the nonrepresentative symbols which function in various ways in both intellectual and practical life.

A further distinction is also necessary. Some symbols, without being themselves directly representative, or standing for any other identifiable thing, except, perhaps, for certain intellectual processes, nevertheless play an important part in activities that are cognitive, that is, which eventuate in knowledge and truth. The body of scientific concepts, hypotheses, and theories is full of such nonrepresentative but *cognitive* symbols. An instance is the notion of "velocity at an instant." In contrast, there are other symbols, like those that play a role in social processes and in art, whose function is not to participate in activities that eventuate in knowledge, but to lead to other kinds of consequences. What is important to recognize is that religious symbols belong with social and artistic symbols, in the group of symbols that are both *nonrepresentative* and *noncognitive*. Such noncognitive symbols can be said to symbolize not some external thing that can be indicated apart from their operation, but rather what they themselves *do*, their peculiar functions.

Just what is it that such noncognitive symbols do? In the first place, all of them, including religious symbols, provoke in men an emotional response, and stimulate appropriate human activities. In traditional terms, they act on the will rather than on the intellect. They act as motives, they lead to action on the part of the men who are influenced by them. They do not, like signs, merely lead the mind to other things; they produce results in conduct.

Secondly, they provoke in a group of men, the community for whom they serve as symbols, a common or shared response. They stimulate joint or cooperative activity. This response can become individualized; but even then its individual form is derivative from what is fundamentally a social or group response. The response is common or shared, although the "meaning" of the symbol, that is, its relations to other elements of men's experience, would receive a different intellectual interpretation from different members of the group or symbol community. Thus a physical social symbol, like the flag, or an intellectual social symbol, like the "state" or "liberty," would be fitted in quite differently with other ideas by different men, though all would be stimulated to patriotic emotions and activities, or to libertarian feelings and attitudes.

Thirdly, noncognitive symbols are able to communicate qualitative or "shared" experience, experience that is difficult to put into precise words or statements, and may well be ineffable. This is particularly clear with artistic symbols: they act powerfully in men's experience, but it is notoriously almost impossible to state exactly what they "mean." Needless to say, such artistic symbols must be carefully distinguished from what are often indeed called "symbols" in works of art, but what are really representative signs—signs of something else. It is just that element in a poetic metaphor that is lost through translation into common prose that distinguishes the symbol that is at work from the element of mere sign.

Religious symbols share with other noncognitive symbols these three characteristics. But in addition, and fourthly, religious symbols in particular can be said to "disclose" or "reveal" something about the world in which they function. It is at just this point that we come to the relation between religious symbols and what is usually called religious "knowledge," which is peculiarly close with those intellectual religious symbols that are religious beliefs or ideas. It is this, for instance, that led Goodenough to say...that "there is a large measure of truth in many of our projections." What is it about religious symbols that drives men who have just rejected the notion that religious beliefs are literally true to go on to say things like this?

Religious symbols are commonly said to "reveal" some "truth" about experience. If we ask what it is that such symbols do reveal or disclose about the world, it is clear that it is not what we should call in the ordinary sense "knowledge," in the sense already defined. This revelation can be styled "knowledge" or "truth" only in a sense that is "equivocal" or metaphorical. It is more like direct acquaintance than descriptive knowledge: it resembles what we call "insight" or "vision." Such symbols do not "tell" us anything that is verifiably so; they rather make us "see" something about our experience and our experienced world.

What such a symbol does disclose can be best approached by asking how it is that we gain "insight" into the character and nature of another human personality. By external observation of his behavior, by watching him act and listening to him talk, we can learn much "knowledge" about him that is clearly gained by methods not essentially different from those by which we gain "knowledge" about the behavior of other things in our natural world. But intimate acquaintance with another human personality acquired through a long experience of friendship or of love, can give us an "insight" into the essence of the man that cannot be won by any merely external observation of his behavior. When certain of his acts or words "reveal" to us what he "really is," as we put it, we often say that they are "symbols" of his true character and nature. The gifted biographer or historian often has such "insight" into the persons he is trying to grasp. Ernst Cassirer had a genius for this kind of insight, and he erected a whole theory of historical knowledge around this process of what he called "symbolic interpretation." What Wilhelm Dilthey called Verstehen has been grossly abused by many German sociologists, but it has a genuine application if anywhere to the knowledge of human personality.

Just what does this process of symbolic interpretation mean? It seems, first, that such symbolic acts or words concentrate and sum up and unify a long and intimate experience we have enjoyed of a person, or a long and close study we have made of a figure's activities. Secondly, they reveal possibilities and powers latent in his nature. For what a man "really is" is not exhausted in what he has already done, in his past behavior that is on the record. It is what he *can* do, the powers he has in him. All knowledge of anything is ultimately a knowledge of its powers and possibilities. But clearly the distinction between what any being has done and what that being can do, is most striking and significant in the case of human personality.

The example of human personality has always seemed the best clue to the way of conceiving the Divine in the world, even when men have gone on to recognize that the religious dimension of existence ultimately transcends personality. Generalizing the function of symbols in coming to know persons, we may say that a religious symbol unifies and sums up and brings to a focus men's long and intimate experience of their universe and of what it offers to human life. As John Dewey says of the work of art in general, it "operates imaginatively rather than in the realm of physical existences. What it does is to concentrate and enlarge an immediate experience."[4]

In so doing, religious symbols seem to disclose or reveal powers and possibilities inherent in the nature of things. They serve, that is, not as instruments of a "knowledge" based on an experience of what the world has done, of how it has behaved and acted in the past, of the resources it has been found to provide for men, but rather as instruments of "insight" and "vision," of what it could do, of what it might offer, of what it might become and be. Religious symbols are thus like Platonic Ideas, which themselves developed from a refinement of the Pythagorean religious symbols: they do not tell us that anything is so, they rather make us see something. They enable us to discern possibilities beyond the actual, powers not yet fully realized; and in so doing they disclose what the nature of things "really is." Like Platonic Ideas, religious symbols are closely connected with the power of intellectual vision, *Nous*, the power of "imagination," if the imagination be the organ of intellectual vision.

And so religious symbols, through concentrating the long experience of a people, and the insights of its prophets and saints, seem to serve as instruments of revelation, of vision—of a vision of the powers and possibilities in the world. They disclose what Paul Tillich calls, in symbolic terms, "the power of Being." They lead to a vision of man in the world, of the human situation in its cosmic setting, and to use Tillich's term again, of man's "ultimate concern." Speaking most generally, they lead to a vision of the Divine, what the Christian symbol has called the *visio Dei* and the *fruitio Dei*. They serve the chief end of man, "to glorify God and enjoy Him forever." It is impossible even to state this function of religious symbols except in symbolic terms. For it is clear that all formulations of these visions, all ways of imagining and conceiving the Divine, all ideas of God, whether those

---

[4]John Dewey, *Art as Experience*, p. 273.

employed in the practice of the religious arts, like worship or prayer, or the refined and subtle concepts of the great philosophical theologians, are religious symbols. Only through symbols can we approach the Divine, only thus can we indicate the religious dimension of life in the world. We cannot see God face to face. This latter is itself a symbolic statement.

Let us then try to express the power of religious vision in another symbolic language. It is man who discerns Perfection shining through the world's imperfections in a dimly reflected splendor. Yet this experience of the Divine splendors suggested in the world, of human life variously illuminated as by a light that is eternal, has seemed to point to a source of that light. In locating this source of splendor, Christianity has alternated over the centuries between expressing a temper of humanism and a temper of humility. At certain periods it has emphasized the humanistic faith of the Greek Fathers, that the source is to be sought in the rationality and moral power of man himself, naturally inhering in him and sustained by the universe about him. At other times it has shared the Augustinian distrust of man, and felt that it is to be sought beyond man and nature, illuminating them and sustaining them from without, wholly beyond man's control, breaking through and grasping him in ecstatic experience.

Our own science and philosophy likewise point in both these two directions. For them also man catches the gleam of an eternal perfection. But "Divinity" they have come to construe as a quality to be discriminated in human experience of the world, the splendor of the vision that sees beyond the actual into the perfected and eternal realm of the imagination. Such a world is human experience purified and recast in the crucible of imaginative vision, an experience that has laid off the garments of time to partake of eternity. Yet for us too this timeless vision is of something inescapably real. And it is no mere dream created by the spirit of man. It is nature herself coming to a fuller realization of her suggested possibilities in the imagination of man.

There is much that suggests that today the twin qualities of power and perfection, the two aspects of the Divine traditionally symbolized as God, have come to impinge upon us from different quarters, and not as from a single ray of light. There are many from whom religion has become a devotion to the ideal, a devotion inspired by a sense of the worth of human personality as its source. They feel intensely the splendor shining through man, so intensely that what is not revealed in the highest human qualities there suggested—mere cosmic power or intelligibility, for instance—cannot for them possess the supreme value of the Divine. Much of our liberal religion, in fact if not yet in symbol, has become such a merely human and social idealism. There are others for whom such purely human values are all too petty and ignoble, to whom salvation comes rather from elevating the spirit to cosmic impartiality, to the majesty and order of the universe. For such, religion is a cosmic sense, a recognition of man's utter dependence on a power which yet satisfies the demand of his intellect for understanding. And for the Spinozas and the Einsteins such a religion does afford a peace intense if austere. There too strikes the splendor of the Divine.

Does the light then fall only on nature, the impartial author of good and evil? Is it through the natural order that the splendor shines most brightly? But it is man alone who realizes, if imperfectly, her highest possibilities, who discerns the cosmic order and beauty. Does it fall only on the ideal which man beholds in vision? Does not the beholder shine even more gloriously than that which is beheld? For the vision fades and passes, but the human spirit advances to fresh vision. Is it then man himself who is the source, man the creature of nature who alone of all her products perfects what she has left imperfect? But is it not nature who reveals her possibilities to man and affords him the power which sustains his vision? Where, indeed, is the Divine to be discerned?

The question remains whether one single symbol can still serve us for the natural order, for its manifestations in the human spirit, and for its perfecting in the vision of that spirit. Our experience seems to have grown more plural: we now respect and use nature, while we consecrate ourselves to its possibilities as transformed in the spirit of man. Our experience of Divinity, in truth, seems manifold: it is only to faith that the Divine is one. The splendor falls on nature, on man, and on that which nature provokes man to discern. But to us it seems a different splendor, and it is on the human spirit in vision calling forth in its fellows answering vision that it seems to fall most gloriously.

In many and diverse places, and through the lens of many and diverse symbols, man has discerned the Divine splendor. To push this symbolic language further, we might speak of the Divine as the "order of splendor," found in our experience of the world, that revealing light which falls so variously upon our life. If the highest it permits us to discern be not the idealized possibilities of nature and of associated human living, but that very gift of vision it brings to the spirit of man, then, still speaking symbolically, God may well be for us the total order of that which has the power to evoke such vision. The Divine awakens our insight in the majesty and system of the universe; it awakens it more directly in the aspiration of our fellow man, dimly striving for contact with the eternal. It awakens it most of all in the vision of a fellow spirit kindling our own vision. And Christianity has found its own most distinctive symbol in the living God revealed to men through incarnation in the vision of Jesus.

It might be better to say, a symbol is functioning religiously, and the vision it makes us see is genuinely religious, only if the symbol does reveal man's ultimate concern, does disclose the Divine. In the last chapter we tried to delimit in a preliminary way what is the distinctive thing that religion and religious symbols do in human life, what is involved in "functioning religiously." We have now come somewhat closer to a statement, not of all the many things religion does for man, but of what the essential religious function is. On the one hand, religion is a practical commitment to certain values. Religious symbols serve to strengthen that kind of religious commitment; to strengthen men's "faith," to intensify and enhance and clarify a practical commitment to one's "ultimate concern." On the other hand, religion is the vision of the Divine; the awareness of the religious dimension of experience and of the world, the awareness of the "order of splendor," and the fostering and clarification of that awareness.

Practical commitment and vision are of course in no sense to be divided or divorced from each other. But men are in the end saved, I am convinced, by vision rather than by works. I find I am not descended from a long line of Calvinists in vain. To be sure, works are the only test of vision, and for most men the vision seems to come only through works and in the midst of works. Our busy and activistic American approach to life leads most of us to emphasize the works, the practical commitment, the function of religious symbols and beliefs in strengthening religious faith. But my own temper and experience have led me to take the vision of God as more inclusive as well as more ultimate than the practical commitment. For the vision does seem to issue necessarily in a commitment, while the practical commitment often fails to include much of a vision. "This is life eternal, that they should know thee the only true God."

But religious symbols not only reveal the powers and possibilities latent in the nature of things. These powers and possibilities are encountered as very complex. In the vision they become unified; in a genuine sense the disclosure is the revelation of their unification. To faith the Divine is one. Hence religious symbols serve not only as instruments of *revelation*, they are at the same time instruments of *unification*. They unify men's experience in terms of what might well be called their "organizing concern"; they unify the world in the light of men's vision of the Divine. To reveal and unify the powers and possibilities inherent in the religious dimension that man's experience of the world discloses, in the "order of splendor," seems to be a way of stating the distinctive function of religious symbols.

We have made it clear that the insight and vision revealed by even intellectual religious symbols, by religious beliefs, can scarcely be called "knowledge" or "truth," except in a Pickwickian and equivocal sense. Yet there still seems to remain something unsatisfactory about the complete denial of all cognitive values to religious beliefs. We do speak about "religious knowledge," and about the "truths" of faith. We speak likewise about the "truth" of the revelations of art, and about an "artistic knowledge" which is denied to the methods of scientific inquiry. Such artistic "knowledge," we are careful to add if we are wise, is very unlike the knowledge that can be expressed in exact statements. And artistic "truth" is so different from the truths that are the product of our elaborate processes of verification that most students of the theory of knowledge today would hold that little but confusion and obliteration of necessary and vital distinctions is generated by calling two such diverse things by the same term. Indeed, there is a philosophic view widespread in our time that "truth" should be restricted to the products of scientific inquiry in a rather narrow sense, so that it is inappropriate, or even "meaningless," to speak even of "moral truth."

Such views, of course, immediately provoke the rejoinder: there must then be many other kinds of "truth" than the scientist's: moral, artistic, religious, and the rest. And this notion that there is a "knowledge" and a "truth" different in kind from that of science, whether of art or of religion, is historically a heritage from the Romantic philosophies that were protesting against just such a rigid, unimaginative, and sterile adherence to a narrow scientific ideal. But after all, this "extranaturalism" or transcendentalism was the great support and the fundamental conviction of all the Romantic philosophies of protest against the limitations of eighteenth-century rationalism. Was there really no significant insight in this protest? Specifically, can the artist, the prophet and the saint show us something that can not inappropriately be called "truth"? Is there any religious "knowledge" significantly different from the verifiable and explanatory knowledge of scientific truths, so that the two never compete but rather supplement each other?

With proper and careful qualification, it seems that the facts do suggest to a sensitive and candid mind that the answer is, yes, there is. That is why, in stating at the outset the three major positions on the place of knowledge and truth in the religious life, it was pointed out that there seem to be essential values in this (then listed as the second position) that could not be lightly abandoned. Just what, then, may be the character of this religious "knowledge" that needs to be carefully set off from knowledge as it is ordinarily understood and as it has so far been here defined—from the explanatory and verifiable truths of common sense and of scientific inquiry?

In trying to answer this question, we can find help by examining the enterprise of art. Indeed, I have discovered that whenever in my thinking I take religion as one art among many others, and being to consider it in the terms appropriate to the other arts or *technai*, things at once begin to happen for me intellectually. I am led on to fruitful and suggestive analogies that illuminate the religious life for me as no other approach seems to do. I should hold, in fact, that all the major human enterprises, those that Santayana admits to "ideal society," and that Hegel held to belong to *Absoluter Geist*, are most fruitfully to be considered as arts, including the art of inquiry, or science; and are most revealingly treated in terms of the concepts that make an art intelligible. I have long found most suggestive the view expressed by John Dewey in the ninth chapter of his *Experience and Nature*, "Experience, Nature and Art," that "art" or techne is the most inclusive metaphysical category. This view is set forth in very similar terms, incidentally, by the early Schelling of the *Identitätsphilosophie*.

What Dewey himself says about the relation between art and knowledge has a most distinct relevance to the art of religion in particular. "The sense of increase of understanding, or a deepened intelligibility on the part of objects of nature and man, resulting from esthetic experience, has led philosophic theorists to treat art as a mode of knowledge, and has induced artists, especially poets, to regard art as a mode of revelation of the inner nature of things that cannot be had in any other way. It has led to treating art as a mode of knowledge superior not only to that of ordinary life but to that of science itself . . . . The assertion has been expressly made by many philosophers . . . . The varieties of incompatible conceptions put forth prove that the philosophers in question were anxious to carry a dialectical development of conceptions framed without regard to art into esthetic experience more than they were willing to allow this experience to speak for itself."[5] This is obviously true in the art of religion: "religious experience" has again and again been made to illustrate and confirm some prevailing philosophical or scientific theory.

"Nevertheless, the sense of disclosure and heightened intelligibility of the world remains to be accounted for . . . . I cannot find in [the remarks of Wordsworth, Shelley, and other Romantic poets] any intention to assert that esthetic experience is to be *defined* as a mode of knowledge. What is intimated to my mind, is, that in both production and enjoyed perception of works of art, knowledge is transformed; it becomes something more than knowledge because it is merged with non-intellectual elements to form an experience worth while as an experience . . . .

"Tangled scenes of life are made more intelligible in esthetic experience: not, however, as reflection and science render things more intelligible by reduction to conceptual form, but by presenting their meanings as the matter of a clarified, coherent, and intensified or 'impassioned' experience." The phrase Dewey uses for what art does with knowledge is peculiarly applicable to what the religious arts do with the secular knowledge they take over and consecrate: "The transformation of knowledge that is effected in emotional and imaginative vision."[6]

What Dewey says about this imaginative vision in all the arts seems to apply with particular force to the art of religion: "Imaginative vision is the power that unifies all the constituents of the matter of a work of art, making a whole out of them in all their variety. Yet all the elements of our being that are displayed in special emphases and partial realizations in other experi-

---

[5]John Dewey, *Art as Experience*, pp. 288–89.
[6]*Ibid.*, pp. 289–90.

ences are merged in esthetic experience. And they are so completely merged in the immediate wholeness of the experience that each is submerged:—it does not present itself in consciousness as a distinct element."[7]

I must confess that my own intellectual experience with the thought of John Dewey has invariably been that, after painfully working out what seemed to me a fairly adequate solution of a philosophic problem, I have then turned to his writings, only to discover that he had already stated my conclusions far better than I had been able to do. But his way of arriving at what is obviously the philosophic truth, since we always seem to agree in the end, has never been mine. And strive as I might, I have never been able to write in the language of John Dewey. In fact, I have not often striven. For these compelling reasons, what I want to say about what the analogy of the other arts suggests to my mind about the art of religion, in this matter of religious "knowledge," will have to make a fresh start.

The aesthetically sensitive painter or poet can notice further features in the seeing of grass, for example, than the mere "green" that suffices for most practical purposes. He brings to the visual transaction an experience, a skill, a trained art of perceiving, that enables him to qualify that transaction in new ways; and he can communicate these newly revealed qualities in his particular language or medium. He can thus reveal unsuspected powers and possibilities of being seen, resident in the visible world—unsuspected qualities in grass, to take our example. Chinese and Japanese painters are notoriously good at this; so, in very different fashion, are the impressionists, and Van Gogh.

This is the source of the enormous fertility of painting or of poetry in revealing new visual, new perceptual powers in things—in "enhancing the significance," as we say, of the visible world—in disclosing "new meanings and consummatory experiences," as Dewey puts it. The painter can qualify, not merely his canvas, and not merely our experience, but also the visible world itself with new qualities hitherto unsuspected. The artist through his products *does* certain things to us, he affects certain changes in us and in our world. He "reconstructs our experience," says our theory: the work of art is to educate and re-educate us. In other words, the artist seems to be teaching us something, about the world and about ourselves, about ourselves in our world. That is why we are tempted, despite all the difficulties and paradoxes to which that leads, to say that he is increasing our "knowledge" and teaching us "truth"—"artistic truth," we sometimes call it. Painting, poetry, music, religion, all the arts, do indeed "teach" us something. They may not teach us *that* anything is so. We have seen the reasons why it seems inappropriate to say that the various arts teach us propositional knowledge. They do not "explain" the world in the sense of accounting for it; rather they "explain" it

---

[7]*Ibid.,* p. 274.

in the sense of making plain its features. But they certainly teach us *how to do* something better. The painter shows us how to see the visible world better, the world of color and form—how to see grass better.

Just what does the artist teach? The painter clearly teaches us how to see selected aspects of the world more adequately than we could without his assistance. Sometimes he teaches us how to see the face of nature or of the works of man; sometimes he teaches us how to see another human being. At bottom he teaches us how to see color, form, their relations and qualities. He reveals possibilities and powers we had not noticed. He enables us to see what can be done with lines, masses, colors, with the features of nature, with the gestures and attitudes of men, with the symbols in terms of which men lead their emotional lives. The composer teaches us how to hear sounds better, how they can be put together, how they can illustrate a pattern of musical logic and dialectic, how they can create a world of pure and unalloyed form. He teaches us how emotion can be expressed, communicated, and resolved through a purge of pity and terror. The poet teaches us the music and the logic of words and language, the feel of words and the feeling of life as lived. He teaches us the emotional intensity of thought.

The work of the painter, the musician, the poet, teaches us how to use our eyes, our ears, our minds, and our feelings with greater power and skill. It teaches us how to become more aware both of what is and of what might be, in the world that offers itself to our sensitive receptivity. It shows us how to discern unsuspected qualities in the world encountered, latent powers and possibilities there resident. Still more, it makes us see the new qualities with which that world, in cooperation with the spirit of man, can clothe itself. For art is an enterprise in which the world and man are most genuinely cooperative, and in which the working together of natural materials and powers and of human techniques and vision is most clearly creative of new qualities and powers.

Is it otherwise with the prophet and the saint? They too can do something to us, they too can effect changes in us and in our world. They too can teach us something, about our world and about ourselves. They teach us how to see what man's life in the world is, and what it might be. They teach us how to discern what human nature can make out of its natural conditions and materials. They reveal latent powers and possibilities not previously noticed. They make us receptive to qualities of the world encountered; and they open our hearts to the new qualities with which that world, in cooperation with the spirit of man, can clothe itself. They enable us to see and feel the religious dimension of our world better, the "order of splendor," and of man's experience in and with it. They teach us how to find the Divine; they show us visions of God.

Is all this properly to be called "knowledge," all that the painter, the composer, the poet, that the prophet and the saint can teach us? It is clearly not "knowledge" as we have so far defined it. It is not the kind of knowledge that can be put into words and statements, and set down in manuals of aesthetics or theology. It cannot be formulated in neat handbooks of "How to Look at the Visible World," or "How to See the Divine." It is not the aesthetician with his analyses, the critic with his rules, the theologian with his propositions, who teaches us these things. It is rather the painter with his painting, the musician with his thematic development, the poet with his sonnet, the prophet with his vision of righteousness, the saint with his quality of holiness, who teaches us how to discern better, who reveals the new qualities and possibilities of the world. The knowledge so taught is not an explanation or account of anything. It is not something that can be formulated as a set of rationally demonstrated conclusions. It cannot even be warranted by any precise method of experimental confirmation, though it clearly has its own standards of adequacy. It is more like an art, a technique, of how to see and discern and feel more fully, of how to use the materials of experience to create what was not before.

But surely we Americans, with our devotion to technical intelligence, would be willing to call this ability "knowledge." "Artistic knowledge," or "religious knowledge," if we are to use the terms at all, it is suggested, must be taken, not as the truth of the propositions of science, but as what we Americans have come to call a "know-how." It is *knowing how* to qualify the world with those qualities appropriate to each art, knowing how to be receptive toward them, and how to make them a part of our experience and of our lives. A "know-how," however, though it may well be said to be "cognitive," does not seem to be appropriately judged as either "true" or "false." That is why it seems preferable to speak of this "know-how" of religion as religious "knowledge" rather than as religious "truth." Its standards are clearly different from those of propositions.

Moreover, such processes of qualification, receiving, and assimilating are, I take it, just what we mean by "revealing" or "disclosing." For the qualities that are the outcome of these processes, qualities that impose themselves upon us and are received, are in a genuine sense qualities of the world. It is not we men who in our wisdom create them. What the painter, the poet, or the prophet has done can be accurately said to be to "reveal" or "disclose" to us authentic powers in things. Just as in the visual situation the grass is qualified by "green," has become "green," and really *is* green, so in the aesthetic situation it has become qualified by aesthetic qualities, and *is* beautiful. Just so, in the religious situation, in religious experience, the world is qualified by "the Divine," has become "Divine," and really *is* Divine. In each case what is revealed is the power of actualizing such a qualification, the world's power of acting upon us, and our power of knowing how to welcome that action—a joint power both of seeing and of being seen, of discerning and of revealing.

Again, as a discoverer of new powers and possibilities the painter has much in common with the scientist. What he does with and makes out of what forces itself upon his attention and what he sees, by selecting from it, manipulating it, reorganizing and reconstructing it by means of his distinctive art, is very much like what the experimentation of the scientist effects. Both the scientist and the artist, by revealing new powers, and by pushing back the limits set to the operation of things, enlarge our horizons, increase our knowledge, and extend our powers. This suggests that, to perform his function successfully, the artist, like the scientist, should be accorded by right the freest possible experimentation with and manipulation of his materials, and that he should likewise recognize the obligation to bring to his manipulation the widest possible past experience and store of resources. Both are essential to the artistic transaction. And dare I add that the activities of the prophet and the saint also resemble the experimentation of the scientist and are subject to the same controlling conditions? We need as many varying visions of God as we can possibly share. Many radically different visions have been beheld, and so long as the world has man in it, many more will be. Every new prophet's vision, like every new poem, will reveal new possibilities in the world. Visions are many, and many are the unified visions to which they can be pushed; but there is no unity of the visions of God. In that sense, the revelation of the Divine is not and can never be completed.

In any event, if we feel justified in speaking of religious "knowledge" at all, this must be carefully and precisely distinguished from the scientific knowledge of descriptive and explanatory statement. The traditional Augustinian distinction is between *scientia* and *sapientia*, between "science" and "wisdom." Paul Tillich, wisely preferring that most philosophic of languages, the Greek, makes the essential distinction between *episteme* and *gnosis*. With his emphasis on religious "knowledge" as what he calls "participating knowledge," he is even willing to compare *gnosis* or religious "knowledge" with what Holy Writ points to when it states that Abraham went in unto Sarah and "knew" her.

The suggestion here is to use the American tongue, and to distinguish between "science," and "technology" or "invention"—between science and "know-how." Religious "knowledge" is not mystic intuition, it is not the awareness of values, it is not the encounter with "the Holy," it is not existential commitment to the will to believe. It is rather a technical skill, an art, a "know-how." Within a broad "knowledge" we shall then distinguish between propositional knowledge, which must be either true or false, and "know-how," which is neither true nor false, but adequate and effective for its purposes or not. And thus the revelation which is the distinctive function of religious symbols, including religious beliefs, turns out in the last analysis to be the disclosing of a "know-how," a revelation of how to become aware of the world's religious dimension, of how to see God and enjoy him forever.

Significantly, also, all these various teachers—painter, poet, musician, prophet, and saint—"know how" to unify their vision. And they can teach us how to unify our own experience. In his artistic product the artist unifies the possibilities he discerns in his materials—in his work of art. And the "work" of that work of art unifies the beholder's experience in turn. The prophet and the saint likewise "know how" to unify their vision of the world's possibilities, and they can teach us how to see the vision that will unify the world for us. Religion gives us a "know-how": how to unify our experience through a unified vision of the Divine, of the religious dimension of the world, of the order of splendor. The distinctive character of religious knowledge, which removes it from any competition with other forms of knowing, is that it is, not a unique experience, not a mystic intuition or "knowledge" of some higher realm, but rather an art, a technique, a "know-how"—for opening one's heart to seeing the Divine, for knowing God, in the midst of the conditions of human life in the natural world.

Does this commit us to a religious "truth"? I think and hope not. It seems more confusing than clarifying to speak in such a way. The best name for the test of religious know-how seems to be "adequacy." It is well to keep "truth" for the knowledge that is science, with all its complex procedures and criteria for verifying propositions that can be stated in words. But perhaps the scientists themselves are today abandoning "truth" as the name for the test of their knowledge, for some other property like "confirmability" or "warranted assertibility." And in calling the knowledge that is "know-how" something that is to be judged by its "adequacy," I remember the old definition of "truth" as "adequation of thing and understanding." Perhaps, after all, we have at last come the full circle. Perhaps it is now the visions of the unified possibilities of the world—of the Divine, of the "order of splendor"— that we are once more permitted to call "true." If so, this "truth" of "know-how" is not to be confused with the warranted knowledge that is science. It is rather that Truth of which it was said of old, "But of all things Truth beareth away the victory," and again, "Ye shall know the Truth, and the Truth shall make you free."

# John Wisdom

John Wisdom (1904–      ), Cambridge philosopher, formerly a pupil
of Wittgenstein's, has written on many philosophical topics, one famous series of articles being reprinted as *Other Minds*.

# 25

# *Gods*

1. *The existence of God is not an experimental issue in the way it was.* An
atheist or agnostic might say to a theist "You still think there are spirits in the
trees, nymphs in the streams, a God of the world." He might say this because
he noticed the theist in time of drought pray for rain and make a sacrifice and
in the morning look for rain. But disagreement about whether there are gods
is now less of this experimental or betting sort than it used to be. This is due
in part, if not wholly, to our better knowledge of why things happen as they
do.

It is true that even in these days it is seldom that one who believes in
God has no hopes or fears which an atheist has not. Few believers now expect
prayer to still the waves, but some think it makes a difference to people and
not merely in ways the atheist would admit. Of course with people, as
opposed to waves and machines, one never knows what they won't do next,
so that expecting prayer to make a difference to them is not so definite a thing
as believing in its mechanical efficacy. Still, just as primitive people pray in a
business-like way for rain, so some people still pray for others with a real
feeling of doing something to help. However, in spite of this persistence of
an experimental element in some theistic belief, it remains true that Elijah's
method on Mount Carmel of settling the matter of what god or gods exist
would be far less appropriate today than it was then.

2. *Belief in gods is not merely a matter of expectation of a world to come.*
Someone may say "The fact that a theist no more than an atheist expects
prayer to bring down fire from heaven or cure the sick does not mean that
there is no difference between them as to the facts, it does not mean that the
theist has no expectations different from the atheist's. For very often those

---

"Gods," *Proceedings of the Aristotelian Society*, 1944–45. Reprinted by courtesy of the Editor
of the Aristotelian Society. The Aristotelian Society, copyright 1944–45.

who believe in God believe in another world and believe that God is there and that we shall go to that world when we die."

This is true, but I do not want to consider here expectations as to what one will see and feel after death nor what sort of reasons these logically unique expectations could have. So I want to consider those theists who do not believe in a future life, or rather, I want to consider the differences between atheists and theists insofar as these differences are not a matter of belief in a future life.

3. *What are these differences? And is it that theists are superstitious or that atheists are blind?* A child may wish to sit awhile with his father and he may, when he has done what his father dislikes, fear punishment and feel distress at causing vexation, and while his father is alive he may feel sure of help when danger threatens and feel that there is sympathy for him when disaster has come. When his father is dead he will no longer expect punishment or help. Maybe for a moment an old fear will come or a cry for help escape him, but he will at once remember that this is no good now. He may feel that his father is no more until perhaps someone says to him that his father is still alive though he lives now in another world and one so far away that there is no hope of seeing him or hearing his voice again. The child may be told that nevertheless his father can see him and hear all he says. When he has been told this the child will still fear no punishment nor expect any sign of his father, but now, even more than he did when his father was alive, he will feel that his father sees him all the time and will dread distressing him and when he has done something wrong he will feel separated from his father until he has felt sorry for what he has done. Maybe when he himself comes to die he will be like a man who expects to find a friend in the strange country where he is going, but even when this is so, it is by no means all of what makes the difference between a child who believes that his father lives still in another world and one who does not.

Likewise one who believes in God may face death differently from one who does not, but there is another difference between them besides this. This other difference may still be described as belief in another world, only this belief is not a matter of expecting one thing rather than another here or hereafter, it is not a matter of a world to come but of a world that now is, though beyond our senses.

We are at once reminded of those other unseen worlds which some philosophers "believe in" and others "deny," while non-philosophers unconsciously "accept" them by using them as models with which to "get the hang of" the patterns in the flux of experience. We recall the timeless entities whose changeless connections we seek to represent in symbols, and the values which stand firm amidst our flickering satisfaction and remorse, and the physical things which, though not beyond the corruption of moth and rust, are yet more permanent than the shadows they throw upon the screen before our minds. We recall, too, our talk of souls and of what lies in their depths and is manifested to us partially and intermittently in our own feelings and the behaviour of others. The hypothesis of mind, of other human minds and of animal minds, is reasonable because it explains for each of us why certain things behave so cunningly all by themselves unlike even the most ingenious machines. Is the hypothesis of minds in flowers and trees reasonable for like reasons? Is the hypothesis of a world mind reasonable for like reasons—someone who adjusts the blossom to the bees, someone whose presence may at times be felt—in a garden in high summer, in the hills when clouds are gathering, but not, perhaps, in a cholera epidemic?

4. *The question "Is belief in gods reasonable?" has more than one source.* It is clear now that in order to grasp fully the logic of belief in divine minds we need to examine the logic of belief in animal and human minds. But we cannot do that here and so for the purposes of this discussion about divine minds let us acknowledge the reasonableness of our belief in human minds without troubling ourselves about its logic. The question of the reasonableness of belief in divine minds then becomes a matter of whether there are facts in nature which support claims about divine minds in the way facts in nature support our claims about human minds.

In this way we resolve the force behind the problem of the existence of gods into two components, one metaphysical and the same which prompts the question "Is there *ever any* behaviour which gives reason to believe in *any* sort of mind?" and one which finds expression in "Are there other mind-patterns in nature beside the human and animal patterns which we can all easily detect, and are these other mind-patterns superhuman?"

Such overdetermination of a question syndrome is common. Thus, the puzzling questions "Do dogs think?" "Do animals feel?" are partly metaphysical puzzles and partly scientific questions. They are not purely metaphysical; for the reports of scientists about the poor performances of cats in cages and old ladies' stories about the remarkable performances of their pets are not irrelevant. But nor are these questions purely scientific; for the stories never settle them and therefore they have other sources. One other source is the metaphysical source we have already noticed, namely, the difficulty about getting behind an animal's behaviour to its mind, whether it is a non-human animal or a human one.

But there's a third component in the force behind these questions, these disputes have a third source, and it is one which is important in the dispute which finds expression in the words "I believe in God," "I do not." This source comes out well if we consider the question "Do flowers feel?" Like the questions about dogs and animals this question about flowers comes partly from the difficulty we sometimes feel over inference from *any* behaviour to thought or feeling and partly from ignorance as to what behaviour is to be found. But these questions, as opposed to a like question about human beings, come also from hesitation as to whether the behaviour in question is *enough* mind-like, that is, is it enough similar to or superior to human behaviour to be called "mind-proving"? Likewise, even when we are satisfied that human behaviour shows mind and even when we have learned whatever mind-suggesting things there are in nature which are not explained by human and animal minds, we may still ask "But are these things sufficiently striking to be called a mind-pattern? Can we fairly call them manifestations of a divine being?"

"The question," someone may say, "has then become merely a matter of the application of a name. And 'What's in a name?' "

5. *But the line between a question of fact and a question or decision as to the application of a name is not so simple as this way of putting things suggests.* The question "What's in a name?" is engaging because we are inclined to answer both "Nothing" and "Very much." And this "Very much" has more than one source. We might have tried to comfort Heloïse by saying "It isn't that Abelard no longer loves you, for this man isn't Abelard"; we might have said to poor Mr. Tebrick in Mr. Garnet's *Lady into Fox* "But this is no longer Silvia." But if Mr. Tebrick replied "Ah, but it is!" this might come not at all from observing facts about the fox which we have not observed, but from noticing facts about the fox which we had missed, although we had in a sense observed all that Mr. Tebrick had observed. It is possible to have before one's eyes all the items of a pattern and still to miss the pattern. Consider the following conversation:

> "And I think Kay and I are pretty happy. We've always been happy."
> Bill lifted up his glass and put it down without drinking.
> "Would you mind saying that again?" he asked.
> "I don't see what's so queer about it. Taken all in all, Kay and I have really been happy."
> "All right," Bill said gently. "Just tell me how you and Kay have been happy."
> Bill had a way of being amused by things which I could not understand.
> "It's a little hard to explain," I said. "It's like taking a lot of numbers that don't look alike and that don't mean anything until you add them all together."
> I stopped, because I hadn't meant to talk to him about Kay and me.
> "Go ahead," Bill said. "What about the numbers." And he began to smile.
> "I don't know why you think it's so funny," I said. "All the things that two people do together, two people like Kay and me, add up to something. There are the kids and the house and the dog and all the people we have known and all the times we've been out to dinner. Of course, Kay and I do quarrel sometimes but when you add it all together, all of it isn't as bad as the parts of it seem. I mean, maybe that's all there is to anybody's life."
> Bill poured himself another drink. He seemed about to say something and checked himself. He kept looking at me.[1]

---

[1] J. P. Marquand, *H. M. Pulham, Esq.* (New York: Little, Brown & Co., 1941), p. 320.

Or again, suppose two people are speaking of two characters in a story which both have read[2] or of two friends which both have known, and one says "Really she hated him," and the other says "She didn't, she loved him." Then the first may have noticed what the other has not although he knows no incident in the lives of the people they are talking about which the other doesn't know too, and the second speaker may say "She didn't, she loved him" because he hasn't noticed what the first noticed, although he can remember every incident the first can remember. But then again he may say "She didn't, she loved him" not because he hasn't noticed the patterns in time which the first has noticed but because though he has noticed them he doesn't feel he still needs to emphasize them with "Really she hated him." The line between using a name because of how we feel and because of what we have noticed isn't sharp. "A difference as to the facts," "a discovery," "a revelation," these phrases cover many things. Discoveries have been made not only by Christopher Columbus and Pasteur, but also by Tolstoy and Dostoievsky and Freud. Things are revealed to us not only by the scientists with microscopes, but also by the poets, the prophets, and the painters. What is so isn't merely a matter of "the facts." For sometimes when there is agreement as to the facts there is still argument as to whether defendant did or did not "exercise reasonable care," was or was not "negligent."

And though we shall need to emphasize how much "There is a God" evinces an attitude to the familiar,[3] we shall find in the end that it also evinces some recognition of patterns in time easily missed and that, therefore, difference as to there being any gods is in part a difference as to what is so and therefore as to the facts, though not in the simple ways which first occurred to us.

6. *Let us now approach these same points by a different road.*

6.1. *How it is that an explanatory hypothesis, such as the existence of God, may start by being experimental and gradually become something quite different can be seen from the following story:*

Two people return to their long neglected garden and find among the weeds a few of the old plants surprisingly vigorous. One says to the other "It must be that a gardener has been coming and doing something about these plants." Upon inquiry they find that no neighbour has ever seen anyone at work in their garden. The first man says to the other "He must have worked while people slept." The other says "No, someone would have heard him and besides, anybody who cared about the plants would have kept down these weeds." The first man says "Look at the way these are arranged. There is purpose and a feeling for beauty here. I believe that someone comes, someone invisible to mortal eyes. I believe that the more carefully we look the more we shall find confirmation of this." They examine the garden ever so carefully

---

[2]E.g., Havelock Ellis's autobiography.

[3]"Persuasive Definitions," *Mind* (July, 1938), by Charles Leslie Stevenson, should be read here. [Also his *Ethics and Language* (New Haven, Conn.: Yale University Press), 1945.]

and sometimes they come on new things suggesting the contrary and even that a malicious person has been at work. Besides examining the garden carefully they also study what happens to gardens left without attention. Each learns all the other learns about this and about the garden. Consequently, when after all this, one says "I still believe a gardener comes" while the other says "I don't," their different words now reflect no difference as to what they have found in the garden, no difference as to what they would find in the garden if they looked further and no difference about how fast untended gardens fall into disorder. At this stage, in this context, the gardener hypothesis has ceased to be experimental, the difference between one who accepts and one who rejects it is now not a matter of the one expecting something the other does not expect. What is the difference between them? The one says "A gardener comes unseen and unheard. He is manifested only in his works with which we are all familiar," the other says "There is no gardener" and with this difference in what they say about the gardener goes a difference in how they feel towards the garden, in spite of the fact that neither expects anything of it which the other does not expect.

But is this the whole difference between them—that the one calls the garden by one name and feels one way towards it, while the other calls it by another name and feels in another way towards it? And if this is what the difference has become then is it any longer appropriate to ask "Which is right?" or "Which is reasonable?"

And yet surely such questions *are* appropriate when one person says to another "You still think the world's a garden and not a wilderness, and that the gardener has not forsaken it" or "You still think there are nymphs of the streams, a presence in the hills, a spirit of the world." Perhaps when a man sings "God's in His heaven" we need not take this as more than an expression of how he feels. But when Bishop Gore or Dr. Joad write about belief in God and young men read them in order to settle their religious doubts the impression is not simply that of persons choosing exclamations with which to face nature and the "changes and chances of this mortal life." The disputants speak as if they are concerned with a matter of scientific fact, or of trans-sensual, trans-scientific and metaphysical fact, but still of fact and still a matter about which reasons for and against may be offered, although no scientific reasons in the sense of field surveys for fossils or experiments on delinquents are to the point.

6.2. *Now can an interjection have a logic?* Can the manifestation of an attitude in the utterance of a word, in the application of a name, have a logic? When all the facts are known how can there still be a question of fact? How can there still be a question? Surely as Hume says " . . . after every circumstance, every relation is known, the understanding has no further room to operate."[4]

---

[4]Hume, *An Enquiry Concerning the Principles of Morals*, Appendix I.

6.3. When the madness of these questions leaves us for a moment *we can all easily recollect disputes which though they cannot be settled by experiment are yet disputes in which one party may be right and the other wrong* and in which both parties may offer reasons and the one better reasons than the other. *This may happen in pure and applied mathematics and logic.* Two accountants or two engineers provided with the same data may reach different results and this difference is resolved not by collecting further data but by going over the calculations again. Such differences indeed share with differences as to what will win a race, the honour of being among the most "settlable" disputes in the language.

6.4. *But it won't do to describe the theistic issue as one settlable by such calculation,* or as one about what can be deduced in this *vertical* fashion from the facts we know. No doubt dispute about God has sometimes, perhaps especially in mediaeval times, been carried on in this fashion. But nowadays it is not and we must look for some other analogy, some other case in which a dispute is settled, but not by experiment.

6.5. *In courts of law* it sometimes happens that opposing counsel are agreed as to the facts and are not trying to settle a question of further fact, are not trying to settle whether the man who admittedly had quarrelled with the deceased did or did not murder him, but are concerned with whether Mr. *A* who admittedly handed his long-trusted clerk signed blank checks did or did not exercise reasonable care, whether a ledger is or is not a document,[5] whether a certain body was or was not a public authority.

In such cases we notice that the process of argument is not a *chain* of demonstrative reasoning. It is a presenting and re-presenting of those features of the case which *severally cooperate* in favour of the conclusion, in favour of saying what the reasoner wishes said, in favour of calling the situation by the name by which he wishes to call it. The reasons are like the legs of a chair, not the links of a chain. Consequently although the discussion is a priori and the steps are not a matter of experience, the procedure resembles scientific argument in that the reasoning is not *vertically* extensive but *horizontally* extensive—it is a matter of the cumulative effect of several independent premises, not of the repeated transformation of one or two. And because the premises are severally inconclusive the process of deciding the issue becomes a matter of weighing the cumulative effect of one group of severally inconclusive items against the cumulative effect of another group of severally

---

[5]*The Times*, March 2, 1945. Also in *The Times* of June 13, 1945, contrast the case of Hannah v. Peel with that of the cruiser cut in two by a liner. In the latter case there is not agreement as to the facts. See also the excellent articles by Dr. Glanville L. Williams in the *Law Quarterly Review*, "Language and the Law" (January and April 1945) and "The Doctrine of Repugnancy" (October 1943, January 1944, and April 1944). The author, having set out how arbitrary are many legal decisions, needs now to set out how far from arbitrary they are—if his readers are ready for the next phase in the dialectic process.

inconclusive items, and thus lends itself to description in terms of conflicting "probabilities." This encourages the feeling that the issue is one of fact—that it is a matter of guessing from the premises at a further fact, at what is to come. But this is a muddle. *The dispute does not cease to be a priori because it is a matter of the cumulative effect of severally inconclusive premises.* The logic of the dispute is not that of a chain of deductive reasoning as in a mathematic calculation. But nor is it a matter of collecting from several inconclusive items of information an expectation as to something further, as when a doctor from a patient's symptoms guesses at what is wrong, or a detective from many clues guesses the criminal. It has its own sort of logic and its own sort of end—the solution of the question at issue is a decision, a ruling by the judge. But it is not an arbitrary decision, though the rational connections are neither quite like those in vertical deductions nor like those in inductions in which from many signs we guess at what is to come; and though the decision manifests itself in the application of a name it is no more merely the application of a name than is the pinning on of a medal merely the pinning on of a bit of metal. Whether a lion with stripes is a tiger or a lion is, if you like, merely a matter of the application of a name. Whether Mr. So-and-So of whose conduct we have so complete a record did or did not exercise reasonable care is not merely a matter of the application of a name or, if we choose to say it is, then we must remember that with this name a game is lost and won and a game with very heavy stakes. With the judges' choice of a name for the facts goes an attitude, and the declaration, the ruling, is an exclamation evincing that attitude. But *it is an exclamation which not only has a purpose but also has a logic*, a logic surprisingly like that of "futile," "deplorable," "graceful," "grand," "divine."

6.6. *Suppose two people are looking at a picture or natural scene.* One says "Excellent" or "Beautiful" or "Divine"; the other says "I don't see it." He means he doesn't see the beauty. And this reminds us of how we felt the theist accuse the atheist of blindness and the atheist accuse the theist of seeing what isn't there. And yet surely each sees what the other sees. It isn't that one can see part of the picture which the other can't see. So the difference is in a sense not as to the facts. And so it cannot be removed by one disputant discovering to the other what so far he hasn't seen. It isn't that the one sees the picture in a different light and so, as we might say, sees a different picture. Consequently the difference between them cannot be resolved by putting the picture in a different light. And yet surely this is just what can be done in such a case—not by moving the picture but by talk perhaps. To settle a dispute as to whether a piece of music is good or better than another we listen again, with a picture we look again. Someone perhaps points to emphasize certain features and we see it in a different light. Shall we call this "field work" and "the last of observation" or shall we call it "reviewing the premises" and "the beginning of deduction (horizontal)"?

If in spite of all this we choose to say that a difference as to whether a thing is beautiful is not a factual difference, we must be careful to remember that there is a procedure for settling these differences and that this consists not only in reasoning and redescription as in the legal case, but also in a more literal re-setting-before with re-looking or re-listening.

6.7. *And if we say, as we did at the beginning, that when a difference as to the existence of a God is not one as to future happenings then it is not experimental and therefore not as to the facts, we must not forthwith assume that there is no right and wrong about it,* no rationality or irrationality, no appropriateness or inappropriateness, no procedure which tends to settle it, *nor even that this procedure is in no sense a discovery of new facts.* After all even in science this is not so. Our two gardeners, even when they had reached the stage when neither expected any experimental result which the other did not, might yet have continued the dispute, each presenting and re-presenting the features of the garden favouring his hypothesis, that is, fitting his model for describing the accepted fact; each emphasizing the pattern he wishes to emphasize. True, in science, there is seldom or never a pure instance of this sort of dispute, for nearly always with difference of hypothesis goes some difference of expectation as to the facts. But scientists argue about rival hypotheses with a vigour which is not exactly proportioned to difference in expectations of experimental results.

The difference as to whether a God exists involves our feelings more than most scientific disputes and in this respect is more like a difference as to whether there is beauty in a thing.

7. *The Connecting Technique.* Let us consider again the technique used in revealing or proving beauty, in removing a blindness, in inducing an attitude which is lacking, in reducing a reaction that is inappropriate. Besides running over in a special way the features of the picture, tracing the rhythms, making sure that this and that are not only seen but noticed, and their relation to each other—besides all this—there are other things we can do to justify our attitude and alter that of the man who cannot see. For features of the picture may be brought out by setting beside it other pictures; just as the merits of an argument may be brought out, proved, by setting beside it other arguments, in which striking but irrelevant features of the original are changed and relevant features emphasized; just as the merits and demerits of a line of action may be brought out by setting beside it other actions. To use Susan Stebbing's example: Nathan brought out for David certain features of what David had done in the matter of Uriah the Hittite by telling him a story about two sheep-owners. This is the kind of thing we very often do when someone is "inconsistent" or "unreasonable." This is what we do in referring to other cases in law. The paths we need to trace from other cases to the case in question are often numerous and difficult to detect and the person with whom we are discussing the matter may well draw attention to connections

which, while not incompatible with those we have tried to emphasize, are of an opposite inclination. *A* may have noticed *B* subtle and hidden likenesses to an angel and reveal these to *C*, while *C* has noticed in *B* subtle and hidden likenesses to a devil which he reveals to *A*.

Imagine that a man picks up some flowers that lie half withered on a table and gently puts them in water. Another man says to him "You believe flowers feel." He says this although he knows that the man who helps the flowers doesn't expect anything of them which he himself doesn't expect; for he himself expects the flowers to be "refreshed" and to be easily hurt, injured, I mean, by rough handling, while the man who puts them in water does not expect them to whisper "Thank you." The skeptic says "You believe flowers feel" because something about the way the other man lifts the flowers and puts them in water suggests an attitude to the flowers which he feels inappropriate although perhaps he would not feel it inappropriate to butterflies. He feels that this attitude to flowers is somewhat crazy *just as it is sometimes felt that a lover's attitude is somewhat crazy even when this is not a matter of his having false hopes about how the person he is in love with will act*. It is often said in such cases that reasoning is useless. But the very person who says this feels that the lover's attitude is crazy, is inappropriate like some dreads and hatreds, such as some horrors of enclosed places. And often one who says "It is useless to reason" proceeds at once to reason with the lover, nor is this reasoning always quite without effect. We may draw the lover's attention to certain things done by her he is in love with and trace for him a path to these from things done by others at other times[6] which have disgusted and infuriated him. And by this means we may weaken his admiration and confidence, make him feel it unjustified and arouse his suspicion and contempt and make him feel our suspicion and contempt reasonable. It is possible, of course, that he has already noticed the analogies, the connections, we point out and that he has accepted them—that is, he has not denied them nor passed them off. He has recognized them and they have altered his attitude, altered his love, but he still loves. We then feel that perhaps it is we who are blind and cannot see what he can see.

8. *Connecting and Disconnecting.* But before we confess ourselves thus inadequate there are other fires his admiration must pass through. For when a man has an attitude which it seems to us he should not have or lacks one which it seems to us he should have, then not only do we suspect that he is not influenced by connections which we feel should influence him and draw his attention to these, but also we suspect he is influenced by connections which should not influence him and draw his attention to these. It may, for a moment, seem strange that we should draw his attention to connections which we feel should not influence him, and which, since they do influence

---

[6]Thus, like the scientist, the critic is concerned to show up the irrelevance of time and space.

him, he has in a sense already noticed. But we do—such is our confidence in "the light of reason."

Sometimes the power of these connections comes mainly from a man's mismanagement of the language he is using. This is what happens in the Monte Carlo fallacy, where by mismanaging the laws of chance a man passes from noticing that a certain colour or number has not turned up for a long while to an improper confidence that now it soon will turn up. In such cases our showing up of the false connections is a process we call "explaining a fallacy in reasoning." To remove fallacies in reasoning we urge a man to call a spade a spade, ask him what he means by "the State" and having pointed out ambiguities and vaguenesses ask him to reconsider the steps in his argument.

9. *Unspoken Connections. Usually, however, wrongheadedness or wrongheartedness in a situation, blindness to what is there or seeing what is not, does not arise merely from mismanagement of language but is more due to connections which are not mishandled in language, for the reason that they are not put into language at all.* And often these misconnections too, weaken in the light of reason, if only we can guess where they lie and turn it on them. Insofar as these connections are not presented in language the process of removing their power is not a process of correcting the mismanagement of language. But it is still akin to such a process; for though it is not a process of setting out fairly what has been set out unfairly, it is a process of setting out fairly what has not been set out at all. And we must remember that the line between connections ill-presented or half-presented in language and connections operative but not presented in language, or only hinted at, is not a sharp one.

Whether or not we call the process of showing up these connections "reasoning to remove bad unconscious reasoning" or not, it is certain that in order to settle in ourselves what weight we shall attach to someone's confidence or attitude we not only ask him for his reasons but also look for unconscious reasons both good and bad; that is, for reasons which he can't put into words, isn't explicitly aware of, is hardly aware of, isn't aware of at all—perhaps it's long experience which he *doesn't* recall which lets him know a squall is coming, perhaps it's old experience which he *can't* recall which makes the cake in the tea mean so much and makes Odette so fascinating.[7]

I am well aware of the distinction between the question "What reasons are there for the belief that S is P?" and the question "What are the sources of beliefs that S is P?" There are cases where investigation of the rationality of a claim which certain persons make is done with very little inquiry into why they say what they do, into the causes of their beliefs. This is so when we have very definite ideas about what is really logically relevant to their claim and what is not. Offered a mathematical theorem we ask for the proof; offered the

---

[7]Proust, *Swann's Way*, Vol. I, 58, Vol. II. Phoenix Edition.

generalization that parental discord causes crime we ask for the correlation coefficients. But even in this last case, if we fancy that only the figures are reasons, we underestimate the complexity of the logic of our conclusion; and yet it is difficult to describe the other features of the evidence which have weight and there is apt to be disagreement about the weight they should have. In criticizing other conclusions, and especially conclusions which are largely the expression of an attitude, we have not only to ascertain what reasons there are for them but also to decide what things are reasons and how much. This latter process of sifting reasons from causes is part of the critical process for every belief, but in some spheres it has been done pretty fully already. In these spheres we don't need to examine the actual processes to belief and distil from them a logic. But in other spheres this remains to be done. Even in science or on the stock exchange or in ordinary life we sometimes hesitate to condemn a belief or a hunch[8] merely because those who believe it cannot offer the sort of reasons we had hoped for. And now suppose Miss Gertrude Stein finds excellent the work of a new artist while we see nothing in it. We nervously recall, perhaps, how pictures by Picasso, which Miss Stein admired and others rejected, later came to be admired by many who gave attention to them, and we wonder whether the case is not a new instance of her perspicacity and our blindness. But if, upon giving all our attention to the work in question, we still do not respond to it, and we notice that the subject matter of the new pictures is perhaps birds in wild places and learn that Miss Stein is a bird-watcher, then we begin to trouble ourselves less about her admiration.

It must not be forgotten that our attempt to show up misconnections in Miss Stein may have an opposite result and reveal to us connections we had missed. Thinking to remove the spell exercised upon his patient by the old stories of the Greeks, the psychoanalyst may himself fall under that spell and find in them what his patient has found and, incidentally, what made the Greeks tell those tales.

10. *Now what happens, what should happen, when we inquire in this way into the reasonableness, the propriety of belief in gods?* The answer is: A double and opposite-phased change. Wordsworth writes:

> . . . And I have felt
> A presence that disturbs me with the joy
> Of elevated thoughts; a sense sublime
> Of something far more deeply interfused,
> Whose dwelling is the light of setting suns,
> And the round ocean and the living air,
> And the blue sky, and in the mind of man:
> A motion and a spirit, that impels

---

[8]Here I think of Mr. Stace's interesting reflections in *Mind* (January 1945), "The Problem of Unreasoned Beliefs."

> All thinking things, all objects of all thought,
> And rolls through all things . . . . [9]

We most of us know this feeling. But is it well placed like the feeling that here is first-rate work, which we sometimes rightly have even before we have fully grasped the picture we are looking at or the book we are reading? Or is it misplaced like the feeling in a house that has long been empty that someone secretly lives there still. Wordsworth's feeling *is* the feeling that the world is haunted, that something watches in the hills and manages the stars. The child feels that the stone tripped him when he stumbled, that the bough struck him when it flew back in his face. He has to learn that the wind isn't buffeting him, that there is not a devil in it, that he was wrong, that his attitude was inappropriate. And as he learns that the wind wasn't hindering him so he also learns it wasn't helping him. But we know how, though he learns, his attitude lingers. It is plain that Wordsworth's feeling is of this family.

Belief in gods, it is true, is often very different from belief that stones are spiteful, the sun kindly. For the gods appear in human form and from the waves and control these things and by so doing reward and punish us. But varied as are the stories of the gods, they have a family likeness and we have only to recall them to feel sure of the other main sources which cooperate with animism to produce them.

What are the stories of the gods? What are our feelings when we believe in God? They are feelings of awe before power, dread of the thunderbolts of Zeus, confidence in the everlasting arms, unease beneath the all-seeing eye. They are feelings of guilt and inescapable vengeance, of smothered hate and of a security we can hardly do without. We have only to remind ourselves of these feelings and the stories of the gods and goddesses and heroes in which these feelings find expression to be reminded of how we felt as children to our parents and the big people of our childhood. Writing of a first telephone call from his grandmother, Proust says:

> . . . it was rather that this isolation of the voice was like a symbol, a presentation, a direct consequence of another isolation, that of my grandmother, separated for the first time in my life, from myself. The orders or prohibitions which she addressed to me at every moment in the ordinary course of my life, the tedium of obedience or the fire of rebellion which neutralized the affection that I felt for her were at this moment eliminated . . . . "Granny!" I cried to her . . . but I had beside me only that voice, a phantom, as unpalpable as that which would come to revisit me when my grandmother was dead. "Speak to me!" but then it happened that, left more solitary still, I ceased to catch the sound of her voice. My grandmother could no longer hear me . . . I continued to call her, sounding the empty night, in which I felt that her appeals also must be straying. I was

---

[9] *Tintern Abbey.*

shaken by the same anguish which, in the distant past, I had felt once before, one day when, a little child, in a crowd, I had lost her.

Giorgio de Chirico, writing of Courbet, says:

The word yesterday envelops us with its yearning echo, just as, on waking, when the sense of time and the logic of things remain a while confused, the memory of a happy hour we spent the day before may sometimes linger reverberating within us. At times we think of Courbet and his work as we do of our own father's youth.

When a man's father fails him by death or weakness how much he needs another father, one in the heavens with whom is "no variableness nor shadow of turning."

We understood Mr. Kenneth Graham when he wrote of the Golden Age we feel we have lived in under the Olympians. Freud says: "The ordinary man cannot imagine this Providence in any other form but that of a greatly exalted father, for only such a one could understand the needs of the sons of men, or be softened by their prayers and be placated by the signs of their remorse. The whole thing is so patently infantile, so incongruous with reality . . . . " "So incongruous with reality"! It cannot be denied.

But here a new aspect of the matter may strike us.[10] For the very facts which make us feel that now we can recognize systems of superhuman, subhuman, elusive beings for what they are—the persistent projections of infantile phantasies—include facts which make these systems less fantastic. What are these facts? They are patterns in human reactions which are well described by saying that we are as if there were hidden within us powers, persons, not ourselves and stronger than ourselves. That this is so may perhaps be said to have been common knowledge yielded by ordinary observation of people,[11] but we did not know the degree in which this is so until recent study of extraordinary cases in extraordinary conditions had revealed it. I refer, of course, to the study of multiple personalities and the wider studies of psychoanalysts. Even when the results of this work are reported to us, that is not the same as tracing the patterns in the details of the cases on which the results are based; and even that is not the same as taking part in the studies oneself. One thing not sufficiently realized is that some of the things shut within us are not bad but good.

Now the gods, good and evil and mixed, have always been mysterious powers outside us rather than within. But they have also been within. It is not

---

[10] I owe to the late Dr. Susan Isaacs the thought of this different aspect of the matter, of this connection between the heavenly Father and "the good father" spoken of in psychoanalysis.

[11] Consider Tolstoy and Dostoievsky—I do not mean, of course, that their observation was ordinary.

a modern theory but an old saying that in each of us a devil sleeps. Eve said: "The serpent beguiled me." Helen says to Menelaus:

> ... And yet how strange it is!
> I ask not thee; I ask my own sad thought,
> What was there in my heart, that I forgot
> My home and land and all I loved, to fly
> With a strange man? Surely it was not I,
> But Cypris there![12]

Elijah found that God was not in the wind, nor in the thunder, but in a still small voice. The kingdom of Heaven is within us, Christ insisted, though usually about the size of a grain of mustard seed, and he prayed that we should become one with the Father in Heaven.

New knowledge made it necessary either to give up saying "The sun is sinking" or to give the words a new meaning. In many contexts we preferred to stick to the old words and give them a new meaning which was not entirely new but, on the contrary, *practically* the same as the old. The Greeks did not speak of the dangers of repressing instincts but they did speak of the dangers of thwarting Dionysos, of neglecting Cypris for Diana, of forgetting Poseidon for Athena. We have eaten of the fruit of a garden we can't forget though we were never there, a garden we still look for though we can never find it. Maybe we look for too simple a likeness to what we dreamed. Maybe we are not as free as we fancy from the old idea that Heaven is a happy hunting ground, or a city with streets of gold. Lately Mr. Aldous Huxley has recommended our seeking not somewhere beyond the sky or late in time but a timeless state not made of the stuff of this world, which he rejects, picking it into worthless pieces. But this sounds to me still too much a looking for another place, not indeed one filled with sweets but instead so empty that some of us would rather remain in the Lamb or the Elephant, where, as we know, they stop whimpering with another bitter and, so far from sneering at all things, hang pictures of winners at Kempton and stars of the 'nineties. Something good we have for each other is freed there, and in some degree and for awhile the miasma of time is rolled back without obliging us to deny the present.

---

[12]Euripides, *The Trojan Women*, Gilbert Murray's translation. Roger Hinks in *Myth and Allegory in Ancient Art* writes (p. 108): "Personifications made their appearance very early in Greek poetry .... It is out of the question to call these terrible beings 'abstractions' .... They are real demons to be worshipped and propitiated .... These beings we observe correspond to states of mind. The experience of man teaches him that from time to time his composure is invaded and overturned by some power from outside, panic, intoxication, sexual desire."

> What use to shoot off guns at unicorns?
> Where one horn's hit another fierce horn grows.
> These beasts are fabulous, and none were born
> Of women who could lay a fable low.
> *The Glass Tower*, Nicholas Moore, p. 100.

The artists who do most for us don't tell us only of fairylands. Proust, Manet, Breughel, even Botticelli and Vermeer show us reality. And yet they give us for a moment exhilaration without anxiety, peace without boredom. And those who, like Freud, work in a different way against that which too often comes over us and forces us into deadness or despair,[13] also deserve critical, patient, and courageous attention. For they, too, work to release us from human bondage into human freedom.

Many have tried to find ways of salvation. The reports they bring back are always incomplete and apt to mislead even when they are not in words but in music or paint. But they are by no means useless; and not the worst of them are those which speak of oneness with God. But insofar as we become one with Him He becomes one with us. St. John says He is in us as we love one another.

This love, I suppose, is not benevolence but something that comes of the oneness with one another of which Christ spoke.[14] Sometimes it momentarily gains strength.[15] Hate and the Devil do too. And what is oneness without otherness?

---

[13]Matthew Arnold, *Summer Night*.

[14]John 16:21.

[15]"The Harvesters" in *The Golden Age*, Kenneth Graham.

# Norman Malcolm

Norman Malcolm (1911–    ) is the author of *Ludwig Wittgenstein: A Memoir, Dreaming, Knowledge and Certainty* and other influential works.

# 26

# The Second Form of the Ontological Argument

## I

I believe that in Anselm's *Proslogion* and *Responsio editoris* there are two different pieces of reasoning which he did not distinguish from one another, and that a good deal of light may be shed on the philosophical problem of "the ontological argument" if we do distinguish them. In Chapter 2 of the *Proslogion*[1] Anselm says that we believe that God is *something a greater than which cannot be conceived*. (The Latin is *aliquid quo nihil maius cogitari possit*. Anselm sometimes uses the alternative expressions *aliquid quo maius nihil cogitari potest, id quo maius cogitari nequit, aliquid quo maius cogitari non valet*.) Even the fool of the Psalm who says in his heart there is no God, when he hears this very thing that Anselm says, namely, "something a greater than which cannot be conceived," understands what he hears, and what he understands is in his understanding though he does not understand that it exists.

Apparently Anselm regards it as tautological to say that whatever is understood is in the understanding (*quidquid intelligitur in intellectu est*): he uses *intelligitur* and *in intellectu est* as interchangeable locutions. The same holds for another formula of his: whatever is thought is in thought (*quidquid cogitatur in cogitatione est*).[2]

---

"Anselm's Ontological Arguments," *The Philosophical Review*, Vol. LXIX, No. 1 (January, 1960), 41–62. Reprinted by permission of the author and of the Editor of *The Philosophical Review*.

[1] I have consulted the Latin text of the *Proslogion*, of *Gaunilonis Pro Insipiente*, and of the *Responsio editoris*, in S. Anselmi, *Opera Omnia*, edited by F. C. Schmitt (Secovii, 1938), vol. I. With numerous modifications, I have used the English translation by S. N. Deane: *St. Anselm* (LaSalle, Illinois, 1948).

[2] See *Proslogion* 1 and *Responsio* 2.

Of course many things may exist in the understanding that do not exist in reality; for example, elves. Now, says Anselm, something a greater than which cannot be conceived exists in the understanding. But it cannot exist *only* in the understanding, for to exist in reality is greater. Therefore that thing a greater than which cannot be conceived cannot exist only in the understanding, for then a greater thing could be conceived: namely, one that exists both in the understanding and in reality.[3]

Here I have a question. It is not clear to me whether Anselm means that (a) existence in reality by itself is greater than existence in the understanding, or that (b) existence in reality and existence in the understanding together are greater than existence in the understanding alone. Certainly he accepts (b). But he might also accept (a), as Descartes apparently does in *Meditation III* when he suggests that the mode of being by which a thing is "objectively in the understanding" is *imperfect*.[4] Of course Anselm might accept both (a) and (b). He might hold that in general something is greater if it has both of these "modes of existence" than if it has either one alone, but also that existence in reality is a more perfect mode of existence than existence in the understanding.

In any case, Anselm holds that something is greater if it exists both in the understanding and in reality than if it exists merely in the understanding. An equivalent way of putting this interesting proposition, in a more current terminology, is: something is greater if it is both conceived of and exists than if it is merely conceived of. Anselm's reasoning can be expressed as follows: *id quo maius cogitari nequit* cannot be merely conceived of and not exist, for then it would not be *id quo maius cogitari nequit*. The doctrine that something is greater if it exists in addition to being conceived of, than if it is only conceived of, could be called the doctrine that *existence is a perfection*. Descartes maintained, in so many words, that existence is a perfection,[5] and presumably he was holding Anselm's doctrine, although he does not, in *Meditation V* or elsewhere, argue in the way that Anselm does in *Proslogion* 2.

When Anselm says, "And certainly, that than which nothing greater can be conceived cannot exist merely in the understanding. For suppose it exists merely in the understanding, then it can be conceived to exist in reality, which is greater,"[6] he is claiming that if I conceived of a being of great excellence, that being would be *greater* (more excellent, more perfect) if it existed than if it did not exist. His supposition that "it exists merely in the understanding"

---

[3] Anselm's actual words are: "Et certe id quo maius cogitari nequit, non potest esse in solo intellectu. Si enim vel in solo intellectu est, potest cogitari esse et in re, quod maius est. Si ergo id quo maius cogitari non potest, est in solo intellectu: id ipsum quo maius cogitari non potest, est quo maius cogitari potest. Sed certe hoc esse non potest." *Proslogion* 2.

[4] Haldane and Ross, *The Philosophical Works of Descartes*, 2 vols. (Cambridge, 1931), I, 163.

[5] *Op. cit.*, p. 182.

[6] *Proslogion* 2; Deane, p. 8.

is the supposition that it is conceived of but does not exist. Anselm repeated this claim in his reply to the criticism of the monk Gaunilo. Speaking of the being a greater than which cannot be conceived, he says:

> I have said that if it exists merely in the understanding it can be conceived to exist in reality, which is greater. Therefore, if it exists merely in the understanding obviously the very being a greater than which cannot be conceived, is one a greater than which can be conceived. What, I ask, can follow better than that? For if it exists merely in the understanding, can it not be conceived to exist in reality? And if it can be so conceived does not he who conceives of this conceive of a thing greater than it, if it does exist merely in the understanding? Can anything follow better than this: that if a being a greater than which cannot be conceived exists merely in the understanding, it is something a greater than which can be conceived? What could be plainer?[7]

He is implying, in the first sentence, that if I conceive of something which does not exist then it is possible for it to exist, and *it will be greater if it exists than if it does not exist.*

The doctrine that existence is a perfection is remarkably queer. It makes sense and is true to say that my future house will be a better one if it is insulated than if it is not insulated; but what could it mean to say that it will be a better house if it exists than if it does not? My future child will be a better man if he is honest than if he is not; but who would understand the saying that he will be a better man if he exists than if he does not? Or who understands the saying that if God exists He is more perfect than if He does not exist? One might say, with some intelligibility, that it would be better (for oneself or for mankind) if God exists than if He does not—but that is a different matter.

A king might desire that his next chancellor should have knowledge, wit, and resolution; but it is ludicrous to add that the king's desire is to have a chancellor who exists. Suppose that two royal councilors, A and B, were asked to draw up separately descriptions of the most perfect chancellor they could conceive, and that the descriptions they produced were identical except that A included existence in his list of attributes of a perfect chancellor and B did not. (I do not mean that B put nonexistence in his list.) One and the same person could satisfy both descriptions. More to the point, any person who satisfied A's description would *necessarily* satisfy B's description and *vice versa!* This is to say that A and B did not produce descriptions that differed in any way but rather one and the same description of necessary and desirable qualities in a chancellor. A only made a show of putting down a desirable quality that B had failed to include.

---

[7]*Responsio* 2; Deane, pp. 157–58.

I believe I am merely restating an observation that Kant made in attacking the notion that "existence" or "being" is a "real predicate." He says:

> By whatever and by however many predicates we may think a thing—even if we completely determine it—we do not make the least addition to the thing when we further declare that this thing *is*. Otherwise, it would not be exactly the same thing that exists, but something more than we had thought in the concept; and we could not, therefore, say that the exact object of my concept exists.[8]

Anselm's ontological proof of *Proslogion* 2 is fallacious because it rests on the false doctrine that existence is a perfection (and therefore that "existence" is a "real predicate"). It would be desirable to have a rigorous refutation of the doctrine but I have not been able to provide one. I am compelled to leave the matter at the more or less intuitive level of Kant's observation. In any case, I believe that the doctrine does not belong to Anselm's other formulation of the ontological argument. It is worth noting that Gassendi anticipated Kant's criticism when he said, against Descartes:

> Existence is a perfection neither in God nor in anything else; it is rather that in the absence of which there is no perfection .... Hence neither is existence held to exist in a thing in the way that perfections do, nor if the thing lacks existence is it said to be imperfect (or deprived of a perfection), so much as to be nothing.[9]

## II

I take up now the consideration of the second ontological proof, which Anselm presents in the very next chapter of the *Proslogion*. (There is no evidence that he thought of himself as offering two different proofs.) Speaking of the being a greater than which cannot be conceived, he says:

> And it so truly exists that it cannot be conceived not to exist. For it is possible to conceive of a being which cannot be conceived not to exist; and this is greater than one which can be conceived not to exist. Hence, if that, than which nothing greater can be conceived, can be conceived not to exist, it is not that than which nothing greater can be conceived. But this is a contradiction. So truly, therefore, is there something than which nothing greater can be conceived, that it cannot even be conceived not to exist. And this being thou art, O Lord, our God.[10]

---

[8]*The Critique of Pure Reason*, tr. by Norman Kemp Smith (London, 1929), p. 505.
[9]Haldane and Ross, II, 186.
[10]*Proslogion* 3; Deane, pp. 8–9.

Anselm is saying two things: first, that a being whose nonexistence is logically impossible is "greater" than a being whose nonexistence is logically possible (and therefore that a being a greater than which cannot be conceived must be one whose nonexistence is logically impossible); second, that *God* is a being than which a greater cannot be conceived.

In regard to the second of these assertions, there certainly is *a* use of the word "God," and I think far the more common use, in accordance with which the statements "God is the greatest of all beings," "God is the most perfect being," "God is the supreme being," are *logically* necessary truths, in the same sense that the statement "A square has four sides" is a logically necessary truth. If there is a man named "Jones" who is the tallest man in the world, the statement "Jones is the tallest man in the world" is merely true and is not a logically necessary truth. It is a virtue of Anselm's unusual phrase, "a being a greater than which cannot be conceived,"[11] to make it explicit that the sentence "God is the greatest of all beings" expresses a logically necessary truth and not a mere matter of fact such as the one we imagined about Jones.

With regard to Anselm's first assertion (namely, that a being whose nonexistence is logically impossible is greater than a being whose nonexistence is logically possible) perhaps the most puzzling thing about it is the use of the word "greater." It appears to mean exactly the same as "superior," "more excellent," "more perfect." This equivalence by itself is of no help to us, however, since the latter expressions would be equally puzzling here. What is required is some explanation of their use.

We do think of *knowledge*, say, as an excellence, a good thing. If A has more knowledge of algebra than B we express this in common language by saying that A has a *better* knowledge of algebra than B, or that A's knowledge of algebra is *superior* to B's, whereas we should not say that B has a better or superior *ignorance* of algebra than A. We do say "greater ignorance," but here the word "greater" is used purely quantitatively.

Previously I rejected *existence* as a perfection. Anselm is maintaining in the remarks last quoted, not that existence is a perfection, but that *the logical impossibility of nonexistence is a perfection*. In other words, *necessary existence* is a perfection. His first ontological proof uses the principle that a thing is greater if it exists than if it does not exist. His second proof employs the different principle that a thing is greater if it necessarily exists than if it does not necessarily exist.

Some remarks about the notion of *dependence* may help to make this latter principle intelligible. Many things depend for their existence on other

---

[11]Professor Robert Calhoun has pointed out to me that a similar locution had been used by Augustine. In *De moribus Manichaeorum* (Bk. II, ch. xi, sec. 24), he says that God is a being *quo esse aut cogitari melius nihil possit* (*Patrologiae Patrum Latinorum*, ed. by J. P. Migne, Paris, 1841–1845, vol. 32: *Augustinus*, vol. 1).

things and events. My house was built by a carpenter: its coming into existence was dependent on a certain creative activity. Its continued existence is dependent on many things: that a tree does not crush it, that it is not consumed by fire, and so on. If we reflect on the common meaning of the word "God" (no matter how vague and confused this is), we realize that it is incompatible with this meaning that God's existence should *depend* on anything. Whether we believe in Him or not we must admit that the "almighty and everlasting God" (as several ancient prayers begin), the "Maker of heaven and earth, and of all things visible and invisible" (as is said in the Nicene Creed), cannot be thought of as being brought into existence by anything or as depending for His continued existence on anything. To conceive of anything as dependent upon something else for its existence is to conceive of it as a lesser being than God.

If a housewife has a set of extremely fragile dishes, then as dishes they are *inferior* to those of another set like them in all respects except that they are *not* fragile. Those of the first set are *dependent* for their continued existence on gentle handling; those of the second set are not. There is a definite connection in common language between the notions of dependency and inferiority, and independence and superiority. To say that something which was dependent on nothing whatever was superior to ("greater than") anything that was dependent in any way upon anything is quite in keeping with the everyday use of the terms "superior" and "greater." Correlative with the notions of dependence and independence are the notions of *limited* and *unlimited*. An engine requires fuel and this is a limitation. It is the same thing to say that an engine's operation is *dependent* on as that it is *limited* by its fuel supply. An engine that could accomplish the same work in the same time and was in other respects satisfactory, but did not require fuel, would be a *superior* engine.

God is usually conceived of as an *unlimited* being. He is conceived of as a being who *could not* be limited, that is, as an absolutely unlimited being. This is no less than to conceive of Him as *something a greater than which cannot be conceived*. If God is conceived to be an absolutely unlimited being He must be conceived to be unlimited in regard to His existence as well as His operation. In this conception it will not make sense to say that He depends on anything for coming into or continuing in existence. Nor, as Spinoza observed, will it make sense to say that something could *prevent* Him from existing.[12] Lack of moisture can prevent trees from existing in a certain region of the earth. But it would be contrary to the concept of God as an unlimited being to suppose that anything other than God Himself could prevent Him from existing, and it would be self-contradictory to suppose that He Himself could do it.

---

[12]*Ethics*, pt. I, prop. 11.

Some may be inclined to object that although nothing could prevent God's existence, still it might just *happen* that He did not exist. And if He did exist that too would be by chance. I think, however, that from the supposition that it could happen that God did not exist it would follow that, if He existed, He would have mere duration and not eternity. It would make sense to ask, "How long has He existed?," "Will He still exist next week?," "He was in existence yesterday but how about today?," and so on. It seems absurd to make God the subject of such questions. According to our ordinary conception of Him, He is an eternal being. And eternity does not mean endless duration, as Spinoza noted. To ascribe eternity to something is to exclude as senseless all sentences that imply that it has duration. If a thing has duration then it would be merely a *contingent* fact, if it was a fact, that its duration was endless. The moon could have endless duration but not eternity. If something has endless duration it will *make sense* (although it will be false) to say that it will cease to exist, and it will make sense (although it will be false) to say that something will *cause* it to cease to exist. A being with endless duration is not, therefore, an absolutely unlimited being. That God is conceived to be eternal follows from the fact that He is conceived to be an absolutely unlimited being.

I have been trying to expand the argument of *Proslogion* 3. In *Responsio* 1 Anselm adds the following acute point: if you can conceive of a certain thing and this thing does not exist then if it *were* to exist its nonexistence would be *possible*. It follows, I believe, that if the thing were to exist it would depend on other things both for coming into and continuing in existence, and also that it would have duration and not eternity. Therefore it would not be, either in reality or in conception, an unlimited being, *aliquid quo nihil maius cogitari possit*.

Anselm states his argument as follows:

> If it [the thing a greater than which cannot be conceived] can be conceived at all it must exist. For no one who denies or doubts the existence of a being a greater than which is inconceivable, denies or doubts that if it did exist its non-existence, either in reality or in the understanding, would be impossible. For otherwise it would not be a being a greater than which cannot be conceived. But as to whatever can be conceived but does not exist: if it were to exist its non-existence either in reality or in the understanding would be possible. Therefore, if a being a greater than which cannot be conceived, can even be conceived, it must exist.[13]

What Anselm has proved is that the notion of contingent existence or of contingent nonexistence cannot have any application to God. His existence must either be logically necessary or logically impossible. The only intelligible way of rejecting Anselm's claim that God's existence is necessary is to

---

[13]*Responsio* 1; Deane, pp. 154–55.

maintain that the concept of God, as a being a greater than which cannot be conceived, is self-contradictory or nonsensical.[14] Supposing that this is false, Anselm is right to deduce God's necessary existence from his characterization of Him as a being a greater than which cannot be conceived.

Let me summarize the proof. If God, a being a greater than which cannot be conceived, does not exist then He cannot *come* into existence. For if He did He would either have been *caused* to come into existence or have *happened* to come into existence, and in either case He would be a limited being, which by our conception of Him He is not. Since He cannot come into existence, if He does not exist His existence is impossible. If He does exist He cannot have come into existence (for the reasons given), nor can He cease to exist, for nothing could cause Him to cease to exist nor could it just happen that He ceased to exist. So if God exists His existence is necessary. Thus God's existence is either impossible or necessary. It can be the former only if the concept of such a being is self-contradictory or in some way logically absurd. Assuming that this is not so, it follows that He necessarily exists.

It may be helpful to express ourselves in the following way: to say, not that *omnipotence* is a property of God, but rather that *necessary omnipotence* is; and to say, not that omniscience is a property of God, but rather that *necessary omniscience* is. We have criteria for determining that a man knows this and that and can do this and that, and for determining that one man has greater knowledge and abilities in a certain subject than another. We could think of various tests to give them. But there is nothing we should wish to describe, seriously and literally, as "testing" God's knowledge and powers. That God is omniscient and omnipotent has not been determined by the application of criteria: rather these are requirements of our conception of Him. They are internal properties of the concept, although they are also rightly said to be properties of God. *Necessary existence* is a property of God in the *same sense* that *necessary omnipotence* and *necessary omniscience* are His properties. And we are not to think that "God necessarily exists" means that it follows necessarily from something that God exists *contingently*. The a priori proposition "God necessarily exists" entails the proposition "God exists," if and only if the latter also is understood as an a priori proposition: in which case the two propositions are equivalent. In this sense Anselm's proof is a proof of God's existence.

---

[14]Gaunilo attacked Anselm's argument on this very point. He would not concede that a being a greater than which cannot be conceived existed in his understanding (*Gaunilonis Pro Insipiente*, secs. 4 and 5; Deane, pp. 148–50). Anselm's reply is: "I call on your faith and conscience to attest that this is most false" (*Responsio* 1; Deane, p. 154). Gaunilo's faith and conscience will attest that it is false that "God is not a being a greater than which is inconceivable," and false that "He is not understood (*intelligitur*) or conceived (*cogitatur*)" (*ibid.*). Descartes also remarks that one would go to "strange extremes" who denied that we understand the words "*that thing which is the most perfect that we can conceive;* for that is what all men call God" (Haldane and Ross, II, 129).

Descartes was somewhat hazy on the question of whether existence is a property of things that exist, but at the same time he saw clearly enough that *necessary existence* is a property of God. Both points are illustrated in his reply to Gassendi's remark, which I quoted above:

> I do not see to what class of reality you wish to assign existence, nor do I see why it may not be said to be a property as well as omnipotence, taking the word property as equivalent to any attribute or anything which can be predicted of a thing, as in the present case it should be by all means regarded. Nay, necessary existence in the case of God is also a true property in the strictest sense of the word, because it belongs to Him and forms part of His essence alone.[15]

Elsewhere he speaks of "the necessity of existence" as being "that crown of perfections without which we cannot comprehend God."[16] He is emphatic on the point that necessary existence applies solely to "an absolutely perfect Being."[17]

### III

I wish to consider now a part of Kant's criticism of the ontological argument which I believe to be wrong. He says:

> If, in an identical proposition, I reject the predicate while retaining the subject, contradiction results; and I therefore say that the former belongs necessarily to the latter. But if we reject subject and predicate alike, there is no contradiction; for nothing is then left that can be contradicted. To posit a triangle, and yet to reject its three angles, is self-contradictory; but there is no contradiction in rejecting the triangle together with its three angles. The same holds true of the concept of an absolutely necessary being. If its existence is rejected, we reject the thing itself with all its predicates and no question of contradiction can then arise. There is nothing outside it that would then be contradicted, since the necessity of the thing is not supposed to be derived from anything external; nor is there anything internal that would be contradicted, since in rejecting the thing itself we have at the same time rejected all its internal properties. "God is omnipotent" is a necessary judgment. The omnipotence cannot be rejected if we posit a Deity, that is, an infinite being; for the two concepts are identical. But if we say, "There is no God," neither the omnipotence nor any other of its predicates is given; they are one and all rejected together with the subject, and there is therefore not the least contradiction in such a judgment.[18]

---

[15]Haldane and Ross, II, 228.

[16]*Ibid.*, I, 445.

[17]E.g., *ibid.*, Principle 15, p. 225.

[18]*Op. cit.*, p. 502.

To these remarks the reply is that when the concept of God is correctly understood one sees that one cannot "reject the subject." "There is no God" is seen to be a necessarily false statement. Anselm's demonstration proves that the proposition "God exists" has the same a priori footing as the proposition "God is omnipotent."

Many present-day philosophers, in agreement with Kant, declare that existence is not a property and think that this overthrows the ontological argument. Although it is an error to regard existence as a property of things that have contingent existence, it does not follow that it is an error to regard necessary existence as a property of God. A recent writer says, against Anselm, that a proof of God's existence "based on the necessities of thought" is "universally regarded as fallacious: it is not thought possible to build bridges between mere abstractions and concrete existence."[19] But this way of putting the matter obscures the distinction we need to make. Does "concrete existence" mean contingent existence? Then to build bridges between concrete existence and mere abstractions would be like inferring the existence of an island from the concept of a perfect island, which both Anselm and Descartes regarded as absurd. What Anselm did was to give a demonstration that the proposition "God necessarily exists" is entailed by the proposition "God is a being a greater than which cannot be conceived" (which is equivalent to "God is an absolutely unlimited being"). Kant declares that when "I think a being as the supreme reality, without any defect, the question still remains whether it exists or not."[20] But once one has grasped Anselm's proof of the necessary existence of a being a greater than which cannot be conceived, no question remains as to whether it exists or not, just as Euclid's demonstration of the existence of an infinity of prime numbers leaves no question on that issue.

Kant says that "every reasonable person" must admit that "all existential propositions are synthetic."[21] Part of the perplexity one has about the ontological argument is in deciding whether or not the proposition "God necessarily exists" is or is not an "existential proposition." But let us look around. Is the Euclidean theorem in number theory, "There exists an infinite number of prime numbers," an "existential proposition"? Do we not want to say that *in some sense* it asserts the existence of something? Cannot we say, with equal justification, that the proposition "God necessarily exists" asserts the existence of something, *in some sense*? What we need to understand, in each case, is the particular sense of the assertion. Neither proposition has the

---

[19]J. N. Findlay, "Can God's Existence Be Disproved?," *New Essays in Philosophical Theology*," ed. by A. N. Flew and A. MacIntyre (London, 1955), p. 47.

[20]*Op. cit.*, pp. 505–6.

[21]*Ibid.*, p. 504.

same sort of sense as do the propositions, "A low pressure area exists over
the Great Lakes," "There still exists some possibility that he will survive,"
"The pain continues to exist in his abdomen." One good way of seeing the
difference in sense of these various propositions is to see the variously
different ways in which they are proved or supported. It is wrong to think
that all assertions of existence have the same kind of meaning. There are as
many kinds of existential propositions as there are kinds of subjects of
discourse.

Closely related to Kant's view that all existential propositions are "synthetic" is the contemporary dogma that all existential propositions are contingent. Professor Gilbert Ryle tells us that "Any assertion of the existence of
something, like any assertion of the occurrence of something, can be denied
without logical absurdity."[22] "All existential statements are contingent," says
Mr. I. M. Crombie.[23] Professor J. J. C. Smart remarks that "Existence is not a
property" and then goes on to assert that "There can never be any *logical
contradiction* in denying that God exists."[24] He declares that "The concept of
a logically necessary being is a self-contradictory concept, like the concept of
a round square .... No existential proposition can be logically necessary," he
maintains, for "the truth of a logically necessary proposition depends only
on our symbolism, or to put the same thing in another way, on the relationship of concepts" (p. 38). Professor K. E. M. Baier says, "It is no longer
seriously in dispute that the notion of a logically necessary being is self-contradictory. Whatever can be conceived of as existing can equally be conceived
of as not existing."[25] This is a repetition of Hume's assertion, "Whatever we
conceive as existent, we can also conceive as non-existent. There is no being,
therefore, whose non-existence implies a contradiction."[26]

Professor J. N. Findlay ingeniously constructs an ontological *disproof* of
God's existence, based on a "modern" view of the nature of "necessity in
propositions": the view, namely, that necessity in propositions "merely reflects our use of words, the arbitrary conventions of our language."[27] Findlay
undertakes to characterize what he calls "religious attitude," and here there
is a striking agreement between his observations and some of the things I
have said in expounding Anselm's proof. Religious attitude, he says, pre-
sumes *superiority* in its object and superiority so great that the worshiper is in
comparison as nothing. Religious attitude finds it "anomalous to worship
anything *limited* in any thinkable manner .... And hence we are led on
irresistibly to demand that our religious object should have an *unsurpassable*

[22]*The Nature of Metaphysics*, ed. by D. F. Pears (New York, 1957), p. 150.
[23]*New Essays in Philosophical Theology*, p. 114.
[24]*Ibid.*, p. 34.
[25]*The Meaning of Life*, Inaugural Lecture, Canberra University College (Canberra, 1957),
p. 8.
[26]*Dialogues Concerning Natural Religion*, pt. IX.
[27]Findlay, *op. cit.*, p. 154.

supremacy along all avenues, that it should tower *infinitely* above all other objects" (p. 51). We cannot help feeling that "the worthy object of our worship can never be a thing that merely *happens* to exist, nor one on which all other objects merely *happen* to depend. The true object of religious reverence must not be one, merely, to which no *actual* independent realities stand opposed: it must be one to which such opposition is totally *inconceivable....*And not only must the existence of *other* things be unthinkable without him, but his own non-existence must be wholly unthinkable in any circumstances" (p. 52). And now, says Findlay, when we add up these various requirements, what they entail is "not only that there isn't a God, but that the Divine Existence is either senseless or impossible" (p. 54). For on the one hand, "if God is to satisfy religious claims and needs, He must be a being in every way inescapable, One whose existence and whose possession of certain excellences we cannot possibly conceive away." On the other hand, "modern views make it self-evidently absurd (if they don't make it ungrammatical) to speak of such a Being and attribute existence to Him. It was indeed an ill day for Anselm when he hit upon his famous proof. For on that day he not only laid bare something that is of the essence of an adequate religious object, but also something that entails its necessary non-existence" (p. 55).

Now I am inclined to hold the "modern" view that logically necessary truth "merely reflects our use of words" (although I do not believe that the conventions of language are always *arbitrary*). But I confess that I am unable to see how that view is supposed to lead to the conclusion that "the Divine existence is either senseless or impossible." Findlay does not explain how this result comes about. Surely he cannot mean that this view entails that nothing can have necessary properties: for this would imply that mathematics is "senseless or impossible," which no one wants to hold. Trying to fill in the argument that is missing from his article, the most plausible conjecture I can make is the following: Findlay thinks that the view that logical necessity "reflects the use of words" implies, not that nothing has necessary properties, but that *existence* cannot be a necessary property of anything. That is to say, every proposition of the form "*x* exists," including the proposition "God exists," must be *contingent.*[28] At the same time, our concept of God requires that His existence be *necessary,* that is, that "God exists" be a necessary truth. Therefore, the modern view of necessity proves that what the concept of God requires *cannot* be fulfilled. It proves that God *cannot* exist.

The correct reply is that the view that logical necessity merely reflects the use of words cannot possibly have the implication that *every* existential proposition must be contingent. That view requires us to *look at* the use of

---

[28]The other philosophers I have just cited may be led to this opinion by the same thinking. Smart, for example, says that "the truth of a logically necessary proposition depends only on our symbolism, or to put the same thing in another way, on the relationship of concepts" (*supra*). This is very similar to saying that it "reflects our use of words."

words and not manufacture a priori theses about it. In the Ninetieth Psalm it is said: "Before the mountains were brought forth, or ever thou hadst formed the earth and the world, even from everlasting to everlasting, thou art God." Here is expressed the idea of the necessary existence and eternity of God, an idea that is essential to the Jewish and Christian religions. In those complex systems of thought, those "languages-games," God has the status of a necessary being. Who can doubt that? Here we must say with Wittgenstein, "This language-game is played!"[29] I believe we may rightly take the existence of those religious systems of thought in which God figures as a necessary being to be a disproof of the dogma, affirmed by Hume and others, that no existential proposition can be necessary.

Another way of criticizing the ontological argument is the following. "Granted that the concept of necessary existence follows from the concept of a being a greater than which cannot be conceived, this amounts to no more than granting the *a priori* truth of the *conditional* proposition, 'If such a being exists then it necessarily exists.' This proposition, however, does not entail the *existence* of *anything*, and one can deny its antecedent without contradiction." Kant, for example, compares the proposition (or "judgment," as he calls it) "A triangle has three angles" with the proposition "God is a necessary being." He allows that the former is "absolutely necessary" and goes on to say:

> The absolute necessity of the judgment is only a conditional necessity of the thing, or of the predicate in the judgment. The above proposition does not declare that three angles are absolutely necessary, but that, under the condition that there is a triangle (that is, that a triangle is given), three angles will necessarily be found in it.[30]

He is saying, quite correctly, that the proposition about triangles is equivalent to the conditional proposition, "If a triangle exists, it has three angles." He then makes the comment that there is no contradiction "in rejecting the triangle together with its three angles." He proceeds to draw the alleged parallel: "The same holds true of the concept of an absolutely necessary being. If its existence is rejected, we reject the thing itself with all its predicates; and no question of contradiction can then arise."[31] The priest, Caterus, made the same objection to Descartes when he said:

> Though it be conceded that an entity of the highest perfection implies its existence by its very name, yet it does not follow that that very existence is anything actual in the real world, but merely that the concept of existence is

---

[29]*Philosophical Investigations* (New York, 1953), sec. 654.
[30]*Op. cit.*, pp. 501–2.
[31]*Ibid.*, p. 502.

inseparably united with the concept of highest being. Hence you cannot infer that the existence of God is anything actual, unless you assume that that highest being actually exists; for then it will actually contain all its perfections, together with this perfection of real existence.[32]

I think that Caterus, Kant, and numerous other philosophers have been mistaken in supposing that the proposition "God is a necessary being" (or "God necessarily exists") is equivalent to the conditional proposition "If God exists then He necessarily exists."[33] For how do they want the antecedent clause, "*If* God exists," to be understood? Clearly they want it to imply that it is *possible* that God does *not* exist.[34] The whole point of Kant's analysis is to try to show that it is possible to "reject the subject." Let us make this implication explicit in the conditional proposition, so that it reads: "If God exists (and it is possible that He does not) then He necessarily exists." But now it is apparent, I think, that these philosophers have arrived at a self-contradictory position. I do not mean that this conditional proposition, taken alone, is self-contradictory. Their position is self-contradictory in the following way. On the one hand, they agree that the proposition "God necessarily exists" is an a priori truth; Kant implies that it is "absolutely necessary," and Caterus says that God's existence is implied by His very name. On the other hand, they think that it is correct to analyze this proposition in such a way that it will entail the proposition "It is possible that God does not exist." But so far from its being the case that the proposition "God necessarily exists" entails the proposition "It is possible that God does not exist," it is rather the case

---

[32]Haldane and Ross, II, 7.

[33]I have heard it said by more than one person in discussion that Kant's view was that it is really a misuse of language to speak of a "necessary being," on the grounds that necessity is properly predicated only of propositions (judgments) not of *things*. This is not a correct account of Kant. (See his discussion of "The Postulates of Empirical Thought in General," *op. cit.*, pp. 239–56, esp. p. 239 and pp. 247–48.) But if he had held this, as perhaps the above philosophers think he should have, then presumably his view would not have been that the pseudo-proposition "God is a necessary being" is equivalent to the conditional "If God exists then He necessarily exists." Rather his view would have been that the genuine proposition " 'God exists' is necessarily true" is equivalent to the conditional "If God exists then He exists" (*not* "If God exists then He *necessarily* exists," which would be an illegitimate formulation, on the view imaginatively attributed to Kant).

"If God exists then He exists" is a foolish tautology which says nothing different from the tautology "If a new earth satellite exists then it exists." If "If God exists then He exists" were a correct analysis of " 'God exists' is necessarily true," then "If a new earth satellite exists then it exists" would be a correct analysis of " 'A new earth satellite exists' is necessarily true." If the *analysans* is necessarily true then the *analysandum* must be necessarily true, provided the analysis is correct. If this proposed Kantian analysis of " 'God exists' is necessarily true" were correct, we should be presented with the consequence that not only is it necessarily true that God exists, but also it is necessarily true that a new earth satellite exists: which is absurd.

[34]When summarizing Anselm's proof (in part II, *supra*) I said: "If God exists He necessarily exists." But there I was merely stating an entailment. "If God exists" did not have the implication that it is possible He does not exist. And of course I was not regarding the conditional as *equivalent* to "God necessarily exists."

that they are *incompatible* with one another! Can anything be clearer than that the conjunction "God necessarily exists but it is possible that He does not exist" is self-contradictory? Is it not just as plainly self-contradictory as the conjunction "A square necessarily has four sides but it is possible for a square not to have four sides"? In short, this familiar criticism of the ontological argument is self-contradictory, because it accepts *both* of two incompatible propositions.[35]

One conclusion we may draw from our examination of this criticism is that (contrary to Kant) there is a lack of symmetry, in an important respect, between the propositions "A triangle has three angles" and "God has necessary existence," although both are a priori. The former can be expressed in the conditional assertion "If a triangle exists (and it is possible that none does) it has three angles." The latter cannot be expressed in the corresponding conditional assertion without contradiction.

## IV

I turn to the question of whether the idea of a being a greater than which cannot be conceived is self-contradictory. Here Leibniz made a contribution to the discussion of the ontological argument. He remarked that the argument of Anselm and Descartes

> is not a paralogism, but it is an imperfect demonstration, which assumes something that must still be proved in order to render it mathematically evident; that is, it is tacitly assumed that this idea of the all-great or all-perfect being is possible, and implies no contradiction. And it is already something that by this remark it is proved that, assuming that God is possible, he exists, which is the privilege of divinity alone.[36]

Leibniz undertook to give a proof that God is possible. He defined a *perfection* as a simple, positive quality in the highest degree.[37] He argued that since perfections are *simple* qualities they must be compatible with one another. Therefore the concept of a being possessing all perfections is consistent.

I will not review his argument because I do not find his definition of a perfection intelligible. For one thing, it assumes that certain qualities or

---

[35]This fallacious criticism of Anselm is implied in the following remarks by Gilson: "To show that the affirmation of necessary existence is analytically implied in the idea of God, would be . . . to show that God is necessary if He exists, but would not prove that He does exist" (E. Gilson, *The Spirit of Medieval Philosophy*, New York, 1940, p. 62).

[36]*New Essays Concerning the Human Understanding*, Bk. IV, ch. 10; ed. by A. G. Langley (LaSalle, Illinois, 1949), p. 504.

[37]See *Ibid.*, Appendix X, p. 714.

attributes are "positive" in their intrinsic nature, and others "negative" or "privative," and I have not been able clearly to understand that. For another thing, it assumes that some qualities are intrinsically simple. I believe that Wittgenstein has shown in the *Investigations* that nothing is *intrinsically* simple, but that whatever has the status of a simple, an indefinable, in one system of concepts, may have the status of a complex thing, a definable thing, in another system of concepts.

I do not know how to demonstrate that the concept of God—that is, of a being a greater than which cannot be conceived—is not self-contradictory. But I do not think that it is legitimate to demand such a demonstration. I also do not know how to demonstrate that either the concept of a material thing or the concept of *seeing* a material thing is not self-contradictory, and philosophers have argued that both of them are. With respect to any particular reasoning that is offered for holding that the concept of seeing a material thing, for example, is self-contradictory, one may try to show the invalidity of the reasoning and thus free the concept from the charge of being self-contradictory *on that ground*. But I do not understand what it would mean to demonstrate *in general*, and not in respect to any particular reasoning, that the concept is not self-contradictory. So it is with the concept of God. I should think there is no more of a presumption that it is self-contradictory than is the concept of seeing a material thing. Both concepts have a place in the thinking and the lives of human beings.

But even if one allows that Anselm's phrase may be free of self-contradiction, one wants to know how it can have any *meaning* for anyone. Why is it that human beings have even *formed* the concept of an infinite being, a being a greater than which cannot be conceived? This is a legitimate and important question. I am sure there cannot be a deep understanding of that concept without an understanding of the phenomena of human life that give rise to it. To give an account of the latter is beyond my ability. I wish, however, to make one suggestion (which should not be understood as autobiographical).

There is the phenomenon of feeling guilt for something that one has done or thought or felt or for a disposition that one has. One wants to be free of this guilt. But sometimes the guilt is felt to be so great that one is sure that nothing one could do oneself, nor any forgiveness by another human being, would remove it. One feels a guilt that is beyond all measure, a guilt "a greater than which cannot be conceived." Paradoxically, it would seem, one nevertheless has an intense desire to have this incomparable guilt removed. One requires a forgiveness that is beyond all measure, a forgiveness "a greater than which cannot be conceived." Out of such a storm in the soul, I am suggesting, there arises the conception of a forgiving mercy that is limitless, beyond all measure. This is one important feature of the Jewish and Christian conception of God.

I wish to relate this thought to a remark made by Kierkegaard, who was speaking about belief in Christianity but whose remark may have a wider application. He says:

> There is only one proof of the truth of Christianity and that, quite rightly, is from the emotions, when the dread of sin and a heavy conscience torture a man into crossing the narrow line between despair bordering upon madness—and Christendom.[38]

One may think it absurd for a human being to feel a guilt of such magnitude, and even more absurd that, if he feels it, he should *desire* its removal. I have nothing to say about that. It may also be absurd for people to fall in love, but they do it. I wish only to say that there *is* that human phenomenon of an unbearably heavy conscience and that it is importantly connected with the genesis of the concept of God, that is, with the formation of the "grammar" of the word "God." I am sure that this concept is related to human experience in other ways. If one had the acuteness and depth to perceive these connections one could grasp the *sense* of the concept. When we encounter this concept as a problem in philosophy, we do not consider the human phenomena that lie behind it. It is not surprising that many philosophers believe that the idea of a necessary being is an arbitrary and absurd construction.

What is the relation of Anselm's ontological argument to religious belief? This is a difficult question. I can imagine an atheist going through the argument, becoming convinced of its validity, acutely defending it against objections, yet remaining an atheist. The only effect it could have on the fool of the Psalm would be that he stopped saying in his heart "There is no God," because he would now realize that this is something he cannot meaningfully say or think. It is hardly to be expected that a demonstrative argument should, in addition, produce in him a living faith. Surely there is a level at which one can view the argument as a piece of logic, following the deductive moves but not being touched religiously? I think so. But even at this level the argument may not be without religious value, for it may help to remove some philosophical scruples that stand in the way of faith. At a deeper level, I suspect that the argument can be thoroughly understood only by one who has a view of that human "form of life" that gives rise to the idea of an infinitely great being, who views it from the *inside* not just from the outside and who has, therefore, at least some inclination to *partake* in that religious form of life. This inclination, in Kierkegaard's words, is "from the emotions." This inclination can hardly be an *effect* of Anselm's argument, but is rather presupposed in the fullest understanding of it. It would be unreasonable to require that the recognition of Anselm's demonstration as valid must produce a conversion.

---

[38]*The Journals*, tr. by A. Dru (Oxford, 1938), sec. 926.

# Antony Flew    R. M. Hare
# Basil Mitchell    I. M. Crombie

The contributors to this symposium are Antony Flew (author of *Hume's Philosophy of Belief* and many other works), R. M. Hare (author of *The Language of Morals, Freedom and Reason*, etc.), Basil Mitchell (author of *Law, Morality and Religion* and other works), and I. M. Crombie (author of *An Examination of Plato's Doctrines* and other writings).

# 27

# *Theology and Falsification*

## Antony Flew

Let us begin with a parable. It is a parable developed from a tale told by John Wisdom in his haunting and revelatory article "Gods." Once upon a time two explorers came upon a clearing in the jungle. In the clearing were growing many flowers and many weeds. One explorer says, "Some gardener must tend this plot." The other disagrees, "There is no gardener." So they pitch their tents and set a watch. No gardener is ever seen. "But perhaps he is an invisible gardener." So they set up a barbed-wire fence. They electrify it. They patrol with bloodhounds. (For they remember how H. G. Wells's *The Invisible Man* could be both smelt and touched though he could not be seen.) But no shrieks ever suggest that some intruder has received a shock. No movements of the wire ever betray an invisible climber. The bloodhounds never give cry. Yet still the Believer is not convinced. "But there is a gardener, invisible, intangible, insensible to electric shocks, a gardener who has no scent and makes no sound, a gardener who comes secretly to look after the garden which he loves." At last the Skeptic despairs, "But what remains of your original assertion? Just how does what you call an invisible, intangible, eternally elusive gardener differ from an imaginary gardener or even from no gardener at all?"

In this parable we can see how what starts as an assertion, that something exists or that there is some analogy between certain complexes of phenomena, may be reduced step by step to an altogether different status, to an expression perhaps of a "picture preference."[1] The Skeptic says there is no gardener. The Believer says there is a gardener (but invisible, etc.). One man talks about sexual behaviour. Another man prefers to talk of Aphrodite (but knows that there is not really a superhuman person additional to, and somehow responsible for, all sexual phenomena). The process of qualification may be checked at any point before the original assertion is completely withdrawn and something of that first assertion will remain (tautology). Mr. Wells's invisible man could not, admittedly, be seen, but in all other respects he was a man like the rest of us. But though the process of qualification may be, and of course usually is, checked in time, it is not always judiciously so halted. Someone may dissipate his assertion completely without noticing that he has done so. A fine brash hypothesis may thus be killed by inches, the death by a thousand qualifications.

And in this, it seems to me, lies the peculiar danger, the endemic evil, of theological utterance. Take such utterances as "God has a plan," "God created the world," "God loves us as a father loves his children." They look at first sight very much like assertions, vast cosmological assertions. Of course, this is no sure sign that they either are, or are intended to be, assertions. But let us confine ourselves to the cases where those who utter such sentences intend them to express assertions. (Merely remarking parenthetically that those who intend or interpret such utterances as crypto-commands, expressions of wishes, disguised ejaculations, concealed ethics, or as anything else but assertions are unlikely to succeed in making them either properly orthodox or practically effective.)

Now to assert that such and such is the case is necessarily equivalent to denying that such and such is not the case. Suppose then that we are in doubt as to what someone who gives vent to an utterance is asserting, or suppose that, more radically, we are skeptical as to whether he is really asserting anything at all, one way of trying to understand (or perhaps it will be to expose) his utterance is to attempt to find what he would regard as counting against, or as being incompatible with, its truth. For if the utterance is indeed an assertion, it will necessarily be equivalent to a denial of the negation of that assertion. And anything which would count against the assertion, or which would induce the speaker to withdraw it and to admit that it had been mistaken, must be part of (or the whole of) the meaning of the negation of that assertion. And to know the meaning of the negation of an assertion is as near as makes no matter to know the meaning of that assertion. And if there is nothing which a putative assertion denies then there is nothing which it asserts either: and so it is not really an assertion. When the Skeptic in the parable asked the Believer, "Just how does what you call an invisible, intan-

---

[1]Cf. J. Wisdom, "Other Minds," *Mind* (1940). [Reading No. 25, above, pp. 334–49.]

gible, eternally elusive gardener differ from an imaginary gardener or even from no gardener at all?" he was suggesting that the Believer's earlier statement had been so eroded by qualification that it was no longer an assertion at all.

Now it often seems to people who are not religious as if there was no conceivable event or series of events the occurrence of which would be admitted by sophisticated religious people to be a sufficient reason for conceding "There wasn't a God after all" or "God does not really love us then." Someone tells us that God loves us as a father loves his children. We are reassured. But then we see a child dying of inoperable cancer of the throat. His earthly father is driven frantic in his efforts to help, but his Heavenly Father reveals no obvious sign of concern. Some qualification is made—God's love is "not a merely human love" or it is "an inscrutable love," perhaps—and we realize that such sufferings are quite compatible with the truth of the assertion that "God loves us as a father (but, of course, . . . )." We are reassured again. But then perhaps we ask: what is this assurance of God's (appropriately qualified) love worth, what is this apparent guarantee really a guarantee against? Just what would have to happen not merely (morally and wrongly) to tempt but also (logically and rightly) to entitle us to say "God does not love us" or even "God does not exist"? I therefore put to the succeeding symposiasts the simple central questions, "What would have to occur or to have occurred to constitute for you a disproof of the love of, or of the existence of, God?"

## R. M. Hare

I wish to make it clear that I shall not try to defend Christianity in particular, but religion in general—not because I do not believe in Christianity, but because you cannot understand what Christianity is, until you have understood what religion is.

I must begin by confessing that, on the ground marked out by Flew, he seems to me to be completely victorious. I therefore shift my ground by relating another parable. A certain lunatic is convinced that all dons want to murder him. His friends introduce him to all the mildest and most respectable dons that they can find, and after each of them has retired, they say, "You see, he doesn't really want to murder you; he spoke to you in a most cordial manner; surely you are convinced now?" But the lunatic replies "Yes, but that was only his diabolical cunning; he's really plotting against me the whole time, like the rest of them; I know it I tell you." However many kindly dons are produced, the reaction is still the same.

Now we say that such a person is deluded. But what is he deluded about? About the truth or falsity of an assertion? Let us apply Flew's test to him. There is no behaviour of dons that can be enacted which he will accept as counting against his theory; and therefore his theory, on this test, asserts nothing. But it does not follow that there is no difference between what he thinks about dons and what most of us think about them—otherwise we should not call him a lunatic and ourselves sane, and dons would have no reason to feel uneasy about his presence in Oxford.

Let us call that in which we differ from this lunatic, our respective *bliks*. He has an insane *blik* about dons; we have a sane one. It is important to realize that we have a sane one, not no *blik* at all; for there must be two sides to any argument—if he has a wrong *blik*, then those who are right about dons must have a right one. Flew has shown that a *blik* does not consist in an assertion or system of them; but nevertheless it is very important to have the right *blik*.

Let us try to imagine what it would be like to have different *bliks* about other things than dons. When I am driving my car, it sometimes occurs to me to wonder whether my movements of the steering-wheel will always continue to be followed by corresponding alterations in the direction of the car. I have never had a steering failure, though I have had skids, which must be similar. Moreover, I know enough about how the steering of my car is made to know the sort of thing that would have to go wrong for the steering to fail—steel joints would have to part, or steel rods break, or something—but how do I know that this won't happen? The truth is, I don't know; I just have a *blik* about steel and its properties, so that normally I trust the steering of my car; but I find it not at all difficult to imagine what it would be like to lose this *blik* and acquire the opposite one. People would say I was silly about steel; but there would be no mistaking the reality of the difference between our respective *bliks*—for example, I should never go in a motor-car. Yet I should hesitate to say that the difference between us was the difference between contradictory assertions. No amount of safe arrivals or bench-tests will remove my *blik* and restore the normal one; for my *blik* is compatible with any finite number of such tests.

It was Hume who taught us that our whole commerce with the world depends upon our *blik* about the world; and that differences between *bliks* about the world cannot be settled by observation of what happens in the world. That was why, having performed the interesting experiment of doubting the ordinary man's *blik* about the world, and showing that no proof could be given to make us adopt one *blik* rather than another, he turned to backgammon to take his mind off the problem. It seems, indeed, to be impossible even to formulate as an assertion the normal *blik* about the world which makes me put my confidence in the future reliability of steel joints, in the continued ability of the road to support my car, and not gape beneath it revealing nothing below; in the general non-homicidal tendencies of dons; in my own continued well-being (in some sense of that word that I may not now fully understand) if I continue to do what is right according to my lights; in the general likelihood of people like Hitler coming to a bad end. But perhaps a formulation less inadequate than most is to be found in the Psalms: "The earth is weak and all the inhabiters thereof: I bear up the pillars of it."

The mistake of the position which Flew selects for attack is to regard this kind of talk as some sort of *explanation*, as scientists are accustomed to use the word. As such, it would obviously be ludicrous. We no longer believe in God as an Atlas—*nous n'avons pas besoin de cette hypothèse*. But it is nevertheless true to say that, as Hume saw, without a *blik* there can be no explanation; for it is by our *bliks* that we decide what is and what is not an explanation. Suppose we believed that everything that happened, happened by pure chance. This would not of course be an assertion; for it is compatible with anything happening or not happening, and so, incidentally, is its contradictory. But if we had this belief, we should not be able to explain or predict or plan anything. Thus, although we should not be *asserting* anything different from those of a more normal belief, there would be a great difference between us; and this is the sort of difference that there is between those who really believe in God and those who really disbelieve in him.

The word "really" is important, and may excite suspicion. I put it in, because when people have had a good Christian upbringing, as have most of those who now profess not to believe in any sort of religion, it is very hard to discover what they really believe. The reason why they find it so easy to think that they are not religious is that they have never got into the frame of mind of one who suffers from the doubts to which religion is the answer. Not for them the terrors of the primitive jungle. Having abandoned some of the more picturesque fringes of religion, they think that they have abandoned the whole thing—whereas in fact they still have got, and could not live without, a religion of a comfortably substantial, albeit highly sophisticated, kind, which differs from that of many "religious people" in little more than this, that "religious people" like to sing Psalms about theirs—a very natural and proper thing to do. But nevertheless there may be a big difference lying behind—the difference between two people who, though side by side, are walking in different directions. I do not know in what direction Flew is walking; perhaps he does not know either. But we have had some examples recently of various ways in which one can walk away from Christianity, and there are any number of possibilities. After all, man has not changed biologically since primitive times; it is his religion that has changed, and it can easily change again. And if you do not think that such changes make a difference, get acquainted with some Sikhs and some Mussulmans of the same Punjabi stock; you will find them quite different sorts of people.

There is an important difference between Flew's parable and my own which we have not yet noticed. The explorers do not *mind* about their garden;

they discuss it with interest, but not with concern. But my lunatic, poor fellow, minds about dons; and I mind about the steering of my car; it often has people in it that I care for. It is because I mind very much about what goes on in the garden in which I find myself, that I am unable to share the explorers' detachment.

## Basil Mitchell

Flew's article is searching and perceptive, but there is, I think, something odd about his conduct of the theologian's case. The theologian surely would not deny that the fact of pain counts against the assertion that God loves men. This very incompatibility generates the most intractable of theological problems—the problem of evil. So the theologian *does* recognize the fact of pain as counting against Christian doctrine. But it is true that he will not allow it—or anything—to count decisively against it; for he is committed by his faith to trust in God. His attitude is not that of the detached observer, but of the believer.

Perhaps this can be brought out by yet another parable. In time of war in an occupied country, a member of the resistance meets one night a stranger who deeply impresses him. They spend that night together in conversation. The Stranger tells the partisan that he himself is on the side of the resistance—indeed that he is in command of it, and urges the partisan to have faith in him no matter what happens. The partisan is utterly convinced at that meeting of the Stranger's sincerity and constancy and undertakes to trust him.

They never meet in conditions of intimacy again. But sometimes the Stranger is seen helping members of the resistance, and the partisan is grateful and says to his friends, "He is on our side."

Sometimes he is seen in the uniform of the police handing over patriots to the occupying power. On these occasions his friends murmur against him: but the partisan still says, "He is on our side." He still believes that, in spite of appearances, the Stranger did not deceive him. Sometimes he asks the Stranger for help and receives it. He is then thankful. Sometimes he asks and does not receive it. Then he says, "The Stranger knows best." Sometimes his friends, in exasperation, say "Well, what *would* he have to do for you to admit that you were wrong and that he is not on our side?" But the partisan refuses to answer. He will not consent to put the Stranger to the test. And sometimes his friends complain, "Well, if *that's* what you mean by his being on our side, the sooner he goes over to the other side the better."

The partisan of the parable does not allow anything to count decisively against the proposition "The Stranger is on our side." This is because he has committed himself to trust the Stranger. But he of course recognizes that the

Stranger's ambiguous behaviour *does* count against what he believes about him. It is precisely this situation which constitutes the trial of his faith.

When the partisan asks for help and doesn't get it, what can he do? He can (*a*) conclude that the stranger is not on our side; or (*b*) maintain that he is on our side, but that he has reasons for withholding help.

The first he will refuse to do. How long can he uphold the second position without its becoming just silly?

I don't think one can say in advance. It will depend on the nature of the impression created by the Stranger in the first place. It will depend, too, on the manner in which he takes the Stranger's behaviour. If he blandly dismisses it as of no consequence, as having no bearing upon his belief, it will be assumed that he is thoughtless or insane. And it quite obviously won't do for him to say easily, "Oh, when used of the Stranger the phrase 'is on our side' *means* ambiguous behaviour of this sort." In that case he would be like the religious man who says blandly of a terrible disaster "It is God's will." No, he will only be regarded as sane and reasonable in his belief, if he experiences in himself the full force of the conflict.

It is here that my parable differs from Hare's. The partisan admits that many things may and do count against his belief: whereas Hare's lunatic who has a *blik* about dons doesn't admit that anything counts against his *blik*. Nothing *can* count against *bliks*. Also the partisan has a reason for having in the first instance committed himself, viz., the character of the Stranger; whereas the lunatic has no reason for his *blik* about dons—because, of course, you can't have reasons for *bliks*.

This means that I agree with Flew that theological utterances must be assertions. The partisan is making an assertion when he says, "The Stranger is on our side."

Do I want to say that the partisan's belief about the Stranger is, in any sense, an explanation? I think I do. It explains and makes sense of the Stranger's behaviour: it helps to explain also the resistance movement in the context of which he appears. In each case it differs from the interpretation which the others put upon the same facts.

"God loves men" resembles "the Stranger is on our side" (and many other significant statements, e.g., historical ones) in not being conclusively falsifiable. They can both be treated in at least three different ways: (1) as provisional hypotheses to be discarded if experience tells against them, (2) as significant articles of faith, (3) as vacuous formulae (expressing, perhaps, a desire for reassurance) to which experience makes no difference and which make no difference to life.

The Christian, once he has committed himself, is precluded by his faith from taking up the first attitude: "Thou shalt not tempt the Lord thy God." He is in constant danger, as Flew has observed, of slipping into the third. But he need not; and, if he does, it is a failure in faith as well as in logic.

## Antony Flew

It has been a good discussion; and I am glad to have helped to provoke it. But now . . . it must come to an end: and [I shall] make some concluding remarks. Since it is impossible to deal with all the issues raised or to comment separately upon each contribution, I will concentrate on Mitchell and Hare, as representative of two very different kinds of response to [my] challenge . . . .

The challenge, it will be remembered, ran like this. Some theological utterances seem to, and are intended to, provide explanations or express assertions. Now an assertion, to be an assertion at all, must claim that things stand thus and thus; *and not otherwise.* Similarly an explanation, to be an explanation at all, must explain why this particular thing occurs; *and not something else.* Those last clauses are crucial. And yet sophisticated religious people—or so it seemed to me—are apt to overlook this, and tend to refuse to allow, not merely that anything actually does occur, but that anything conceivably could occur, which would count against their theological assertions and explanations. But insofar as they do this their supposed explanations are actually bogus, and their seeming assertions are really vacuous.

Mitchell's response to this challenge is admirably direct, straightforward, and understanding. He agrees "that theological utterances must be assertions." He agrees that if they are to be assertions, there must be something that would count against their truth. He agrees, too, that believers are in constant danger of transforming their would-be assertions into "vacuous formulae." But he takes me to task for an oddity in my "conduct of the theologian's case. The theologian surely would not deny that the fact of pain counts against the assertion that God loves men. This very incompatibility generates the most intractable of theological problems, the problem of evil." I think he is right. I should have made a distinction between two very different ways of dealing with what looks like evidence against the love of God; the way I stressed was the expedient of qualifying the original assertion; the way the theologian usually takes, at first, is to admit that it looks bad but to insist that there is—there must be—some explanation which will show that, in spite of appearances, there really is a God who loves us. His difficulty, it seems to me, is that he has given God attributes which rule out all possible saving explanations. In Mitchell's parable of the Stranger it is easy for the believer to find plausible excuses for ambiguous behaviour; for the Stranger is a man. But suppose the Stranger is God. We cannot say that he would like to help but cannot; God is omnipotent. We cannot say that he would help if he only knew; God is omniscient. We cannot say that he is not responsible for the wickedness of others; God creates those others. Indeed an omnipotent, omniscient God must be an accessory before (and during) the fact to every human misdeed; as well as being responsible for every non-moral defect in the universe. So, though I entirely concede that Mitchell was absolutely right to insist against me that the theologian's first move is to look for an *explanation*, I still think that in the end, if relentlessly pursued, he will have to resort to the avoiding action of *qualification*. And there lies the danger of that death by a thousand qualifications, which would, I agree, constitute "a failure in faith as well as in logic."

Hare's approach is fresh and bold. He confesses that "on the ground marked out by Flew, he seems to me to be completely victorious." He therefore introduces the concept of *blik*. But while I think that there is room for some such concept in philosophy, and that philosophers should be grateful to Hare for his invention, I nevertheless want to insist that any attempt to analyze Christian religious utterances as expressions or affirmations of a *blik* rather than as (at least would-be) assertions about the cosmos is fundamentally misguided. First, because thus interpreted they would be entirely unorthodox. If Hare's religion really is a *blik*, involving no cosmological assertions about the nature and activities of a supposed personal creator, then surely he is not a Christian at all? Second, because thus interpreted, they could scarcely do the job they do. If they were not even intended as assertions, then many religious activities would become fraudulent, or merely silly. If "You ought *because* it is God's will" asserts no more than "You ought," then the person who prefers the former phraseology is not really giving a reason, but a fraudulent substitute for one, a dialectical dud check. If "My soul must be immortal *because* God loves his children, etc." asserts no more than "My soul must be immortal," then the man who reassures himself with theological arguments for immortality is being as silly as the man who tries to clear his overdraft by writing his bank a check on the same account. (Of course neither of these utterances would be distinctively Christian; but this discussion never pretended to be so confined.) Religious utterances may indeed express false or even bogus assertions: but I simply do not believe that they are not both intended and interpreted to be or at any rate to presuppose assertions, at least in the context or religious practice, whatever shifts may be demanded, in another context, by the exigencies of theological apologetic.

One final suggestion. The philosophers of religion might well draw upon George Orwell's last appalling nightmare, *1984*, for the concept of *doublethink*. "*Doublethink* means the power of holding two contradictory beliefs simultaneously, and accepting both of them. The party intellectual knows that he is playing tricks with reality, but by the exercise of *doublethink* he also satisfies himself that reality is not violated." Perhaps religious intellectuals too are sometimes driven to doublethink in order to retain their faith in a loving God in face of the reality of a heartless and indifferent world. But of this more another time, perhaps.

## I. M. Crombie[2]

There are some who hold that religious statements cannot be fully meaningful, on the ground that those who use them allow nothing to count decisively against them, treat them, that is, as incapable of falsification. This paper is an attempted answer to this view; and in composing it I have had particularly in mind [the above] article by Antony Flew. I shall offer only a very short, and doubtless tendentious, summary of my opponents' views.

Briefly, then, it is contended that there are utterances made from time to time by Christians and others, which are said by those who make them to be statements, but which are thought by our opponents to lack some of the properties which anything must have before it deserves to be called a statement. "There is a God," "God loves us as a father loves his children," "He shall come again with glory . . ." are examples of such utterances. *Prima facie* such utterances are neither exhortations, nor questions, nor expressions of wishes; *prima facie* they appear to assert the actuality of some state of affairs; and yet (and this is the objection) they are allowed to be compatible with any and every state of affairs. If they are compatible with any and every state of affairs, they cannot mark out some one state of affairs (or group of states of affairs); and if they do not mark out some one state of affairs, how can they be statements? In the case of any ordinary statement, such as "It is raining," there is at least one situation (the absence of falling water) which is held to be incompatible with the statement, and it is the incompatibility of the situation with the statement which gives the statement its meaning. If, then, religious "statements" are compatible with anything and everything, how can they be statements? How can the honest inquirer find out what they mean, if nobody will tell him what they are incompatible with? Are they not much more like such exhortations as "Keep smiling," whose confessed purpose is to go on being in point whatever occurs? Furthermore, is it not true that they only appear to be statements to those of us who use them, because we deceive ourselves by a sort of conjuring trick, oscillating backwards and forwards between a literal interpretation of what we say when we say it, and a scornful rejection of such anthropomorphism when anybody challenges us? When we *say:* "He shall come again with glory . . . ," do we not picture real angels sitting on real clouds; when asked whether we really mean the clouds, we hedge; offer perhaps another picture, which again we refuse to take literally; and so on indefinitely. Whatever symbolism we offer, we always insist that only a crude man would take it literally, and yet we never offer him anything but

---

[2]This paper was composed to be read to a non-philosophical audience. In composing it I have also filched shamelessly (and shamefully no doubt distorted) some unpublished utterances of Dr. A. M. Farrer's.

symbolism; deceived by our imagery into supposing that we have something in mind, in fact there is nothing on which we are prepared to take our stand.

This is the position I am to try to criticize. It is, I think, less novel than its clothes; but nonetheless it is important. I turn to criticism.

Let us begin by dismissing from our inquiry the troublesome statement "There is a God" or "God exists." As every student of logic knows, all statements asserting the existence of something offer difficulties of their own, with which we need not complicate our embarrassment.

That being dismissed, I shall want to say of statements about God that they consist of two parts. Call them, if you like, subject and predicate. Whatever you call them, there is that which is said, and that which is said about—namely God. It is important to make this distinction, for different problems arise about the different parts. As a first approximation towards isolating the difference, we may notice that the predicate is normally composed of ordinary words, put to unordinary uses, whereas the subject-word is "God," which has no other use. In the expression "God loves us," the word "God" is playing, so to speak, on its home ground, the phrase "loves us" is playing away. Now there is one set of questions which deal with the problem of why we say, and what we mean by saying, that God loves us, rather than hates us, and there is another set of questions concerned with the problem of what it is that this statement is being made about.

To approach the matter from an angle which seems to me to afford a good view of it, I shall make a few observations about the epistemological nature of religious belief. Let me caution the reader that, in doing so, I am not attempting to describe how religious belief in fact arises.

Theoretically, then, not in how it arises, but in its logical structure, religious belief has two parents; and it also has a nurse. Its logical mother is what one might call *undifferentiated theism*, its logical father is particular events or occasions interpreted as theophanic, and the extraparental nurture is provided by religious activity.

A word, first, about the logical mother. It is in fact the case that there are elements in our experience which lead people to a certain sort of belief, which we call a belief in God. (We could, if we wished, call it rather an attitude than a belief, so long as we were careful not to call it an attitude to life; for it is of the essence of the attitude to hold that nothing whatever in life may be identified with that towards which it is taken up.) Among the elements in experience which provoke this belief or attitude, perhaps the most powerful is what I shall call a sense of contingency. Others are moral experience, and the beauty and order of nature. Others may be actual abnormal experience of the type called religious or mystical. There are those to whom conscience appears in the form of an unconditional demand; to whom the obligation to one's neighbour seems to be something imposed on him and on me by a third party who is set over us both. There are those to whom the beauty and order of nature appears as the intrusion into nature of a realm of beauty and order beyond it. There are those who believe themselves or others to be enriched by moments of direct access to the divine. Now there are two things that must be said about these various theistic interpretations of our experience. The first is that those who so interpret need not be so inexpert in logic as to suppose that there is anything of the nature of a deductive or inductive argument which leads from a premise asserting the existence of the area of experience in question to a conclusion expressing belief in God. Nobody who takes seriously the so-called moral argument need suppose that the *prima facie* authority of conscience cannot be naturalistically explained. He can quite well acknowledge that the imperativeness which so impresses him could be a mere reflection of his jealousy of his father, or a vestigial survival of tribal taboo. The mystic can quite well acknowledge that there is nothing which logically forbids the interpretation of the experience which he enjoys in terms of the condition of his liver or the rate of his respiration. If, being acquainted with the alternative explanations, he persists in rejecting them, it need not be, though of course it sometimes is, because he is seized with a fallacious refutation of their validity. All that is necessary is that he should be honestly convinced that, in interpreting them, as he does, theistically, he is in some sense facing them more honestly, bringing out more of what they contain or involve that could be done by interpreting them in any other way. The one interpretation is preferred to the other, not because the latter is thought to be refutable on paper, but because it is judged to be unconvincing in the light of familiarity with the facts. There is a partial parallel to this in historical judgment. Where you and I differ in our interpretation of a series of events, there is nothing outside the events in question which can overrule either of us, so that each man must accept the interpretation which seems, on fair and critical scrutiny, the most convincing to him. The parallel is only partial, however, for in historical (and literary) interpretation there is something which to some extent controls one's interpretation, and that is one's general knowledge of human nature; and in metaphysical interpretation there is nothing analogous to this. That, then, is my first comment on theistic interpretations; for all that these journeys of the mind are often recorded in quasi-argumentative form, they are not in any ordinary sense arguments, and their validity cannot be assessed by asking whether they conform to the laws either of logic or of scientific method. My second comment upon them is that, in stating them, we find ourselves saying things which we cannot literally mean. Thus the man of conscience uses some such concept as the juridical concept of authority, and locates his authority outside nature; the man of beauty and order speaks of an intrusion from another realm; the mystic speaks of experiencing God. In every case such language lays the user open to devastating criticism, to which he can only retort by pleading that such language, while it is not to be taken strictly, seems to him to be the natural language to use.

To bring these points into a somewhat stronger light, let me say something about the sense of contingency, the conviction which people have, it may be in blinding moments, or it may be in a permanent disposition of a man's mind, that we, and the whole world in which we live, derive our being from something outside us. The first thing I want to say about this is that such a conviction is to no extent like the conclusion of an argument; the sense of dependence feels not at all like being persuaded by arguments, but like seeing, as it were, through a gap in the rolling mists of argument, which alone, one feels, could conceal the obvious truth. One is not *persuaded* to believe that one is contingent; rather one feels that it is only by persuasion that one could ever believe anything else. The second thing I want to say about this conviction of contingency is that in expressing it, as Quinton has admirably shown, we turn the word "contingent" to work which is not its normal employment, and which it cannot properly do.

For the distinction between necessity and contingency is not a distinction between different sorts of entities, but between different sorts of statement. A necessary statement is one whose denial involves a breach of the laws of logic, and a contingent statement is one in which this is not the case. (I do not, of course, assert that this is the only way in which these terms have been used in the history of philosophy; but I do assert that this is the only use of them which does not give rise to impossible difficulties. I have no space to demonstrate this here; and indeed I do not think that it is any longer in need of demonstration.) But in this, the only coherent, sense of "contingent," the existence of the world may be contingent fact, but so unfortunately is that of God. For *all* existential statements are contingent; that is to say, it is never true that we can involve ourselves in a breach of the laws of logic by merely denying of something that it exists. We cannot therefore in this sense contrast the contingent existence of the world with the necessary existence of God.

It follows that if a man persists in speaking of the contingency of the world, he must be using the term in a new or transferred sense. It must be that he is borrowing[3] a word from the logician and putting it to work which it cannot properly do. Why does he do this, and how can he make clear what precisely this new use is? For it is no good saying that when we are talking about God we do not use words in their ordinary senses unless we are prepared to say in what senses it is that we do use them. And yet how can we explain to the honest inquirer what is the new sense in which the word

---

[3]It might be argued that, historically, the borrowing was the other way round. To decide that we should have to decide where the frontier between logic and metaphysics really comes in the work of those whose doctrine on the relationship between these disciplines is unsatisfactory.

"contingent" is being used when we use it of the world? For if it is proper to use it, in this sense, of everything with which we are acquainted, and improper to use it only of God, with whom we are not acquainted, how can the new use be learnt? For we normally learn the correct use of a word by noticing the differences between the situations in which it may be applied and those in which it may not; but the word "contingent" is applicable in all the situations in which we ever find ourselves. If I said that everything but God was flexible, not of course in the ordinary sense, but in some other, how could you discover what the new sense was?

The answer must be that when we speak of the world as contingent, dependent, an effect or product, and so contrast it with a necessary, self-existent being, a first cause or a creator, we say something which on analysis will not do at all (for devastating criticisms can be brought against all these formulations), but which seems to us to be the fittest sort of language for our purpose. Why we find such language appropriate, and how, therefore, it is to be interpreted, is not at all an easy question; that it does in some way, it may be in some logically anomalous way, convey the meaning of those who use it, seems however to be an evident fact. How it is that the trick is worked, how it is that this sort of distortion of language enables believers to give expression to their beliefs, this it is the true business of the natural theologian to discuss. Farrer, for example, in *Finite and Infinite*, has done much to elucidate what it is that one is striving to express when one speaks of the contingency of the world, and so to enlighten the honest inquirer who wishes to know how the word "contingent" is here being used.

What I have said about contingency and necessity applies also to obligation and its transcendent ground (or goodness and its transcendent goal), to design and its transcendent designer, to religious experience and its transcendent object. In all these cases we use language which on analysis will not do, but which seems to us to be appropriate for the expression of our beliefs; and in all these cases the question can be, and is, discussed, why such language is chosen, and how it is to be understood.

That then is the logical mother of religious belief; call her natural theism, or what you will, she is a response, not precisely logical, and yet in no sense emotional or evaluative, to certain elements in our experience, whose characteristic is that they induce us, not to make straightforward statements about the world, but to strain and distort our media of communication in order to express what we make of them. In herself she is an honest woman; and if she is sometimes bedizened in logical trappings, and put out on the streets as an inductive argument, the fault is hardly hers. Her function is not to prove to us that God exists, but to provide us with a "meaning" for the word "God." Without her we should not know whither statements concerning the word were to be referred; the subject in theological utterances would be unattached. All that we should know of them is that they were not to be referred to anything with which we are or could hope to be acquainted; that, and also that they were to be understood in terms of whatever it is that people suppose themselves to be doing when they build churches and kneel down in them. And that is not entirely satisfactory; for while there is much to be said in practice for advising the honest inquirer into the reference of the word "God" to pursue his inquiry by familiarizing himself with the concrete activity of religion, it remains true that the range and variety of possible delusions which could induce such behaviour is theoretically boundless, and, as visitors to the Pacific coast of the United States can testify, in practice very large.

The logical father of religious belief, that which might bring us on from the condition of merely possessing the category of the divine, into the condition of active belief in God, this consists, in Christianity (and if there is nothing analogous in other religions, so much the worse for them), in the interpretation of certain objects or events as a manifestation of the divine. It is, in other words, because we find that, in thinking of certain events in terms of the category of the divine, we can give what seems to us the most convincing account of them, that we can assure ourselves that the notion of God is not just an empty aspiration. Without the notion of God we could interpret nothing as divine, and without concrete events which we felt impelled to interpret as divine we could not know that the notion of divinity had any application to reality. Why it is that as Christians we find ourselves impelled to interpret the history of Israel, the life and death of Christ, and the experience of his Church as revelatory of God, I shall not here attempt to say; it is an oft-told tale, and I shall content myself with saying that we can hardly expect to feel such an impulsion so long as our knowledge of these matters is superficial and altogether from without. Whyever we feel such an impulsion, it is not, of course, a logical impulsion; that is, we may resist it (or fail to feel it) without thereby contravening the laws of logic, or the rules of any pragmatically accredited inductive procedure. On the anthropological level the history of Israel, Old and New, is certainly the history of a religious development from its tribal origins. We may decide, or we may not, that it is something more, something beyond the wit of man to invent, something which seems to us to be a real and coherent communication from a real and coherent, though superhuman, mind. We may decide, or we may not; neither decision breaks the rules, for in such a unique matter there are no rules to conform to or to break. The judgment is our own; and in the language of the New Testament it judges us; that is, it reveals what, up to the moment of our decision, the Spirit of God has done in us—but that, of course, is to argue in a circle.

Belief, thus begotten, is nurtured by the practice of the Christian life—by the conviction so aroused (or, of course, not aroused; but then it is starvation and not nurture) that the Christian warfare is a real warfare. Something will have to be said about this later on, but for the moment I propose to dismiss it, and to return to the consideration of the significance of religious utterances in the light of the dual parentage of religious belief.

I have argued that unless certain things seem to us to be signs of divine activity, then we may hope that there is a God, but we cannot properly believe that there is. It follows from this that religious belief must properly involve treating something as revelatory of God; and that is to say that it must involve an element of authority (for to treat something as divine revelation is to invest it with authority). That what we say about God is said on authority (and, in particular, on the authority of Christ) is of the first importance in considering the significance of these statements. In what way this is so, I shall hope to make clear as we go along.

If we remember that our statements about God rest on the authority of Christ, whom we call His Word, we can see what seems to me the essential clue to the interpretation of the logical nature of such utterances, and that is, in a word, the notion of parable. To elucidate what I mean by "parable" (for I am using the word in an extended sense) let us consider Christ's action on Palm Sunday, when he rode into Jerusalem on an ass. This action was an act of teaching. For it had been said to Jerusalem that her king would come to her riding upon an ass. Whoever, therefore, deliberately chose this method of entry, was saying in effect: "What you are about to witness (namely my Passion, Death and Resurrection) is the coming of the Messianic King to claim his kingdom." The prophecy of Messiah's kingdom was to be interpreted, not in the ordinary sense, but in the sense of the royal kingship of the Crucified. To interpret in this way is to teach by violent paradox, indeed, but nonetheless it is to teach. Part of the lesson is that it is only the kings of the Gentiles that lord it over their subjects; if any man will be a king in Israel (God's chosen people), he must humble himself as a servant; part of it is that the Crucifixion is to be seen as Messianic, that is as God's salvation of His chosen people. Now the logical structure which is involved here is something like this: You are told a story (Behold, thy king cometh, meek and lowly, and riding upon an ass). You will not know just what the reality to which the story refers will be like until it happens. If you take the story at its face value (an ordinary, though humble, king, bringing an ordinary political salvation), you will get it all wrong. If you bring to bear upon its interpretation all that the Law and the Prophets have taught you about God's purposes for His people, though you will still not know just what it will be like until it happens, nonetheless you will not go wrong by believing it; for then you will know that Christ ought to have suffered these things, and to enter into his glory, and so you will learn what the story has to tell you of God's purposes for man, and something therefore, indirectly, of God. If you remember what Isaiah says about humility and sacrifice, you will see that what is being forecast is that God's purposes will be accomplished by a man who fulfills the Law and the Prophets in humble obedience.

This story is . . . one that can be fairly fully interpreted. There are others than cannot. There is, for example, Hosea's parable in which he likens himself to God, and Israel to his unfaithful wife, and expresses his grief at his wife's unfaithfulness. If, now, you ask for this to be fully interpreted, if you ask Hosea to tell you what he supposes it is like for the Holy One of Israel, of whom no similitude may be made, to be grieved, demanding to know, not what would happen in such a case to the unfaithful sinner who had provoked the divine wrath, but what was the condition of the divine mind in itself, then no doubt he would have regarded the very question as blasphemous. As an inspired prophet, he felt himself entitled to say that God was grieved, without presuming to imagine what such a situation was like, other than in its effects. What he said was said on authority; it was not his own invention, and therefore he could rely on its truth, without supposing himself to understand its full meaning. Insofar as Hosea's parable is "interpreted," the interpretation is confined to identifying the *dramatis personae* (Hosea = God, his wife = Israel). It is noteworthy that the interpretation which is sometimes given to the parables of the New Testament is usually of the same sketchy kind (the reapers are the angels). In Plato's famous parable of prisoners in a cave, it is quite possible to describe the situation which the parable seeks to illuminate. One can describe how a man can begin by being content to establish rough laws concerning what follows what in nature, how he may proceed from such a condition to desire explanation of the regularities which are forced on his attention, rising thus to more abstract and mathematical generalizations, and then, through the study of mathematics, to completely abstract speculation. One cannot similarly describe the situation which the parable of the Prodigal Son is intended to illustrate (or rather one can only describe the human end of it); and no attempt is ever made to do so.

I make no apology for these paragraphs about the Bible; after all the Bible is the source of Christian belief, and it cannot but illuminate the logical nature of the latter to consider the communicational methods of the former. But we must turn back to more general considerations. It is, then, characteristic of a parable that the words which are used in it are used in their ordinary senses. Elsewhere this is not always so. If you speak of the virtues of a certain sort of car, the word "virtue," being applied to a car, comes to mean something different from what it means in application to human beings. If you speak of hot temper, the word "hot" does not mean what it means in the ordinary way. Now many people suppose that something of the latter sort is happening in religious utterances. When God is said to be jealous, or active in history, it is felt that the word "jealous" or "active" must be being used here in a transferred sense. But if it is being used in a transferred sense, some means or other must be supplied whereby the new sense can be taken. The activity of God is presumably not like the activity of men (it does not make Him hot or tired); to say then that God is active must involve modifying the meaning of the word. But, if the word is undergoing modification, it is essential that we should know in what direction. In the case of ordinary transfers, how do we know what sort of modification is involved? This is a large question, but roughly, I think, the answer is in two ways. Firstly there is normally a certain appropriateness, like the appropriateness of "hot" in "hot temper"; and secondly we can notice the circumstances in which the word gets used and withheld in its transferred sense. If I hear the phrase "Baroque music," the meaning of the word "Baroque" in its normal architectural employment may set me looking in a certain direction; and I can clinch the matter by asking for examples, "Bach? Buxtehude? Beethoven?" But for either of these ways to be of any use to me, I must know something about *both* ends of the transfer. I must know something about Baroque architecture, *and* I must be able to run through musical styles in my head, to look for the musical analogue of Baroque features. If I cannot stumble on your meaning without assistance, I can still do so by eliciting from you that Bach and Buxtehude are, Handel and Mozart are not, examples of the sort of music you have in mind. This is informative to me if and only if I know something of Buxtehude and Bach, Handel and Mozart.

Now we all know what it is like for a man to be active. We can quote examples, decide correctly, and so forth. But what about divine activity? Surely we cannot have it both ways. Either God can be moderately like a man, so that the word "active," used of Him, can set us looking in the right direction; or He can be quite unlike a man, in which case it cannot. Nor can we be helped by the giving of examples, unless it is legitimate to point to examples of divine activity—to say, "Now here God is being active, but not there." This constitutes the force of Flew's demand that we should tell him how statements about God can be falsified. In essence Flew is saying: "When you speak about God, the words which occur in the predicate part of your statements are not being used in the ordinary sense; you make so great a difference between God and man that I cannot even find that the words you use set me looking in anything that might perhaps be the right direction. You speak of God as being outside time; and when I think what I mean by 'activity,' I find that that word, as used about a timeless being, suggests to me nothing whatsoever. There is only one resort left; give me examples of when one of your statements is, and is not, applicable. If, as no doubt you will say, that is an unfair demand, since they are always applicable (e.g., God is always active, so that there are no cases of His inactivity to be pointed to), I will not insist on actual examples; make them up if you like. But do not point to *everything* and say, '*That* is what I mean'; for *everything* is not *that*, but this and this and this and many other mutual incompatibles; and black and white and red and green and kind and cruel and coal and ink and everything else together cannot possibly elucidate to me the meaning of a word."

As I have said, the answer must be that when we speak about God, the words we use are intended in their ordinary sense (for we cannot make a transfer, failing familiarity with both ends of it), although we do not suppose that in their ordinary interpretation they can be strictly true of Him. We do not even know how much of them applies. To some extent it may be possible to take a word like "activity" and whittle away that in it which most obviously does not apply. It is, however, an exaggeration, at the least, to suppose that this process of whittling away leaves us in the end with a kernel about which we can say that we know that it does apply. A traditional procedure is to compose a scale on which inanimate matter is at the bottom, the characteristically human activities, such as thinking and personal relationship, at the top, and to suppose that the scale is pointing towards God; and so on this assumption the first thing to do is to pare away from the notion of human activity whatever in it is common to what stands below it on the scale—for example actual physical moving about. Taking the human residue, we try to decide what in it is positive, and what is negative, mere limitation. The tenuous ghost of a concept remaining we suppose to be the essential structure of activity (that structure which is common to running and thinking) and so to be realized also in divine activity. Perhaps this is how we imagine our language to be related to the divine realities about which we use it; but such ghostly and evacuated concepts are clearly too tenuous and elusive to be called the meanings of the words we use. To think of God thus is to think of Him not in our own image, but in the rarefied ghost of our own image; and so we think of Him in our own image, but do not suppose that in so thinking of Him we begin to do Him justice. What we do, then, is in essence to think of God in parables. The things we say about God are said on the authority of the words and acts of Christ, who spoke in human language, using parable; and so we too speak of God in parable—authoritative parable, authorized parable; knowing that the truth is not literally that which our parables represent, knowing therefore that now we see in a glass darkly, but trusting, because we trust the source of the parables, that in believing them and interpreting them in the light of each other, we shall not be misled, that we shall have such knowledge as we need to possess for the foundation of the religious life.

So far so good. But it is only the predicates of theological utterances which are parabolic; it is only in what is *said about* God that words are put to other than customary employment. When we say "God is merciful," it is "merciful" that is in strange company—deprived of its usual escort of human sentiments. But the word "God" only occurs in statements about God. Our grasp of this word, therefore, cannot be derived from our grasp of it in ordinary human contexts, for it is not used in such contexts. How then is our grasp of it to be accounted for? In other words, if I have given some account of how, and in what sense, we understand the meaning of the things we say about God, I have still to give some account of how, and in what sense, we know what it is that we are saying them about.

In thus turning back from the predicate to the subject of religious utterances, we are turning from revealed theology to natural theology, from the logical father to the logical mother of religious belief. And the answer to the question: "What grasp have we of the meaning of the word 'God'?" must be dealt with along the following lines. Revelation is important to the believer not for what it is in itself (the biography of a Jew, and the history of his forerunners and followers), nor because it is revelation of nothing in particular, but because it is revelation of God. In treating it as something important, something commanding our allegiance, we are bringing to bear upon it the category of the transcendent, of the divine. Of the nature of that category I have already spoken. In other words, there must exist within a man's mind the contrast between the contingent and the necessary, the derivative and the underivative, the finite and the infinite, the perfect and the imperfect, if anything is to be for him a revelation of God. Given that contrast, we are given also that to which the parables or stories are referred. What is thus given is certainly not knowledge of the object to which they apply; it is something much more like a direction. We do not, that is, know to what to refer our parables; we know merely that we are to refer them out of experience, and out of it *in which direction*. The expression "God" is to refer to that object, whatever it is, and if there be one, which is such that the knowledge of it would be to us knowledge of the unfamiliar term in the contrast between finite and infinite.

Statements about God, then, are in effect parables, which are referred, by means of the proper name "God," out of our experience in a certain direction. We may, if we like, by the process of whittling away, which I have mentioned, try to tell ourselves what part of the meaning of our statements applies reasonably well, what part outrageously badly; but the fact remains that, in one important sense, when we speak about God, we do not know what we mean (that is, we do not know what that which we are talking about is like), and do not need to know, because we accept the images, which we employ, on authority. Because our concern with God is religious and not speculative (it is contemplative in part, but that is another matter), because our need is not to know what God is like, but to enter into relation with him, the authorized images serve our purpose. They belong to a type of discourse—parable—with which we are familiar, and therefore they have communication value, although in a sense they lack descriptive value.

If this is so, how do we stand with regard to verification and falsification? Must we, to preserve our claim to be making assertions, be prepared to say what would count against them? Let us see how far we can do so. Does anything count against the assertion that God is merciful? Yes, suffering. Does anything count decisively against it? No, we reply, because it is true.

Could anything count decisively against it? Yes, suffering which was utterly, eternally, and irredeemably pointless. Can we then design a crucial experiment? No, because we can never see all of the picture. Two things at least are hidden from us; what goes on in the recesses of the personality of the sufferer, and what shall happen hereafter.

Well, then, the statement that God is merciful is not testable; it is compatible with any and every tract of experience which we are in fact capable of witnessing. It cannot be verified; does this matter?

To answer this, we must make up our minds why the demand for verification or falsification is legitimate. On this large matter I shall be summary and dogmatic, as follows. (1) The demand that a statement of fact should be verifiable is a conflation of two demands. (2) The *first* point is that all statements of fact must be verifiable in the sense that there must not exist a *rule of language* which precludes testing the statement. That is to say, the way the statement is to be taken must not be such that to try to test it is to show that you do not understand it. If I say that it is wrong to kill, and you challenge my statement and adduce as evidence against it that thugs and headhunters do so out of religious duty, then you have not understood my statement. My statement was not a statement of fact, but a moral judgment, and your statement that it should be tested by anthropological investigations shows that you did not understand it. But so long as there exists no *logical* (or we might say *interpretational*) ban on looking around for verification, the existence of a *factual* ban on verification does not matter. "Caesar had mutton before he crossed the Rubicon" cannot in fact be tested, but by trying to devise ways of testing it you do not show that you have not understood it; you are merely wasting your time. (3) The *second* point is that, *for me fully* to understand a statement, *I* must know what a test of it would be like. If I have no idea how to test whether somebody had mutton, then I do not know what "having mutton" means. This stipulation is concerned not with the logical nature of the expression, but with its communication value for me. (4) There are then two stipulations, and they are different. The first is a logical stipulation, and it is to the effect that nothing can be a statement of fact if it is untestable in the sense that the notion of testing it is precluded by correctly interpreting it. The second is a communicational stipulation, and it is to the effect that nobody can fully understand a statement, unless he has a fair idea how a situation about which it was true would differ from a situation about which it was false.

Now with regard to these two stipulations, how do religious utterances fare? With regard to the first, there is no language rule implicit in a correct understanding of them which precludes putting them to the test (there may be a rule of faith, but that is another matter). If a man says, "How can God be loving, and allow pain?" he does *not* show that he has misunderstood the statement that God is loving. There *is* a *prima facie* incompatibility between the love of God, and pain and suffering. The Christian maintains that it is *prima facie* only; others maintain that it is not. They may argue about it, and the issue cannot be decided; but it cannot be decided, not because (as in the case of, e.g., moral or mathematical judgments) the appeal to facts is *logically* the wrong way of trying to decide the issue, and shows that you have not understood the judgment; *but* because, since our experience is limited in the way it is, we cannot get into position to decide it, any more than we can get into position to decide what Julius Caesar had for breakfast before he crossed the Rubicon. For the Christian the operation of getting into position to decide it is called dying; and, though we can all do that, we cannot return to report what we find. By this test, then, religious utterances can be called statements of fact; that is their *logical* classification.

With regard to the second stipulation, the case is a little complicated, for here we are concerned with communication value, and there are the two levels, the one on which we remain within the parable, and the other on which we try to step outside it. Now, on the first level we know well enough how to test a statement like "God loves us"; it is, for example, like testing "My father loves me." In fact, of course, since with parents and schoolmasters severity is notoriously a way of displaying affection, the decisive testing of such a statement is not easy; but there is a point beyond which it is foolish to continue to have doubts. Now, within the parable, we are supposing "God loves us" to be a statement like "My father loves me," "God" to be a subject similar to "My father," "God loves us" being thus related to "My father loves me" as the latter is related to "Aristotle's father loved him." We do not suppose that we can actually test "God loves us," for reasons already given (any more than we can test the one about Aristotle); but the communication value of the statement whose subject is "God" is derived from the communication value of the statement with a different proper name as subject. If we try to step outside the parable, then we must admit that we do not know what the situation about which our parable is being told is like; we should only know if we could know God, and know even as also we have been known; see, that is, the unfolding of the divine purposes in their entirety. Such ignorance is what we ought to expect. We do not know how what we call the divine wrath differs from the divine mercy (because we do not know how they respectively resemble human wrath and mercy); but we do know how what *we mean* when we talk about the wrath of God differs from what *we mean* when we talk about His mercy, because then we are within the parable, talking within the framework of admitted ignorance, in language which we accept because we trust its source. We know what is meant *in* the parable, when the father of the Prodigal sees him coming a great way off and runs to meet him, and we can therefore think in terms of this image. We know that we are here promised that whenever we come to ourselves and return to God, He will come to meet us. This is enough to encourage us to return, and to make us alert to catch the signs of the divine response; but it does not lead us to presume to an understanding of the mind and heart of God. In talking we remain within the parable, and so our statements communicate; we do not know how the parable applies, but we believe that it does apply, and that we shall one day see how. (Some even believe, perhaps rightly, that in our earthly condition we may by direct illumination of our minds be enabled to know progressively more about the realities to which our parables apply, and in consequence about the manner of their application.)

Much of what I have said agrees very closely with what the atheist says about religious belief, except that I have tried to make it sound better. The atheist alleges that the religious man supposes himself to know what he means by his statements only because, until challenged, he interprets them anthropomorphically; when challenged, however, he retreats rapidly backwards towards complete agnosticism. I agree with this, with two provisos. The first is that the religious man does not suppose himself to know what he means by his statements (for what religious man supposes himself to be the Holy Ghost?); he knows what his statements mean within the parable, and believes that they are the right statements to use. (Theology is not a science; it is a sort of art of enlightened ignorance.) The second proviso is that the agnosticism is not complete; for the Christian, under attack, falls back not in any direction, but in one direction; he falls back upon the person of Christ, and the concrete realities of the Christian life.

Let us consider this for a moment with regard to the divine love. I could be attacked in this sort of way: "You have contended," my opponent might argue, "that when we say that God loves us the communication value of the statement is determined by the communication value of a similar statement about a human subject; and that we know the statement to be the right statement, but cannot know *how* it is the right statement, that is, what the divine love is like. But this will not do. Loving is an activity with two poles, the lover and the loved. We may not know the lover, in the case of God, but we *are*, and therefore *must know*, the loved. Now, to say that the image or parable of human love is the right image to use about God must imply that there is some similarity or analogy between human and divine love. Father's love may be superficially very unlike mother's, but unless there is some similarity of structure between them, we cannot use the same word of both. But we cannot believe that there is any similarity between the love of God and human love, unless we can detect some similarity between being loved by God and being loved by man. But if being loved by God is what we experience all the time, then it is not like being loved by man; it is like being let down right and left. And in the face of so great a discrepancy, we cannot believe that God loves us, if that is supposed to be in any sense a statement of sober fact."

I cannot attempt to answer this objection; it involves the whole problem of religion. But there is something I want to say about it, which is that the

Christian does not attempt to evade it either by helter-skelter flight, or by impudent bluff. He has his prepared positions onto which he retreats; and he knows that if these positions are taken, then he must surrender. He does not believe that they can be taken, but that is another matter. There are three main fortresses behind which he goes. For, first, he looks for the resurrection of the dead, and the life of the world to come; he believes, that is, that we do not see all of the picture, and that the parts which we do not see are precisely the parts which determine the design of the whole. He admits that if this hope be vain then we are of all men the most miserable. Second, he claims that he sees in Christ the verification, and to some extent also the specification, of the divine love. That is to say, he finds in Christ not only convincing evidence of God's concern for us, but also what sort of love the divine love is, what sort of benefits God is concerned to give us. He sees that, on the New Testament scale of values, it is better for a man to lose the whole world if he can thereby save his soul (which means his relationship to God); and that for that hope it is reasonable to sacrifice all that he has, and to undergo the death of the body and the mortification of the spirit. Third, he claims that in the religious life, of others, if not as yet in his own, the divine love may be encountered, that the promise "I will not fail thee nor forsake thee" is, if rightly understood, confirmed there. If, of course, this promise is interpreted as involving immunity from bodily suffering, it will be refuted; but no reader of the New Testament has any right so to interpret it. It is less glaringly, but as decisively, wrong to interpret it as involving immunity from spiritual suffering; for in the New Testament only the undergoing of death (which means the abdication of control over one's destiny) can be the beginning of life. What then does it promise? It promises that to the man who begins on the way of the Christian life, on the way that is of seeking life through death, of seeking relationship with God through the abdication of the self-sovereignty claimed by Adam, that to him the fight will be hard but not impossible, progress often indiscernible, but real, progress which is towards the paring away of self-hood, and which is therefore often given through defeat and humiliation, but a defeat and humiliation which are not final, which leave it possible to continue. This is the extra-parental nurture of religious belief of which I spoke earlier, and it is the third of the prepared positions onto which the Christian retreats, claiming that the image and reflection of the love of God may be seen not only hereafter, not only in Christ, but also, if dimly, in the concrete process of living the Christian life.

One final word. Religion has indeed its problems; but it is useless to consider them outside their religious context. Seen as a whole religion makes rough sense, though it does not make limpidity.

# John Hick

John Hick (1922–    ) is the author of numerous influential works on
the philosophy of religion, including *An Interpretation of Religion*, *Evil
and the God of Love*, and *Death and Eternal Life*.

# 28

# *An Irenaean Theodicy*

Can a world in which sadistic cruelty often has its way, in which selfish
lovelessness is so rife, in which there are debilitating diseases, crippling
accidents, bodily and mental decay, insanity, and all manner of natural
disasters be regarded as the expression of infinite creative goodness? Certainly all this could never by itself lead anyone to believe in the existence of
a limitlessly powerful God. And yet even in a world which contains these
things innumerable men and women have believed and do believe in the
reality of an infinite creative goodness, which they call God. The theodicy
project starts at this point, with an already operating belief in God, embodied
in human living, and attempts to show that this belief is not rendered
irrational by the fact of evil. It attempts to explain how it is that the universe,
assumed to be created and ultimately ruled by a limitlessly good and limitlessly powerful Being, is as it is, including all the pain and suffering and all
the wickedness and folly that we find around us and within us. The theodicy
project is thus an exercise in metaphysical construction, in the sense that it
consists in the formation and criticism of large-scale hypotheses concerning
the nature and process of the universe.

Since a theodicy both starts from and tests belief in the reality of God, it
naturally takes different forms in relation to different concepts of God. In this
essay I shall be discussing the project of a specifically Christian theodicy; I
shall not be attempting the further and even more difficult work of comparative theodicy, leading in turn to the question of a global theodicy.

The two main demands upon a theodicy hypothesis are (1) that it be
internally coherent, and (2) that it be consistent with the data both of the
religious tradition on which it is based, and of the world, in respect both of
the latter's general character as revealed by scientific enquiry and of the

From *Encountering Evil*, ed. by Stephen T. Davis, © 1981. Used by permission of Westminster / John Knox Press.

specific facts of moral and natural evil. These two criteria demand, respectively, possibility and plausibility.

Traditionally, Christian theology has centered upon the concept of God as both limitlessly powerful and limitlessly good and loving; and it is this concept of deity that gives rise to the problem of evil as a threat to theistic faith. The threat was definitively expressed in Stendhal's bombshell, "The only excuse for God is that he does not exist!" The theodicy project is the attempt to offer a different view of the universe which is both possible and plausible and which does not ignite Stendhal's bombshell.

Christian thought has always included a certain range of variety, and in the area of theodicy it offers two broad types of approach. The Augustinian approach, representing until fairly recently the majority report of the Christian mind, hinges upon the idea of the fall, which has in turn brought about the disharmony of nature. This type of theodicy is developed today as "the free will defense." The Irenaean approach, representing in the past a minority report, hinges upon the creation of humankind through the evolutionary process as an immature creature living in a challenging and therefore person-making world. I shall indicate very briefly why I do not find the first type of theodicy satisfactory, and then spend the remainder of this essay in exploring the second type.

In recent years the philosophical discussion of the problem of evil has been dominated by the free-will defense. A major effort has been made by Alvin Plantinga and a number of other Christian philosophers to show that it is logically possible that a limitlessly powerful and limitlessly good God is responsible for the existence of this world. For all evil may ultimately be due to misuses of creaturely freedom. But it may nevertheless be better for God to have created free than unfree beings; and it is logically possible that any and all free beings whom God might create would, as a matter of contingent fact, misuse their freedom by falling into sin. In that case it would be logically impossible for God to have created a world containing free beings and yet not containing sin and the suffering which sin brings with it. Thus it is logically possible, despite the fact of evil, that the existing universe is the work of a limitlessly good creator.

These writers are in effect arguing that the traditional Augustinian type of theodicy, based upon the fall from grace of free finite creatures—first angels and then human beings—and a consequent going wrong of the physical world, is not logically impossible. I am in fact doubtful whether their argument is sound, and will return to the question later. But even if it should be sound, I suggest that their argument wins only a Pyrrhic victory, since the logical possibility that it would establish is one which, for very many people today, is fatally lacking in plausibility. For most educated inhabitants of the modern world regard the biblical story of Adam and Eve, and their temptation by the devil, as myth rather than as history; and they believe that so far from having been created finitely perfect and then falling, humanity evolved out of lower forms of life, emerging in a morally, spiritually, and culturally primitive state. Further, they reject as incredible the idea that earthquake and flood, disease, decay, and death are consequences either of a human fall, or of a prior fall of angelic beings who are now exerting an evil influence upon the earth. They see all this as part of a pre-scientific world view, along with the stories of the world having been created in six days and of the sun standing still for twenty-four hours at Joshua's command. One cannot, strictly speaking, disprove any of these ancient biblical myths and sagas, or refute their confident elaboration in the medieval Christian picture of the universe. But those of us for whom the resulting theodicy, even if logically possible, is radically implausible, must look elsewhere for light on the problem of evil.

I believe that we find the light that we need in the main alternative strand of Christian thinking, which goes back to important constructive suggestions by the early Hellenistic Fathers of the Church, particularly St. Irenaeus (A.D. 120–202). Irenaeus himself did not develop a theodicy, but he did—together with other Greek-speaking Christian writers of that period, such as Clement of Alexandria—build a framework of thought within which a theodicy became possible which does not depend upon the idea of the fall, and which is consonant with modern knowledge concerning the origins of the human race. This theodicy cannot, as such, be attributed to Irenaeus. We should rather speak of a type of theodicy, presented in varying ways by different subsequent thinkers (the greatest of whom has been Friedrich Schleiermacher), of which Irenaeus can properly be regarded as the patron saint.

The central theme out of which this Irenaean type of theodicy has arisen is the two-stage conception of the creation of humankind, first in the "image" and then in the "likeness" of God. Re-expressing this in modern terms, the first stage was the gradual production of *homo sapiens*, through the long evolutionary process, as intelligent ethical and religious animals. The human being is an animal, one of the varied forms of earthly life and continuous as such with the whole realm of animal existence. But the human being is uniquely intelligent, having evolved a large and immensely complex brain. Further, the human being is ethical—that is, a gregarious as well as an intelligent animal, able to realize and respond to the complex demands of social life. And the human being is a religious animal, with an innate tendency to experience the world in terms of the presence and activity of supernatural beings and powers. This then is early *homo sapiens*, the intelligent social animal capable of awareness of the divine. But early *homo sapiens* is not the Adam and Eve of Augustinian theology, living in perfect harmony with self, with nature, and with God. On the contrary, the life of this being must have been a constant struggle against a hostile environment, and capable of savage violence against one's fellow human beings, particularly outside one's own immediate group; and this being's concepts of the divine were primitive and often bloodthirsty. Thus existence "in the image of God" was a potentiality for knowledge of and relationship with one's Maker rather than such knowledge and relationship as a fully realized state. In other words, people were created as spiritually and morally immature creatures, at the beginning of a long process of further growth and development, which constitutes the second stage of God's creative work. In this second stage, of which we are a part, the intelligent, ethical, and religious animal is being brought through one's own free responses into what Irenaeus called the divine "likeness." The human animal is being created into a child of God. Irenaeus' own terminology (*eikon, homoiosis; imago, similitudo*) has no particular merit, based as it is on a misunderstanding of the Hebrew parallelism in Genesis 1:26; but his conception of a two-stage creation of the human, with perfection lying in the future rather than in the past, is of fundamental importance. The notion of the fall was not basic to this picture, although it was to become basic to the great drama of salvation depicted by St. Augustine and accepted within western Christendom, including the churches stemming from the Reformation, until well into the nineteenth century. Irenaeus himself however could not, in the historical knowledge of his time, question the fact of the fall; though he treated it as a relatively minor lapse, a youthful error, rather than as the infinite crime and cosmic disaster which has ruined the whole creation. But today we can acknowledge that there is no evidence at all of a period in the distant past when humankind was in the ideal state of a fully realized "child of God." We can accept that, so far as actual events in time are concerned, there never was a fall from an original righteousness and grace. If we want to continue to use the term fall, because of its hallowed place in the Christian tradition, we must use it to refer to the immense gap between what we actually are and what in the divine intention is eventually to be. But we must not blur our awareness that the ideal state is not something already enjoyed and lost, but is a future and as yet unrealized goal. The reality is not a perfect creation which has gone tragically wrong, but a still continuing creative process whose completion lies in the eschaton.

Let us now try to formulate a contemporary version of the Irenaean type of theodicy, based on this suggestion of the initial creation of humankind, not as a finitely perfect, but as an immature creature at the beginning of a long process of further growth and development. We may begin by asking why one should have been created as an imperfect and developing creature rather than as the perfect being whom God is presumably intending to create? The answer, I think, consists in two considerations which converge in their practical implications, one concerned with the human's relationship to God and the other with the relationship to other human beings. As to the first, we could have the picture of God creating finite beings, whether angels or persons, directly in God's own presence, so that in being conscious of that which is other than one's self the creature is automatically conscious of God, the limitless divine reality and power, goodness and love, knowledge and wisdom, towering above one's self. In such a situation the disproportion between Creator and creatures would be so great that the latter would have no freedom in relation to God; they would indeed not exist as independent autonomous persons. For what freedom could finite beings have in an immediate consciousness of the presence of the one who has created them, who knows them through and through, who is limitlessly powerful as well as limitlessly loving and good, and who claims their total obedience? In order to be a person, exercising some measure of genuine freedom, the creature must be brought into existence, not in the immediate divine presence, but at a "distance" from God. This "distance" cannot of course be spatial; for God is omnipresent. It must be an epistemic distance, a distance in the cognitive dimension. And the Irenaean hypothesis is that this "distance" consists, in the case of humans, in their existence within and as part of a world which functions as an autonomous system and from within which God is not overwhelmingly evident. It is a world, in Bonhoeffer's phrase, *etsi deus non daretur*, as if there were no God. Or rather, it is religiously ambiguous, capable both of being seen as a purely natural phenomenon and of being seen as God's creation and experienced as mediating God's presence. In such a world one can exist as a person over against the Creator. One has space to exist as a finite being, a space created by the epistemic distance from God and protected by one's basic cognitive freedom, one's freedom to open or close oneself to the dawning awareness of God which is experienced naturally by a religious animal. This Irenaean picture corresponds, I suggest, to our actual human situation. Emerging within the evolutionary process as part of the continuum of animal life, in a universe which functions in accordance with its own laws and whose workings can be investigated and described without reference to a creator, the human being has a genuine, even awesome, freedom in relation to one's Maker. The human being is free to acknowledge and worship God; and is free—particularly since the emergence of human individuality and the beginnings of critical consciousness during the first millennium B.C.—to doubt the reality of God.

Within such a situation there is the possibility of the human being coming freely to know and love one's Maker. Indeed, if the end state which God is seeking to bring about is one in which finite persons have come in their own freedom to know and love God, this requires creating them initially in a state which is not that of their already knowing and loving God. For it is logically impossible to create beings already in a state of having come into that state by their own free choices.

The other consideration, which converges with this in pointing to something like the human situation as we experience it, concerns our human moral nature. We can approach it by asking why humans should not have been created at this epistemic distance from God, and yet at the same time as morally perfect beings? That persons could have been created morally perfect and yet free, so that they would always in fact choose rightly, has been argued by such critics of the free-will defense in theodicy as Antony Flew and J. L. Mackie, and argued against by Alvin Plantinga and other upholders of that form of theodicy. On the specific issue defined in the debate between them, it appears to me that the criticism of the freewill defense stands. It appears to me that a perfectly good being, although formally free to sin, would in fact never do so. If we imagine such a being in a morally frictionless environment, involving no stresses or temptation, then we must assume that one would exemplify the ethical equivalent of Newton's first law of motion, which states that a moving body will continue in uniform motion until interfered with by some outside force. By analogy, a perfectly good being would continue in the same moral course forever, there being nothing in the environment to throw one off it. But even if we suppose the morally perfect being to exist in an imperfect world, in which one is subject to temptations, it still follows that, in virtue of moral perfection, one will always overcome those temptations—as in the case, according to orthodox Christian belief, of Jesus Christ. It is, to be sure, logically possible, as Plantinga and others argue, that a free being, simply as such, may at any time contingently decide to sin. However, a responsible free being does not act randomly, but on the basis of moral nature. And a free being whose nature is wholly and unqualifiedly good will accordingly never in fact sin.

But if God could, without logical contradiction, have created humans as wholly good free beings, why did God not do so? Why was humanity not initially created in possession of all the virtues, instead of having to acquire them through the long hard struggle of life as we know it? The answer, I suggest, appeals to the principle that virtues which have been formed within the agent as a hard-won deposit of her own right decisions in situations of challenge and temptation, are intrinsically more valuable than virtues created within her ready made and without any effort on her own part. This principle expresses a basic value judgment, which cannot be established by argument but which one can only present, in the hope that it will be as morally plausible, and indeed compelling, to others as to oneself. It is, to repeat, the judgment that a moral goodness which exists as the agent's initial given nature, without ever having been chosen by her in the face of temptations to the contrary, is intrinsically less valuable than a moral goodness which has been built up through the agent's own responsible choices through time in the face of alternative possibilities.

If, then, God's purpose was to create finite persons embodying the most valuable kind of moral goodness, God would have to create them, not as already perfect beings but rather as imperfect creatures who can then attain to the more valuable kind of goodness through their own free choices as in the course of their personal and social history new responses prompt new insights, opening up new moral possibilities, and providing a milieu in which the most valuable kind of moral nature can be developed.

We have thus far, then, the hypothesis that one is created at an epistemic distance from God in order to come freely to know and love the Maker; and that one is at the same time created as a morally immature and imperfect being in order to attain through freedom the most valuable quality of goodness. The end sought, according to this hypothesis, is the full realization of the human potentialities in a unitary spiritual and moral perfection in the divine kingdom. And the question we have to ask is whether humans as we know them, and the world as we know it, are compatible with this hypothesis.

Clearly we cannot expect to be able to deduce our actual world in its concrete character, and our actual human nature as part of it, from the general concept of spiritually and morally immature creatures developing ethically in an appropriate environment. No doubt there is an immense range of possible worlds, any one of which, if actualized, would exemplify this concept. All that we can hope to do is to show that our actual world is one of these. And when we look at our human situation as part of the evolving life of this planet we can, I think, see that it fits this specification. As animal organisms, integral to the whole ecology of life, we are programmed for survival. In pursuit of survival, primitives not only killed other animals for food but fought other human beings when their vital interests conflicted. The life of prehistoric persons must indeed have been a constant struggle to stay alive, prolonging an existence which was, in Hobbes' phrase, "poor, nasty, brutish and short." And in his basic animal self-regardingness humankind was, and is, morally imperfect. In saying this I am assuming that the essence of moral evil is selfishness, the sacrificing of others to one's own interests. It consists, in Kantian terminology, in treating others, not as ends in themselves, but as means to one's own ends. This is what the survival instinct demands. And yet we are also capable of love, of self-giving in a common cause, of a conscience which responds to others in their needs and dangers. And with the development of civilization we see the growth of moral insight, the glimpsing and gradual assimilation of higher ideals, and tension between our animality and our ethical values. But that the human being has a lower as well as a higher nature, that one is an animal as well as a potential child of God, and that one's moral goodness is won from a struggle with one's own innate selfishness, is inevitable given one's continuity with the other forms of animal life. Further, the human animal is not responsible for having come into existence as an animal. The ultimate responsibility for humankind's existence, as a morally imperfect creature, can only rest with the Creator. The human does not, in one's own degree of freedom and responsibility, choose one's origin, but rather one's destiny.

This then, in brief outline, is the answer of the Irenaean type of theodicy to the question of the origin of moral evil: the general fact of humankind's basic self-regarding animality is an aspect of creation as part of the realm of organic life; and this basic self-regardingness has been expressed over the centuries both in sins of individual selfishness and in the much more massive sins of corporate selfishness, institutionalized in slavery and exploitation and all the many and complex forms of social injustice.

But nevertheless our sinful nature in a sinful world is the matrix within which God is gradually creating children of God out of human animals. For it is as men and women freely respond to the claim of God upon their lives, transmuting their animality into the structure of divine worship, that the creation of humanity is taking place. And in its concrete character this response consists in every form of moral goodness, from unselfish love in individual personal relationships to the dedicated and selfless striving to end exploitation and to create justice within and between societies.

But one cannot discuss moral evil without at the same time discussing the non-moral evil of pain and suffering. (I propose to mean by "pain" physical pain, including the pains of hunger and thirst; and by "suffering" the mental and emotional pain of loneliness, anxiety, remorse, lack of love, fear, grief, envy, etc.). For what constitutes moral evil as evil is the fact that it causes pain and suffering. It is impossible to conceive of an instance of moral evil, or sin, which is not productive of pain or suffering to anyone at any time. But in addition to moral evil there is another source of pain and suffering in the structure of the physical world, which produces storms, earthquakes, and floods and which afflicts the human body with diseases—cholera, epilepsy, cancer, malaria, arthritis, rickets, meningitis, etc.—as well as with broken bones and other outcomes of physical accident. It is true that a great deal both of pain and of suffering is humanly caused, not only by the 'inhumanity of man to man' but also by the stresses of our individual and corporate lifestyles, causing many disorders—not only lung cancer and cirrhosis of the liver but many cases of heart disease, stomach and other ulcers, strokes, etc.—as well as accidents. But there remain nevertheless, in the natural world itself, permanent causes of human pain and suffering. And we have to ask why an unlimitedly good and unlimitedly powerful God should have created so dangerous a world, both as regards its purely natural hazards of earthquake and flood, etc., and as regards the liability of the human body to so many ills, both psychosomatic and purely somatic.

The answer offered by the Irenaean type of theodicy follows from and is indeed integrally bound up with its account of the origin of moral evil. We have the hypothesis of humankind being brought into being within the evolutionary process as a spiritually and morally immature creature, and then growing and developing through the exercise of freedom in this religiously ambiguous world. We can now ask what sort of a world would constitute an appropriate environment for this second stage of creation? The development of human personality—moral, spiritual, and intellectual—is a product of challenge and response. It does not occur in a static situation demanding no exertion and no choices. So far as intellectual development is concerned, this is a well-established principle which underlies the whole modern educational process, from preschool nurseries designed to provide a rich and stimulating environment, to all forms of higher education designed to challenge the intellect. At a basic level the essential part played in learning by the learner's own active response to environment was strikingly demonstrated by the Held and Heim experiment with kittens.[1] Of two litter-mate kittens in the same artificial environment one was free to exercise its own freedom and intelligence in exploring the environment, while the other was suspended in a kind of "gondola" which moved whenever and wherever the free kitten moved. Thus the second kitten had a similar succession of visual experiences as the first, but did not exert itself or make any choices in obtaining them. And whereas the first kitten learned in the normal way to conduct itself safely within its environment, the second did not. With no interaction with a challenging environment there was no development in its behavioral patterns. And I think we can safely say that the intellectual development of humanity has been due to interaction with an objective environment functioning in accordance with its own laws, an environment which we have had actively to explore and to cooperate with in order to escape its perils and exploit its benefits. In a world devoid both of dangers to be avoided and rewards to be won we may assume that there would have been virtually no development of the human intellect and imagination, and hence of either the sciences or the arts, and hence of human civilization or culture.

The fact of an objective world within which one has to learn to live, on penalty of pain or death, is also basic to the development of one's moral nature. For it is because the world is one in which men and women can suffer harm—by violence, disease, accident, starvation, etc.—that our actions affecting one another have moral significance. A morally wrong act is, basically, one which harms some part of the human community; while a morally right action is, on the contrary, one which prevents or neutralizes harm or which preserves or increases human well being. Now we can imagine a paradise in which no one can ever come to any harm. It could be a world which, instead of having its own fixed structure, would be plastic to human wishes. Or it could be a world with a fixed structure, and hence the possibility of damage

---

[1] R. Held and A. Heim, "Movement-produced stimulation in the development of visually guided behaviour," *Journal of Comparative and Physiological Psychology*, Vol. 56 (1963), pp. 872–876.

and pain, but whose structure is suspended or adjusted by special divine action whenever necessary to avoid human pain. Thus, for example, in such a miraculously pain-free world one who falls accidentally off a high building would presumably float unharmed to the ground; bullets would become insubstantial when fired at a human body; poisons would cease to poison; water to drown, and so on. We can at least begin to imagine such a world. And a good deal of the older discussion of the problem of evil—for example in Part xi of Hume's *Dialogues Concerning Natural Religion*—assumed that it must be the intention of a limitlessly good and powerful Creator to make for human creatures a pain-free environment; so that the very existence of pain is evidence against the existence of God. But such an assumption overlooks the fact that a world in which there can be no pain or suffering would also be one in which there can be no moral choices and hence no possibility of moral growth and development. For in a situation in which no one can ever suffer injury or be liable to pain or suffering there would be no distinction between right and wrong action. No action would be morally wrong, because no action could have harmful consequences; and likewise no action would be morally right in contrast to wrong. Whatever the values of such a world, it clearly could not serve a purpose of the development of its inhabitants from self-regarding animality to self-giving love.

Thus the hypothesis of a divine purpose in which finite persons are created at an epistemic distance from God, in order that they may gradually become children of God through their own moral and spiritual choices, requires that their environment, instead of being a pain-free and stress-free paradise, be broadly the kind of world of which we find ourselves to be a part. It requires that it be such as to provoke the theological problem of evil. For it requires that it be an environment which offers challenges to be met, problems to be solved, dangers to be faced, and which accordingly involves real possibilities of hardship, disaster, failure, defeat, and misery as well as of delight and happiness, success, triumph and achievement. For it is by grappling with the real problems of a real environment, in which a person is one form of life among many, and which is not designed to minister exclusively to one's well-being, that one can develop in intelligence and in such qualities as courage and determination. And it is in the relationships of human beings with one another, in the context of this struggle to survive and flourish, that they can develop the higher values of mutual love and care, of self-sacrifice for others, and of commitment to a common good.

To summarize thus far:

(1) The divine intention in relation to humankind, according to our hypothesis, is to create perfect finite personal beings in filial relationship with their Maker.

(2) It is logically impossible for humans to be created already in this perfect state, because in its spiritual aspect it involves coming freely to an

uncoerced consciousness of God from a situation of epistemic distance, and in its moral aspect, freely choosing the good in preference to evil.

(3) Accordingly the human being was initially created through the evolutionary process, as a spiritually and morally immature creature, and as part of a world which is both religiously ambiguous and ethically demanding.

(4) Thus that one is morally imperfect (i.e., that there is moral evil), and that the world is a challenging and even dangerous environment (i.e., that there is natural evil), are necessary aspects of the present stage of the process through which God is gradually creating perfected finite persons.

In terms of this hypothesis, as we have developed it thus far, then, both the basic moral evil in the human heart and the natural evils of the world are compatible with the existence of a Creator who is unlimited in both goodness and power. But is the hypothesis plausible as well as possible? The principal threat to its plausibility comes, I think, from the sheer amount and intensity of both moral and natural evil. One can accept the principle that in order to arrive at a freely chosen goodness one must start out in a state of moral immaturity and imperfection. But is it necessary that there should be the depths of demonic malice and cruelty which each generation has experienced, and which we have seen above all in recent history in the Nazi attempt to exterminate the Jewish population of Europe? Can any future fulfillment be worth such horrors? This was Dostoyevski's haunting question: "Imagine that you are creating a fabric of human destiny with the object of making men happy in the end, giving them peace and rest at last, but that it was essential and inevitable to torture to death only one tiny creature—that baby beating its breast with its fist, for instance—and to found that edifice on its unavenged tears, would you consent to be the architect on those conditions?"[2] The theistic answer is one which may be true but which takes so large a view that it baffles the imagination. Intellectually one may be able to see, but emotionally one cannot be expected to feel, its truth; and in that sense it cannot satisfy us. For the theistic answer is that if we take with full seriousness the value of human freedom and responsibility, as essential to the eventual creation of perfected children of God, then we cannot consistently want God to revoke that freedom when its wrong exercise becomes intolerable to us. From our vantage point within the historical process we may indeed cry out to God to revoke his gift of freedom, or to overrule it by some secret or open intervention. Such a cry must have come from millions caught in the Jewish Holocaust, or in the yet more recent laying waste of Korea and Vietnam, or from the victims of racism in many parts of the world. And the thought that humankind's moral freedom is indivisible, and can lead eventually to a consummation of limitless value which could never be attained without that

---

[2]Fyodor Dostoyevsky, *The Brothers Karamazov*, trans. by Constance Garnett (New York: Modern Library, n.d.), Bk. V, chap. 4, p. 254.

freedom, and which is worth any finite suffering in the course of its creation, can be of no comfort to those who are now in the midst of that suffering. But while fully acknowledging this, I nevertheless want to insist that this eschatological answer may well be true. Expressed in religious language it tells us to trust in God even in the midst of deep suffering, for in the end we shall participate in his glorious kingdom.

Again, we may grant that a world which is to be a person-making environment cannot be a pain-free paradise but must contain challenges and dangers, with real possibilities of many kinds of accident and disaster, and the pain and suffering which they bring. But need it contain the worst forms of disease and catastrophe? And need misfortune fall upon us with such heartbreaking indiscriminateness? Once again there are answers, which may well be true, and yet once again the truth in this area may offer little in the way of pastoral balm. Concerning the intensity of natural evil, the truth is probably that our judgments of intensity are relative. We might identify some form of natural evil as the worst that there is—say, the agony that can be caused by death from cancer—and claim that a loving God would not have allowed this to exist. But in a world in which there was no cancer, something else would then rank as the worst form of natural evil. If we then eliminate this, something else; and so on. And the process would continue until the world was free of all natural evil. For whatever form of evil for the time being remained would be intolerable to the inhabitants of that world. But in removing all occasions of pain and suffering, and hence all challenge and all need for mutual care, we should have converted the world from a person-making into a static environment, which could not elicit moral growth. In short, having accepted that a person-making world must have its dangers and therefore also its trage-dies, we must accept that whatever form these take will be intolerable to the inhabitants of that world. There could not be a person-making world devoid of what we call evil; and evils are never tolerable—except for the sake of greater goods which may come out of them.

But accepting that a person-making environment must contain causes of pain and suffering, and that no pain or suffering is going to be acceptable, one of the most daunting and even terrifying features of the world is that calamity strikes indiscriminately. There is no justice in the incidence of disease, accident, disaster and tragedy. The righteous as well as the unrigh-teous are struck down by illness and afflicted by misfortune. There is no security in goodness, but the good are as likely as the wicked to suffer "the slings and arrows of outrageous fortune." From the time of Job this fact has set a glaring question mark against the goodness of God. But let us suppose that things were otherwise. Let us suppose that misfortune came upon humankind, not haphazardly and therefore unjustly, but justly and therefore not haphazardly. Let us suppose that instead of coming without regard to moral considerations, it was proportioned to desert, so that the sinner was punished and the virtuous rewarded. Would such a dispensation serve a person-making purpose? Surely not. For it would be evident that wrong deeds bring disaster upon the agent whilst good deeds bring health and prosperity; and in such a world truly moral action, action done because it is right, would be impossible. The fact that natural evil is not morally directed, but is a hazard which comes by chance, is thus an intrinsic feature of a person-making world.

In other words, the very mystery of natural evil, the very fact that disasters afflict human beings in contingent, undirected and haphazard ways, is itself a necessary feature of a world that calls forth mutual aid and builds up mutual caring and love. Thus on the one hand it would be completely wrong to say that God sends misfortune upon individuals, so that their death, maiming, starvation or ruin is God's will for them. But on the other hand God has set us in a world containing unpredictable contingencies and dangers, in which unexpected and undeserved calamities may occur to anyone; because only in such a world can mutual caring and love be elicited. As an abstract philosophical hypothesis this may offer little comfort. But translated into religious language it tells us that God's good purpose enfolds the entire process of this world, with all its good and bad contingencies, and that even amidst tragic calamity and suffering we are still within the sphere of God's love and are moving towards God's kingdom.

But there is one further all-important aspect of the Irenaean type of theodicy, without which all the foregoing would lose its plausibility. This is the eschatological aspect. Our hypothesis depicts persons as still in course of creation towards an end state of perfected personal community in the divine kingdom. This end state is conceived of as one in which individual egoity has been transcended in communal unity before God. And in the present phase of that creative process the naturally self-centered human animal has the opportunity freely to respond to God's non-coercive self-disclosures, through the work of prophets and saints, through the resulting religious traditions, and through the individual's religious experience. Such response always has an ethical aspect; for the growing awareness of God is at the same time a growing awareness of the moral claim which God's presence makes upon the way in which we live.

But it is very evident that this person-making process, leading eventually to perfect human community, is not completed on this earth. It is not completed in the life of the individual—or at best only in the few who have attained to sanctification, or moksha, or nirvana on this earth. Clearly the enormous majority of men and women die without having attained to this. As Eric Fromm has said, "The tragedy in the life of most of us is that we die before we are fully born."[3] And therefore if we are ever to reach the full realization of the potentialities of our human nature, this can only be in a continuation of our lives in another sphere of existence after bodily death. And it is equally evident that the perfect all-embracing human community, in which self-regarding concern has been transcended in mutual love, not only has not been realized in this world, but never can be, since hundreds of generations of human beings have already lived and died and accordingly could not be part of any ideal community established at some future moment of earthly history. Thus if the unity of humankind in God's presence is ever to be realized it will have to be in some sphere of existence other than our earth. In short, the fulfillment of the divine purpose, as it is postulated in the Irenaean type of theodicy, presupposes each person's survival, in some form, of bodily death, and further living and growing towards that end state. Without such an eschatological fulfillment, this theodicy would collapse.

A theodicy which presupposes and requires an eschatology will thereby be rendered implausible in the minds of many today. I nevertheless do not see how any coherent theodicy can avoid dependence upon an eschatology. Indeed I would go further and say that the belief in the reality of a limitlessly loving and powerful deity must incorporate some kind of eschatology according to which God holds in being the creatures whom God has made for fellowship with himself, beyond bodily death, and brings them into the eternal fellowship which God has intended for them. I have tried elsewhere to argue that such an eschatology is a necessary corollary of ethical monotheism; to argue for the realistic possibility of an afterlife or lives, despite the philosophical and empirical arguments against this; and even to spell out some of the general features which human life after death may possibly have.[4] Since all this is a very large task, which would far exceed the bounds of this essay, I shall not attempt to repeat it here but must refer the reader to my existing discussion of it. It is that extended discussion that constitutes my answer to the question whether an Irenaean theodicy, with its eschatology, may not be as implausible as an Augustinian theodicy, with its human or angelic fall. (If it is, then the latter is doubly implausible; for it also involves an eschatology!)

There is however one particular aspect of eschatology which must receive some treatment here, however brief and inadequate. This is the issue of "universal salvation" versus "heaven and hell" (or perhaps annihilation instead of hell). If the justification of evil within the creative process lies in

---

[3]Erich Fromm, "Values, Psychology, and Human Existence," in *New Knowledge of Human Values*, ed. A. H. Maslow (New York: Harper & Row, 1959), p. 156.

[4]John Hick, *Death and Eternal Life* (New York: Harper & Row; and London: Collins, 1976; revised, London: Macillan, 1987).

the limitless and eternal good of the end state to which it leads, then the completeness of the justification must depend upon the completeness, or universality, of the salvation achieved. Only if it includes the entire human race can it justify the sins and sufferings of the entire human race throughout all history. But, having given human beings cognitive freedom, which in turn makes possible moral freedom, can the Creator bring it about that in the end all his human creatures freely turn to God in love and trust? The issue is a very difficult one; but I believe that it is in fact possible to reconcile a full affirmation of human freedom with a belief in the ultimate universal success of God's creative work. We have to accept that creaturely freedom always occurs within the limits of a basic nature that we did not ourselves choose; for this is entailed by the fact of having been created. If then a real though limited freedom does not preclude our being endowed with a certain nature, it does not preclude our being endowed with a basic Godward bias, so that, quoting from another side of St. Augustine's thought, "our hearts are restless until they find their rest in Thee."[5] If this is so, it can be predicted that sooner or later, in our own time and in our own way, we shall all freely come to God; and universal salvation can be affirmed, not as a logical necessity but as the contingent but predictable outcome of the process of the universe, interpreted theistically. Once again, I have tried to present this argument more fully elsewhere, and to consider various objections to it.[6]

On this view the human, endowed with a real though limited freedom, is basically formed for relationship with God and destined ultimately to find the fulfillment of his or her nature in that relationship. This does not seem to me excessively paradoxical. On the contrary, given the theistic postulate, it seems to me to offer a very probable account of our human situation. If so, it is a situation in which we can rejoice; for it gives meaning to our temporal existence as the long process through which we are being created, by our own free responses to life's mixture of good and evil, into "children of God" who "inherit eternal life."

---

[5]*The Confessions of St. Augustine*, trans. by F. J. Sheed (New York: Sheed and Ward, 1942), Bk. 1, chap. 1, p. 3.

[6]Hick, *Death and Eternal Life*, chap. 13.

# 29

## *Religious Faith as Experiencing-As*

The particular sense or use of the word "faith" that I am seeking to understand is that which occurs when the religious man, and more specifically the Christian believer, speaks of "knowing God" and goes on to explain that this is a knowing of God by faith. Or again, when asked how she professes to know that God, as spoken about in Christianity, is real, her answer is "by faith." Our question is: what does "faith" mean in these contexts? And what I should like to be able to do is to make a descriptive (or if you like phenomenological) analysis that could be acceptable to both believers and non-believers. A Christian and an atheist or agnostic should equally be able to say, Yes, that is what, phenomenologically, faith is—though they would of course then go on to say radically different things about its value.

The modes of cognition have been classified in various ways. But the distinction that is most relevant to our present purpose is that between what I shall call cognition in presence and cognition in absence; or acquaintance (using this term less restrictedly than it was used by Russell) and holding beliefs-about. We cognize things that are present before us, this being called perception; and we also cognize things in their absence, this being a matter of holding beliefs about them. And the astonishing fact is that while our religious literature—the Bible, and prayers, hymns, sermons, devotional meditations, and so on—confidently presuppose a cognition of God by acquaintance, our theological literature in contrast recognizes for the most part only cognition in absence. That is to say, whereas the Bible itself, and other writings directly expressing the life of faith, are full of human encounters with God and our personal dealings with the divine Thou, the dominant systems of Christian theology nevertheless treat faith as belief, as a propositional attitude. In the Catholic tradition deriving from St. Thomas, and no less in the Protestant orthodoxy that supervened upon the Reformation movement, faith has been quite explicitly defined as believing on God's authority certain truths, i.e. propositional truths, that he has revealed. Thus faith, instead of being seen as a religious response to God's redemptive action in

Reprinted, with permission, from *Talk of God*, ed. Godfrey Vesey (London: Macmillan, 1969).

the life of Jesus of Nazareth, has been seen instead as primarily an assent to theological truths. For good or ill this was a very major and radical step, taken early on in the church's history and displaying its implications over the centuries in many different aspects of the life of Christendom. I believe that it was a wrong step, which the Reformers of the sixteenth century sought to correct. If this is so, we want to find a viable way, or perhaps even ways (in the plural), of thinking of faith as a form of cognition by acquaintance or cognition in presence. Instead of assimilating faith to propositional belief—whether such belief be produced by reasoning or act of will or both—we must assimilate it to perception. I therefore want to explore the possibility that the cognition of God by faith is more like perceiving something, even perceiving a physical object, that is present before us than it is like believing a statement about some absent object, whether because the statement has been proved to us or because we want to believe it.

But surely—if I may myself at once voice an inevitable protest—the cognition of God can no more be like sense perception than God is like a physical object. It is true that Christian tradition tells of an ultimate beatific vision of God, but we are not now speaking of this but of the ordinary believer's awareness of God in our present earthly life. And this is not a matter of perceiving him, but of believing, without being able to perceive him, that he nevertheless exists. It is in fact, as it has traditionally been held to be, a case of cognition in absence, or of holding beliefs-about.

However the hypothesis that we want to consider is not that religious faith *is* sense perception, but that as a form of cognition by acquaintance it is *more like* sense perception than like propositional belief. That propositions may be validly founded upon the awareness of God, and that they then play an indispensable and immensely valuable part in the religious life, is not in question. But what we are interested in now is the awareness of God itself; for this is faith—that is to say, distinctively religious cognition—in its primary sense.

It is today hardly a contentious doctrine requiring elaborate argumentation that seeing—to confine ourselves for the moment to this one mode of perceiving—is not a simple straightforward matter of physical objects registering themselves on our retinas and thence in our conscious visual fields. There are complexities, and indeed a complex variety of complexities. The particular complexity that concerns us now was brought to the attention of philosophers by Wittgenstein's discussion of seeing-as in the *Philosophical Investigations*.[1] Wittgenstein pointed to puzzle pictures and ambiguous diagrams of the kind that are found in abundance in some of the psychological texts—for instance the Necker cube, Jastrow's duck-rabbit, and Köhler's goblet-faces. The cube diagram, for instance, can be seen as a cube viewed

---

[1] Pt. II, sec. xi.

either from below or from above, and the perceiving mind tends to alternate between these two perspectives. The goblet-faces diagram can be seen as the outline of a goblet or vase or as the outlines of two faces looking straight into each other's eyes. The duck-rabbit can be seen as the representation of a rabbit's head facing to the left or of a duck's head facing to the right. In these cases every line of the diagram plays its part in both aspects (as Wittgenstein called them) and has equal weight in each: these may accordingly be called cases of total ambiguity. Another sort, artistically more complex, might be called cases of emergent pattern; for example, those puzzle pictures in which you are presented with what at first seems to be a random and meaningless scattering of lines and dots, but in which as you look at it you come to see, say, a face; or again, as another example, the well-known "Christ in the snow" picture. And in between there are various other sorts of intermediate cases which we need not however take account of here. We speak of seeing-as when that which is objectively there, in the sense of that which affects the retina, can be consciously perceived in two different ways as having two different characters or natures or meanings or significances; and very often, in these two-dimensional instances, we find that the mind switches back and forth between the alternative ways of seeing-as.

Let us at this point expand the notion of seeing-as into that of experiencing-as. The elements of experiencing-as are the purely visual seeing-as which we have thus far been discussing, plus its equivalents for the other senses. For as well as seeing a bird as a bird, we may hear it as a bird—hear the bird's song as a bird's song, hear the rustle of its wings as a bird in flight, hear the rapping of the woodpecker as just that; and so on. Again, a carpenter may not only see the wood as mahogany but also feel it as mahogany; he may recognize it tactually as well as visually. Or again, we may taste the wine as Burgundy and smell the cheese as Gorgonzola. Not of course that the different senses normally function in isolation. We perceive and recognize by means of all the relevant senses cooperating as a single complex means of perception; and I suggest that we use the term "experiencing-as" to refer to the end product of this in consciousness.

The next step is from these two-dimensional pictures and diagrams to experiencing-as in real life—for example, seeing the tuft of grass over there in the field as a rabbit, or the shadows in the corner of the room as someone standing there. And the analogy to be explored is with two contrasting ways of experiencing the events of our lives and of human history, on the one hand as purely natural events and on the other hand as mediating the presence and activity of God. For there is a sense in which the religious person and the atheist both live in the same world and another sense in which they live consciously in different worlds. They inhabit the same physical environment and are confronted by the same changes occurring within it. But in its actual concrete character in their respective "streams of consciousness" it has for each a different nature and quality, a different meaning and significance; for one does and the other does not experience life as a continual interaction with the transcendent God. Is there then any true analogy or parallel between, on the one hand, these two ways of experiencing human life, *as* an encounter with God or *as* an encounter only with a natural order, and on the other hand the two ways of seeing the distant shape, *as* a rabbit or *as* a tuft of grass?

An immediate comment might be: if there is any such analogy, so much the worse for religious cognition! For does not the analogy between seeing a puzzle picture in a certain way and experiencing human life in a certain way underline once again the purely subjective and gratuitous character of religious knowledge claims in contrast with the compelling objectivity of ordinary sense perception?

So far as the argument has thus far gone, perhaps it does. But the next point to be introduced must considerably affect the upshot of what has gone before. This is the thesis that *all* experiencing is experiencing-as—not only, for example, seeing the tuft of grass, erroneously, as a rabbit, but also seeing it correctly as a tuft of grass. On the face of it this sounds paradoxical. One might put the difficulty in this way: we may if we like speak of seeing the tuft of grass *as* a tuft of grass because it is evidently possible to misperceive it as a sitting rabbit. But what about something utterly familiar and unmistakable? What about the fork on the table? Would it not be absurd to say that you are seeing it *as* a fork? It must be granted that this particular locution would be distinctly odd in most circumstances. However we have more acceptable names for ordinary seeing-as in real life; we call it "recognizing" or "identifying." Of course we are so familiar with forks that normally we recognize one without encountering even enough difficulty to make us notice that we are in fact performing an act of recognition. But if the fork were sufficiently exotic in design I might have occasion to say that I can recognize the thing before me on the table as a fork—that is, as a man-made instrument for conveying food into the mouth. And, going further afield, a Stone Age savage would not be able to recognize it at all. He might identify it instead as a marvellously shining object which must be full of *mana* and must not be touched; or as a small but deadly weapon; or as a tool for digging; or just as something utterly baffling and unidentifiable. But he would not have the concept of a fork with which to identify it as a fork. Indeed to say that he does not have this concept and that he cannot perform this act of recognition are two ways of saying the same thing. That there is no ambiguity or mystery about forks for you or me is simply due to the contingent circumstance that forks are familiar parts of the apparatus of our culture. For the original nature or meaning of an artifact is determined by the purpose for which it has been made, and this purpose necessarily operates within a particular cultural context. But simply as a physical object of a certain size and shape an artifact does not bear its meaning stamped upon it. To recognize or identify is to be experiencing-as in terms of a concept; and our concepts are social products having their life within a particular linguistic environment.

Further, this is as true of natural objects as it is of artifacts. Here, too, to recognize is to apply a concept; and this is always to cognize the thing as being much more than is currently perceptible. For example, to identify a moving object in the sky as a bird is not only to make implicit claims about its present shape, size and structure beyond what we immediately observe but also about its past (for instance, that it came out of an egg, not a factory), about its future (for instance, that it will one day die), and about its behavior in various hypothetical circumstances (for instance, that it will tend to be frightened by loud noises). When we thus equate experiencing-as with recognizing it is I think no longer a paradoxical doctrine that all conscious experiencing is experiencing-as.

But—if I may raise a possible objection—is it not the case that "She recognizes $x$" entails that the thing recognized is indeed $x$, while "She is experiencing $a$ as $x$" does not entail that $a$ is indeed $x$: and must we not therefore acknowledge a distinction between recognizing and experiencing-as? As a matter of the ordinary use of these words the objection is, I think, in order. But what it indicates is that we lack a term to cover both recognition and misrecognition. We are accordingly driven to use "recognition" generically, as "knowledge" in "theory of knowledge" is used to cover error as well as knowledge, or as "morality" in "theory of morality" is used to cover immorality also. I have been using "recognition" here in an analogous way to include unjustified as well as justified identification assertions.

I proceed, then, from the proposition that all conscious experiencing involves recognitions which go beyond what is given to the senses and is thus a matter of experiencing-as. This means that ordinary secular perceiving shares a common epistemological character with religious experiencing. We must accordingly abandon the view—if we ever held it—that sense perception at the highly sophisticated human level is a mere automatic registering by the mind of what is on the retina, while religious perception is, in contrast, a subjective response which gratuitously projects meanings into the world. We find instead that all conscious perceiving goes beyond what the senses report to a significance which has not as such been given to the senses. And the religious experience of life as a sphere in which we have continually to do with God and God with us is likewise an awareness in our experience as a whole of a significance which transcends the scope of the senses. In both cases, in a classic statement of John Oman's, "knowing is not knowledge as an effect of an unknown external cause, but is knowledge as we so interpret that our meaning is the actual meaning of our environment."[2] And, as Oman also taught, the claim of the religious believer is that in his religious commit-

---

[2]*The Natural and the Supernatural* (Cambridge: Cambridge University Press, 1931), p. 175.

ment he is relating himself to his total environment in its most ultimate meaning.

The conclusion that *all* experiencing is experiencing-as enables us to meet a fundamental objection that might be made against the analogy between experiencing-as in ordinary life and in religious awareness. It might be pointed out that it is only possible to see, let us say, a tuft of grass as a rabbit if one has previously seen real rabbits; and that in general to see *A* as a *B* presupposes acquaintance with *B*s. Analogously, in order to experience some event, say a striking escape from danger or a healing, as an act of God it would seem that we must first know by direct acquaintance what an act of God is like. However, all that has ever been witnessed in the way of divine actions are earthly events which the religious mind has seen as acts of God but which a sceptical observer could see as having a purely natural explanation. In other words, we never have before us unambiguously divine acts, but only ambiguous events which are capable of taking on religious significance to the eyes of faith. But in that case, it will be said, we have no unproblematic cases of divine actions available to us, as we have in abundance unproblematic instances of rabbits and forks; and consequently we can never be in a position to recognize any of these ambiguous events *as* acts of God. Just as it would be impossible for one who had never seen rabbits to see anything *as* a rabbit, so it must be impossible for us who have never seen an undeniable act of God, to see an event *as* an act of God. This seems on the face of it to be a conclusive objection.

However, the objection collapses if, as I have been arguing, *all* experiencing, involving as it does the activity of recognizing, is to be construed as experiencing-as. For although the process of recognizing is mysterious, there is no doubt that we do continually recognize things, and further that we can learn to recognize. We have learned, starting from scratch, to identify rabbits and forks and innumerable other kinds of things. And so there is thus far in principle no difficulty about the claim that we may learn to use the concept "act of God," as we have learned to use other concepts, and acquire the capacity to recognize exemplifying instances.

But of course—let it at once be granted—there are obvious and indeed immense differences between the concept of a divine act and such concepts as rabbit and fork. For one thing, rabbits and forks are objects—substances, if you like—whereas a divine act is an event. This is already a considerable conceptual contrast. And we must proceed to enlarge it still further. For the cognition of God recorded in the Bible is much wider in scope than an awareness of particular isolated events as being acts of God. Such divine acts are but points of peculiarly intense focus within a much wider awareness of existing in the presence of God. Indeed, the biblical cognition of God is typically mediated through the whole experience of the prophet or apostle after his call or conversion, even though within this totality there are specially vivid moments of awareness of God, some of which are evoked by striking or numinous events which thereby becomes miracles or theophanies. However, we are primarily concerned here with the wider and more continuous awareness of living within the ambience of the unseen God—with the sense of the presence of God—and this is surely something very unlike the awareness of forks and rabbits.

But although the sense of the presence of God is indeed very far removed from the recognition of forks and rabbits, it is already, I think, clear that there are connecting links in virtue of which the religious awareness need not be completely unintelligible to us. In its epistemological structure it exhibits a continuity with our awareness in other fields.

In seeking further to uncover and investigate this continuity we must now take note of another feature of experiencing-as, namely the fact that it occurs at various levels of awareness. By this I mean that as well as there being values of $x$ and $y$ such that to experience $A$ as $x$ is incompatible with experiencing it as $y$, because $x$ and $y$ are mutually exclusive alternatives, there are also values of $x$ and $y$ such that it is possible to experience $A$ as simultaneously $x$ and $y$. Here $y$ is supplementary to $x$, but on a different level. What is meant by "levels" in this context? That $y$ is on a higher level than $x$ means that the experiencing of $A$ as $y$ presupposes but goes beyond the experiencing of it as $x$. One or two examples may be useful at this point. As an example, first, of mutually exclusive experiencings-as, one cannot see the tuft of grass simultaneously as a tuft of grass and as a rabbit; or the person whose face we are watching as both furiously angry and profoundly delighted. On the other hand, as an example of supplementary experiencings-as, we may see what is moving above us in the sky as a bird; we may further see it as a hawk; and we may further see it as a hawk engaged in searching for prey; and if we are extremely expert bird watchers we may even see it as a hawk about to swoop down on something on the far side of that low hump of ground. These are successively higher-level recognitions in the sense that each later member of the list presupposes and goes beyond the previous one.

Now let us call the correlate of experiencing-as "significance," defining this by means of the notion of appropriate response. That is to say, to recognize what is before us as an $x$ involves being in a dispositional state to act in relation to it in a certain distinctive way or range of ways. For example, to recognize the object on the table as a fork is to be in a different dispositional state from that in which one is if one recognizes it as a fountain pen. One is prepared in the two cases for the object to display different characteristics, and to be surprised if it doesn't; and one is prepared to use it in different ways and on different occasions, and so on; and in general to recognize something as a this or a that (i.e. as significant in this way or in that way) involves being in a certain dispositional state in relation to it.

Our next step must be to shift attention from isolated objects as units of significance to larger and more complex units, namely situations.

A situation is composed of objects; but it is not simply any random collocation of objects. It is a group of objects which, when attended to as a group, has its own distinctive significance over and above the individual significances of its constituent members. That is to say, the situation evokes its own appropriate dispositional response.

As in the case of object significance there can be different levels of situational significance, with higher levels presupposing lower. An example that is directly relevant is the relation between the ethical significance of a human situation and its purely natural or physical significance. Think of any situation involving an element of moral obligation. Suppose, for example, that someone is caught at the foot of a steep cliff by an incoming tide and I at the top hear her cries for help. She asks me to run to the nearest telephone, ring the police and ask them to call out the lifeboat to rescue her. Consider this first at the purely natural or physical level. There are the cliff and the sea, a human creature liable in due course to be submerged by the rising tide, and her shouted appeals for help. And, morality apart, that is all that there is—just this particular pattern of physical events. However, as moral beings we are aware of more than that. As well as experiencing the physical events as physical events we also experience them as constituting a situation of moral claim upon ourselves. We experience the physical pattern as having ethical significance; and the dispositional response that it renders appropriate is to seek to help the trapped person in whatever way seems most practicable. We can, however, conceive of someone with no moral sense at all, who simply fails to be aware of the ethical significance of this situation. He would be interpreting or recognizing or experiencing-as only at the physical level of significance. And there would be no way of proving to someone who was thus morally defective that there is any such thing as moral obligation. No doubt an amoral creature could be induced by threats and promises to conform to a socially desirable pattern of behavior, but he could never be turned by these means into a moral being. In the end we can only say, tautologously, that a person is aware of the ethical significance of situations because one is a moral being; one experiences in moral terms because one is built that way.

The ethical is experienced as an order of significance which supervenes upon, interpenetrates and is mediated through the physical significance which it presupposes. And if on some occasion the moral character of a situation is not at first apparent to us, but dawns upon as we contemplate it, something happens that is comparable to the discovery of an emergent pattern in a puzzle picture. As the same lines and marks are there, but we have now come to see them as constituting an importantly new pattern, so the social situation is there with the same describable features, but we have now come to be aware of it as laying upon us an inescapable moral claim.

Now consider religious significance as a yet higher level of significance. It is a higher level of significance, adding a new dimension which both includes and transcends that of moral judgement, and yet on the other hand it does not form a simple continuation of the pattern we have already noted. As between natural and ethical significance it is safe to say that every instance of the latter presupposes some instance of the former; for there could be no moral situations if there were no physical situations to have moral significance. But as between ethical and religious significance the relationship is more complex. Not every moment of religious awareness is superimposed upon some occasion of moral obligation. Very often—and especially in the prophetic type of religion that we know in Judaism and Christianity—the sense of the presence of God does carry with it some specific or general moral demand. But we may also be conscious of God in solitude, surrounded only by the natural world, when the divine presence is borne in upon us by the vastness of the starry heavens above or the majestic beauty of a sunrise or a mountain range or some lake or forest scene, or other aspect of earth's marvelously varied face. Again, the sense of the presence of God may occur without any specific environmental context, when the mind is wrapt in prayer or meditation; for there is a contemplative and mystical awareness of God which is relatively independent of external circumstances. And indeed even within the prophetic type of religious experience there are also moments of encounter with God in nature and through solitary prayer as well as in the claims of the personal world. But on the other hand even when the sense of the presence of God has dawned upon us in solitude it is still normally true that it leads us back to our neighbors and often deepens the ethical significance of our relations with them. Thus the dispositional response which is part of the awareness of God is a response in terms of our involvement with our neighbours within our common environment. Even the awareness of God through nature and mystical contemplation leads eventually back to the service of God in the world.

Let us then continue to think here primarily of the prophetic awareness of God, since although this is not the only form of religious cognition it is the typically Judaic-Christian form. And let us test the notion of faith as religious experiencing-as by applying it to the particular history of faith which is reflected in the biblical records.

The Old Testament prophets were vividly conscious of Jahweh as acting in relation to the people of Israel in certain of the events of their time. Through the writings which recall their words and deeds we feel their overwhelmingly vivid consciousness of God as actively present in their contemporary history. It was God who, in the experience of Amos, was threatening selfish and complacent Israel with Assyrian conquest, while also offering mercy to such as should repent. It was God in his holy anger who, in the experience of Jeremiah, was bringing up the Babylonian army against Jerusalem and summoning his people to turn from their greed and wickedness. It is equally true of the other great prophets of the Old Testament that they were experiencing history, as it was taking place around them, as having a distinctively religious significance. Humanly explicable events were experienced as also acts of God, embodying his wrath or his mercy or his calling of the Jewish nation into covenant with him. The prophets experienced the religious significance of these events and declared it to the people; and this religious significance was always such that to see it meant being conscious of a sacred demand to behave in a new way towards one's neighbours.

It is, I think, important to realize that this prophetic interpretation of Hebrew history was not in the first place a philosophy of history, a theoretical pattern imposed retrospectively upon remembered or recorded events. It was in the first place the way in which the great prophets actually experienced and participated in these events at the time. Hosea did not *infer* Jahweh's mercy; second Isaiah did not *infer* his universal sovereignty; Jeremiah did not *infer* his holy righteousness—rather they were conscious of the Eternal as acting towards them, and towards their nation, in his mercy, in his holy righteousness, in his absolute sovereignty. They were, in other words, experiencing-as.

Again, in the New Testament, the primary instance of faith, the rock on which Christianity is based, consisted in seeing Jesus as the Christ. This was the faith of the disciples, epitomized in Peter's confession at Caesarea Philippi, whereby their experience of following Jesus was also an experience of being in the presence of God's personal purpose and claim and love. They may or may not at the time have used any of the terms that were later used in the New Testament writings to express this awareness—Messiah, Son of God, divine Logos. However, these terms point back to that original response, and the faith which they came to express must have been implicit within it. And once again this primary response of the first disciples to Jesus as Lord and Christ was not a theory about him which they adopted, but an experience out of which christian language and theory later grew. That he was their Lord was a fact of experience given in their personal dealings with him. And the special character of their way of seeing and responding to him, in contrast to that of others who never found him to be their Lord, is precisely the distinctive essence of christian faith.

The experiencing of Jesus of Nazareth as Lord—Jesus of Nazareth, that is to say, not as a theological symbol but in his historical concreteness, including his teaching concerning God and man—meant coming to share in some degree both his experiencing of life as the sphere of God's redemptive activity and his practical response to God's purposes in the world. What that involved for Jesus himself is spelled out in his life, and especially in the drama of his death. What it involves for Christians—for those who have begun to share Jesus' vision of the world in its relation to God—is indicated in his moral teaching. For this is simply a general description, with concrete examples drawn from the life of first-century Palestine, of the way in which someone tends spontaneously to behave who is consciously living in the presence of God as Jesus has revealed him.

I have now, I hope, offered at least a very rough outline of a conception of faith as the interpretative element within our cognitive religious experience. How is one to test such a theory, and how decide whether to accept or reject it? All that can be done is to spell out its consequences as fully as possible in the hope that the theory will then either founder under a weight of implausible corollaries, or else show its viability as it proceeds and float triumphantly on to acceptance. I have already tried to indicate its epistemological basis in the thesis that all experiencing is experiencing-as, and the way in which this thesis is relevant to the stream of distinctively religious experience recorded in the Bible. Let me now sketch some of its lines of implication in other directions.

It suggests, as I have already mentioned, a view of the Christian ethic as the practical corollary of the distinctively Christian vision of the world. Taking a hint from the modern dispositional analysis of belief we may say that to experience the world as having a certain character is, among other things, to be in a dispositional state to live in it in the manner which such a character in our environment renders appropriate. And to experience it in a way derived from Christ's own experience is accordingly to tend to live in the kind of way that he both taught and showed forth in his own life.

Another implication of this theory of faith concerns the nature of revelation. For in Christian theology revelation and faith are correlative concepts, faith being a human response to the divine activity of self-revelation. If faith is construed as a distinctively religious experiencing of life as mediating God's presence and activity, this clearly fits and even demands a *heilsgeschichtliche* conception of revelation as consisting in divine actions in human history. God is self-revealingly active within the world that he has made. But his actions are not overwhelmingly manifest and unmistakable; for then men would have no cognitive freedom in relation to their maker. Instead God always acts in such a way that man is free to see or fail to see the events in question as divine acts. The prophets were conscious of God at work in the happenings of their time; but many of their contemporaries were not. Again, the disciples were conscious of Jesus as the Christ; but the scribes and pharisees and the Romans were not. Thus revelation, as communication between God and man, only becomes actual when it meets an answering human response of faith; and the necessity for this response, making possible an uncompelled cognition of God's presence and activity, preserves the freedom and responsibility of the finite creature in relation to the infinite creator.

This in turn suggests an understanding of the special character of the Bible and of its inspiration. The Bible is a record of the stream of revelatory events that culminated in the coming of the Christ. But it differs from a secular account of the same strand of history in that the Bible is written throughout from the standpoint of faith. It describes this history as it was experienced from within by the prophets and then by the apostles. And the faith of the writers, whereby they saw the revelatory events *as* revelatory, is their inspiration. The uniqueness of the Bible is not due to any unique mode or quality of its writing but to the unique significance of the events of which it is the original documentary expression, which became revelatory through the faith of the biblical writers. As such the Bible mediates the same revelation to subsequent generations and is thus itself revelatory in a secondary sense, calling in its own turn for a response of faith.

This theory of faith can also be used to throw light on the nature of the miraculous. For a miracle, whatever else it may be, is an event through which we become vividly and immediately conscious of God as acting towards us. A startling happening, even if it should involve a suspension of natural law, does not constitute for us a miracle in the religious sense of the word if it fails to make us intensely aware of being in God's presence. In order to be miraculous, an event must be experienced as religiously significant. Indeed we may say that a miracle is any event that is experienced as a miracle; and this particular mode of experiencing-as is accordingly an essential element in the miraculous.

Finally, yet another application of this theory of faith is to the sacraments. In the sacraments some ordinary material object, bread or wine or water, is experienced as a vehicle of God's grace and becomes a focus of specially intense consciousness of God's overshadowing presence and purpose. A sacrament has in fact the same religious quality as a miracle but differs from other miracles in that it occurs within a liturgical context and is a product of ritual. In themselves, apart from the sacramental context of worshipping faith, the bread and wine or the water are ordinary material things; they have no magical properties. What happens in the sacramental event is that they are experienced as channels of divine grace. They thus invite a peculiarly direct moment of religious experiencing-as, fulfilling for subsequent believers the faith-eliciting and faith-nourishing function of the person of Christ in the experience of the first disciples.

Now I must repeat something that I said near the beginning of this chapter. What I have been attempting to formulate is an epistemological analysis of religious faith, not an argument for the validity of that faith. Faith, I have been suggesting, is the interpretative element within what the religious man reports as his experience of living in the presence of God. But whether that experience is veridical or illusory is another question. My own view is that it is as rational for the religious man to treat his experience of God as veridical as it is for him and others to treat their experience of the physical world as veridical. But that requires another argument, which I have not attempted to supply here.[3]

---

[3]I have, however, attempted to supply it in the last chapter of *Arguments for the Existence of God* (London: Macmillan, 1970, and New York: Herder and Herder, 1971), and more fully in *An Interpretation of Religion* (London: Macmillan, and New Haven: Yale University Press, 1989).

# 30

# *A Philosophy of Religious Pluralism*

Wilfred Cantwell Smith in his work on the concepts of religion and of religions has been responsible, more than any other one individual, for the change which has taken place within a single generation in the way in which many of us perceive the religious life of mankind.

Seen through pre–Cantwell Smith eyes there are a number of vast, long-lived historical entities or organisms known as Christianity, Hinduism, Islam, Buddhism, and so on. Each has an inner skeletal framework of beliefs, giving shape to a distinctive form of religious life, wrapped in a thick institutional skin which divides it from other religions and from the secular world within which they exist. Thus Buddhism, Islam, Christianity, and the rest, are seen as contraposed socio-religious entities which are the bearers of distinctive creeds; and every religious individual is a member of one or other of these mutually exclusive groups.

This way of seeing the religious life of humanity, as organized in a number of communities based upon rival sets of religious beliefs, leads to the posing of questions about religion in a certain way. For the beliefs which a religion professes are beliefs about God, or the Ultimate, and as such they

---

Reprinted, with the publisher's permission, from *The World's Religious Traditions: Essays in Honour of Wilfred Cantwell Smith*, ed. Frank Whaling (Edinburgh: T. & T. Clark, 1984).

define a way of human salvation or liberation and are accordingly a matter of spiritual life and death. Looking at the religions of the world, then, in the plural we are presented with competing claims to possess the saving truth. For each community believes that its own gospel is true and that other gospels are false in so far as they differ from it. Each believes that the way of salvation to which it witnesses is the authentic way, the only sure path to eternal blessedness. And so the proper question in face of this plurality of claims is, which is the true religion?

In practice, those who are concerned to raise this question are normally fully convinced that theirs is the true religion; so that for them the task is to show the spiritual superiority of their own creed and the consequent moral superiority of the community which embodies it. A great deal of the mutual criticism of religions, and of the derogatory assessment of one by another, has been in fulfilment of this task.

This view of mankind's religious life as divided into great contraposed entities, each claiming to be the true religion, is not however the only possible way of seeing the religious situation. Cantwell Smith has offered an alternative vision.

He shows first that the presently dominant conceptuality has a history that can be traced back to the European Renaissance. It was then that the different streams of religious life began to be reified in western thought as solid structures called Christianity, Judaism, and so forth. And having reified their own faith in this way westerners have then exported the notion of "a religion" to the rest of the world, causing others to think of themselves as belonging to the Hindu, or the Confucian, or the Buddhist religion, and so on, over against others. But an alternative perception can divide the scene differently. It sees something of vital religious significance taking different forms all over the world within the contexts of the different historical traditions. This "something of vital religious significance" Cantwell Smith calls faith. I would agree with some of his critics that this is not the ideal word for it; for "faith" is a term that is more at home in the Semitic than in the Indian family of traditions and which has, as his own historical researches have shown, become badly overintellectualized. But I take it that he uses the term to refer to the spiritual state, or existential condition, constituted by a person's present response to the ultimate divine Reality. This ranges from the negative response of a self-enclosed consciousness which is blind to the divine presence, whether beyond us or in the depths of our own being, to a positive openness to the Divine which gradually transforms us and which is called salvation or liberation or enlightenment. This transformation is essentially the same within the different religious contexts within which it occurs: I would define it formally as the transformation of human existence from self-centeredness to Reality-centeredness. This is the event or process of vital significance which one can see to be occurring in individuals all over the world, taking different forms within the contexts of the different perceptions of the Ultimate made available by the various religious traditions.

These cumulative traditions themselves are the other thing that one sees with the aid of the new conceptuality suggested by Cantwell Smith. They are distinguishable strands of human history in each of which a multitude of religious and cultural elements interact to form a distinctive pattern, constituting, say, the Hindu, Buddhist, Confucian, Jewish, Christian, or Muslim tradition. These traditions are not static entities but living movements; and they are not tightly homogeneous but have each become in the course of time internally highly various. Thus there are large differences between, for example, Buddhism in the time of Gautama and Buddhism after the development of the Mahāyāna and its expansion northwards into China; or between the Christian movement in Roman Palestine and that in medieval Europe. And there are large differences today between, say, Zen and Amida Buddhism in Japan, or between Southern Baptist and Northern Episcopalian Christianity in the United States. Indeed, since we cannot always avoid using the substantives, we might do well to speak of Buddhisms, Christianities, and so on, in the plural. A usage consonant with Cantwell Smith's analysis has however already become widespread, and many of us now often prefer to speak not of Christianity but of the Christian tradition, the Hindu tradition, and so on, when referring to these historically identifiable strands of history.

These cumulative traditions are composed of a rich complex of inner and outer elements cohering in a distinctive living pattern which includes structures of belief, lifestyles, scriptures and their interpretations, liturgies, cultic celebrations, myths, music, poetry, architecture, literature, remembered history and its heroes. Thus the traditions constitute religious cultures, each with its own unique history and ethos. And each such tradition creates human beings in its own image. For we are not human in general, participating in an eternal Platonic essence of humanity. We are human in one or other of the various concrete ways of being human which constitute the cultures of the earth. There is a Chinese way of being human, an African way, an Arab way, a European way, or ways, and so on. These are not fixed molds but living organisms which develop and interact over the centuries, so that the patterns of human life change, usually very slowly but sometimes with startling rapidity. But we are all formed in a hundred ways of which we are not normally aware by the culture into which we were born, by which we are fed, and with which we interact.

Let us then enter, with Cantwell Smith, into the experiment of thinking, on the one hand, of "faith," or human response to the divine, which in its positive and negative forms is salvation and non-salvation and, on the other hand, of the cumulative religious traditions within which this occurs; and let us ask what the relation is between these two realities—on the one hand salvation/liberation and on the other the cumulative traditions.

In various different forms this question has been much discussed within the Christian world, particularly during the last hundred and fifty years or so as Christians have become increasingly conscious of the continuing reality of the other great religious traditions. For this period has seen renaissances within the Hindu and Buddhist worlds—to an important extent, it would seem, in reaction to eighteenth- and nineteenth-century Christian imperialism—and a resurgence of Islam is currently taking place. These developments have precipitated intense debate among Christian thinkers in which many different options have been and are being canvassed. Both because of the fullness of this discussion within Christianity, and because I am myself a Christian and am concerned with the problem from a Christian point of view, I propose to describe the main options in Christian terms. They are three in number.

The first, which we may call "exclusivism," relates salvation/liberation exclusively to one particular tradition, so that it is an article of faith that salvation is restricted to this one group, the rest of mankind being either left out of account or explicitly excluded from the sphere of salvation. The most emphatic and influential expression of such a faith occurred in the Catholic dogma *Extra ecclesiam nulla salus* (outside the Church, no salvation) and the corresponding assumption of the nineteenth-century Protestant missionary movement: outside Christianity, no salvation. In these developments Christian thought went beyond a mere overlooking of non-Christian humanity—which might perhaps simply be attributed to restricted vision—to a positive doctrine of the unsaved status of that wider human majority. Exclusiveness of this strong kind was supported by a juridical conception of salvation. If salvation consists in a change of status in the eyes of God from the guilt of participation in Adam's original sin to a forgiveness made possible by Christ's sacrifice on the cross, the appropriation of which is conditional upon a personal response of faith in Christ, this salvation can very naturally be seen as restricted to the Christian faith community. If on the other hand salvation is understood as the actual transformation of human life from self-centeredness to Reality-centeredness, this is not necessarily restricted within the boundaries of any one historical tradition. One cannot know *a priori* where or to what extent it occurs; one can only look at the living of human life in its endlessly varied circumstances and try to discern the signs of this transformation. Except in those whom we call saints, in whom the transformation is sufficiently advanced to be publicly evident, such discernment is often extremely difficult; for salvation/liberation, understood in this way, is to be found in many stages and degrees in the varying qualities of true humanity, often realized more in some areas of life than in others, and with advances and regressions, efforts and lapses in all the respects in which human beings develop and change through the experience of life in time. There may of course—as the Hindu and Buddhist traditions generally teach—be a final moment of enlightenment in which the transformation is completed and Reality-centeredness definitively supersedes the last remnants of self-centeredness. But, even if this should be a universal pattern, the journey leading towards that final moment must be long and slow; and progress on the journey can to some extent be humanly discerned as the process of salvation gradually taking place. This understanding of salvation/liberation as the actual transformation of human beings is more easily open than is the juridical understanding of it to the possibility that the salvific process may be taking place not only within one tradition but within a number of traditions.

Christian exclusivism has now largely faded out from the "mainline" churches, but is still powerful in many of the "marginal" fundamentalistic sects; and it should be added that the "margins" of Christianity are probably more extensive today than ever before.

However, we may now turn to a second Christian answer to our question, which can be labeled "inclusivism." This can be expressed in terms either of a juridical or of a transformation-of-human-existence conception of salvation. In the former terms it is the view that God's forgiveness and acceptance of humanity have been made possible by Christ's death, but that the benefits of this sacrifice are not confined to those who respond to it with an explicit act of faith. The juridical transaction of Christ's atonement covered *all* human sin, so that all human beings are now open to God's mercy, even though they may never have heard of Jesus Christ and why he died on the cross of Calvary. I take it that it is this form of inclusivism that the present Pope was endorsing in his first encyclical when he said that "man—every man without any exception whatever—has been redeemed by Christ, and because with man—with each man without any exception whatever—Christ is in a way united, even when man is unaware of it."[1] This statement could however also be an expression of the other form of Christian inclusivism, which accepts the understanding of salvation as the gradual transformation of human life and sees this as taking place not only within Christian history but also within the contexts of all the other great world traditions. It regards this, however, wherever it happens, as the work of Christ—the universal divine Logos, the Second Person of the divine Trinity, who became incarnate in Jesus of Nazareth. Thus we can speak of "the unknown Christ of Hinduism" and of the other traditions, and indeed the unknown Christ within all creative transformations of individuals and societies. And, if we ask how this differs from simply saying that within all these different streams of human life there is a creative and re-creative response to the divine Reality, the answer of this kind of Christian inclusivism is that Christians are those,

---

[1] *Redemptor Hominis,* Vatican Polyglot Press trs. (London: Catholic Truth Society, 1979), para. 14.

uniquely, who are able to identify the source of salvation because they have encountered that source as personally incarnate in Jesus Christ.

Both forms of inclusivism do, however, involve certain inner strains and certain awkward implications. How are they to be combined with the traditional *Extra ecclesiam* dogma? The best known attempt is that of Karl Rahner, with his concept of the "anonymous Christian." Those who do not have an explicit Christian faith but who nevertheless seek, consciously or unconsciously, to do God's will can be regarded as, so to speak, honorary Christians—and this even though they do not so regard themselves and even though they may insist that they are not Christians but Muslims, Jews, Hindus, or whatever. Rahner's is a brave attempt to attain an inclusivist position which is in principle universal but which does not thereby renounce the old exclusivist dogma. But the question is whether in this new context the old dogma has not been so emptied of content as no longer to be worth affirming. When salvation is acknowledged to be taking place without any connection with the Christian Church or Gospel, in people who are living on the basis of quite other faiths, is it not a somewhat empty gesture to insist upon affixing a Christian label to them? Further, having thus labeled them, why persist in the aim of gathering all humankind into the Christian Church? Once it is accepted that salvation does not depend upon this, the conversion of the people of the other great world faiths to Christianity hardly seems the best way of spending one's energies.

The third possible answer to the question of the relation between salvation/liberation and the cumulative religious traditions can best be called pluralism. As a Christian position this can be seen as an acceptance of the further conclusion to which inclusivism points. If we accept that salvation/liberation is taking place within all the great religious traditions, why not frankly acknowledge that there is a plurality of saving human responses to the ultimate divine Reality? Pluralism, then, is the view that the transformation of human existence from self-centeredness to Reality-centeredness is taking place in different ways within the contexts of all the great religious traditions. There is not merely one way but a plurality of ways of salvation or liberation. In Christian theological terms, there is a plurality of divine revelations, making possible a plurality of forms of saving human response.

What, however, makes it difficult for Christians to move from inclusivism to pluralism, holding the majority of Christian theologians today in the inclusivist position despite its evident logical instability, is of course the traditional doctrine of the Incarnation, together with its protective envelope, the doctrine of the Trinity. For in its orthodox form, as classically expressed at the Councils of Nicaea and Chalcedon, the incarnational doctrine claims that Jesus was God incarnate, the Second Person of the Triune God living a human life. It is integral to this faith that there has been (and will be) no other divine incarnation. This makes Christianity unique in that it, alone among the religions of the world, was founded by God in person. Such a uniqueness would seem to demand Christian exclusivism—for must God not want all human beings to enter the way of salvation which he has provided for them? However, since such exclusivism seems so unrealistic in the light of our knowledge of the wider religious life of mankind, many theologians have moved to some form of inclusivism, but now feel unable to go further and follow the argument to its conclusion in the frank acceptance of pluralism. The break with traditional missionary attitudes and long-established ecclesiastical and liturgical language would, for many, be so great as to be prohibitive.

There is, however, the possibility of an acceptable Christian route to religious pluralism in work which has already been done, and which is being done, in the field of Christology with motivations quite other than to facilitate pluralism, and on grounds which are internal to the intellectual development of Christianity. For there is a decisive watershed between what might be called all-or-nothing Christologies and degree Christologies. The all-or-nothing principle is classically expressed in the Chalcedonian Definition, according to which Christ is "to be acknowledged in Two Natures," "Consubstantial with the Father according to his Deity, Consubstantial with us according to his Humanity." Substance is an all-or-nothing notion, in that A either is or is not composed of the same substance, either has or does not have the same essential nature, as B. Using this all-or-nothing conceptuality Chalcedon attributed to Christ two complete natures, one divine and the other human, being in his divine nature of one substance with God the Father. Degree Christologies, on the other hand, apply the term "incarnation" to the activity of God's Spirit or of God's grace in human lives, so that the divine will is done on earth. This kind of reinterpretation has been represented in recent years by, for example, the "paradox of grace" Christology of Donald Baillie (in *God Was in Christ*, 1948) and the "inspiration Christology" of Geoffrey Lampe (in *God as Spirit*, 1977). In so far as a human being is open and responsive to God, so that God is able to act in and through that individual, we can speak of the embodiment in human life of God's redemptive activity. And in Jesus this "paradox of grace"—the paradox expressed by St. Paul when he wrote "it was not I, but the grace of God which is in me" (1 Corinthians 15:10)—or the inspiration of God's Spirit, occurred to a startling extent. The paradox, or the inspiration, are not however confined to the life of Jesus; they are found, in varying degrees, in all free human response to God. Christologies of the same broad family occur in the work of Norman Pittenger (*The Word Incarnate*, 1957), John Knox (*The Humanity and Divinity of Christ*, 1967), and earlier in John Baillie (*The Place of Jesus Christ in Modern Christianity*, 1929), and more recently in the authors of *The Myth of God Incarnate* (1977).

These modern degree Christologies were not in fact for the most part developed in order to facilitate a Christian acceptance of religious pluralism.

They were developed as alternatives to the old substance Christology, in which so many difficulties, both historical and philosophical, had become apparent. They claim to be compatible with the teachings of Jesus and of the very early Church, and to avoid the intractable problem, generated by a substance Christology, of the relation between Jesus' two natures. But, as an unintended consequence, degree Christologies open up the possibility of seeing God's activity in Jesus as being of the same kind as God's activity in other great human mediators of the divine. The traditional Christian claim to the unique superiority of Christ and of the Christian tradition is not of course precluded by a degree Christology; for it may be argued (as it was, for example, by both Baillie and Lampe) that Christ was the *supreme* instance of the paradox of grace or of the inspiration of the Spirit, so that Christianity is still assumed to be the *best* context of salvation/liberation. But, whereas, starting from the substance Christology, the unique superiority of Christ and the Christian Church are guaranteed *a priori*, starting from a degree Christology they have to be established by historical evidence. Whether this can in fact be done is, clearly, an open question. It would indeed be an uphill task today to establish that we know enough about the inner and outer life of the historical Jesus, and of the other founders of great religious traditions, to be able to make any such claim; and perhaps an even more uphill task to establish from the morally ambiguous histories of each of the great traditions, complex mixtures of good and evil as each has been, that one's own tradition stands out as manifestly superior to all others.

I think, then, that a path exists along which Christians can, if they feel so drawn, move to an acceptance of religious pluralism. Stated philosophically such a pluralism is the view that the great world faiths embody different perceptions and conceptions of, and correspondingly different responses to, the Real or the Ultimate from within the major variant cultural ways of being human; and that within each of them the transformation of human existence from self-centeredness to Reality-centeredness is manifestly taking place—and taking place, so far as human observation can tell, to much the same extent. Thus the great religious traditions are to be regarded as alternative soteriological "spaces" within which, or "ways" along which, men and women can find salvation/liberation/enlightenment/fulfilment.

But how can such a view be arrived at? Are we not proposing a picture reminiscent of the ancient allegory of the blind men and the elephant, in which each runs his hands over a different part of the animal, and identifies it differently, a leg as a tree, the trunk as a snake, the tail as a rope, and so on? Clearly, in the story the situation is being described from the point of view of someone who can observe both elephant and blind men. But where is the vantage point from which one can observe both the divine Reality and the different limited human standpoints from which that Reality is being variously perceived? The advocate of the pluralist understanding cannot pretend to any such cosmic vision. How then does he profess to know that the situation is indeed as he depicts it? The answer is that he does not profess to *know* this, if by knowledge we mean infallible cognition. Nor indeed can anyone else properly claim to have knowledge, in this sense, of either the exclusivist or the inclusivist picture. All of them are, strictly speaking, hypotheses. The pluralist hypothesis is arrived at inductively. One starts from the fact that many human beings experience life in relation to a limitlessly greater transcendent Reality—whether the direction of transcendence be beyond our present existence or within its hidden depths. In theory such religious experience is capable of a purely naturalistic analysis which does not involve reference to any reality other than the human and the natural. But to participate by faith in one of the actual streams of religious experience—in my case, the Christian stream—is to participate in it as an experience of transcendent Reality. I think that there is in fact a good argument for the rationality of trusting one's own religious experience, together with that of the larger tradition within which it occurs, so as both to believe and to live on the basis of it; but I cannot develop that argument here.[2] Treating one's own form of religious experience, then, as veridical—as an experience (however dim, like "seeing through a glass, darkly") of transcendent divine Reality—one then has to take account of the fact that there are other great streams of religious experience which take different forms, are shaped by different conceptualities, and embodied in different institutions, art forms, and lifestyles. In other words, besides one's own religion, sustained by its distinctive form of religious experience, there are also other religions, through each of which flows the life blood of a different form of religious experience. What account is one to give of this plurality?

At this point the three answers that we discussed above become available again: exclusivism, inclusivism and pluralism. The exclusivist answer is that only one's own form of religious experience is an authentic contact with the Transcendent, other forms being delusory: the naturalistic interpretation applies to those other forms, but not to ours. This is a logically possible position; but clearly it is painfully vulnerable to the charge of being entirely arbitrary. It thus serves the cause of general scepticism, as David Hume noted with regard to claims that the miracles of one's own religion are genuine whilst those of others are spurious.[3]

Moving to the inclusivist answer, this would suggest that religious experience in general does indeed constitute a contact with the Transcendent, but that this contact occurs in its purest and most salvifically effective form within one's own tradition, other forms having value to the varying extents

---

[2] See Michael Goulder and John Hick, *Why Believe in God?* (London: SCM Press, 1983).
[3] David Hume, *An Enquiry Concerning Human Understanding*, x. ii. 95. Para. 95.

to which they approximate to ours. This is a more viable position than the previous one, and less damaging to the claim that religion is not a human projection but a genuine human response to transcendent Reality. There is however a range of facts which do not fit easily into the inclusivist theory, namely the changed and elevated lives, moving from self-centeredness towards Reality-centeredness, within the other great religious traditions. Presumably there must be a strong correlation between the authenticity of the forms of religious experience and their spiritual and moral fruits. It would then follow from the inclusivist position that there should be a far higher incidence and quality of saintliness in one tradition—namely, that in which contact with the Transcendent occurs in "its purest and most salvifically effective form"—than in the others. But this does not seem to be the case. There is of course no reliable census of saints! Nor indeed is the concept of a saint by any means clear and unproblematic; very different profiles of saintliness have operated at different times and in different places. But if we look for the transcendence of egoism and a recentering in God or in the transcendent Real, then I venture the proposition that, so far as human observation and historical memory can tell, this occurs to about the same extent within each of the great world traditions.

If this is so, it prompts us to go beyond inclusivism to a pluralism which recognizes a variety of human religious contexts within which salvation/liberation takes place.

But such a pluralistic hypothesis raises many questions. What is this divine Reality to which all the great traditions are said to be oriented? Can we really equate the personal Yahweh with the non-personal Brahman, Shiva with the Tao, the Holy Trinity with the Buddhist Trikāya, and all with one another? Indeed, do not the Eastern and Western faiths deal incommensurably with different problems?

As these questions indicate, we need a pluralistic theory which enables us to recognize and be fascinated by the manifold differences between the religious traditions, with their different conceptualisations, their different modes of religious experience, and their different forms of individual and social response to the divine. I should like in these final pages to suggest the ground plan of such a theory—a theory which is, I venture to think, fully compatible with the central themes of Cantwell Smith's thought.

Each of the great religious traditions affirms that in addition to the social and natural world of our ordinary human experience there is a limitlessly greater and higher Reality beyond or within us, in relation to which or to whom is our highest good. The ultimately real and the ultimately valuable are one, and to give oneself freely and totally to this One is our final salvation/liberation/enlightenment/fulfilment. Further, each tradition is conscious that the divine Reality exceeds the reach of our earthly speech and thought. It cannot be encompassed in human concepts. It is infinite, eternal, limitlessly rich beyond the scope of our finite conceiving or experiencing. Let us then both avoid the particular names used within the particular traditions and yet use a term which is consonant with the faith of each of them—Ultimate Reality, or the Real.

Let us next adopt a distinction that is to be found in different forms and with different emphases within each of the great traditions, the distinction between the Real *an sich* (in him/her/itself) and the Real as humanly experienced and thought. In Christian terms this is the distinction between God in God's infinite and eternal self-existent being, "prior" to and independent of creation, and God as related to and known by us as creator, redeemer and sanctifier. In Hindu thought it is the distinction between *nirguna* Brahman, the Ultimate in itself, beyond all human categories, and *saguna* Brahman, the Ultimate as known to finite consciousness as a personal deity, Isvara. In Taoist thought, "The Tao that can be expressed is not the eternal Tao" (*Tao-Te Ching*, 1). There are also analogous distinctions in Jewish and Muslim mystical thought in which the Real *an sich* is called *en Soph* and *al Haqq*. In Mahāyāna Buddhism there is the distinction between the *dharmakāya*, the eternal cosmic Buddha-nature, which is also the infinite Void (*sūnyatā*), and on the other hand the realm of heavenly Buddha figures (*sambhogakāya*) and their incarnations in the earthly Buddhas (*nirmānakāya*). This varied family of distinctions suggests the perhaps daring thought that the Real *an sich* is one but is nevertheless capable of being humanly experienced in a variety of ways. This thought lies at the heart of the pluralistic hypothesis which I am suggesting.

The next point of which we need to take account is the creative part that thought, and the range of concepts in terms of which it functions, plays in the formation of conscious experience. It was above all Immanuel Kant who brought this realization into the stream of modern reflection, and it has since been confirmed and amplified by innumerable studies, not only in general epistemology but also in cognitive psychology, in the sociology of knowledge, and in the philosophy of science. The central fact, of which the epistemology of religion also has to take account, is that our environment is not reflected in our consciousness in a simple and straightforward way, just as it is, independently of our perceiving it. At the physical level, out of the immense richness of structure and detail around us, only that minute selection that is relevant to our biological survival and flourishing affects our senses; and these inputs are interpreted in the mind/brain to produce our conscious experience of the familiar world in which we live. Its character as an environment within which we can learn to behave appropriately can be called its *meaning* for us. This all-important dimension of meaning, which begins at the physical level as the habitability of the material world, continues at the personal, or social, level of awareness as the moral significance of the situations of our life, and at the religious level as a consciousness of the ultimate meaning of each situation and of our situation as a whole in relation to the divine Reality. This latter consciousness is not however a general consciousness of the divine, but always takes specific forms; and, as in the case of the awareness of the physical and of the ethical meaning of our environment, such consciousness has an essential dispositional aspect. To experience in this way rather than in that involves being in a state of readiness to behave in a particular range of ways, namely that which is appropriate to our environment having the particular character that we perceive (or of course misperceive) it to have. Thus to be aware of the divine as "the God and Father of our Lord Jesus Christ," in so far as this is the operative awareness which determines our dispositional state, is to live in the kind of way described by Jesus in his religious and moral teaching—in trust towards God and in love towards our neighbours.

How are these various specific forms of religious awareness formed? Our hypothesis is that they are formed by the presence of the divine Reality, this presence coming to consciousness in terms of the different sets of religious concepts and structures of religious meaning that operate within the different religious traditions of the world. If we look at the range of actual human religious experience and ask ourselves what basic concepts and what concrete images have operated in its genesis, I would suggest that we arrive at something like the following answer. There are, first, the two basic religious concepts which between them dominate the entire range of the forms of religious experience. One is the concept of Deity, or God, i.e., the Real as personal; and the other is the concept of the Absolute, i.e., the Real as non-personal. (The term "Absolute" is by no means ideal for the purpose, but is perhaps the nearest that we have.) We do not, however, in actual religious experience, encounter either Deity in general or the Absolute in general, but always in specific forms. In Kantian language, each general concept is schematized, or made concrete. In Kant's own analysis of sense experience the schematisation of the basic categories is in terms of time; but religious experience occurs at a much higher level of meaning, presupposing and going beyond physical meaning and involving much more complex and variable modes of dispositional response. Schematization or concretization here is in terms of "filled" human time, or history, as diversified into the different cultures and civilizations of the earth. For there are different concrete ways of being human and of participating in human history, and within these different ways the presence of the divine Reality is experienced in characteristically different ways.

To take the concept of God first, this becomes concrete as the range of specific deities to which the history of religion bears witness. Thus the Real as personal is known in the Christian tradition as God the Father; in Judaism as Adonai; in Islam as Allah, the Qur'ānic Revealer; in the Indian traditions as Shiva, or Vishnu, or Paramātmā, and under the many other lesser images of deity which in different regions of India concretise different aspects of the divine nature. This range of personal deities who are the foci of worship within the theistic traditions constitutes the range of the divine *personae* in relation to mankind. Each *persona*, in his or her historical concreteness, lives within the corporate experience of a particular faith community. Thus the Yahweh *persona* exists and has developed in interaction with the Jewish people. He is a part of their history, and they are a part of his; and he cannot be extracted from this historical context. Shiva, on the other hand, is a quite different divine *persona*, existing in the experience of hundreds of millions of people in the Shaivite stream of Indian religious life. These two *personae*, Yahweh and Shiva, live within different worlds of faith, partly creating and partly created by the features of different human cultures, being responded to in different patterns of life, and being integral to different strands of historical experience. Within each of these worlds of faith great numbers of people find the ultimate meaning of their existence, and are carried through the crises of life and death; and within this process many are, in varying degrees, challenged and empowered to move forward on the way of salvation/liberation from self-centeredness to Reality-centeredness. From the pluralist point of view Yahweh and Shiva are not rival gods, or rival claimants to be the one and only God, but rather two different concrete historical *personae* in terms of which the ultimate divine Reality is present and responded to by different large historical communities within different strands of the human story.

This conception of divine *personae*, constituting (in Kantian language) different divine phenomena in terms of which the one divine noumenon is humanly experienced, enables us to acknowledge the degree of truth within the various projection theories of religion from Feuerbach through Freud to the present day. An element of human projection colors our mental images of God, accounting for their anthropomorphic features—for example, as male or female. But human projection does not—on this view—bring God into existence; rather it affects the ways in which the independently existing divine Reality is experienced.

Does this epistemological pattern of the schematization of a basic religious concept into a range of particular correlates of religious experience apply also to the non-theistic traditions? I suggest that it does. Here the general concept, the Absolute, is schematized in actual religious experience to form the range of divine *impersonae*—Brahman, the Dharma, the Tao, *nirvāna, sūnyatā,* and so on—which are experienced within the Eastern traditions. The structure of these *impersonae* is, however, importantly different from that of the *personae*. A divine *persona* is concrete, implicitly finite, sometimes visualizable and even capable of being pictured. A divine *impersona*, on the other hand, is not a "thing" in contrast to a person. It is the infinite being—consciousness—bliss (*saccidānanda*) of Brahman; or the beginningless and endless process of cosmic change (*pratītya samutpāda*) of

Buddhist teaching; or again the ineffable "further shore" of *nirvāna*, or the eternal Buddha nature (*dharmakāya*); or the ultimate Emptiness (*sūnyatā*) which is also the fullness or suchness of the world; or the eternal principle of the Tao. It is thus not so much an entity as a field of spiritual force, or the ultimate reality of everything, that which gives final meaning and joy. These non-personal conceptions of the Ultimate inform modes of consciousness varying from the advaitic experience of becoming one with the Infinite, to the Zen experience of finding a total reality in the present concrete moment of existence in the ordinary world. And according to the pluralistic hypothesis these different modes of experience constitute different experiences of the Real as non- or trans-personal. As in the case of the divine *personae,* they are formed by different religious conceptualities which have developed in inter-action with different spiritual disciplines and methods of meditation. The evidence that a range of *impersonae* of the one Ultimate Reality are involved in the non-theistic forms of religious experience, rather than the direct unme-diated awareness of Reality itself, consists precisely in the differences be-tween the experiences reported within the different traditions. How is it that a "direct experience" of the Real can take such different forms? One could of course at this point revert to the exclusivism or the inclusivism whose limitations we have already noted. But the pluralist answer will be that even the most advanced form of mystical experience, as an experience undergone by an embodied consciousness whose mind/brain has been conditioned by a particular religious tradition, must be affected by the conceptual framework and spiritual training provided by that tradition, and accordingly takes these different forms. In other words the Real is experienced not *an sich,* but in terms of the various non-personal images or concepts that have been generated at the interface between the Real and different patterns of human consciousness.

These many different perceptions of the Real, both theistic and non-the-istic, can only establish themselves as authentic by their soteriological effi-cacy. The great world traditions have in fact all proved to be realms within which or routes along which people are enabled to advance in the transition from self-centeredness to Reality-centeredness. And, since they reveal the Real in such different lights, we must conclude that they are independently valid. Accordingly, by attending to other traditions than one's own one may become aware of other aspects or dimensions of the Real, and of other possibilities of response to the Real, which had not been made effectively available by one's own tradition. Thus a mutual mission of the sharing of experiences and insights can proceed through the growing network of inter-faith dialogue and the interactions of the faith communities. Such mutual mission does not aim at conversion—although occasionally individual con-versions, in all directions, will continue to occur—but at mutual enrichment and at cooperation in face of the urgent problems of human survival in a just and sustainable world society.

There are many topics which I have not had space to take up in this chapter. I have spoken of "the great world traditions"; but what about the other smaller ones, including the many new religious movements which are springing up around us today? And what about the great secular faiths of Marxism and Maoism and humanism? Again, I have spoken of salvation/liberation as the transformation of human existence from self-centeredness to Reality-centeredness; but what about the social and political dimensions of this transformation? These are among the many important questions which any complete philosophy of religious pluralism must answer. But I hope that in this paper I may have said enough to indicate the possible fruitfulness of this general standpoint, a standpoint to which Wilfred Cantwell Smith's work has contributed so centrally and so notably.

# Sallie McFague

Sallie McFague (1933–     ) is an influential contemporary feminist
theologian and philosopher of religion.

## 31

# *Toward a Metaphorical Theology*

There is a God. There is no God. Where is the problem? I am quite sure that there
is a God in the sense that I am sure my love is no illusion. I am quite sure there
is no God in the sense that I am sure there is nothing which resembles what I
can conceive when I say that word.[1]

Simone Weil, in her book *Waiting for God,* states the problem of religious
language in the classic way. As a religious person, she is certain that her love
for God is not an illusion, but she is equally certain that none of her conceptions of the divine resembles God. Her comments are in the great tradition of
deeply religious people, and especially the mystics of all religious traditions,
who feel conviction at the level of experience, at the level of worship, but great
uncertainty at the level of words adequate to express the reality of God.

Augustine, the great Bishop of Hippo, notes that even the person who
says the most about God is but "dumb," and yet, he adds, our only alternatives are to speak in halting, inadequate words or to remain silent. The
Judeo-Christian tradition, more than many other religious traditions, has
chosen not to remain silent. In fact, this tradition and especially Christianity,
and within Christianity especially Protestantism, has focused on and at times
been obsessed by words, both "the Word of God" and human words about
God.

---

Reprinted by permission from *Metaphorical Theology* by Sallie McFague, copyright © 1982
Fortress Press (paper $11.95). Sallie McFAgue, *Metaphorical Theology: Models of God in
Religious Language* (Philadelphia: Fortress Press, 1982), Chapter 1. Reprinted with permis-
sion.

[1]Simone Weil, *Waiting for God* (New York: Harper & Row, 1973), p. 32.

## THE PROBLEM OF RELIGIOUS LANGUAGE

Increasingly, however, religious language is a problem for us, a problem of a somewhat different kind than the classical one. For most of us, it is not a question of being sure of God while being unsure of our language about God. Rather, we are unsure both at the experiential and the expressive levels. We are unsure at the experiential level because we are, even the most religious of us, secular in ways our foremothers and forefathers were not. We do not live in a sacramental universe in which the things of this world, its joys and catastrophes, harvests and famines, births and deaths, are understood as connected to and permeated by divine power and love. Our experience, our daily experience, is for the most part nonreligious. Most of us go through the days accepting our fortunes and explaining our world without direct reference to God. If we experience God at all it tends to be at a private level and in a sporadic way; the natural and public events of our world do not stand for or image God.

Certainly we cannot return to the time of the sacramental universe; but apart from a *religious context* of some kind, religious language becomes both idolatrous and irrelevant. It becomes *idolatrous* because without a sense of awe, wonder, and mystery, we forget the inevitable distance between our words and the divine reality. It becomes *irrelevant* because without a sense of the immanence of the divine in our lives, we find language about God empty and meaningless. It is no accident, then, that the mystics in all religious traditions have been the most perceptive on the question of religious language. Aware as they are of the transcendence of God, they have not been inclined to identify our words with God; in fact, their tendency is more often to refuse any similarity between our words and the divine reality. Simone Weil stands foursquare in this tradition when she says there is "nothing" which resembles her thoughts about God. The mystics, however, have also been the most imaginative and free in their language about God, finding all sorts of language relevant. As Augustine notes, we must use all the best images available to us in order to say *something* about the divine. The mystics have also not restricted their language about God to biblical or traditional imagery, for the experience of God, the certainty and the immediacy of it, has been the basis for new and powerful religious language.

The *primary context*, then, for any discussion of religious language is worship. Unless one has a sense of the mystery surrounding existence, of the profound inadequacy of all our thoughts and words, one will most likely identify God with our words: God *becomes* father, mother, lover, friend. Unless one has a sense of the nearness of God, the overwhelming sense of the way God pervades and permeates our very being, one will not find religious images significant: the power of the images for God of father, mother, lover, friend will not be appreciated. Apart from a religious context, religious language will inevitably go awry either in the direction of idolatry or irrelevancy or both.

There is, however, another critical context for religious language, one that has not been as central in the classical tradition and that does not surface in the quotation by Weil. In the broadest sense, we could call this the *interpretive context*. It is the context that recognizes that we who attempt to speak about God are social, cultural, and historical beings with particular perspectives influenced by a wide range of factors. The interpretive context within religious faiths has usually been limited to the "tradition," meaning the church or another institution which has set the interpretive precedents for what is proper (orthodox) or improper (heretical) religious language. In the last two hundred years, however, the interpretive context has increased greatly as people have realized the relativity of perspectives. With the introduction of historical criticism of religious texts, we became aware of the relativity of the words and images in sacred Scriptures, that these texts were written by limited people who expressed their experiences of divine reality in the manners and mores of their historical times.

Most recently, we have become conscious, by deepening our awareness of the *plurality* of perspectives, of dimensions of interpretation which had been largely submerged. That is to say, it is not only our time and place in history that influences our religious language, but also our class, race, and sex; our nationality, education, and family background; our interests, prejudices, and concerns. We have become aware, for instance, of the varying interests that determined the perspectives of New Testament writers. They not only saw their religious experience through the glasses of first-century Palestine but also through the refractions provided by their own individual histories and concerns. Consciousness of the relativity and plurality of interpretations forces us to recognize that religious language is not just the halting attempts by "Christians" to say something appropriate about God, but is the halting attempts by specific individuals: by Paul, a first-century convert from Judaism, who had great empathy with the problems of Jewish Christians but little sympathy for women or slave Christians; by Julian of Norwich, a medieval woman mystic, who spoke of "our tender Mother Jesus"; by Reinhold Niebuhr, a twentieth-century preacher from Detroit, whose experience with American capitalism caused him to see human sinfulness as the basis for political "realism"; by Mary Daly, a twentieth-century, Catholic-educated feminist, who sees the history of the world's religions as an exercise in misogyny. If we lose sight of the relativity and plurality of the interpretive context, our religious language will, as with the loss of the religious context, become idolatrous or irrelevant. It will become idolatrous, for we will absolutize one tradition of images for God; it will become irrelevant, for the experiences of many people will not be included within the canonized tradition.

The issues that emerge, then, from both the worship and the interpretive contexts of religious language, are *idolatry* and *irrelevance*: either we take our language about God literally or we find it meaningless. Another way to phrase these issues is to ask the questions: How does religious language refer to God and which religious images are central? Is there a way of speaking of religious language as referring to God without identifying it with the divine? Are there images which are central to a religious tradition *and* are there revolutionary possibilities within that tradition aiding new images to emerge? These are very complex questions, for they focus on the heart of language—its truth and its meaning. Does religious language refer to anything; if so, to what and how? Does religious language mean anything; if so, what and to whom? Our route to suggesting modest answers to these questions will be slow and indirect, as I believe is appropriate to the subject matter; but a beginning can be made by illustrating the issues of idolatry and irrelevance, truth and meaning, through contemporary movements within our culture that find them especially problematic.

### THE IDOLATRY OF RELIGIOUS LANGUAGE

On the issue of the truth of religious language, there are continuing, powerful, conservative religious movements which insist on the literal reference of language to God. Religious conservatism is a widespread tendency within contemporary culture, not restricted to groups which call themselves "evangelicals" or "fundamentalists." This tendency is linked with fear of relativizing Scripture through historical criticism and a refusal to accept a plurality of interpretive perspectives. The Bible, says this movement, *is* the Word of God; the Bible is inerrant or divinely inspired; the words and images of the Bible are the authoritative and appropriate words and images for God. The Bible is a sacred text, different from all other texts, and not relative and pluralistic as are all other human products. The Bible becomes an idol: the fallible, human words of Scripture are understood as referring correctly and literally to God. Even where these sentiments are not expressed clearly or in such extreme fashion, religious literalism remains a powerful current in our society. And it does not stem only from a fear of relativism and plurality. It also derives from the understanding of what counts as "true" in our culture. What is "true" in our positivistic, scientifically oriented society is what corresponds with "reality," with the "facts." Translated into artistic terms, this means realistic art; the "true" painting or sculpture is a copy of what it represents. Translated into religious terms, "true" religious language is also a copy of what it represents; in other words, a literal or realistic representation of God's nature. If the Bible says that God is "father" then God is literally, really, "father"; the word "father" and the associations of that word truly refer to God's nature. In the same way that the law of gravity refers to the way things really are in the world, so "father" refers to the way God really is.

But there is, I believe, an even deeper reason why religious literalism runs rampant in our time. It is not only that many people have lost the practice of religious contemplation and prayer, which alone is sufficient to keep literalism at bay, or that positivistic scientism has injected a narrow view of truth into our culture. While both are true, it is also the case that we do not think in symbols in the way our forebears did. That is to say, we do not see the things of this world as standing for something else; they are simply what they are. A symbolic sensibility, on the contrary, sees multilayered realities, with the literal level suggestive of meanings beyond itself. While it may have been more justified for people in earlier times to be biblical literalists since they were less conscious of relativity, as symbolic thinkers, they were *not* literalists. From the third century on, the "fourfold method of exegesis"—in which three levels of interpretation followed the literal level—permitted and encouraged the exercise of the imagination in the interpretation of Scripture. While many of the "anagogical" and "tropological" interpretations were fanciful, the abandonment of the four levels in the Protestant Reformation, with the claim that the text was self-explanatory, eventually resulted in literalism.[2] The claim can be made that our time is *more* literalistic than any other time in history. Not only were double, triple, and more meanings once seen in Scripture (and Scripture considered richer as a consequence), but our notion of history as the recording of "facts" is alien to the biblical consciousness. The ancients were less literalistic than we are, aware that truth has many levels and that when one writes the story of an influential person's life, one's perspective will color that story. Ours is a literalistic mentality; theirs was a symbolical mentality. There can be no return to a symbolical mentality in its earlier forms; we no longer believe in four levels of scriptural exegesis or in a three-tiered universe.

Nor can many of us return to a symbolical mentality in its sacramental form; for instance, belief that natural and human objects and events are "figures" of the divine. For a traditional sacramental sensibility, the bread and wine of the Eucharist are symbols of divine nurture; they do not merely "point to" spiritual food, but really and truly *are* spiritual food. The things of this world participate in and signify what transcends our world. The sacramental sensibility depends upon a belief that everything is connected, that the beings of this world are analogously related to God (Being-Itself), and hence can be sacramentally related to God. The analogy of being by which all that is *is*

---

[2]See Frank Kermode, *The Classic: Literary Images of Permanence and Change* (New York: Viking Press, 1975).

because of its radical dependence on God ties everything together in a silent ontological web which reverberates with similarity within dissimilarity out to its farthest reaches. Even a corpse, says Augustine, is like God to the extent that it still has some degree of order left in its decaying flesh and emerging skeleton. In such a universe, everything holds together, everything fits, everything is related.

For a genuine symbolical sensibility such as Dante embraced in his *Divine Comedy*, the symbol—the finite object which signifies the infinite by participating in it—is neither literalized nor spiritualized. It does not become an idol or a mere sign. In our time, however, when there is skepticism concerning the unity of all that is, symbols tend either to be literalized (as in fundamentalism or the doctrine of transubstantiation) or spiritualized (as in Feuerbach or Protestant liberalism).

The medieval sacramental sensibility is not ours, either in theory or practice. Our time is characterized by disunity, by skepticism that anything is related to anything else, and by secularity. If there is to be any fresh understanding of the truth of images as a counter to literalistic truth, it will have to be one that takes seriously the characteristics of the contemporary sensibility.[3]

Before we leave this preliminary overview of literalism and the truth of religious language, it is necessary to add a word from social anthropology about *why* people cling to religious systems with such fervor, especially if they appear threatened by a secularized, relativistic, and pluralistic culture. As Clifford Geertz points out, human beings are "unfinished" at birth and must construct and order their world in ways that no other animals must do. Monkeys and bees are born into a monkey or bee "world" respectively—which is simply there for them. Having to construct our world, we are

---

[3]James Hillman in *Re-Visioning Psychology* (New York: Harper & Row, 1977) claims Protestantism denied the imagination and myth and killed off fantasy. See the article by Lucy Bregman, "Religious Imagination: Polytheistic Psychology Confronts Calvin," *Soundings* 63 (1980): 36–60. Bregman also suggests an intriguing list that includes the "left" and "right" brains, equating literalism with the left and symbolism with the right.

| | |
|---|---|
| Rational | Imaginative |
| Technology | Art |
| Literal | Symbolic |
| History | Myth |
| Western | Eastern, primitive |
| Masculine | Feminine |
| Left-brain | Right-brain |
| Reformation | Renaissance |
| Repressive | Liberating |
| Sacred text | Myth |
| Work ethic | Spontaneous pleasure |

necessarily (if only subconsciously) protective of it and extremely anxious if it is threatened. We depend, says Geertz, so deeply on our constructions for our most basic sense of sanity that any threat to them is a threat to our very being.[4] Thus, one can conclude that people will be less open, less imaginative, less flexible during times of threat. They will be more literalistic, absolutist, dogmatic when the construction which orders their world is relativized, either through pluralistic perspectives from within the tradition or competing systems from without. Given the pressures against the traditional Christian imagistic system from, for instance, both the liberation theologies and from other world religions, this retreat into literalistic, absolutist hibernation is no surprise.

But literalism will not do. Much of this essay will be devoted to trying to show why it will not do and what the alternative is. Two thoughtful theologians point us in the right direction on the matter of religious language, the first with a straightforward admonition, the second with an analogy of religious language with poetic. British theologian Ian T. Ramsey has written:

> Let us always be cautious of talking about God in straightforward language. Let us never talk as if we had privileged access to the diaries of God's private life . . . so that we may say quite cheerfully why God did what, when and where.[5]

This admonition is never necessary for deeply religious people or persons aware of their own relative and limited perspectives. Old Testament scholar Phyllis Trible has written:

> To appropriate the metaphor of a Zen sutra, poetry is "like a finger pointing to the moon." It is a way to see the light that shines in darkness, a way to participate in transcendent truth and to embrace reality. To equate the finger with the moon or to acknowledge the finger and not perceive the moon is to miss the point.[6]

Or, to rephrase Trible's words for our subject, either to equate human words with the divine reality or to see no relationship between them is inappropriate. Rather, the proper way is "like a finger pointing to the moon." Is *this* the way "to participate in transcendent truth and to embrace reality"? I would

---

[4]Clifford Geertz, "Religion as a Cultural System," in *Reader in Comparative Religion*, 2d ed. rev., ed. William Lessa and Evon Vogt (New York: Harper & Row, 1965), p. 209.

[5]Ian T. Ramsey, *Religious Language* (New York: Macmillan Co., 1963), p. 107.

[6]Phyllis Trible, *God and the Rhetoric of Sexuality*, Overtures to Biblical Theology (Philadelphia: Fortress Press, 1978), p. 16.

agree with Trible that it is; I would call it the "metaphorical" way and will be elaborating on it as the form of religious language.

## THE IRRELEVANCE OF RELIGIOUS LANGUAGE

Turning now to the second problem facing religious language in our time—irrelevancy—we note that it also is a widespread phenomenon. In a secularized culture where the practice of regular public and private prayer is not widespread, this is bound to be the case. For many, the images in the Bible have sentimental significance from childhood days and happier times; for some, the biblical language creates a world of its own in sharp distinction from the evil modern world. But for many people, religious language, biblical language, has become, like a creed repeated too many times, boring and repetitious. We are essentially indifferent to it. And this is true despite the fact that biblical imagery is often vivid, powerful, shocking, and revolutionary. But all of the reasons given thus far for the "meaninglessness" of religious language have probably always been current. What distinguishes our time is various groups of people who are saying that traditional religious language is meaningless to them because it excludes them in *special* ways. In a more general sense, religious language in the Judeo-Christian tradition excludes us all, for it is largely biblical language; hence, its assumptions concerning social, political, and cultural matters are not ours. Entering the biblical world for many people is like going into a time warp in which one is transported to a world two thousand years in the past. We are aware of significant connections since both worlds are inhabited by human beings, but the images, problems, issues, and assumptions are different. In one way or another, we are all excluded from the biblical world and the tradition that has been formed from it: few if any of us identify easily or enthusiastically with images of demons, vineyards, Messiah and Son of man, kings, Pharisees, and so on. But the issues are much sharper and more painful for some groups: it is not simply that they do not identify; rather, they feel *specifically* excluded. The indifference and irrelevance that many people feel with regard to religious language is clarified by the critique of the more revolutionary groups, for their particular difficulties with religious language highlight issues that point directly to some of its basic characteristics. The feminist critique of religious language is especially relevant in this regard, for more than any of the other liberation theologies, feminist theology has focused on language, its power and its abuses. Three points in this critique stand out as significant.

First, feminists generally agree that whoever names the world owns the world. The Genesis story, according to the traditional, patriarchal interpretation, sees Adam naming the world without consulting Eve. For many feminists, this is a model of Western culture, including Christianity, which has been and still is a "man's world."[7] The feminist critique of religious language is an extremely sophisticated one, for it is based on a recognition of the fundamental importance of language to human existence. With Ludwig Wittgenstein, feminists would say, "The limits of one's language are the limits of one's world," and with Martin Heidegger, "Language is the house of being." We do not so much use language as we are used by it. Since we are all born into a world which is already linguistic, in which the naming has already taken place, we only own our world to the extent that the naming that has occurred is our naming. Feminist theologians are claiming that the world of Western religion is not their world; it was named by men and excludes women. The world of Western religion can become a world for women only if it is open to their naming. New naming, changes in language, are, however, no minor matters, for if one believes that language and "world" are coterminous, then changes in the one will involve changes in the other, and such changes are often revolutionary. The current resistance to inclusive or unbiased language, for instance, both at the social and religious level, indicates that people know instinctively that a revolution in language means a revolution in one's world.

Second, feminists are saying that the particular problem they have with Western religious language is its patriarchal character. It is not just that "God the father" is a frequent appellation for the divine, but that the entire structure of divine-human and human-human relationships is understood in a patri-

---

[7]The following quotation by Carol Christ and Judith Plaskow is an excellent summary of the feminist critique of language and the importance of naming.

> Consciousness-raising . . . leads to a critique of culture and to the tasks of transforming or recreating it. Feminists have called their task a "new naming" of self and world. It is through naming that humans progress from childhood to adulthood and learn to understand and shape the world about them. Under patriarchy, men have reserved to themselves the right to name, keeping women in a state of intellectual and spiritual dependency. Mary Daly suggests that the Genesis creation story, in which Adam names the animals and woman, is the paradigm of false naming in Western culture. If the world has been named by Adam without Eve's consultation, then the world has been named from the male point of view. As women begin to name the world for themselves, they will upset the order that has been taken for granted throughout history. They will call themselves and the world into new being. Naming women's experience thus becomes the model not only for personal liberation and growth, but for the feminist transformation of culture and religion (Carol Christ and Judith Plaskow, eds., *Womanspirit Rising: A Feminist Reader in Religion* [New York: Harper & Row, 1979], p. 7).

archal framework.[8] "God the father," as we shall see, has become a model which serves as a grid or screen through which to see not only the nature of God but also our relations to the divine and with one another. "Patriarchy" then is not just that most of the images of the deity in Western religion are masculine—king, father, husband, lord, master—but it is the Western way of life: it describes patterns of governance at national, ecclesiastical, business, and family levels. We shall investigate this model in some detail at a later time, for it is one of the most prominent in the Judeo-Christian tradition. But the point I am stressing now is the total, overarching character of patriarchalism which contributes to the sense of exclusion on the part of women and hence prompts their criticism of the irrelevance of much of Western religious language to them. They say the model of "God the father" has become an idol. When a model becomes an idol, the hypothetical character of the model is forgotten and what ought to be seen as *one* way to understand our relationship with God has become identified as *the* way. In fact, as happens when a model becomes an idol, the distance between image and reality collapses: "father" becomes God's "name" and patriarchy becomes the proper description of governing relationships at many levels. The transformation of the paternal model into the patriarchal is an important case in point concerning what can happen to models when *one* dominates. Feminist theologians are insisting that many models of God are necessary, among them feminine models, in order both to avoid idolatry and to include the experience of all peoples in our language about God.

Third, feminist theologians are saying that religious language is not only religious but also human, not only about God but also about us. The tradition says that we were created in the image of God, but the obverse is also the case, for we imagine God in *our* image. And the human images we choose for the divine influence the way we feel about ourselves, for these images are "divinized" and hence raised in status. For instance, earthly

---

[8] The reasons for patriarchy undoubtedly derive in part from the fact that as Elaine Pagels, along with many other scholars, points out, the God of Israel, unlike most other deities in the ancient Near East, shared his power with no female divinity. She writes,

he scarcely can be characterized in any but masculine epithets: King, Lord, Master, Judge, and Father. Indeed, the absence of feminine symbolism of God marks Judaism, Christianity, and Islam in striking contrast to the world's other religious traditions, whether in Egypt, Babylonia, Greece, and Rome, or Africa, Polynesia, India, and North America. Jewish, Christian, and Islamic theologians, however, are quick to point out that God is not to be considered in sexual terms at all. Yet the actual language they use in worship and prayer conveys a different message and gives the distinct impression that God is thought of in exclusively *masculine* terms ("What Became of God the Mother? Conflicting Images of God in Early Christianity," in *Womanspirit Rising*, ed. Christ and Plaskow, p. 107).

kingship gains in importance when the image of king is applied to God.[9] On the contrary, images that are excluded are not legitimated and honored; for instance, as feminists have pointed out, the paucity of feminine imagery for God in the Judeo-Christian tradition means a lower self-image for women in that tradition. The relationship between feminine imagery for the divine and the status of women in a society has been well documented in the history of religions.[10] One of the functions, therefore, of religious language is "naming ourselves" as we "name" God. Those who are conscious of being excluded from a religious tradition are most likely to recognize this important and often forgotten function of religious language.

In a number of ways, then, feminist theologians (and a similar case could be made by black and third world theologians) have shown why religious language is not meaningful in our time. Language which is not our language, models which have become idols, images which exclude our experience are three common failings of religious language, but they are especially evident to groups of people who feel excluded by the classical tradition of a religious faith.

## CAN RELIGIOUS LANGUAGE BE REVITALIZED?

If idolatry and irrelevance are the critical issues for religious language in our time, what remedies are possible for its revitalization? The crisis is too deep for patchwork solutions, for the problem lies in our most basic sense of "how things hold together." That is, many of us no longer believe in a symbolic, sacramental universe in which the part stands for the whole, the things of this world "figure" another world, and all that is is connected by a web of being. No longer believing in connections of this sort and hence afraid that our images refer to nothing, we literalize them, worshiping the icon in our desperation. Furthermore, we find them irrelevant for they connect us to nothing transcending ourselves: they are "just symbols." The question that looms before us is, I believe, a critical one for religious faith and expression: is it possible to have significant religious language, language that is true and meaningful, without classic sacramentalism? If we can no longer believe in a "figural" world—our world as a whole and in all its parts as a symbol of another world, a microcosm of it—can we still believe that our words about the divine are significant?

Let us consider this question more carefully. What are the characteristics of the classic sacramental perspective? The basis of the sacramental universe

---

[9]This point is made at length in the classic study by Peter Berger, *The Social Reality of Religion* (London: Faber & Faber, 1969).

[10]See, for example, Rita M. Gross, ed., *Beyond Androcentrism: New Essays on Women and Religion* (Missoula, Mont.: Scholars Press, 1977).

within Christianity (and there are similar perspectives in other religions) is the incarnation: the sense of divine immanence in the Hebrew tradition is brought to its apotheosis in the Johannine assertion that "the Word became flesh and dwelt among us." The full presence of God in an otherwise ordinary person, Jesus of Nazareth—as the Chalcedonian statement puts it, "fully God and fully man"—was the basis for a thoroughgoing sacramentalism. If God can be fully present in a particular human being, then all creation has the potential for serving as a symbol of divine immanence.[11] The natural and human orders of creation are not flat but two dimensional: each thing is itself, but as itself, it is also something else—"news of God" as Gerard Manley Hopkins says. The world is alive with the presence of God; it "figures," shows forth, the divine in all its myriad particularity. Sacramentalism of this sort tends to be static and focused on the natural, not the historical, order. Incarnationalism, as the word indicates, is centered on the body, the flesh, not on human being as restless, moving, growing. The most extreme example of sacramentalism, the eucharistic doctrine of transubstantiation, illustrates clearly both the static and fleshly characteristics of the perspective. The bread and wine *become* the body and blood of Christ: two items of the naturalistic order are changed into what they symbolize. Actually, in this extreme case symbolization gives over to realism; the symbol is consumed by what it represents. But elsewhere in the symbolic perspective, the two dimensions exist in a hierarchical order of macrocosm-microcosm, spirit-body, Christ-church, man-woman, and so on. All is ordered, statically and hierarchically, with the body always "below," but permeated by spirit and capable of expressing and imaging spirit.[12]

In such a universe, of course, the meaning and truth of religious language are no problem. If the entire earthly order is a "figure" of the divine order, if each and every scrap of creation, both natural and human, participates in and signifies the divine order according to its own particularities, its

---

[11]Incarnational theology, based on "the Word became flesh," eventuated in the orthodox christology which has always been cryptically Docetic. In spite of the formula, "fully God and fully man," the human partnership was never taken with full seriousness, for again and again the church has been unwilling to deal with such matters as growth and change in Jesus of Nazareth as evidenced by its uneasiness about admitting the possibility of sin in him. An incarnational christology is inevitably static and nature-oriented, rather than dynamic and human-oriented. A thoughtful debate on incarnational christology can be found in John Hick, ed., *The Myth of God Incarnate* (Philadelphia: Westminster Press; London: SCM Press, 1977).

[12]There are of course many fine studies of sacramentalism and it is not necessary or appropriate here to list them. A particularly interesting one, however, is Mary Douglas's *Natural Symbols* (New York: Pantheon Books, 1970) because she sees a direct connection both in primitive and advanced cultures between attitudes toward the body and the ability to think sacramentally. She finds Protestantism especially alienated in this regard, for its stress on inner experience, denigration of ritual, and rejection of mediating institutions make it impossible to see the body and hence the world from a symbolic perspective. I find her analysis of our problematic situation—one in which all connections have been broken—illuminating, but her solution—a return to organic sacramentalism with the full paraphernalia of medieval orthodox incarnationalism—insupportable.

own way of being in the world, then all that is "refers" to Being-Itself and has "meaning," both in itself and as a symbol. Everything is connected hierarchically; hence, everything here below is meaningful both in itself and as a symbol of the divine.

Symbolic sacramentalism received systematic interpretation and ordering in the medieval doctrine of *analogia entis*, the analogy of being. This doctrine says, in essence, that every existing thing participates in Being-Itself, but analogously. That is, being is differentiated absolutely, so that while everything is connected as beings immediately and radically dependent on God, each thing has, is, its own act of being and hence is radically particular. The analogy of being does not paint the world all the same color; on the contrary, it stresses the glory of difference. Beneath the distinctions, however, everything is connected and this is the reason why everything in such a universe can be a symbol of everything else and, most especially, of God, who created everything out of the divine plenitude as a mirror and a reflection of the divine self. The analogical way, the symbolic way, rests on a profound *similarity* beneath the surface dissimilarities; what we see and speak of must be the differences, but we rest in the faith that all is empowered by the breath of God, Being-Itself.[13] The vision of God, the goal of all creation, is the belief that one day all of creation shall be one. The many shall return to the One, for the many are in secret one already.[14]

---

[13]The medieval doctrine of analogical predication rests on the analogy of being. We can predicate human characteristics of God (goodness, wisdom, etc.) because our being was created by and is dependent upon God's being. In the order of knowing, we proceed from the creature to the creator for we must start from the concrete and empirical; in the order of being we proceed from the creator to the creature, for God possesses the characteristics we attribute absolutely and truly, though we do not know the *mode* in which they are realized in the divine being. The two prominent types of analogical predication in medieval philosophy were analogy of attribution and of proper proportionality. Both are necessary for one provides the *content*, the other the *form*, of predication. The analogy of attribution allows that we can attribute certain qualities to God because God is the ground of being and hence everything that is participates in God—*what* we say, therefore, is based on the creature as caused by, dependent upon, the creator. The analogy of proper proportionality insists that we do not know *how* such qualities are realized in God and hence this form of analogy serves as a negation of all forms of literalism and idolatry. Another way of expressing the necessity and relationship of the two types is to say that analogies of attribution are "models" licensing certain language for God and analogies of proper proportionality are "qualifiers" insisting on the necessary distance in all talk of God. In order to say *anything* we must use models from concrete, human experience, but in order to say anything *appropriately*, we must qualify our language for we do not know how these terms refer to God. For a fuller elaboration of models and qualifiers, see the works of Ian T. Ramsey.

[14]The Neoplatonic background of this synthesis is obvious, but so is the Aristotelian. The stress on the independence of each particular thing and the insistence that each glorifies God *only* as it seeks its own rightful end is the contribution of Aristotle; the stress on the relationship of the many to the One as an emanation and a return is from Neoplatonism via Augustine. The issue here (and the interpretation of *analogia entis*) is very complex; my suggestions are meant not as a contribution to that debate but solely to depict in a general way some of the characteristics of a sacramental mentality. For a careful interpretation along the above lines, see Etienne Gilson, *The Christian Philosophy of St. Thomas Aquinas* (New York: Random House, 1956).

Now, try as we might, many if not most of us cannot work ourselves back into this mentality. If the destiny of religious language rests on a return to the traditional sacramental universe, if the significance of imagistic language depends on a belief that symbols participate in a transcendent reality, the future for religious language is grim. I do not believe either is the case—that we must or can return to such a sacramental universe or that the significance of images rests on symbolic participationism. In fact, we have not had a classic sacramental mentality for a long time (even though it hangs on in many quarters and, improperly understood, is the source of much literalistic realism in religious language). In effect, however, we have not had such a sensibility since at least the Protestant Reformation. One way to describe what occurred in the Reformation is a profound questioning of the symbolic mentality, a loosening of the connections between symbol and its reference. The eucharistic debate between Luther and the proponents of transubstantiation on the one hand, and between Luther and Zwingli on the other hand, reveals as much. Luther took a mediating position between the bread and wine as one with the body and the blood and these elements as a mere sign recalling them.[15] To Luther, the bread and the wine were still symbols of Christ's body and blood, still participated in that reality, but in a way that I would call "metaphorical," for the assertions "This is my body" and "This is my blood" were not viewed as identity statements, but as including a silent but present negative. One critical difference between symbolic and metaphorical statements is that the latter always contain the whisper, "it is *and it is not*."

I suggest, therefore, that one of the distinctive characteristics of Protestant thought is its insistence on the "and it is not." It is the iconoclastic tendency in Protestantism, what Paul Tillich calls the "Protestant Principle," the fear of idolatry, the concern lest the finite ever be imagined to be capable of the infinite. We see it in Martin Luther's "masks" of God, that God is revealed and veiled in all symbols; in John Calvin's notion of divine "accommodation" by which God stoops to our level by speaking in signs and images; and in an extreme form in Karl Barth's concept of *analogia fidei*, which insists that our language refers to God only as God from time to time causes our words to conform to the divine being.

The Protestant tradition is, I would suggest, "metaphorical"; the Catholic, "symbolical" (or "analogical" for contemporary Catholicism). I do not mean to suggest a hard and fast distinction here, but only a characteristic sensibility. The Protestant sensibility tends to see dissimilarity, distinction, tension and hence to be skeptical and secular, stressing the transcendence of

---

[15]For a fine discussion and elaboration of this point, see Erich Heller, *The Disinherited Mind: Essays in Modern German Literature and Thought* (Cleveland: World Publishing, 1961), pp. 261–68.

God and the finitude of creation. The Catholic sensibility tends to see similarity, connection, harmony and, hence, to be believing and religious, stressing the continuity between God and creation. These caricatures are not meant to be directly related to the Protestant and Catholic ecclesiastical institutions or even to the theologies supported by these bodies. Not only are many Protestants "catholic" and many Catholics "protestant," but it is obvious that either tendency without the other would be insupportable. They are complementary. However, a sacramentalism of the medieval sort—the classic Catholic mentality—is not viable today, nor is it supported by most Catholics who seek a revitalization of this tradition. The most sophisticated revitalizations of the symbolic, sacramental tradition interpret it analogically, that is, in a way that stresses many of the characteristics of the metaphorical sensibility: its emphasis on the negativities, on the distance between image and what it represents, on its refusal of easy harmonies. Obversely, a Protestant sensibility which failed to see any connections or unity between God and the world would be totally negative and agnostic. A metaphorical perspective *does* see connections but they are of a tensive, discontinuous, and surprising nature.

One of the interesting and important characteristics of contemporary ecumenical theology is that it is neither traditionally Catholic nor Protestant, emphasizing neither easy continuities nor radical discontinuities, but some form of both. However, as David Tracy points out in his recent book, *The Analogical Imagination*, there are characteristic differences in the Christian community between those for whom experience in the world engenders primarily a sense of wonder and trust and those for whom it engenders primarily a need for healing and transformation.[16] The first moves from an awareness of harmony, taking the negativities into account, while the second moves from an awareness of the negativities, reaching toward a future harmony. They are two "ways," one not necessarily better than the other; it is the contention of this essay, however, that the Protestant sensibility is more

---

[16]David Tracy's impressive new work, *The Analogical Imagination: Christian Theology and the Culture of Pluralism* (New York: Crossroad; London: SCM Press, 1981), presents a contemporary interpretation of the analogical sensibility that in no way falls into either heavy sacramentalism or easy harmonies oblivious of the negativities. In fact, his view of the analogical imagination is in many ways identical with my understanding of the metaphorical sensibility. At one point he quotes Aristotle on *metaphor* as support for the analogical imagination:

> The power of the analogical imagination was honored by Aristotle in his famous dictum "to spot the similar in the dissimilar is the mark of poetic genius." That same power—at once participatory in the originating event of wonder, trust, disclosure and concealment by the whole, and positively distancing itself from that event by its own self-constituting demands of critical reflection—releases the analogical imagination of the systematic theologian to note the profound similarities-in-difference in all reality (p. 410).

characteristic of our time and is the place from which many of us must start. What we seek, then, is a form of theology, a form for our talk about God both at the primary religious level of images and the secondary theological level of concepts, which takes the Protestant sensibility seriously.


## METAPHORICAL THEOLOGY

If modernity were the only criterion, our task would be relatively easy. But such is never the case in theology. Christian theology is always an interpretation of the "Gospel" in a particular time and place. So the other task of equal importance is to show that a *metaphorical theology* is indigenous to Christianity, not just in the sense that it is permitted, but is called for. And this I believe is the case. The heart of the Gospel in the New Testament is widely accepted to be the "kingdom of God"; what the kingdom is or means is never expressed but indirectly suggested by the parables of the kingdom.[17]

---

As Tracy notes, all post-Enlightenment attempts to revive analogy as a basic Christian sensibility must take with absolute seriousness the skepticism, relativity, negativities, and indeed chaos that characterize contemporary life at intellectual, personal, and political levels. Nonetheless, I believe there is a difference between even Tracy's analogical imagination and what I am calling the metaphorical sensibility: the former, as Tracy says, is in the tradition of "manifestation," a tradition in which a sense of trust, wonder, grace is primary even when profoundly aware of the suffering, evil, and discontinuity that pervade that basic harmony. The other two traditions which he notes as comprising Christianity—"proclamation" and "prophetic action"—are less conscious of that underlying grace, more conscious of the distance between the human and the divine and of the negativities of existence. It is my contention that while all three perspectives are necessary for a full Christian theology, the proclamation/prophetic is not only a necessity for many people in our time but is also an authentic Christian perspective. The different perspectives, as Tracy notes, need to be intensified and articulated in their concrete particularity, as long as such intensification and articulation are carried on in conversation and openness to the other perspectives.

Another case in point is the work of David Burrell who, in his book *Analogy and Philosophical Language* (New Haven, Conn.: Yale Univ. Press, 1973) comes out in favor of metaphor as lying behind analogy and serving as the justification for analogy. His main thesis is to show with the help of Wittgenstein that ordinary language is deeply metaphorical; hence, the use of analogy in predicating of God is not a medieval, esoteric exercise but an extension of ordinary usage. What lies behind analogical predication for Burrell, then, is not *analogia entis* or the analogy of attribution but the metaphorical character of ordinary language—its dialectical, multi-faceted nature in which borrowings and cross-sortings, judgments of aptness and appropriateness are all common characteristics. Analogical predication of God is, says Burrell, the same *kind* of language.

[17]Leander Keck voices the position of many New Testament exegetes in the following statement: "The whole network of words, deeds, and death which we call 'Jesus' was pulled into a pattern by the magnetic power of the kingdom and hence reflected the impingement of that kingdom on his life and work. This was not simply a matter of Jesus working out the implications of a root idea. Rather, it was a matter of being grasped by a perception in such a way that the whole career became a celebration of the kingdom's coming and thereby its vanguard as well" (*A Future for the Historical Jesus: The Place of Jesus in Preaching and Theology* [Philadelphia: Fortress Press, 1981], pp. 218–19).

The parables are by no means the only form in the New Testament which deals with the kingdom and we must be cautious lest we make an idol of them. However, as the dominant genre of Jesus' teaching on the kingdom, they suggest some central, albeit indirect, clues to its reality. As a form of religious language, the parables of the New Testament are very different from symbolic, sacramental language. They do not assume a believing or religious perspective on the part of the listeners to whom they are addressed; they do not assume continuity between our world and a transcendent one; they do not see similarity, connection, and harmony between our ways and the ways of God. On the contrary, they are a secular form of language, telling stories of ordinary people involved in mundane family, business, and social matters; they assume a nonbelieving or secular attitude on the part of their audience; they stress the discontinuity between our ways and the ways of the kingdom; they focus on the dissimilarity, incongruity, and tension between the assumptions and expectations of their characters and another set of assumptions and expectations identified with the kingdom. In other words, they are a form peculiarly suited to what I have called the Protestant sensibility.

They are so suited because they are metaphors, not symbols. They are metaphorical statements about religious matters, about what both transcends and affects us at the deepest level of our existence. What is it about a religious metaphorical statement which makes it more powerful than a symbolical statement? The answer to this question centers on the nature of metaphor and especially of metaphorical statements. To many people "metaphor" is merely a poetic ornament for illustrating an idea or adding rhetorical color to abstract or flat language. It appears to have little to do with ordinary language until one realizes that most ordinary language is composed of "dead metaphors," some obvious, such as "the arm of the chair" and others less obvious, such as "tradition," meaning "to hand over or hand down." Most simply, a metaphor is seeing one thing *as* something else, pretending "this" is "that" because we do not know how to think or talk about "this," so we use "that" as a way of saying something about it. Thinking metaphorically means spotting a thread of similarity between two dissimilar objects, events, or whatever, one of which is better known than the other, and using the better-known one as a way of speaking about the lesser known.

Poets use metaphor all the time because they are constantly speaking about the great unknowns—mortality, love, fear, joy, guilt, hope, and so on. Religious language is deeply metaphorical for the same reason and it is therefore no surprise that Jesus' most characteristic form of teaching, the parables, should be extended metaphors. Less obvious, but of paramount importance, is the fact that metaphorical thinking constitutes the basis of human thought and language. From the time we are infants we construct our world through metaphor; that is, just as young children learn the meaning of the color red by finding the thread of similarity through many dissimilar objects (red ball, red apple, red cheeks), so we constantly ask when we do not know how to think about something, "What is it like?" Far from being an esoteric or ornamental rhetorical device superimposed *on* ordinary language, metaphor *is* ordinary language. It is the *way* we think. We often make distinctions between ordinary and poetic language, assuming that the first is direct and the second indirect, but actually both are indirect, for we always think by indirection. The difference between the two kinds of language is only that we have grown accustomed to the indirections of ordinary language; they have become conventional. Likewise, conceptual or abstract language is metaphorical in the sense that the ability to generalize depends upon seeing similarity within dissimilarity; a concept is an abstraction of the similar from a sea of dissimilars. Thus, Darwin's theory of the survival of the fittest is a high-level metaphorical exercise of recognizing a similar pattern amid an otherwise incredibly diverse set of phenomena.

The primary answer to the question of why religious metaphorical statements are so powerful is that they are in continuity with the way we think ordinarily. We are not usually conscious of the metaphorical character of our thought, of seeing "this" in terms of "that," of finding the thread of similarity amid dissimilars, but it is the only way a child's world can be constructed or our worlds expanded and transformed. Of course, there are important differences between ordinary and religious metaphorical statements which we shall fully note, but the first thing is to insist on their continuity. Symbolic statements, on the other hand, are not so much a way of knowing and speaking as they are sedimentation and solidification of metaphor. For in symbolical or sacramental thought, one does not think of "this" *as* "that," but "this" as *a part of* "that." The tension of metaphor is absorbed by the harmony of symbol.

Another way to discern the distinction between metaphorical and sacramental thinking is to say that in metaphorical statements we always make judgments. That is, we make assertions; we say "I am thinking about 'this' in terms of 'that.' " The only times we do not think this way is when we have already accepted a particular way of thinking of something. When we already know something, that is, when we have accepted a perspective on something, then we see and think about it "directly," or so it seems. Actually, it is not the case that anything can be known or thought of directly or literally; rather, we have simply acquired a way of looking at it which is acceptable to us. Even as simple a statement as "this is a chair" means only that I have made a judgment that I will think about this object *as* a chair because there is sufficient similarity between this object and other objects which I have called "chairs" in the past that I believe my assertion is justified. The example may appear ridiculous but it was chosen because it illustrates metaphorical thinking at its most common, continuous, and instantaneous level. It is the same *kind* of thinking as the assertion "Jesus is the savior," inasmuch as here again one is making a decision to think of one thing in terms of another; in both cases, a judgment is involved that similarity is present. The differences between the two statements are vast and important, such as the degree of existential involvement and the much greater ignorance of the subject matter, as well as the novelty of the assertion in the second statement. The point to stress, however, is that human thought is of a piece, it is indirect, and it involves judgments.[18]

We have remarked that metaphor finds the vein of similarity in the midst of dissimilars, while symbol rests on similarity already present and assumed. But the difference is even more marked: metaphor not only lives in the region of dissimilarity, but also in the region of the unconventional and surprising. Both humor and the grotesque are distinctly metaphorical.[19] Humor is the recognition of a *very* unlikely similarity among dissimilars and we laugh because we are surprised to discover that such unlikes are indeed alike in at least one respect. A great many jokes take the form, "How is a ___ like a ___?" Likewise, the grotesque forces us to look at radical incongruity, at what is outside, does not fit, is strange and disturbing. Both are extreme metaphorical forms which point up a crucial characteristic of metaphor: good metaphors shock, they bring unlikes together, they upset conventions, they involve tension, and they are implicitly revolutionary. The parables of Jesus are typically metaphorical in this regard, for they bring together dissimilars (lost coins, wayward children, buried treasure, and tardy laborers with the kingdom of God); they shock and disturb; they upset conventions and expectations and in so doing have revolutionary potential. In this regard, one could characterize symbolic, sacramental thinking as priestly and metaphorical thinking as prophetic. The first assumes an order and unity already present

---

[18]Jean Piaget's pattern of "assimilation" and "accommodation" to define the character of learning is similar to what we have presented. Hugh Petrie writes of Piaget's theory, "during assimilation, we learn by changing experience to fit our concepts and modes of understanding. During accommodation, we learn by changing our concepts and modes of understanding to fit our experience" ("Metaphor and Learning," in *Metaphor and Thought*, ed. Andrew Ortony [New York and Cambridge: Cambridge Univ. Press, 1979], p. 440). In assimilation, we stay with existing frameworks, with the familiar; but in accommodation, we pass from the known to the unknown—we change our concepts—and this process is accomplished by means of metaphor: "The crucial use of metaphor is our moving from one conceptual scheme with its associated way of knowing to another conceptual scheme with *its* associated way of knowing" (p. 460). Thus, metaphor is not just heuristic or illustrative, but epistemologically necessary if new learning is to take place. What we discover is an anomaly: the old framework no longer can encompass our experience and only metaphor—which connects both with what we already know *and* with what we are groping to know—provides the movement that is the distinctive mark of learning.

[19]See Kenneth Burke, *Permanence and Change: An Anatomy of Purpose* (New York: New Republic, 1935).

waiting to be realized; the second projects, tentatively, a possible transformed order and unity yet to be realized.[20]

Perhaps the most striking evidence of the revolutionary character of the New Testament parables is the redefinition they give to conventional understandings of the monarchical, hierarchical metaphors of "kingdom" and "rule." God's "kingdom," we discover from the parables, is not like any worldly reign; in fact, its essence is its opposition to the power of the mighty over the lowly, the rich over the poor, the righteous over the unrighteous. It is a *new* rule which is defined by the extraordinary reversal of expectations in the parables as well as in the life and death of Jesus.

The characteristics of metaphorical thinking we have suggested—ordinariness, incongruity, indirection, skepticism, judgment, unconventionality, surprise, and transformation or revolution—especially as they are realized in Jesus' parables, have persuaded many people to think of Jesus as a parable of God.[21] That is to say, the life and death of Jesus of Nazareth can be

---

[20]I am indebted to F. W. Dillistone for his distinction between analogical and metaphorical thinking. Of analogy he writes: "In any organic system the single member is related to the whole according to some pattern of order and proportion; no figure of speech is more fitted to express this relation than analogy" (*Christianity and Symbolism* [London: William Collins, 1955], p. 152). He notes that one can move from the known to the unknown because the part participates in the whole and is similar to it. Analogical thought is positive, comprehensive, and systematic. Analogy has links with the simile, metaphor with the contrast. Metaphor focuses attention on variety and the openness of reality, and on dissimilarity rather than similarity. Metaphor holds together similarity and dissimilarity in a resolution:

> The resolution is not final, for there are ever wider areas of conflict to embrace. But every metaphor which holds together two disparate aspects of reality in creative tension assumes the character of a prophecy of the final reconciliation of all things in the kingdom of God. It is the favorite tool of all the great poets.... Through it the imagination performs its task, the task which Coleridge describes as dissolving, diffusing, dissipating in order to recreate, as reconciling opposite or discordant qualities, as struggling to idealise and to unify. Through it the prophet leaps outside the circle of present experience, the realm of the factual and the commonsense, the typical and the regular. He parts company with those who are travelling the surer and steadier road of analogical comparison. By one act of daring he brings into creative relationship the apparently opposite and contrary and, if his metaphorical adventure proves successful, gains new treasure both for language and for life (*Ibid.*, p. 161).

Finally, Dillistone notes that while analogy tends toward petrification, metaphor moves toward renovation and that Jesus was a metaphorical thinker, disrupting the old by seeing it in a new light.

[21]Among the several New Testament critics who see Jesus as a parable of God are Leander Keck and John Donahue. Keck writes: "Jesus concentrated on parabolic speech because he himself was a parabolic event of the kingdom of God" (*A Future for the Historical Jesus*, p. 244). Donahue writes: "Responding to the parable of Jesus in Mark is engagement in the ultimate paradox of the Christian life ("Jesus as the Parable of God in the Gospel of Mark," *Interpretation* 32 [1978]: 386). Both exegetes substantiate their claim by a comparison of Jesus' life with the characteristics of parables: their metaphoricity, mundanity, realism, strangeness, indirection, shocking disclosive power, and existential engagement.

understood as itself a "parable" of God; in order to understand the ways of God with us—something unfamiliar and unknown to us, about which we do not know how to think or talk—we look at that life as a metaphor of God. What we see through that "grid" or "screen" is at one level an ordinary, secular story of a human being, but also a story shot through with surprise, unconventionality, and incongruities which not only upset our conventional expectations (for instance, of what a "savior" is and who gets "saved"), but also involve a judgment on our part—"Surely this man is the Christ." In contrast to incarnational christology, however, parabolic christology does not involve an assumption of continuity or identity between the human and the divine; it is not a "Jesusolatry," a form of idolatry. It is, I believe, a christology for the Protestant sensibility and the modern mentality.

All the foregoing comments on metaphor, parable, and Jesus as a parable require considerable elaboration. Perhaps, however, these brief introductory remarks are sufficient for us to attempt to advance a case for a metaphorical theology. If metaphor is the way by which we understand as well as enlarge our world and change it—that is, if the only way we have of dealing with the unfamiliar and new is in terms of the familiar and the old, thinking of "this" as "that" although we know the new thing is both like *and* unlike the old—if all this is the case, then it is no surprise that Jesus taught in parables or that many see him as a parable of God. For he introduced a new, strange way of being in the world, a way that could be grasped only through the indirection of stories of familiar life which both "were and were not" the kingdom. And he himself was in the world in a new, strange way which was in many respects an ordinary life but one which also, as with the parables, called the mores and conventions of ordinary life into radical question.

A metaphorical theology, then, starts with the parables of Jesus and with Jesus as a parable of God. This starting place does not involve a belief in the Bible as authoritative in an absolute or closed sense; it does not involve acceptance of a canon or the Bible as "the Word of God." In fact, such a perspective reverses the direction of authority suitable both to Scripture and to the Protestant sensibility. For what we have in the New Testament are confessions of faith by people who, on the basis of their experience of the way their lives were changed by Jesus' Gospel and by Jesus, *gave* authority to him and to the writings about him. The New Testament writings are foundational; they are classics; they are a beginning. But if we take seriously the parables of Jesus and Jesus as a parable of God as our starting point and model, then we cannot say that the Bible is absolute or authoritative in any sense except the way that a "classic" text is authoritative: it continues to speak to us. What must always be kept in mind is that the parables as metaphors and the life of Jesus as a metaphor of God provide characteristics for theology: a theology guided by them is open ended, tentative, indirect, tensive, iconoclastic, transformative. Some of these characteristics appear "negative," in the sense that they qualify any attempts at idolatry, whether this be the idolatry of the Bible, of tradition, of orthodoxy, or of the Church. In such a theology *no* finite thought, product, or creature can be identified with God and this includes Jesus of Nazareth, who as parable of God both "is and is not" God. Against all forms of literalistic realism and idolatry, a metaphorical theology insists that it is not only in keeping with the Protestant sensibility to be open, tentative, and iconoclastic but that these are the characteristics of Jesus' parables and of Jesus' own way of being in the world.

On the other hand, metaphorical theology is not just a modern version of the *via negativa* or an exercise in iconoclasm. It not only says "is not" but "is," not only no but yes. If the parables of Jesus and Jesus himself as a parable of God are genuine metaphors, then they give license for language about life with God; they point to a real, an assumed similarity between the metaphors and that to which they refer. The many parables of the kingdom tell us something about the rule of God, of what it means to live in the world according to God's way. Jesus as a parable of God tells us actually and concretely (though, of course, indirectly) about God's relationship to us. In other words, a metaphorical theology is "positive" as well as "negative," giving license for speech about God as well as indicating the limits of such speech. Such a theology, as is true of all theologies, must be concerned not only with *how* we speak of God but *what* we say of God. On the question of how we speak of God, a metaphorical theology is firmly opposed to literalism and idolatry of all kinds; on the question of what we say about God, metaphorical theology again turns to the parables and to Jesus as a parable for beginning, foundational clues.

The parables of the New Testament are united by a number of characteristics, of which one of the most outstanding is their concern with *relationships* of various kinds. What is important in the parables is not *who* the characters are (a static notion) but *what they do* (a dynamic one). The plot is always the heart of a parable, what a character or several characters decide in matters having to do with their *relationships with each other*. Whether one thinks of the parable of the Prodigal Son, the Good Samaritan, the Unjust Steward, or the Great Supper, it is relationships and decisions about them that are critical.[22] Just as the central Old Testament religious language is relational—focused on the covenant between God and Israel; so the central New Testament language is relational—focused on persons and their way of being in the world in community. Likewise, if we look at Jesus as a parable of God, we have no alternative but to recognize personal, relational language as the most appropriate language about God. Whatever more one may wish

---

[22]Not all parables are of this sort: the kingdom parables of the buried treasure, lost coin, and mustard seed are not, for instance, but as we shall see, relational language, while the dominant model for God, ought to be balanced and is balanced in the Bible by nonrelational, impersonal, naturalistic language.

to say about him, he was a person relating to other persons in loving service and transforming power.

I have emphasized the word "person" for two reasons. First, as we were made *in the image of God* (Gen. 3:27), so we now, with the model of Jesus, have further support for imagining God in *our* image, the image of persons. This means that personal, relational images are central in a metaphorical theology—images of God as father, mother, lover, friend, savior, ruler, governor, servant, companion, comrade, liberator, and so on. The Judeo-Christian tradition has always been personalistic and relational in its religious languages. This need not be seen as crude anthropomorphism, but as foundational language, the dominant model, of God-talk. Such language, however, is not the only appropriate religious language: no *one* model can ever be adequate. We find—both in Scripture and in our tradition—naturalistic, impersonal images balancing the relational, personal ones: God as rock, fortress, running stream, power, sun, thunder, First Cause, and so on. The Judeo-Christian tradition has had a decidedly personalistic rather than naturalistic tendency, with appalling consequences for the exploitation of the natural environment. This tradition is personalistic, however, not in an individualistic but in a relational sense, and it is therefore appropriate and required that a revolutionary hermeneutic of this tradition broaden relationship to its widest dimensions, including the entire natural world. In any case, a metaphorical theology will insist that *many* metaphors and models are necessary, that a piling up of images is essential, both to avoid idolatry and to attempt to express the richness and variety of the divine-human relationship.

The second reason for stressing the word "person" is to underscore, in as strong and definitive a way as possible, that it is not patriarchal language which is licensed by Jesus as parable of God. The Christian tradition, and the Jewish as well, have been and still are deeply patriarchal. We will be giving substantial time to this issue, for the profound penetration of the patriarchal model not only in theology but also in the structures of Western culture makes it a critical one for any metaphorical theology to consider. What is stressed in the parables and in Jesus' own life focuses on persons and their relationships; therefore, the dominance of the patriarchal model in the Christian tradition must be seen as a perversion in its hegemony of the field of religious models and its exclusion of other personal, relational models. The dominance of the patriarchal model is idolatrous in its assumption of privileged appropriateness. To put the issue in its simplest form, God's name is not "father" although many Christians use "God" and "father" interchangeably as if "father" were a literal description of God.

A metaphorical theology, then, will emphasize personal, relational categories in its language about God, but not necessarily as the tradition has interpreted these categories. On the contrary, if one looks to the parables and

Jesus as a parable to gain some preliminary understanding of what "person" means and what "relationship" means, both applied to us and to God, one finds not a baptizing of conventional hierarchies of relationships, whether these be of class, race, sex, or whatever, but a radical transformation of our expectations. For instance, if we are to say "God is father" it is both true *and* untrue, and even where true, it is different from conventional views of patriarchal fatherhood. If we are to call ourselves "children" in relationship to God, this is a limited and in some respects false image. There are personal, relational models which have been suppressed in the Christian tradition because of their social and political consequences; they are, however, as appropriate as the fatherhood model and are necessary both to qualify it and to include the images of personal, relational life of large numbers of people whose experiences have been excluded from traditional Christian language. To mention but two examples in passing, "mother" and "liberator" are metaphors of profound personal relationships with vast potential as models for God. They arise out of the depths of human relational existence and are licensed by the parabolic dimension of the New Testament, not in a literal way (the words do not appear), but in the sense that the characteristics we associate with "mother" and "liberator" fit with (and, of course, also do not fit with) the surprising rule of God as we have it in the parables and the parable of Jesus.

But a metaphorical theology cannot stop with metaphors, with the parables and the life and death of Jesus as extended metaphors of God's rule. Metaphor, parables, and Jesus as parable *fund* theology, but are not theology. If we wish to be precise, we must make a distinction between primary and secondary religious language, between metaphorical and conceptual language. But it is impossible to keep the distinction clear because most primary religious language is implicitly conceptual and most secondary theological language is latently imagistic. The parables of Jesus cry out for interpretation—not for *one* interpretation, but nonetheless for answers to the question, "What does this parable mean?" The richness of imagistic language means that it will always spawn many interpretations. Likewise, the biblical story of Jesus' life and death, an extended metaphor itself and packed with many supporting metaphors (Jesus as Messiah, as Son of man, as Suffering Servant, and so on), is not just a story but is already highly interpreted. What the story *means* is the perspective from which it is told and not something tacked on to pure, unadulterated images. Or if we think of Paul's letters, we see a mixture of images and concepts, the images moving in the direction of concepts in the sense that, for instance, when Paul tells us we are buried with Christ so that we might rise with him, he also tells us what this means (baptism, or the newness of the Christian life). Or if one considers the Nicene Creed, one sees a mixture of imagistic and conceptual language: the phrase "God of God, Light of Light, Very God of Very God, Begotten not made, Being of one substance with the Father" and so on was deemed necessary to interpret the imagistic language "one Lord Jesus Christ" and "Son of God." Whether the interpretations are good ones, are appropriate, or are still meaningful to us is beside the point. What is critical at the moment is that *some* interpretation is necessary; imagistic language does not just tolerate interpretation but *demands* it.

Thus, metaphorical theology does not stop with metaphors but must deal with the entire gamut of religious/theological language. Robert Funk has noted that it is a tortuous route between Jesus' parables and systematic theology.[23] Indeed it is, but that route must be traversed, for to stop at the level of images, of metaphor, of story is inevitably to give over either to baptizing certain images (usually biblical ones) as alone appropriate or to finding religious images sterile and meaningless. In other words, in terms of the twin issues of idolatry and irrelevance in religious language, *moving beyond* metaphors is necessary both to avoid literalizing them and to attempt significant interpretations of them for our time. It is impossible just to tell "the simple story of Jesus" and it was not told that way in the first place, for the many "stories" of Jesus in the New Testament are each told within several layers of interpretation.

In the continuum of religious language from primary, imagistic to secondary, conceptual, a form emerges which is a mixed type: *the model*. The simplest way to define a model is as a dominant metaphor, a metaphor with staying power. Metaphors are usually the work of an individual, a flash of insight which is often passing. But some metaphors gain wide appeal and become major ways of structuring and ordering experience. Thus, T. S. Eliot's Wasteland or W. H. Auden's Age of Anxiety became perspectives from which modern culture was perceived. There are many kinds of models—scale models, picture models, analogue and theoretical models, as well as root-metaphors which are similar to models but of wider range. For our preliminary purposes, however, the main point is that models are a further step along the route from metaphorical to conceptual language. They are similar to metaphors in that they are images which retain the tension of the "is and is not" and, like religious and poetic metaphors, they have emotional appeal insofar as they suggest ways of understanding our being in the world. The example we have used before, "God the father," comes readily to mind: it is a metaphor which has become a model. As a model it not only retains characteristics of metaphor but also reaches toward qualities of conceptual thought. It suggests a comprehensive, ordering structure with impressive interpretive potential. As a rich model with many associated commonplaces as well as a host of

---

[23]Robert W. Funk, "The Parables: A Fragmentary Agenda," in *Jesus and Man's Hope*, 2 vols., ed. Donald G. Miller and Dikran Y. Hadidian (Pittsburgh: Pittsburgh Theological Seminary, 1971), vol. 2, pp. 287–303.

supporting metaphors, an entire theology can be worked out from this model. Thus, if God is understood on the model of "father," human beings are understood as "children," sin is rebellion against the "father," redemption is sacrifice by the "elder son" on behalf of the "brothers and sisters" for the guilt against the "father" and so on.[24]

Models, as is true of metaphors but in an organic, consistent, and comprehensive manner, give us a way of thinking about the unknown in terms of the known. As Max Black says, a model gives us a "grid," "screen," or "filter" which helps us to organize our thoughts about a less familiar subject by means of seeing it in terms of a more familiar one. He gives the example of seeing a military battle in terms of a chess game. The chess model will help to understand tactics and the movement of armies; as he shrewdly notes, however, it also "screens out" certain other aspects of battle—for instance, we will not think of blood and death if we use only the chess analogy.[25] Models are necessary, then, for they give us something to think about when we do not know what to think, a way of talking when we do not know how to talk. But they are also dangerous, for they exclude other ways of thinking and talking, and in so doing they can easily become literalized, that is, identified as *the* one and only way of understanding a subject. This danger is more prevalent with models than with metaphors because models have a wider range and are more permanent; they tend to object to competition in ways that metaphors do not. In many Old Testament psalms the psalmist will pile up metaphors for God in a riotous *melée*, mixing "rock," "lover," "fortress," "midwife," "fresh water," "judge," "helper," "thunder," and so on in a desperate attempt to express the richness of God's being. But models do not welcome such profusion; even in the case of models of the same *type* (for instance, "God the mother" along with "God the father") there is often great resistance. This is due, in part, to the literalization of models and it is probably the single greatest risk in their use.

It should be evident by now, however, that in all matters except the most conventional (where widely accepted perspectives or models are already operating), thinking by metaphor and hence by models is not optional but necessary. And this is true in the sciences as well as in the humanities. It is

---

[24]One thoroughgoing version of such a theology is in Sigmund Freud's *Moses and Monotheism* (New York: Alfred A. Knopf, 1947) where the Judeo-Christian tradition is reduced to an exercise in which adherents attempt to rid themselves of latent guilt from the tribal horde's murder of the father of the clan. The Oedipus complex is the individual's version, while Western religion deals with the same issue of coming to terms with guilt from the childhood of the race. But one does not need to accept Freud's somewhat esoteric views on the subject, for there are many examples of mainline Christian theologies where the dominant categories are familiar ones derived from the structural possibilities of patriarchy. The imagistic language in both the trinitarian and christological controversies is principally "Father" and "Son" with the relationships between God and Jesus of Nazareth largely determined by the potential of these images.

[25]See Max Black's fine chapters 3 and 13 in his *Models and Metaphors* (Ithaca, N.Y.: Cornell Univ. Press, 1962).

sometimes supposed that science deals with its subject matter directly, empirically; science is "factual" whereas poetry and religion are "spiritual, emotional, or imaginative." Unlike them, science does not need the indirection of metaphor but can move inductively from empirical observations to theory and from theory to verification in the "real" world. This positivistic view of science is fortunately no longer the only force in science; rather, what one finds is that much of the most interesting and suggestive work on models is being done by scientists, especially physicists. Relatively little has been written by theologians on models in religion; however, the literature on models in science is enormous, going back a good twenty-five years. As physics comes increasingly to deal with invisibles such as subatomic particles, behaviors of entities that must be imagined rather than observed, it finds itself in a position similar to poetry and religion in that it must attempt to understand the unknown in terms of known models. Also, as more and more conclusions in physics (as well as in many of the other sciences) are expressed in mathematical formulas, models become the only way of connecting scientific knowledge both with ordinary language and with other domains of science. Finally, and most importantly, scientists need models for discovering the new; to think of the new in terms of the old, so long as one does not collapse the two, can often, through the dialectic of similarity and dissimilarity, provide a breakthrough.

There are other uses of models in science as well. But the critical point for our preliminary purposes is to note the widespread acceptance of models in science as well as in many other disciplines. One finds thinking by models in biology, computer science, education theory, political science, ethics, psychology, sociology, and so on. The self-conscious use of models, in regard to both their benefits and their risks, is a common phenomenon in most fields of study. What this means, among other things, is that poetry and religion, the two fields which have always known they must think via metaphor (and as a consequence have been denied by many as dealing in knowledge—truth and meaning), now find that their way of metaphor and indirection is widely accepted as necessary in all creative, constructive thought. A scientist doing a routine experiment does not need models, but a scientist devising an experiment to test a hypothesis may very well need to try out various models in order to locate what is unfamiliar about the present case. And so it is in all creative ventures. What we do not know, we must simulate through models of what we do know.

Because of the centrality of models in science and the amount of analysis available on scientific models, we will be looking carefully at some of this material for possible insights into the ways models function in theology. We will discover, for instance, that as interpretive, explanatory devices religious models share structural characteristics with scientific models; but because models in religion emerge from existential experience, they have affectional dimensions as do poetic metaphors. But a metaphorical theology cannot stop at the level of models. To be sure, considerable interpretive activity takes place at such a stage: as dominant metaphors, models manifest priorities within a religious tradition; as organizing networks of images, they are well on the way to systematic thought; as comprehensive ways of envisioning reality, they implicitly raise questions of truth and reference; as metaphors that control the ways people envision both human and divine reality, they cannot avoid the issue of criteria in the choice of certain models and the exclusion of others. A further step of interpretation, however, is called for: conceptual interpretation and criticism.

Concepts and theories arise from metaphors and models; they are an attempt to generalize at the level of abstraction concerning competing and, at times, contradictory metaphors and models. By "concept" we mean an abstract notion; by "theory" we mean a speculative, systematic statement of relationships underlying certain phenomena. A concept is an idea or thought; a theory organizes ideas into an explanatory structure. Concepts, unlike metaphors, do not create new meaning, but rely on conventional, accepted meanings. Theories, unlike models, do not systematize one area in terms of another, but organize concepts into a whole. These definitions are only minimally helpful, however, for they are too neat and compartmentalized for a metaphorical theology. If our thesis holds that *all* thought is indirect, then all concepts and theories are metaphorical in the sense that they too are constructions; they are indirect attempts to interpret reality, which never can be dealt with directly. Concepts and theories, however, are at the far end of the continuum and rarely expose their metaphorical roots. These distinctions mainly show the different functions of metaphor, model, and concept or theory in the *one* task of interpreting our being in the world.

Conceptual language tends toward univocity, toward clear and concise meanings for ambiguous, multileveled, imagistic language. In this process something is lost and something is gained: richness and multivalency are sacrificed for precision and consistency. Conceptual thought attempts to find similarities among the models while models insist on dissimilarities among themselves. The relationship, however, is symbiotic. Images "feed" concepts; concepts "discipline" images. Images without concepts are blind; concepts without images are sterile. In a metaphorical theology, there is no suggestion of a hierarchy among metaphors, models, and concepts: concepts are not higher, better, or more necessary than images, or vice versa. Images are never free of the need for interpretation by concepts, their critique of competing images, or their demythologizing of literalized models. Concepts are never free of the need for funding by images, the affectional and existential richness of images, and the qualification against conceptual pretensions supplied by the plurality of images. In no sense can systematic thought be said to *explain* metaphors and models so that they become mere illustrations for concepts; rather, the task of conceptual thought is to generalize (often in philosophical language, *the* generalizing language), to criticize images, to raise questions of their meaning and truth in explicit ways.

An example of the movement from parable toward conceptual thought can be illustrated briefly by the career of "the kingdom of God." I would call "the kingdom of God" the root-metaphor of Christianity which is supported and fed by many extended metaphors, the various parables. No *one* parable is adequate as a way of seeing the kingdom, and all the parables together undoubtedly are not either, but they are all that is provided. Many extended metaphors are necessary to give meaning to the model of the kingdom; taken together they display certain common features which are not illustrations of the kingdom so much as exemplifications of it. The process of understanding and interpreting these common features is not deductive or inductive but dialectical: "the rule of God" at this stage *is* all of the parabolic exemplifications. In the hands of Paul and his notion of "justification by faith," however, we move to a higher level of interpretation by a concept generalizing on that rule. Paul Ricoeur points out, and I believe rightly, that Paul's notion is in continuity with the foundational language of "the kingdom of God" and the underlying parables, but it is less particular, more generalized; less concrete, more abstract; less imagistic, more univocal. Ricoeur calls Paul's concept a "translation language," a semi-conceptual mode of discourse which remains under the control of the hermeneutical potential of metaphor *because* it preserves the tension of the foundational language.[26]

For another example of the relationship among metaphors, models, and concepts, one must remember that metaphors and models of God will range widely and have various degrees of dominance within a tradition: person, king, rock, mother, savior, father, fortress, lover, liberator, helper, and many more. We must ask questions of these models. Which ones are dominant? Why should certain ones be dominant? Are they consistent? Are the central models comprehensive? To whom are they significant? To whom are they meaningless or objectionable? Are they fruitful in the sense that they help us to understand our lives better, and are they commensurate with other matters we hold to be important? Do they fit with lived experience or do they have to be rationalized in order to be held? All of these questions and more fall under the heading of the critique of metaphors and models that is the task of conceptual thought.

Systematic thought also tries to organize all the dominant models in a tradition into an overarching system with a key model of its own. For instance, for Paul it was justification by grace through faith; for Augustine, the radical dependence of all that is on God; for Aquinas, the analogy of being whereby each creature participates in and glorifies God through realizing its proper finite end; for Schleiermacher, the feeling of absolute dependence; for

---

[26]Paul Ricoeur, "Biblical Hermeneutics," *Semeia* 4 (1975): 138.

Barth, the election of all people to salvation in the election of Jesus Christ
before the foundation of the world. Each of these is a radical model, which
could be called a "root-metaphor": "a root-metaphor is the most basic assumption about the nature of the world or experience that we can make when
we try to give a description of it."[27] Each root-metaphor is a way of seeing
"all that is" through a particular key concept. It is also thinking by models
and, as is evident, even these root-metaphors are still metaphors: at the
highest level of abstraction and generalization one does not escape metaphor
(the exceptions are symbolic logic and higher mathematics which do not
pretend to refer to reality as lived).

Therefore, we will focus on *models* because, as mediators between
metaphors and concepts, they partake of the characteristics of each and are
an especially fruitful type of expression to investigate for a metaphorical
theology. The aim of a metaphorical theology, as we recall, is to envision ways
of talking about the relationship between the divine and the human which
are nonidolatrous but relevant: ways which can be said to be true without
being literal; ways which are meaningful to all peoples, the traditionally
excluded as well as the included. Such a theology, I believe, is appropriate to
the Protestant sensibility and I have suggested clues to its character from the
parables of Jesus and Jesus as parable. In this framework, moreover, models
are critical because models are dominant *metaphors:* they retain the tension of
metaphor—its "is and is not" quality which refuses all literalization. Models
are also *dominant* metaphors: they are dominant within a tradition both
because they have earned that right as "classics" which speak to people across
many ages and because they have usurped that right to the false exclusion of
other metaphors. Both their right and their usurpation of right must be taken
into account.

The tasks of a metaphorical theology will become clear: to understand
the centrality of models in religion and the particular models in the Christian
tradition; to criticize literalized, exclusive models; to chart the relationships
among metaphors, models, and concepts; and to investigate possibilities for
transformative, revolutionary models.[28] The goal of this analysis can then be

---

[27]The term "root-metaphor" is Stephen Pepper's from his book *World Hypotheses* (Berkeley
and Los Angeles: Univ. of California Press, 1942). The quotation is from Earl R. MacCormac,
*Metaphor and Myth in Science and Religion* (Durham, N.C.: Duke Univ. Press, 1976), p. 93.

[28]I have used the term "metaphorical theology" rather than "parabolic theology" because
the latter limits theological discourse to the primary level. I have tried to show that, to varying
degrees, all constructive thought is implicitly or explicitly metaphorical (which is not to say that
"everything is metaphor," for much philosophical as well as most scientific and ordinary
language is at most mainly dead metaphor and does not function as alive metaphorical language).
Hence, metaphorical theology can refer to the entire spectrum from parable to concept, though
by using this term stress is put on the foundational, primary language that I believe is appropriate
and necessary to theology. Moreover, by retaining the term "metaphorical," the characteristics
of metaphor that I find critical to a theology in keeping with the Protestant sensibility, are
constantly called to mind—tentativeness, open-endedness, secularity, projected rather than
realized unity, tension, transformation, revolution, skepticism, and so on.

thought of as an attempt to question the *didactic* tradition of orthodoxy over the more flexible, open, *kerygmatic* point of view epitomized in the parables and Jesus as parable. What must be done in a metaphorical theology is to open up the relationships among metaphor, model, and concept for the purpose both of justifying dominant, founding metaphors as true but not literal *and* of discovering other appropriate dominant metaphors which for cultural, political, and social reasons have been suppressed.

The final task of a metaphorical theology will be a reforming, transforming one. As metaphorical, such theology can never be simply a baptizing of the tradition, for that would mean giving up the *tension* which is at the heart of metaphor. The classic models of the Christian tradition have been and still are hierarchical, authoritarian ones which have been absolutized. As feminist theologians have become increasingly aware, the orthodox tradition did a thorough job of plumbing the depths of one such model, the patriarchal, as a way of being articulate about God. Feminists have become conscious of the profound structural implications of this model as a form of ecclesiastical, social, political, economic, and personal oppression. The problem does not lie with the model itself of "God the father," for it is a profound metaphor and as true as any religious model available, but it has established a hegemony over the Western religious consciousness which it is the task of metaphorical theology to break. The "outsiders" to the mainline Christian tradition—women, blacks, third world people—are questioning the hierarchical, authoritarian, patriarchal models of Western theology. If Christianity is a universal religion (and not a tribal one for white, middle-class males), such voices are legitimate and necessary. As an example of one such voice, we will look at new religious images and models being suggested by women and we will do so in the spirit of openness to the future and to the unity that lies in the future, a spirit appropriate to a metaphorical theology. As Ursula LeGuin, a fantasy and science-fiction writer, says, truth lies in the imagination.[29] This may be only half a truth, but it is the half we most often forget.

---

[29] Ursula K. LeGuin, *The Language of the Night: Essays on Fantasy and Science Fiction*, ed. Susan Wood (New York: G.P. Putnam's Sons, 1979), p. 159.

# William Alston

William Alston (1921–      ) is the author of numerous articles on the
philosophy of religion which have proven highly influential.

# 32

# Religious Experience as a Ground of Religious Belief

## I

The question I wish to consider is whether religious experience can
provide any ground or basis for religious belief, whether it can serve to justify
religious belief, or make it rational. This essay will differ from many others
in the literature by virtue of looking at this question in the light of basic
epistemological issues. Throughout we will be comparing the epistemology
of religious experience with the epistemology of sense experience.

First, we must distinguish between experience directly providing justification for a belief and indirectly providing justification. It indirectly provides justification for belief $B_1$ when it provides justification for some other
beliefs, which in turn provide justification for $B_1$. Thus I have learned indirectly from experience that Beaujolais wine is fruity, because I have learned
from experience that this, that, and the other bottle of Beaujolais is fruity, and
these propositions support the generalization. Experience will diretcly justify
a belief when the justification does not go through other beliefs in this way.
There are quite different views as to just how experience can directly provide
justification, and some epistemologists deny that it can happen at all. In this
essay I shall think of direct experiential justification in terms of the subject's
being justified, by virtue of having the experience, in taking what he is
experiencing to be so-and-so. Thus if I am justified, by virtue of having the
visual experiences I am now having, in supposing what I am experiencing to
be a typewriter situated directly in front of me, then the belief that there is a
typewriter directly in front of me is directly justified by that experience. Less

---

From *Religious Experience and Religious Belief*, ed. Joseph Runzo and Craig Ihara (New York:
University Press of America, 1986). Reprinted with permission.

controversially, I may be directly justified by my experience in taking it that I feel upset.

On the explanation just given, any justification by reasons where the chain of reasons will eventually lead to beliefs justified directly by experience, will count as indirect experiential justification. I don't really want to cast the net that wide, but for our purposes it will not be necessary to draw a precise line. Let's just say that under the heading of indirect justification by experience we will restrict ourselves to cases in which direct experiential justification comes into the picture not very far back.

We find claims to both direct and indirect justification of religious beliefs by religious experience. Where someone believes that her new way of relating herself to the world after her conversion is to be explained by the Holy Spirit imparting supernatural graces to her, she supposes her belief that *the Holy Spirit imparts graces to her* to be indirectly justified by her experience. What she directly learns from experience is that she sees and reacts to things differently; this is then taken as a reason for supposing that the Holy Spirit is imparting graces to her. When, on the other hand, someone takes himself to be experiencing the presence of God, he thinks that his experience justifies him in supposing that God is *what* he is experiencing. Thus he supposes himself to be directly justified by his experience in believing God to be present to him.

No doubt this distinction is often difficult to draw, especially with respect to religious experience. Nevertheless there is a real distinction to be drawn here. A good way to get at the distinction is this. Suppose the subject was asked: "Just what were you aware of?" where it is clear that this asks for a specification of the object of awareness (consciousness) rather than how one is interpreting it or explaining it, or what suppositions one is forming about it. Then if the subject answers that question by saying "the presence of God" or "God sustaining my being," rather than, for example, "a profound sense of peace," or "a feeling of being filled with power," we may say that the subject takes himself to directly experience the presence of God, and to be directly justified by his experience in believing that God is present to him. If he answers in the second way, then he is, at most, indirectly justified by his experience in supposing God to be present to him. The crucial difference lies in what the subject takes to be the most basic way of specifying what he was experiencing, what he was aware of. That is, this is what is crucial to what he *takes* himself to be directly justified in believing on the basis of experience. Whether he *is* so justified is a further question.

In this essay I am going to confine myself to the question of whether religious experience can provide *direct* justification for religious belief. This has some implications for the class of experiences we shall be considering. In the widest sense, "religious experience" ranges over any experiences one has in connection with one's religious life, including any joys, fears, longings, or whatever one has in a religious context. But here I am concerned with experiences that could be taken to *directly* justify religious beliefs. Given the preceding explanation of that notion, this means that we are confining ourselves to experiences the subject takes to involve a direct awareness of what the religious belief is about. To focus the discussion further, let's confine ourselves to beliefs to the effect that God, as conceived in theistic religions, is doing something that is directed to the subject of the experience—that God is speaking to him, comforting him, strengthening him, enlightening him, giving him courage, guiding him, pouring out His love or joy into him, sustaining him in being, or just being present to him. Call these *M-beliefs* ("M" for "manifestation"). I want to focus on M-beliefs because they seem the best candidates for theistic beliefs that are directly justified by experience. Relatively abstract theological beliefs in the trinity, the incarnation, and the details of the divine nature would seem to be no more susceptible of direct justification by experience than are high-level scientific theories. Just as the public facts we can glean directly from sense experience consist, at most, in facts about the nature and situation of particular physical objects in the immediate vicinity, so it would seem that the theological facts I could learn directly from religious experience would consist, at most, in facts about how God impinges on my life. And, to continue the analogy, just as we would never reach any knowledge of "theoretical scientific facts" unless we had access to humble facts about particular middle-sized objects in the immediate vicinity, so it may be contended that we would never learn anything about the existence and nature and plans of God unless we could be aware of His operations in my life-space.

Finally, I will confine myself to religious experiences enjoyed by ordinary devout believers who have not undertaken a major contemplative or ascetic discipline, and who have not sacrificed all else to the attainment of an immediate vision of God. This means that I sacrifice the most obvious continuity with the bulk of the philosophical literature on the epistemology of religious experience, which concentrates, much too narrowly, on highly developed mystical experience. It is not surprising that so splashy and so easily demarcated a phenomenon as classical mystical experience should have attracted so much attention, but such experience, because of the extreme immediacy and ineffability allegedly involved, poses very special problems not generated by its humbler relatives; and the obsession with mystical experience has led to a serious neglect of the epistemology of the person in the pew.


## II

Let's call the view that religious experience can directly justify M-beliefs *religious empiricism*. Religious empiricism is compatible with a wide variety of views on the place of religious experience in a complete epistemology of religious belief. For example, it is compatible both with the view that experience merely serves to confirm or disconfirm other independent, and perhaps more basic, sources of justification, and with the view that the experiential justification of M-beliefs is basic to the whole edifice of religious belief. I will not be going into these wider questions in this essay.

What is our highest reasonable aspiration for being directly justified by experience? Being justified no matter what else is the case? A brief consideration of sense perception would suggest a negative answer. I may be justified in believing that there is a tree in front of me by virtue of the fact that I am currently having a certain kind of sense experience, but this will be true only in "favorable circumstances." If I am confronted with a complicated arrangement of mirrors, I may not be justified in believing that there is an oak tree in front of me, even though it looks for all the world as if there is. Again, it may look for all the world as if water is running uphill, but the general improbability of this greatly diminishes the justification the corresponding belief receives from that experience. What this shows is that the justification provided by one's sense experience is only *prima facie* or defeasible. It is inherently liable to be overridden, diminished, or canceled by stronger considerations to the contrary.

It would seem that direct experiential justification for M-beliefs is also, at most, *prima facie*. Beliefs about the nature and ways of God are often used to override M-beliefs, particularly beliefs concerning communications from God. If I report that God told me to kill all Wittgensteinians, fellow Christians will, no doubt, dismiss the report on the grounds that God wouldn't give me any such injunction as that. I shall take it that both sensory experience and religious experience provide, at most, *prima facie* justification.

Religious empiricism consists of a general principle of justification, a principle that specifies conditions under which beliefs of a certain sort are *prima facie* justified. Let's formulate the principle as follows.

(I) An M-belief is *prima facie* justified if *it arises from an experience that seems to the subject to be an experience of what is believed*. (Call the italicized condition C.)

(I) implies, for example, that if I come to believe that God is sustaining me in being because I seem to experience myself being sustained in being by God, then that belief is *prima facie* justified. In considering whether (I) is true, acceptable, rational, or whatever, we shall have to go on some assumptions, explicit or implicit, about what it is for a belief to be justified. Let's be explicit about this.

### III

First, the justification about which we are asking is an "epistemic" rather than a "moral" or "prudential" justification. What makes a justification *episte-*

*mic?* As the name implies, it has something to do with knowledge or, more broadly, with the aim at attaining truth and avoiding falsity. At a first approximation, I am justified in believing that *p* when, from the point of view of that aim, there is something okay, all right, to be approved, about the fact that I believe that *p*. But when we come to spell this out further, we find that a fundamental distinction must be drawn between two different ways of being in an epistemically commendable position.

On the one hand there is what we may call a "normative" concept of epistemic justification (*Jn*), normative because it has to do with how we stand vis-à-vis norms that specify our intellectual obligations, obligations that attach to one *qua* truth seeker. Stated most generally, to be *Jn* in believing that *p* consists in not having violated one's intellectual obligations in believing that *p*. We have to say "not having violated" rather than "having fulfilled" because in all normative spheres, *being justified* is a negative status; it amounts to one's behavior not being in violation of the norms. For example, to say that my expenditures on the trip were justified is not to say that I was obliged to make those expenditures (e.g., for taxis), but only that it was all right for me to do so, that in doing so I was not in violation of any relevant rules or regulations. If belief is under voluntary control, we may think of intellectual obligations as attaching directly to believing, as most advocates of a normative conception do. Thus one might be obliged to refrain from believing in the absence of adequate evidence. But if, as seems obvious to me, belief is not under voluntary control, obligations cannot attach directly to believing. However, I do have voluntary control over moves that can influence a particular belief formation, such as looking for more evidence, and moves that can affect my belief-forming habits or tendencies, such as training myself to be more critical of testimony. This suggests that we might think of the relevant normative principles as governing what we can do voluntarily to influence our beliefs. One will be doing one's intellectual duty if one engages in such belief-influencing activities as the norms require. We can then think of being-in-the-clear, normatively, as consisting, roughly, in the fact that the belief does not stem from violations of such intellectual obligations. It would be like the way in which one is or isn't to blame for other conditions or processes that are not themselves under voluntary control. I am subject to reproach for being overweight (being irritable, being in poor health, being without friends) only if the condition is in some way due to my own past failures to do what I should to limit my intake or to exercise or whatever. If I were still overweight even if I had done everything I could and should have done about it, then I can hardly be blamed for it. Similarly, we may say that I am subject to reproach for believing that *p* only if there are things I could and should have done, such that if I had done them I would not now be believing that *p*. If that is the case, I am normatively *unjustified* in that belief. If that is not the case, if my believing that *p* does not depend on violation of intellectual obligations, then I am normatively *justified*, *Jn*, in believing that *p*. I will be restricting myself to this "involuntaristic" version of *Jn*, the one that does not assume belief to be under direct voluntary control.

Some epistemologists, on the other hand, use the term "justified" in such a way that it has to do not with how the subject stands vis-a-vis obligations, but rather with the strength of her epistemic position in believing that *p*, with how likely it is that a belief of that sort acquired or held in that way is true. In what ways can one's "position" in believing that *p* be a strong one, vis-à-vis the aim at truth? How can the way in which one believes that *p* be "truth-conducive"? For one thing, *p* might be well supported by reasons that one has, by other things one knows or is justified in believing. (I) could not be true on this "reasonableness" account of justification, just as no other claim to direct justification by experience could be. For to say that a belief is directly supported by experience is to say that, given the appropriate experience (plus the absence of defeaters, if that is needed), the belief is justified whether or not the subject has adequate reasons for the belief. A less *ad hoc* reason for dismissing this understanding of justification is that it ignores the way in which the belief originated and/or is sustained; on the "reasonableness" conception one might *have* adequate reasons for a belief, whatever produces or sustains the belief. But any set of conditions that leaves open the possibility that a belief arose as a sheer guess, or on the basis of wishful thinking, cannot be sufficient for epistemic justification.

There is a "truth-conduciveness" conception of justification that is more interesting for our purposes. This is the "reliability" conception, according to which a belief is justified *iff* it arose from a process of belief formation and/or sustenance that is a generally reliable one, that can be generally relied on to produce true beliefs.[1] This is the most obvious way in which a subject can believe that *p* in a way that is generally truth-conducive. Where the belief is due to a process that is a generally reliable one, it is not just a matter of hitting the mark in this particular instance. Let us dub this "reliability" conception of justification *Jr*. In discussing (I), I will restrict myself to *Jr* and *Jn*.

To underscore the difference between *Jn* and *Jr*, let's consider some cases in which a practice is justified in the one sense but not in the other. Consider a naive member of an isolated primitive tribe who, along with his fellows, unhesitatingly accepts the traditions of the tribe. That is, he engages in the practice of believing *p* wherever the traditions of the tribe, as recited by the elders, include the assertion that *p*. He is normatively justified in doing so, for he has no reason whatsoever to doubt these traditions. Everyone he knows accepts them without question, and they do not conflict with anything else he believes. And yet, let us suppose, this is in fact not a reliable procedure of

---

[1] Being *based* on adequate reasons is one form of this, but not the only possible form. There can also be reliable ways in which a belief arises from experience.

belief formation, and so he is not justified in the *Jr* sense. Conversely, a procedure may be in fact reliable, though I have strong reasons for regarding it as unreliable and so would not be normatively justified in engaging in it; to do so would be to ignore those reasons and so would be a violation of an intellectual obligation. Suppose that I have been presented with overwhelming, though spurious, evidence that for about half the time over the last ten years I have, without realizing it, been in a physiological laboratory where my sensory experience was artificially produced. In this case I have strong reasons for supposing that I cannot tell at a given moment whether I am engaging in normal perception or not; and so I have strong reasons for regarding my perceptual belief-forming processes as unreliable. Nevertheless, they are as reliable as any normal person's.

## IV

If (I) is interpreted in terms of *Jr*, then the question of its truth is just the question of whether the "epistemic practice,"[2] as we might say, of forming M-beliefs on the basis of religious experience is a generally reliable one. I will consider in due time what can be said on this score. But first, let's see what the issue amounts to if (I) is understood in terms of *Jn*.

Remember that being *Jn* in believing that *p* hangs on whether that belief depends on some failure to carry out intellectual obligations. But here we are talking not about the justification of a particular belief; we are considering whether all M-beliefs that satisfy condition *C* are justified. If that is the case, then, understanding justification as *Jn*, no M-belief that satisfies *C* depends on any failure of intellectual obligation. The question of whether all M-beliefs that satisfy *C* are *Jn* is just the question of whether the satisfaction of *C* by an M-belief ensures that the belief does not stem from a failure to carry out intellectual obligations.

Whether this is so is going to depend, *inter alia*, on what intellectual obligations we have. Let's take it that our most fundamental aim as intellectual beings is to believe the true and to avoid believing the false. Now if belief were under voluntary control, that would mean that our most fundamental obligation would be, for each proposition *p* we consider, to believe that *p iff* it is true, or, more realistically, to believe that *p iff* we have sufficient reason to suppose it to be true. But since we are not taking belief to be under voluntary control, our intellectual obligations will have to be thought of as applying to things that we can do voluntarily to affect our belief-forming practices, what we are calling "epistemic practices." Keeping in mind the fundamental aim at truth and the avoidance of falsity, we can then say that

---

[2]It should be abundantly clear that, contrary to what might be the suggestion of the term, we are *not* taking epistemic practices to involve *voluntary* actions.

our basic intellectual obligation is to try to make our epistemic practice as *reliable* as possible, as well designed as possible to produce true and only true beliefs.[3]

Because our belief-forming processes are only imperfectly under our (indirect) control, the obligation had to be stated in terms of *trying* to bring it about that we engage only in reliable practices. To avoid tedious circumlocutions I shall henceforth make the simplifying assumption that belief-forming processes are wholly within our (indirect) control. Thus we can speak of being obliged to restrict ourselves to reliable practices, rather than of being obliged to *try* to so restrict ourselves.[4] This gives us the following formulation of our basic intellectual obligation.

> (II) One is obliged to refrain from engaging in an epistemic practice *iff* it is not reliable.[5]

However, to put it this way overestimates our capacity to determine the reliability of practices. If we could always or usually ascertain reliability on inspection, (II) would be a satisfactory formulation. But in fact the most we have, all too often, are reasons that are far from conclusive. This suggests that the condition for our being obliged to refrain should be couched in terms of reasons we have that bear on unreliability, rather than in terms of unreliability itself. But when we set out to make this revision we find that there are two candidates for a sufficient condition for an obligation to refrain. On the one

---

[3]This indicates a crucial connection between *Jn* and *Jr*. Even though one can be *Jn* without being *Jr*, still one can be *Jn* only if one's belief doesn't stem from failures to attempt to make one's belief-forming practices reliable and hence to make one's beliefs *Jr*. Being *Jn*, we might say, is to have aimed as one should at being *Jr*.

[4]The main difference between this idealized formulation and the more realistic one is that where we are unable to prevent ourselves from engaging in an epistemic practice, we will thereby be *Jn* in the beliefs that emerge from it, whatever its reliability and whatever we have reason to think of its reliability. Whereas on the simplifying assumption, that complexity is washed out.

[5]The reader will note that our fundamental intellectual obligation, according to (II), has to do only with refraining from epistemic practices; nothing is said as to conditions under which we are obliged to engage in practices. I don't want to deny that we have a purely intellectual obligation to engage in belief-forming practices, but the conditions under which one is so obliged would be very difficult to spell out. It obviously won't do to take the simplest tack and say that one is obliged to engage in a practice *iff* it is reliable. Assuming that there are several reliable practices, that would leave us with an intolerable multiplicity of jointly unfulfillable obligations. (That same point would hold on the "reasons" formulation to be presented next, provided there is a multiplicity of practices concerning which we have the appropriate reasons.) Of course, one could say that we have a *prima facie* obligation to engage in each reliable practice at any given time, but that this is often overridden by more pressing obligations. But even this is untenable. Suppose that at this moment I have no other pressing obligations at all. It still seems false that I am obliged to engage in the practice of acquiring information about Attic vase painting from the Encyclopaedia Britannica, just on the grounds that this is a reliable epistemic practice and/or one that I have adequate reason to regard as reliable. What we want in the way of a positive obligation is, roughly speaking, an obligation to engage in practices of the proper sort a reasonable proportion of the time. For the purposes of this paper I do not need to get into all that. The obligation to refrain will be sufficient to generate the problems I need to consider here.

hand there are adequate reasons for taking a practice, $P$, to be unreliable; and on the other hand there is the lack of adequate reasons for taking $P$ to be reliable. Everyone who has gone along with the argument up to this point will agree that the former generates an intellectual obligation to refrain; if that doesn't, nothing does. But there will be controversy over the latter. Suppose that I do actually engage in practice $P$, or have a considerable tendency to do so. And suppose that I have sufficient reasons neither for a judgment of reliability nor for a judgment of unreliability. Am I obliged to refrain (remembering our assumption of effective control)? This issue is reminiscent of the famous Clifford-James confrontation over the ethics of belief. There it was the question of whether one is justified in believing only when in possession of adequate reasons for the proposition believed, or whether the mere absence of adequate reasons for the contradictory entitles one to believe. Are beliefs to be held guilty until proven innocent, or innocent until proven guilty? We are now considering a precisely parallel issue concerning epistemic practices. Those who take the hard, Cliffordian line hold that one is obliged to refrain unless one has adequate reasons for reliability; while the partisans of the more permissive, Jamesian line hold that one is obliged to refrain only if one has adequate reasons for unreliability. They agree that one is obliged to refrain where one has adequate reasons for unreliability, and they agree that one is not so obliged where one has adequate reasons for reliability. But they disagree over the case in which one has adequate reasons for neither.

The Jamesian position might be supported by bringing in our need to guide our behavior by our beliefs. Suppose that we have adequate reasons for the reliability of none, or very few, epistemic practices. (The further course of this essay will indicate that this is a live possibility.) In that case, the stricter line would have us form no, or very few, beliefs; and that is hardly a defensible position. But it is not my aim in this essay to settle this issue. Instead, I want to recognize both these positions and consider the application of each to our central problem concerning religious empiricism. Let's formulate each principle of obligation as follows. The stricter one will read:

(III) One is obliged to refrain from engaging in an epistemic practice *iff* it is not the case that one has adequate reasons for taking that practice to be reliable.

And the more permissive one will read:

(IV) One is obliged to refrain from engaging in an epistemic practice *iff* one has adequate reasons for taking that epistemic practice to be unreliable.[6]

---

[6]There are, of course, various positions that are intermediate between these pure extremes. Thus one might hold that one is obliged to abstain from a practice if one has *some* reason to regard it as unreliable, and no reason to regard it as reliable. In this short discussion we shall have to restrict ourselves to the simplest alternatives.

Now let's apply all this to the question of the truth of I. on a *Jn* construal. Let's use the term *Jns* for *Jn* with the strong principle of obligation, (III), and the term *Jnw* for *Jn* with the weaker principle of obligation, IV. Now we can say that M-beliefs that satisfy C are *Jns* provided there are adequate reasons for the reliability of the practice of forming M-beliefs in the presence of C. (Call this practice *RE*, for "religious experience.") For if there are such reasons, then one has not violated any intellectual obligations in engaging in *RE*, and so beliefs formed from that practice are *Jn*. Whereas M-beliefs that satisfy C are *Jnw*, provided that there are no adequate reasons for the unreliability of *RE*. For in that case one has not violated (IV) in engaging in *RE*, and so beliefs formed by *RE* are *Jn*. Thus the question of whether M-beliefs that satisfy C are *Jn* boils down to the question of whether there are adequate reasons for the reliability or for the unreliability of *RE*.

We have just been making an additional idealization. Whether a given person is *Jn* in believing that *p* does not depend on what reasons there are (in the abstract, in general) for or against the reliability of the appropriate practice; it depends on what reasons that person has. And this can, and will, vary a great deal from person to person. But in this paper we are not interested in individual variations. We want to know whether one *can* be justified by one's experience in holding an M-belief; we want to know whether there are conditions, satisfiable currently by actual human beings, under which one would be so justified. In order to bypass individual variation we shall be thinking in terms of an idealized subject that is *au courant* with whatever relevant reasons are available to a reasonably educated, intelligent, and reflective person today. With that idealization the question of *Jn* will hang on what reasons are available.

Hearkening back to *Jr*, we remember that whether M-beliefs that satisfy C are *Jr* depends on whether *RE is* reliable. But in discussing that issue, there is nothing for us to do except to determine what reasons there are for and against the reliability of *RE*. It is not as if it is self-evident, or otherwise immediately knowable, that *RE* is or is not reliable. But that is just what we have to consider to determine whether I is true on a *Jn* construal. So, whatever concept of justification we pick, the issue will hang on what reasons there are for the reliability or unreliability of *RE*.

## V

I want to set my discussion of reasons for or against the reliability of *RE* in the context of a *general* discussion of the evaluation of epistemic practices. For only in that way can we assess the significance of the results we will obtain for the restricted question of *RE*.

First, let's distinguish between what we may call practices of belief creation (C-practices) and practices of belief transformation (T-practices). A

C-practice "creates" beliefs out of something other than beliefs, whereas T-practices produce new beliefs from old beliefs (perhaps along with other conditions).[7] A C-practice, so to say, *creates* beliefs out of non-doxastic materials, whereas a T-practice might be thought of as simply *transforming* an initial set of beliefs into other beliefs with different contents. (If this picture gives you trouble, just take the terms as arbitrary labels.) *RE* is a C-practice, since the operative condition involves a certain kind of experience and the *absence* of defeaters; it does not include other beliefs. More generally, any practice of forming beliefs "directly" from experience will count as a C-practice.

To simplify and focus the discussion, I will restrict myself to C-practices. In particular, I will concentrate on comparing the epistemic status of *RE* with a much more thoroughly explored C-practice, that of forming beliefs about the immediate physical environment on the basis of sense experience. Let's call such a practice *PP* (for "perceptual practice"). *PP* gives rise to the same epistemological questions as *RE*. We may ask whether a perceptual belief about the immediate environment (P-belief)—for example, the belief that there is a maple tree in front of me—is justified by virtue of arising from a certain kind of sense experience. And again our highest reasonable aspiration will be a *prima facie* justification. The principle of justification for P-beliefs, parallel to (I) for M-beliefs, will be:

(V) A P-belief is *prima facie* justified if *it arises from a sense experience that seems to the subject to present the fact believed.* (Call the italicized condition D.)

And in deciding whether (V) is true, on various concepts of justification, we will, by the line of reasoning just sketched for (I), be driven back to parallel problems about what reasons there are for the reliability or unreliability of *PP*. Thus the comparison of the epistemic statuses of *RE* and *PP* will boil down to an investigation of the reasons for the reliability or unreliability of the two practices.[8]

---

[7] T-practices might be called "inferential" practices, but because of persistent unclarity over the boundaries of that term I have avoided it.

[8] Before considering *PP* and *RE* specifically, let's note that it is not possible to demonstrate reliability, or to provide reasons of any sort for or against, *all* our epistemic practices. For in order to provide non-circular reasons for the reliability of a practice, *P*, we have to use some other practice to acquire those reasons. Whatever practice we use, we are assuming *it* to be reliable in putting forward those reasons; and so if it were *P* that we were using, we would be assuming its reliability in order to establish its reliability. But if we are using some other practice, *Q*, then in order to provide reasons for its reliability we have to use some practice other than *P* or *Q*, if we are not to fall into circularity. It is easy to see that unless we are to generate an infinite regress or fall at some point into circularity, we must at some point simply rely on the reliability of a practice without being able to show that it is reliable. Nor does this argument presuppose a foundationalist conception of the structure of knowledge. Assume a coherence theory. Then to show that *P* is reliable we would show that the assumption of its reliability coheres with *S* (the system coherence with which is our supreme test). Now if *P* is *not* *C*, the practice of accepting beliefs on the basis of coherence with *S*, all is well so far. But now what about the question of the reliability of *C*? If that reliability is shown by alleging coherence with *C*, we are involved in circularity. If not, we must use another practice to garner support for *C*, and we are off to the races again.

## VI

Let's begin with reasons for the reliability of *PP*, and first let's note a reason for pessimism about our chances. We may distinguish between "basic" and "derived" epistemic practices. As far as C-practices are concerned, the gut idea of a basic practice is that it is one that constitutes our basic access to its subject matter, so that any other access presupposes it. Of course, if we put it that way we would seem to be presupposing the validity of the practice in question, so let's put it negatively. A C-practice, *P*, is *basic* provided there is no other practice that yields beliefs about its subject matter and provided its reliability is independent of the reliability of *P*. It would seem that *PP* is basic in this sense. Any other way of finding out about the physical world presupposes the reliability of *PP*. The use of instruments such as thermometers presupposes the reliability of *PP*, both because we have to use *PP* to get the thermometer reading and because our confidence in those readings is ultimately based on data obtained by *PP*.

Here is why this is a reason for pessimism. We are unable to marshal the most direct conceivable reasons for the reliability of *PP*, viz., a comparison of its deliverances with the facts in question. For we would have to ascertain those facts either by *PP* itself or some other practice. And in either case, since *PP* is basic, we would be *presupposing* the reliability of *PP* and the reasoning would be circular.

Before proceeding further, we should specify the kind of circularity just alluded to. It is not logical circularity. Even if one uses *PP* itself to provide reasons for the claim that *PP* is reliable, that claim does not itself appear among the premises of one's argument. For example, suppose that I argue for the reliability of *PP* by citing the fact that by engaging in *PP* we are enabled to gain some considerable success in predicting the future course of events. Here we use *PP*, of course, to ascertain that this is the case. We tell what people predict by listening to what they say and reading what they write. And we tell whether things come out as they predict by taking a look or a listen. But the claim of the reliability of *PP* does not appear among our premises. Those premises just contain claims of predictive success. Then where is the circularity? It comes in the fact that, in supposing ourselves entitled to those premises, we are relying (in practice) on the reliability of *PP*. The reliability of *PP* is a presupposition of our adducing those premises.[9] Let's term this mode of circularity "epistemic circularity." We may say that an argument is epistemically circular *iff* the conclusion is assumed (at least in practice) by the arguer in supposing himself to *know*, or to be *justified* in believing, the premises.

---

[9] This could be flushed out by a challenge to our procedure. If we were asked why we supposed ourselves to know that such and such a prediction was made and borne out, if the inquiry were pushed sufficiently far, and if we were sufficiently reflective and candid, we would eventually be forced to claim the reliability of PP in supporting our procedure.

It is not obvious that epistemic circularity is a fatal flaw in an argument.[10] But if epistemic circularity is to be allowed, then it will be too easy to mount an acceptable argument for the reliability of *any* C-practice. We simply compare the deliverances of that practice with the facts, as determined by that practice. The practice being tested will always score 100 percent. Moreover, epistemically circular arguments are dialectically impotent in a context in which the reliability of a practice is in question. If I doubt that *P* is reliable, or if I am just trying to determine whether there are any reasons for supposing it to be, I am unlikely to be impressed with the point that it can be shown to be reliable if we use *it* to produce the premises. In this essay we are examining the reliability of *RE* in a context in which its reliability is not taken for granted. And we want, by comparison, to see what could be done to show the reliability of *PP* in a context in which that was not taken for granted. Therefore we shall disallow epistemically circular arguments. From now on, "circular" is to be read "epistemically circular."

Since we are unable, without circularity, to check the testimony of *PP* against the facts attested to, how could we establish its reliability? There have been a number of ingenious attempts to use other practices, usually purely rational ones, to establish facts that will provide support for taking *PP* to be reliable. Thus Descartes appealed to the veracity and benevolence of God, which he took himself to have established *a priori*. Wittgenstein, Strawson, and others have employed transcendental arguments to the effect that the reliability of *PP* is a necessary condition of having a conception of oneself or attributing states of consciousness to oneself or using a language.[11] More recently, Michael Slote and Richard Brandt have argued on methodological grounds that relying on *PP* is the most rational move to make. Some of these arguments exhibit epistemic circularity, albeit in a less blatant form than, for example, the appeal to predictive success. Others suffer from a variety of other defects. I believe that none of them succeeds, and I see little hope that

---

[10]In a recent article ("Foundationalism, Epistemic Principles, and the Cartesian Circle," *Philosophical Review*, 88 (1979), pp. 55–91.) James van Cleve (1979) has sought to absolve Descartes from the famous charge of circularity. He points out that when Descartes uses clear and distinct perceptions to obtain the premises he then uses to prove the existence of God, from which he derives the conclusion that clear and distinct perceptions are reliable, he is not guilty of logical circularity, since the claim of the reliability of clear and distinct perception does not itself appear among the premises. Van Cleve does not seem to find the epistemic circularity involved to be disturbing. And, indeed, something is to be said for this position. As van Cleve points out, if it is merely *true* that all clear and distinct perceptions are true, then Descartes will be *justified* in accepting propositions because he clearly and distinctly perceives them, even if he does not know, and is not justified in believing, the proposition that all clear and distinct perceptions are true. Thus Descartes could become justified by this procedure in accepting the general principle, provided it was *true* all along; he wouldn't have had to be justified antecedently in believing it.

[11]These arguments have not generally been explicitly cast as arguments for the reliability of *PP*, but something like that is part of what the argument seeks to establish.

others will do better. If I had a general argument for the impossibility of success, I would certainly unveil it at this point, but in the absence of such an argument my position can be supported only by unmasking each pretender in turn. Obviously I have no time for that here; I am forced to simply assume that there are no adequate non-circular reasons for the reliability of *PP*. Given that assumption, it follows that our P-beliefs are not *Jns* by sense experience. And though they *may* be *Jr*, we lack sufficient positive reason for supposing them to be.

What about reasons for the unreliability of *PP*? Here there will be little controversy. Except for those who, like Parmenides and Bradley, have argued that there are ineradicable inconsistencies in the conceptual scheme involved in *PP*, philosophers have not supposed that we can show that sense perception is an unreliable guide to our immediate surroundings. Sceptics about sense perception have generally confined themselves to arguing that we can't show that sense perception is reliable; that is, they have argued that *PP* is not *Jns*. I shall assume without further argument that we do not have adequate reasons for taking *PP* to be unreliable, and hence that our P-beliefs are *Jnw* by sense experience.

Thus it would seem that *Jnw* is the most we have sufficient reason to attribute to P-beliefs, on the basis of sense experience. In other words, we have adequate reason to take V to be true only on the *Jnw* interpretation. Now let's turn to M-beliefs and begin there, too, by asking whether we have adequate reasons for the reliability of *RE*.

## VII

The first thing to ask in this connection is whether *RE* is a basic C-practice. Many would suppose that it is not. We may neutralize partisans of revelation as an independent source of knowledge about God by maintaining that revelation must be received through the experience of revelatees, so that this is just a special form of *RE*. But there still remains the claim that we can gain knowledge of God by reasoning from premises that make no appeal to *RE*. And even if *RE* is basic, there could still be parallels to the attempts to show *PP* to be reliable. Since this is something else I will not have time to go into, I shall just assume that a thorough examination would reveal that here too there are no adequate non-circular reasons for the reliability of *RE*, and hence that M-beliefs are not *Jns* by experience. And once more, though they may be *Jr*, we have no sufficient positive reason for supposing them to be.

This brings us once more to *Jnw*. If M-beliefs are *Jnw*, then their epistemic status is quite parallel to that of P-beliefs. And they will be, provided that there are no adequate reasons for regarding *RE* as unreliable. Are there such reasons? What might they be?

First, we can have the most direct and unquestionably relevant reason for regarding an epistemic practice as unreliable if we have ascertained that its outputs are generally incorrect, or not generally correct. Now to the extent that RE yields beliefs about matters that we also have some other, perhaps more favored way of discovering, its unreliability could be shown in this way. Perhaps something like this is involved when fundamentalist Christians take it on the "inward testimony of the Holy Spirit" that the Bible is the word of God and then suppose that in the Bible God is telling us about the physical history and constitution of the universe. However, one who engages in RE need not get involved in anything like that. I shall restrict the discussion to a kind of RE that only yields beliefs about God, His nature and His doings, the truth or falsity of which are not assessable on empirical or scientific grounds.

That still leaves the possibility that we might establish conclusions by philosophical reasoning that contradict all or many of the products of RE. For example, we might demonstrate the non-existence of God. Or, contrariwise, we might be able to show that God's nature is such that He couldn't be doing what He is frequently represented in RE as doing. Finally, we might be able to show that RE yields a system of belief that is ineradicably internally inconsistent. (I am not speaking of isolated and remediable inconsistencies that continually pop up in every area of thought and experience.) I don't believe that we are able to bring off any of this, but again I won't have time to argue the point.[12] Instead, I will pass on to some other putative grounds for unreliability, where the considerations alleged are relatively uncontroversial; it is their relevance to the question of reliability that is dubious.

I believe that many people are inclined to take RE to be discredited by certain ways in which it differs from PP, by the lack of certain salient features of PP. These include the following.

(1) Within PP there are standard ways of checking the accuracy of any particular perceptual belief.

(2) By engaging in PP we can discover regularities in the behavior of the objects putatively observed, and on this basis we can, to a certain extent, effectively predict the course of events.

(3) Capacity for PP, and practice of it, is found universally among normal adult human beings.

(4) All normal adult human beings, whatever their culture, use basically the same conceptual scheme in objectifying their sense experience.

---

[12]Unfortunately, the argument of this essay depends on three assumptions I have not been able to support. (1) There are no adequate reasons for the reliability of PP. (2) There are no adequate reasons for the reliability of RE. (3) We cannot use philosophical reasoning to establish conclusions that generally disconfirm the deliverances of RE.

It is the first of these features that has been most often invoked in this connection by twentieth-century philosophers. Nevertheless, it is just a special case of (2). Our standard checking procedures in *PP* presuppose that we know a good deal about the ways in which things can be expected to behave in the physical world. Consider the appeal to other observers. Suppose I think I see a fir tree across the street from my house. What would count as intersubjective corroboration? Not *any* report of seeing a fir tree. If someone reports seeing a fir tree in Nepal, that will not tend to show that there is a fir tree across from my house. Nor will the failure of someone in Nepal, or across town, to see a fir tree have any tendency to disconfirm my report. Nor if a blind man stands just where I was standing and fails to see a fir tree, would that disconfirm my report. The point is, of course, that only observers that satisfy certain conditions as to location, condition, state of the environment, etc., can qualify as either confirming or disconfirming my report. And how do we know what conditions to specify? We do it in the light of presumed regularities in the interaction of physical objects and sentient subjects. Persons in certain circumstances, and only in those circumstances, will count as possible confirmers or disconfirmers of my claim, because given what we know about the way things go, it is only persons in such circumstances that could be expected to see a fir tree if there is one there. Similar points can be made about the other modes of testing. Since (1) is just a special case of (2), we can concentrate on the latter.

It would seem that theistic practice does not exhibit these features.

(1) and (2). Religious experience does not put us in a position to make predictions about the divine, despite the persistent claims of apocalyptic groups. God, so far as we can tell from our experience, does not operate in accordance with any regularities discernible by us. We are not able to anticipate God's punishment or forgiveness, the granting or withdrawing of His grace. No more are we able to anticipate where, when, or under what conditions He will enter into a human being's experience. Hence we are not in a position to devise checking procedures, to specify what experiences some other subject would have under certain conditions if what the first subject reported of God is correct.

(3). *RE* is not a common possession of mankind in the way *PP* is. This divides into two points. (a) Many people do not engage in *RE* at all. This includes both those who do not take themselves to be experiencing any divine or transcendent reality at all (some of whom are religious believers), and those who objectify religious experience with schemes quite different from those of theistic religions. (b) Most of the practitioners of *RE* are aware of the presence of God only fleetingly and, for the most part, uncertainly. Awareness of God is usually a dim, elusive matter, lacking in detail and vividness and eminently subject to doubt. It is like seeing something in a dense fog, or, in a more traditional phrase, through a glass, darkly. All this is in sharp contrast to the clarity, detail, persistence, and irresistible convincingness of sense perception.

(4). It hardly requires mention that religious experience gets objectified in terms of radically different conceptual schemes in different religious traditions. The same general sort of experience that a Christian takes to be an awareness of the presence of a supreme personal deity might be taken in Hindu circles as an experienced identity of the self with a supreme undifferentiated unity. Where individuals experience God as communicating something to them, these messages will differ in ways that, generally but not invariably, correspond to the locally dominant theology.

Before coming to grips with the alleged epistemic bearing of these differences, I want to make two preliminary points. (1) We have to engage in *PP* to determine that this practice has features 1–4, and that *CP* lacks them. Apart from observation, we have no way of knowing that, for example, whereas all cultures agree in their way of cognizing the physical environment, they differ in their ways of cognizing the divine, or that *PP* puts us in a position to predict while *CP* doesn't. It might be thought that this is loading the dice in favor of my opponent. If we are to use *PP*, rather than some neutral source, to determine what features *it* has, shouldn't the same courtesy of self-assessment be accorded *CP*? Why should *it* be judged on the basis of what we learn about it from another practice, while that other practice is allowed to grade itself? To be sure, this is a serious issue only if answers to these questions *are* forthcoming from *CP* that differ from those we arrive at by engaging in *PP*. Fortunately, I can avoid getting involved in these issues by ruling that what I am interested in here is how *CP* looks from the standpoint of *PP*. The person I am primarily concerned to address is one who, like all the rest of us, engages in *PP* and supposes it to be generally reliable. My aim is to show this person that, on his own grounds, *CP* enjoys basically the same epistemic status as *PP*. Hence it is consonant with my purposes to allow *PP* to determine the facts of the matter with respect to both practices. (2) I could quibble over whether the contrast is as sharp as is alleged. Questions could be raised about both sides of the putative divide. On the *PP* side, is it really true that all cultures have objectified sense experience in the same way? Many anthropologists have thought not. And what about the idea that all *normal* adult human beings engage in the same perceptual practice? Aren't we loading the dice by taking participation in what we regard as standard perceptual practice as our basic criterion for normality? On the *CP* side, is it really the case that this practice reveals no regularities to us, or only that they are very different from regularities in the physical world? What about the point that God is faithful to His promises? Or that the pure in heart will see God? However, I believe that when all legitimate quibbles have been duly registered there will still be very significant difference between the two practices in these respects. So rather than contesting the factual allegations, I will concentrate on the *de jure* issue as to what bearing these differences have on epistemic status.

Why suppose that the lack of these features constitutes an adequate, or even a significant, reason for taking *RE* to be unreliable? I can see that (1)–(4) are desiderata for an epistemic practice. If we were shaping the world to our heart's desire, we would arrange for our practices to exhibit these features. Since *PP* possesses them and *RE* does not, the former is, to that extent and in that way, superior. But, granting all that, why should we suppose that the lack of these features is incompatible with reliability?

Presumably, one who thinks this is reasoning as follows. In the case of *PP*, these features are manifestations of reliability.[13] It is because *PP* is reliable that it yields successful predictions, that its practitioners tend to agree, and so on. These are ways in which its reliability shows itself. Therefore, when we encounter a practice that lacks these manifestations, we can conclude that it also lacks reliability; otherwise analogous manifestations would be forthcoming.

The trouble with this reasoning is that it assumes that reliability will manifest itself in these ways wherever and whenever it is found, and without specific reasons for assuming that we are not entitled to the assumption. It is certainly not true in general that when a state or condition manifests itself by *M* in certain cases, it will yield *M wherever* it is found. Being a good philosopher sometimes, but not always, manifests itself by the production of many important writings. Anger sometimes, but not always, shows itself in increased volume of speech. And so on. Why should we suppose that the reliability of an epistemic practice always shows itself in features like (1)–(4)? I can see no warrant for any such supposition. So far as I can see, it is just a kind of parochialism that makes the lack of (1)–(4) seem to be token unreliability. One uncritically takes salient features of *PP*, ways in which reliability shows itself there, as necessary conditions of reliability.

I will now, in conclusion, support this judgment by indicating how *RE*, in particular, could well be reliable in the absence of (1)–(4). I shall sketch out a possible state of affairs in which *RE* is quite trustworthy while lacking (1)–(4), and then suggest that we have no reason to suppose that this state of affairs does not obtain.

Suppose, then, that (A) God is too different from created beings, too "wholly other," for us to be able to grasp any regularities in His behavior. Suppose further that (B) for the same reasons we can only attain the faintest, sketchiest, and most insecure grasp of what God is like. Finally, suppose that (C) God has decreed that a human being will be aware of His presence in any

---

[13]This point must not be put by saying: "These features give us an adequate reason for taking *PP* to be reliable." Since we can only ascertain these features by using *PP*, any such reasoning would be infected with epistemic circularity.

clear and unmistakable fashion only when certain special and difficult conditions are satisfied. If all this is the case, then it is the reverse of surprising that RE should lack 1–4 even if it does involve a genuine experience of God. It would lack 1–2 because of (A). It is quite understandable that it should lack 4 because of (B). If our cognitive powers are not fitted to frame an adequate conception of God, it is not at all surprising that there should be wide variation in attempts to do so. This is what typically happens in science when investigators are grappling with a phenomenon no one really understands. A variety of models, analogues, metaphors, hypotheses, hunches are propounded, and it is impossible to secure universal agreement. Feature (3) is missing because of (C). If very difficult conditions are set, it is not surprising that few are chosen. Now it is compatible with (A)–(C) that (D) religious experience should, in general, constitute a genuine awareness of the divine, and that (E) although any particular articulation of such an experience might be mistaken to a greater or lesser extent, indeed even though all such articulations might miss the mark to some extent, still such judgments will for the most part contain some measure of truth; and that (F) God's designs contain provision for correction and refinement, for increasing the accuracy of the beliefs derived from religious experience. If something like (A)–(F) is the case, then RE is trustworthy even though it lacks features (1)–(4). This is a conceivable way in which RE would constitute a road to the truth, while differing from PP in respects (1)–(4). Therefore, unless we have adequate reason for supposing that (A)–(F) does not obtain, as we do not, we cannot infer the unreliability of RE from the lack of (1)–(4).

Moreover, it is not just that (A)–(C) constitute a bare possibility. In the practice of RE we seem to learn that this is the way things are. As for (A) and (B), it is the common teaching of all the higher religions that God is of a radically different order of being from finite substances and, therefore, that we cannot expect to attain the grasp of His nature and His doings that we have of worldly objects. As for (C), it is a basic theme in Christianity, and in other religions as well, that one finds God within one's experience, to any considerable degree, only as one progresses in the spiritual life. God is not available for *voyeurs*. Awareness of God, and understanding of His nature and His will for us, is not a purely cognitive achievement; it requires the involvement of the whole person; it takes a practical commitment and a practice of the life of the spirit, as well as the exercise of cognitive faculties.

To be sure, if in the last paragraph I were arguing for the reliability of RE by alleging that (A)–(C) obtain, then that argument would be vitiated with circularity since we have no reason for supposing that (A)–(C) obtain, apart from assuming the reliability of RE, or some other religious epistemic practice. But that was not the point. In calling attention to the fact that RE yields (A)–(C), I was merely reinforcing the negative point that we lack adequate reason for supposing that these conditions do not obtain. So far from that being the case, insofar as any epistemic practice claims to tell us anything about the matter, what it tells us is that they do obtain. Thus the basic point is still the negative one. We do not have adequate reason for supposing that (A)–(F) do not obtain, and, therefore, we are not justified in taking the absence of (1)–(4) to establish the unreliability of *RE*.


## VIII

I conclude that M-beliefs have basically the same epistemic status as P-beliefs, and that one who regards the latter as *prima facie* justified by experience is in no position to deny that status to the former.

# Alvin Plantinga

Alvin Plantinga (1932–      ) is the author of many influential works on
the philosophy of religion, including *God and Other Minds* and *God,
Freedom and Evil*.

# 33

# *On Taking Belief in God as Basic*

### I. THE EVIDENTIALIST OBJECTION TO THEISTIC BELIEF

Many philosophers—Clifford, Blanshard, Russell, Scriven, and Flew, to
name a few—have argued that belief in God is irrational, or unreasonable, or
not rationally acceptable, or intellectually irresponsible, or somehow noetic-
ally below par because, as they say, there is *insufficient evidence* for it.[1] Bertrand
Russell was once asked what he would say if, after dying, he were brought
into the presence of God and asked why he hadn't been a believer. Russell's
reply: "I'd say, 'Not enough evidence, God! Not enough evidence!' "[2] I don't
know just how such a response would be received; but Russell, like many
others, held that theistic belief is unreasonable because there is insufficient
evidence for it. We all remember W. K. Clifford, that delicious *enfant terrible*,
as William James called him, and his insistence that it is immoral, wicked,
and monstrous, and maybe even impolite to accept a belief for which you
don't have sufficient evidence:

> Who so would deserve well of his fellows in this matter will guard the purity
> of his belief with a very fanaticism of jealous care, lest at any time it should rest
> on an unworthy object, and catch a stain which can never be wiped away.

From *Religious Experience and Religious Belief*, ed. Joseph Runzo and Craig Ihara (New York:
University Press of America, 1986). Reprinted with permission.

[1]See, for example, Blanshard, *Reason and Belief*, pp. 400ff; Clifford, "The Ethics of Belief,"
pp. 345ff; Flew, *The Presumption of Atheism*, p. 22; Russell, "Why I Am Not a Christian," pp. 3ff;
and Scriven, *Primary Philosophy*, pp. 87ff. In Plantinga, "Is Belief in God Rational?" I consider and
reject the evidentialist objection to theistic belief.

[2]W. Salmon, "Religion and Science: A New Look at Hume's Dialogues," *Philosophical
Studies* 33 (1978), p. 176.

He adds that if a

> belief has been accepted on insufficient evidence, the pleasure is a stolen one. Not only does it deceive ourselves by giving us a sense of power which we do not really possess, but it is sinful, because it is stolen in defiance of our duty to mankind. That duty is to guard ourselves from such beliefs as from a pestilence which may shortly master our body and spread to the rest of the town.

and finally:

> To sum up: it is wrong always, everywhere, and for anyone to believe anything upon insufficient evidence.

(It is not hard to detect, in these quotations, the "tone of robustious pathos" with which James credits him.) Clifford, of course, held that one who accepts belief in God *does* accept that belief on insufficient evidence, and has indeed defied his duty to mankind. More recently, Bertrand Russell has endorsed the evidentialist injunction "Give to any hypothesis which is worth your while to consider, just that degree or credence which the evidence warrants."

More recently, Anthony Flew[3] has commended what he calls Clifford's "luminous and compulsive essay" (perhaps "compulsive" here is a misprint for "compelling"); and Flew goes on to claim that there is, in his words a "presumption of atheism." What is a presumption of atheism, and why should we think there is one? Flew puts it as follows:

> The debate about the existence of God should properly begin from the presumption of atheism . . . the onus of proof must lie upon the theist. The word "atheism," however, has in this contention to be construed unusually. Whereas nowadays the usual meaning of "atheist" in English is "someone who asserts there is no such being as God," I want the word to be understood not positively but negatively. I want the original Greek prefix "a" to be read in the same way in "atheist" as it is customarily read in such other Greco-English words as "amoral," "atypical," and "asymmetrical." In this interpretation an atheist becomes: not someone who positively asserts the non-existence of God; but someone who is simply not a theist.
>
> What the protagonist of my presumption of atheism wants to show is that the debate about the existence of God ought to be conducted in a particular way, and that the issue should be seen in a certain perspective. His thesis about the onus of proof involves that it is up to the theist: first to introduce and to defend his proposed concept of God; and second, to provide sufficient reason for believing that this concept of his does in fact have an application.

---

[3] A. G. N. Flew, *The Presumption of Atheism* (London: Pemberton Publishing Co., 1976).

How shall we understand this? What does it mean, for example, to say that the debate "should properly begin from the presumption of atheism"? What sorts of things do debates begin from, and what is it for one to begin from such a thing? Perhaps Flew means something like this: to speak of where a debate should begin is to speak of the sorts of premises to which the affirmative and negative sides can properly appeal in arguing their cases. Suppose you and I are debating the question whether, say, the United States has a right to seize Mideast oil fields if the OPEC countries refuse to sell us oil at what we think is a fair price. I take the affirmative, and produce for my conclusion an argument one premise of which is the proposition that the United States has indeed a right to seize these oil fields under those conditions. Doubtless that maneuver would earn me very few points. Similarly, a debate about the existence of God cannot sensibly start from the assumption that God does indeed exist. That is to say, the affirmative can't properly appeal, in its arguments, to such premises as that there is such a person as God; if it could, it'd have much too easy a time of it. So in this sense of "start," Flew is quite right: the debate can't start from the assumption that God exists.

Of course, it is also true that the debate can't start from the assumption that God does *not* exist; using "atheism" in its ordinary sense, there is equally a presumption of aatheism (which, by a familiary principle of logic, reduces to theism). So it looks as if there is in Flew's sense a presumption of atheism, all right, but in that same sense an equal presumption of aatheism. If this is what Flew means, then what he says is entirely correct, if something of a truism.

In another passage, however, Flew seems to understand the presumption of atheism in quite another different fashion:

> It is by reference to this inescapable demand for grounds that the presumption of atheism is justified. If it is to be established that there is a God, then we have to have good grounds for believing that this is indeed so. Until or unless some such grounds are produced we have literally no reason at all for believing; and in that situation the only reasonable posture must be that of either the negative atheist or the agnostic.

Here we have the much more substantial suggestion that it is unreasonable or irrational to accept theistic belief in the absence of sufficient grounds or reasons. And of course Flew, along with Russell, Clifford, and many others, holds that in fact there aren't sufficient grounds or evidence for belief in God. The evidentialist objection, therefore, appeals to the following two premises:

(A) It is irrational or unreasonable to accept theistic belief in the absence of sufficient evidence or reasons.

and

(B) There is no evidence, or at any rate not sufficient evidence, for the proposition that God exists.

(B), I think, is at best dubious. At present, however, I'm interested in the objector's other premise—the claim that it is irrational or unreasonable to accept theistic belief in the absence of evidence or reasons. Why suppose *that's* true? Why suppose a theist must have evidence or reason to think there *is* evidence for this belief, if he is not to be irrational? This isn't just *obvious*, after all.

Now many Reformed thinkers and theologians[4] have rejected *natural theology* (thought of as the attempt to provide proofs or arguments for the existence of God). They have held not merely that the proffered arguments are unsuccessful, but that the whole enterprise is in some way radically misguided. I have argued (1980) that the Reformed rejection of natural theology is best construed as an inchoate and unfocused rejection of (A). What these Reformed thinkers really mean to hold, I think, is that belief in God is properly basic: it need not be based on argument or evidence from other propositions at all. They mean to hold that the believer is entirely within his intellectual right in believing as he does, even if he doesn't know of any good theistic argument (deductive or inductive), even if he doesn't believe that there is any such argument, and even if in fact no such argument exists. They hold that it is perfectly rational to accept belief in God without accepting it on the basis of any other beliefs or propositions at all. Why suppose that the believer must have evidence if he is not to be irrational? Why should anyone accept (A)? What is to be said in its favor?

Suppose we begin by asking what the objector means by describing a belief as *irrational*. What is the force of his claim that the theistic belief is irrational and how is it to be understood? The first thing to see is that this claim is rooted in a *normative* contention. It lays down conditions that must be met by anyone whose system of beliefs is *rational*; and here "rational" is to be taken as a normative or evaluative term. According to the objector, there is a right way and a wrong way with respect to belief. People have responsibilities, duties and obligations with respect to their believings just as they do with respect to their actions—or if we think believings are a kind of action, their *other* actions. Professor Brand Blanshard puts this clearly:

> everywhere and always belief has an ethical aspect. There is such a thing as a general ethics of the intellect. The main principle of that ethic I hold to be the same inside and outside religion. This principle is simple and sweeping: Equate your assent to the evidence. (*Reason and Belief*, p. 401)

---

[4]A Reformed thinker or theologian is one whose intellectual sympathies lie with the Protestant tradition going back to John Calvin (not someone who was formerly a theologian and has since seen the light).

and according to Michael Scriven:

> Now even belief in something for which there is no evidence, i.e., a belief which
> goes beyond the evidence, although a lesser sin that a belief in something which
> is contrary to well-established laws, is plainly irrational in that it simply
> amounts to attaching belief where it is not justified. So the proper alternative,
> when there is no evidence, is not mere suspension of belief, e.g., about Santa
> Claus, it is disbelief. It most certainly is not faith. (*Primary Philosophy*, p. 103)

Perhaps this sort of obligation is really a special case of a more general moral
obligation; or perhaps, on the other hand, it is *sui generis*. In any event, says
the objector, there are such obligations: to conform to them is to be rational
and to go against them is to be irrational.

Now here the objector seems right; there are duties and obligations with
respect to beliefs. One's own welfare and that of others sometimes depends
on what one believes. If we're descending the Grand Teton and I'm setting
the anchor for the 120-foot rappel into the Upper Saddle, I have an obligation
to form such beliefs as *this anchor point is solid* only on the basis of careful
scrutiny and testing. One comissioned to gather intelligence—the spies
Joshua sent into Canaan, for example—has an obligation to get it right. I have
an obligation with respect to the belief that Justin Martyr was a Latin apologist—an obligation arising from the fact that I teach medieval philosophy,
must make a declaration on this issue, and am obliged not to mislead my
students here. The precise *form* of these obligations may be hard to specify:
am I obliged to believe that J. M. was a Latin apologist if and only if J. M. *was*
a Latin apologist? Or to form a belief on this topic only after the appropriate
amount of checking and investigating? Or maybe just to tell the students the
truth about it, whatever I myself believe in the privacy of my own study? Or
to tell them what's generally thought by those who should know? In the
rappel case: Do I have a duty to believe that the anchor point is solid if and
only if it is? Or just to check carefully before forming the belief? Or perhaps
there's no obligation to believe at all, but only to *act on* a certain belief only
after appropriate investigation. In any event, it seems plausible to hold that
there are obligations and norms with respect to belief, and I do not intend to
contest this assumption.

The objector begins, therefore, from the plausible contention that there
are duties or obligations with respect to belief: call them *intellectual duties*.
These duties can be understood in several ways. First, we could construe
them teleologically; we could adopt an intellectual utilitarianism. Here the
rough idea is that our intellectual obligations arise out of a connection
between our beliefs and what is intrinsically good and intrinsically bad; and
our intellectual obligations are just a special case of the general obligation so
to act to maximize good and minimize evil. Perhaps this is how W. K. Clifford
thinks of the matter. If people accepted such propositions as *this DC-10 is*

*airworthy* when the evidence is insufficient, the consequences could be disastrous: so perhaps some of us, at any rate, have an obligation to believe that proposition only in the presence of adequate evidence. The intellectual utilitarian could be an ideal utilitarian; he could hold that certain epistemic states are intrinsically valuable—knowledge, perhaps, or believing the truth, or a skeptical and judicial temper that is not blown about by every wind of doctrine. Among our duties, then, is a duty to try to bring about these valuable states of affairs. Perhaps this is how Professor Roderick Chisholm is to be understood when he says

> Let us consider the concept of what might be called an "intellectual requirement." We may assume that every person is subject to a purely intellectual requirement: that of trying his best to bring it about that, for every proposition that he considers, he accepts it if and only if it is true. (*Theory of Knowledge*, 2nd ed., p. 9)

Secondly, we could construe intellectual obligations *aretetically;* we could adopt what Professor Frankena calls a "mixed ethics of virtue" with respect to the intellect. There are valuable noetic or intellectual states (whether intrinsically or extrinsically valuable); there are also the corresponding intellectual virtues, the habits of acting so as to produce or promote or enhance those valuable states. One's intellectual obligations, then, are to try to produce and enhance these intellectual virtues in oneself and others.

Thirdly, we could construe intellectual obligations *deontologically;* we could adopt a *pure* ethics of obligation with respect to the intellect. Perhaps there are intellectual obligations that do not arise from any connection with good or evil, but attach to us just by virtue of our having the sorts of noetic powers human beings do in fact display. The quotation from Chisholm could also be understood along these lines.

Intellectual obligations, therefore, can be understood teleologically or aretetically or deontologically. And perhaps there are purely intellectual obligations of the following sorts. Perhaps I have a duty not to take as basic a proposition whose denial seems self-evident. Perhaps I have a duty to take as basic the proposition *I seem to see a tree* under certain conditions. With respect to certain kinds of propositions, perhaps I have a duty to believe them only if I have evidence for them, and a duty to proportion the strength of my belief to the strength of my evidence.

Of course, these would be *prima facie* obligations. One presumably has an obligation not to take bread from the grocery store without permission and another to tell the truth. Both can be overridden, in specific circumstances, by other obligations—in the first case, perhaps, an obligation to feed my starving children and in the second, an obligation to protect a human life. So we must distinguish *prima facie* duties or obligations from *all-things-considered* or *on-balance* (*ultima facie?*) obligations. I have a *prima facie* obligation to tell the truth;

in a given situation, however, that obligation may be overridden by others, so that my duty, all things considered, is to tell a lie. This is the grain of truth contained in situation ethics and the ill-named "new morality."

And *prima facie* intellectual obligations can conflict, just as obligations of other sorts. Perhaps I have a *prima facie* obligation to believe what seems to me self-evident, and what seems to me to follow self-evidently from what seems to me self-evident. But what if, as in the Russell paradoxes, something that seems self-evidently false apparently follows, self-evidently, from what seems self-evidently true? Here *prima facie* intellectual obligations conflict, and no matter what I do I will violate a *prima facie* obligation. Another example: in reporting the Grand Teton rappel, I neglected to mention the violent electrical storm coming in from the southwest; to escape it we must get off in a hurry, so that I have a *prima facie* obligation to inspect the anchor point carefully, but anchor to set up the rappel rapidly, which means I can't spend a lot of time inspecting the anchor point.

Thus lightly armed, suppose we return to the evidential objector. Does he mean to hold that the theist without evidence is violating some intellectual obligation? If so, which one? Does he claim, for example, that the theist is violating his *ultima facie* intellectual obligation in thus believing? Perhaps he thinks anyone who believes in God without evidence is violating his all-things-considered intellectual duty. This, however, seems unduly harsh. What about the fourteen-year-old theist brought up to believe in God in a community where everyone believes? This fourteen-year-old theist, we may suppose, doesn't believe on the basis of evidence. He doesn't argue thus: everyone around here says God loves us and cares for us; most of what everyone around here says is true; so probably *that's* true. Instead, he simply believes what he's taught. Is he violating an all-things-considered intellectual duty? Surely not. And what about the mature theist—Thomas Aquinas, let's say—who thinks he *does* have adequate evidence? Let's suppose he's wrong; let's suppose all of his arguments are failures. Nevertheless, he has reflected long, hard, and conscientiously on the matter and thinks he *does* have adequate evidence. Shall we suppose he's violating an all-things-considered intellectual duty here? I should think not. So construed, the objector's contention is totally implausible.

Perhaps, then, he is to be understood as claiming that there is a *prima facie* intellectual duty not to believe in God without evidence. This duty can be overridden by circumstances, of course; but there is a *prima facie* obligation to believe propositions of this sort only on the basis of evidence. But here too there are problems. The suggestion is that I now have the *prima facie* obligation to believe propositions of this sort only on the basis of evidence. I have a *prima facie* duty to comply with the following command: either have evidence or don't believe. But this may be a command I can't comply with. The objector thinks there *isn't* adequate evidence for this belief, so presumably I can't *have* adequate evidence for it, unless we suppose I could create some. And it is also not within my power to refrain from believing this proposition. My beliefs aren't for the most part directly within my control. If you order me now, for example, to cease believing that the earth is very old, there's no way I can comply with your order. But in the same way it isn't within my power to cease believing in God now. So this alleged *prima facie* duty is one it isn't within my power to comply with. But how can I have a *prima facie* duty to do what isn't within my power to do?

Presumably, then, the objector means to be understood in still another fashion. Although it is not within my power now to cease believing now, there may be a series of actions now, such that I can now take the first, and after taking the first, will be able to take the second, and so on; and after taking the whole series of actions, I will no longer believe in God. Perhaps the objector thinks it is my *prima facie* duty to undertake whatever sort of regimen will at some time in the future result in my not believing without evidence. Perhaps I should attend a Universalist Unitarian Church, for example, and consort with members of the Rationalist Society of America. Perhaps I should read a lot of Voltaire and Bertrand Russell. Even if I can't now stop believing without evidence, perhaps there are other actions I can now take, such that if I do take them, then at some time in the future I won't be in this deplorable condition.

There is still another option available to the objector. He need not hold that the theist without evidence is violating some duty, *prima facie, ultima facie* or otherwise. Consider someone who believes that Venus is smaller than Mercury, not because he has evidence, but because he finds it amusing to believe what everyone disbelieves—or consider someone who holds this belief on the basis of an outrageously bad argument. Perhaps there is no obligation he has failed to meet; nevertheless his intellectual condition is defective in some way; or perhaps alternatively there is a commonly achieved excellence he fails to display. Perhaps he is like someone who is easily gulled, or walks with a limp, or has a serious astigmatism, or is unduly clumsy. And perhaps the evidentialist objection is to be understood, not as the claim that the theist without evidence has failed to meet some obligation, but that he suffers from a certain sort of intellectual deficiency. If this is the objector's view, then his proper attitude towards the theist would be one of sympathy rather than censure.

These are some of the ways, then, in which the evidentialist objection could be developed; and of course there are still other possibilities. For ease of exposition, let us take the claim deontologically; what I shall say will apply *mutatis mutandis* if we take it one of the other ways. The evidentialist objector, then, holds that it is irrational to believe in God without evidence. He doesn't typically hold, however, that the same goes for *every* proposition; for given certain plausible conditions on the evidence relation it would follow that if we believe anything, then we are under obligation to believe infinitely many propositions. Let's say that proposition *p* is *basic* for a person *S* if *S* believes *p* but does not have evidence for *p*; and let's say that p is *properly basic* for *S* if *S* is within his epistemic rights in taking *p* as basic. The evidentialist objection, therefore, presupposes some view about what sorts of propositions are correctly or rightly or justifiably taken as basic; it presupposes a view about what is properly basic. And the minimally relevant claim for the evidentialist objector is that belief in God is *not* properly basic. Typically this objection has been rooted in some form of *classical foundationalism*, an enormously popular picture or total way of looking at faith, knowledge, justified belief, rationality and allied topics. This picture had been widely accepted ever since the days of Plato and Aristotle; its near relatives, perhaps, remain the dominant ways of thinking about these topics. According to the classical foundationalist, some propositions are *properly* or *rightly* basic for a person and some are not. Those that are not are rationally accepted only on the basis of *evidence* where the evidence must trace back, ultimately, to what is properly basic. Now there are two varieties of classical foundationalism. According to the ancient and medieval variety, a proposition is properly basic for a person *S* if and only if it is either self-evident to *S* or "evident to the senses," to use Aquinas' term for *S*; according to the modern variety, a proposition is properly basic for *S* if and only if it is either self-evident to *S* or incorrigible for him. For ease of exposition, let's say that classical foundationalism is the disjunction of ancient and medieval with modern foundationalism; according to the classical foundationalist, then, a proposition is properly basic for a person *S* if and only if it is either self-evident to *S* or incorrigible for *S* or evident to the senses for *S*.

Now I said that the evidentialist objection to theistic belief is typically rooted in classical foundationalism. Insofar as it is so rooted, it is *poorly* rooted. For classical foundationalism is self-referentially incoherent. Consider the main tenet of classical foundationalism:

(C)   *p* is properly basic for *S* if and only if *p* is self-evident, incorrigible, or evident to the senses for *S*.

Now of course the classical foundationalist accepts (C) and proposes that we do so as well. And either he takes (C) as basic or he doesn't. If he doesn't, then if he is rational in accepting it, he must by his own claims have an argument for it from propositions that are properly basic, by argument forms whose corresponding conditionals are properly basic. Classical foundationalists do not, so far as I know, offer such arguments for (C). I suspect the reason is that they don't know of any arguments of that sort for (C). It is certainly hard to see what such an argument would be. Accordingly, classical foundationalists probably take (C) as basic. But then according to (C) itself, if (C) is properly taken as basic, it must be either self-evident, incorrigible, or evident to the senses for the foundationalist, and clearly it isn't any of those. If the foundationalist takes (C) as basic, therefore, he is self-referentially inconsistent. We must conclude, I think, that the classical foundationalist is in self-referential hot water—his own acceptance of the central tenet of his view is irrational by his own standards.

## II. OBJECTIONS TO TAKING BELIEF IN GOD AS BASIC

Insofar as the evidentialist objection is rooted in classical foundationalism, it is poorly rooted indeed; and so far as I know, no one has developed and articulated any other reason for supporting that belief in God is not properly basic. Of course it doesn't follow that it *is* properly basic; perhaps the class of properly basic propositions is broader than classical foundationalists think, but still not broad enough to admit belief in God. But why think so? What might be the objections to the Reformed view that belief in God is properly basic?

I've heard it argued that if I have no evidence for the existence of God, then if I accept that proposition, my belief will be *groundless*, or *gratuitous*, or *arbitrary*. I think this is an error; let me explain.

Suppose we consider perceptual beliefs, memory beliefs, and beliefs ascribing mental states to other persons: such beliefs as

(1) I see a tree.
(2) I had breakfast this morning.
(3) That person is angry.

Although beliefs of this sort are typically and properly taken as basic, it would be a mistake to describe them as *groundless*. Upon having experience of a certain sort, I believe that I am perceiving a tree. In the typical case I do not hold this belief on the basis of other beliefs; it is nonetheless not groundless. My having that characteristic sort of experience—to use Professor Chisholm's language, my being appeared treely to—plays a crucial role in the formation and justification of that belief. We might say this experience, together, perhaps, with other circumstances, is what *justifies* me in holding it; this is the *ground* of my justification, and, by extension, the ground of the belief itself.

If I see someone displaying typical pain behavior, I take it that he or she is in pain. Again, I don't take the displayed behavior as *evidence* for that belief; I don't infer that belief from others I hold; I don't accept it on the basis of other beliefs. Still, my perceiving the pain behavior plays a unique role in the formation and justification of that belief; as in the previous case, it forms the ground of my justification for the belief in question. The same holds for memory beliefs. I seem to remember having breakfast this morning; that is, I have an inclination to believe the proposition that I had breakfast, along with a certain past-tinged experience that is familiar to all but hard to describe. Perhaps we should say that I am appeared to pastly; but perhaps that insufficiently distinguishes the experience in question from that accompanying beliefs about the past not grounded in my own memory. The phenomenology of memory is a rich and unexplored realm; here I have no time to explore it. In this case as in the others, however, there is a justifying circumstance present, a condition that forms the ground of my justification for accepting the memory belief in question.

In each of these cases, a belief is taken as basic, and in each case properly taken as basic. In each case there is some circumstance or condition that confers justification; there is a circumstance that serves as the *ground* of justification. So in each case there will be some true proposition of the sort:

> (4) In condition C, S is justified in taking p as basic. Of course C will vary with p.

For a perceptual judgment such as

> (5) I see a rose-colored wall before me,

C will include my being appeared to in a certain fashion. No doubt C will include more. If I'm appeared to in the familiar fashion but know that I am wearing rose-colored glasses, or that I am suffering from a disease that causes me to be thus appeared to, no matter what the color of the nearby objects, then I am not justified in taking (5) as basic. Similarly for memory. Suppose I know that my memory is unreliable; it often plays me tricks. In particular, when I seem to remember having breakfast, then, more often than not, I *haven't* had breakfast. Under these conditions I am not justified in taking it as basic that I had breakfast, even though I seem to remember that I did.

So being appropriately appeared to, in the perceptual case, is not sufficient for justification; some further condition—a condition hard to state in detail—is clearly necessary. The central point, here, however, is that a belief is properly basic only in certain conditions; these conditions are, we might say, the ground of its justification and, by extension, the ground of the belief itself. In this sense, basic beliefs are not, or are not necessarily, *groundless* beliefs.

Now similar things may be said about belief in God. When the Reformers claim that this belief is properly basic, they do not mean to say, of course, that there are no justifying circumstances for it, or that it is in that sense groundless or gratuitous. Quite the contrary. Calvin holds that God "reveals and daily discloses himself in the whole workmanship of the universe," and the divine art "reveals itself in the innumerable and yet distinct and well-ordered variety of the heavenly host." God has so created us that we have a tendency or disposition to see his hand in the world about us. More precisely, there is in us a disposition to believe propositions of the sort *this flower was created by God* or *this vast and intricate universe was created by God* when we contemplate the flower or behold the starry heavens or think about the vast reaches of the universe.

Calvin recognizes, at least implicitly, that other sorts of conditions may trigger this disposition. Upon reading the Bible, one may be impressed with a deep sense that God is speaking to one. Upon having done what I know is cheap, or wrong, or wicked, I may feel guilty in God's sight and form the belief *God disapproves of what I've done*. Upon confession and repentance, I may feel forgiven, forming the belief *God forgives me for what I've done*. A person in grave danger may turn to God, asking for His protection and help; and of course he or she then forms the belief that God is indeed able to hear and help if He sees fit. When life is sweet and satisfying, a spontaneous sense of gratitude may well up within the soul; someone in this condition may thank and praise the Lord for His goodness, and will of course form the accompanying belief that indeed the Lord is to be thanked and praised.

There are therefore many conditions and circumstances that call forth belief in God: guilt, gratitude, danger, a sense of God's presence, a sense that He speaks, perception of various parts of the universe. A complete job would explore the phenomenology of all these conditions and of more besides. This is a large and important topic; but here I can only point to the existence of these conditions.

Of course, none of the beliefs I mentioned a moment ago is the simple belief that God exists. What we have instead are such beliefs as

(6) God is speaking to me.
(7) God has created all this.
(8) God disapproves of what I have done.
(9) God forgives me.
(10) God is to be thanked and praised.

These propositions are properly basic in the right circumstances. But it is quite consistent with this to suppose that the proposition *there is such a person as God* is neither properly basic nor taken as basic by those who believe in God. Perhaps what they take as basic are such propositions as (6)–(10), believing in the existence of God on the basis of such propositions. From this point of view, it isn't exactly right to say that belief in God is properly basic; more exactly, what are properly basic are such propositions (6)–(10), each of which self-evidently entails that God exists. It isn't the relatively high level and general proposition *God exists* that is properly basic, but instead propositions detailing some of His attributes or actions.

Suppose we return to the analogy between belief in God and belief in the existence of perceptual objects, other persons, and the past. Here too it is relatively specific and concrete propositions rather than their more general and abstract colleagues that are properly basic. Perhaps such items as

(11) There are trees.
(12) There are other persons.
(13) The world has existed for more than 5 minutes

are not properly basic; it is instead such propositions as

(14) I see a tree.
(15) That person is pleased.
(16) I had breakfast more than an hour ago

that deserve the accolade. Of course, propositions of the latter sort immediately and self-evidently entail propositions of the former sort; and perhaps there is thus no harm in speaking of the former as properly basic, even though so to speak is to speak a bit loosely.

The same must be said about belief in God. We may say, speaking loosely, that belief in God is properly basic; strictly speaking, however, it is probably not that proposition but such propositions as (6)–(10) that enjoy that status. But the main point, here, is this: belief in God or (6)–(10) are properly basic; to say so, however, is not to deny that there are justifying conditions for these beliefs, or conditions that confer justification on one who accepts them as basic. They are therefore not groundless or gratuitous.

A second objection I've often heard: If belief in God is properly basic, why can't *just any* belief be properly basic? What about voodoo or astrology? What about the belief that the Great Pumpkin returns every Halloween? Could I properly take *that* as basic? And if I can't, why can I properly take belief in God as basic? Suppose I believe that if I flap my arms with sufficient vigor, I can take off and fly about the room; could I defend myself against the charge of irrationality by claiming this belief is basic? If we say that belief in God is properly basic, won't we be committed to holding that just anything, or nearly anything, can properly be taken as basic, thus throwing wide the gates to irrationalism and superstition?

Certainly not. What might lead one to think the Reformed epistemologist is in this kind of trouble? The fact that he rejects the criteria for proper basicality purveyed by classical foundationalism? But why should *that* be thought to commit him to such tolerance or irrationality? Consider an analogy. In the palmy days of positivism, the positivists went about confidently wielding their verifiability criterion and declaring meaningless much that was obviously meaningful. Now suppose someone rejected a formulation of that criterion—the one to be found in the second edition of A. J. Ayer's *Language, Truth and Logic*, for example. Would that mean she was committed to holding that

(17)  'Twas brillig; and the slithy toves did gyre and gimble in the wabe

contrary to appearances, makes good sense? Of course not. But then the same goes for the Reformed epistemologist; the fact that he rejects the Classical Foundationalist's criterion of proper basicality does not mean that he is committed to supposing just anything is properly basic.

But what then is the problem? Is it that the Reformed epistemologist not only rejects those criteria for proper basicality, but seems in no hurry to produce what he takes to be a better substitute? If he has no such criterion, how can he fairly reject belief in the Great Pumpkin as properly basic?

This objection betrays an important misconception. How do we rightly arrive at or develop criteria for meaningfulness, or justified belief, or proper basicality? Where do they come from? Must one have such a criterion before one can sensibly make any judgments—positive or negative—about proper basicality? Surely not. Suppose I don't know of a satisfactory substitute for the criteria proposed by Classical Foundationalism; I am nevertheless entirely within my rights in holding that certain propositions are not properly basic in certain conditions. Some propositions seem self-evident when in fact they are not; that is the lesson of some of the Russell paradoxes. Nevertheless it would be irrational to take as basic the denial of a proposition that seems self-evident to you. Similarly, suppose it seems to you that you see a tree; you would then be irrational in taking as basic the proposition that you don't see a tree, or that there aren't any trees. In the same way, even if I don't know of some illuminating criterion of meaning, I can quite properly declare (17) meaningless.

And this raises an important question—one Roderick Chisholm has taught us to ask. What is the status of the criteria for knowledge, or proper basicality, or justified belief? Typically, these are universal statements. The modern foundationalist's criterion for proper basicality, for example, is doubly universal:

(18)  For any proposition *A* and person *S*, *A* is properly basic for *S* if and only if *A* is incorrigible for *S* or self-evident to *S*.

But how could one know a thing like that? What are its credentials? Clearly enough, (18) isn't self-evident or just obviously true. But if it isn't, how does one arrive at it? What sorts of arguments would be appropriate? Of course, a foundationalist might find (18) so appealing, he simply takes it to be true, neither offering argument for it, nor accepting it on the basis of other things he believes. If he does so, however, his noetic structure will be self-referentially incoherent. (18) itself is neither self-evident nor incorrigible; hence in accepting (18) as basic, the modern foundationalist violates the condition of proper basicality he himself lays down in accepting it. On the other hand, perhaps the foundationalist will try to produce some argument for it from premises that are self-evident or incorrigible: it is exceedingly hard to see, however, what such an argument might be like. And until he has produced such arguments, what shall the rest of us do—we who do not find (18) at all obvious or compelling? How could he use (18) to show us that belief in God, for example, is not properly basic? Why should we believe (18), or pay it any attention?

The fact is, I think, that neither (18) nor any other revealing necessary and sufficient condition for proper basicality follows from clearly self-evident premises by clearly acceptable arguments. And hence the proper way to arrive at such a criterion is, broadly speaking, *inductive*. We must assemble examples of beliefs and conditions such that the former are obviously properly basic in the latter, and examples of beliefs and conditions such that the former are obviously *not* properly basic in the latter. We must then frame hypotheses on the necessary and sufficient conditions of proper basicality and test these hypotheses by reference to those examples. Under the right conditions, for example, it is clearly rational to believe that you see a human person before you: a being who has thoughts and feelings, who knows and believes things, who makes decisions and acts. It is clear, furthermore, that you are under no obligation to reason to this belief from others you hold; under those conditions that belief is properly basic for you. But then (18) must be mistaken; the belief in question, under those circumstances, is properly basic, though neither self-evident nor incorrigible for you. Similarly, you may seem to remember that you had breakfast this morning, and perhaps you know of no reason to suppose your memory is playing you tricks. If so, you are entirely justified in taking that belief as basic. Of course it isn't properly basic on the criteria offered by classical foundationalists; but that fact counts not against you but against those criteria.

Accordingly, criteria for proper basicality must be reached from below rather than above; they should not be presented as *obiter dicta*, but argued to and tested by a relevant set of examples. But there is no reason to assume, in advance, that everyone will agree on the examples. The Christian will of course suppose that belief in God is entirely proper and rational; if he doesn't accept this belief on the basis of other propositions, he will conclude that it is basic for him and quite properly so. Followers of Bertrand Russell and Madelyn Murray O'Hare may disagree, but how is that relevant? Must my criteria, or those of the Christian community, conform to their examples?

Surely not. The Christian community is responsible to *its* set of examples, not to theirs.

Accordingly, the Reformed epistemologist can properly hold that belief in the Great Pumpkin is not properly basic, even though he holds that belief in God *is* properly basic and even if he has no full-fledged criterion of proper basicality. Of course he is committed to supposing that there is a relevant *difference* between belief in God and belief in the Great Pumpkin, if he holds that the former, but not the latter, is properly basic. But this should prove no great embarrassment; there are plenty of candidates. These candidates are to be found in the neighborhood of the conditions I mentioned in the last section that justify and ground belief in God. Thus, for example, the Reformed epistemologist may concur with Calvin in holding that God has implanted in us a natural tendency to see his hand in the world around us; the same cannot be said for the Great Pumpkin, there being no Great Pumpkin and no natural tendency to accept beliefs about the Great Pumpkin.

By way of conclusion, then: being self-evident, or incorrigible, or evident to the senses is not a necessary condition of proper basicality. Furthermore, one who holds that belief in God *is* properly basic is not thereby committed to the idea that belief in God is groundless or gratuitous or without justifying circumstances. And even if he lacks a general criterion of proper basicality, he is not obliged to suppose that just any, or nearly any, belief—belief in the Great Pumpkin, for example—is properly basic. Like everyone should, he begins with examples; and he may take belief in the Great Pumpkin, in certain circumstances, as a paradigm of irrational basic belief.

## BIBLIOGRAPHY

BLANSHARD, BRAND. *Reason and Belief* (London: Allen & Urwin, 1974).

CLIFFORD, W. K. "The Ethics of Belief," in *Lectures and Essays* (London: MacMillan, 1879).

FLEW, A. G. N. *The Presumption of Atheism* (London: Pemberton Publishing Co., 1976).

PLANTINGA, A. "Is Belief in God Rational?" in *Rationality and Religious Belief*, ed. C. Delaney (Indiana: University of Notre Dame Press, 1979).

PLANTINGA, A. "The Reformed Objection to Natural Theology," in *Proceedings of the American Catholic Philosophical Association* (1980).

RUSSELL, BERTRAND. "Why I Am Not a Christian," in *Why I Am Not a Christian* (New York: Simon & Schuster, 1957).

SCRIVEN, MICHAEL. *Primary Philosophy* (New York: McGraw-Hill, 1966).

# Appendix

## *Introductory Notes and Bibliographies*

### I
### *The Ontological Argument*

The ontological argument was first explicitly propounded by Anselm (Selection 3). As recent writers on the subject have emphasized, two forms of the argument are to be found in Anselm, one in *Proslogion* 2, and the other in *Proslogion* 3 and the *Reply to Gaunilo*. Both start from the concept of God as "that than which no greater can be conceived" (*aliquid quo maius cogitari nequit*). "Greater" here means "more perfect." Even "the Fool who says in his heart, There is no God" (Psalm 14:1) can possess this idea of a greatest conceivable being. The question, then, is whether such a being exists only in our minds (*in intellectu*) or in extra-mental reality (*in re*) as well.

In its first form the argument proceeds: suppose that that than which no greater can be conceived exists only in our minds. We should then have the paradox that it is possible to conceive of something greater than it— greater by virtue of existing in reality as well as in the mind. But this is impossible; there cannot be anything greater than that than which no greater can be conceived! Therefore, that than which no greater can be conceived *must* exist in reality.

Gaunilo objected that the same argument could be used to prove the existence of, for example, "the most excellent island" and that therefore the Anselmic reasoning is absurd. It is not clear on the basis of the text whether Anselm himself offered any serious reply to this. (The author of the Anselm translation used here believes that he did not. See his discussion in the Introduction to *The Many-Faced Argument: Recent Studies on the Ontological Argument for the Existence of God*, eds. John Hick and Arthur McGill [New York: Macmillan, 1967].) There is, however, a good reply to Gaunilo inherent in the second form of Anselm's argument, and to the present writer it appears psychologically likely that Anselm saw this. The second form of the argument claims that it is more perfect to have necessary existence than merely contingent existence; hence the most perfect conceivable being must have necessary existence, and must therefore exist. But an island, or any other material object, cannot have *necessary* existence. By its very nature an island is a part of the physical universe, and its existence is contingent upon other elements of the universe. Hence the Anselmic argument only applies to the unique case of the most perfect conceivable being.

After a long period during which the ontological argument was comparatively little considered, it was reformulated by Descartes in the seventeenth century as the argument that a supremely perfect being must possess, among many other perfections, that of existing. As the idea of the equality of its internal angles to two right angles is part of the concept of a triangle, so the idea of existence is part of the concept of the supremely perfect being. But while there is nothing in the concept of a triangle which entails that any triangle exists, there is something in the concept of God which entails that God exists, namely the attribute of existence, without which the idea in question would be less than that of the supremely perfect being (selection 7).

Kant's famous critique of the argument (selection 10) was directed against this Cartesian form of it and consists of a single thesis expressed in two different ways. (1) A concept cannot be so formed as to guarantee its own instantiation (i.e., its having an instance) in extra-mental reality. The nature of ideas on the one hand, and of the realm of existence (other than ideas) on the other, and of the radical difference between them, is such that whether a concept is exemplified in reality is a question of fact, and must be determined on the basis of experience. The *idea* of existence is indeed analytically connected with the *idea* of a supreme being; but whether the complex idea of an (existent) supreme being corresponds to any reality outside the human mind cannot be settled a priori. (2) Although existence is a grammatical predicate, it differs from all other predicates in that its logical function is not to add a further component to a concept, but to posit something answering to the concept.

This latter point was further developed in twentieth-century logic, especially by Bertrand Russell. To say, for example, "Horses exist but dragons don't exist" is not to say of horses that they possess and of dragons that they do not possess a special characteristic, namely existence. It is to say of the concept of a horse that this concept has instances, and of the concept of a dragon that it has no instances. But if existence is thus not a characteristic that something may have or lack we cannot argue, as the ontological argument seeks to do, that a supremely perfect being, or a being than which no more perfect can be conceived, must possess this particular characteristic. The question whether the concept of the most perfect conceivable being applies to extra-mental reality remains an open question.

Note the quite different Hegelian-type use of the argument expounded by Tillich (p. 254).

The second form of the argument (selection 3) occurs in Chapter 3 of Anselm's *Proslogion* and in his *Reply to Gaunilo*, and has recently been re-emphasized by some philosophers who claim that it is not subject to the criticisms that have undermined the first form (see selection 26 by Norman Malcolm). They argue that while "existence" is not a predicate, "necessary existence" is, and must be a predicate of an insurpassably perfect being. Thus if the notion of an insurpassably perfect being is nonself-contradictory, such a being necessarily exists; while if the notion is self-contradictory it is impossible that any such being should exist. But it has not been shown that this notion is self-contradictory, and so we must conclude that such a being necessarily exists.

This reasoning has been much criticized. The concept of a *logically* necessary being is ruled out by modern empiricist philosophy. But the kind of necessary existence of which Anselm speaks, and which Christian theology has always attributed to God, is not logical but *factual* or *ontological* necessity: an ontologically necessary being is one that exists without beginning or end and without depending for its existence upon anything other than itself. If there is such a being, it cannot cease to exist but exists necessarily, and if there is no such being none can come into existence. Thus its existence is either necessary or impossible. But we cannot add to this the final phase of Malcolm's argument—that divine existence is impossible only if the concept of God is self-contradictory. For divine existence would also be (ontologically) impossible if it is not the case that there is an eternal, self-existent being. (For a fuller development of this criticism, see "Critique of the 'Second Argument' " in Hick and McGill, *op. cit.*)

*For further reading:* Russell's analysis of the word "exists" can be found in "The Philosophy of Logical Atomism," sec. V, in *Logic and Language*, R. C. March, ed. (London: George Allen and Unwin, 1956); or more briefly in Russell, *History of Western Philosophy* (London: George Allen and Unwin, 1946), pp. 859–60. For an illuminating discussion of the question, see Jerome Shaffer, "Existence, Predication and the Ontological Argument," *Mind*, LXXI (July, 1962), 307–25.

For the Hegelian use of the ontological argument, see Edward Caird, "Anselm's Argument for the Being of God," *Journal of Theological Studies*, I (October, 1899), 23–39; and for a critique and defense, see Gilbert Ryle, "Mr. Collingwood and the Ontological Argument," *Mind*, XLIV (April, 1935), 137–51, and E. E. Harris, "Mr. Ryle and the Ontological Argument," *Mind*, XLV (October, 1936), 474–80, together with Ryle's reply, "Back to the Ontological Argument," *Mind*, XLVI (January, 1937), 53–57.

For yet another different use of the argument, see Nicholas Rescher, "The Ontological Argument Revisited," *The Australasian Journal of Philosophy*, XXXVII (August, 1959), 138–48.

There are good critical discussions of the ontological argument in H. J. Paton, *The Modern Predicament* (New York: Macmillan, 1955), chap. 12; and in Wallace I. Matson, *The Existence of God* (Ithaca, N.Y.: Cornell University Press, 1965), part II.

For the recent defense of Anselm's "second form" of the argument, see, as well as Malcolm's article (selection 26), Charles Hartshorne, *The Logic of Perfection* (LaSalle, Ill.: Open Court Publishing Co., 1962), chap. 2, *Anselm's Discovery* (LaSalle, Ill.: Open Court Publishing Co., 1965), and Alvin Plantinga, *God, Freedom and Evil* (Grand Rapids, MI.: William B. Eerdmans Publishing Co., 1974), part II.

Much of the above material, together with further items, can be found in *The Many-Faced Argument*, John Hick and Arthur McGill, eds. (New York: Macmillan, 1967). *The Ontological Argument, from St. Anselm to Contemporary Philosophers*, ed. Alvin Plantinga (Garden City, N.Y.: Doubleday & Co., 1965), contains a useful selection of readings.

## II

# *The Cosmological Argument*

This name is generally assigned to the third of Aquinas' Five Ways, the argument from the contingency of the world, although this and the previous two ways can all be regarded as variations on a common basic theme (selection 4). This theme first appears in Plato's doctrine that motion as we observe it presupposes an ultimate spontaneous source of motion that must be of the nature of soul (*Laws*, Book X). Aristotle developed this reasoning into the form in which it was later to influence Aquinas, and through him Christian and especially Catholic thought. Aristotle contended that the fact of motion points to an ultimate originating unmoved Mover. He says, "But if there is nothing eternal, then there can be no becoming; for there must be something which undergoes the process of becoming, that is, that from which things come to be; and the last member of this series must be ungenerated, for the series must start with something, since nothing can come from nothing" (*Metaphysics*, 999b).

The key terms of the argument as we find it in Aquinas are "contingent" and "necessary." To say of something, e.g., my pen, that it exists contingently is to say that there are other things or events apart from which my pen would not now exist. For example, if the machinery by which it was made had not been constructed, or if the raw materials of which it is composed had not existed, my pen, as it now is, could not be. Further, so far as we can observe, everything in the universe shares this status of contingency. Everything points to sources of its existence beyond itself. Now as we trace contingent entities back to the conditions upon which they depend and these to the further conditions upon which *they* depend, and so on in a regressive series, we realize that there must either be an infinite regress or, behind and supporting the entire realm of contingent beings, a reality that is not contingent. This noncontingent reality would be God, conceived as ultimate in that God does not depend for existence upon any other entity. God simply *is* as the self-existent One, without beginning or end, the uncreated Creator of everything other than God.

Given these alternatives of an endless regress of contingent things and events, or an ultimate self-existent Being, why should we choose the latter? The answer of the proponents of the cosmological argument is that only on this basis can we regard the universe as intelligible. We explain a contingent entity by referring to its conditions, and we explain these in turn by reference to further conditions; but if this process never terminates, nothing is ever finally explained. The universe would then be a sheer inexplicable fact. But as rational beings we cannot without self-contradiction accept such a possibility. We are driven to postulate an ultimate, unconditioned (or "necessary") being.

To this the critic replies that the sense in which a God-less universe is inexplicable and unintelligible is a sense that is compatible with the entire enterprise of scientific research and the growing understanding and control of our environment in which this issues. But it may be that in a more ultimate sense the universe *is* "unintelligible." That is to say, it may be that the physical universe itself has always existed in some form and is the most ultimate reality that there is, to be accepted as such without reference to any imagined entity beyond it. The cosmological argument does not prove that this is not the case, but only points to the alternative as some form of theism.

This dialectic comes out in the debate between Bertrand Russell and Father Copleston (selection 17), in which Copleston argues that "what we call the world is intrinsically unintelligible, apart from the existence of God," and Russell replies, "I should say that the universe is just there, and that's all." The discussion has now reached an impasse. For, as Copleston acknowledges in another context (his Pelican *Aquinas*, p. 124), "If one does not wish to embark on the path which leads to the affirmation of transcendent being, however the latter may be described (if it is described at all), one has to deny the reality of the problem, assert that things 'just are' and that the existential problem in question is a pseudo-problem. And if one refuses even to sit down at the chessboard and make a move, one cannot, of course, be checkmated."

*For further reading:* Much of the history of the argument is well described by William Craig in *The Cosmological Argument from Plato to Leibniz* (London: Macmillan, 1980). There are lucid commentaries on Aquinas' Five Ways in F. C. Copleston, *Aquinas* (London: Penguin Books, 1955), chap. 3, and Anthony

Kenny, *The Five Ways* (London: Routledge & Kegan Paul, 1969). For further Thomist treatments, see D. J. B. Hawkins, *The Essentials of Theism* (London: Sheed & Ward, Ltd., 1949), and E. Gilson, *The Christian Philosophy of St. Thomas* (London: Victor Gollancz, Ltd., 1957), part 1. There is an interesting sympathetic discussion in E. L. Mascall, *He Who Is* (London: Longmans, Green & Company, Ltd., 1943), chap. 5. For more critical treatments, see Wallace I. Matson, *The Existence of God* (Ithaca, N.Y.: Cornell University Press, 1965), part II, and William Rowe, *The Cosmological Argument* (Princeton University Press, 1975). A brilliant recent independent use of the argument occurs in Richard Taylor, *Metaphysics* (Englewood Cliffs, N.J.: Prentice-Hall, Inc., 1963), Chap. 7. For another recent work supporting the argument, see William Craig, *The Kalam Cosmological Argument* (London: Macmillan, 1979).

## III

# The Design Argument

The design (or teleological) argument is, as Kant acknowledged even as he criticized it, of all the traditional theistic proofs "the oldest, the clearest, and the most accordant with the common reason of mankind" (p. 136). It was much used in the eighteenth and nineteenth centuries, perhaps the most widely read exposition of it being that of Archdeacon William Paley in his *Natural Theology, or Evidences of the Existence and Attributes of the Deity Collected from the Appearances of Nature* (1802). Paley elaborated in great detail the thesis that the innumerable complex adaptations between one element of nature and another, and particularly between a living organism and its environment, are direct evidences of divine forethought. The eye, for example, must represent an intelligent creator's design. It would, he argued, be as absurd to attribute the formation of the eye to "chance" as to suppose that a watch found lying on the ground on an open heath had been formed by the accidental operations of wind and rain and other natural forces. Paley's argument, convincing though it seems as first view, had already been devastatingly criticized by David Hume in his *Dialogues Concerning Natural Religion* (1779), much of which appears in selection 8, and it was further undermined in the second half of the nineteenth century by the influence of Darwin's theories tracing the ways in which nature itself brings about these marvelous adaptations.

The most impressive twentieth-century restatement of the design argument is that of Richard Swinburne in *The Existence of God* (Oxford: Oxford University Press, 1979), offering a complex argument based upon Bayes's theorem in probability logic. It is unfortunately impossible to present this in a selection which would be intelligible on its own. The more advanced student, however, should read Swinburne's book. For a critique of his argument, see John Hick, *An Interpretation of Religion* (New Haven: Yale University Press, and London: Macmillan, 1989), chap. 6. For an earlier twentieth-century version of the design argument, see F. R. Tennant, *Philosophical Theology*, vol. II (Cambridge University Press, 1930). Instead of dealing with this or that specific instance of "design" (which can, he acknowledges, individually be given a naturalistic explanation) Tennant argues that "the multitude of interwoven adaptations by which the world is constituted a theatre of life, intelligence, and morality, cannot reasonably be regarded as an outcome of mechanism, or of blind formative power, or of aught but purposive intelligence" (*ibid.*, 121).

Perhaps the major problem facing the design argument as thus reformulated centers upon the concept of probability that it involves. Tennant's conclusion is that in view of the various considerations which he presents, it is much more probable that there is a God than that there is not. But what does "probable" mean in this context? Granting (as Tennant does) that theistic and naturalistic explanations are alike possible, both for each individual case of adaptation in nature and for the conjunction of these cases constituting the world as a whole, in what sense is the theistic option alleged to be more "probable" than its naturalistic alternative?

It has often been pointed out that the statistical concept of probability which is used in the sciences cannot be applied to the unique case of the universe as a whole. In order to be warranted in saying that the probability of our universe being God-produced is $1/n$, we should have to know that there are a number of universes with similar characteristics and that $1/n$ of them are God-produced. But clearly, questions of statistical probability do not arise in relation to the *universe* in the comprehensive sense of "the totality of all that is (other than any possible creator of everything other than the creator)," since there can here be no plurality of cases upon which to found statistical generalizations. The probability of theism must accordingly be an "alogical" type of probability, and any estimation of it must represent a judgment of general human reasonableness or common sense. The formation of such a judgement will be a matter of weighing various contrary considerations against each other; for a major part of the critique of the design argument consists in an appeal to counter-indications, such as the fact of evil in its many forms. Are there, then, any objective scales in which to weigh the appearance of purpose in the universe against the suffering of so much sentient life within it; or the positive factor of man's moral life against the no less real factor of human wickedness and cruelty; or the beauties of the natural scenery against the destructiveness of disease, tornado, earthquake, and drought? Can conclusions on these matters express anything other than purely personal responses and individual weightings? Can they claim to register any kind of objective probability-characteristic, whether logical or alogical? Such purely personal responses to the universe may well provide an appropriate basis for theistic, or atheistic, convictions; but precisely because of their unavoidably personal character they cannot constitute an argument having objective validity in the sense that it must convince everyone insofar as he or she is rational. An exposition of "the probability of God" will be convincing to those in whose view the theistic evidence already deserves greater emphasis and shines with a wider luminosity than the anti-theistic evidence; and it will remain unconvincing to those other persons in whose minds the weighting is reversed.

*For further reading:* For a recent presentation of the now rather antiquated Paleyian type of argument, see Robert E. D. Clark, *The Universe—Plan or Accident?* (Philadelphia: Muhlenberg Press, 1961); for a hard-hitting attack, see Clarence Darrow's autobiography, *The Story of My Life* (New York: Grosset & Dunlap, 1932), chap. 44. Lecomte du Noüy's rather crude probability argument is to be found in his *Human Destiny* (New York: Longmans, Green & Co., 1947), chap. 3, and is thoroughly criticized by Wallace I. Matson in *The Existence of God* (Ithaca, N.Y.: Cornell University Press, 1965), part II.

There is an ingenious form of the design argument in Richard Taylor, *Metaphysics* (Englewood Cliffs, N.J.: Prentice-Hall, 1963), chap. 7. The attempt to show that modern scientific cosmology points to God is presented in Hugh Montefiore, *The Probability of God* (London: SCM Press, 1985).

## IV

# *The Moral Argument*

Immanuel Kant, having declared invalid the traditional attempts to prove the existence of God by means of the ontological, cosmological, and design arguments (selection 10), indicated a different ground for assurance as to the reality of God, namely as a postulate or presupposition of the moral life (selection 11). Kant did not present his reasoning as another theistic proof, since it does not profess to establish the existence of God as a theoretically certain conclusion. It rather points to a supreme being as an implicate of the fact of moral obligation, an implicate that is unavoidable by anyone who acknowledges such obligation as having an absolute and unconditional authority.

Kant takes as his starting point the idea of the highest good (*summum bonum*)—that intrinsically valuable state of affairs which a moral being, *qua* moral, must want to establish or promote to such extent as is within one's power. The highest good in its fullness includes both moral goodness, or virtue, and happiness as the appropriate reward of virtue, and would thus consist in a society of perfect moral beings enjoying full and secure happiness.

Since it is our duty to seek to further the realization of the highest good, that goal must itself be capable of realization. But it can be capable of realization only if there exists a sovereign moral Being who has the power to bring about this coincidence of happiness with morality. Accordingly, it belongs to our character as moral agents, acknowledging the commands of duty and believing in the ultimate realizability of the highest good, which it is our duty to promote, to postulate, or assume, the existence of God.

In the nineteenth and early twentieth centuries the "moral argument" was employed by a number of thinkers. The essence of the argument, as such Idealist philosophers as Hastings Rashdall or W. R. Sorley presented it, is that while certain other conceptions of morality are compatible with atheism, a belief in moral absolutes is not. If morality were a human creation, consisting in the adoption by a group of people of rules of behavior designed to safeguard their common life, it would not presuppose any ground beyond humanity considered as an intelligent and gregarious animal species. But if we are sometimes aware of moral claims upon us that are absolute in the sense that no considerations of personal self-interest can lift them from our conscience, then something more than a gregarious animal must be involved. In acknowledging such claims upon our lives we are recognizing a source of moral obligation that is higher than ourselves in the scale of values and that rightfully summons us to faithful obedience. It is characteristic of the moral prophet or saint that he or she is vividly conscious of an obligation that is unconditional and that cannot rightfully be set in the balance with any other interest whatever, not even life itself. If there are such moral absolutes—and it is claimed that most of us in our heart of hearts acknowledge that there are—one cannot consistently accord to them the allegiance they demand and at the same time be satisfied with a naturalistic analysis of our obedience. So it is claimed, to quote another twentieth-century writer who uses this type of moral argument, that "Our moral consciousness, when taken in earnest, involves us in a whole realm of religious truth" (D. M. Baillie, *Faith in God* [Edinburgh: T. & T. Clark, 1927], p. 171).

In trying to evaluate this position, much would seem to depend upon the credibility of a naturalistic theory of ethics from the standpoint of the person who is engaged in any exceptional and critically demanding response to the claims of duty. There is no doubt that a variety of naturalistic ethical theories are possible. But could one *rationally* risk life as, let us say, a French underground fighter in World War II, or embark on a career of poverty and hardship in the struggle to win social justice for others, or sacrifice oneself to save another, if one believed that there is ultimately nothing more to human morality than group compulsions which are basically akin to those of an ant-hill? It may be said that self-sacrificial action is not usually based upon rational calculation at all, but expresses some altruistic impulse of our nature. But why, from a naturalistic point of view, should we not try to suppress such an impulse? Why should we respect it? The answer of the moral conscious-ness itself seems to be that in the call of some special and costing moral duty we are aware of a valid claim upon our lives, a demand that is authoritative and absolute. And it may be considered less than rational to acknowledge such an absolute claim in practice while denying it in theory.

For further reading: On Kant's argument, see L. W. Beck, *A Commentary on Kant's Critique of Practical Reason* (Chicago: University of Chicago Press, 1960). For a somewhat Kantian twentieth-century moral argument, see H. J. Paton, *The Modern Predicament* (London: George Allen and Unwin, and New York: Macmillan, 1955).

The kind of moral argument that was widely used earlier in the present century is eloquently presented in Hastings Rashdall, *The Theory of Good and Evil* (Oxford: The Clarendon Press, 1907), book III, chap. 1, sec. 4; W. R. Sorley, *Moral Values and the Idea of God* (Cambridge: Cambridge University Press, 1918), chap. 13; and D. M. Baillie, *Faith in God* (Edinburgh: T. & T. Clark, 1927), chap. 5. For the rather wooden argument of Newman, see Adrian J. Boekraad, *The Argument from Conscience to the Existence of God, According to J. H. Newman* (Louvain, Belgium: Nauwelaerts, 1961).

For useful discussions of the whole subject, see H. P. Owen, *The Moral Argument for Christian Theism* (London: George Allen and Unwin, 1965) and W. G. Maclagan, *The Theological Frontier of Ethics* (New York: Macmillan, 1961), chap. 3.

## V

# *The Religious Rejection of the Theistic Proofs*

The basic "rationalist" dogma of a great deal of modern philosophy, from Descartes to the present time, has been that to *know* means to be able to prove. It was assumed by Descartes that we cannot properly claim to know even that a real material world exists around us or that our friends and neighbors have an independent personal existence, still less that there is a divine Creator, until we can support these beliefs with logically compelling arguments. And a considerable investment of philosophical endeavor since Descartes has been devoted to the quest for such proofs.

Although some philosophers would dissent from this judgment, most today would agree that the last four centuries of philosophical work have shown that there are and can be no proofs to satisfy the rationalist desire. We live from the dawn of our consciousness within an environing material world in which we interact with other people, and no verbal proof could ever provide us with a greater or more rational assurance of its reality than we have already received from the massive consistency of our experience. But if any were seriously to doubt the reality of the world in which they live, they could never be rescued from such a state of radical doubt by logically compelling philosophical demonstrations.

In further opposition to the rationalist equation of knowledge with proof the rival philosophical tradition of empiricism sees strict logical demonstrations as operating exclusively within the realm (in Hume's phrases) of "the relations between ideas" and not extending to "matters of fact and existence." From this philosophical standpoint, the reality of God, as a matter of fact and existence, necessarily lies outside the province of logical demonstration. Like other questions of fact, it must be determined primarily on the basis of experience. If there is a God, and if God is to be known to us humans, God must somehow enter into the sphere of our experience.

It is therefore perhaps not surprising that the rationalist program, which has widely come to be regarded as mistaken in relation to our knowledge of the natural environment, should also prove unfruitful in relation to the divine presence and purpose, which (according to the claim of theistic religion) constitutes the supernatural environment of human life. We may therefore note without astonishment that the Bible, as the primary source document of western religion, contains no attempted proofs of the existence of God. Such proofs would have been as pointless to the biblical writers as proofs of the reality of their physical surroundings or of the existence of their neighbors. God was to them an encountered personal will, and their pages resound and vibrate with the divine presence and with the shocks of God's commands as a building might reverberate from the tread of some great being walking through it. Theistic proofs would have been as purely and merely academic to the prophets and apostles as a philosophical proof offered to a husband or wife of the existence of the spouse.

The theistic arguments have accordingly been of far more interest to philosophers (including religious philosophers) than to the person of faith as such. And the successive failures of these arguments, as they have been subjected to philosophical criticism, have seemed more significant to those for whom they might have established something new than to those others who believe that they have already come to know God by another route.

Going beyond this lack of interest in the traditional arguments, it has been urged that a theistic proof, even though it be logically flawless, could still never lead us to the God of Christian, Jewish, or Islamic faith. It could at most establish an abstract philosophical conception—an Unmoved Mover, a First Cause, a Necessary Being, or a Mind behind Evolution.

Some theologians have further argued that there is a positive reason why, in the divine arrangement, we are unable to prove God's existence. This inability, they say, helps to preserve human personal autonomy in relation to the infinite divine Person. Instead of being compelled by force of logic to acknowledge a higher Being, our awareness of God represents a free response to our whole nature to the moral claim and the freely proffered love of a personal reality infinitely higher than us in worth, in power, and in intensity and richness of being.

The chapter included here from Kierkegaard (selection 13) is a classical expression of certain aspects of the religious rejection of the theistic proofs.

*For further reading:* On Kierkegaard, see James D. Collins, *The Mind of Kierkegaard* (Chicago: University of Chicago Press, 1953) or Gregor Malantschuk, *Kierkegaard's Thought* (Princeton, N.J.: Princeton University Press, 1971). On the theological rejection of theistic proofs, see Emil Brunner, *Revelation and Reason* (London: Student Christian Movement Press, 1947), chap. 22.

On the breakdown of Cartesian Rationalism, see, e.g., William Temple, *Nature, Man and God* (New York: St. Martin's Press, 1934), chap. 3.

## VI
# Miracles

Reports of miracles are common among the religions of the world and, until well into the nineteenth century, such reports were almost universally regarded within Christianity as conclusive evidence of the truth of the Christian gospel. In Roman Catholic theology miracles occupy an important place among the "preambles to faith" by which the reality of divine revelation is held to be proved. Part of the Oath against Modernism which was imposed upon the Catholic clergy by Pope Pius X in 1910 reads: "Secondly, I accept and acknowledge the external proofs of revelation, that is, divine acts and especially miracles and prophecies as the surest signs of the divine origin of the Christian religion and I hold that these same proofs are well adapted to the understanding of all eras and all men, even of this time" (Denzinger, *Enchiridion Symbolorum*, 2145). In previous centuries miracle stories were regularly put to the same apologetic use by Protestant writers. John Locke's statement in his *Discourse on Miracles* can stand for hundreds that could be quoted: "he who comes with a message from God to be delivered to the world cannot be refused belief if he vouches his mission by a miracle."

In these contexts a miracle was regularly conceived as a breach or suspension of natural law by special divine action. Hume is using this same conception ("A miracle is a violation of the laws of nature," p. 110 above) when he argues in selection 9 that there can never in the nature of the case be human testimony strong enough to render it rational to believe that events have occurred directly in conflict with the whole working of the natural order.

He argues that the testimony for a miracle story, however good, must be outweighed by the counterevidence that we have in favor of the universal operation of natural law. "There must, therefore, be a uniform experience against every miraculous event, otherwise the event would not merit that appellation. And as a uniform experience amounts to a proof, there is here a direct and full *proof*, from the nature of the fact, against the existence of any miracle" (pp. 110-11 above). In the second part of his essay Hume buttresses his case by listing some of the many ways in which false testimony for the miraculous can come to be given, honestly as well as dishonestly.

It has been pointed out in criticism of Hume's essay that the conclusion to which all his arguments point is simply that we should never believe in miracles at second hand—not that miracles cannot occur, or that anyone who has witnessed one ought to refuse to believe the evidence of one's senses. As A. E. Taylor remarks in the course of his criticism of Hume's argument, "It is quietly forgotten [by Hume] that, on the premises, there cannot be said to be 'uniform experience' against the resuscitation of the dead man or any other sequence of events. At best I have only a uniformity within the range of *my own* experience to urge; a narrator who professes to have seen the resuscitation is actually appealing to *his own* experience as the foundation of his story. Thus, unless I am to assume that my own personal experiences are the standard of the credible—and if I do assume this, there is an end of all correction of expectations—it is a *petitio principii* [a begging of the question] to say that there is 'uniform experience' against any event to which any man claims to be able to testify" ("David Hume and the Miraculous," *Philosophical Studies* [London: Macmillan, 1934], chap. 9, p. 336).

The definition of "miracle," however, which is operative in all these discussions is not the only one used today. There has long been a tendency to move from a purely physical definition of miracle, as a breach or suspension of natural law, to a religious account of it as some striking and mysterious event (whether arising from coincidence, or from the operation of laws of nature not yet formulated) which mediates to some who witness it the purposeful presence of God.

On this view a miraculous event does not have to be "scientifically impossible" or in principle inexplicable; although we tend not to apply the notion of miracle to an event that was entirely expected in the ordinary course of nature and that in no way creates a shock of astonishment. But the notion is compatible with the assumption that *all* events exemplify general laws and are in principle explicable, even though there are realms, such as that studied by parapsychology, in which we cannot as yet formulate the laws. But when, unexpectedly, someone becomes vividly conscious of the reality, the glory, the goodness, or the claim of God, the situation is to that person miraculous. Such religiously momentous occasions touch the depths of human life and are usually moments of deliverance from danger, disease, or spiritual darkness. Thus the crossing of the Red Sea by the Israelites as they escaped from Egypt, or Jesus' healings, or healings at Lourdes today, or a profound religious conversion have been experienced as miraculous events, and have this character regardless of the extent to which they are or are not "scientifically explicable."

*For further reading:* On the place of miracles in Protestant apologetics, see John Dillenberger, *Protestant Thought and Natural Science* (Garden City, N.Y.: Doubleday, 1960). On Hume's discussion of miracles see Antony Flew, *Hume's Philosophy of Belief* (London: Routledge & Kegan Paul, 1961), chap. 8, and A. E. Taylor, "David Hume and the Miraculous" in his *Philosophical Studies* (London: Macmillan, 1934).

For a defense of a somewhat traditional view of miracles, see Richard Swinburne, *The Concept of Miracle* (London: Macmillan and New York: St. Martin's Press, 1970) and C. S. Lewis, *Miracles* (London: The Centenary Press, 1947). *Signs and Wonders: A Study of the Miraculous Element in Religion* by Louis Monden S.J. (New York: Desclee Company, 1966, English translation) is an important modern Roman Catholic treatment.

For a development of the view of miracle as a purely religious category, see H. H. Farmer, *The World and God* (New York: Harper & Row, 1936) chaps. 7, 9, and 10.

## VII

# *Religious Experience and Knowledge*

How is God known, or claimed to be known? According to philosophical rationalism (see Note V above), to know that there is a supreme Being means to possess a logically cogent proof of God's existence. If, as many philosophers and theologians now believe, this is a mistaken conception of religious knowledge, arising from a mistaken conception of knowledge in general, what alternative offers itself? In general, we come to know "what there is" and "how things are" in the world outside us as a result of that world's impinging upon us through our various organs of perception. Does religion claim, then, that there is some kind of perceptual awareness of God? The answer is Yes. Indeed, if there were no such thing as religious experience—which is, directly or indirectly and in one form or another, a putative experience of the divine—there would be no such thing as religion. Religious experience is the living spring out of which the vast and complex phenomenon of religion has grown and from which it continues to draw its vitality.

The forms of religious experience are very various, but can nevertheless be seen as forming a continuous series or, perhaps one should rather say, spectrum. At one end there are states of consciousness in which the religious content or object fills the entire field of awareness, temporarily blotting out the material world. In one of the many meanings of the term, this is mystical experience. William James, writing as a psychologist with a sensitive appreciation of mysticism, sympathetically discusses a number of the reports given by mystics of the absorbing depths of experience which have opened before them (selection 14). In considering the wider philosophical implications of mysticism, note Paul Tillich's important essay (selection 19) entitled "The Two Types of Philosophy of Religion"; what Tillich calls the ontological type of philosophy is closely related to mysticism.

Moving through the spectrum away from mysticism toward more ordinary forms of experience, there is the widespread sense of what Rudolf Otto calls the *numinous*, a sense that is constitutive of primal religion and that gives its emotional depth and life to the experiences of worship in all religions.

At a still further point along the spectrum there occurs the kind of religious experience that William Temple once described as "the whole experience of religious persons." We are now no longer speaking of religious in contrast to secular experience, but rather of a religious mode of experiencing life in both its "secular" and its "religious" aspects. This spreading of religious experience over the whole field of perception is well described by H. Richard Niebuhr: "Now every day is the day that the Lord has made; every nation is a holy people called by Him into existence in its place and time to His glory; every person is sacred, made in His image and likeness; every living thing, on earth, in the heavens, and in the waters is His creation and points in its existence toward Him; the whole earth is filled with His glory; the infinity of space is His temple where all creation is summoned to silence before Him" (*Radical Monotheism and Western Culture* [New York: Harper & Row, 1960], pp. 52–53). The selection from Martin Buber (selection 18) is a now classic description of human experience as a medium of personal relationship with the divine Thou.

A theory of the nature of religious knowledge that gives central place to this type of religious experience is suggested in selection 29 by John Hick. Religious awareness is there presented as a distinctive way of experiencing and responding to human existence in all its breadth and depth—seeing all of one's life in relation to God, and responding to God in and through all life's relationships and responsibilities. This in turn suggests a conception of religious faith as the interpretative element within the distinctively religious mode of experience. Religious faith is thus a name for that which differentiates a religious from a non-religious way of experiencing and participating in our human existence.

Within the total field of religious awareness, in which any or all of life's moments may become illuminated by a religious meaning, there are especially impressive and memorable events that focus a peculiarly intense religious consciousness. These function as centers of meaning, or points of revelation, casting a light upon wide ranges of human experience. In Judaism these revelatory events are the great high points of the national story, and especially the providential deliverance from Egypt under Moses. In Christianity the revelatory moments are those constituting the life of Jesus and the first days of the Church. These events are seen as central to the entire *Heilsgeschichte*, or salvation-history, recorded in the Bible. As William Temple ways, "There is event and appreciation; and in the coincidence of these the revelation consists." This view stands in contrast to the "propositional" conception of revelation as consisting in the divine disclosure of certain religious truths, a view that is classically expressed in selection 6 by Thomas Aquinas.

The view of religious faith as the interpretative element within the religious person's awareness of God, as having to do with one in and through the whole of life, likewise contrasts with that presented by Aquinas in selection 6. According to Aquinas, faith is a believing acceptance of certain truths that God has revealed, this acceptance being a voluntary act motivated by such external evidences as prophecies and miracles. The voluntarist emphasis thus introduced by Aquinas is carried further and made central in the conception of faith as willed belief argued in William James' famous essay "The Will to Believe" (selection 15).

*For further reading:* Two major studies of mysticism are Evelyn Underhill, *Mysticism* (New York: New American Library, 1955), and Baron F. von Hügel, *The Mystical Element of Religion*, 2nd ed., 2 vols. (London: J. M. Dent & Sons Ltd., 1923). See also Richard Woods, ed., *Understanding Mysticism* (New York: Image Books, 1980).

On Buber, see Maurice S. Friedman, *Martin Buber, The Life of Dialogue* (New York: Harper & Row, 1960); Arthur A. Cohen, *Martin Buber* (New York: Hilary House, 1957); and Malcolm L. Diamond, *Martin Buber: Jewish Existentialist* (New York: Oxford University Press, 1960). Of Buber's many works available in English, the next to be read after *I and Thou* might well be *Between Man and Man* (Boston: Beacon Press, 1955).

One conception of faith as interpretation is to be found in John Oman, *The Natural and the Supernatural* (Cambridge: Cambridge University Press, 1931); John Baillie, *The Sense of the Presence of God* (London: Oxford University Press, 1962); and John Hick, *Faith and Knowledge*, 2nd ed. (London: Macmillan 1966, reissued 1988). H. D. Lewis's *Our Experience of God* (New York: Macmillan, 1959) is an important treatment of religious experience and knowledge.

On the contemporary non-propositional conception of revelation, see H. Richard Niebuhr, *The Meaning of Revelation* (New York: Macmillan, 1959).

For contemporary critiques of the philosophical use of religious experiences, see C. B. Martin, *Religious Belief* (Ithaca, N.Y.: Cornell University Press,

1959), chap. 5, and Ronald Hepburn, *Christianity and Paradox* (London: C. A. Watts & Co., 1958), chaps. 3–4.

For recent philosophical discussions, see Joseph Runzo and Craig Ihara, eds., *Religious Experience and Religious Belief* (New York: University Press of America, 1986), containing articles by Alson, Plantinga, Hick, and others, and Alvin Plantinga and Nicholas Wolterstorff, eds., *Faith and Rationality* (Notre Dame and London: University of Notre Dame Press, 1983).

## VIII
# *The Problem of Evil*

The reality of evil in its many forms probably presents theistic faith with its most serious challenge. This challenge has traditionally been formulated as a dilemma: If God is omnipotent, God can prevent all evil; if God is perfectly good, God must want to prevent all evil; but evil exists; therefore God is either not omnipotent or not perfectly good. Either of these alternatives would amount to the collapse of traditional Hebrew-Christian monotheism.

In order to divide the problem for purposes of reflection a distinction has commonly been drawn between, on the one hand, moral evil or sin, which is evil apparently originating in the human agent and, on the other hand, non-moral or natural evil, which is pain suffered by sentient creatures, human and sub-human.

St. Augustine's thought concerning the problem of evil has been more influential than that of anyone else in the Western world. Two main themes are woven together in his discussions (selection 2). (1) Evil as privation of good: Augustine insists (against the contemporary sect of the Manichaeans) that evil is not any kind of positive substance with an independent status and power of its own. On the contrary, it always consists in the going wrong of something that is in itself good. Being, as such, is good, and evil has a parasitic status as the privation, corruption, or perversion of a good substance. The point at which evil first enters into God's good creation is through the misused freedom of finite creatures. And yet even this evil-willing has a negative character; it is a turning away from a higher to a lower good, from the supreme Good to created goods. Evil has thus no positive (or, in Aristotelian terms, "efficient") cause, but only a "deficient" cause. (2) The "aesthetic" theme: This is Augustine's affirmation of faith that, viewed in its totality from the ultimate divine standpoint, the universe is seen as perfectly good. Evil exists within it like the black patches in a painting that contribute in their own way to the beauty of the whole. Augustine applies this aesthetic conception to sin by invoking a principle of moral balance that was later to play an important part in Christian atonement theories. According to this principle, a universe in which there is sin, but in which this sin is exactly cancelled out by just punishment, is as good in the sight of God as one in which there is neither sin nor punishment. Connected with the aesthetic conception is what Arthur Lovejoy (in *The Great Chain of Being*, Cambridge, Mass.: Harvard University Press, 1936) has called the principle of plenitude—the idea that a created universe which contains the fullest variety of creatures, extending from the highest down to the lowest, is a richer and better universe than one consisting only of the highest kind of creatures—say archangels. Further, the lower forms of existence, such as snakes and baboons, are not to be considered evil just because they have a lowly place in the scale of being; they only become evil when the order of nature, in which they have their proper place, is upset.

In selection 28 an alternative to the Augustinian standpoint reappears, an alternative tradition that can be traced through Schleiermacher in the nineteenth century back to some of the early Hellenistic Fathers of the Christian Church, especially Irenaeus. In this non-Augustinian tradition what is mythologically called the Fall of Man is seen as a virtually inevitable, and divinely anticipated, aspect of man's growth into moral self-consciousness and personal responsibility; and the "rough edges" of the world, which we call its natural evils, are integral to its character as an environment in which the moral values of human life have a practical meaning and function, and in which they may accordingly undergo development—an interpretation which requires the postulation of a life after death in which this process may be continued and eventually brought to full fruition.

*For further reading:* For historical treatments of the subject, see R. A. Tsanoff, *The Nature of Evil* (New York: Macmillan, 1931) and John Hick, *Evil and the God of Love*, 2nd ed. (New York: Harper & Row, 1978). Austin Farrer's *Love Almighty and Ills Unlimited* (Garden City, N.Y.: Doubleday, 1961) is a brilliant recent Augustinian treatment. For a contemporary Roman Catholic discussion, see François Petit, *The Problem of Evil* (New York: Hawthorn Books, Inc., 1959) or Charles Journet, *The Meaning of Evil* (London: Geoffrey Chapman, 1963).

The "Irenaean" type of theodicy is to be found in Friedrich Schleiermacher, *The Christian Faith* (1921), Part I, section 3, and Part II, section 1; and in the present century in F. R. Tennant, *Philosophical Theology*, II (Cambridge: Cambridge University Press, 1930), chap. 7; William Temple, *Nature, Man and God* (London: Macmillan, 1934), chap. 14; and John Hick, *Evil and the God of Love, op. cit.* For a classic discussion of the topics indicated in its title, see N.P. Williams, *The Ideas of the Fall and of Original Sin* (London: Longmans, Green & Company, 1927).

For a response to the problem of evil from process theology, see David Griffin, *God, Power and Evil* (Philadelphia: Westminster Press, 1976).

Some important recent articles are J. L. Mackie, "Evil and Omnipotence," *Mind*, LXIV (April, 195); Antony Flew, "Divine Omnipotence and Human Freedom," *New Essays in Philosophical Theology* (New York: The Macmillan Company, 1955); Ninian Smart, "Omnipotence, Evil and Supermen," *Philosophy*, XXXVI, No. 137 (April and July, 1961); discussions by Mackie, Flew, and Smart in *Philosophy* (January, 1962, and April, 1962); and Alvin Plantinga, *God, Freedom and Evil* (Grand Rapids, MI: William B. Eerdmans Publishing Co., 1983). Nelson Pike, ed., *God and Evil* (Englewood Cliffs, N.J.: Prentice-Hall, Inc., 1964) is a useful anthology of such articles.

## IX

# *Immortality*

The main contrast that is commonly drawn is between the Greek conception of a natural "immortality of the soul" and the Hebraic conviction as to the "resurrection of the dead."

In Plato's *Phaedo*, some central arguments of which appear in selection 1, we have a classic and unforgettable picture of the "otherworldly" attitude to the body and to earthly life, which can be summed up in the Greek pun *sōma-sēma* (body-tomb). The *Phaedo* memorably articulates an aspect of the human response to existence that is dominant in the world-renouncing strands of Indian religion and that has also been strongly present in the ascetic and monastic tradition within Christianity.

By the "soul" Plato means the mind considered as a rational and moral agent. His basic argument for the immortality of the soul, worked out in the dialogue in various specific arguments, is that the soul can, if it will, relate itself to the eternal realities or values, the Forms or Ideas, and that, insofar as this relationship is determinative for the life of the soul, it ensures for it an immortal existence. The soul is apparently thought of by Plato as enjoying a disembodied immortality, although this is also presented as a social immortality in company with the souls of other "just men made perfect" and, further, the myths by means of which Plato describes the life to come are necessarily cast in spatial terms.

Thus Plato's (or Socrates') arguments are predicated upon a radical separability of soul and body, such that the former can exist and function entirely independently of the latter. In contrast, the Hebraic view, which is pervasively dominant in the Bible, sees the human being as an indissoluble psychophysical unity. A man or woman is not a material body plus an immaterial soul, but a creature fashioned out of the dust of the earth and yet at the same time made as person in the "image of God." When, toward the end of the Old Testament period, elements within Judaism came to affirm the reality of a life after death, what was affirmed was not the immortality of a disembodied soul but a divine raising up of the whole person from the grave. In Christianity, while this very earthly conception of resurrection has persisted among some of the unsophisticated to the present day, we already find in the thought of St. Paul the conception of a "spiritual body" (*soma pneumatikon*). There has been discussion and disagreement among New Testament scholars as to how Paul's references to the *soma pneumatikon* are to be understood, but one way of construing them is as follows. The resurrection body, as it might perhaps more aptly be called, is initially an exact replica of the earthly person as he was a moment before death, complete with memories, dispositions, and all other mental and bodily characteristics. This resurrection person, however, is not a part of the physical universe of which we are presently aware by means of our sense organs. He is part of a resurrection world occupying its own space: that is to say, objects in the resurrection world are spatially related to one another, as are objects in this world, but an object in the resurrection world is not spatially related to any object in this world.

Any such notion is repudiated in the mystical thoughts, included in selection 20, with which the most radically original of twentieth-century philosophers, Ludwig Wittgenstein, ends his *Tractatus*. However, while Wittgenstein is no doubt right in feeling that a mere continuance of human existence beyond the grave would not in itself solve any of life's deepest problems, it does not follow that there is in fact no life after death, nor that such life could not be a sphere of crucially significant qualitative developments of human personality.

The notion of continued conscious life after death is also repudiated in the article by Charles Hartshorne (selection 21) and replaced by an idea of immortality as perpetual presence to the divine memory. Each human life, from the cradle to the grave, stands totally recorded in God's consciousness and has an immortal existence in this form. Hartshorne is explicit that on his view there is no human *life* after death, no continued consciousness, no continued interaction with other people and with an environment. What continues to exist is not Tom Jones or Mary Williams, or anything that is in any way different from and yet continuous with their present earthly existence, but rather an unfailing memory of their lives, a memory which is part of the eternal consciousness of God.

One criticism that is made of this "social immortality" is that what it signifies is not immortality at all. For to live involves not only being remembered but also being capable of remembering and of creating fresh and different material for memory. But in Hartshorne's view the book of a person's life is closed at death so that nothing can thereafter be added to or subtracted from it, even though the book itself is eternally preserved in the heavenly library which is the universal divine memory. We do not exist in an after-life; but after we have ceased to exist the record of our lives will exist as part of the continually expanding cosmic record of everything that has occurred in the whole universe throughout past time.

It has also been questioned whether the basic process theme of life as continual change, development, and growth is as adequately expressed in Hartshorne's theory as in the more traditional doctrine of the continued existence of the living human personality after bodily death. For Hartshorne's doctrine postulates a static, frozen immortality: the last page of the book of life has been filled, and all that happens subsequently is that the completed volume is preserved for ever, unchanged and unchangeable.

A further question touches upon the problem of evil. On a divine memory view it seems that not only is all the good that has been realized within human experience immortalized in the divine memory, but also and equally all the pain, suffering, and misery. All alike will be perpetuated in the divine consciousness. It is as though God's eternity were filled with a continual playing over again and again of the records of this world, just as it has been, without selection, abridgment, or editing. Evil is eternalized together with good, and in the same proportions as before. There is no final resolving of evil in the gradual creation of an ultimate good. In contrast to this, traditional Christian thought sees our temporal existence as moving toward a far distant goal in which universal good will finally have been brought out of evil; and evil will not be immortalized in the static hell formed by its eternal retention in the divine memory.

In our contemporary western scientific culture, most people (including most members of the various churches) find it almost impossible to take seriously the thought of a life after death. For this reason, the bold attempt of a distinguished recent philosopher to develop one possible conception of "personal survival and the idea of another world" (selection 22) can reveal coherent and intriguing possibilities that may have a liberating effect upon the mind.

*For further reading:* There are good commentaries on Plato's *Phadeo* in A. E. Taylor, *Plato: The Man and His Work,* 4th ed. (London: Methuen, 1937) and, with a valuable philosophical critique, I. M. Crombie, *An Examination of Plato's Doctrines,* Vol. I (New York: Humanities Press, 1962).

Baron F. von Hügel's *Eternal Life,* 2nd ed. (Edinburgh: T. & T. Clark, 1913) is a classic on the history of the subject. Bishop Butler, *Analogy of Religion,* 1736 (Part I, chap. 1), presents rational arguments for the immortality of the soul. A more recent and more tentative discussion is that of John Hick in *Death and Eternal Life* (San Francisco: Harper & Row, and London: Macmillan, 1976, reissued 1987). For arguments for immortality from the standpoint of Idealist philosophy see Josiah Royce, *The Conception of Immortality* (Boston: Houghton Mifflin Company, 1900) and J. M. E. McTaggart, *Some Dogmas of*

*Religion* (London: Arnold, 1906). Corliss Lamont, *The Illusion of Immortality* (New York: Wisdom Library, 1959) is a strong attack upon all forms of belief in personal survival after death.

F. W. H. Myers, *Human Personality and Its Survival of Bodily Death* (London: Longmans, Green, & Company, 1903) is a classic of psychical research or parapsychology. For a more recent general discussion, see Benjamin Wolman, ed., *Handbook of Parapsychology* (New York: Van Nostrand, 1977). For an excellent work on immortality that takes account of parapsychology, see C. J. Ducasse, *A Critical Examination of the Belief in a Life after Death* (Springfield, Ill.: Charles C Thomas, Publishers, 1961). See also C. D. Broad, *Lectures on Psychical Research* (New York: The Humanity Press, 1962), which is still perhaps the best philosophical work on the subject.

## X
## *The Rejection of Theism, and New Forms of Religious Naturalism*

There have been philosophical criticisms and rejections of theism ever since some of the Epicureans propounded the theory that it was originally fear that created the gods (*primus in orbe deos fecit timor*). The personal God of the Judaic and Christian faiths is regarded, in this critical tradition, as a projection of the human mind—whether a projection of our common ideals or of the individual's buried infancy memories of father as a great overarching protective power. Feuerbach's exposition of the projection theory (selection 12) is unsurpassed in the literature of atheism for its philosophical and literary quality.

From this view of God as a projection of the human psyche, and of theistic religion as being accordingly based upon illusion, it by no means follows that religion in all its phases and aspects is to be rejected as false or harmful. Feuerbach did not thus reject it; and in the contemporary humanism of J. H. Randall, Jr. (selection 24) religion, understood as an appreciation of the mysteries and depths of human experience, is highly valued. Such humanism or naturalism advocates a religion without God, religion as an instrument for the conservation and enhancement of human values, and sees it as playing an important role in our management of our own nature and destiny.

Another form of humanism—though it does not generally identify itself as such—uses the traditional language of religion, and seeks to retain its emotional power while jettisoning its claims to refer to realities transcending the empirical world. We see the seeds of this development in Part XXI of

Hume's *Dialogues* (in selection 8), and its contemporary flowering in two quite different forms in writings by John Wisdom (selection 25) and R. B. Braithwaite (selection 23).

One of the chief considerations that has been urged against the orthodox Western religious conception of God is its anthropomorphic character. God, it is said, is conceived as an enormously magnified human person, with the mental and moral but not the physical properties of human personality. So far from God having created us in the divine image, as the Book of Genesis affirms, it seems to be humanity which has created God in its own image. The following poem by Rupert Brooke (1887–1915) suggests this thought, together with the allied thought that religious faith is wishful thinking, in a more succinct and effective way than could be achieved by many pages of polemical prose:

Heaven.

Fish (fly-replete, in depth of June,
Dawdling away their wat'ry noon)
Ponder deep wisdom, dark or clear,
Each secret fishy hope or fear.
Fish say, they have their Stream and Pond;
But is there anything Beyond?
This life cannot be All, they swear,
For how unpleasant, if it were!
One may not doubt that, somehow, Good
Shall come of Water and of Mud;
And, sure, the reverent eye must see
A Purpose in Liquidity.
We darkly know, by Faith we cry,
The future is not Wholly Dry.
Mud unto mud!—Death eddies near—
Not here the appointed End, not here!
But somewhere, beyond Space and Time,
Is wetter water, slimier slime!
And there (they trust) there swimmeth One
Who swam ere rivers were begun,
Immense, of fishy form and mind,
Squamous, omnipotent, and kind;
And under that Almighty Fin,
The littlest fish may enter in.
Oh! never fly conceals a hook,
Fish say, in the Eternal Brook,
But more than mundane weeds are there,
And mud, celestially fair;
Fat caterpillars drift around,
And Paradisal grubs are found;
Unfading moths, immortal flies,

And the worm that never dies.
And in that Heaven of all their wish,
There shall be no more land, say fish.[1]

*For further reading:* Among the older classics in criticism of traditional theism are Thomas Paine, *The Age of Reason* (1791–1792) and Baron d'Holbach, *The System of Nature* (1795–1796). In the same tradition and style, but by contemporary writers, are Bertrand Russell, *Why I Am Not a Christian* (New York: Simon and Schuster, 1957); Walter Kaufmann, *Critique of Religion and Philosophy* (Garden City, N.Y.: Doubleday, 1958) and *The Faith of a Heretic* (Garden City, N.Y.: Doubleday & Company, Inc., 1961); and Julian Huxley, *Religion Without Revelation*, 2nd ed. (London: Max Parrish & Company, 1957).

Today two major critical standpoints are those of Marxism and of Freudian psychology. For Marxist critiques of religion, see Karl Marx and Frederick Engels, *On Religion* (London: Lawrence & Wishart, 1958) and Maurice Cornforth, *Dialectical Materialism: An Introductory Course*, vol. 3 (London: Lawrence & Wishart, 1954). For Freud's criticism of religion see his *Totem and Taboo, Moses and Monotheism*, and *The Future of an Illusion*.

The contemporary philosophical criticism of religious belief begins with A. J. Ayer, *Language, Truth and Logic*, 2nd ed. (London: Victor Gollancz, Ltd., 1946). There is important material in *New Essays in Philosophical Theology*, Antony Flew and Alasdair MacIntyre, eds. (London: Student Christian Movement Press, 1955). More recent works are J. L. Mackie, *The Miracle of Theism* (London: Oxford University Press, 1982) and Anthony Kenny, *The God of the Philosophers* (London: Oxford University Press, 1979).

# XI

# *Religious Language*

It is evident even to the most preliminary reflection that the words traditionally used to describe God, such as "good," "loving," "just," "wise," and "powerful," are not meant in their religious context to bear the sense that they have in their application to human beings. When, for example, we describe human beings as "good" we mean, among other things, that they recognize the authority over them of a moral law, that they are relatively successful in resisting temptation, and that they are concerned about other people, whose interests they tend to consider equally with their own. But only an anthropomorphic deity could be good in this sense. God, as described in

---

[1]*The Poetical Works of Rupert Brooke* (London: Faber & Faber, Ltd., 1946). Reprinted by permission of the publishers.

the developed theology of the West, does not exist under the moral law as we do; God's relation to human beings, as their Creator, is necessarily different from their relation to each other as fellow creatures; and God is not subject to temptations to be resisted or conflicting urges to be internally arbitrated. How then can we properly attribute to God either moral goodness or any other quality of human personality?

The classic answer to this question was formulated by Thomas Aquinas in his doctrine of analogy, to be found in selection 5. The central thread of Aquinas' reasoning is as follows. A good quality, or an excellence, exists in a given being in a manner appropriate to the nature of that being; and accordingly the excellencies of all finite creatures are themselves finite and limited qualities. But in God, the infinite Being, these excellencies must be present in their unlimited perfection (*Summa contra Gentiles*, Book I, Chapter 28). Since God is the creative cause of both the existence and the nature of God's creatures, they share some of God's attributes, and can thus be said to be like God, although in a vastly diminished manner (Chapter 29). Thus those perfections of the creature (e.g., according to Aquinas, "being" and "good") that we can define without tying them to their specifically creaturely forms can be attributed to God on the understanding that they are present in God in whatever may be their appropriately divine form (Chapter 30). Further, the excellencies that are distinguishable in humanity, and that are accordingly given different names ("good," "wise," "knowing," etc.) are all, as they exist in God, aspects of a single simple essence constituting the indivisible divine nature (Chapter 31). For all these reasons, when we call both God and a human being "good" we are not using the word "good" in precisely the same sense (univocally) (Chapter 32). Nor on the other hand are we using it in totally different and unrelated senses (equivocally), as for example when we use the word "club" both for a weapon and for an association of people (Chapter 33). In the case of Creator and creatures a common term is predicated neither univocally nor equivocally but analogically. Analogies are of two kinds. In the first kind (called "the analogy of proportion" or "attribution") two different things are said to be analogous to one another in virtue of their common relation to some third thing (which is the "prime analogate"). But God and humans cannot be analogous to one another in this way, for there is no third reality prior to them both that could serve as the prime analogate. In the second kind (called "the analogy of proportionality") a term is applied in basically the same sense to two different things, but it applies to each of them in a sense appropriate to the nature of that thing. It is in this way that God and humans are alike called "good," "wise," etc. The divine goodness is like human goodness in that God has created our human nature in God's own image; but at the same time the divine goodness differs from our human goodness as the eternal, immutable, self-existent nature of God differs from our human nature. There is, however, still a proportionality between them: as human goodness is to human nature, so is divine goodness to the divine nature (Chapter 34).

Another aspect of the problem of religious language that is currently under active discussion concerns its realist or non-realist intent. More specifically, this question is raised regarding those sentences that appear to constitute factual assertions about God—e.g., "God loves mankind" or "God was in Christ reconciling the world to God's self." Traditionally these have been intended by religious speakers as factual statements (i.e., statements that purport to give a true account of how things are), though of course they have readily been recognized to be about a kind of fact other than that investigated by the sciences. But a number of contemporary philosophers, impressed by the difficulty of showing that statements about God are factual in the sense of being in principle open to experimental verification or falsification, have offered non-realist theories of religious language. They see its function as other than that of making a special kind of factual assertion. Wisdom's subtle and thought-provoking essay (selection 25, in connection with which read Pt. XII of Hume's *Dialogues* in selection 8) was the first of a series of explorations of possible non-realist uses of religious language. Randall's position (selection 24) has interesting affinities with Wisdom's. Braithwaite's lecture (selection 23) develops with challenging lucidity an alternative view to Wisdom's. Hare's piece (selection 27) offers yet another. In Flew's paper (selection 27) the verification-falsification issue is brought into sharp focus; and a defense of the realist use of the core religious statements is offered by Mitchell and, on a fuller scale, by Crombie.

Another type of religious non-realism is developed by such contemporary Wittgensteinian philosophers as D. Z. Phillips, for whom God is not an objective reality to which theistic language intends to refer; rather God-talk expresses a distinctive way of seeing life and of responding to its unpredictable mixture of good and evil (see, e.g., his *Religion Without Explanation* [Oxford: Blackwell, 1976]). Don Cupitt also eloquently represents this rejection of 'objective theism' together with a continued use of standard religious language and practice (see, e.g., his *Taking Leave of God* [London: SCM Press, 1980]).

In contrast to these non-realist views stands religious realism. In its contemporary forms this is not the "naive realism" which believes that religious statements are all literally true but the "critical realism" which affirms a transcendent divine reality about which our human discourse often has to be metaphorical or mythological or analogical (see, for example, selection 31).

*For further reading:* On the Thomist doctrine of analogy, see E. L. Mascall, *Existence and Analogy* (London: Longmans, Green & Company, Ltd., 1949), chap. 5. Cardinal Cajetan's *The Analogy of Names*, 2nd ed. (Pittsburgh:

Duquesne University Press, 1959) is a classic, but difficult, work on the subject.

Tillich's doctrine of religious language as symbolic occurs in a number of his writings, including *Dynamics of Faith* (New York: Harper & Row, 1957), chap. 3, and in two papers, "The Religious Symbol" and "The Meaning and Justification of Religious Symbols," in *Religious Experience and Truth*, ed. Sidney Hood (New York: New York University Press, 1961), which volume also contains an important critique by William Alston entitled "Tillich's Conception of a Religious Symbol."

There are good surveys of the modern debate concerning the cognitive or non-cognitive character of religious language in Frederick Ferré, *Language, Logic and God* (New York: Harper & Row, 1961); and James Alfred Martin,*The New Dialogue Between Philosophy and Theology* (New York: The Seabury Press, 1966). For another treatment, see John Macquarrie, *God-Talk* (London: SCM Press and New York: Harper & Row, 1967).

On the broader realist/non-realist debate, see John Hick, *An Interpretation of Religion* (Yale University Press, 1989, chapters 11–12) and Dale Breitkrentz, ed., *Is God Real?* (London: Macmillan, and New York: St. Martin's Press, 1990).

There are further articles by Crombie and other upholders of the traditional cognitive and realist understanding of theological statements in *Faith and Logic*, Basil Mitchell, ed. (London: George Allen and Unwin, 1957). See also John Hick, "Theology and Verification," *Theology Today* (April, 1960), reprinted in *The Existence of God*, John Hick, ed. (New York: Macmillan, 1964), and *God and the Universe of Faiths* (London: Macmillan, and New York: St. Martin's Press, 1973, reissued 1988), chaps. 1, 2.

## XII

# Religious Pluralism

Epistemological issue arising from the fact of religious plurality have only recently begun to attract the attention of western philosophers of religion. This no doubt reflects the circumstance that it is only since World War II that any large section of western society has become acutely conscious of the reality and spiritual depth of the great world faiths other than Christianity and Judaism.

Philosophical issues are provoked particularly by the conflicting truth-claims of the different traditions. Many philosophers today hold that the rationality of religious belief depends upon the rationality of the practice of basing our beliefs upon our experience, including distinctively religious experience (see selections 29, 32, and 33). From this point of view those who, in moments of worship or in some crisis or turning point of life, experience themselves as "existing in God's presence" are rationally entitled to believe in the reality of God and to proceed to live on that basis. Or again, those who, in a more specifically Christian mode, experience the presence of the risen cosmic Christ are entitled on this basis to believe in Christ as (in J. A. T. Robinson's phrase) "the human face of God" and to proceed to acquire a Christian system of beliefs. But clearly, if Christian religious experience justifies Christian beliefs, then on the same principle Jewish religious experience justifies Jewish beliefs, Islamic religious experience justifies Muslim beliefs, Hindu religious experience justifies Hindu beliefs, and so on. And so immediately we have the paradox of these different, and at many points incompatible, systems of belief all claiming to be justified in the same way.

One obvious solution flows from the naturalistic understanding of religious experience as delusory. From this point of view all the varying sets of religious belief are alike and equally false; and the very fact of their variety can be brought as supporting evidence. Thus David Hume, noting that almost every religion produces its own miracle stories, laid down the principle "that, in matters of religion, whatever is different is contrary; and that it is impossible the religions of ancient Rome, of Turkey, of Siam, and of China should, all of them, be established on any solid foundation" (p. 115 above).

A religious interpretation of the situation, on the other hand, starts from the premis that religious experience is not as such and *in toto* human projection, but constitutes the field of human responses (though always in complexly mediated ways) to a transcendent reality. Such an interpretation cannot be as simple and straightforward as its naturalistic alternative. For how can the ultimate divine Reality be both the personal Adonai, and the Holy Trinity, and Allah, and Visnu . . . and also the non-personal Brahman, and Tao, and Dharmakaya? And yet the reports of religious experience across the different traditions present this bewildering plurality. Further, each tradition in its most orthodox form has been accustomed to assume that it alone knows the divine Reality, whereas the others worship false gods or pursue illusory ultimates. Such claims to unique validity are, however, hard to justify philosophically. For if—as seems to be the case—the major streams of religious experience and spiritual life all produce, apparently to more or less the same extent, the fruits of human transformation from self-centeredness to a new orientation centered in the divine Reality, it is manifestly arbitrary to hold that one form constitutes a valid human response to that Reality while the others do not.

One promising line for the development of a religious interpretation of religious plurality is suggested by a distinction that occurs in some form in each of the great traditions. Christianity, for example, distinguishes between God in God's infinite, eternal self-existent being, transcending all our human ideas and definitions, and God in relation to humanity and as known by human beings. Again, advaitic Hinduism distinguishes between *nirguna* Brahman, the absolute reality in itself, beyond the scope of our concepts, and *saguna* Brahman, that same reality humanly encountered as a personal deity. If we refer to the supposed ultimate object of religious thought simply as the Real, the distinction is between the Real in itself and the Real as conceived and experienced from within the different cultural forms of human life. The model that suggests itself is that of the same infinite reality being variously perceived through varying human receptivities. From this point of view the great world faiths constitute different ways of thinking of the Real, and hence different modes of experiencing the Real, and hence different ways of responding to the Real in spiritual practices and in personal and communal moral codes and lifestyles. The religions are then different human "lenses" through which we regard the Real, these "lenses" being rich historical complexes composed of concepts, modes of thought, liturgies, methods of prayer or meditation, cultural assumptions, sacred scriptures, historical memories and sagas, myths, saintly figures, and institutional forms. (For a fuller outline of this approach, see selection 30).

*For further reading:* There are as yet few philosophical treatments of this topic. The October 1988 issue of the journal *Faith and Philosophy*, however, contains a variety of contemporary approaches. Important background material can be found in R. C. Zaehner, *Concordant Discord* (London: Oxford University Press, 1970); Huston Smith, *The Religions of Man* (New York: Harper & Row, 1958); Keith Ward, *Images of Eternity: Concepts of God in Five Religious Traditions* (London: Darton, Longman and Todd, 1987); John Hick, *Problems of Religious Pluralism* (New York: St. Martin's Press and London: Macmillan, 1985); and *An Interpretation of Religion* (New Haven: Yale University Press and London: Macmillan, 1989).

On the issue posed from the point of view of Christian theology, see Paul Knitter, *No Other Name?* (Maryknoll: Orbis and London: SCM Press, 1985); Alan Race, *Christians and Religious Pluralism* (Maryknoll: Orbis and London: SCM, 1983); Gerald H. Anderson and Thomas F. Stransky, *Christ's Lordship and Religious Pluralism* (Maryknoll, Orbis, 1981); and, for a volume of readings representing the major points of view, John Hick and Brian Hebblethwaite, eds., *Christianity and Other Religions* (Philadelphia: Westminster Press and London: Collins, 1980). See also Leonard Swidler, ed., *Towards a Universal Theology of Religion* (Maryknoll: Orbis, 1987). Hans Küng's *Christianity and the World Religions* (New York: Doubleday, 1986) is valuably informative.

Hendrik Kraemer's *The Christian Message in a Non-Christian World* (London: Edinburgh House Press, 1938) is a classic statement of a Barthian point of view.

# Index